THE SOCIAL SYSTEM

Talcott Parsons

THE

SOCIAL

SYSTEM

THE FREE PRESS, *New York*

COLLIER-MACMILLAN LIMITED, *London*

Collier-Macmillan Canada, Ltd., Toronto, Ontario

FIRST FREE PRESS PAPERBACK EDITION 1964

printing number
5   6   7   8   9   10

To Helen

WHOSE HEALTHY AND PRACTICAL
EMPIRICISM HAS LONG BEEN AN
INDISPENSABLE BALANCE-WHEEL
FOR AN INCURABLE THEORIST

PREFACE

THE present volume is an attempt to bring together, in systematic and generalized form, the main outlines of a conceptual scheme for the analysis of the structure and processes of social systems. In the nature of the case, within the frame of reference of action, such a conceptual scheme must focus on the delineation of the system of institutionalized roles and the motivational processes organized about them. Because of this focus and the very elementary treatment of processes of economic exchange and of the organization of political power, the book should be regarded as a statement of general sociological theory, since this is here interpreted to be that part of the theory of the social system which is centered on the phenomena of the institutionalization of patterns of value-orientation in roles.

The title, *The Social System,* goes back, more than to any other source, to the insistence of the late Professor L. J. Henderson on the extreme importance of the concept of system in scientific theory, and his clear realization that the attempt to delineate the social system as a system was the most important contribution of Pareto's great work.[1] This book therefore is an attempt to carry out Pareto's intention, using an approach, the "structural-functional" level of analysis, which is quite different from that of Pareto, and, of course, taking advantage of the very considerable advances in our knowledge at many points, which have accumulated in the generation since Pareto wrote.

For the reader's orientation it is important to relate the present

[1] Cf. L. J. Henderson, *Pareto's General Sociology.*

vii

book both to the author's previously published work and to his nearly simultaneously appearing contribution to the volume *Toward a General Theory of Action* by members of the Harvard University Department of Social Relations and their collaborators.

The author's *Structure of Social Action* was not a study in *sociological* theory in a strict sense, but an analysis, in relation to the work of a group of authors, of the nature and implications of the action frame of reference. Since its publication in 1937 there has been gradually taking shape a formulation of a systematic approach to the narrower tasks of sociological theory as such, stimulated by empirical work in a variety of fields and by the writings of other authors, particularly Merton.[2] Various steps in this development are documented in the papers published in the collection *Essays in Sociological Theory*.

For some years I have intended, when opportunity offered and the time seemed ripe, to attempt to pull these strands of thought together in a general book. In the fall of 1947 I held at Harvard a seminar on the Theory of Social Systems. The clarification of thought achieved there was documented in exceedingly condensed form in the paper *The Position of Sociological Theory* (*Essays*, Chapter I). Then an invitation to deliver the University Lectures in Sociology at the University of London in January-February 1949 provided an occasion for further systematic consideration of the problem. In a rather rough sense those lectures, which were not published as such, constituted the outline of the present book. Then in connection with a collaborative attempt to clarify some of the theoretical fundamentals of the whole field involved in sociology, social anthropology and social psychology, I was given leave of absence from Harvard teaching for the fall term of 1949-50. Starting in the summer of 1949, and continuing in the fall while group discussions were proceeding, I made it my principal contribution to the early phase of this project to work on the first draft of the long projected book.

The work of this broader project, particularly since it proceeded in such a stimulating atmosphere of group discussion, entailed reappraisal of many of the fundamentals of the action frame of reference as they underlay, not only sociological theory, but the

[2] See esp. *Social Theory and Social Structure*.

other disciplines of the social relations field. Late in November of 1949 this rethinking of the underlying frame of reference reached a culmination out of which the volume to be published as the most direct result of the broader theoretical project mentioned above took shape. My principal personal contribution to that, the monograph written together with Edward Shils under the title *Values, Motives and Systems of Action* constitutes essentially a new and extended statement of the theoretical subject matter of the *Structure of Social Action*. Indeed, if that title had not already been preempted it might have been the most appropriate for the monograph.

The work which has resulted in the writing of the general monograph on systems of action thus bears a critically important relation to the present volume. In the first place it has necessitated far more extensive revision of the first draft of the present book (more than three fourths of what had been projected stood in first draft) than would ordinarily have been the case. As a result this is a greatly different and I think a far better book than it would have been. The monograph also provides, in readily accessible form, a careful and systematic analysis of many of the methodological problems, and general problems of the theory of action and of its personality and cultural phases, which underlie or are intimately related to, the subject of this book at many points. It thus relieves this volume of a serious burden and frees it for concentration on its central problems. In a sense this book should, therefore, be treated as a second volume of a systematic treatise on the theory of action of which the monograph would serve as the first.

The body of the monograph consists of four long chapters. The first outlines the fundamentals of the general conceptual scheme of action, the other three spelling it out for each of the three modes of systematization of action, Personality, Cultural Systems with special reference to systems of Value-orientation, and Social Systems. Thus in a sense the present volume is to be regarded as an expansion of the chapter on the Social System in the monograph, though it also impinges on other important parts of the latter.

When an author is involved in two such closely related and nearly simultaneous publications, each of which is designed to be read independently, it would seem that a certain amount of overlapping is inevitable. An attempt, however, has been made to minimize this. The first chapter of the present book contains a condensed statement of the essentials of the structure of action and of action systems, and of the basic interrelations of personality, culture and social systems. The reader who finds this statement overly condensed will find the problems much more extensively discussed in the monograph. Obviously, further, much of the content of the chapter in the monograph on the Social System finds its place in this volume also, but this time in greatly expanded form, and with much more illustrative material. Finally, a special attempt has been made in this volume to deal systematically with the interrelations of the social system both with personality and with culture. Here the main difference from the monograph lies in the consistent maintenance of the perspective of relevance to the structure and functioning of social systems wherever personality and culture are discussed. A complete treatment of the theory of basic social science as here conceived would require two further volumes parallel to the present one.

Another difference between the two publications lies in the fact that most of the material of the present book was, in its final form, written somewhat later than the text of the monograph. The development of theoretical ideas has been proceeding so rapidly that a difference of a few months or even weeks in time may lead to important changes, so there are some differences in the positions taken in the two publications. Indeed this process of development is such that it inevitably affects even the internal consistency of the present book. It is not possible to work intensively on one part without implications of the changes introduced arising for other points; the process of revision thus never fully catches up with itself. In general the reader may expect to find some of this less than perfect consistency. I have thought it better to run this risk and get the book published, rather than to work it over and over for too long. It can then get the benefit of critical discussion, and then, within a relatively short time, a revision may be attempted. It is fully expected that such a revision in, say, about five years, will lead to substantial changes. The field is in a process of such rapid development as to make this inevitable.

A volume produced under the circumstances just outlined owes more than the usual debt to others. My heaviest direct obligation is to Edward Shils, co-author of the monograph on *Values, Motives and Systems of Action*. It is quite impossible to disentangle our individual contributions to the monograph and much of this joint thinking has spilled over into the present volume. Also very important is the debt to Edward Tolman in the many long discussions we had during the collaborative project, and to Richard Sheldon who participated in many of them.

In the background of course lies the immense influence of the great founders of modern social science, of whom the three major figures of my previous studies, Pareto, Durkheim and Max Weber, stand out, and in addition to them especially Freud. Over the years there has been an outstandingly important influence of association with colleagues, especially with Clyde and Florence Kluckhohn, in the problems of culture and its relation to society and of Henry A. Murray and Gordon W. Allport in relation to personality and social psychology. In the more centrally sociological field many discussions with Samuel A. Stouffer, Robert K. Merton, Florence Kluckhohn, and Robert Freed Bales and Francis X. Sutton in particular have been most fruitful.

Not least important have been many discussions with a succession of able students—these are too numerous for more than a few to be mentioned, but a sub-committee of a seminar on Social Structure which included François Bourricaud, Renée Fox, Miriam Massey, Rev. John V. Martin, Robert N. Wilson and Dr. Lyman Wynne may be especially singled out, since as a group we canvassed together many of the problems of motivational process in the social system.

A considerable part of the work of this volume was done as part of the general project on the theoretical foundations of the field of Social Relations in connection with which Professors Tolman and Shils were brought to Harvard. It therefore shared the benefits of the financial support given to that project by the Carnegie Corporation of New York and the Harvard Laboratory of Social Relations. This help is hereby gratefully acknowledged.

Finally, the secretary of the Department of Social Relations, Miss Weymouth Yelle, competently supervised the clerical work involved in processing of the manuscript, the actual processing being done by Mr. Seymour Katz and Mrs. Norman F. Geer. The index was prepared by Mr. Stuart Cleveland. The author's gratitude for effective performance of these indispensable services is hereby recorded.

TALCOTT PARSONS.

Cambridge, Mass.
February, 1951

CONTENTS

xiii

Contents

I THE ACTION FRAME OF REFERENCE AND THE GENERAL THEORY OF ACTION SYSTEMS: CULTURE, PERSONALITY AND THE PLACE OF SOCIAL SYSTEMS

THE subject of this volume is the exposition and illustration of a conceptual scheme for the analysis of social systems in terms of the action frame of reference. It is intended as a theoretical work in a strict sense. Its direct concern will be neither with empirical generalization as such nor with methodology, though of course it will contain a considerable amount of both. Naturally the value of the conceptual scheme here put forward is ultimately to be tested in terms of its usefulness in empirical research. But this is not an attempt to set forth a systematic account of our empirical knowledge, as would be necessary in a work on general sociology. The focus is on a theoretical scheme. The systematic treatment of its empirical uses will have to be undertaken separately.

The fundamental starting point is the concept of social systems of action. The *interaction* of individual actors, that is, takes place under such conditions that it is possible to treat such a process of interaction as a system in the scientific sense and subject it to the same order of theoretical analysis which has been successfully applied to other types of systems in other sciences.

The fundamentals of the action frame of reference have been extensively dealt with elsewhere and need only to be briefly sum-

3

marized here.[1] The frame of reference concerns the "orientation" of one or more actors—in the fundamental individual case biological organisms—to a situation, which includes other actors. The scheme, that is, relative to the units of action and interaction, is a *relational* scheme. It analyzes the structure and processes of the systems built up by the relations of such units to their situations, including other units. It is not as such concerned with the *internal* structure of the units except so far as this directly bears on the relational system.

The situation is defined as consisting of objects of orientation, so that the orientation of a given actor is differentiated relative to the different objects and classes of them of which his situation is composed. It is convenient in action terms to classify the object world as composed of the three classes of "social," "physical," and "cultural" objects. A social object is an actor, which may in turn be any given other individual actor (alter), the actor who is taken as a point of reference himself (ego), or a collectivity which is treated as a unit for purposes of the analysis of orientation. Physical objects are empirical entities which do not "interact" with or "respond" to ego. They are means and conditions of his action. Cultural objects are symbolic elements of the cultural tradition, ideas or beliefs, expressive symbols or value patterns so far as they are treated as situational objects by ego and are not "internalized" as constitutive elements of the structure of his personality.

"Action" is a process in the actor-situation system which has motivational significance to the individual actor, or, in the case of a collectivity, its component individuals. This means that the orientation of the corresponding action processes has a bearing on the attainment of gratifications or the avoidance of deprivations of the relevant actor, whatever concretely in the light of the relevant personality structures these may be. Only in so far as his relation to the situation is in this sense motivationally relevant will it be treated in this work as action in a technical sense. It is presumed that the ultimate source of the energy or "effort" factor of action processes is derived from the organism, and correspondingly that in

---

[1] Cf. especially Parsons and Shils, *Values, Motives and Systems of Action* in *Toward a General Theory of Action.* Also Parsons, *Structure of Social Action,* and *Essays in Sociological Theory,* and, of course, Weber, *Theory of Social and Economic Organization.*

some sense all gratification and deprivation have an organic significance. But though it is rooted in them the concrete organization of motivation cannot for purposes of action theory be analyzed in terms of the organic needs of the organism. This organization of action elements is, for purposes of the theory of action, above all a function of the relation of the actor to his situation and the history of that relation, in this sense of "experience."

It is a fundamental property of action thus defined that it does not consist only of ad hoc "responses" to particular situational "stimuli" but that the actor develops a *system* of "expectations" relative to the various objects of the situation. These *may* be structured only relative to his own need-dispositions and the probabilities of gratification or deprivation contingent on the various alternatives of action which he may undertake. But in the case of interaction with social objects a further dimension is added. Part of ego's expectation, in many cases the most crucial part, consists in the probable *r*eaction of alter to ego's possible action, a reaction which comes to be anticipated in advance and thus to affect ego's own choices.

On both levels, however, various elements of the situation come to have special "meanings" for ego as "signs" or "symbols" which become relevant to the organization of his expectation system. Especially where there is social interaction, signs and symbols acquire common meanings and serve as media of communication between actors. When symbolic systems which can mediate communication have emerged we may speak of the beginnings of a "culture" which becomes part of the action systems of the relevant actors.

It is only with systems of interaction which have become differentiated to a cultural level that we are here concerned. Though the term social system may be used in a more elementary sense, for present purposes this possibility can be ignored and attention confined to systems of interaction of a plurality of individual actors oriented to a situation and where the system includes a commonly understood system of cultural symbols.

Reduced to the simplest possible terms, then, a social system consists in a plurality of individual actors interacting with each other in a situation which has at least a physical or environmental aspect, actors who are motivated in terms of a tendency to the "optimization of gratification" and whose relation to their situations, including each other, is defined and mediated in terms of a system of culturally structured and shared symbols.

Thus conceived, a social system is only one of three aspects of the structuring of a completely concrete system of social action. The other two are the personality systems of the individual actors and the cultural system which is built into their action. Each of the three must be considered to be an independent focus of the organization of the elements of the action system in the sense that no one of them is theoretically reducible to terms of one or a combination of the other two. Each is indispensable to the other two in the sense that without personalities and culture there would be no social system and so on around the roster of logical possibilities. But this interdependence and interpenetration is a very different matter from reducibility, which would mean that the important properties and processes of one class of system could be theoretically *derived* from our theoretical knowledge of one or both of the other two. The action frame of reference is common to all three and this fact makes certain "transformations" between them possible. But on the level of theory here attempted they do not constitute a single system, however this might turn out to be on some other theoretical level.

Almost another way of making this point is to say that on the present level of theoretical systematization our dynamic knowledge of action-processes is fragmentary. Because of this we are forced to use these types of empirical system, descriptively presented in terms of a frame of reference, as an indispensable point of reference. In relation to this point of reference we conceive dynamic processes as "mechanisms"[2] which influence the "functioning" of the system. The descriptive presentation of the empirical system must be made in terms of a set of "structural" categories, into which the appropriate "motivational" constructs necessary to constitute a usable knowledge of mechanisms are fitted.

Before going further into some of these broad methodological problems of the analysis of systems of action with special reference to the social system, it is advisable to say something more about the

[2] A mechanism as the term will here be used is an empirical generalization about motivational processes stated in terms of its relevance to the functional problems of an action system. See below, Chapter VI.

more elementary components of action in general. In the most general sense the "need-disposition" system of the individual actor seems to have two most primary or elementary aspects which may be called the "gratificational" aspect and the "orientational" aspect. The first concerns the "content" of his interchange with the object world, "what" he gets out of his interaction with it, and what its "costs" to him are. The second concerns the "how" of his relation to the object world, the patterns or ways in which his relations to it are organized.

Emphasizing the relational aspect we may refer to the former as "cathectic" orientation which means the significance of ego's relation to the object or objects in question for the gratification-deprivation balance of his personality. The most elementary and fundamental "orientational" category on the other hand, seems to be the "cognitive" which in its most general sense may be treated as the "definition" of the relevant aspects of the situation in their relevance to the actor's "interests." This is then the cognitive orientation aspect, or cognitive mapping in Tolman's sense.[3] Both these aspects must be present in anything which could be considered a unit of an action system, a "unit act."

But acts do not occur singly and discretely, they are organized in systems. The moment even the most elementary system-level is brought under consideration a component of "system integration" must enter in. In terms of the action frame of reference again this integration is a selective ordering among the possibilities of orientation. Gratification needs have alternatively possible objects presented in the situation. Cognitive mapping has alternatives of judgment or interpretation as to what objects are or what they "mean." There must be ordered selection among such alternatives. The term "evaluation" will be given to this process of ordered selection. There is, therefore, an evaluative aspect of all concrete action orientation. The most elementary components of any action system then may be reduced to the actor and his situation. With regard to the actor our interest is organized about the cognitive, cathectic and evaluative modes of his orientation; with regard to the situation, to its differentiation into objects and classes of them.

The three basic modes of motivational orientation along with
[3] Cf. E. C. Tolman, *Purposive Behavior in Animals and Men.*

the conception of an object system categorize the elements of action on the broadest level. They are all three implicated in the structure of what has been called "expectation." Besides cathectic interests, cognitive definition of the situation and evaluative selection, an expectation has, as the term suggests, a time aspect in the orientation to future development of the actor-situation system and to the memory of past actions. Orientation to the situation is *structured,* that is, with reference to its developmental patterns. The actor acquires an "investment" in certain possibilities of that development. It matters to him how it occurs, that some possibilities should be realized rather than others.

This temporal dimension of the actor's concern with the development of the situation may be differentiated along an activity-passivity coordinate. The actor may at one extreme simply "await developments" and not actively attempt to "do anything about it," or he may actively attempt to control the situation in conformity with his wishes or interests. A future state of the actor-situation system in which the actor takes merely a passive interest, may be called an "anticipation," while a future state which he attempts actively to bring about (including the prevention of events he does not want to happen) may be called a "goal." The goal-directedness of action is, as we shall see, particularly when the bases of normative orientation have been discussed, a fundamental property of all action-systems. Analytically, however, it seems to stand on the next level "down" from the concept of expectations because of the logical possibility of passively anticipatory orientation. Both types must be clearly distinguished from "stimulus-response" in that the latter does not make the orientation to the future development of the situation explicit. The stimulus may be conceived that is, as coming completely "out of the blue" without affecting the theoretical analysis.

The fundamental concept of the "instrumental" aspects of action is applicable only to cases where the action is positively goal-oriented. It formulates those considerations about the situation and the actor's relations to it, the alternatives open to him and their probable consequences, which are relevant to the attainment of a goal.[4]

[4] In *The Structure of Social Action,* the exposition of the action frame of reference was made largely on the level of goal-direction and thus an "end" as it

A word may be said about the problem of the ultimate structuring of "gratification-needs." A general theory of action will, of course, eventually have to come to decisions about the unity or the qualitative plurality of the ultimate genetically given needs and their classification and organization. Particularly, however, for a work concerned with the social system level of action theory it is highly advisable scrupulously to observe the rule of parsimony in such controversial areas. It is, however, necessary to assume an ultimate polarity of this need structure which is incorporated in the concept of the gratification-deprivation balance, and has its derivatives in such antitheses as attraction-aversion. Beyond this, however, and certain general statements about the relations of need-gratification and the other aspects of action it does not, for our purposes, seem necessary to go in highly general terms.

The major reason for this is that in their sociologically relevant forms, "motivations" come to us as organized on the personality level. We deal, that is, with more concrete structures which are conceived as products of the interaction of genetically given need-components with social experience. It is the uniformities on this level which are empirically significant for sociological problems. To make use of knowledge of such uniformities it is generally not necessary to unravel the genetic and the experiential components underlying them. The principal exception to this statement arises in connection with problems of the limits of social variability in the structure of social systems which may be imposed by the biological constitution of the relevant population. Of course when such problems arise it is necessary to mobilize all the available evidence to form a judgment about more specific gratification needs.

A related problem is that of the relevance not only of gratification needs, but of capacities or abilities. Every empirical analysis of action presumes biologically given capacities. We know that these

---

was there called, was made an essential component of the "unit act." It seems that it is necessary to push the analysis to a still more elementary level especially in order to clarify the place in which many of the problems of motivation as analyzed in terms of modern psychology must be fitted in. However, no fundamental change has been made. The analysis has simply been carried to a more generalized level. The unit act of *The Structure of Social Action* is a special case of the unit of action as portrayed here and in *Values, Motives, and Systems of Action*.

are highly differentiated as between individuals. But for the most general theoretical purposes the same rule of parsimony may be applied. The soundness of this procedure is confirmed by the knowledge that individual variations are by and large more important than those between large populations so that it is relatively unlikely that the most important differences of large-scale social systems are primarily determined by biological differences in the capacities of their populations. For most sociological purposes the resultant of the genes and life experience is adequate without attempting to segregate out the factors.

It was pointed out that even the most elementary orientation of action on animal levels involves signs which are at least the beginning of symbolization. This is inherent in the concept of expectation which involves some sort of "generalization" from the particularities of an immediately current stimulus-situation. Without signs the whole "orientational" aspect of action would be meaningless, including the conceptions of "selection" and underlying it, of "alternatives." On the human level certainly the step is taken from sign-orientation to true symbolization. This is the necessary condition for the emergence of culture.

In the basic scheme of action, symbolization is clearly involved both in cognitive orientation and in the concept of evaluation. Further elaboration of the role and structure of symbol systems in action involves considerations of differentiation in relation to the various aspects of the action system, and the aspect of sharing and its relation to communication and to culture. The latter may be dealt with first.

Whatever the importance of neurological prerequisites may be, it seems probable that true symbolization as distinguished from the use of signs, cannot arise or function without the interaction of actors, and that the individual actor can acquire symbolic systems only through interaction with social objects. It is at least suggestive that this fact may well be connected with the element of "double contingency" involved in the interaction process. In the classical animal learning situations the animal has alternatives between which he makes a selection and develops expectations which can be "triggered" by certain signs or "cues." But the sign is part of a situation which is stable independently of what the animal does;

the only "problem" presented to him is whether he can "interpret" it correctly, e.g., that the black panel means food, the white one no food. But in social interaction alter's possible "reactions" may cover a considerable range, selection within which is contingent on ego's actions. Thus for the interaction process to become structured, the meaning of a sign must be further abstracted from the particularity of the situation. Its meaning, that is, must be stable through a much wider range of "ifs," which covers the contingent alternatives not only of ego's action, but of alter's and the possible permutations and combinations of the relation between them.

Whatever may be the origins and processes of development of symbol systems it is quite clear that the high elaboration of human action systems is not possible without relatively stable symbolic systems where meaning is not predominantly contingent on highly particularized situations. The most important single implication of this generalization is perhaps the possibility of communication, because the situations of two actors are *never* identical and without the capacity to abstract meaning from the most particular situations communication would be impossible. But in turn this stability of a symbol system, a stability which must extend between individuals and over time, could probably not be maintained unless it functioned in a communication process in the interaction of a plurality of actors. It is such a shared symbolic system which functions in interaction which will here be called a *cultural tradition*.

There is a fundamental relation between this aspect and the "normative orientation" of action as it is often called. A symbolic system of meanings is an element of order "imposed" as it were on the realistic situation. Even the most elementary communication is not possible without some degree of conformity to the "conventions" of the symbolic system. Put a little differently, the mutuality of expectations is oriented to the shared *order* of symbolic meanings. In so far as ego's gratifications become dependent on the reactions of alter, a conditional standard comes to be set up of what conditions will and what will not call forth the "gratifying" reactions, and the relation between these conditions and the reactions becomes as such part of the meaning system of ego's orientation to the situation. The orientation to a normative order, and the mutual interlocking of expectations and sanctions which will be fundamental to our analysis of social systems is rooted, therefore, in the deepest fundamentals of the action frame of reference.

This fundamental relationship is also common to all types and modes of interactional orientation. But nevertheless it is important to work out certain differentiations in terms of the relative primacies of the three modal elements, the cathectic, the cognitive and the evaluative, which have been outlined above. An element of a shared symbolic system which serves as a criterion or standard for selection among the alternatives of orientation which are intrinsically open in a situation may be called a value.

In one sense "motivation" consists in orientation to improvement of the gratification-deprivation balance of the actor. But since action without cognitive and evaluative components in its orientation is inconceivable within the action frame of reference, the term motivation will here be used to include all three aspects, not only the cathectic. But from this motivational orientation aspect of the totality of action it is, in view of the role of symbolic systems, necessary to distinguish a "value-orientation" aspect. This aspect concerns, not the meaning of the expected state of affairs to the actor in terms of his gratification-deprivation balance but the content of the selective standards themselves. The concept of value-orientations in this sense is thus the logical device for formulating one central aspect of the articulation of cultural traditions into the action system.

It follows from the derivation of normative orientation and the role of values in action as stated above, that all values involve what may be called a social reference. In so far as they are cultural rather than purely personal they are in fact shared. Even if idiosyncratic to the individual they are still by virtue of the circumstances of their genesis, defined in relation to a shared cultural tradition; their idiosyncrasies consist in specifiable departures from the shared tradition and are defined in this way.

However, along with this social reference, value standards may also be differentiated in terms of their functional relations to the action of the individual. The social reference implies, from the motivational side, an evaluative significance for all value standards. But still the *primary* relevance of a standard may be to cognitive definitions of the situation, to cathectic "expressions" or to the integration of the action system as a system or of some part of it. Hence on the value-orientation side we may repeat the three-fold classification of "modes" of orientation as *cognitive* standards, *appreciative* standards and *moral* standards of value-orientation.

A word of explanation of these terms is in order. The classification, as noted, corresponds to that of the modes of motivational orientation. In the cognitive case there is not much difficulty. On the motivational side the concern is with the cognitive interest in the situation and its objects, the motivation to define the situation cognitively. On the value-orientation side, on the other hand, concern is with the standards by which the validity of cognitive judgments is assessed. Some of these, like the most elementary standards of logic or correctness of observation may be cultural universals, while other elements are culturally variable. In any case it is a matter of selective evaluation, of standards of preference between alternative solutions of cognitive problems, or alternative interpretations of phenomena and objects.

The normative aspect of cognitive orientation is readily taken for granted. In the case of cathexes this is not so obvious. There is of course a sense in which the actor's relation to an object just is or is not gratifying in a given way. But it must not be forgotten that gratification takes place as part of an action system where actors are in general normatively oriented. It is out of the question that this one aspect should be exempted from the relevance of normative standards of valuation. There is always a question of the rightness and the propriety of the orientation in this respect, in terms of choice of object, and of attitude toward the object. This, therefore, also involves standards by which selections among the possibilities of cathectic significance can be made.

Finally the evaluative aspect of motivational orientation also has its value-orientation counterpart. Evaluation is concerned with the problem of integrating the elements of an action system, fundamentally the "you can't eat your cake and have it" problem. Both cognitive and appreciative value standards are of course relevant to this. But every act has both cognitive and cathectic aspects. A primacy of cognitive interests, therefore, still leaves the problem of integrating the concrete action in terms of the relevance of cathectic interests and vice versa. There must, therefore, in an action system, be a paramount focus of evaluative standards which are neither cognitive as such nor appreciative as such, but involve a synthesis of both aspects. It has seemed appropriate to call these moral standards. In a sense they constitute the standards in terms of which more particular evaluations are themselves evaluated.

It should also be clear from the general character of action systems that moral standards in this sense have peculiarly a social relevance. This is because every action system, concretely is in one aspect a social system, even though the focus on personality is very important for certain purposes. The moral reference is by no means exclusively social, but without the social reference it is impossible to conceive a concrete action system as integrated in an overall sense. In particular from the point of view of any given actor, the definition of the patterns of mutual rights and obligations, and of the standards governing them in his interaction with others, is a crucial aspect of his general orientation to his situation. Because of this special relevance to the social system, moral standards become that aspect of value-orientation which is of greatest direct importance to the sociologist. We shall have much to say about them in the chapters which follow.

Though there is a direct parallel between this classification of value-orientation patterns and the classification of motivational orientations it is very important to be clear that these two basic aspects, or components of the action system are logically independent, not in the sense that both are not essential, but in the sense that the content under the two classifications may be independently variable. From the fact of a given "psychological" cathectic significance of an object one cannot infer the specific appreciative standards according to which the object is evaluated or vice versa. The classification of the modes of motivational orientation provides essentially a framework for analyzing the "problems" in which the actor has an "interest." Value-orientation, on the other hand, provides the standards of what constitute satisfactory "solutions" of these problems. The clear recognition of the independent variability of these two basic modes or levels of orientation is at the very basis of a satisfactory theory in the field of "culture and personality." Indeed it can be said that failure to recognize this independent variability has underlain much of the difficulty in this field, particularly the unstable tendency of much social science to oscillate between "psychological determinism" and "cultural determinism." Indeed, it may be said that this independent variability is the logical foundation of the independent significance of the theory of the social system vis-à-vis that of personality on the one hand and of culture on the other.

Perhaps the point may first be discussed briefly in relation to the problem of culture. In anthropological theory there is not what could be called close agreement on the definition of the concept of culture. But for present purposes three prominent keynotes of the discussion may be picked out: first, that culture is *transmitted*, it constitutes a heritage or a social tradition; secondly, that it is *learned*, it is not a manifestation, in particular content, of man's genetic constitution; and third, that it is *shared*. Culture, that is, is on the one hand the product of, on the other hand a determinant of, systems of human social interaction.

The first point, transmissibility, serves as a most important criterion for distinguishing culture from the social system, because culture can be diffused from one social system to another. Relative to the particular social system it is a "pattern" element which is both analytically and empirically abstractable from that particular social system. There is crucially important interdependence between cultural patterns and the other elements of the social system, but these other elements are not completely "pattern-integrated" with culture or with each other.

On the basis of the approach to culture taken above, the broad reasons for this complication are not far to seek. A symbolic system has modes of integration of its own, which may be called "pattern consistency." The most familiar example is the logical consistency of a cognitive system, but art styles and systems of value-orientation are subject to the same kind of criteria of integration as a system in pattern terms. Examples of such symbolic systems are, of course, empirically familiar as in a philosophical treatise or a work of art.

But as an integral part of a concrete system of social interaction this norm of pattern-consistent integration of a cultural system can only be approximately realized, because of strains arising out of the imperatives of interdependence with the situational and motivational elements of concrete action. This problem may be approached through certain considerations having to do with the "learning" of a culture pattern.

This very common expression in anthropological literature seems to derive originally from the model of the learning of intellectual content. But it has been extended to become the common term for the process by which the requisite integration of an element of culture in the concrete action of an individual comes to be motivated. One can in these terms learn to read a language, to solve mathematical problems by use of the differential calculus. But one also learns to conform with a norm of behavior or to value an art style. Learning in this broad sense, then, means the incorporation of cultural pattern elements into the action-systems of individual actors.

The analysis of capacity to learn then comes up against the problem of the place the cultural item in question can assume in the personality system. *One* aspect of this problem is its compatibility with the other elements of culture which the same individual has already learned or is expected to learn. But there are others. Each individual actor is a biological organism acting in an environment. Both the genetic constitution of the organism and the non-socio-cultural environment set limits to this learning, though these limits are very difficult to specify. And finally each individual actor is subject to the exigencies of interaction in a social system. This last consideration is peculiarly important to the problem of culture because of the shared aspect of a cultural tradition. Such a tradition must be "borne" by one or more concrete social systems and can only be said to "function" when it is part of their actual action systems.

In action terms this problem may be summed up as that of whether a completely pattern-consistent cultural system can be related to the exigencies both of personalities and of the social system in such a way that complete "conformity" with its standards can be adequately motivated among all the individual actors in the social system. Here it may be merely asserted without any attempt to demonstrate, that such a limiting case is incompatible with the fundamental functional imperatives both of personalities and of social systems. The integration of the total action system, partial and incomplete as it is, is a kind of "compromise" between the "strains to consistency" of its personality, social and cultural components respectively, in such a way that no one of them closely approaches "perfect" integration. With respect to the relation between culture and the social system this problem will have to be discussed in some detail below. The crucial point for the present is that the "learning" and the "living" of a system of cultural patterns by the actors in a social system, cannot be understood without the analysis of motivation in relation to concrete situations, not only on the level of personality theory, but on the level of the mechanisms of the social system.

There is a certain element of logical symmetry in the relations of the social system to culture on the one hand and to personality on the other, but its implications must not be pressed too far. The deeper symmetry lies in the fact that both personalities and social systems are types of empirical action system in which both motivational and cultural elements or components are combined, and are thus in a sense parallel to each other. The basis of integration of the cultural system is, as has been noted, pattern-consistency. But that of personality is its structural pattern-consistency *plus* functional adequacy of motivational balance in a concrete situation. A cultural system does not "function" except as part of a concrete action system, it just "is."

It should be made quite clear that the relevance of interaction is not what distinguishes the social system from that of personality. Most emphatically interaction is just as much constitutive of personality as it is of a social system. It is rather the functional focus of organization and integration which is the basis of the difference between personalities and social systems. Personality is the relational system of a living organism interacting with a situation. Its integrative focus is the organism-personality unit as an empirical entity. The mechanisms of the personality must be understood and formulated relative to the functional problems of this unit. The system of social relationships in which the actor is involved is not merely of situational significance, but is directly constitutive of the personality itself. But even where these relationships are socially structured in a uniform way for a group of individuals, it does not follow that the ways in which these uniform "roles" are structured are constitutive of each of the different personalities in the same way. Each is integrated into a different personality system, and therefore does not in a precise sense "mean the same thing" to any two of them. The relation of personality to a uniform role structure is one of interdependence and interpenetration but not one of "inclusion" where the properties of the personality system are constituted by the roles of which it is allegedly "made up."

There are, as we shall see, important homologies between the personality and the social system. But these are homologies, not a macrocosm-microcosm relationship—the distinction is fundamental. Indeed, failure to take account of these considerations has lain at the basis of much of the theoretical difficulty of social psychology, especially where it has attempted to "extrapolate" from the psychology of the individual to the motivational interpretation of mass phenomena, or conversely has postulated a "group mind."

It follows from these considerations that both the structure of social systems and the motivational mechanisms of their functioning must be categorized on a level independent both of personality and of culture. Roughly stated, tempting though such a procedure is, trouble arises from the attempt either to treat social structure as a part of culture or to treat "social motivation" as applied psychology in the sense that it is a direct application of personality theory.

The correct formula is different. It is that the fundamental building stones of the theory of social systems, like those of personality and culture theory, are common to *all* the sciences of action. This is true *not of some of them but of all of them.* But the ways in which these conceptual materials are to be built into theoretical structures is not the same in the cases of the three major foci of action theory. Psychology, as the science of personality, is thus not the "foundation" of the theory of social systems, but *one* main branch of the great tree of action theory of which the theory of social systems is another. The common foundation is not the theory of the individual as the unit of society, but of action as the "stuff" out of which both personality systems and social systems are built up. It will be the task of later chapters to document this statement from the special point of view of analyzing certain aspects of the interdependence of social systems both with personalities and with cultural systems.

The focus of this work, then, is, within the action frame of reference as just outlined, on the theory of social systems. It is concerned both with personality and with culture, but not for their own sakes, rather in their bearing on the structure and functioning of social systems. Within systems of action the social system is, as has been noted, an independent focus both of realistic empirical organization of action and of theoretical analysis.

Because empirical organization of the system is a fundamental focus, the norm, as it were, must be the conception of an empirically self-subsistent social system. If we add the consideration of duration sufficiently long to transcend the life span of the normal human individual, recruitment by biological reproduction and socialization of the oncoming generation become essential aspects of such a social system. A social system of this type, which meets all the essential functional prerequisites of long term persistence from within its own resources, will be called a *society*. It is not essential to the concept of a society that it should not be in any way empirically interdependent with other societies, but only that it should contain all the structural and functional fundamentals of an independently subsisting system.

Any other social system will be called a "partial" social system. Obviously most empirical sociological studies are concerned with partial social systems rather than with societies as wholes. This is entirely legitimate. But using the society as a "norm" in the theory of social systems ensures that a conceptual scheme will be developed for explicitly and systematically placing the partial social system in question in the setting of the society of which it is a part. It thereby becomes much more unlikely that the investigator will overlook essential features of the society outside the partial social system which are prerequisites of the properties of the latter. It goes almost without saying that it is always of the greatest importance to specify what the system is which is being used as the object for a sociological analysis, whether or not it is a society, and if not, just how this particular partial social system is located in the society of which it is a part.

It has been remarked several times above that we are not in a position to develop a complete dynamic theory in the action field and that, therefore, the systematization of theory in the present state of knowledge must be in "structural-functional" terms. A brief elucidation of the meaning and implications of this proposition is advisable before turning to the substantive analysis.

It may be taken for granted that all scientific theory is concerned with the analysis of elements of uniformity in empirical processes. This is what is ordinarily meant by the "dynamic" interest of theory. The essential question is how far the state of theory is developed to the point of permitting deductive transitions from one aspect or state of a system to another, so that it is possible to say that if the facts in A sector are W and X, those in B sector must be Y and Z. In some parts of physics and chemistry it is possible to extend the empirical coverage of such a deductive system quite widely. But in the sciences of action dynamic knowledge of this character is highly fragmentary, though by no means absent.

In this situation there is danger of losing all the advantages of systematic theory. But it is possible to retain some of them and at the same time provide a framework for the orderly growth of dynamic knowledge. It is as such a second best type of theory that the structural-functional level of theoretical systematization is here conceived and employed.

In the first place completely raw empiricism is overcome by describing phenomena as parts of or processes within systematically conceived empirical systems. The set of descriptive categories employed is neither ad hoc nor sheer common sense but is a carefully and critically worked out system of concepts which are capable of application to all relevant parts or aspects of a concrete system in a coherent way. This makes comparability and transition from one part and/or state of the system to another, and from system to system, possible. It is of the greatest importance that this set of descriptive categories should be such that the dynamic generalizations which will explain processes are directly a part of the theoretical system. This essentially is what the "motivational" aspect of the action frame of reference accomplishes. By conceiving the processes of the social system as action processes in the technical sense of the above discussion, it becomes possible to articulate with the established knowledge of motivation which has been developed in modern psychology and thereby, as it were, to tap an enormous reservoir of knowledge.

A particularly important aspect of our system of categories is the "structural" aspect. We simply are not in a position to "catch" the uniformities of dynamic process in the social system except here and there. But in order to give those we can catch a setting and to be in the most advantageous position to extend our dynamic knowledge we must have a "picture" of the system within which they fit, of the given relationships of its parts in a given state of the system, and, where changes take place, of what changes into what through what order of intermediate stages. The system of structural categories is the conceptual scheme which gives this setting for dynamic analysis. As dynamic knowledge is extended the *independent* explanatory significance of structural categories evaporates. But their scientific function is nonetheless crucial.

Therefore, one primary concern of this work must be with the categorization of the structure of social systems, the modes of structural differentiation within such systems, and the ranges of variability with reference to each structural category between systems. Precisely because of the fragmentary character of our dynamic knowledge, careful and systematic attention to these problems is of the highest urgency to sociology. But at the same time it should be made quite clear that this morphological interest is not an end in itself, but its products constitute an indispensable tool for other purposes.

If we have a sufficiently generalized system of categories for the systematic description and comparison of the structure of systems, then we have a setting within which we can mobilize our dynamic knowledge of motivational processes to maximum effect. But precisely relative to the problems which are of significance in social system terms, the knowledge we possess is both fragmentary and of very uneven and unequal analytical status. The most effective way of organizing it for our purposes is to bring it into relation to a scheme of points of reference relative to the social system. This is where the much-discussed concept of "function" comes in. We must, of course, "place" a dynamic process structurally in the social system. But beyond that we must have a test of the significance of generalizations relative to it. That test of significance takes the form of the "functional" relevance of the process. The test is to ask the question, what would be the differential consequences for the system of two or more alternative outcomes of a dynamic process? Such consequences will be found to fit into the terms of maintenance of stability or production of change, of integration or disruption of the system in some sense.

It is placing dynamic motivational processes in this context of functional significance for the system which provides the basis for the formulation of the concept mechanism as introduced above. Motivational dynamics in sociological theory, then, must take the form in the first instance of the formulation of mechanisms which "account for" the functioning of social systems, for the maintenance or breakdown of given structural patterns, for a typical process of transition from one structural pattern to another.

Such a mechanism is always an empirical generalization about the operation of motivational "forces" under the conditions stated. The analytical basis of such generalizations may, however, be extremely variable. Sometimes we may just know empirically that it goes this way, in other cases there may be deeper foundations for the generalization as in application of established laws of learning or operation of the mechanisms of defense on the personality level. But the formulation of the motivational problem in mechanism terms is essential to establish the *relevance* of whatever level of motivational knowledge may be available to the problems of functioning of a social system. For the scientific fruitfulness of a generalization this problem of relevance is just as important as is that of the soundness of the generalization itself.

We may now outline the organization of the volume. Following the very brief presentation in the present chapter of the fundamentals of the frame of reference of action, the next chapter will take up the most essential components and points of reference for analysis of social systems as such, and will show the most general way in which these components come to be organized through the institutionalization of roles. There will then follow three chapters on the structure of social systems. The first of these will be concerned with the principal types of subsystem which enter into more complex social systems while the second and third will attempt to analyze the modes of differentiation and the ranges of structural variation of societies.

When this framework for the analysis of social process in relation to the structure of social systems and their variability has been laid down, attention will be turned to the analysis of process itself. This analysis will occupy two chapters, of which the first will be on the mechanisms of socialization, that is, the learning of patterns of orientation in social roles. The second of the two will then turn to the analysis of tendencies to deviant behavior, and of the mechanisms of social control which tend to counteract them.

Chapters VI and VII will thus be concerned with the motivational aspects of social behavior. The two chapters which follow these will turn to the cultural aspects. Patterns of value-orientation are so fundamental to the social system that they will have been dealt with throughout the general analysis of social structure. But to complete the analysis of the relations of culture to the social system it is necessary to discuss explicitly the place of the other two principal components of a cultural tradition, systems of beliefs or ideas, and systems of expressive symbols. These will be the subject-matter of Chapters VIII and IX respectively. There is a certain arbitrariness in the decision of whether the motivational or the cultural aspect should be treated first. The choice taken here is primarily dictated by the fact that in dealing with social structure value-orientation patterns had already been extensively analyzed. Before carrying the analysis of the relations of culture to the social system farther, it seemed advisable to give explicit attention to motivational process in order to make the significance of these other two classes of culture pattern for action clearer.

At this point a pause will be taken in the high level of sustained abstract analysis, to illustrate what has gone before in terms of a kind of case study, the analysis of certain highlights of modern medical practice considered as a partial social system. After this the last major theoretical task will be undertaken, the analysis of the problem of social change, with some illustrations of types of processes of such change.

The book will close with a very brief methodological stock-taking which will be concerned primarily with consideration of a definition of the scope of sociological theory and its relations to other conceptual schemes among the sciences of the action field.

II
THE MAJOR POINTS OF REFERENCE AND STRUCTURAL COMPONENTS OF THE SOCIAL SYSTEM

AS WE have seen in the preceding chapter, a social system is a mode of organization of action elements relative to the persistence or ordered processes of change of the interactive patterns of a plurality of individual actors. Regardless of the enormous variability in degrees of stability and structural integration of these interaction patterns, of their static character or involvement in processes of structural development or change, it is necessary for the present type of theoretical analysis to develop a scheme for the explicit analysis of the structure of such systems. This scheme must provide a fundamental set of points of reference for the analysis of motivational processes.

In the preceding chapter we outlined the general character of systems of action and their major components. Now we must undertake the specific spelling out of the theory of action in relation to social systems as such. The present chapter will focus on the general problems of the constitution of social systems and the bases of their structure, while those which follow it will deal with the problems of structural differentiation and variability.

First a word should be said about the units of social systems. In the most elementary sense the unit is the act. This is of course true, as was shown in the last chapter, of *any* system of action. The act then becomes a unit in a social system so far as it is part of a process of interaction between its author and other actors.

Secondly, for most purposes of the more macroscopic analysis of social systems, however, it is convenient to make use of a higher order unit than the act, namely the status-role as it will here be called. Since a social system is a system of processes of interaction between actors, it is the structure of the *relations* between the actors as involved in the interactive process which is essentially the structure of the social system. The system is a network of such relationships.

Each individual actor is involved in a plurality of such interactive relationships each with one or more partners in the complementary role. Hence it is the *participation* of an actor in a patterned interactive relationship which is for many purposes the most significant unit of the social system.

This participation in turn has two principal aspects. On the one hand there is the positional aspect—that of where the actor in question is "located" in the social system relative to other actors. This is what we will call his *status*, which is his place in the relationship system considered as a structure, that is a patterned system of *parts*. On the other hand there is the processual aspect, that of what the actor does in his relations with others seen in the context of its functional significance for the social system. It is this which we shall call his *role*.

The distinction between status and role is at the root very closely related to that between the two reciprocal perspectives inherent in interaction. On the one hand each actor is an *object* of orientation for other actors (and for himself). In so far as this object-significance derives from his position in the social relationship system, it is a status significance. On the other hand each actor is oriented *to* other actors. In this capacity he is acting, not serving as an object—this is what we mean by his playing a role.

It should be made quite clear that statuses and roles, or the status-role bundle, are not in general attributes of the actor, but are *units* of the social system, though having a given status may sometimes be treated as an attribute. But the status-role is analogous to the particle of mechanics, not to mass or velocity.

Third, a word should be said about the sense in which the actor himself is a unit of the social system. As a *point of reference,* as he who holds a status or performs a role, the individual actor is always a significant unit which, however, for purposes of the analysis of social systems is to be treated as a higher order unit than the status-role. The actor in this sense is a composite *bundle* of statuses and roles. But this social actor must be distinguished from the personality as itself a system of action. This distinction derives from the mutual irreducibility of personality and social systems as discussed in the last chapter.

We have, then, three different units of social systems referable to the individual actor ranging from the most elementary to the most composite. The first is the social act, performed by an actor and oriented to one or more actors as objects. The second is the status-role as the organized sub-system of acts of the actor or actors occupying given reciprocal statuses and acting toward each other in terms of given reciprocal orientations. The third is the actor himself as a social unit, the organized system of all the statuses and roles referable to him as a social object and as the "author" of a system of role-activities.

Finally, cutting across the individual actor as a composite unit is the collectivity as actor and as object. Here the particular sectors of the action-systems of the relevant individual actors are abstracted from their other status-roles and treated together. Part of the significance of the status-role as a unit derives from the fact that it is the unit which is a unit both for the action system of the individual and for that of the collectivity. It thus serves to articulate the two cross-cutting modes of organization of social systems.

It is naturally extremely important to be clear which of these four units is meant when a social structure is broken down into units.

§ THE FUNCTIONAL PREREQUISITES OF SOCIAL SYSTEMS[1]

INTERACTIVE relationships analyzed in terms of statuses and roles occur as we have seen in systems. If such a system is to

[1] On the general problem of functional prerequisites of the social system see Aberle, Cohen, Davis, Levy, Sutton, "The Functional Prerequisites of a Society," *Ethics,* IX (January, 1950), 100-111. The present treatment is indebted to their paper but departs from it rather radically.

constitute a persistent order or to undergo an orderly[2] process of developmental change, certain functional prerequisites must be met. A brief discussion of these functional prerequisites is in order because it provides the setting for a more extended analysis of the points of reference for analyzing the structure of social systems.

The problem of functional prerequisites is a protean problem because of the variety of different levels on which it may be approached. What we propose here is to start on the most general and therefore formal level of action theory and proceed to introduce specifications step by step. It should be possible to do this in a sufficiently orderly fashion.

The broadest framework of such an analysis is directly deducible from the considerations about action in general which were put forward in the last chapter. The basis of this is the insight that action systems are structured about three integrative foci, the individual actor, the interactive system, and a system of cultural patterning.[3] Each implies the others and therefore the variability of any one is limited by its compatibility with the minimum conditions of functioning of each of the other two.

Looked at from the perspective of any one integrate of action such as the social system there are in turn two aspects of this reciprocal interrelation with each of the others. First, a social system cannot be so structured as to be radically incompatible with the conditions of functioning of its component individual actors as biological organisms and as personalities, or of the relatively stable integration of a cultural system. Secondly, in turn the social system, on both fronts, depends on the requisite minimum of "support" from each of the other systems. It must, that is, have a sufficient proportion of its component actors adequately motivated to act in accordance with the requirements of its role system, positively in the fulfillment of expectations and negatively in abstention from too much disruptive, i.e., deviant, behavior. It must on the other hand avoid commitment to cultural patterns which either fail to

[2] An orderly process in this sense is contrasted with the disintegration of a system. Disintegration in this sense means disappearance of the boundaries of the system relative to its environment. Cf. *Values, Motives, and Systems of Action*, Chapter I.

[3] And also in a different sense about the non-action environment, the physical aspects of the situation.

define a minimum of order or which place impossible demands on people and thereby generate deviance and conflict to a degree which is incompatible with the minimum conditions of stability or orderly development. These problems may be briefly taken up in turn.

We have tried to make clear that there is no simple relation between personalities and social systems. Because of this fact, in the present state of knowledge it is not possible to define precisely what are the minimum needs of individual actors, so only certain rather general things can be said. From the point of view of functioning of the social system, it is not the needs of all the participant actors which must be met, nor all the needs of any one, but only a sufficient proportion for a sufficient fraction of the population. It is indeed a very general phenomenon that social forces are directly responsible for injury to or destruction of some individuals and some of the wants or needs of all individuals, and though this may be reduced it is highly probable that it cannot be eliminated under realistic conditions. To cite a very simple case, a war cannot be won without casualties, and acceptance of war is sometimes a condition of survival of a social system as a distinctive system.

The elements of this class of functional prerequisites may be said to begin with the biological prerequisites of individual life, like nutrition and physical safety. They go on to the subtler problems of the conditions of minimum stability of personality. It seems to be reasonably well established that there are minimum conditions of socialization with respect for instance to the relation between affectional support and security, without which a functioning personality cannot be built up. The present task is not to attempt to analyze these borderline problems, but only to make clear where they fit in relation to the theory of the social system. These minimum needs of individual actors constitute a set of conditions to which the social system must be adapted. If the variation of the latter goes too far in a given direction this will tend to set up repercussions which will in turn tend to produce deviant behavior in the actors in question, behavior which is either positively disruptive or involves withdrawal from functionally important activities. Such a need, as a functional prerequisite, may be likened to a spring. The less adequately it is met, the more "pressure" it will take to realize certain patterns of social action in the face of it, and hence the less energy will be available for other purposes. At certain points for certain individuals or classes of them then the pressure may become too great and the spring may break—such persons no longer participate in the inter-active system of personality and social system.[4]

The obverse of the functional prerequisite of meeting a mini-mum proportion of the needs of the individual actors, is the need to secure adequate participation of a sufficient proportion of these actors in the social system, that is to motivate them adequately to the performances which may be necessary if the social system in question is to persist or develop. Indeed it is because it is a condi-tion of this that the need to satisfy minimum needs of actors is a prerequisite at all.

The prerequisite of adequate motivation in turn subdivides into two main aspects, a negative and a positive. The negative is that of a minimum of control over potentially disruptive behavior. This means action which interferes with the action of others in their roles in the social system. It may involve either aggressive action toward others or merely action which has deleterious consequences for others or for an aspect of the system, without aggressive intent.

The field is highly complex but perhaps one particular aspect of it may be singled out for special mention. This is that in terms of functional significance relative to the social system, the significance of an action or class of them is to be understood not directly and primarily in terms of its motivation but of its actual or probable consequences for the system. In this sense the pursuit of "private interests" may be highly disruptive under certain circumstances

[4] It is, of course, highly important not to invent ad hoc generalizations about these prerequisites which allegedly explain certain classes of concrete social phenomena. This procedure is especially tempting because such an ad hoc hypothe-sis can serve to absolve the investigator from the difficult analysis of the internal balances and processes of the social system itself. In its cruder forms this pro-cedure has played a very prominent part in the history of social thought, as in the currency of theories that virtually all social phenomena were determined by the genetic constitution of populations or their geographical environments. It is an index of the increasing maturity of our science that such sweeping formulae are no longer considered to merit even serious discussion. Both the positive role of such conditioning factors and of internal social processes are in general terms fully established. But the general formulae do not solve the specific problems. The task is to unravel the complex patterns of interaction between the two classes of factors.

even though the content of the interests, for example in religious terms, may be such as to be rather generally ethically approved. Similarly conflict as such may be highly disruptive. If it becomes sufficiently severe the functional problem for the system becomes the control of the conflict as such. In such a case the merits of the "case" of one or the other of the parties may become of quite secondary importance.

In general terms the functional problem for a social system of minimizing potentially disruptive behavior and the motivation to it, may be called the "motivational problem of order." Because of certain further features of social systems which will be analyzed in the following chapters the present discussion should lead up to consideration of certain relatively specific classes of potential disruption, notably the problem of opportunity, the problem of prestige allocation, and the problem of power. There is, that is to say, an immense variety of particular acts which are disruptive in that they interfere with the role-performance of one or more other actors. So long, however, as they remain nearly randomly distributed they may reduce the efficiency of the system by depressing levels of role performance, but still not constitute a threat to its stability. This latter may develop when disruptive tendencies become organized as a sub-system in such a way as to impinge on strategic points in the social system itself. It is as such strategic points that the problems of opportunity, prestige and power will be treated below.[5]

The distinction between the negative and the positive aspects of the problem of adequate motivation is relative and gradual. Both present functional problems in terms of the operation of the social system, which focus attention on the mechanisms which fit into the relevant context. But in spite of this relativity there is an important distinction between action which is positively disruptive of a going system of social relationships, and simple withdrawal of the individual from performance of his obligations. The principal criterion

---

[5] It is in this kind of a context that the distinction between manifest and latent function becomes significant. In general only within limited ranges and to a limited extent are the consequences which the sociologist takes as his standard for the analysis of the systemic significance of actions explicitly intended by the actor, individual or collective. It is these unintended consequences which constitute the latent functions or dysfunctions of the actions. Cf. Robert K. Merton, *Social Theory and Social Structure*, Chapter I.

would be that in the latter case the only interference with others would consist in forcing them to do without the benefits expected from a person's actions. The possibility of withdrawal in fact defines one of the most important directions of deviant behavior, and enters as we shall see in most important ways into the structure of the problems and mechanisms of social control. Illness is for example one of the most important types of withdrawal behavior in our society, which will be extensively discussed below.

Again in relation to withdrawal as a type of failure to be motivated to adequate role performance, it must be made clear that the negative aspect of withdrawal is *not* defined in motivational terms but in functional terms relative to the social system. Precisely because people are dependent on each other's performances, simple withdrawal from fulfillment of expectations may, motivationally speaking, be a highly aggressive act, and may in fact injure the other severely. But in part precisely because it does not correspond to the motivational distinction the functional distinction is highly significant as will become evident. It provides a point of reference for the analysis of the directions of deviant behavior and hence places such behavior in relation to problems of the mechanisms of operation of the social system.

The prerequisite of adequate motivation gives us one of the primary starting points for building up to the concepts of role and of institutionalization. Fundamentally the problem is, will the personalities developed within a social system, at whatever stage in the life cycle, "spontaneously" act in such ways as to fulfill the functional prerequisites of the social systems of which they are parts, or is it necessary to look for relatively specific mechanisms, that is, modes of organization of the motivational systems of personalities, which can be understood in direct relation to the socially structured level or role behavior? The older "psychological" view that societies are resultants of the independently determined "traits" of individuals would take the first alternative. The modern sociological view tends to emphasize the second.

Statement of the problem of adequate motivation not only poses in general the problems of the mechanisms of socialization and of social control and their relation to the dynamics of the social system, but it provides the setting for an approach to the analysis of the relevant mechanisms. Personality psychology, as we have seen, is becoming highly oriented to the actor's relational system, that is, his orientation to objects. When this fact is combined with the fundamental place of the concept of expectations in the theory of action, it becomes clear that one central aspect of the general and especially the cathectic orientation of the actor is his set of need-dispositions toward the fulfillment of role expectations, in the first place those of other significant actors but also his own. There is, in the personality structure of the individual actor a "conformity-alienation" dimension in the sense of a disposition to conform with the expectations of others or to be alienated from them. When these relevant expectations are those relative to the fulfillment of role-obligations, this conformity-alienation balance, in general or in particular role contexts, becomes a central focus of the articulation of the motivational system of the personality with the structure of the social system.

It is furthermore in the present context of the problem of adequate motivation of role-expectation fulfillment that the basic significance for the social system of two fundamental properties of biological "human nature" may best be briefly brought to attention. The first of these is the much discussed "plasticity" of the human organism, its capacity to learn any one of a large number of alternative patterns of behavior instead of being bound by its genetic constitution to a very limited range of alternatives. It is of course within the limits of this plasticity that the independent determinant significance of cultural and social factors in action must be sought. The clear demonstration of determination in terms of the genes automatically narrows the range of relevance of the factors which are of theoretical interest in the sciences of action, except for their possible bearing on the problems of assortative mating which influence the processes of combination and recombination of genetic strains. The limits of plasticity are for the most part still unknown.[6]

[6] From the point of view of action theory and specifically that of the social system it may be said that the burden of proof rests upon him who would assert that what has been considered an action theory problem is adequately solved by invoking the role of such sub-action determinants of behavior. This will often turn out to be the case, but resort to ad hoc hypotheses on this level which have failed to stand up under criticism and further investigation, has been so prominent in the history of social science that we must insist on this burden of proof maxim.

The second characteristic of human nature in the biological sense is what may be called "sensitivity." By this is meant the accessibility of the human individual to influence by the attitudes of others in the social interaction process, and the resulting dependence on receiving relatively particular and specific reactions. What this provides essentially is the motivational basis for accessibility to influence in the learning process. Thus the attitudes of others are probably of first rate importance in all human learning, but are particularly crucial in motivating the acceptance of value-orientation patterns, with their legitimation of the renunciations which are essential to the achievement of a disciplined integration of personality. Without this discipline the stability of expectations in relation to their fulfillment which is essential for a functioning social system would not be possible. It is highly probable that one of the principal limitations on the social potentialities of animals on other than an instinct basis, lies in the absence or weakness of this lever. The physiological dependency of the human infant is associated with its capacity for developing emotional dependency which in turn is an essential condition of much of social learning.

It has not been common in discussions of the functional prerequisites of social systems to include explicit treatment of cultural prerequisites, but the need to do so seems to follow directly from the major premises of action theory as set forth above. The integration of cultural patterns as well as their specific content involve factors which at any given time are independent of the other elements for the action system and yet must be articulated with them. Such integration imposes "imperatives" on the other elements just as truly as is the case the other way around. This major functional problem area of the social system may be subdivided along the same lines as in the case of the motivational problem.

In the first place there are minimum social conditions necessary for the production, maintenance and development of cultural systems in general and of particular types of cultural system. It may be presumed that disruption of the communication system of a society is ultimately just as dangerous as disruption of its system of order in the above sense of motivational integration. This is an aspect of "anomie" which deserves much more explicit analysis than it has received. Perhaps the most obvious specific example is provided by the role of language. We know quite definitely that the individual does not develop language spontaneously without undergoing a socially structured learning process in relation to others. It is quite definite that this process must be part of a system of social relations which is orderly within certain limits, however difficult it may be to specify the limits in detail. It is altogether probable that many protohuman groups failed to make the transition to the human socio-cultural level of action because of failure to fulfill the prerequisites of the emergence of language or of some other functionally essential aspects of culture.

Thus a social system in the present sense is not possible without language, and without certain other minimum patterns of culture, such as empirical knowledge necessary to cope with situational exigencies, and sufficiently integrated patterns of expressive sym-bolism and of value orientation. A social system which leads to too drastic disruption of its culture, for example through blocking the processes of its acquisition, would be exposed to social as well as cultural disintegration.

We do not accurately know the cultural limits of "human so-ciety," so exactly what the above limits may be remains to be deter-mined. With respect to certain more specific types of cultural pat-tern, however, we have relatively detailed knowledge—we shall, for example, discuss modern science from this point of view below. In any case the determination of these conditions is an important field of sociological research.

One final remark in orientation to the general problem. Culture may of course be "embodied" in physical form independently of par-ticular actors, e.g., knowledge in books, but it is a cardinal principle of the theory of action that culture is not merely "situational" rela-tive to action but becomes directly constitutive of personalities as such through what personality psychologists now tend to call "in-ternalization." The minimum cultural prerequisites of a social sys-tem may thus be said to operate at least in part through the functions of culture for personality. Without the requisite cultural resources to be assimilated through internalization it is not possible for a human level of personality to emerge and hence for a human type of social system to develop.

The other aspect of the problem of prerequisites on the cultural side is that of adequate cultural resources and organization for the maintenance of the social system. This has already been touched upon in the discussions above, but a few additional remarks may be made. Perhaps the most obvious type of case is instrumental knowledge. Without a minimum of technical lore which makes it possible to deal with the physical environment and with other human beings no human society would be possible. This in turn presupposes language. But similar considerations also apply to the other departments of culture, to non-empirical existential ideas, to expressive symbol systems and above all to patterns of value-orientation about which much will have to be said in what follows.

It was pointed out above that tendencies to deviant behavior on the part of the component actors pose functional "problems" for the social system in the sense that they must be counteracted by "mechanisms of control" unless dysfunctional consequences are to ensue. The parallel on the cultural side is the case where the maintenance of certain cultural patterns as integral parts of the going system of action imposes certain strains. This may be true both on the personality and the social system levels. The most obvious cases are those of a value-orientation pattern and of cognitive beliefs which are motivationally difficult to conform with. Such difficulty might be attributable to a conflict with reality. Thus within the area covered by well established medical science the maintenance of and action upon some beliefs of Christian Science may impose a serious strain on the actor especially where he cannot escape knowing the medical views. Or it may be a matter of difficulty in attaining conformative motivation, as in the case where certain types of socialization tend to generate deeply anti-authoritarian sentiments so that at least some kinds of authority cannot be tolerated by some people. In particular a utopian ideal if accepted and institutionalized imposes strains on the social system.

Though the limits in this as in the other cases are in general not known, it is safe to say not only that the social system must be able to keep a minimum of culture going, but vice versa, any given culture must be compatible with a social system to a minimum degree if its patterns are not to become extinct, and if the latter is to continue functioning unchanged. Analysis of the mediating mechanisms between the cultural patterns and the concrete action systems in its motivational aspect constitutes one of the most important problem areas of action theory and specifically of the theory of social systems. This subject will be further explored in Chapters VIII and IX below.

§ THE INSTITUTIONAL INTEGRATION OF ACTION ELEMENTS

A CONCRETE action system is an integrated[7] structure of action elements in relation to a situation. This means essentially integration of motivational and cultural or symbolic elements, brought together in a certain kind of ordered system.

The analysis of the general features of action in the previous chapter, combined with the immediately preceding analysis of the functional prerequisites of social systems, yield certain specifications which can guide us to strategic features of this ordered structure.

It is inherent in an action system that action is, to use one phrase, "normatively oriented." This follows, as was shown, from the concept of expectations and its place in action theory, especially in the "active" phase in which the actor pursues goals. Expectations then, in combination with the "double contingency" of the process of interaction as it has been called, create a crucially imperative problem of order. Two aspects of this problem of order may in turn be distinguished, order in the symbolic systems which make communication possible, and order in the mutuality of motivational orientation to the normative aspect of expectations, the "Hobbesian" problem of order.

The problem of order, and thus of the nature of the integration of stable systems of social interaction, that is, of social structure, thus focuses on the integration of the motivation of actors with the normative cultural standards which integrate the action system, in

[7] We are here concerned with what has been called the "boundary-maintaining" type of system (*Values, Motives, and Systems of Action*, op. cit.). For this type of system, as noted there, the concept integration has a double reference: a) to the compatibility of the components of the system with each other so that change is not necessitated before equilibrium can be reached, and b) to the maintenance of the conditions of the distinctiveness of the system within its boundaries over against its environment. Integration may be relative to a moving equilibrium, i.e., an orderly process of change of the system, as well as to a static equilibrium.

our context interpersonally. These standards are, in the terms used in the preceding chapter, patterns of value-orientation, and as such are a particularly crucial part of the cultural tradition of the social system.[8]

The orientation of one actor to the contingent action of another inherently involves evaluative orientation, because the element of contingency implies the relevance of a system of alternatives. Stability of interaction in turn depends on the condition that the particular acts of evaluation on both sides should be oriented to common standards since only in terms of such standards is "order" in either the communication or the motivational contexts possible.

There is a range of possible modes of orientation in the motivational sense to a value-standard. Perhaps the most important distinction is between the attitude of "expediency" at one pole, where conformity or non-conformity is a function of the instrumental interests of the actor, and at the other pole the "introjection" or internalization of the standard so that to act in conformity with it becomes a need-disposition in the actor's own personality structure, relatively independently of any instrumentally significant consequences of that conformity. The latter is to be treated as the basic type of integration of motivation with a normative pattern-structure of values.

In order to justify this last proposition it is necessary to go somewhat further into the nature of the interaction process. In the case of a given actor, ego, there is soon built up a system of expectations relative to a given other, alter. With respect to alter's action this implies for ego hopes and anxieties, that is, some of alter's possible reactions will be favorable from ego's point of view and others unfavorable. By and large we are on psychological grounds justified in saying ego's orientation will on balance tend to be oriented to stimulating the favorable, gratification-producing reactions and avoiding provocations for the unfavorable, deprivation-producing reactions.

Generally, in so far as the normative standards in terms of which ego and alter are interacting are shared and clear, favorable reactions on the part of alter will tend to be stimulated by ego's action conforming with the standards in question, and the unfavorable, by his

[8] The other components of the cultural tradition pose somewhat different problems which will be taken up in the following section.

deviating from them (and vice versa of course). The result of this circumstance is the tendency for the conformity-deviation dimension and the favorable-unfavorable or the gratification-deprivation dimension to coincide. In other words the basic condition on which an interaction system can be stabilized is for the interests of the actors to be bound to conformity with a shared system of value-orientation standards.

There is in turn a two-fold structure of this "binding in." In the first place, by virtue of internalization of the standard, conformity with it tends to be of personal, expressive and/or instrumental significance to ego. In the second place, the structuring of the reactions of alter to ego's action as sanctions is a function of his conformity with the standard. Therefore conformity as a direct mode of the fulfillment of his own need-dispositions tends to coincide with conformity as a condition of eliciting the favorable and avoiding the unfavorable reactions of others. In so far as, relative to the actions of a plurality of actors, conformity with a value-orientation standard meets *both* these criteria, that is from the point of view of any given actor in the system, it is both a mode of the fulfillment of his own need-dispositions and a condition of "optimizing" the reactions of other significant actors, that standard will be said to be "institutionalized."

A value pattern in this sense is always institutionalized in an *inter*action context. Therefore there is always a double aspect of the expectation system which is integrated in relation to it. On the one hand there are the expectations which concern and in part set standards for the behavior of the actor, ego, who is taken as the point of reference; these are his "role-expectations." On the other hand, from his point of view there is a set of expectations relative to the contingently probable *re*actions of others (alters)—these will be called "sanctions," which in turn may be subdivided into positive and negative according to whether they are felt by ego to be gratification-promoting or depriving. The relation between role-expectations and sanctions then is clearly reciprocal. What are sanctions to ego are role-expectations to alter and vice versa.

A role then is a sector of the total orientation system of an individual actor which is organized about expectations in relation to a particular interaction context, that is integrated with a particular set of value-standards which govern interaction with one or more alters in the appropriate complementary roles. These alters need not be a defined group of individuals, but can involve any alter if and when he comes into a particular complementary interaction relationship with ego which involves a reciprocity of expectations with reference to common standards of value-orientation.

The institutionalization of a set of role-expectations and of the corresponding sanctions is clearly a matter of degree. This degree is a function of two sets of variables; on the one hand those affecting the actual sharedness of the value-orientation patterns, on the other those determining the motivational orientation or commitment to the fulfillment of the relevant expectations. As we shall see a variety of factors can influence this degree of institutionalization through each of these channels. The polar antithesis of full institutionalization is, however, *anomie,* the absence of structured complementarity of the interaction process or, what is the same thing, the complete breakdown of normative order in both senses. This is, however, a limiting concept which is never descriptive of a concrete social system. Just as there are degrees of institutionalization so are there also degrees of *anomie.* The one is the obverse of the other.

An *institution* will be said to be a complex of institutionalized role integrates[9] which is of strategic structural significance in the social system in question. The institution should be considered to be a higher order unit of social structure than the role, and indeed it is made up of a plurality of interdependent role-patterns or components of them. Thus when we speak of the "institution of property" in a social system we bring together those aspects of the roles of the component actors which have to do with the integration of action-expectations with the value-patterns governing the definition of rights in "possessions" and obligations relative to them. An institution in this sense should be clearly distinguished from a collectivity. A collectivity is a system of concretely interactive specific roles. An institution on the other hand is a complex of patterned elements in role-expectations which may apply to an indefinite number of collectivities. Conversely, a collectivity may be the focus of a whole series of institutions. Thus the institutions of marriage and of par-

---

[9] Or status-relationships. There are no roles without corresponding statuses and vice versa.

enthood are both constitutive of a particular family as a collectivity.

It is now necessary to go back to certain aspects of the integration of action elements in institutionalized roles. The starting point is the crucial significance of interaction and the corresponding complementarity of expectations. *What are expectations to ego are sanctions to alter and vice versa,* for among the expectations of any role, indeed the central part of them, are definitions of how its incumbent should act toward others, and these definitions are structured along the conformity-deviance dimension. The question of how far sanctions are *intended* by the actor who imposes them to influence the behavior of the other, or to "reward" his conformity and to "punish" his deviance, may remain an open question for the moment. The important point is that such intention is *not a criterion* of the concept of sanctions as here used. The criterion is merely that they are meaningful reactions of alter to what ego does.

Certain empirical generalizations seem to be established which can carry us somewhat farther in interpreting the dynamic significance of this reciprocal integration of role-expectations. The first derives from what was above called the "sensitivity" of the human personality to the attitudes of others. From this it follows that only in limiting cases will the significance of sanctions be purely instrumental, that is, will the probability of a given reaction be significant only as a set of expected conditions of the situation which influence the probability of successful attainment of a particular goal or the probable cost of its attainment. Conformity with role-expectations will always to a greater or less degree involve motivational elements of the character referred to in psychological discussions as composing the "ego-ideal" or the superego, elements of "self-respect," adequacy or "security" in the psychological sense. Such elements are not of course necessarily central for every concrete actor in every concrete situation which is connected with a set of institutionalized role-expectations. A particular individual or class of them may well become involved in an interaction situation in which their own "sentiments" are only very peripherally involved. But in a general sense in social situations, the circumstances of socialization and other factors preclude that this should be the predominant situation in permanent social systems which involve the major motivational interests of the participant actors. The focal case is that where the actor "cares" how others react to him in much more than a purely instrumental sense.

Considering that we are talking about the conditions of relatively stable interaction in social systems, it follows from this that the value-standards which define institutionalized role-expectations assume to a greater or less degree a moral significance. Conformity with them becomes, that is, to some degree a matter of the fulfillment of obligations which ego carries relative to the interests of the larger action system in which he is involved, that is a social system. The sharing of such common value patterns, entailing a sense of responsibility for the fulfillment of obligations, then creates a solidarity among those mutually oriented to the common values. The actors concerned will be said to constitute, within the area of relevance of these values, a *collectivity*.

For some classes of participants the significance of collectivity membership may be predominantly its usefulness in an instrumental context to their "private" goals. But such an orientation cannot be constitutive of the collectivity itself, and so far as it predominates, tends to disrupt the solidarity of the collectivity. This is *most emphatically not* to say that participation in a solidary collectivity tends in general to interfere with the attainment of the individual's private goals, but that without the attachment to the constitutive common values the collectivity tends to dissolve. If this attachment is given, there is room for much fulfillment of private interests.

Attachment to common values means, motivationally considered, that the actors have common "sentiments"[10] in support of the value patterns, which may be defined as meaning that conformity with the relevant expectations is treated as a "good thing" relatively independently of any specific instrumental "advantage" to be gained from such conformity, e.g., in the avoidance of negative sanctions. Furthermore, this attachment to common values, while it may fit the immediate gratificational needs of the actor, always has also a "moral" aspect in that to some degree this conformity defines the "responsibilities" of the actor in the wider, that is, social action system in which he participates. Obviously the specific focus of re-

[10] The term "sentiments" is here used to denote culturally organized cathectic and/or evaluative modes or patterns of orientation toward particular objects or classes of objects. A sentiment thus involves the internalization of cultural patterns.

sponsibility is the collectivity which is constituted by a particular common value-orientation.

Finally, it is quite clear that the "sentiments" which support such common values are not ordinarily in their specific structure the manifestation of constitutionally given propensities of the organism. They are in general learned or acquired. Furthermore, the part they play in the orientation of action is not predominantly that of cultural objects which are cognized and "adapted to" but the culture patterns have come to be internalized; they constitute part of the structure of the personality system of the actor itself. Such sentiments or "value-attitudes" as they may be called, are therefore genuine need-dispositions of the personality. It is only by virtue of internalization of institutionalized values that a genuine motivational integration of behavior in the social structure takes place, that the "deeper" layers of motivation become harnessed to the fulfillment of role-expectations. It is only when this has taken place to a high degree that it is possible to say that a social system is highly integrated, and that the interests of the collectivity and the private interests of its constituent members can be said to approach[11] coincidence.

This integration of a set of common value patterns with the internalized need-disposition structure of the constituent personalities is the core phenomenon of the dynamics of social systems. That the stability of any social system except the most evanescent interaction process is dependent on a degree of such integration may be said to be the fundamental dynamic theorem of sociology. It is the major point of reference for all analysis which may claim to be a dynamic analysis of social process.

It is the significance of institutional integration in this sense which lies at the basis of the place of specifically sociological theory in the sciences of action and the reasons why economic theory and other versions of the conceptual schemes which give predominance to rational instrumental goal-orientation cannot provide an adequate model for the dynamic analysis of the social system in general terms.

[11] Exact coincidence should be regarded as a limiting case like the famous frictionless machine. Though complete integration of a social system of motivation with a fully consistent set of cultural patterns is empirically unknown, the conception of such an integrated social system is of high theoretical significance.

It has been repeatedly shown that reduction of motivational dynamics to rational instrumental terms leads straight to the Hobbesian thesis, which is a reduction ad absurdum of the concept of a social system. This reductio was carried out in classic form by Durkheim in his *Division of Labor*. But Durkheim's excellent functional analysis has since been enormously reinforced by the implications of modern psychological knowledge with reference to the conditions of socialization and the bases of psychological security and the stability of personality, as well as much further empirical and theoretical analysis of social systems as such.

The theory of institutional behavior, which is essentially sociological theory, is precisely of the highest significance in social science because by setting the problems of social dynamics in a context of institutional structure and drawing the implications of the theorem of institutional integration which has just been stated, this theory is enabled to exploit and extend the knowledge of modern psychology about the non- and irrational aspects of motivation in order to analyze social processes. It follows also that any conceptual scheme which utilizes only the motivational elements of rational instrumental goal-orientation can be an adequate theory only of certain relatively specialized processes *within* the framework of an institutionally structured social system.

The basic theorem of institutional integration like all such basic theorems, explains very little in detail. It provides rather a point of reference in relation to which it is possible in an orderly fashion to introduce successively the more detailed distinctions which are necessary before an adequate analysis of complex behavioral processes can be approached. The present exposition has chosen the deductive approach. Hence it should be clearly understood that empirical applications of the conceptual scheme will be possible only after a much more advanced stage of elaboration has been reached.

There are above all two main directions in which this further elaboration must be carried out. In the first place institutionalized role behavior has been defined as behavior oriented to a value-orientation pattern or system of them. But there are many different kinds of such patterns and many different ways in which role-expectations may be structured relative to them. In place of this extremely general formula then it is necessary to put a differentiated account of at least some of the most important of these differentiated possibilities. Secondly, the oversimplified "ideal case" depicts complete motivational integration with a given value-pattern in the sense that this pattern as internalized is conceived to produce a need-disposition for conformity with it which insures adequate motivation for conforming behavior. This is obviously a highly simplified model. Before approaching realistic levels it is essential to analyze the complications involved in the possibilities of alienative as well as conformative need-dispositions, of conflicts and ambivalence and the like. An introduction to the elaboration of the cultural aspects of this problem will constitute the remainder of the present chapter.

Before embarking on these considerations, however, a brief discussion is in order of the implications of this theorem of institutional integration for the articulation of social role structure with personality structure. The starting point is that stated above, that the role expectation is structured around a specific interaction context. To whatever extent adequate motivation for the fulfillment of such expectations is achieved, where a set of expectations for those playing the "same" role is uniform there is every reason why in personality terms the motivational significance of this uniform behavior cannot be the same for all the personalities concerned. Three crucial reasons for this may be cited. First, the role in question is only one of several in which each individual is involved. Though the expectations for each may be identical with respect to *this* role, the total role systems would only in a limiting case be identical. In each case then the particular role must fit into a different total system of role expectations. Since all the different roles in which an individual is involved are interdependent in his motivational system, the combination of motivational elements which produces the uniform behavior will be different for different personalities.

Secondly, role-involvements do not exhaust the orientation or interest system of any personality. He has internal or "narcissistic" and individually creative foci of interest, and orientations to nonsocial aspects of his situation. Again for two different personalities only in a limiting case would these non-social aspects of the total orientation system be identical. Since this non-social sector of his personality is interdependent with the social sector, differences in this realm would have repercussions in the field of social motivation.

Finally third, there is every reason to believe that it is strictly impossible for the distribution of constitutional differences in the population of a complex social system to correspond directly with the distribution of roles. Therefore the *relation* between the constitutional basis of role-behavior and the overt behavior will be different with different individuals in the same role. Fulfillment of a given set of expectations will impose a greater "strain" on one actor than on another.

For all these reasons and possibly others, it is not possible to infer directly back and forth from personality structure to role behavior. The uniformities of role behavior as well as their differentiations are problematical even *given* the personality constitutions of the participants in the social system. Analysis of the motivational dynamics of role behavior therefore implies the formulation of mechanisms specific to the *sociological* problem level. It is not possible simply to "extrapolate" from the personality mechanisms of the one to those of the many as participants in the social system. This circumstance introduces frightful complications into the task of the sociologist, but unfortunately its implications cannot be evaded.

These considerations should not, however, give the impression that what are ordinarily called "psychological" concepts have no relevance to sociological theory. Just what the scope of the term psychological should be is a question discussion of which may be deferred to the final chapter. But it is of the greatest importance that *motivational* categories should play a central role in sociological theory. Essentially the dynamic elements of personalities and of social systems are made up of the same "stuff." This material must, however, conceptually be differently organized for the purposes of analysis of the two types of system.

§ THE POINTS OF REFERENCE FOR THE
CLASSIFICATION OF INSTITUTIONAL
PATTERNS

SO FAR in this chapter we have accomplished two important things. The first section outlined the basic functional problems of an ordered system of social relationships. This defined a set of "imperatives" which are imposed on the variability of social systems if the minimum conditions of stability are to be fulfilled. They will be of the first importance in setting the stage for analyzing the ranges of variation of social structures and the bases of their internal differentiation. Secondly, in the foregoing section we analyzed the nature of the most important structural unit of the social system, the status-role, and showed the nature of the integration of the elementary components of action which was involved in it.

The next step is to begin to lay the groundwork for dealing systematically with the differentiation of roles. This involves careful analysis of the points of reference with respect to which they become differentiated. For only with a systematic analysis of these points of reference is any orderly derivation of the bases and ranges of such differentiation possible. The analysis of such points of reference will have to proceed through several stages in the development of this and the following two chapters.

It should be evident from the nature of the role as a unit that a most crucial structural focus of differentiation of role types is to be found in differentiations among the cultural patterns which are institutionalized in roles. But the classification of cultural patterns in the relevant respects cannot be carried out without relating it to the general system of points of reference which is inherent in the structure of action. Hence the present section will be concerned with that general system of points of reference in its relevance to the structuring of roles, that is, of social relationships. When this groundwork has been laid the analysis will proceed to consider the relevant differentiations between types of culture patterns themselves. Finally, from this will be derived a classification of general role- or institutionalization types, general, that is, in that it will distinguish components which enter into the role structure of any social system, but will not attempt to approach the problem of the determinants of the specific combinations in which they are put together to form a particular system, or type of system.

First, as we saw in Chapter I, what we have called the primary points of reference for the organization of action-orientations, consist on the one hand of the three modes of motivational orientation, cognitive, cathectic and evaluative, and the basic differentiations in the structure of the situation. Of the latter the most important for present purposes is the distinction between social and non-social objects, the social being those with which ego is in *inter*action in the specifically social sense. In the non-social sphere, the case which is at present important is that of physical objects, since the cultural will presently be "pulled out" as it were and placed in a special position. The fundamental reason for this special treatment is that culture patterns have a dual relation to action, they may be objects of the situation or they may be internalized to become components of the actor's orientation pattern. This peculiarity of culture is indeed the main basis for treating it in a special category, and for dealing with actor, situation *and* culture pattern, not only the first two.

Since culture patterns may become internalized as part of the actor's orientation system, the first basis of their differentiation which is relevant here is that according to their relation to the three basic orientation modes. There are those culture patterns which function primarily as symbolic forms for the organization of the actor's cognitive orientation, those which serve a similar function in relation to the cathectic aspect of this orientation and finally those which mediate or structure his evaluative orientations. It should be remembered that these are analytically distinguished modes, *all three* of which are found in *all* concrete orientations to *all* objects. There is no such thing as a "purely" cognitive or cathectic orientation in the sense that in the first case there is no cathexis of an object or in the second no cognitive definition of the situation.

However, there is such a thing as relative *primacy* of the different modes. Indeed in a structural sense the cultural aspect of this primacy is crucial because it defines the order of priorities in the relevance of the selective criteria in each primary type of orientation. This basis of classification yields three primary *types* of orientation, as distinguished from the modal aspects of all orientations. In the first type cognitive *interests* are primary, the salient orientation problem is a cognitive problem, and cathexes and evaluations are secondary to this cognitive interest. "Gratification" consists in a solution of the cognitive problem, in coming to *know*. In the second type cathectic interests are primary, the problem is one of "adjustment," of attaining the appropriate gratificatory relation to the object. Cognitive and evaluative considerations are secondary and instrumental. Gratification is measured in affective or "emotional" terms. Finally in the third type evaluative interests have primacy.

The problem here is the *integration* of the cognitive and cathectic factors involved. Gratification consists in the achievement of an integration which resolves or minimizes conflict, actual or anticipated.

What defines each type is the *combination* of the primacy of one of the three modes of motivational orientation *and* the primacy of one type of culture pattern. Therefore from the same fundamental roots we derive *both* a typology of action orientations or interests *and* a typology of culture patterns. The three types on the cultural level are: 1) systems of cognitive ideas or beliefs; 2) systems of adjustive patterns or expressive symbols; and 3) systems of integrative patterns or value-orientation standards.

The objects toward which any of the three types of interest is oriented, and in relation to which the corresponding types of culture pattern "define the situation" may be of any class, including the cultural. All three basic classes of objects present cognitive problems for solution, constitute basic possibilities for cathexis with selective problems of the patterning of the corresponding adjustments, and present problems for evaluation. Social objects are, however, particularly strategic in this respect because of the complementary character of the orientation process and patterning. Perhaps this special significance of social objects can be put in terms of the paramount significance of evaluation and hence of the evaluative primacy which is present in both motivational orientation and culture in the context of social relationships. This in turn derives from the double contingency of interaction which has been discussed above. Essentially this double contingency introduces an extra hazard of conflict which makes adherence to relatively specific evaluative standards a paramount condition of order.

A further differentiation of the organization of action occurs when the time dimension is taken into account. Action may be oriented to the achievement of a goal which is an anticipated future state of affairs, the attainment of which is felt to promise gratification; a state of affairs which will not come about without the intervention of the actor in the course of events. Such instrumental or goal-orientation introduces an element of discipline, the renunciation of certain immediately potential gratifications, including that to be derived from passively "letting things slide" and awaiting the outcome. Such immediate gratifications are renounced in the interest of the prospectively larger gains to be derived from the attainment of the goal, an attainment which is felt to be contingent on fulfillment of certain conditions at intermediate stages of the process.

In these terms instrumental orientation may be interpreted to be a special case of evaluative primacy and therefore such action belongs to the third type of action-orientation. It involves the *givenness* of a goal, but given the goal, the evaluative selection gives primacy to cognitive considerations; that is, knowledge of the conditions necessary to attain the goal over immediate cathectic interests, defined as interests in taking advantage of the immediately available gratification opportunities in the meantime, even though they might interfere with the attainment of the goal. But in spite of the cognitive primacy of instrumental orientation, this differs from the case of the primacy of the cognitive interest as such in that *in addition* to the cognitive interest itself, there is the interest in the attainment of the given goal.

There is a corresponding type on the adjustive side which may be called *expressive* orientation. Here the primary orientation is not to the attainment of a goal anticipated for the future, but the organization of the "flow" of gratifications (and of course the warding off of threatened deprivations). This also is a version of evaluative primacy, but with the relationship of the two elementary components reversed. *Given* the cognitive definition of the situation the primacy is cathectic. The "burden of proof" is on the side of the contention that a given gratification *will* upset the expressive order whereas in the instrumental case it is the other way around, the burden of proof is on the side that a given gratification *will not* interfere with attainment of the goal. This secondary type differs from the type of primacy of cathectic interests as such in the primary classification in that the orientation is not to the specific adjustment problem as such, but on a higher level of the organization of action, to an evaluative *order* among gratification-potentialities.

Hence just as there may be an authentic system of instrumental values, so there may in this sense be an authentic system of expressive values, that is, the definition of an order in which gratification-interests have primacy, but nevertheless an order which organizes the different components of action-orientation in determinate relations to each other.

There is a third logical possibility of the structuring of order, namely that in which neither cognitive nor cathectic but evaluative interests themselves have primacy. In so far as this is the case, the focus is on the system of order itself, not on the goals transcendent to it nor on the gratification-interests of the actor. This may be called the "moral" aspect of the ordering of action and the cultural values which have primacy in relation to it, moral values. This integrative focus may be relative to the integrative problems of any system or sub-system of action. In general terms, however, it is important to distinguish the two principal foci, the integrative aspects of personality and those of social systems. The social system focus (including of course any sub-system, i.e., collectivity) may be called the "relational" orientation of action while that to the integration of personality may be called the "ego-integrative." This is of course of paramount significance in relation to the system of social relationships because of the very special importance of the element of order which has several times been mentioned.

Indeed it is this, in a sense "derivative," element of evaluation and of cultural value-patterns which is brought into play with institutionalization. Institutionalization contributes a "superadded" element in addition to the primary value-orientations of the actors, which is integrative for a specifically social aspect of the ordering of action. For, because of the complementarity of expectations, the significance of an actor's action can never be evaluated solely in terms of his "personal" values independently of the relational system in which he is implicated. His action orientations, that is, the selections he makes among alternatives, inevitably impinge on the "personal" interests of the other actors with whom he is in interaction, and of the collectivities of which he is a member, so far as these interests cannot be distributively discriminated. To the extent to which his "responsibility" for these other and collectivity defined interests is evaluated, the actor is concerned with a "moral" problem. The value-orientation patterns which define his orientation are moral values. The type of action where moral considerations have primacy in the social context is that where the actor is in a role of specific responsibility for the interests of a collectivity. But even where this is not the case the moral aspect is a highly important aspect or component of the orientation of actors in social roles generally, because it defines the institutional limits of permissiveness for action.

§ TYPES OF INSTITUTIONALIZATION RELATIVE TO THE SOCIAL SYSTEM

THERE are, as we have seen, certain common features of the phenomenon of institutionalization of cultural patterns wherever it occurs, by virtue of which these patterns become integrated with the motivational interests of individual actors. The distinctions which have been made in the preceding section, however, give us a basis for differentiating three different modes or types of institutionalization in terms of their different relationships to the structure of the social system itself.

It has been made clear above that institutionalization itself is in the nature of the case an evaluative phenomenon, a mode of the organization of the system of action. Therefore the patterns which are institutionalized in the nature of the case involve an element of value-orientation on the social system level, that is, they involve moral commitments on the part of the actors in the social-integrative as distinguished from the ego-integrative sense. But institutionalized value-patterns may still be classified in terms of different modes of relation of the commitments in question to the social relationship system itself.

The social system is, as we have seen, essentially a network of interactive relationships. The most central institutions therefore are those directly constitutive of the patterning of these relationships themselves through the definition of the statuses and roles of the parties to the interactive process. This first category will hence be called *relational* institutions. Secondly, particular actors, individual or collective, act in terms of interests which may to a greater or less degree be independent of the moral-integrative patterning of the social system, i.e., the overall collectivity itself. Hence in terms of collectivity-integration the functional problem in social system terms is *regulation* of the pursuit of these interests rather than constitutive definition of the goals and means. Instrumental, expressive and ego-integrative interests may be involved in any combination. But there are distinct problems of institutionalization in this area. This class of institutions will be called *regulative*. Finally there is a third class, still more peripheral to the social relationship structure as such. This is the case where the content of the institutions concerned consists only of patterns of cultural orientation as such, not directly of commitments to overt action. It is a question of beliefs, of particular systems of expressive symbols, or even of patterns of moral value-orientation when only "acceptance" rather than commitment in action is involved. These will be called *cultural* institutions. Each of the three classes will be briefly commented upon.

The nature and significance of relational institutions must be understood in terms of the fundamental paradigm of social interaction, and the way in which the theorem of institutional integration has been derived from that. We have seen that such institutional integration in terms of the internalization of common value-patterns is a condition of the stability of the interaction process. But further specification of this condition leads us to see that the *content* of the common patterns of value-orientation must be such that the reciprocal orientations of the interacting actors will mesh with each other. There is a variety of different patterns according to which such meshing is conceivable, but in *any given* system of interactive relationships the patterns must have been selected from among these possibilities in such a way as to be compatible with the stability of the interaction process.

The content of these value-orientation patterns will be discussed in the following section. They center about the fundamental possibilities of organizing the mutual attitudes of actors to each other, which means essentially selection from among the inherent possibilities of mutual orientation.

These relational institutions are of course differentiated both for different roles within the same social system and for different social systems; these differentiations will be analyzed in subsequent chapters. But essentially they constitute the structural core of the social system, and the institutionalization of the value-orientation patterns concerned is the primary mechanism of the stabilization of the social system itself.

By virtue of the internalization of these primary value-orientation patterns, certain fundamental components of the need-disposition structure and hence of the interests of the actors in a social system are determined. But these need-dispositions most directly integrated with the relational structure are not exhaustive of the needs and interests of individual actors. The latter have interests which within limits may vary independently of the relational structure as such, with respect to which the basic institutional patterns of the social system are conditional rather than constitutive. This is, as noted above, true of all the basic types of interests, the instrumental, the expressive and the ego-integrative.

The obverse of the conditional significance of such patterns for the action of the individual (and the sub-collectivity) is their regulative significance from the point of view of the social system. There are two primary aspects of this regulative function of institutions. First they concern the definition of the value-standards according to which the directions of acceptable activity in pursuit of "private" interests are defined. They constitute an element in the definition of goal orientations. Secondly, they concern definition of the limits to the acceptable choice of means or other action procedures in pursuit of the realization of the goals and values in question.

This may first be illustrated for the instrumental case. In contemporary American society the pursuit of financial profit is sanctioned as a type of goal appropriate for either an individual, or a certain type of collectivity, for example, a "business firm," to pursue. On the other hand according to the values of socialism this is not treated as a legitimate direction of pursuit of interests, or at least only within much narrower limits. But even within our own "business economy" there is specification in value-terms of the technical production goals with which the profit interest may legitimately be fused. Many things for which there might well be a market may either not be produced at all for profit, for example, certain types of morally censorable entertainment, or only under varying degrees of strictness of regulation, as in the case of weapons or certain public utility services. Thus in the sense of selection of goals within the sphere of "private" interest-oriented activity, there is a set of institutionalized limitations of the pursuit of goals and of the conditions under which they may be pursued. Essentially the same type of considerations is involved in relation to the selection of means with respect to the pursuit of private interests. Most notable are the limitations placed on the choice of means as they involve the interests of others. The most general formula concerns the exclusion or strict regulation of attaining a goal by the exercise of force or fraud upon others. But in many societies there are still more radical limitations on individual "freedom" imposed, for example in our own, the prohibition that anyone should by contract infringe not only the personal freedom of others but his own; no matter how advantageous the "bargain" offered, a man may not sell himself into slavery.

There is a similar set of regulative institutions relative to expressive interests. Expressive activities are, as we shall see, not cast directly into the means-end form as is the case with the instrumental. Hence the distinction between goals and means is not so important. But in part such institutions regulate expressive activities by specifying the legitimate relationships and contexts for them. Thus with respect to erotic activities, incest and homosexuality are drastically tabooed in most societies, and normal heterosexual activity is regulated both by selection of partner (e.g., within marriage) and by occasion (e.g., the requirement of privacy). Similarly aggressive feeling toward others may in general be expressed only within strictly defined limits, and many types of aggression are almost wholly tabooed. Obviously the killing of members of the in-group must be forbidden and drastically punished in every society, except under very special conditions.

Essentially the same, finally, is true of ego-integrative orientations. One of the most familiar examples is the fact that, in our society, the institutions of religious toleration regulate the pursuit of religiously founded moral interests so far as they are not commonly shared in the society as a whole. The members of denominational groups may act upon their religious convictions only so far as they do not infringe the regulative norms in other respects (e.g., norms defining standards of decency—hence the difficulty of tolerating the Dokhubors) and so far as they do not infringe on the rights of others to their share of religious freedom, for example by using the role of teacher in a public school to attempt to indoctrinate children with a special religious point of view.

There is in a social system a gradual transition between its relational and its regulative institutions rather than a rigid line. All social action involves relationships and mutuality of orientation. Furthermore it is a functional requirement of the culturally integrative aspect of the social system that there should be a degree of consistency in the value-patterns which have been institutionalized in both spheres. The distinction is essentially in terms of the functional relation to the integration of the social system. The greater the degree to which interests acquire independence relative to the main institutionalized value system, the greater the importance of the regulative functions of the institutional structure. This distinction between spheres of permissiveness for private interests and of collectivity-obligations is of such fundamental importance that it must be conceptualized as part of the fundamental value-pattern system itself. The place of the distinction will be brought out in the following section. Regulative institutions are of particular significance where private interests become "ecologically" structured in market systems and power systems. These will be further analyzed in Chapters III, IV and V below.

The distinction between patterns of value-orientation and the other components of the cultural tradition is in part one of degrees of commitment to the implications of the pattern for action. Evaluation is the integration of the components of orientation in a functioning whole. This functioning whole must *include* overt action. This is an essential part of the significance of what, in the last section, we have called the evaluative level of the organization of the components of action orientation, the types of action. Of the requisite levels of such evaluative integration, however, the highest is, as we have seen, the moral, because the scope of the evaluative integration is the broadest in that case.

Short of this moral level of integration, however, there may be a mode of evaluative interest in cultural patterns which we may call that of *acceptance* as distinguished from commitment. This is perhaps most evident in the case of belief systems. We may accept a belief as "true" without it becoming integrated in the system of action in any other respect. This would be the case for example of the popularization of much of scientific knowledge for those who are not "professionally" involved with it, either as scientists, or as having special commitments in fields of its application. The same is true with respect to patterns of expressive symbolism We may assent to the validity of certain canons of taste without making a commitment to make conformity with them part of our own way of life. Thus we may "appreciate" works of art in this sense. The absence of commitment in this field is signalized by the possibility of being appreciative of different kinds of works of art which comply with incompatible standards.

A more special case is that of the uninstitutionalized acceptance of moral standards. The essential point would seem to be that these standards are thereby put into the sphere of socially sanctioned (in the sense of permissible) "personal" morality. The most notable case is that of what may be called the "utopian" standards which are often current in a society. For example, in countries with a Christian tradition the ethic of the Sermon on the Mount is in this sense socially accepted. It is rather generally felt to be a higher standard than that currently institutionalized and anyone who actually lived up to it would be admired, though certainly not unanimously or without ambivalence. But clearly it is not institutionalized in the sense that literal conformity is expected in everyday affairs, and that he who does not "turn the other cheek" but resists aggression against him, is not stigmatized by negative sanction, so long as his resistance is within certain limits. Indeed, the acceptance of this pattern is in conflict with other elements of our value system such as the obligation to "stand up for one's rights," so the situation is far from simple. But it is important to note the possibility of such acceptance of moral value-patterns without full institutionalization.

The relations between belief systems and expressive symbols and the social system will be more fully discussed in Chapters VIII and IX below. Here it is sufficient to note that, though by itself acceptance of them does not necessarily involve direct commitments to action, in certain circumstances through institutionalization such a commitment may arise. The most familiar example is the institutionalization of belief, so that subscription to a system of belief becomes a criterion of loyalty to a collectivity, such as a religious group. There is room for wide variations in the extent to which, and the ways in which, this occurs. At one pole we may have the enforcement of detailed doctrinal conformity on pain of expulsion from the collectivity as in the case of the Catholic Church. At the other is the situation of "liberal" society where no specific beliefs are institutionalized. But here there are still institutionalized values relative to the belief system. There is an obligation to approach as closely as possible to rationality of belief, to be open-minded toward evidence and the like. It is not acceptable within the national collectivity to believe "anything one pleases." For example, the prestige of education would not be understandable without this institutionalized attitude toward beliefs.

The situation is similar with respect to expressive symbols. In some social systems, highly specific expressive symbols are positively institutionalized only within sub-collectivities, such as specific rituals in specific denominational groups, and specific aesthetic commitments in specific circles of artistic enthusiasts. But in spite of the lack of institutionalization on a broad level of specific expressive symbols in our society, there are still broadly accepted canons of "good taste" which are integrated with the general system of expressive symbolism, and hence the reward system.

Hence the cultural institutions of a social system are always present, though they are much more specifically defined and rigorously enforced in some social systems than in others. The distinction of these three main functional references of institutionalization will be used throughout the subsequent analysis.

The series of distinctions of levels of commitments and their relation to integration and institutionalization which has been reviewed in the last two sections is rather complex. Hence an outline of the main categories is presented for convenience of reference.

*Outline of Modes and Types of Action-Orientation,
Culture Patterns and Institutions*

A. Modes of *Motivational Orientation* of Action.
   1. Cognitive.
   2. Cathectic.
   3. Evaluative.
B. Modes of *Value-Orientation* of Action.
   1. Cognitive.
   2. Appreciative.
   3. Moral (system-integrative).
      a. Ego-integrative (personal).
      b. Collectivity-integrative (social-relational).
C. Types of *Culture Pattern*.
   1. Belief Systems (primacy of cognitive significance).
   2. Systems of Expressive Symbolism (Cathectic primacy).
   3. Systems of Value-orientation Standards (Evaluative primacy).
D. Types of *Action-Interests* (Primacy of *one* motivational mode *combined with* the corresponding type of culture pattern).
   1. Cognitive interests (in "knowing").

2. Adjustive interests (in securing gratification from objects).
3. Integrative interests (in minimizing and resolving conflicts).
E. Types of *Evaluative Action-Orientation* (Evaluative or integrative synthesis with primacy of one type of interest).
   1. Instrumental (given cathexis of a goal, cognitive primacy).
     a. Investigative (cognitive problem solution as the goal).
     b. Creative (new expressive symbolic forms as the goal).
     c. Applied (use of knowledge—hence primacy of cognitive interest, in interest of any goal not defined under a or b).
   2. Expressive ("acting out" of a need-disposition in terms of a pattern of expressive symbolism).
   3. Moral.
     a. Ego-integrative.
     b. Collectivity-integrative.
F. Types of *Institution*, embodying value-orientation patterns.
   1. Relational institutions (defining reciprocal role-expectations as such, independent of interest content).
   2. Regulative institutions (defining limits of the legitimacy of "private" interest-pursuit with respect to goals and means).
     a. Instrumental (integration of private goals with common values, and definition of legitimate means).
     b. Expressive (regulating permissible expressive actions, situations, persons, occasions, and canons of taste).
     c. Moral (defining permissible areas of moral responsibility to personal code or sub-collectivity).
   3. Cultural institutions (defining obligations to acceptance of culture patterns—converting private acceptance into institutionalized commitment).
     a. Cognitive beliefs.
     b. Systems of expressive symbols.
     c. Private moral obligations.

§ THE PATTERN-ALTERNATIVES OF VALUE-ORIENTATION AS DEFINITIONS OF RELATIONAL ROLE-EXPECTATION PATTERNS

THE role-partner in a social relationship is a social object. To develop a systematic scheme of points of reference for the analysis of orientations in roles it is then essential first to analyze those basic alternatives of selection which are particularly significant in defining the character of relations to such a social object, and which are constitutive of the character of the relationship pattern itself rather than of its "content" in interest terms, its cultural or motivational aspects in any sense other than as constitutive of relational patterns. In other words the analysis of the differentiation of a social structure must start with the patterns which enter into its relational institutions. The following discussion is posited on the view that there is on a given level of generality a strictly limited and defined set of such alternatives, and that the relative primacies given to choices between them can be treated as constitutive of the patterning of relational institutions.[12]

It should be made as clear as possible exactly what the following discussion is attempting to do. We are concerned with the patterning of the collectivity-integrative sub-type of the moral type of evaluative action-orientation (E-3-b in the outline). Within this we are concerned with analyzing the structure of an actor's relations to social objects in order to identify the points of reference which define the strategically significant limits of variability of this category of orientations. We will bring out a limited number of such ranges which, in their simplest form, can be defined as polar alternatives of possible orientation-selection. These alternatives will be defined in terms of relative primacies among the types of orientation possibilities which have been discussed in previous sections.

It should again be emphasized that we are here dealing with the foci for the patterning of relational institutions. We are therefore concerned with primacy relations among the possibilities of evaluative action-orientations and the correlative modes of value-orientation, not with the types of interest or with culture-pattern types as such. The first problem then is that of primacy relations as between instrumental, expressive and moral orientations (including the sub-types of the latter). In motivational terms it may be presumed that the "ultimate" interest of any actor is in the optimization of gratification. The most *direct* path to gratification in an organized action system is through expressive orientations; hence relative to the expressive, both the instrumental and the moral modes of orientation impose renunciations or discipline. The social object is always actually and potentially to some degree an object of cathexis.

---

[12] A more extensive discussion of the following conceptual scheme will be found in *Values, Motives, and Systems of Action*, Chapter I.

Hence in patterning the orientation to that object it is always a problem whether, in certain relevant respects, expressive orientation in terms of relatively immediate gratification interests is permissible, or is to be renounced in favor of instrumental or moral, that is certain types of evaluative interests. The first alternative may be defined as that of "affectivity," the second of "affective neutrality." This basic alternative is grounded in the nature of action systems. No actor can subsist without gratifications, while at the same time no action system can be organized or integrated without the renunciation of *some* gratifications which are available in the given situation. The polarity of affectivity-neutrality formulates the patterning out of action with respect to this basic alternative, in direct orientations to the social objects with whom an actor interacts in a role, and in its relevance to the structure of the expectations of his action in that role.

This first alternative-pair focuses on the permissibility or non-permissibility of gratifying the actor's *immediate* adjustive interests by expressive activity. The second concerns the same intrinsic problem approached from the other end, as it were, namely the permissibility of his pursuing *any* interests "private" to himself[13] as distinguished from those shared with the other members of the collectivity in which he plays a role. Thus not only his expressive, but his instrumental and ego-integrative orientations and the corresponding interests are defined as "private" in so far as they do not coincide with those recognized as collective by the collectivity. A role, then, may define certain areas of pursuit of private interests as legitimate, and in other areas obligate the actor to pursuit of the common interests of the collectivity. The primacy of the former alternative may be called "self-orientation," that of the latter, "collectivity-orientation."

Both these alternative-pairs raise an important problem of interpretation. It may rightly be said that just as every actor must both have immediate gratifications and accept discipline, so must every role both provide for pursuit of private interests and ensure the interests of the collectivity. This circumstance is not a paradox, because, defined as a matter of orientation-primacy in role-expectations

---

[13] This includes the interests of a sub-collectivity as actor relative to a more inclusive collectivity.

these alternatives apply to specifically relevant selection-contexts, not necessarily to every specific act within the role. Thus where effective instrumental pursuit of a certain class of goals is institutionalized as part of the role, *only* the gratification of expressive interests which might interfere with the attainment of these goals must be subordinated; the role is defined in affectively neutral terms in *this* context but not necessarily in all others. In the relevant choice-dilemma one alternative is prescribed. But this prescription is always relative to a specified context in which the dilemma arises. Similarly we would only speak of a role as collectivity-oriented if the pursuit of *certain* private interests which were relevant possibilities in the *given* type of situation was subordinated to the collective interest. Thus the public official has an interest in his own financial well-being, which for example he may take into account in deciding between jobs, but he is expected not to take this into consideration in his specific decisions respecting public policy where the two potentially conflict. This is the subordination of an instrumental (or ego-integrative) personal value.

The first two alternative pairs have been concerned with the expression-discipline problem which confronts all action systems on two levels: first, the obligation to acceptance of discipline by the individual actor vis-à-vis his expressive interests, the gratification of which would, in *this* role context, be felt to be disruptive; second the same dilemma reappears in relation to the pursuit of *any* sort of private interests, no matter how highly disciplined in a personality sense vis-à-vis the definition of obligations to the collectivity. Indeed, in this context often the most highly disciplined pursuit of private interests may be the most dysfunctional in collectivity terms. The third alternative pair concerns not subordination to vs. freedom from certain value standards whatever their content, but the *type* of value-standard which is defined as relevant to the role-expectation. Here recourse must be had to primacy relations among the modes of value-orientation themselves, since these define types of standard by which action-orientations are evaluated. For this purpose the moral category may be neglected since it is not an "autonomous" type, but concerns orientation to the integration of the action system, *given* commitment to the standards involved. Hence the basic alternative is between the primacy of cognitive and appreciative standards. What does this mean in the present context?

Cognitive orientation is, it may be said, essentially orientation to the element of generalization in the object-world. Cathectic orientation on the other hand, is inherently particularized, to particular objects and ordered combinations of them. If generalization is paramount in cognitive orientation, then the standards characterized by cognitive primacy cannot be particular to the specific relational system (with non-social as well as social objects) in which the actor is involved. It transcends this relational context. Normatively its orientation is to universal canons of validity.

In the case of cathectic orientation and the cognate modes of action- and value-orientation, there is an inherently "subjective" reference to gratification-significance. But the gratificational significance of an orientation can never transcend the particular relational system of which it is a part. The standard must be couched in terms of significance *for this particular actor in these particular relations with these particular objects*. The primacy of cognitive values then may be said to imply a *universalistic* standard of role-expectation, while that of appreciative values implies a *particularistic* standard.[14] In the former case the standard is derived from the validity of a set of existential ideas, or the generality of a normative rule, in the latter from the particularity of the cathectic significance of an object or of the status of the object in a relational system. Thus definitions of role-expectations in terms of a universally valid moral precept, e.g., the obligation to fulfill contractual agreements, an empirical cognitive generalization, or a selection for a role in terms of the belief that technical competence in the relevant respects will increase the effectiveness of achievement in the role, are universalistic definitions of roles. On the other hand definitions in such terms as "I must try to help him because he is my friend," or of obligations to a kinsman, a neighbor, or the fellow-member of any solidary group *because of this membership as such* are particularistic.

There is one common source of confusion in this field which must be cleared up at once. It derives from the fact that a particu-

[14] The primacy of appreciative over cognitive standards in particularism means that generalization is relativized to the particular relational system.

laristic role-obligation may be formulated in terms of a general rule in the sense that it states *in general terms* the particularistic obligations of all those in the relevant class of roles. Thus "honor thy father and thy mother" is stated as a general rule of morality. But it is its form that is general. The *content* of the obligation is particularistic, namely for each child, toward *his particular* parents. If the rule were, on the other hand, "pay honor to parents because of their quality of parenthood as such, regardless of whose parents they are," it would be a universalistic norm. *All* norms are capable of generality of statement and application (though varying greatly in degree of generality). The question is whether or not a *discrimination* is made between those objects with which ego stands in a particularistic relationship and *other objects possessing the same attributes*. Such a discrimination is incompatible with the conception of a universalistic norm. If parenthood is the relevant attribute, then the norm, if it is universalistic, applies equally to all objects possessing that attribute.

The first three alternative-pairs have been defined in terms of relative primacy relations of the orientational components of action, that is, with reference to ego as actor. In terms of primary functional significance for the patterning of role-orientations these three are exhaustive of the major possibilities, *on the same level of generality*. But they have not taken account of the total frame of reference. There remain alternatives with respect to the *characteristics* of social objects themselves, that is, from ego's point of view of the *alter* in the complementary role-orientation structure or to ego himself as an object, and with reference to the *scope* of relevance of alter an an object. These contexts produce two further alternative-pairs.

In both cases it is essential to strike just the right level of generality which is coordinate with that of the relevance of the first three pairs. Applying this criterion it seems that there is one dilemma which is of the most generalized significance in each context. With respect to characteristics of the object it is that of the focus on its qualities or attributes as distinguished from focus on its performances. "Performance" in this sense is a characteristic which, by definition, we have confined to the category of social objects. But the "alter" who is the complementary member of a reciprocal role-orientation system is also by definition a social object, and therefore is characterized by performance.

Orientation to the actor's performance (which may be either ego's or alter's or both) means that the focus is on his achievement. The expectation is that the actor is committed to the achievement of certain goals or expressive performances and that expectations are oriented to his "effectiveness" or "success" in achieving them, hence that positive sanctions will reward such success and negative sanctions will ensue in case of failure to achieve. There are of course all manner of complications such as the definition of what constitute "extenuating circumstances," but this is the major axis of the expectation structure.

On the other hand, even though actors can and do perform in the above sense, the major focus of a particular role-expectation need not be on this performance. All objects have attributes, they not only *do* this or that, but they *are* such and such. They have attributes of sex, age, intelligence, physical characteristics, statuses in relational systems, e.g., collectivity memberships. The focus of orientation then may be what the object *is* in this sense, e.g., *that* he is ego's father, that he is a physician, or that he is over six feet tall. Such attributes or quality-complexes may be conditions of a variety of performances, for physical or social reasons, but even so the orientation focus may still be the quality as such. This may be the criterion for differentiation of treatment and of expectations of his behavior.

This distinction has become current in the sociological literature in Linton's terms of achieved and ascribed status and hence it seems advisable to adopt those terms here. Achievement-oriented roles are those which place the accent on the performances of the incumbent, ascribed roles, on his qualities or attributes independently of specific expected performances.

The incidence of the alternative as between qualities and performances involves a further set of ramifications beyond the ascription-achievement distinction with reference to role-expectations, which because of their general importance in the theory of action may be brought to attention here. These concern its application to the definition of ideal states of affairs where they differ from a given initial state. Where performances are the focus of value-orientation the emphasis may be on the goal as the "expression," as it were, of the valued achievement-process. On the other hand the valuation of the goal-state as such may emphasize its qualities independently of the processes of its achievement. We shall see that this distinction is of considerable significance in defining different patterns of orientation to "ideal" states of affairs.

The achievement-ascription alternative-pair concerns characteristics of the object which may be selected as the focus of orientation. There remains the question of the scope of ego's "interest" in the object. It has been noted above how crucially important is the differentiation of modes of orientation of action and the corresponding differentiation of types of orientations in terms of primacies. But this differentiation has been treated in terms of the orientation of an actor taken as a point of reference without regard to the question of whether the different modes of orientation were segregated out in relation to different objects, or combined in orientation to the same object. This question of the relative incidence of "fusions" and "segregations" of action-orientation types will be seen to be of the greatest importance for the analysis of social structure.

When many empirical differences are taken into account it will prove to be possible to derive very complex permutations and combinations in this respect. But on the present level of generality the starting point should again be the evaluative types of action-orientation as such. Here a particular instrumental or expressive orientation or interest has a certain specificity such that is capable of clear analytical segregation from the other or from moral orientations. Hence one horn of the dilemma will be the definition of the role as orienting to the social object in *specific* terms, that is in terms of a specific instrumental or expressive interest. This is, it will be noted, a definition of the scope of the object's (alter's) significance to ego. Since it is defined in terms of a moral value-pattern it means that he is held to be *entitled* or even obligated to confine the relevance of this particular object or class of them within these limits. Hence the burden of proof rests on him who would suggest that ego has obligations vis-à-vis the object in question which transcend this specificity of relevance.

The alternative is to treat the object as significant in an indefinite plurality of specific orientation contexts. This always implies a moral element because the problem of evaluative integration of the different components of the total orientation to the object is by definition involved. Conversely the binding together of such a plurality of such specific interests in a single object-relation always implies a moral component in the orientation (note, this may be only ego-integrative, not relational. It does not imply consideration for the welfare of the object—a range of variation which is conceptualized in terms of self- vs. collectivity-orientation). Hence the clear antithesis of the specific, interest-segregated type of orientation is a *diffuse* mode, where the burden of proof is on the side of the exclusion of an interest or mode of orientation as outside the range of obligations defined by the role-expectation. This proof can be furnished by invoking an obligation higher in a scale of evaluative priority.

As in the cases of the other alternative-pairs it is essential here to keep in mind the relativity of this conceptualization. Like the others it applies at the choice-point to *directions* of orientation. It is a question at such a point of confining relevance and hence obligation to a specific interest (definable on various levels of generality) or of admitting the *possible* relevance in terms of integrative evaluation and subject to a priority scale, of any contingency which might arise.

If the derivation of these five alternative pairs from possibilities of the combination of the basic components of the action system has been correct, if they are in fact all on the same level of generality and are exhaustive of the relevant logical possibilities on that level, they may be held to constitute a system. Then, on the relevant level which, as we shall see is *only one* which needs to be considered, their permutations and combinations should yield a system of types of possible role-expectation pattern, on the relational level, namely defining the pattern of orientation to the actors in the role relationship. This system will consist of thirty-two types, which may in turn be grouped into a smaller number of more fundamental ones. These problems will be taken up in the following chapter.

For the convenience of the reader these five concept-pairs, which will be called the *pattern variables* of role-definition, may be schematically outlined as follows:

I. The Gratification-Discipline Dilemma
   Affectivity vs. Affective Neutrality
II. The Private vs. Collective Interest Dilemma
   Self-Orientation vs. Collectivity-Orientation
III. The Choice Between Types of Value-Orientation Standard
   Universalism vs. Particularism
IV. The Choice between "Modalities" of the Social Object
   Achievement vs. Ascription
V. The Definition of Scope of Interest in the Object
   Specificity vs. Diffuseness.

That these five pattern variables are focused on the relational aspect of the role structure of the social system does not mean that they are irrelevant to the definition of the patterns of regulative and of cultural institutions. They cannot be, if only because of the element of consistency of pattern which must run throughout a system of value-orientations in a cultural tradition. But for us the system of relational institutions is the core of the social structure and it will facilitate development of the analysis to start from this core and work out from there.

The main body of the book thus falls into two principal parts. After the principal components of the social system have been outlined in Chapter II, the following three chapters, III-V are concerned with the elaboration of the analysis of social structure, pushing it to the point of considerable refinement of detail. Chapter VI, on the Mechanisms of Socialization then returns to the central paradigm of interaction. This and the following three chapters are mainly concerned with the elements of this paradigm as they are outlined in Chapter II. The refinements of the analysis of social structure developed in Chapters III to V are for the most part not directly used.

It is suggested that the reader keep this clearly in mind as he proceeds, and keep continually referring back to the fundamental conceptual elements of Chapter II. It may well be that if he finds the elaborateness of Chapters III to V confusing he would be well advised to skim over them and resume his careful reading in Chapter VI, coming back to Chapters III to V after he has finished Chapter X.

III

THE STRUCTURE OF THE SO-CIAL SYSTEM, I: THE ORGANIZATION OF THE COMPONENTS INTO SUB-SYSTEMS

THE two foregoing chapters have been designed to prepare the ground for the task of the present one. The first developed an outline of the general frame of reference of action and showed the character of its components and of the types of system into which they are organized. The second carried this development further with reference to those features of action most directly relevant to the social system. It analyzed the basic functional problems and prerequisites of social systems, the points of reference relative to which their principal components must be analyzed, and the nature and place in the action scheme of those components themselves, the types of action-orientation of roles, institutions and their component value-patterns. We are now in a position to take a first major step toward showing how these components become organized to constitute a social system.

We shall begin by analyzing certain features of what may be called the "relational context" of types of action-orientation relative to which these actions must be institutionalized. We have so far dealt with these crucial evaluative action-orientation types only in the context of particular roles, not in their combinations in differentiated reciprocal interaction systems. It is this step which must now be taken. After that we must go into further detail with respect to the analysis of the points of reference which differentiate objects, that is, the differentiation of their ascriptive quality-complexes which are significant for role-structure, and of their achievement pattern-types.

Then in the following chapter we shall place the results of this analysis into the setting of the major functional problem-foci of the social system which will be classified as the allocative and the integrative problems respectively, and will be further differentiated. Finally, then, we will be in a position to raise the question of the actual constitution of a systematically differentiated role-structure which is adequate to the functional requirements of a society. The starting point of this will be the treatment of the combinations of the values of the pattern variables which were put forward in the last main section of the foregoing chapter. These primary pattern elements of role structure will be seen to be of necessity unevenly distributed in different parts of the same social system. Finally, the primary patterns will be related to further "adaptive" structures which bridge the gap, as it were, between the rather abstract formalism of the primary patterns and the more specific adjustment problems of action in particular situations within the relevant sector of the social system. It will be shown that from these same starting points it is possible to carry out the analysis *both* of the bases of internal differentiation within the structure of a given social system, *and* of the definition of the ranges of variation between social systems.

§ THE STRUCTURE OF THE RELATIONAL CONTEXT OF EVALUATIVE ACTION-ORIENTATIONS

THE types of action-orientation are, it will be remembered, the instrumental, the expressive and the moral. In the last chapter we considered them only in terms of their relevance to the structure of a *particular* role, not of systems of roles. We will now proceed to this step. It will simplify matters to take the cases of systems of each of the first two types in turn by itself before attempting to put them together into a composite system. We will start with the instrumental.

Fortunately a long tradition of thought has worked out most of the problems in this area and all that is necessary is to take over the results and place them in the proper setting. The key concept is that of the "division of labor" as developed by Adam Smith and his successors in utilitarian, especially economic theory. The starting point is the conception of a given actor, ego, as instrumentally oriented to the attainment of a goal, a goal which may be of any desired degree of specificity or generality. The relational problems enter in when alter becomes significant not only passively as a means or condition of the attainment of ego's goal, but his reactions become a constitutive part of the system which includes ego's own goal-striving.

If we conceive a system of such instrumentally oriented inter-action, the simplest case is that of reciprocity of goal orientation, the classical economic case of exchange, where alter's action is a means to the attainment of ego's goal, and vice versa, ego is a means to the attainment of alter's. Exchange in this sense may be confined to a highly ad hoc particular transaction, but it may become elaborated into a highly organized and durable system of interaction. As this occurs ego may become specialized in the process of attaining his own goals by the "production" of means to the attainment of the goals of one or a class of alters. Reciprocally the attainment of his own goals is enmeshed in expectations of (to him) instrumentally significant results of the actions of these alters.

The attainment of ego's goals then becomes dependent on the relational context in a double way. What he gets depends not only on what he himself "produces" in the sense in which this is inde-pendent of what the alters do, but on the "terms of exchange," that is, the patterning of his relationship in certain respects to the rele-vant alters. There are, in turn, two aspects of this relational system: first, the regulation of structuring (through settlement of terms) of the "outflow" process which may be called that of "disposal" of the product of his efforts to a class of alters; and second, the regulation of the "inflow" process, the settlement of the terms on which he receives contributions to his own goals from alters, which may be called his "remuneration." Of course in a single ad hoc transaction the two will coincide. Even in a complex reciprocal relationship between two actors they may continue to coincide. But it is a criti-cally important feature of the further differentiation of action systems that they need not do so; the recipients for the disposal of ego's "products" may be entirely distinct from the sources of his remuneration. Of course, if this is the case, there must be some mechanism by which the two aspects of the total interaction system in which ego is involved are adjusted to each other. The most conspicuous such mechanism operates through the ramifications of a system of monetary exchange. To account for such a mechanism would introduce additional steps into the differentiation of the system which need not be considered at this point of our analysis.

Two centrally significant foci of the problem of order in social systems are brought to light immediately by the foregoing considerations. First, and most obvious, is that of the regulation of the settlement of the terms of exchange. Because some of what every man does is potentially a means (including hindrance) to the attainment of every other man's goals, it is vitally important to the conception of social order that there should be mechanisms through which the terms on which ego will or will not make his "services" available to alter are settled in such a way as to be compatible with the conditions of stability of the system. This is the famous Hobbesian aspect of the problem of order.

Somewhat less obvious is the fact, secondly, that for there to be exchange there must be "something" which changes hands in the course of a transaction, something which is "disposed of" and "received." This something may be control of a physical object in certain respects, including power to destroy it (e.g., food through "consumption"). It may be an agreement to do certain things in the future, positive as contributing to alter's goals, or negative as refraining from interfering with alter's goals. This something will be called a *possession*. There are cogent reasons why the structure of the "rights" defining the conditions under which possessions are "held" and may be disposed of cannot in a complex social system be settled ad hoc as part of each exchange transaction. A stable system of exchange presupposes *a priori* settlement among possible alternative ways of defining such rights, that is, an institutionalization of them. The institutionalization of rights in such possessions is, in one major aspect, what we mean by the institution of property.

These are the most elementary features of a relational complex of instrumental orientations, but two further aspects of differentiation are so important that they need to be brought in at this point. First, any elaborated system of continuous and specialized instrumentally oriented activity, especially with the degree of specialization which precludes self-consumption and therefore is inevitably enmeshed in a relational context, requires "facilities" which extend beyond those features of the situation available at any time on a purely ad hoc basis. Facilities, i.e., materials, equipment, premises and the like are possessions in a special mode of significance to action; they are possessions devoted to the "production" of further "utilities," that is, destined to be used as means to some future goal rather than as objects of immediate gratification. Regulation of rights to facilities or of access to them, and of the possibilities of the acquisition of these rights through exchange is therefore another of the fundamental functional problem foci of a relational system of instrumental orientation.

Finally, the elementary paradigm provides only for that type of instrumental activity which ego can, to the point of exchange, carry out entirely alone. But very generally, the exchangeable entity, the significant "product" or possession, is not the product of a single actor's activity, but of the *cooperation* of a plurality of individual actors. Cooperation is a closer mode of the integration of instrumental activities than is exchange. It means the meshing of activities or "contributions" in such a way that the outcome is a *unit which as a unit can enter into the exchange process.* (Of course the terms on which cooperative relationships are entered into or continued may also be settled by an exchange transaction, a "contract.") According to the nature of the cooperative goal, the "unit product," and of other features of the system of cooperative activity (e.g., the numbers involved), the imperatives of a functioning process of cooperative activity, will differ. But they are always more stringent than those imposed on a system of exchange relationships. A system of cooperative relationships may be called an *organization*.

A given actor, ego, then is within an "instrumental complex" as it may be called, confronted with four major types of problems of the ordering of his relations to the significant alters. There is, first, the problem of "disposal," the settlement of terms on which his non-self-consumed product is made available to others. Secondly, there is the problem of "remuneration," of settlement of terms on which he receives the significant products of the activities of other actors (individually or collective as organizations). Third there is the problem of his access to facilities, and the regulation of his relations to competitors, actual and potential, for use of the same facilities. Underlying all three problems of exchange is that of the definition of rights in possessions and their limits, and of their differentiation according to classes of possessions. Finally there is the problem of his relationships of cooperation with others in the same "productive" process, which may include assumption of authority over some others and/or acceptance of subjection to the authority of others. These elements and their relations are diagrammatically represented as follows:

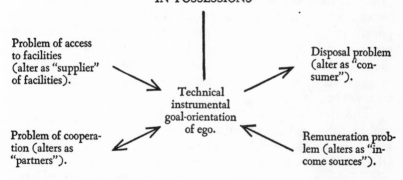

PROBLEM OF EGO'S AND ALTER'S RIGHTS
IN POSSESSIONS

Problem of access
to facilities
(alter as "supplier"
of facilities).

Disposal problem
(alter as "consumer").

Technical
instrumental
goal-orientation
of ego.

Problem of cooperation (alters as "partners").

Remuneration problem (alters as "income sources").

These relational problem-contexts may in any way be fused with each other in the same concrete relationships, or segregated, in that they involve different relations to different alters *with different roles* of and vis-à-vis ego. The ways in which these differentiations take place or fail to do so provide highly important criteria for classification of different types of social structure, and will be analyzed below.

This paradigm also provides important points of reference for analyzing the organization and dynamics of complex social systems. The access to "markets" and to facilities are among the most important conditions for the pursuit of any type of instrumentally oriented activity the more so the more specialized, while the "remuneration" receivable through the relational system is obviously of crucial importance to the motivation of such a type of instrumental activity.

What we have done in the foregoing pages is to describe, from the point of view of ego's role taken as point of reference, the main outline of the structure of a *differentiated system* of instrumentally oriented activity, involving an indefinite plurality of interacting actors. In so far as such a system develops, the institutional patterns of the component roles must do more than describe the value-orientations of the component actors. They constitute, rather, a set of value-orientation patterns *relative to* a specifically structured interaction situation. They define expectations of ego's action as follows: 1) in the processes of fulfilling his own technical goals; 2) in exchange relations with a series of alters relative to disposal, remuneration and facilities; and 3) in cooperative relations with alters. (Each of these can of course be further differentiated.) In such a system, concretely, there is necessarily a relational orientation component and, so far as the interests of the actors are not all interests in common goals, a regulative component, especially with reference to the settlement of terms and to rights in possessions. There may also be elements of cultural institutionalization, e.g., with reference to common beliefs.

The specifically sociological problem focus with reference to such a sub-system of social action concerns the kinds of value-orientations which are institutionalized in it, and the degrees to which and ways in which they are institutionalized to define the roles of the component actors. It concerns the mechanisms of learning of these patterns, and of social control where tendencies to deviance from them exist. With special reference to these factors thus the concern of sociological analysis with such a system is with their bearing on processes within the system, e.g., recruitment and status-change of personnel; and with processes of change in the institutional structure of the system itself, e.g., further elaboration of the division of labor.

The same paradigm, however, underlies certain problem-areas of other social sciences, notably economics and political science. The economic problem is two-fold. On the one hand, *within a given institutional role-structure*, it concerns the processes of allocation of resources, i.e., "labor power" and facilities within the system. On the other hand, it concerns in motivational terms the processes of balancing advantages and cost with special reference to the settlement of terms and within a given role-structure and a given set of power conditions. Political science, on the other hand, is concerned with the power relations within the institutional system and with a broader aspect of settlement of terms. These problems will be further discussed in the next chapter after a more extensive groundwork for them has been laid.

There is a closely parallel paradigm of the relational context involved in a differentiated system of expressively oriented actions. In this case, it will be remembered, the motivational significance of the action is given in the immediate gratification of a need-disposition, that is, through the action itself, not through the attainment of a goal beyond the particular action-process. Such orientation is, of course, organized in terms of a cultural pattern of value-orientation as well as of its motivational significance, hence it is expressive, not *only* cathectic.

The type of case of motivational orientation which is most directly relevant here is that where alter is a cathected object and this cathectic significance is the primary focus of the orientation on the motivational side. Here ego has a problem homologous with that of disposal, namely, that of ensuring alter's "acceptance" of his orientation, of his willingness to serve as an object of the relevant type of expressive interest on ego's part. This may be called the problem of alter's "receptiveness" to ego's orientation. It only arises, of course, when from ego's point of view alter is an "appropriate" object for him.[1] Secondly, however, expressive interaction is generally not a "one-way street." Alter is not only a passively receptive object but the gratification of ego's need-disposition may depend on an active "response" from alter. It may not, for example, be enough to "love" alter as an object; it may be very important to "be loved" in return. Response, thus, would seem to be homologous with the remuneration aspect of an instrumental system.

It is probable that the psychological characteristics of expressive interests are such that more generally than in the instrumental case

[1] Of course, some expressive orientations do not require receptiveness, e.g., a "hero" may be "worshipped" without even being aware of the identity of many of his admirers.

receptiveness and response are and must be found in the same social object. Nevertheless differentiation in this respect is by no means unknown even in an intimately "affective" object relationships. The most familiar case perhaps is the case of needing to be loved without the capacity for loving in return. But the separation of the two elements in relation to two different objects is certainly by no means unknown to clinical experience.[1a] Furthermore it must not be forgotten that the category of expressive orientation is by no means confined to such intimate relationships. It may, for example, be a matter of attitudes toward collectivities.

Expressive action is not oriented to the attainment of a goal outside the immediate action situation and process itself in the same sense as is instrumental action. But this does not mean that objects in the situation other than the immediate object of focus are indifferent from the expressive point of view. On the contrary an indefinite range of situational objects may be significant to ego as objects of cathexis and as expressive symbols which provide an appropriate context or "occasion" for the expressive activity. This includes such matters as the appropriateness of time and place for an expressive activity, the significance of surrounding physical objects, including the embodiments of cultural symbolism, e.g., works of art, the presence and role of third parties and the relation to collectivities as social objects. Hence the selection and regulation of the components of the occasion in this sense constitutes a third major problem area of ego's relational system of expressive orientation. The various objects in and aspects of the situation apart from the focal object are symbolically integrated with that focal object and its significance in ego's orientation patterning, and hence there is a need to have them "fit" with the central expressive interest. In one important aspect this may be spoken of as the need for an integrated "style" patterning for the context of expressive activities.

It should be quite clear that the same concrete objects of the situation may function both as objects of instrumental orientation and as cathectic-expressive symbolic objects. In particular, the processes of acquisition of objects which are significant in the expressive context are generally best analyzed in instrumental terms, not as themselves processes of expressive activity.

[1a] The problem of the interpretation of ambivalent orientations toward the same object introduces complications which will be taken up later. Cf. Chapter VII.

Finally, there is also a clear expressive homologue of the instrumental category of cooperation in the cathectic-expressive aspect of ego's integration with alter; where this integration is institutionalized we will call it *solidarity*,[2] short of this it will be called *loyalty*. There are two aspects of this loyalty. In the purely cathectic sense alter may be an object of *attachment*. This means that the relation to alter is the source, not merely of discrete, unorganized, ad hoc gratifications for ego, but of an organized *system* of gratifications which include expectations of the future continuance and development of alter's gratificatory significance. In the normally integrated case, as between individual actors, there would, of course, be a mutuality of this attachment significance. What the attachment does is to organize a plurality of need-dispositions in relation to a particular object into an integrated system.

The second aspect of the loyalty derives from the fact that the attachment is organized in terms of a cultural pattern which, in the first instance, will be a pattern of expressive symbols, the meanings of which are shared between ego and alter. This will involve value-orientations at least on the level of appreciative standards; whether it will go beyond that to involve a moral level of value-orientation is an open question. It will do so if the loyalty between ego and alter becomes institutionalized and is thus shifted to solidarity. Thus between two lovers a system of shared erotic symbolism will be developed which is an inherent aspect of the relationship and a condition of its integration.[3] When institutionalized in the form of marriage, however, this symbolism acquires the further dimension of moral sanction and obligation in terms of the common value system of the society. A relationship of expressive loyalty then organizes a set of need-dispositions in an attachment to the particular object and integrates it with a system of commonly shared expressive symbols which are appropriate to the cathectic interests in question. It is this loyalty integrated with a social object which is the homologue of cooperation in the instrumental case.

By extension of this conception of expressive loyalty between individual actors we derive the further important concept of the loyalty of the individual actor to a collectivity of which he is a member. The collectivity may be treated as an object of attach-

[2] See below, pp. 96 ff.
[3] See Chapter IX below for a further analysis of this problem.

ment, as when we speak of "love of country" in what is clearly more than a metaphorical sense. In such a case it is clearly the collectivity, not its members as individuals, which is the significant object. It is quite possible to love one's country and at the same time to be highly selective about loving one's fellow-countrymen as individuals. By essentially the same token, attachment to a collectivity is integrated with a system of expressive symbolism which in its application to ego signifies membership, status within the collectivity and perhaps meritorious services on behalf of the collectivity. On the side of the collectivity itself there are symbols such as flags, emblems, buildings and leaders in their expressive capacity which are foci for the expressive orientation of the members of the collectivity.

In the nature of the case the relation between an individual actor and a collectivity in terms of expressive loyalty cannot be symmetrical in the same sense as that between two individual actors. A collectivity can act only *through* the actions of its members, particularly those in roles of responsibility. It does not itself have affective "feelings" toward its members, it can only symbolize the *common* feelings of its members. It is of the highest importance to be clear about these fundamental differences between a collectivity and an individual actor. Nevertheless the conception of attachment to and loyalty to a collectivity is an exceedingly important tool of sociological analysis. It is the focus for the analysis of the cathectic-expressive relation of the individual to the group.

There are, furthermore, homologies with respect to the problems both of settlement of the terms of exchange, and of rights to possessions, between the instrumental and the expressive cases. Possessions in their expressive significance will be called *rewards*, the category of rewards being treated as directly parallel with that of facilities. The reward-object is always an object of immediate gratification, but its gratificatory significance depends not only on its properties as an object as such, but also on its specific relation to ego. That specific relation, so far as it is contingent on the organization of the interaction between ego and the relevant alters, is the focus of the sociological problem of rewards. But just as rewards are objects of gratification so in a culturally patterned action system they must *at the same time* be significant as expressive symbols.

Concretely rewards may consist in the possession of physical objects or specific relations to cultural objects. But a special significance attaches to one class of rewards, namely, the "possession" of contingent relations to other actors. Above all, because of the significance of the mutuality of attitudes involved in attachments and of loyalty and solidarity, to be in a position to "count on" the favorable attitudes of alter—of the appropriate type—may be regarded as the primary core of the reward system. Alter, that is, may give or withdraw his responsiveness, his love, or his esteem; ego, therefore, acquires and retains his place in alter's orientation system only under specific conditions. The institutionalization of these conditions is an aspect of the ordering of the social system.

As in the case of the acquisition and use of facilities, the social system need not and very generally does not prescribe by institutionalization precisely what rewards should be allocated to what actors. But both with regard to the terms on which rights to various kinds of rewards are held and exercised, and with regard to the settlement of the terms of exchange for the acquisition and disposal of reward-possessions there is an inherent problem of order for the social system. Institutionalization in this sphere is as much an imperative of social order as it is with respect to facilities.

Indeed, it is in relation to the differentiation of the relational contexts both of instrumental and of expressive activities, that the most fundamental regulative problems of the social system arise, and that regulative institutions are primarily focused. The implications of this situation will be taken up at a variety of points in the chapters which follow.

The paradigm for the analysis of the structure of the relational context of an expressive orientation is as follows:

PROBLEM OF RIGHTS IN RELATIONAL POSSESSIONS

Problem of appropriate context of occasions (involving third parties).

Problem of social objects as appropriately receptive.

Orientation to a specific gratification within a pattern of expressive symbolism.

Problem of expressive loyalty (involving cathectic attachment and loyalty symbolism).

Problem of social objects as appropriately responsive.

We may now turn to the moral aspect of the structure and ordering of ego's relational system. It is quite clear that this raises problems on a different plane from the instrumental and expressive because moral orientation is directly of integrative significance with reference to the components of an action system. We may, therefore, say that the problem is that of establishing the patterns of order both *within* the instrumental and the expressive complexes respectively, and *between* them, since every actor must have relationships of both types.

We have here reached a vantage point for making clear the difference in one crucial respect between the ego-integrative and the relational aspect of the moral orientation problem. Any given individual actor is, in both instrumental and expressive respects, involved in a complex *system* of relationships to other actors. The composition of this system is, because no other person occupies exactly the same place in the total society, largely idiosyncratic to him. Its organization and integrative stabilization as a system with his physiological organism and his particular environmental situation, presents a distinctive integrative focus not reducible to that of any other individual nor to that of the social system. The integration of the structures of the relational system of one actor, which will in some of the most important cases constitute his roles, represents one of the most important foci of the problems of the theory of personality.

But our concern is only indirectly with this. Directly it is with the correlative integrative problem of the relational system itself as a system, for as between social objects or actors this is by definition a social system. The focus of this problem concerns the conditions of order in such a system; in such systems generally and in each particular differentiated type of such system.

At present our interest is in the bases of structural differentiation, so we may follow up from this point of view. It is to be remembered that we are considering this structure in terms of the relational system as a system of roles, and hence we are concerned with the relevance of differentiation or role-pattern types.

In terms of the two paradigms presented above and the relations between them there seem to be two ranges of variability to consider. The first concerns the differentiations and integrations *within* each one of the orientation systems. The second concerns the possibilities of segregation and fusion of components of both in the same role.

Certain of the pattern variables outlined in the last chapter provide us with a basis for classifying these possibilities. Three of them, namely affectivity-neutrality, specificity-diffuseness and universalism-particularism, are all relevant to the problem on the most elementary level. The fourth and fifth fit into different contexts which will be taken up in due course.

The definition of a role in terms of affective neutrality excludes any expressive interest[4] from primacy in the orientation structure and gives the primacy either to instrumental or to moral considerations. This does not mean that, concretely, the actor does not receive any direct gratifications through the performance of such a role, far from it, but that in the definition of the role-expectations, these interests, *whatever they may be*, are in the case of conflict, to be subordinated to one or both of the other types of consideration. If there is no conflict it is another matter. *By itself*, this variable does not discriminate between instrumental and moral orientations, nor between private and collective interests. It serves only to discriminate the legitimacy of relative primacies of expressive and non-expressive orientations.

However, there are important respects in which the discrimination between instrumental and ego-integrative moral orientation is secondary if not indifferent from the point of view of the ordering of the *social* system. The functional problem in these terms is that of moral integration on the social level, not that of personality. But this brings us into ground not yet worked out. This variable defines quite clearly the relative primacy as between expressive and instrumental orientations.

It will be convenient next to take up the application of the specificity-diffuseness variable. Specificity in a role-expectation "segregates" out one specific element of an instrumental *or* an expressive complex from the rest of its relational context. Thus the content of

---

[4] The extent to which a cathectic interest is or is not integrated with a pattern of expressive symbolism may be neglected for purposes of the following analysis. In general we shall assume this integration and deal with the evaluative action-orientation level.

the role may be confined to the "productive" process itself without reference to responsibility for disposal or for the provision of facilities or regulation of cooperative relationships, or it may be concerned with the gratification of a need-disposition without reference to the context of occasions or its combination with others in an attachment. It would seem that the possibilities of segregation in the expressive field were intrinsically more limited than in the instrumental.

In any case, however, diffuseness refers to such a fusion of relational aspects or relevant need-dispositions into a single "bundle." The important point to remember is that a pattern variable in the present context defines role-expectations, that is, rights and obligations vis-à-vis others, and hence the structuring of sanctions. Therefore, a "specific" role is one in which obligations are expected to be confined to the specifically defined relational content, while in a "diffuse" role the expectation is that no claim to obligation arising out of a contingency of the situation will be *a priori* irrelevant; its irrelevance must be justified in terms of conflict with a *higher* obligation in terms of a priority scale.

There is a certain relativity in defining what is a segregated aspect which is apt to give rise to confusion unless it is clearly recognized. In the instrumental case it derives from the fact that *any* desired future state of affairs may be conceived as a goal. Therefore, when we speak of the productive (or "functional") goal of an instrumental orientation, disposal, adequate remuneration, etc., may each serve as such a goal. What, therefore, is to be considered the "technical" goal at the center of an instrumental system of division of labor as indicated in the paradigm, is *relative* to the position of ego in the system of division of labor. What is from ego's point of view the technical goal, may, seen from the perspective of the wider *system*, be the performance of a disposal *function* (e.g., he may be a "salesman") or some other function. This should not be a serious source of difficulty if the frame of reference within which a statement belongs is always made clear.

In the expressive case it is somewhat different. The system into which a need-disposition gratification is to be fitted, must be taken to include other need-dispositions of the same actor as well as his relations to objects. Hence a "fusion" may mean either the organization of a system of need-dispositions relative to the same object, or the organization of a system of objects relative to gratification of the same need-disposition or both.

It would seem to be clear that an object-orientation which includes both expressive and instrumental elements, defined as positively expected rather than only permissively legitimate in the role-expectation, should be treated as diffuse. However, this would not seem to be possible unless on either the instrumental or the expressive side diffuseness were already involved. The most obvious type of case is that where an instrumentally specific expectation is bound up with an expressively diffuse one, in orientation to another person or to a collectivity. Solidarity, which will be further discussed below, necessarily has a component of this diffuse character. But in the absence of the collectivity-orientation involved in solidarity we may speak of the obligation of loyalty to alter or to a collectivity, as defined above, when the instrumental orientation is fitted into the context of a diffuse relation of reciprocal expressive significance.

It is also evident that there are important relations of the variable universalism-particularism to this context. The standards governing instrumental orientations are, *given the goal,* as we have seen inherently universalistic. They have to do with the intrinsic, relationally indifferent criteria of effective goal-attainment. The primacy of an instrumental orientation, *even a diffuse one,* is, therefore, *always* a primacy of universalistic standards. The same may, but need not, be true of an expressive orientation. Here it depends on whether the orientation is inherently to the *specific* object or to a universalistically defined *class* of objects. If *any* object of the generally defined class is appropriate, the standard is universalistic.

However, the orientation is more likely, in the expressive case, to be particularistic. This is especially, indeed overwhelmingly, so unless the object is an abstract, cultural object which contains the property of universality within itself or a class of other objects in their symbolic significance. Perhaps, for instance, universal love in the religious sense is an example of a universalistically defined attachment, to *all* men without discrimination. It is, however, evident that it is extremely difficult of realization. It may be surmised that the universalistic orientation is more likely to be to the abstraction "humanity," that is, to a symbol, than it is to all concrete human beings.

Table 1 presents a cross-classification of the values of these three pattern variables, yielding eight types. It can be seen from this that there is a considerable, though not a complete correspondence with the outcome of the analysis of the instrumental and expressive paradigms. The table is formulated in such a way that the neutrality-affectivity variable is consistently used to discriminate the primacy of instrumental and expressive orientations respectively, and the specificity-diffuseness variable to distinguish limitation to a specific component of the relational system from the integration of the system in question as a system. These lines of discrimination seem to be quite clear. The main difficulty with them is that the classification does not as such take account of the combinations of instrumental and expressive elements in the same role-expectation pattern. The best way to do this appears to be to conceive such a combined pattern as covering two cells in the table, for example, both the affective and the neutral cell where the combination of the other two variables is still the same. Such a combined type could then be further differentiated according to whether the instrumental or the expressive (or possibly a moral) element were given primacy. This is highly important in the case of cells 6 and 8 which define—so far as these variables are concerned—the very important cases where a diffuse attachment is integrated with expectations of reciprocal instrumental performances. A major example is that of kinship roles.

Another complication arises where the primary interest is expressive on one side and instrumental on the other. This would, for instance, be true in the relation between performer and audience in commercial entertainment, where the member of the audience is directly gratifying a need-disposition whereas the performer is in an occupational role.[5] In such an asymmetrical role interaction system it seems necessary to classify one role in one box, the other in another. Thus the role of the performer in the above case would belong in cell 1 while that of the spectator would belong in cell 3.

[5] To account for the integration of such an interaction pattern it seems necessary to assume that there is institutionalization of a *common* pattern of expressive symbolism between performer and audience, a pattern which would be internalized in the performer's personality. Then the latter's instrumental orientation to "getting across" and/or to remuneration would operate within this value-orientation matrix. This problem will be further analyzed in Chapter IX, pp. 408 ff.

It is still significant that the complementary pair belong in two adjacent cells out of the eight possibilities. It would not be possible to build up complementary pairs of role-patterns by random combinations of the eight cells.

Another set of problems arises in connection with the place of the variable universalism-particularism. Row 1 (cells 1 and 2) which defines the primary components of both technical and executive roles in the instrumental complex, is clear and unambiguous. With respect to all of the others there are problems. Cell 3 is certainly important with respect to specific gratifications. But if the object is a social object there is a strong pressure to shift the emphasis in a particularistic and diffuse direction, the more so the more lasting the relation and the more strategic the cathectic interest. There seems to be an inherent instability in this combination of orientation interests. It never appears as central to the structure of a social system (where the object must be a social object) but mainly in "safety valve" or deviant phenomena, e.g., prostitution.

The instability of the orientation defined by cell 4 has also been commented upon. Here the difficulty is in maintaining the universalism of the pattern in the face of the pressures to particularism of the affective expressive primacy. Thus religious universalism very easily shifts into a denominational particularism where the primary loyalty is to the particular religious collectivity, e.g., the church, rather than to "all men," especially, of course, where men outside the church refuse to recognize the definition of the situation espoused by the denomination in question.

To take one further example, cell 8 formulates the "ideal type" of the romantic love relationship. But it seems to be in the nature of a concrete love attachment that if it is intense and durable it will come to involve realistic common and reciprocal activities outside the core of expressive symbolism itself. Though also possessing symbolic significance many of these activities will possess or acquire instrumental significance as well. The actual role pattern, then, will tend to "spill over" into cell 6 and to fuse the two. With integration in a larger functional system including the presence of offspring and responsibility for their care the love relationship shades into that of marriage. Kinship roles in all societies involve a fusion of the pattern-elements formulated in cells 6 and 8.

These cases are not exhaustive of the implications of the table but will suffice for the present. The fundamental reason why we do not find a "perfect fit" between the logically elaborated scheme of pattern variable combinations and the results of analyzing the

TABLE 1

Universalism

	SPECIFICITY	DIFFUSENESS
Neutrality	**1** Expectation of specific instrumental performances segregated from the relational context and subordinating expressive interests.	**2** Expectation of diffuse instrumental coordinations relative to a relational context subordinating expressive interests.
Affectivity	**3** Pursuit of a segregated specific expressive interest segregated both from diffuse attachments and from instrumental expectations vis-à-vis any one of a *class* of objects.	**4** Fusion of a plurality of expressive interests in a loyalty-attachment to a *class* of objects or an abstract cultural object, e.g., love of all mankind or of God.

Particularism

	SPECIFICITY	DIFFUSENESS
Neutrality	**5** Expectation of specifically delimited instrumental obligation to a person or collectivity, subordinating expressive interests.	**6** Expectation of diffuse instrumental obligation to a person or collectivity subordinating ego's expressive interests.
Affectivity	**7** Pursuit of a segregated specific expressive interest segregated to above vis-à-vis a particular object, individual or collective.	**8** Fusion of a plurality of expressive interests in a relation of diffuse loyalty to a particular object without instrumental expectations.

relational complexes of instrumental and expressive action lies in the fact that the former is a *cultural* pattern element, and the types derived in these terms are governed by the rules of pattern consistency and symmetry. The relational paradigms on the other hand analyze the structure of social relations on another level. We see here some of the beginnings of the sources of tensions between cultural patterns and the realistic conditions of functioning of a social system.

It must not be forgotten that in Table 1 two of the pattern variables have been omitted, namely achievement-ascription and self-collectivity orientation. Especially the latter variable will be found to modify the results of this table considerably. But we are not yet ready to introduce these modifications.

In a very tentative way it will be useful to bring together the results of the above analysis of the instrumental and expressive orientation systems, by setting up a classification of types of fusion and segregation of the components of these paradigms. These will not suffice to characterize concrete role types but will provide some very important elements in them, and in particular will lay the basis for a series of highly important discriminations in the field of social structure to be utilized further in Chapter IV below.

1. The segregation of specific cathectic-expressive interests, both from diffuse attachments or loyalties and from instrumental expectations, e.g., the role of spectator at an unpaid entertainment (cells 3 and 7 of Table 1).

2. The fusion of a plurality of specific cathectic-expressive interests in a diffuse object attachment, e.g., the "pure" type of romantic love role. (Cell 8.)

3. The conditioning of the gratification of a specific cathectic-expressive interest on a specific instrumental performance (asymmetrical) e.g., the role of spectator at a commercial entertainment (involves all of left hand—specificity—column in Table 1).

4. The fusion of a diffuse attachment and loyalty with a diffuse complex of expected instrumental performances, e.g., kinship roles (cells 6 and 8).

5. The segregation of specific instrumental performances, both from expressive orientations other than the specifically appropriate rewards and from other components of the instrumental complex, e.g., "technical" roles (cell 1).

6. The fusion of a diffuse plurality of instrumental functions with the specifically appropriate rewards in a complex segre-

gated from other expressive interests, e.g., "artisan" and "executive" roles (cell 2).

7. The fusion of a plurality of expressive interests in a diffuse attachment to a *class* of objects or an abstract cultural object, e.g., "universal love" in a religious sense (cell 4).

§ THE MODALITIES OF OBJECTS AS FOCI OF ROLE-EXPECTATIONS

THE foregoing section was concerned with differentiations in patterns relevant to the structuring of social relationships and hence of roles. The bases of differentiation, that is, were found in the motivational structure of the actor's orientation and in the cultural value-standards which are built into his action orientation. It is now necessary to take up the relevance of differentiation within the object itself which may serve as a focus for selective differentiation of orientation, that is, relative primacies among alternatives. We are concerned here, it will be remembered, with role-pattern structure and hence the mutual orientations of actors to each other. The relevant object is for this purpose always a *social* object.

This immediately suggests the usefulness of building the analysis around the pattern variable of ascription-achievement as this is nothing other than the formulation of the most significant differentiation running through the constitution of the social object world. In orienting to an actor as object, then (including ego's own personality) primacy may be given on the one hand to his attributes or qualities, independently of specific expected performances, or on the other, it may be given to his performances, completed, in process, or expected in the future. The relevant context, it will be remembered, is always the *evaluation* of the object as a whole in the relevant respects. This evaluation may be applied to the *selection* of the object, from among alternative possibilities, or to the structuring of expectations relative to the object once a relationship is established, that is, the "treatment" he receives in a role.

The nature of the general differentiation should be clear. The main problem of this section is to bring out its relevance by spelling out some of the more empirical considerations that are involved under each of the two main alternatives. We may start with the analysis of quality-complexes, or ascriptive criteria.

It seems essential at the start to differentiate between two classes of such criteria. For convenience they may be called primary and secondary. The former are those which are logically prior to the social system, the latter those which derive from the relevant features of social systems. Relative to both classes, for purposes of making the relevance to social structure clear, it is useful to make a further initial distinction, namely between *classificatory* and *relational* criteria. By classificatory criteria is meant those which orient the actor to the object by virtue of the fact that it belongs to a universalistically defined class which *as a class* has special significance for ego. By relational criteria, on the other hand, is meant those by which the object as a particular object is placed in a specific significant *relation* to ego and thus to other significant objects. Thus the sex of the object is a classificatory criterion while a specific biological relationship to ego, e.g., as parent, is relational. The relevance of this distinction to relating ascriptive criteria to the incidence of the universalism-particularism variable seems to be obvious.

The relevant primary ascriptive criteria may be classified as attributes of organisms (ego's and alter's) or attributes of personalities (again both ego's and alter's). Collectivities are excluded as belonging only to the secondary class. Physical and cultural objects are likewise excluded. Apart from their relations to social objects they are by definition irrelevant to our present discussion. Cultural objects as internalized are part of personality, as institutionalized patterns of the social system, they are secondary. Physical objects (other than organisms of actors) are only *indirectly* relevant. They may, that is, be involved in relational criteria, because of the object's relation to his environment, as in the case of spatial location.

We have, then, the classificatory and the relational attributes of the organism. The former are his biological or, as it is sometimes expressed, "physical" traits. Two of these, because of their universality and their relevance to certain intrinsic functional problems of social systems stand out from the others, they are sex, and age, or more precisely, stage of the biological life cycle. The fact that all human populations are classifiable by sex into two and only two categories (with negligible exceptions) forms a crucial focus of orientation to human individuals. Similarly with age. Beside these two we may refer only to a residual category of numerous physical or somatic traits which will include stature, body weight and shape, skin and eye color and the rest of the familiar catalogue. Traits which are manifested only or mainly in behavior and where the physiological basis and the socio-culturally acquired element can only be distinguished by sophisticated analysis if at all, are best treated as traits of personality rather than of the organism, e.g., "intelligence."

Turning to the relational category, there seem to be three primary relational attributes of the organism which stand out as of primary significance, namely "biological position," spatial or territorial location and temporal location. By biological position is meant the place of alter *relative* to ego in the concatenations of sexual reproduction and descent, what is sometimes called the "biological structure of kinship." Descent through bisexual reproduction is the essential fact. Alter is always related to ego, if any relationship can be traced at all, through specific lines of descent from specific common ancestors, with, of course, the possibility of more than one line being involved. For reasons which will be discussed in the following chapters biological position is a fundamental ascriptive criterion in all known societies, defining the focus of the social structures known as kinship.

Territorial location is equally important. By this is meant, *given* the spatial position of ego as organism at a given time, the relation to this of the position in space at which alter is located. With ego himself as object, of course, the identity of spatial position is itself a crucial fact. He cannot, that is, be spatially separated from "himself." Since all individual actors are organisms this focus of orientation can never be left out, it is always there by implication if not explicitly dealt with. It always creates a "problem" for action. If ego and alter are out of sight and hearing there must be specific physical mechanisms which enable them to communicate, e.g., mail or telephone. Or if communication is not enough to accomplish ego's goal, he must somehow be able to "get at" alter in the place where he is located, or bring about a change in the location of one or both. It should be quite clear that territorial location, in this context, is always a relational attribute of the organism of an actor. Though obviously influenced by past action and subject to altera-

tion through a projected course of action, at any given time it simply
is a given fact.

Though relative territorial location inherently enters into all
action it is of particularly crucial significance in two contexts. One
is that of residential location. The plurality of roles of any individual actor implies a time-allocation between them, and conditions
are such that the time-segments cannot be long enough to permit
more than limited spatial mobility in the course of the change-over
between at least some of them, e.g., family and job. This means that
the main "bases of operations" of the action of an individual must
be within a limited territorial area, though "commuting" by mechanical means has considerably extended the range. This base of
operations requirement is at the basis of the grouping we call a
"community." A community is that collectivity the members of
which share a common territorial area as their base of operations
for daily activities.

The second crucial context is that of the use of force. Force
operates on the actor through the organism, by limiting its freedom,
e.g., of motion or communication, or by inflicting injury on it. In
order to use force against an actor it is necessary to "get at him" *in
the place where he is* or would like to be. Since the use of force is
an ultimate means of prevention of action (a dead man does not
act), and since as a component of power the use of force *must* be
controlled in a society, the territorial organization of force and its
contingent use is always a focus of the structure of the society.

Time relations may be treated as the third set of relational criteria relative to the organism. All action is, of course, in one of its
major aspects, temporal sequence. For interaction the crucial implication is that the impact of ego's action on alter is always specifically
located in that sequence. "Timing" of actions is always possible
within limits, but when an act has been performed its consequences
flow into the temporal sequence, as part of the "experience" of alter
as well as of ego. Ego is, therefore, always related to alter in time in
the sense that they co-exist in the temporal continuum, and the
relevant state of either for interaction orientation is the state "at
the time."

But action is not only "located" in time, it "ranges" through
time. The consequences of past actions are situationally given and

thus *always* of ascriptive significance. Action itself, as involving expectation, however, is oriented to the future. The assessment of "how long it will take" and "when is the proper time" are inherently parts of any action problem. In relation to the structuring of action perhaps the most important relevance of these considerations is to the proliferation of instrumental orientations in systems. The more complex the instrumental system the more are goals, which as goals are meaningful in the present, capable of *attainment* only in a more or less distant future. An instrumentally elaborated social system is one in which orientations are to a high degree "time-extended." Its members cannot simply live "for the moment." In particular the significance of alter for ego clearly has a highly important time dimension.

Turning now to personality (ego's own or alter's) as object we have the immense field of personality traits. It is perhaps questionable how far it is legitimate to treat these as primary ascriptive criteria at all, since they are so intimately bound up with the social system itself. Hence there is a possible arbitrariness in where they should be classified. But provisionally they may be put here. The most important distinction within the classificatory category seems to be between those traits which are primarily significant to performances and those which are not. The former may be called "performance-capacities." Admittedly the line is difficult to draw and is probably relative to context, but it is an important line. Such traits as physical strength or agility, as intelligence or responsibility, are primarily ways of formulating the kind of performances which may be expected under certain conditions. On the other hand such traits as cheerfulness or "attractiveness" seem relatively independent of specific performances.

In any case it is important to emphasize that performance capacities are attributes which may function as ascriptive criteria. Even though, as is frequently the case, past performance serves as the empirical criterion, still persons regarded as having the trait in question, or having it in the requisite degree, are *classified* together, and belonging to this class may be taken as the criterion of status-ascription, independently of any specific expected performances. Indeed every performance, once it has been accomplished, becomes in its consequences an aspect of a *given* situation and the person who has done it has the attribute of being the one who did. This is the basis of certain dynamic relations between achievement and ascription.

It is evident that there are no *relational* attributes of personalities which are "primary," that is, are neither attributes of the organism of the sorts just discussed, nor secondary attributes derived from the social system. This is merely another way of saying that the relational system in which personalities as personalities are involved is *by definition* the social system.

Turning then to secondary criteria of ascription, in the classificatory category the most important ones are status-classes or categories. Though a large proportion of statuses also involve collectivity memberships, it is highly important to distinguish the two. High School graduates, or married persons, or professional men, for example, constitute status classes. The members of a status class are classed together by virtue of a common attribute of their place or "location" in the social structure, or of a common attribute which is relevant to such status as a determinant or a symbol of status. Thus "rich men" or the "indigent" constitute a status class. Such an attribute is not a personality trait in the usual sense, though again admittedly the line is indistinct when personality characteristics are in fact made the focus of status ascription. But generally there is room for considerable variability in the personality traits of the members of a status class.

To be distinguished from membership in a status-class are the two types of secondary relational criteria, participation in an "ecological" system and membership in a collectivity. By an ecological system is meant a state of mutually oriented interdependence of a plurality of actors who are not integrated by bonds of solidarity to form a collectivity but who are objects to one another. The "customers" of a commercial firm constitute such a category as do in general the participants in a market. Another example is the antagonists in a contest. Of course their interaction is oriented to a system of "rules of the game" and in their orientation to these rules they are members of the collectivity which upholds them. For ecological interactors in this capacity the only "sanction" is failure to achieve the goal or to avoid injury to self. Only the rules, not the specific orientations thus are institutionalized, and the relevant institutions are regulative not relational. As a relational category such participants must belong to the *same* concrete system of interaction. Classed as customers in general they constitute a status class.

Membership in a collectivity is also a secondary relational criterion. Such a collectivity may, like a kinship group or a community, be constituted by primary relational criteria, but it *need* not be. Even where membership is achieved *by* the individual actor, not ascribed *to* him, *once he is a member* this becomes a basis of further ascription.

We may now turn to achievement criteria of object selection or discriminative orientation. Such a criterion does not refer to an attribute of a given state of the object as such, but to actual or expected specific performance. The significant aspect is the contingency; being what he is, is not enough, in addition to this the critical thing is what the actor does. The evaluation is always *relative* to an ascriptively given base. The actor might have done otherwise, worse or better, but the focus is on what he actually does, not on the ascriptive base.

That this possibility is inherent in the theory of action is clear from the most elementary analysis of interaction, with its emphasis on the contingency element of alter's reactions to what ego does. Achievement orientation, then, is related to ascriptive through the addition of the *second* contingency factor which results in double contingency. The expectation is not defined "*Being* what I am, alter's treatment of me must take one of the following alternatives" but "Depending on *which of several alternatives open to me I take*, I will set *alter* a problem to which he will react in terms of the alternative system of his own which is oriented to my action." It is this involvement in the fundamental paradigm of interaction which makes the pattern variable of ascriptive-achievement so crucial in the whole theory of action.

In approaching the problem of sub-classification the first remark to be made is that primary achievement criteria relative to the organism drop out; achievements are specifically defined as those of an *actor*. However, it seems best, parallel with the place of personality traits, to treat the achievements of the individual actor as primary rather than secondary criteria for orientation. This leaves only the achievements of collectivities considered as actors as secondary achievement foci. Such collective achievements as the record of games won by a team or the profits of a business firm would be cases in point.

The next important point is that achievement criteria as such are in the nature of the case *always* classificatory, never relational. They are always abstractable from context, to be "measured" by a universalistic standard. Achievement primacy is always universalistic, so far as the criteria of achievement are directly applicable. There are, however, certain difficulties in the interpretation of this statement. Performance is always relative to a goal; performance criteria are, therefore, limited in their direct applicability to the relations of means and conditions to a *given* goal, in such terms as effectiveness, efficiency, economy. They are thus intrinsically limited to instrumental orientations. But while instrumental orientation may be a *component* of a concrete role-expectation system, it need not exhaust it. The value-orientations in terms of which the goals themselves are defined need not be universalistic. There is, therefore, such a thing as performance in the interest of particularistic values. Furthermore other things than performances may be involved in the sanction system, and the achievement of certain responses on alter's part may be part of the goal. These may be expressive orientations on alter's part. There is thus in many cases an intricate web to unravel before the significance of the above propositions can be properly assessed.

A particularly important case of this is the secondary type of achievement criterion, namely collective achievement, that is, achievement imputable to a collectivity as an actor. Membership in a collectivity is, we have seen, inherently a relational quality. This has certain implications for the structure of a role of "responsibility" in relation to a collectivity, notably a leadership role which may be defined as a role of diffuse responsibility relative to a collectivity. The focus of that responsibility is *always* in one sense particularistic because of the relational involvement. Yet, the leadership role may be achievement-oriented and "success" measured in universalistic terms, *given* the goal, which must in some sense include "promotion of the welfare of the collectivity."

It is in the light of considerations such as these that it is necessary to assess the implications of a value-orientation system which combines achievement values and particularism for the structure of the social system in which it is institutionalized. The particularistic component of the value-system places stringent limitations on the choice of goals to which achievement values may legitimately be applied. Above all the emphasis is thrown on collective achievements and roles involving responsibility toward collectivities. This, for example, underlies the "collectivism" of traditional Chinese values as distinguished from our own type of individualism.

To sum up, we may say that the ascription-achievement variable defines the major axis of differentiation of actors in a social system in their capacity as *objects* of orientation, as distinguished from their capacity as actors whose own orientations are to be analyzed. Since all statuses in the social system have to be entered into by the individual actor, if only by the fact of being born, in the first place these criteria are relevant to classifying the discriminations by which actors are distributed among the statuses and roles of the social system. They thus define criteria of *eligibility*, and therefore in what roles ego may or may not appear vis-à-vis alter. Furthermore, they define patterns of *differential treatment* within a role, once the actor is an incumbent of it. They are foci for the definition of expectations for deciding between alternative evaluations. They constitute the framework for defining in what respects the actor as object (again both ego and alter) is significant, in the sense that is relevant to ego's orientation.

§ THE SOLIDARITY OF THE COLLECTIVITY

WE have so far dealt with the structure of role complexes, first treating the differentiation of the different roles composing such a complex in terms of the orientational content of the expectations and then in terms of selectivity as between the basic modalities of the objects of the orientations, of quality and performance. It remains to discuss the relevance of the problem of the specific *commonness* of the value-orientation patterns of the participants in a system of social interaction. This constitutes one primary aspect of the integration of such a system.

In one aspect or sense, of course, any actually existent system is "integrated" in that its parts have somehow to "intermesh." This is true of a system of roles in the same sense as any other type of system. Going one step further, there is, as we have seen, a norma-tive aspect of *any* system of social interaction. There is an element of common value-orientation, therefore, in any system of social inter-action. These values may, for example, be cognitive standards governing communication, or appreciative standards governing the appropriateness of expressive symbols. But the present concern is with the next "higher" level of integration, the "moral" in its rela-tional or social system relevance.

On this level, it is not determined by the fact of interaction alone, or by the presence of common values in the more general sense, whether with respect to a given orientation-alternative choice, there is a "moral issue" involved or not. The problem may be purely an instrumental one of efficiency, or an expressive one of appropri-ate object choice and attitude. There is a moral issue only when the alternatives involve a presumption of relevance to the "integrity" or the "solidarity" of an interaction system when the preservation of that integrity or solidarity is itself a value. The fifth of the pattern variables constitutes the conceptualization of this alternative with reference to the integration of *social* systems. The case of self-orientation is the case where, in the choice in question, which alternative is chosen is felt to be or defined as *indifferent* as far as the integrity of a valued social system of action is concerned. That of collectivity-orientation on the other hand is that where such in-tegrity is defined as being involved, so that the actor who chooses one side is violating his *responsibilities,* to the system as a unit and its participant members. It is only when as action system involves *solidarity*[6] in this sense that its members define certain actions as required in the interest of the integrity of the system itself, and others as incompatible with that integrity—with the result that sanc-tions are organized about this definition. Such a system will be called a "collectivity." Collectivity-orientation, as it were, involves posing the "question of confidence"; "are you one of us or not? your atti-tude on this question decides."

It will be noted that solidarity in this sense involves going a step beyond "loyalty" as that concept was defined above. Loyalty is, as it

---

[6] It will be, evident that the present conception of patterns defining social morality and solidarity in this sense is congruent with Sumner's concept of the *mores* and Durkheim's of *moral constraint.*

were, the uninstitutionalized precursor of solidarity, it is the "spilling over" of motivation to conform with the interests or expectations of alter beyond the boundaries of any institutionalized or agreed obligation. Collectivity-orientation on the other hand converts this "propensity" into an institutionalized obligation of the role-expectation. Then whether the actor "feels like it" or not, he is obligated to act in certain ways and risks the application of negative sanctions if he does not.

It is exceedingly important to be clear about the relativity of the concepts of solidarity and collectivity and hence the applicability of the self-collectivity variable. Only in the limiting case would a collectivity constitute an aggregate of persons as *total* individuals—that of a completely self-subsistent society. The type case is rather the aggregate as participants in a particular interactive system organized as a system of complementary roles, i.e., a partial social system. Therefore, an actor may be a member of as many collectivities as he has roles—there is no inherent limitation to that number. With regard to personnel of collectivities it follows that while some may be completely separate with no overlap, others overlap, with some members in common, others not, while still others are related as more and less inclusive collectivities. Thus in this country residents of a town or city are also residents of a state, and in turn also of the United States; they thus have the role of "citizen" in each of these three levels of governmental organization, that is, are members of all three collectivities.

Every role, so far as it is *institutionalized,* involves a pattern of solidarity obligations; it entails, that is, membership in at least one collectivity. But in the *particular* orientation within the role these obligations may or may not be involved. The range of orientation alternatives relative to which they are not invoked is defined by the concept self-orientation, that where they are invoked by collectivity-orientation. Thus, to take a familiar example, the participants in a commercial market are members of a collectivity, the state, which has "rules of law." In their particular orientations to actual or potential exchange partners, within certain limits, they may be "self-oriented," for example, with reference to negotiating agreements on particular prices. But beyond those limits solidarity obligations come to be invoked in the form of insistence on compliance with certain common rules, e.g., with respect to refraining from fraudulent misrepresentations about the nature of commodities. The obligation to observe these rules is a collectivity-orientation element of the total role. When we speak of the system of market relations as "governed by self-interest" we mean that within a range of permissiveness defined by such a set of (formal and informal) rules, decisions can be made on grounds which are treated as irrelevant or indifferent in terms of solidarity obligations. To reiterate the crucial point: *All* institutionalization involves common moral as well as other values. Collectivity obligations are, therefore, an aspect of every institutionalized role. But in certain contexts of orientation-choice these obligations may be latent, while in others they are "activated" in the sense that the actor faces the choice either of choosing the alternatives which conform with these values or of accepting the negative sanctions which go with violation.

There is another aspect of latency which is particularly applicable to collectivity-orientations or solidarity obligations but is also more widely relevant. Many obligations are contingent on certain specific situational conditions. In the absence of such conditions they may remain latent—e.g., a professor has an obligation to teach. An observer who knew him only in the summer months and did not see him teaching would obviously not be entitled to conclude that he was violating his obligation to teach or did not "recognize it." It is only that the obligation is latent when the university is not "in session." The only test, therefore, of the recognition of an obligation is the reaction of the actor in the *specific situation* to which it applies. Of course a secondary but not always reliable test is the verbal response to a question such as "what would you do in such and such a situation?"

Conformity with expectations of collectivity-orientation may be called taking "responsibility" as a member of the collectivity. But it is a further step of elaboration to conceive of the collectivity "acting as a unit," or "in concert." Such action is, in a latent sense, a constitutive property of any collectivity—at a minimum a system which would in no sense ever "defend itself," that is, mobilize some kind of resistance to a threat to its integrity, could not be called a collectivity in the present sense. But only in certain types of situation will this latent property of action in concert be mobilized or activated.

A collectivity in which expressive interests have primacy in its orientation to continual action in concert may for lack of a better term, be called a *Gemeinschaft;* one in which instrumental interests have primacy is an "organization" in the sense defined above. In so far as either type has explicit and formalized rules and differentiated organs of implementation of collective action (including interpretation and enforcement of rules) it is an "association."*

When the association level of the organization of collectivities is reached, and to some degree short of this, it certainly involves an internal differentiation of roles with respect to the functions of the collectivity as a unit, as well as those of what may be called its primary division of labor. This differentiation is about the axis of "responsibility" relative to the possibilities of "action in concert." Internally this may be called a leadership role. When the special concern is with relations of the collectivity and its members outside itself, to other persons and collectivities, it may be called a "representative" role.

In terms of the discussion of the division of labor earlier in this chapter it should be clear that, while there is a good deal of room for differences of specification, relative to specialized "contributions" to a cooperative action system, leadership roles are *always* diffuse. Responsibility in the present sense can never be confined to the efficient performance of a specialized function, but involves in some sense coordinating a variety of factors and contingencies in the interest of the collective goals. Like so many of the distinctions involved in this discussion, there is an important relativity about this one. But the focus on relational context as distinguished from technical goal, is the essential criterion of a leadership or executive role.

At the limiting pole of completely uninstitutionalized fluidity a system of social interaction would involve no collectivities in the technical sense of the present discussion; it would be *only* an ecological complex. But this is definitely a limiting case. No actual society approaches close to it. The only concretely relevant cases

---

* This terminology is similar to, but a somewhat modified version of, that of Max Weber. Cf. *The Theory of Social and Economic Organization,* Chapter I.

which do are certain classes of partial social systems within an institutionalized society, such as ad hoc small groups set up for purposes of observation. Such a group will not yet have attained an institutionalized structure peculiar to itself, and, therefore, until a certain stage of its integration as a group is reached, it does not make sense to apply the variable of self-collectivity orientation to it. This case is empirically important as calling attention to the fact that the collectivity-structure of a larger social system is always more or less fluid, though societies differ greatly in this respect. But there is a continual process of dissolution of old collectivities and formation of new ones, and this is one of the most important processes of social change. It does not, of course, preclude that there should also be processes of change within a collectivity which do not destroy its identity.

In one sense a social system, except for the above limiting case, may be regarded as *a* collectivity. But in a much more important sense a society or any at all complex partial social system is to be regarded as a net-work of collectivities, side by side, overlapping and larger-smaller. The concept of collectivity has here been introduced as one of the most important of the sub-structures of the structure of social systems, not as a name for the overall characterization of such systems.

§ TYPES OF SOCIAL VALUE-ORIENTATION

THE main thread of the organization of material of this chapter has been the pattern variables and their context of applicability to the different modes of organization of the components of relational systems. In conclusion we may bring together this material by showing how all five of the variables can be used to set forth a classification of value-pattern types defining role-orientations. This is done in Table 2. The organization of this table of classification requires some comment.

When the pattern variables are seen in the context of the general action scheme, they fall into a pattern of mutual interrelations; they do not, that is, simply constitute a list, but they have important systematic interrelations. There is a certain symmetry in the scheme which revolves about an axis which has two primary aspects of significance. This axis is that of the polarity between motivational orientation on the one hand, and cultural orientation on the other. In the presently relevant sense, as will be evident from the above analysis, it is the value-orientation aspect of culture which is of crucial significance here.

TABLE 2a

Types of Combination of Value-Orientation Components[7]

Major Social Value-Orientations

	UNIVERSALISM	PARTICULARISM
	A. Universalistic Achievement Pattern	**B.** Particularistic Achievement Pattern
Achievement	Expectation of active achievements in accord with universalized standards and generalized rules relative to other actors.	Expectation of active achievements relative to and/or on behalf of the particular relational context in which the actor is involved.
	C. Universalistic Ascription Pattern	**D.** Particularistic Ascription Pattern
Ascription	Expectation of orientation of action to a universalistic norm defined either as an ideal state or as embodied in the status-structure of the existing society.	Expectation of orientation of action to an ascribed status within a given relational context.

This polarity of the reference points of action systems in general is reflected on the next level of derivation "down" toward their concrete structure, that is, in the pattern variables, in that two of them are of particular relevance to one pole of the reference system, two to the other, and the fifth is, as it were, "neutral" between them. These relations are diagrammatically represented in Chart I.

The first section of the present chapter built up certain ele-

[7] For simplicity the pattern variable of self vs. collectivity orientation is omitted from these tables. Because of its symmetrical relation to the whole scheme it can be used to subdivide any cell in the tables.

TABLE 2b

Types of Value-Orientation Components of Social Role-Expectation

Universalism

	AFFECTIVITY	NEUTRALITY
Universalistic Achievement Patterns →	1	2
Specificity	Expectation of specific affective expressions toward a class of objects designated on basis of achievement.	Expectation of specific disciplined action in relation to a class of objects designated on basis of achievement.
Achievement		
	3	4
Diffuseness	Expectation of diffuse affective expression toward classes of objects on basis of achievement.	Expectation of diffuse disciplined action toward classes of objects on basis of achievement.
	9	10
Specificity	Expectation of specific affective expression toward class of objects on basis of qualities.	Expectation of specific disciplined action toward class of objects on basis of qualities.
Ascription		
	11	12
Diffuseness **Universalistic Ascriptive Patterns →**	Expectation of diffuse affective expression toward class of objects on basis of qualities.	Expectation of diffuse disciplined action toward class of objects on basis of qualities.

TABLE 2b—(*Continued*)

Types of Value-Orientation Components of Social Role-Expectation

Particularism

AFFECTIVITY	NEUTRALITY	
		Particularistic Achievement ← Patterns
5	6	
Expectation of specific affective expression vis-à-vis a particular object or one in particular relationship on basis of performance.	Expectation of specific disciplined action toward an object in particularistic relation to ego on basis of performances.	Specificity
		Achievement
7	8	
Expectation of diffuse affective expression toward object in particularistic relation to ego on basis of performance.	Expectation of diffuse disciplined action toward object in particularistic relation to ego on basis of performance.	Diffuseness
13	14	
Expectation of specific affective expression toward object in particularistic relation to ego on basis of qualities.	Expectation of specific disciplined action toward object in particularistic relation to ego on basis of qualities.	Specificity
		Ascription
15	16	
Expectation of diffuse affective expression toward object in particularistic relation to ego on basis of qualities.	Expectation of diffuse disciplined action toward object in particularistic relation to ego on basis of qualities.	Diffuseness
		Particularistic Ascriptive ← Patterns

mentary types of social sub-system from the organization of types of action-orientation in different relational systems. This analysis started out from the pole of motivational orientations. It used them, not on the most elementary level, but on that of organization *with* cultural elements which was called, in Chapter II, evaluative *action* orientation. The two pattern variables of affectivity-neutrality and specificity-diffuseness were the ones most directly relevant to that

CHART I

Grouping of Pattern Variables

Value-Orientation

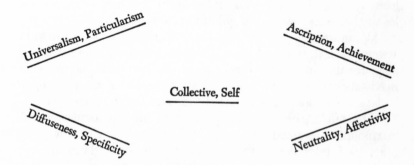

Collective, Self

Motivational-Orientation

motivational focus and may be said to be the keynote of value-orientation relevance on that level. The universalism-particularism variable was then brought in as introducing further specification into the structuring of these orientations, above all because of its relevance to the primacy of cognitive elements in instrumental orientations, once goals are assumed as given.

This consideration, combined with their relevance to the structure of personality which will be discussed in Chapter V below, justifies putting this pair of variables together. They may, indeed, be considered as the major axes of the organization of action with reference to the needs of personality, that is, in the *first* context of the problems of functional prerequisites of social systems discussed in Chapter II, the Hobbesian problem of order. They formulate the necessity of balances in two fundamental respects. On the one hand the actor must have gratifications; without them he can neither subsist nor be adequately motivated for the performance of social roles. On the other hand he must also accept discipline, both in the interest of his own longer run gratification-deprivation balance, and in the social interest, that of his role-performance. Secondly in its psychological reference the specificity-diffuseness variable in the first place formulates the significance of diffuse loyalties, but at the same time conversely the necessity of limitations on such loyalties, in the interest of instrumental performances and kinds of gratification which cannot be integrated with attachments. In relation to collectivities solidarity with its diffusion of responsibility to the collectivity, involving diffuseness, is the institutionalized counterpart of loyalty between individuals without institutionalization.

We must keep in mind that we are here dealing with the social system context, not with action in general. Hence these two variables for us concern the mechanisms which mediate between the needs and capacities of the personalities which as actors compose social systems, and the structure of the social systems themselves.

The other pair of variables is universalism-particularism and ascription-achievement. These variables have, by contrast with the other pair, reference to the social system as such. They are concerned, as we have seen, respectively with the type of value-norms which enter into the structure of the social system, and with the ways in which the characteristics of actors as objects of orientation are "taken account of" in the selective processes through which social structures are built up. *Both* pairs of variables are constitutive of the structure of the relational system, otherwise they would not be relevant to the present analysis. But the second pair is concerned more with the social-system pole of functional reference. There is a sense in which the motivational adequacy of a social system to the needs of individuals can be more nearly accounted for in terms of the first pair, ignoring the second. But this is not true of the bases of *structural* differentiation and variability of social systems. In a sense, therefore, the second pair will have primacy for analysis of the variability of social systems as structural types, the combinations of the first pair being, as it were, resultants of the fact that a given society is structured in a given way with respect to the second pair. On the other hand, for analysis of adjustive and personality problems, and of the variability of these phenomena *within* a given social structure, the first pair will have primacy.

Finally the fifth variable, self-collectivity-orientation has been placed "in the middle." This is because it does not as such have primary structural significance, but rather its significance is integrative. It is, to be sure, just as the others are, a component of the structure of social systems, otherwise it would not belong here. But the reference points for this variable are "internal" to the social system itself, they are relational as it were, while the reference points for the other four variables are "external" in the sense of referring to features of the action-components which are logically prior to their organization in social systems.

For these reasons, in Table 2 the fourfold table of possible combinations of the variables, universalism-particularism and ascription-achievement are given primacy as yielding a classification of four *major* types of *social* value-orientation. Each of the cells of this first part of the table may, however, be regarded not as a single cell but as a summary designation for a "block" of eight cells of the full table which details all the thirty-two possibilities of combination of polar values of the five variables. However, for most purposes of classification of social structure, it seems justified to regard these latter as "sub-types" of the four major types. This point should not, however, be overemphasized. The most important thing is the classification itself, and the possibility of deriving a systematic classification of this sort from the most general considerations of the structure of action and its elaboration in social systems. It constitutes the *fundamental starting point* for a classification of possible types of social structure and eventually of societies. It should, however, be *quite* clear that *as such* it does not constitute such a classification because it includes only the value-orientation element and does not account for the rest of the components of the social system.

A very brief comment on each of the four major types is in order to give the classification some kind of concrete relevance; fuller discussion will be reserved to Chapter V. Cell 1, the "Universalistic Achievement Pattern" is best exemplified in the dominant

American ethos. The combination of universalism and achievement-orientation puts the primary emphasis on universalistically defined goal-achievement and on the dynamic quality of continuing to achieve particular goals. It does not emphasize a "final" goal-state,

TABLE 2c

Major Types of Value-Orientation of Personal Attitudes

	AFFECTIVITY	NEUTRALITY
	A. Receptiveness-Responsiveness Attitude	**B.** Approval Attitude
Specificity	Disposition to be receptive to and respond to alter's attitude of expectation of mutual gratifications within a specific sphere or context.	Disposition to approve alter's action within a specific sphere conditional on his performances in terms of a standard.
	C. Love Attitude	**D.** Esteem Attitude
Diffuseness	Disposition to be receptive to and to reciprocate a diffuse affective attachment to alter and accept the obligation of loyalty accompanying it.	Disposition to evaluate alter as a total personality relative to a set of standards.

which once achieved is to be maintained in perpetuity. The combination of universalism with achievement values puts the primary universalistic accent on process, that is, on means-choice and particular goal-choice, leaving the goal-system fluid. In some such sense the philosophy of Pragmatism epitomizes this orientation.

When universalism is combined with an ascriptive emphasis in Cell 3 on the other hand, to constitute the "Universalistic Ascriptive Pattern" the primary relevance of universalistic standards shifts to the validation of the quality-ideal. The focus is on the attainment of an ideal state of affairs, which once attained is considered to be permanently valid. But the universalistic element introduces a factor of strain since, in its main lines, it is scarcely possible to maintain

TABLE 2d

Types of Value-Orientation Components of Need-Dispositions (Attitudes) of Personality

Affectivity

	UNIVERSALISM	PARTICULARISM
Receptiveness-Responsiveness Block →	**1**	**2**
Ascription	Disposition to receive and give specific gratifications vis-à-vis any member of a class of quality-selected objects.	Disposition to receive and give specific gratifications in reciprocal relation with a particular object possessing special qualities.
Specificity		
Achievement	**3** Disposition to receive and give specific gratifications to any object in a class characterized by a type of performance.	**4** Disposition to receive and give specific gratifications in interaction with a particular object on the basis of mutual performances.
Ascription	**9** Disposition to love and be loved by any person belonging to a class defined by specified qualities.	**10** Disposition to love and be loved by a particular object by virtue of specific qualities.
Diffuseness		
Achievement	**11** Disposition to love and be loved by any object conforming to standards of performance.	**12** Disposition to love and be loved by a particular object by virtue of its specific performance record or prospects.
Love Block →		

TABLE 2d—(*Continued*)

*Types of Value-Orientation Components of Need-Dispositions (Attitudes)
of Personality*

Neutrality

UNIVERSALISM	PARTICULARISM	
		Approval ← Block
5 Disposition to approve and be approved by object possessing or on a basis of specific qualities.	**6** Disposition to approve and be approved in reciprocal relation to particular object on basis of specific qualities.	Ascription
		Specificity
7 Disposition to approve and be approved by any of class of objects with specific performance records or capacities.	**8** Disposition to approve and be approved in reciprocal relationship with particular object on basis of mutual specific performances.	Achievement
13 Disposition to esteem and want to be esteemed by any object possessed of certain qualities.	**14** Disposition to esteem and want to be esteemed by a particular object by virtue of possession of specific qualities.	Ascription
		Diffuseness
15 Disposition to esteem and want to be esteemed by any object conforming to given standards.	**16** Disposition to esteem and want to be esteemed by a particular object on basis of given performances or prospects.	Achievement
		Esteem ← Block

that any status quo of a social system conforms with any sharply defined ideal state. Hence a tendency to a dualism of ideal and real. Broadly the philosophy of "idealism" and the German cultural ideal seem to conform with this pattern.

When we move to Cell 2, the combination of particularism and achievement which is called the "Particularistic Achievement Pattern" there is a great mitigation of this tension between ideal and real, for the focus is no longer on an absolutely ideal state, but on a *given* dynamic relational system. But with the accent on achievement the actor's relation to this is "dynamically" conceived. It is not something which "comes automatically," but which must be achieved, and may, if not enough care is taken, deteriorate and have to be re-achieved. An excellent example seems to be the Classical Chinese cultural pattern, with its concept of a harmonious order for the maintenance or restoration of which men are held to be responsible. There is truth in the common saying that the Confucian Chinese were above all concerned with morality, namely responsibility for the maintenance of a given social structure as a going concern. But, by contrast with both universalistic types of pattern this is, as Max Weber said, a doctrine of "adaptation *to* the world" not of "mastery *over* the world."

Finally, the combination of ascription and particularism yields what may be called the "Particularistic Ascriptive Pattern." Here the order is conceived as given in a more radical sense, in that man is thought of as adapting his action within an order for which he cannot be held responsible. The accent, therefore, is on "making the most" of expressive opportunities, using the social order as a kind of "stage" for the play. The Spanish-American pattern seems to be a close approximation to this type.

One or two interesting relations between these four types may be called to attention. First they involve an order of "tension" which may be put roughly as Cells 3, 1, 2, 4 from high to low. This order is changed, however, when the focus is on responsibility for the social system as such, that is, the accent is on collectivity-orientation. Here it seems that there are two pairs. Cells 2 and 3 place a strong accent on such responsibility because a *system* as such is in the center of attention. Cells 1 and 4 on the other hand tend to be much more "individualistic" but of very different types in the two cases.

In the first case it is a kind of "goal-achievement" individualism which is not bound into a particularistic nexus as in Cell 2, in that the accent on achievement tends to preclude subordinating the achieving unit to a system in any sense, and the ascriptive focus on an absolute ideal is lacking. In the case of cell 4, on the other hand, the individualism has an expressive focus, because it has to take place within a framework treated as given.

Relationships of this character will be further discussed later. Next, however, it is essential to place these cultural ideal patterns in their *adaptive* context in relation to the functional problems of social systems. In a very broad way the differentiations between types of social system do correspond to this order of cultural value pattern differentiation, but *only* in a very broad way. Actual social structures are not value-pattern types, but *resultants* of the integration of value-patterns with the other components of the social system.

IV
THE STRUCTURE OF THE SO-CIAL SYSTEM, II: INVARIANT POINTS OF REFER-ENCE FOR THE STRUCTURAL DIFFERENTIATION AND VARIATION OF SOCIETIES

THE foregoing chapter brought us a step farther toward the conception of an operating social system. Instead of dealing only with the more elementary components of such a system, as was done in Chapter II, it showed how these elementary components could be organized into relational complexes and collectivities, and how the structure of these complexes could vary about the fundamental foci of crystallization of the social system. The task of the present chapter is to show how, in turn, these "sub-systems" are brought together to constitute more complex social systems, approaching the level of concreteness with which the empirical sociologist is concerned.

The norm for this discussion will be the society as defined above, that is, the social system which is potentially or, "in principle" self-subsistent. This is essential because only with reference to this norm can the problems of differentiation of a total system be analyzed. However, the results of the analysis will be applicable to any partial social system once it can be satisfactorily "located" within the society of which it is a part, and its boundaries relative to the rest of the society determined.

We shall have to start by analyzing still another set of points of reference, the functional foci for the structural differentiation of the social system. These points of reference may be regarded as the derivatives, on the requisite level of concreteness, of the points of reference for the analysis of action-orientations dealt with above, and many specific connections with that foregoing analysis will be established.

§ THE FOCI OF CRYSTALLIZATION FOR SOCIAL STRUCTURE

A SOCIAL system is, with respect to its structurally signifi-cant components, a *differentiated* system. For our purposes we can assume that what is differentiated is the unit of structure with which so much of the foregoing discussion has been concerned, the role in-cluding the object-significances of actors as well as their orientation patterns. Hence the fundamental focus for the analysis of the system as a differentiated system concerns the ways in which roles within it are differentiated and, in turn, these differentiated roles are inte-grated together, that is "mesh" to form a functioning system. At the same time it is not only roles which are differentiated. The indi-vidual and collective actors must be distributed between the various roles and role-clusters in the social system. Furthermore, so far as the roles involve instrumental orientations there must be facilities, and, so far as they involve expressive orientations, rewards.

The differentiation of the social system may then be treated under two main headings. First, it is a system of differentiated roles. The types of which it is composed, how they are distributed within the social system and how integrated with each other must be analyzed. This is what we mean by the social structure in the nar-rower sense of the term. Secondly, however, *given* the role struc-ture, we must analyze the processes of distribution of "movable" elements as between statuses and roles. This process of distribution of significant objects within the role-system will be called allocation.[1] There are three contexts of the problem of allocation which we will have to consider: 1) the allocation of personnel, i.e., of actors, be-tween roles; 2) the allocation of facilities; and 3) the allocation of rewards. The last two can, for certain purposes, be treated together

[1] The term is taken from economics and means essentially distribution in the perspective of functional significance to the system.

as constituting the allocation of possessions. Each of these will be discussed in turn, but first a few words need to be said about the general significance of allocation itself.

Allocation is, as noted, essentially an economic concept, and as here used is concerned with the "economic" aspect of the social system, but this is treated in a somewhat broader sense than is customary in the discipline of economics. The basic concept is the dilemma of scarcity which is always relative to demand. This is, in turn, a version of the still more general dilemma of "wanting to eat your cake and have it," that is of the incompatibilities of two or more things which, from some point of view, are both desired. The most obvious cases of allocation are those of quantifiable entities, which must somehow be divided up between claims and claimants. Money is of course a type case since the question "how much?" has a completely unambiguous meaning. But even where quantification reaches only the level of rank-ordering, essentially the same basic problem arises.

The distribution of role-types within the social system has been separated off from the three problems of allocation of "movable" elements within the system. There is, however, an allocative aspect to this distribution which is in a sense the obverse of the other three allocations. Roles are, from the point of view of the functioning of the social system, the primary mechanisms through which the essential functional prerequisites of the system are met. There is the same order of relationship between roles and functions relative to the system in social systems, as there is between organs and functions in the organism. There is not, with certain exceptions to be noted, an inherently limited supply of roles which has to be allocated among claimants. However, if the role is to serve the requisite functions in the social system, it must be adapted to the capacities and needs of the incumbents. The role structure must be adapted to such conditions as the possibility of the same individual combining a given set of roles in his own activity; e.g., with respect to time limitations, to requirements of geographical location of the activities, with respect to psychological compatibility, as in the case of requiring both decisive action and reflective thought from the incumbent of the same role.

Subject to such conditions the performance of the various functions essential to the system comes to be allocated among the population of the system through the patterning of their roles, and must, as noted, be adapted to the human material. But precisely because in the larger scale social systems the role structure itself is the stabler element it is for most purposes more convenient to consider a given role structure as the major point of reference for the analysis of the three allocative processes we have distinguished.

There is one specific scarcity aspect relative to the distribution of role-content between persons. In a given social system, with a given type and level of differentiation, if the functions of a role are specialized relative to the social system, there will not be "room" for an indefinite number of the particular class of roles in the same system. There is a wide variation between types of roles in this respect. If, as is always empirically the case, socialization is organized largely about kinship, there is necessarily "room" for as many mother roles as there are conjugal family units in the society, generally approaching the number of adult couples in the society; in other words practically any adult woman will be "eligible" for a mother role. But at the other end of the distribution there may be some types of role which in the nature of the case must be extremely limited in numbers in the same society. There seem to be essentially two types of these. One is the type of role which is near the "top" in a scale of responsibility or prestige or both—e.g., there can be only one President of the United States at a time—the other is the type of role which is extremely specialized in other respects—hence there are severe limitations on the "market" for the relevant products or services. An example would be the role of theoretical physicist.

The existence of different types of roles in the same society distributed among the population in different ways is of course also limited by their mutual compatibility in the system, whether they mesh or generate conflict. This, however, is an integrative, not an allocative aspect of the problems of social structure.

We have noted that this distribution of role types is itself the basic structure of the social system as a system. This structure is described by the answers to such questions as of what types of roles is it made up, in what proportions and how distributed in "clusters"? But to develop a conception of the social system it is highly important to relate this role structure to the three allocative problem-foci of the social system.

The first of these is the allocation of personnel.[2] From the point of view of the analysis of personality, roles are, as it were, *allocated* to actors. But from the point of view of the social system the primary allocative problem is the obverse, the regulation of the "flow" of personnel within the role-system. It is of course possible that the two processes should coincide as in the development of a new social structure. But the larger, stabler social structures obviously transcend the life-span of the human individual, or that sector of it which is suitable for incumbency of a given role. Social structures, even relatively stable ones, change too, but their rhythms and periodicities of change are not the same as those of the individual life cycle. There must from the point of view of the going social system, therefore, be a continual process of "replacement" of the personnel in the roles of the social system. It is of course essential to stability in most cases that this should not come all at once, and it seldom does but nevertheless it is always going on.

The first allocative "decision" about a given individual of course concerns where he is going to start off. This is, in all known societies determined by the fact that he is an infant of a given sex, *and* that he is born as a child into a particular position in a particular kinship unit. The initial allocative criteria, therefore, are in the nature of the case *ascriptive,* both classificatory, with respect to age and sex, which presumably *cannot* be changed, and relational, with respect to kinship unit membership, which conceivably might. Why kinship ascription should be universal constitutes an empirical problem.

In some respects in all societies, and overwhelmingly in some, status by birth continues as an allocative criterion throughout the life cycle. But in some respects which are functionally of the highest significance, there is in all societies a series of status changes in the course of the life cycle. The sequence may be ascriptively pre-determined or it may not, that is, there may be selection-points where a sorting out process takes place at various stages.

Besides the automatically ascriptive mechanism of which allo-

---

[2] Collectivities as actors are within limits also subject to allocation as units. The following discussion will, however, be confined to individual actors.

cation of status and role by birth is the type case, there are two other principally relevant possibilities, the second of which falls into two major sub-types. The first is the allocation by explicit decision of other persons, what is usually called the system of *appointment*.

The second is allocation as the outcome of an unplanned selective process. Such a selective process may be competitive to a greater or less degree. In one sub-type those who "happen" to reach a certain position are automatically selected. In the other sub-type the actor "tries for" a given role-status as a goal of intentional endeavor and in order to reach his goal must win out over his competitors. The type case of the latter which may be called competitive allocation is of course the process of economic competition in the market situation.

All three of these types are continually involved in social systems and occur in varying combinations. Allocation by appointment very generally is combined with selective processes in that appointment is from among those who have qualified for it by some criterion of eligibility. Fulfillment of the criteria may or may not be the result of a competitive endeavor to meet them. Thus it may be laid down that a high Government appointment should go to a prominent businessman. But it would be extremely unlikely that any of those considered for it became prominent businessmen in order to qualify for this type of appointment. On the other hand, certainly most graduate students directly seek the Ph.D. degree in part at least in order to qualify for a certain class of academic or research appointment.

Analysis of what above has been called the Hobbesian problem of order shows conclusively that competitive allocation cannot operate without institutionalization of a set of norms defining the limits of legitimate action, particularly in this case with regard to legitimacy of means of attaining the goal. Both appointive and selective allocation are associated with primacy of achievement-orientation over ascriptive. The "power of appointment" may indeed be regarded as a further specification of the regulation of competition in terms of rules. The raison d'etre of appointment is often to ensure the closest possible approximation to an achievement norm. But both types are, in different ways, open to possibilities of "bias" of any given selective criteria, the competitive through the "loopholes" of the system of regulatory norms and of their enforcement, the appointive through biases in the action of the appointing "authorities" (often of course a reflection of "pressures").

Facilities, it will be remembered from the last chapter, are possessions which are significant as means to further goals in complexes of instrumental orientation. The criteria of a facility are therefore intrinsic transferability between actors, individual or collective, and relevance to instrumental orientation. The former distinguishes it from the modality of an actor as object; neither his qualities nor his performances are intrinsically transferable, they are always and indelibly "his." Facilities must also be distinguished from rewards. Rewards may or may not be the same concrete possessions in another aspect. But in any case analytically the distinction is crucial. Rewards are always to be understood as part of the complex of expressive symbolism not part of the instrumental means-end complex.

A possession has been defined as an entity which is transferable from one actor to another, which can change hands through the process of exchange. This entity, the possession as such, is *always* a right or a bundle of rights. In other words, it is a set of expectations relative to social behavior and attitudes. It is never as such a physical object, but always consists in *rights in* or relative to physical, social, or cultural objects, rights of use or of control of disposal. At the very least ego's right implies the negative obligation of alter to refrain from interfering with ego's use or control of the object of his rights of possession; on occasion it may go further to require positive performances from alter, such as relinquishment of a mode of control which "rightfully belongs" to ego.

It is true that physical objects "change hands," but in terms of the social system this is not the essential but a derivative phenomenon. In innumerable cases of transfer of possessions in a physical sense nothing changes hands, or only a symbolic entity, e.g., a "piece of paper." This is true even with respect to rights in physical objects, where, as in the case of land, the object "stays put" and what changes is the relation to it of the previous "owner" on the one hand and the new one on the other. But many of the most important objects in which there are rights of possession are not physical at all, but may be cultural objects, e.g., the "book" an author has written. Another exceedingly important class is that of *relational* possessions. By this is meant the incumbency of given positions in the social system to which certain advantages attach and which may be relinquished in favor of another. Thus eligibility for a status, e.g., a "job," or a claim to the services of another, may be a possession.

Every social system must have mechanisms for the allocation of possessions as facilities, because their possession is desirable and they are inherently limited in supply relative to demand. The next question concerns the sources of this scarcity, and the implications of these facts for the social system. For present purposes it is sufficient to classify these sources as relational and non-relational.

The non-relational sources are extrinsic to the social system as such. They concern for example physical and biological limitations on the availability of physical objects or the fact that though they can be produced, this is at a cost in the economic sense of the term. Thus buildings, machines and the like are limited in supply for cost reasons. This whole subject has been so fully treated in the literature of economics that it need not detain us further here.

Similar considerations apply to a certain class of cultural possessions which may be important as facilities. Thus specialized technical knowledge can be acquired only through labor, and often through access to other special facilities as well, such as the services of teachers and various types of equipment, e.g., books. When such knowledge can only be attained at a cost, or far more effectively by utilizing such facilities, the possessor of the specialized knowledge may acquire rights in it as a possession, for example the right to use an academic degree, which may even as in the case of the M.D. degree, be the prerequisite of practicing a given profession.

An intermediate case is that of physical possessions which are for physical reasons intrinsically incapable of increase and cannot therefore be produced at any case. The most familiar example is space on the surface of the earth. A particularly desirable location, e.g., an urban business site, must therefore be allocated to some user, and many competitors for it excluded. The same is essentially true of time limitations. Because of the finitude of the human life span it is strictly impossible for anyone ever to "find the time" to do everything he might want to do. These two bases of intrinsic limitation alone are sufficient to preclude the notion sometimes put forward that we are on the verge of an "economy of abundance" where scarcity in the economic sense would come to be in principle meaningless.

The most fundamental limitation, however, is the directly relational one, as distinguished from the indirectly relational character of space and time limitations on the freedom of action. The relational limitation rests upon the fact that it is inherent in the nature of social interaction that the gratification of ego's need-dispositions is contingent on alter's action and vice versa. The action system of each actor is a finite system of limited possibilities. Therefore alter in the nature of the case cannot do everything ego might want him to do, and vice versa. Relational possessions in the sense of rights of any actor to count on certain reciprocal actions (and attitudes) of others, must in the nature of the case be organized into a patterned system. Every actor must distribute his actions which are significant to others in a determinate way, as between the various claimants, as between types of action, and as between occasions, and this determinate organization must be mutual. Ego, for example, cannot, in the sense of what we mean by an occupational role, "work for" an indefinite number of clients or employers. The fact that he must choose is reflected in the fact that not all the alters who might like to have his services can do so.

So far as it concerns the problem of the allocation of facilities this basically relational problem of order we shall, following Hobbes, call the problem of *power*. With one qualification Hobbes' own famous definition of power "a man's present means to any future good" fits the case. We would add the qualification, that such means constitute his power, so far as these means are dependent on his relations to other actors; the correlative is the obligation of alter to respect ego's rights. Hence *in one aspect* all possession of facilities is possession of power because it is at least in an implied and contingent sense a control over the actions of others, at least in the sense of ability to count on their non-interference. There is a complete shading off between this negative, contingent aspect of power, and the positive aspect, ego's capacity to influence the action of others in the interest of attainment of his positive goal beyond merely counting on their otherwise expected non-interference.

Power and its bases may be highly specific and particularized. Thus possession of a particular bit of land may have no further social implications than the "power" to forestall trespass. But the significance of power in the social system, besides the institutionalization of rights to particularized possessions, is dependent on the fact of its generalization and, as a consequence of this, of its quantification. This generalization and quantification is a matter of degree with highly different levels of development in different social systems. It seems to depend above all on three conditions. The first is the inherent significance of what we have called the exchange problem in all systems of differentiated roles. The higher the degree of differentiation of the role system, the more extended the network of exchange relationships must become, the more that is, there must be processes of settlement of terms between the incumbents of different roles. It is in these processes of the settlement of terms that the opportunity to exercise power arises, and that its significance to goal-achievement resides. This is essentially another way of stating the fact of the inherently relational character of possessions, including facilities. The significance of power to the realization of any given goal-orientation of one or more actors within the social system is a function of the extensity of the system of actual or potential exchange relationships through which it ramifies.

The second condition is the incidence of universalistic orientations within the social system. This and the elaboration of role differentiation are inherently linked. The more extensive the relational context of an instrumental orientation in which exchange processes take place freely, and hence can become of prime functional significance, the more it is essential for these processes to be governed by generalized norms which in their applicability transcend the particularity of each specific set of relationships within which they occur. It is only on this condition that a restriction of the range of exchanges which would in itself lead to constriction of the differentiation of roles can be overcome. The more narrowly particularistic the institutional structure is then the greater the barriers to extension of ego's influence to alters beyond the immediate range of the particular associations in which he is implicated. Breakdown of particularistic ties is the first condition of extension of the power system. But this taken alone leads to instability which can only be met either by reversion to particularistic restrictions or by the institutionalization of universalistic norms.

The third condition is what may be called a gradient of effectiveness or "drasticness" of means. All institutionalization of exchange relations involves, as was pointed out in the last chapter, the definition of legitimate limits on the choice of means. The fundamental functional basis of the need for such institutionalization lies in the fact that resort to certain means would give ego "too much power" in the sense that, unless his power can be generalized to others he could gain his ends at the expense of alter. In individual exchange relationships there are above all two classes of means which are the focus of this institutional regulation, fraud and force. The Hobbesian analysis shows in classic form why their unregulated use would lead to the "war of all against all." There is, however a third equally basic problem concerned with the control of organization, since so many goals can be attained through organization which would be impossible without it. This is of course preeminently true of the use of force.[3] The essential point is that power can always in the short run be increased by going farther along the gradient of more and more drastic means. But, of course, since power, being relational, is by definition relative, ego can enhance his power by resort to more drastic means, only so long as alter fails to take "countermeasures" by resort to the corresponding means on his side. It is this interactive resort to more and more drastic means which is the source of the "struggle for power" and the inherent vicious-circle character of this struggle. Only by some sort of control operating on both parties to a conflict can the vicious circle be broken.

The generalization and quantification of power in social systems seems to occur in two principal interdependent but distinct modes or directions, which may be called the *economic* and the *political* respectively. The economic type consists in the extension of the range of actually and potentially available exchange relationships, and hence of the range of any given actor's choice relative to the acquisition and disposal of rights of possession of facilities—and of course rewards so far as these are "negotiable." This extension is

[3] On a somewhat subtler level capacity to play on the "sentiments" of others is another means of attainment of goals which must be subject to institutionalized control. This problem belongs, however, primarily under the heading of the institutionalization of expressive symbolism and the reward system rather than of the organization and allocation of facilities.

possible only under relatively rigidly defined conditions which include on the negative side primarily the "emancipation" of the exchange context from diffuse and particularistic involvements so that criteria of instrumental efficiency may have primacy, and on the positive side the institutionalization of restrictions on resort to means of gaining advantage which would be disruptive of the operation of such an exchange system, notably fraud and force, and the "abuse" (defined in the requisite functional terms) of the control of organization. In this sense the situation of the exercise of economic power must be specific, not diffuse in its pattern.

Power which is in this sense laterally extended through a ramified exchange system, but at the same time sharply restricted in scope in the above sense is economic or "purchasing" power. This potential scope is of course enormously extended through the cultural invention of money which, in present terms, may be treated as the symbolic generalization of purchasing power, indeed one of the most remarkable and important of all human symbolizations. The essence of this symbolization is that, within the sharply defined limits of relevance to this particular type of exchange transaction relationship, a certain quantity of money can "stand for" or "mean" a whole complex of particular physical or cultural "goods" or relational "services" to use the traditional terminology of economics.

Economic power, particularly as culturally defined and shaped through the institutionalization of money, has remarkable properties not shared by any other phenomenon of the whole system of social interaction. The most interesting of these properties, for present purposes, is the fact that it can, within the requisite limits, be treated as a *lineally* quantitative element or variable in the total equilibrium of social systems—perhaps it is the only variable on a comparable level of generalized significance which possesses this property. Obviously such concepts as wealth and income can be treated as special cases of the more general category of economic power.

Here we find the point of departure of economic theory as a special branch of the theory of social systems. Economic theory is the conceptual scheme dealing with the phenomenon of economic power in this sense, and in the most technical sense, with the complex interdependences involved in a *system* of such power relations in an "economy." The relevance of these interdependencies in turn to the processes of allocation of facilities and personnel within a social system should be obvious in the light of the foregoing discussion.

It should also be clear that the empirical relevance of economic theory in a technical sense is very strictly a function of the *type* of social system to which it is applied. This relevance depends upon the scope of exchange relationships where the settlement of terms can operate independently of the institutional variables of the social system and of political power. These relationships must operate within a framework of regulative institutions which both enforce the degree of emancipation from particularism and diffuseness which are prerequisite to the independent orientational significance of "economic considerations," and enforce observance of the limitations on choice of goals and means which prevent the merging of an economic into a political problem. In so far as these conditions fail to be fulfilled economic theory loses its independent relevance as an explanatory scheme. Its relevance, that is, must be confined to the sphere where what may in motivational terms be legitimately called "economizing" actually takes place, and in the absence of the above conditions this is a narrow sphere. But in such a case economic theory may still retain another order of significance as a canon of functional interpretation. Action that is, however oriented, may still have economic *consequences*, with regard to the allocation of facilities in the social system, and analysis of the significance of these consequences in terms of the social system regarded as a hypothetical "economy" may still be of very great importance.

The second direction of generalization and quantification of power has been called the political. The range of potential exchange relations to which the possibility of "influence" is extended is relevant here as in the economic case. But what is distinctive about political power is not this, but extension of the *scope* of considerations relevant to its definition and exercise. Economic power, that is, is focused on the possession of *means* (the use of the term in such expressions as "a man of means" is significant) to maximize advantage in a range of alternatively possible exchange transactions under very strictly defined conditions through the offer of balancing advantages. Political power, on the other hand, is generalized through the broadening of the scope of relevance to the whole relational context of a given goal. On the level of the particular relational context political power is capacity to control the relational system as a system, whether it be an organization or a diffuser, less integrated system.

The principle of generalization of political power then is its extension to more and more comprehensive relational systems which must as power systems be integrated in this sense into master systems and sub-systems. While the structure of economic power is, as we have noted, lineally quantitative, simply a matter of *more and less,* that of political power is *hierarchical;* that is, of *higher and lower levels.* The greater power is power *over* the lesser, not merely *more* power *than* the lesser. Political power is relational, not merely in reference, that is to *n* potential exchange partners, but in direct significance. This is perhaps another way of stating the diffuseness of political power, in that it is a *mobilization of the total relational* context as a facility relative to the goal in question.

This diffuse character of political power explains the peculiar relevance to it of the gradient of drasticness of means. Since ability to use force in its relation to territoriality is one ultimate focus of power in this sense, the control of the use and organization of force relative to territory is always a crucial focus of the political power system, in one sense the crucial focus. It is this which gives the state its central position in the power system of a complex society. It is in turn the functional need to organize the power system relative to force and territory which gives control of the machinery of governmental organization its strategic position as a proximate goal of emulation for power.

These considerations throw some light on the problems of the status of political science as a discipline which will be developed further in the final chapter. Neither power in the political sense nor the operation of government as a sub-system of the social system can be treated in terms of a specifically specialized conceptual scheme of the same order as that of economic theory, precisely for the reason that the political problem of the social system is a focus for the integration of *all* of its analytically distinguishable components, not of a specially differentiated *class* of these components. Political science thus tends to be a synthetic science, not one built about an analytical theory as is the case with economics.

In conclusion we may reiterate that the generalization of power in the economic direction is dependent on the institutionalization of universalistic and functionally specific institutions which are regulative institutions *par excellence*. The institutionalization of economic power is focused on the maintenance of the conditions, on the one hand of its generalization, on the other of its insulation from other components of the system of facilities, above all from political power. This includes preventing large concentrations of economic power from having "undue influence" as facilities for the exercise of political power. Political power, on the other hand, is inherently diffuse, and is greater in proportion to the scope of the relational context which is involved. Its generalization is, however, dependent on the level of univeralism. The problem of control of political power is above all the problem of *integration,* of building the power of individuals and sub-collectivities into a coherent system of legitimized authority where power is fused with collective responsibility.

By rewards we mean those transferable entities or possessions which are desired as objects of immediate gratification by actors. A possession is a facility so far as the actor's orientation to it is primarily instrumental (and it is not itself an ultimate "goal-object"). It is a reward so far as the actor's orientation (i.e., basis of interest) is predominantly expressive. This means that so far as ego's interest is in alter because the object can be "got from" alter, the orientation to alter should be treated as instrumental. Only when alter *himself* is, in some relevant aspect, the object, is it expressive. Ego's relation to alter as a means to a goal, e.g., the mother as the source of food, is one in terms of which the rights vis-à-vis alter should be classified as facilities. This example shows the fundamental character of the reciprocal interdependence of human beings on each other in an instrumental context.

All classes of objects may, as objects of cathexis, function as rewards, and the problem of the allocation of rights in their possession may enter into the allocative processes of the social system for all of them. This is obviously true of "consumer goods" in the terminology of economics. Such goods are both cathected objects in the sense of their significance to the gratification processes of the actor, and they are expressive symbols. In the latter capacity they come to be evaluated in terms of their conformity with appreciative standards as well as their immediate role as need-disposition gratifiers. It is above all in this connection that so many physical artifacts are more significantly cultural than physical objects, because their style-patterning is more important than any other aspect of them. A good example would be style in clothing or in house furnishings.

But just as in the case of facilities, perhaps even more so, a central significance attaches to the relational aspects of the reward system. Just as alter's reaction to ego's action can be of fundamental instrumental significance for the attainment or the blocking of ego's goals, so alter's reactions may be of fundamental expressive significance so far as alter is cathected as an object. We have seen in the last chapter that there is generalization from the cathexis of particular acts on alter's part, to that of alter's attitudes. This implies the establishment of expectations on both sides that actions toward the other will fit a certain pattern. Where the cathexis is positive, this involves an attachment, and where there is a common evaluative standard of expressive symbolism, we have spoken of a relation of "loyalty" between ego and alter.

The expectation of a continuing pattern of attitude on alter's part, with the exceptions of appropriate behavior, may be regarded as a relational possession of ego. It is intrinsically transferable in the sense first that the element of contingency means that either party may "withdraw" his loyalty from the other if his expectations are not met (or from other motives). The fulfillment of his expectations by alter can therefore only conditionally be counted upon by ego, and is not an intrinsic property of ego's situation. Furthermore, most attitudes toward actors are capable of being transferred from one actor to another.

This is true above all because from one point of view the cathexis of any one actor is the result of a selection among possibilities. There is always implicit if not explicit a comparative reference in a loyalty relationship, namely, "I am more loyal to A than to B because of a differential evaluation of their respective significances to me." This may be a wholly particularistic evaluation, e.g., because A is my mother whereas B is only a cousin, or it may be because A ranks higher by a universalistic standard of evaluation than does B, e.g., has a higher level of technical competence in a relevant field. But in any case this differential evaluation is as it were the obverse of the contingency of the particular loyalty; that is, the latter is contingent on ego retaining his place in accordance with the evaluative criteria.

Then relational reward-possessions present an allocative problem just as do facilities, that is, through the power problem, and in the homologous way. The conditions on which ego has a right to a certain attitude of loyalty on alter's part cannot be left unstructured and random. Indeed because of the crucial significance of the mutual orientation of ego and alter in interaction for the social system, it may be said that relational rewards are the core of the reward system of a society. The first principle of its organization is the institutionalization of the possession of relational rewards themselves. Physical and cultural reward-objects then come to be built into an integrated reward system in the first instance through their symbolic association with relational rewards; that is, on the level of expressive symbolism.[4]

Before putting forward a few considerations about this integration it is best to raise the question of whether there is any basis of generalization and quantification in the reward system which is comparable to that in the system of facilities. This raises the question of the basis of classification of relational rewards.

This in turn is the problem of classification of the fundamental types of attachment and hence of loyalty. Because these are so deeply involved in the fundamental attitude structure of the personality, it seems justified to take as the basis of this classification the two pattern variables of affectivity-neutrality and specificity-diffuseness. This, as was shown in the last chapter, yields the following fourfold table:

[4] This type of symbolic integration will be further analyzed in Chapter IX below.

	SPECIFICITY	DIFFUSENESS
Affectivity	Receptiveness-Responsiveness	Love
Neutrality	Approval	Esteem

The bases for the significance of this classification have been laid in the discussion in the last chapter of the relational context of expressive action-orientation. It remains here to draw a few of the implications for the structure of the reward system.

There seem to be inherent empirical connections between diffuse love attachments and particularism. This means that through love attachments an actor is likely to be bound only to a small circle of persons "close" to him. However, the same order of attachment may be involved, as we have seen, in his integration with collectivities, including very large ones such as the nation. But a very important feature of such attachment to a collectivity is that it is not a basis of *differential* reward as between those who share membership, though there may of course be differential rewards in the form of statuses and other symbolically significant things *within* the collectivity—but this is different from the significance of membership as such. Furthermore, love attachments become attenuated into "casual" friendliness as they go down in the order of precedence of obligation, but precisely because of this attenuation, to be treated in a friendly way is not a focally significant reward in most situations from the point of view of personality.

The attitudes of receptiveness and responsiveness in specific expressively significant contexts are considerably more capable of generalization. Indeed by virtue of their specificity they are in certain respects comparable with the pattern of economic exchange. It is of course well known that under certain circumstances mutual erotic gratification may be made to fit such a context, though this is never the central pattern of the institutionalization of this class of rewards. Similarly with the type of expressively oriented activity we may call recreation or entertainment. Indeed in all probability what is usually thought of as friendliness should probably be placed in this category. It is a kind of "recreational penumbra" of orientations, the core of which belongs on another level.

In societies with a primacy of expressive orientations it is probable that the primary focus of the total reward system is to be sought on this level (i.e., of love and receptiveness-response). In this case institutionalization will tend to prescribe the limits and the scope of obligations involved in legitimate love attachments, as well as defining the range of legitimacy of the expressive interests and activities. The proliferation of recreational activities and of art would be expected in such a society.

There would, however, appear to be considerably greater possibilities of generalization where the balance is shifted from affectivity to the affectively neutral side. For evident reasons rewards in the form of attitudes of approval and esteem would be more prominent in societies and subsystems of any society where either universalism or achievement values or both were prominent.

There is an interesting parallel between the distinction between economic and political power on the one hand, and approval and esteem rewards on the other. Approval is an attitude focused on a specific context, a quality complex or a type of performance. It is therefore capable of abstraction to a relatively high degree from the other features of the object. We can approve or admire competent performance even though we are far from admiring other things about the person in question. Approval-rewards are clearly of great importance to the reward system of a society which institutionalizes universalistic-achievement values and which gives a prominent place to roles defined in these terms and those of functional specificity. The great difference from economic power, however, lies in the fact that there is no symbolic quantification of the objects of approval to compare with money with respect to simplicity and lack of ambiguity. This, however, is one principal reason why money tends to acquire such a prominent status as a *symbol* of approved qualities or achievements in such a situation. It is a peculiarly appropriate symbol.

The case of esteem is more closely analogous with political

power. Approval may be given without the implication of a generalized rank-ordering. Esteem, because of the element of diffuseness, however, makes segregation of particular contexts more difficult. Hence there is at least a tendency to a hierarchical ordering in terms of esteem. This hierarchical ordering we may call *prestige*, which is the relative esteem in which an individual is held in an ordered total system of differentiated evaluation.

There is, therefore, a sense in which all the elements of the relational reward system come to be integrated in terms of a ranking system in terms of esteem, just as the control of facilities is ordered in a political power system. This ranking system in terms of esteem is what we may call the system of *stratification* of the society. It is the general resultant of many particular bases of differential evaluation. Non-relational reward-objects naturally have to be integrated with the prestige system in one aspect of their significance as expressive symbols. Hence many elements of the "style of life" come to have significance, among other things, as symbols of prestige in the system of stratification.

One further general point needs to be made. Affective neutrality in general terms means, as we saw in the last chapter, primacy either of instrumental or of moral orientations. In the case of approval and esteem it *must* mean the latter because only this is directly relevant to expressive orientations. This is the fundamental analytical basis of the place of moral sentiments in the institutionalization of the reward allocation systems of societies on which Durkheim and Max Weber laid such great stress. Both affective and affectively neutral attitudes play a fundamental part in the sanction system of role-orientations. The present analysis gives us a basis for discriminating their respective places, and their relation to the instrumental aspect of sanctions.

We may now turn to the integrative foci of the functional problems of the social system. These fall, in accordance with the discussions of the last chapter, into two well defined classes. First are the negative problems of defining the limits of permissiveness for "private" interests or self-orientation, both of individual actors and of sub-collectivities. The second is that of the institutionalization of the positively integrative functions of the social system considered as *a* collectivity; that is, the definition of the gradations of responsibility, and the structuring of leadership, including executive and representative roles.

In approaching this problem area it should first be called to mind that the institutionalization of roles is itself a mode of integration of the social system. It is the most elementary level of putting together of the units. Our concern now is with the higher reaches of integration of many sub-integrations. This conception of a hierarchy of integrations may be carried a step farther. A collectivity is a system of roles integrated in certain ways, which were discussed in the last chapter. But a social system is in one aspect a network of sub-collectivities, connected by "interstitial" patternings and mechanisms. At the same time a society, and many though not all types of partial social system, is itself *a* collectivity of a higher order of organization. Thus our fundamental starting point has to be the general nature of the collectivity and hence of its possibilities of differentiation. Conversely the problems of the society are referable back to *any* collectivity, with the appropriate allowance for its partiality.

The first basic integrative reference then is to the limitations on permissiveness for orientation in terms of private interests. These limitations are referable to functional "problem" contexts of the social system as a collectivity. These are in turn classifiable as the regulation of the allocative processes, and adequate provision for collective needs. This is the functional focus of the significance of what we have called regulative institutions.

The problem of the regulation of allocative processes may be broken down in terms of the foregoing classification. There must be regulation of the processes by which roles themselves and their relationships change within the system. Only in a limiting case is the role-structure of a system completely fixed. Most social systems are dynamically changing in this as in other respects. But room for change does not mean that any actor or group of them can "innovate" by redefining their roles in any way they may happen to desire. Some types of such innovation are compatible with the stability of the social system while others are not. Hence the institutionalization of patterns of legitimation of private role-innovation is one important context of regulation of permissiveness.

The second context is regulation of the processes of allocation of personnel where the problem is to see that the "right" people get into the right roles, and that people stay "where they belong" in terms of status. Essentially the same is to be said about the regulation of the allocation of facilities and of rewards, heading as they do up to the political power problem and the prestige problem. In all three of these contexts there is not only the problem of protecting a status quo but of the institutionalization of regulated innovation. This is extremely closely connected with regulation of what have been called the competitive aspects of the processes of allocation.

A stable equilibrium of purely competitive orientation is, of course, as economic theory has shown, fully conceivable. Nonetheless such interaction systems must be presumed to be in general more unstable than the automatically ascriptive type and probably more so than the appointive or decision-selection type. The prediction of just how personnel, facility and reward allocation will come out when left to a freely competitive process may be highly uncertain. A social system in which such processes are prominent must therefore presumably have a considerable range of tolerance for differences of outcome. At the same time the disruptive potentialities are so great that there must also be limits to this range, even though they are flexible. It seems probable that an "individualistic" society of this sort will also have to be able to tolerate considerable deviations from any abstract standard of "justice."

With respect to any or all of the above integrative problems there is a range of possibilities as to how this set of norms limiting permissiveness, that is, the system of regulative institutions, is both patterned and institutionalized in the sense of the structure of the sanction system. Here there seem to be two most significant poles of variability on the latter basis, the "informal" and the "formal." In the first case sanctions are left in "private" hands alone. They are a matter of the "spontaneous" reaction of alter to what ego does. There is no differentiation of roles about the axis of implementation of the common value patterns as a collective interest. This informal mode of institutionalization is, the evidence seems to show, the fundamental foundation of "social control" in all societies next to the institutionalization of roles in general. There is little hope of a formal sanction system operating effectively in most cases unless it is backed by such a system of moral sentiments as on the whole favor the institutionalized pattern system so that alter is inclined spontaneously to react favorably to conformity and unfavorably to deviance on ego's part.

The second polar type, however, is that of formalized sanctions. This implies, as noted, differentiation of roles relative to responsibility vis-à-vis the collectivity for maintenance of the integrity of a normative system. There are, in turn, two main functions in such differentiated roles, namely, *interpretation,* which is important because of the frequent range of uncertainty as to just what role-obligations are and how generalized rules apply, and *enforcement.* Enforcement here should not be interpreted to mean only the application of negative sanctions in case of deviance, but special responsibility for use of any and all sanctions, positive or negative. The difference from the spontaneous informal case is that in that case sanctions are a matter of "private morality," whereas in the formal case they are a matter of specific role-obligation.

Most larger-scale social systems of course have important elements of both types of institutionalization. As noted, the fundamental groundwork tends to be informal, but the more complex and dynamic the social system, the more this tends to be supplemented by the differentiation of roles carrying collective responsibility, which thus have directly integrative functions in this sense.

The other aspect of the foci for integrative structuring is that of the positive promotion of collective goals or interests. Again in a limiting case this may be informally structured, with completely spontaneous collective reactions. But the limits of this informality, according to size of group and other factors, are extremely narrow. Very soon "leadership" roles appear, which in most complex social systems become of very great significance. As we noted above such roles may in turn be differentiated according to functions internal to the collectivity as "administrative" roles, and those external to it in relations outside, in "representative" roles.

There is of course a wide variety of functional problems concerned with the relation between leadership roles and the rest of the collectivity, problems which have been intensively worked over in studies in the field of government, and elsewhere. Following Max Weber here we may put primary stress on the basis of the legitimacy of "authority" to take action which is "binding" on the collectivity as a unit and hence its members. Authority to bind and to coerce a member of the collectivity is, in this respect, of the same fundamental character as authority to assume a treaty obligation. In other words, the primary starting point for the analysis of

TABLE 3
PARADIGM FOR THE ANALYSIS OF SOCIAL SYSTEMS

Prerequisites of Social Structure: 1) Motivational Resources for Role-behavior requirements. 2) Situational Resources and Conditions. 3) Cultural Accumulation: knowledge, artifacts, etc.

STRUCTURE OF THE OBJECT SITUATION (AS ENTERING INTO THE DEFINITIONS OF ROLE-EXPECTATIONS)		FUNCTIONAL FOCI FOR STRUCTURING OF THE SOCIAL SYSTEM	SELECTIVE CHOICE-ALTERNATIVE FOCI FOR THE STRUCTURING OF ROLE-EXPECTATIONS (PATTERN VARIABLES)
Organisms	Social objects oriented to selectivity by quality or performance modalities	1. Allocative Foci. a) Distribution of role-content types. b) Distribution of personnel between roles, including memberships in collectivities. c) Distribution of facilities, among roles and actors. d) Distribution of Rewards among roles and actors.	1. Primarily relevant to status-structure patterning. a) Universalism—Particularism. b) Ascription—Achievement.
Ego as Personality			
Alter as Personality			2. Primarily relevant to attitude-orientation within roles. c) Affectivity—Affective Neutrality. d) Specificity—Diffuseness
Collectivities	All objects as of Cognitive-Cathectic significance and as instrumental means or conditions	2. Integrative Foci. a) Sub-collectivity solidarities. b) Society - wide solidarity (Relation to the Ethos of the Culture).	3. Primarily relevant to integration of the collectivity. e) Self-Orientation—Collectivity - Orientation.
Physical Objects			
Cultural Objects			

variability lies in the nature of the value-orientation patterns which define this aspect of the role.

These functional foci of crystallization of the structure of the social system discussed in this section are shown in relation to the pattern variables and to the structure of the situation in Table 3.

§ THE INTERNAL DIFFERENTIATION OF SOCIAL SYSTEMS

WE have now reached the point where an attempt must be made to work out a basis for the structural description of a social system as a whole, showing the basis of the differentiation of its units from each other, the ranges of that differentiation, and the structural relations of the units which constitute the system.

We will classify these possible sources of structural differentiation under six headings as follows:

RELATIONAL INSTITUTIONS

1. The Categorization of actor-units as *objects* of orientation. Their classificatory differentiation and distribution, i.e., their object-roles (statuses), within the social system.
   a. Individual actors as objects
   b. Collective actors as objects
2. The Classification of role-orientation types and their distribution within the social system.
   a. Roles of individual actors
   b. Roles of collective actors

REGULATIVE INSTITUTIONS

3. The "Economy" of instrumentally oriented relationships; classification and distribution of facilities and the organization of the power system.
4. The "Economy" of expressively oriented relationships; the classification and distribution of rewards and the organization of the reward system.

CULTURAL INSTITUTIONS

5. The Cultural Orientation System
   The patterning of cultural orientations in relation to the social structure; ideology, religious beliefs, expressive symbol-systems and their syntheses including mechanisms of enforcement and positive implementation.

RELATIONAL AND REGULATIVE INSTITUTIONS

6. The Integrative Structures
   Social-relational integration (moral); the social system as itself a collectivity; regulative norms and their enforcement. Roles institutionalizing special responsibilities for collective interests.

It will be maintained that filling in the above outline with the requisite detail of properly conceptualized statements of empirical fact will constitute an adequate description of a concrete social system, the amount of detail required depending on the problem. This of course implies that under each main heading there is available an adequate classification of the ranges of possible variability and then that the facts under each heading and the proper sub-classes can be put together to describe the system coherently. Working out at least the starting points for these sub-classifications will be the principal task of the present section. But before entering upon it a few remarks about the rationale of the classification as a whole are needed.

Perhaps the most familiar feature of the classification is the distinction between the first and second categories, namely, the classification of actors *as objects,* and the classification of orientation role-types. The employment of this distinction and its relevance to the analysis of social structure, along with the relevance of the concept of "possessions" to categories three and four, makes it possible to clarify a number of what have hitherto been baffling problems.

The classification of object-units is concerned with what has sometimes been called "categorization" in the analysis of social structure, what in the last chapter were called the ascriptive qualities and the performance capacities. The ascription-achievement variable was, it has been seen, concerned with the *modalities of objects;* it is therefore the major axis around which the classification under this heading must be worked out. Such categories of social structure as age and sex differentiations clearly belong here. But just as clearly *both* individual and collective actors must be included, of course with due attention to the differences. It has been evident throughout the development of the present conceptual scheme from early in Chapter I that collectivities must in certain contexts be treated as actors.[5] If this is true in general two obvious conclusions follow for the present context. First they are objects just as are individual actors and must be included in any classification of social objects. Second, the classification and distribution of collec-

---

[5] This view is also extensively discussed in *Values, Motives and Systems of Action.*

tivity types, that is what, relative to the social system in question are its *sub*-collectivities, must be treated as part of the structure of the social system.

The second main heading concerns the classification and distribution of role-orientation types. These are, as we have seen, basic units of the social system. But they are units seen in one of the two possible perspectives, that of the *orientations* of actors, while the object-position of *the same* actors is the other perspective. The attempt to combine *both* in the formulation of the role concept without making allowance for the difference of perspective has been the source of considerable difficulty in the analysis of social structures. The essential point is perhaps that the total unit of social structure is an interactive relationship. Such a relationship includes, at the minimum, two actors, each in two capacities, first as an orienting actor, second as an object, *but the same actor does not operate in both capacities in the same relationship from the same orientation point of reference.*[6]

In a completely "free" orientation relationship ego is free to "define" alter as an object any way he sees fit, within limits of what "makes sense." But here we are talking about social structures. It is taken for granted that social structure through institutionalization places limits on the range of legitimized *orientation* of an actor in a given status of ego. By exactly the same token it places limits on the ranges within which he may legitimately define alter as an object. In other words alter as object is institutionally "categorized." Only certain of the intrinsically possible meanings permitted of alter as an object are to be acted upon in this particular social system or the relevant part of it.

The first heading then concerns the categorization of *alters*. *What,* in an "existential" sense, *are* they within this social system and its relevant parts? The second heading deals with *exactly the same* concrete actors, but as *egos*, with the structuring of their orientations to the given object-world, the alters. Each actor is a "bundle" in each respect. For each social relationship in which he is involved he has, that is, what may be called an object-role *and* an orientation-

[6] Ego may for certain purposes be located as an object to himself—but this special case does not affect the above statements.

role. Just as in orientation terms he is not a single unitary entity, he has for instance an instrumental role toward one object, and an expressive role toward another, so in his object-roles he can also be "broken down," he may be an ascriptively significant object for one, an achieving object for the other and so on. This separation of the object-role and the orientation-role of course involves a special type of abstraction. It must never be forgotten that these are both abstractions from the same concrete roles of the same concrete actors.

The second pair of main headings of the classification also call for preliminary comment. Their rationale rests heavily on the analysis of the nature of facilities and of rewards and of "rights" to them put forward in the preceding section. Besides the allocative distribution of actors themselves as object-units, what is in fact allocated as part of the *social structure* consists in *rights* to these two categories of possessions, which in the specifically relational category of possessions comes to be identical with (or at least inseparable from) the possessions themselves. The concept of rights to possessions (and the obverse, the obligations to respect these rights) *constitutes the relational link between the orientation-role aspect of social structure and the object-role aspect.* Under these two categories, therefore, are treated the specifically relational structures or aspects, as distinguished from the classification and distribution of structural units.

The possibility of reducing this relational aspect of the organization of rights to the two categories of facilities and to rewards means an enormous simplification of the usual common sense ways of handling such problems. It is derived directly from the classification of evaluative action-orientations themselves, reserving the moral class for special treatment in the integrative context. Of course as a classification of concrete relational nexi it must be put in terms of primacies, since all the concrete elements are inherently involved in every concrete social relationship.

The fifth category is the cultural orientation system as such, so far as it is not already taken account of in the value-orientation patterns which are involved in the preceding four categories. Primarily, that is, this concerns belief systems and systems of expressive symbols. They cannot, in the nature of their place in systems of action generally, vary at random relative to the structure of the social system itself and must like the other elements vary within determinate ranges relative to definite foci of crystallization.[7]

The sixth category concerns the overall integrative structure of the social system as a whole. It has already been made clear that in this connection it is necessary to consider the society itself as a collectivity, or perhaps (as in the case of Medieval Europe with church and state) of two (or even more) interpenetrating and partially integrated collectivities. Many partial social systems of course, such as a market complex, may be lacking such an integrative structure within themselves.

Finally we may point out the relation of the present classification of the primary elements of social structure to the classification of the types of institutions presented in Chapter II above. Very clearly the primary relational institutions fall under categories one and two. Categories three and four are the focus of the primary regulative institutions and five of the cultural institutions. Category six, finally, has relevance to both of the first two classes of institutions. The structure of leadership roles itself may be regarded as a relational structure—but in addition the overall collectivity has regulative functions including those toward beliefs and expressive symbols. It must not be forgotten that relative to all these categories of structural elements there may be any degree of institutionalization from complete *anomie* at one pole to "perfect integration" at the other.

The procedure will be next to present a sub-classification under each of the six main headings with a brief commentary in connection with each, and then in the next chapter to enter into a discussion of how these can be put together to describe a total social system. For filling in the first heading we take up the discussion of ascriptive and achievement criteria in the last chapter.[8]

[7] Fuller analysis of these problems will be presented in Chapters VIII and IX below.

[8] What we are presenting here, it should be made clear, is a scheme of the invariant points of reference or foci of crystallization relative to which concrete social structures become patterned and organized.

I. *Categorization of actor-units in object-roles:*

A. Individual actors

    1. Ascriptive Quality foci

        a. Classificatory

            Sex

            Age

            Organic and personality traits

        b. Relational

            Biological position

            Spatial location

            Temporal location

            "Ecological" situation

            Collectivity memberships

    2. Performance-capacity foci (all classificatory)

        a. Instrumental primacy

            Technical competence

            Instrumental leadership capacity (executive and representative)

        b. Expressive primacy

            Capacity to elicit receptiveness and response

            Capacity to form and maintain diffuse attachments and loyalties

            Expressive leadership capacity

        c. Moral primacy

            "Private" moral "character"   } both eliciting

            Moral leadership capacity (charisma)   } approval and esteem

B. Collectivities as actors

    1. Ascriptive Qualities as foci

        a. Classificatory

            Size (number of participant individual actors)

            Composition (object-role types, distribution of relevant qualities of constituent individuals as detailed under A).

            Constituent orientation-role types (as under II below).

            Traits as a collectivity-unit (e.g., "rationalism" or "traditionalism," "individualism" or "collectivism").

        b. Relational

            Territorial location focus (is membership territorially bound or not? how?).

            Temporal location

            Inclusiveness (relative to any given other collectivity is

    membership mutually exclusive, are the two overlapping, or is collectivity B a sub-collectivity of collectivty A?).

2. Performance-capacity foci
    a. Instrumental primacy (e.g., a "productive" organization, a military unit).
    b. Expressive primacy (e.g., a theatrical troupe, certain types of propaganda agency).
    c. Moral primacy (e.g., a church).

This is a somewhat elaborate classification but a simpler one will not do justice to the complexity of the subject-matter. At any rate, in the main, it is systematically derived and should serve to order empirically descriptive materials. It is, from one point of view not as elaborate as it seems in that it incorporates generally significant variables which have played a critical part throughout the development of the present conceptual scheme, namely, ascription-achievement, universalism-particularism through its relation to the classificatory-relational distinction, and the classification of types of action-orientation. It is by virtue of such connections that the detail of such a classification can be given generalized significance.

Of course, there remains the task of classifying the possible and significant ranges of variation with reference to each of these foci and certain of their combinations. For example, biological position in combination with sex and age, give the points of reference for the classification of the actual possibilities of kinship structures. If this problem of classification of concrete types were approached solely in terms of logically possible permutations and combinations it would very quickly become impossible complex. It will be necessary, therefore, to look for possibilities of simplification; a problem which will be raised in the following chapter.

II. *Classification of orientation-role types*
  A. Individual actors
    1. Primacy of "private" interests (self-orientation).
      a. Instrumental—orientation to alter primarily as a source of facilities, i.e., acquisition of rights to instrumental possessions or services, "contractual" or cooperative.
      b. Expressive—orientation to alter primarily as a source of rewards, i.e., rights to relational possessions and other possessions as symbolic of them.

    c. Moral—orientation to alter primarily in terms of "private morality," i.e., their respective ego-integrative standards. These may or may not be deviant relative to institutionalized collective moral standards.

    (In all three cases if there is institutionalization at all, it is regulative institutionalization in terms of "rules of the game," the conditions on which rights may be established and relinquished as limits of *permissiveness*.)

2. Primacy of collective obligations (collectivity-orientation). Ego's role that of collectivity member.

    a. Instrumental primacy of orientation with performance of instrumental functions sanctioned as obligation to the collectivity. Orientation to alter *within* the collectivity primarily as a "cooperating" colleague, to any alter outside, ego takes a *representative* role. Facilities are *for the collectivity*, not individualized.

    b. Expressive primacy of orientation with performance of expressive functions sanctioned as obligation to the collectivity. Orientation to alter within the collectivity as "comrade" with whom reciprocity of sentiment is shared, orientation outside the collectivity in a representative role. Rewards are *for the collectivity*, not individualized. In the case of an individual they symbolize status in and services to the collectivity.

    (In both the above two cases the focus is not on the limits of permissiveness for private interests, but on the positive obligations of fulfillment of membership expectations. But the focus is not on the significance of the collectivity in the larger social system, that comes under B below; it is on ego's orientation *to the collectivity*.)

    c. Moral primacy. Expectation of both instrumental and expressive content of obligations to the collectivity (e.g., most kinship roles). With clear cut primacy in either direction this type would slip over to a or b type. Both rewards and facilities are for the collectivity and orientation to any alter *outside* is in a representative role. Obligation to collectivity is not merely a matter of "performance of duty" but of solidarity in sentiment.

B. Collectivities as Actors

  1. Primacy of "private interests," i.e., of the particular collectivity vis-à-vis the wider social system.

    a. Instrumental—orientation to other actors, collective and individual primarily as facilities (including prospective members as contributors of "services") and including enhancement of power position of the collectivity as a possible goal.

    b. Expressive—orientation to other actors, collective and individual, primarily as rewards, including above all enhancement of the collectivity's prestige as a focus.

    c. Moral—orientation to other actors, collective and individual in terms of their respective moral standards and of the possibility or lack of it of solidarity with them, i.e., of merging into a wider collectivity.

2. Primacy of collective obligations to a larger collectivity of which the first is defined as a part. Primacy of the "functions" of the sub-collectivity for the larger collectivity.

    a. Instrumental primacy of orientation, with instrumental functions on behalf of the larger collectivity sanctioned as obligations to the latter, e.g., the army's obligations to the "state" of which it is an organizational part.

    b. Expressive primacy of orientation with expressive functions for the larger collectivity sanctioned as obligations, e.g., the choir as part of the organization of the church.

    c. Moral primacy—essentially parallel to the individual case.

The above classification, it is evident, is organized about the types of evaluative action orientation, and the variable of self-collectivity orientation. This, as distinguished from category I, is not merely a classification of foci of crystallization but of *actual role-orientation types* because it is concerned with the fabric of the relational structure itself, not the properties of the objects which enter into those relationships as in the case of Heading I. It is therefore in fact a classification of the possibilities of variation of social structures.

III. *The "Economy" of Instrumental Orientations*
    (Here, instrumentally oriented roles of the types delineated under II, A and B are thought of as integrated to from differentiated complexes. These are of three types: 1) "ecological" complexes of division of labor without organization as collectivities, 2) collectivities and 3) the instrumental economy of the social system as a whole considered as an ecological system. The fourth possibility, the social system as a whole as an instrumentally oriented collectivity

does not require special treatment because in its fundamental structure it is the same as any other collectivity.)

A. The "instrumental ecological complex," seen with any given ego as a point of reference.

   1. Ego's technical role.

   2. Structuring of ego's "disposal" relations.

   3. Structuring of ego's "remuneration" relations.

   4. Structuring of ego's facility-procurement relations.

   5. Structuring of ego's cooperative relations.

(Structural variability occurs especially with regard to the segregation of one from all the other functions, or the fusion of one or more of them into the same role. Segregation extreme: technical role—fusion extreme; without organization artisan, independent professional role.)

(The content of the technical role or its fused counterparts will vary enormously, and such roles must always also be classified by content of "production" goal which are as various as "functions" on behalf either of actors or of a social system can be. The social system can, within the limits of permissiveness for private interests, be conceived as a "seamless web" of such instrumental ecological complexes each with an ego as its referential center. Certain such groups of complexes may be singled out as "markets" or "fields of competition," etc., i.e., as units of a sort.)

B. The instrumentally oriented sub-collectivity or "organization" (II-B-2a), as a system of differential instrumental roles.

   1. Differentiated technical roles—"contributions" to the cooperative production process.

   2. "Policy roles," decision-making with regard to the goal-orientations of the organization, "what to produce," quantities, timing, "public relations," etc.

   3. Administrative or "implementation" roles.

      a. Internal to organization.

         Allocative—budget, facilities, etc.

         Supervisory—"seeing that things get done" (instrumental authority).

      b. External to organization (representative).

         Disposal functions.

         Income-securing and facility-securing functions.

         Cooperation arranging and implementing roles.

(Except so far as the collectivity is an "organ" or an "agency" of a more inclusive collectivity, such collectivities constitute foci of ecological complexes relative to the larger social system. They operate within the range of permissiveness for self-orientation for collectivities—which may of course be differentiated by type of collectivity. Each one is the point of reference for such a complex. Similarly there is differentiation of functional content relative to the social system, and grouping as in "industries" or "institutions of higher education." Such terms may designate either a status class of actors or an ecological complex or both.)

C. The instrumental economy as a differentiated and integrated system.
    1. Types of unit and their distribution; individual actors, organizations by size, composition, role-constitution type, etc.
    2. Functional content-differentiation of units.
    Production, product distribution, income distribution, facility provision, cooperation.
    3. The instrumental units as a power system.
    (Institutionalization of power relations and "regulation of competition.")

Obviously the subject-matter under this heading has been intensively dealt with in economics and political science. The present attempt is limited to taking over a few of the familiar concepts of these fields in such a way as to facilitate connecting them with the general analytical framework of this work. This would be the primary starting point for an analysis of economic and political institutions, though in the political case considerable attention needs to be devoted to the expressive and integrative elements as well as the instrumental.

IV. *The "Economy" of Expressive Orientations*
    A. The "ecological" complex of expressive reciprocities with any given ego as a point of reference.
        1. Ego's specific gratification and expressive-symbolic orientation to a particular object, or class of objects.
        2. Structuring of ego's receptiveness relations.
        3. Structuring of ego's response relations.
        4. Structuring of occasions.
        5. Structuring of ego's diffuse attachments and loyalties.
(As in the instrumental case structural variability will be in terms of fusion-segregation with respect to the elements of this complex. The economy of "private" individual expressive orientations is

another "seamless web" with each individual ego as a point of reference.)

(Also, again, the "content" of the expressive interest will vary, and there must also [C below] be a classification by content.)

B. The expressively oriented sub-collectivity (the *Gemeinschaft*) (II-B-2b) as a system of differentiated expressive roles.

    1. Differentiated expressive "contributions" to the collectivity, rewarding different members and the collectivity as a whole in different ways.

    2. Expressive leadership roles, eliciting receptiveness and response, becoming focus of attachments and loyalties.

        a. Internally—symbolic foci of loyalty.

        b. Externally—representative roles, e.g., as "propagandist."

(Fundamentally this is exactly parallel to the instrumental case, but of course structural elaboration does not go so far, and it is much rarer to find anything approaching "pure" cases of expressive primacy, than of instrumental primacy.)

C. The expressive economy as a differentiated and integrated system.

    1. Types of unit; individual actors, collectivities by size, composition, role-orientation type, etc.

    2. Functional content-differentiation of units.
    Fusions and segregations, receptiveness-responsiveness, love, approval, esteem orientations.

    3. The expressive units as a prestige system (when institutionalized, stratification of the social system).

As noted, pure expressive primacy is relatively rare in the more conspicuous social structures. It is therefore essential to "dissect out" the elements of this expressive interaction structure. It is highly conspicuous in affectively accented relationships such as much of kinship or friendship, and of certain types of solidarity and leader-follower relations.

V. *The Cultural Orientation System*

A. Belief Systems.

    1. Existential Beliefs.

        a. Empirical—Science and empirical lore.

        b. Non-Empirical—Philosophy and supernatural lore.

        c. Specialization of roles with respect to investigative interests (e.g., scientist and philosopher).

　　2. Evaluative Beliefs.
　　　　a. Ideologies.
　　　　b. Religious ideas.
　　　　c. Role differentiation with respect to responsibility for evaluative beliefs (roles of religious and ideological "authorities").
　B. Systems of Expressive Symbols.
　　1. Purely expressive symbol systems.
　　　　a. Expressive of accepted attitude system.
　　　　b. Expressive of adjustive needs in response to strain.
　　　　c. Specialization of roles with respect to symbolism (e.g., artist or performer).
　　2. Evaluative symbolism.
　　　　a. Symbolization of collective solidarity.
　　　　b. Symbolization of meaning-adjustment patterns; religious symbolism.
　　　　c. Differentiation of roles with respect to evaluative symbolism—moral-expressive leadership or priesthood.

In addition to providing a set of foci of crystallization for cultural institutions as such, the above classification calls attention to the fact that roles may be differentiated with respect to the special significances of cultural problems other than those of value-orientation as such in their general bearing on role-structure. The roles of scientist, philosopher, theologian, artist and priest—in the sense of "cult administrator"—fit in here. As noted above, this whole aspect of the relation of cultural patterns to the social system will be dealt with more in detail in Chapters VIII and IX below.

VI. *Integrative Structures*
　　The system of moral value-orientation patterns on the social relational level in their relevance to the institutionalization of the social system as an overall collectivity.
　A. Institutionalization of the regulative patterns governing and defining the limits of the private sphere of orientations—for individuals and sub-collectivities. (The interests will be classifiable as instrumental, expressive and moral in the sense either of ego-integrative or sub-collectivity integrative.)
　　1. Through spontaneous action and informal sanctions.
　　2. Through formalized enforcement machinery.
　　　　a. Differentiation of roles with respect to enforcement functions.

B. Institutionalization of positive collective functions, instrumental or expressive.
   1. Informally.
   2. Through differentiation of leadership roles and institutionalization of their authority.
      a. Oriented to internal coordination functions—administrative roles.
      b. Oriented to the situation external to the collectivity—representative roles.

(In content the above classification should be the same as III-B and hence is not elaborated again here. Among the problems are those of the extent to which the integration of cultural orientations is fused with that of value-orientations in general, e.g., are "church" and "state" the same structures or are they differentiated from one another?)

The above classification is somewhat elaborate, and especially in the finer details, highly provisional. Such taxonomy is, of course, not profitable if undertaken only for its own sake. It is essentially a tool. Only in rather exceptional cases will any one research study involve very large parts of the total scheme. But it is extremely important to have such a scheme and to have it coherently worked out, to serve as a system of points of reference within which to locate any more specialized study and to begin to establish connections between the different parts. Such a scheme is, furthermore, the basis from which the comparative analysis of different social structures must start. It is the main outline, in short, of the structural framework to what has been called a "structural-functional" level of theoretical analysis.[9]

---

[9] Far more than any other single source this scheme derives from that of Max Weber as outlined in Chapter I of *The Theory of Social and Economic Organization.*

V
THE STRUCTURE OF THE SOCIAL
SYSTEM, III: EMPIRICAL DIFFERENTIATION AND
VARIATION IN THE STRUCTURE OF SOCIETIES

THE classification presented in the last section of the
foregoing chapter brings us a long step nearer to the possibility of
treating systematically the concrete structure of societies in terms
of the internal differentiations in the structure of any particular
society and the ranges of variability between societies. At this point,
however, we encounter a serious difficulty. From a certain abstract
theoretical point of view a systematic treatment of these problems
could only be attained by methodically spelling out all the logically
possible permutations and combinations of all the elements which
have been distinguished in the outline of points of reference, or
which could be derived by further subdivision of the categories.

Certainly far more work along these lines should be carefully
and systematically undertaken than has so far been the case. Such
an undertaking is, however, far beyond the possible scope of the
present work. Many particular phases of it will prove to be of great
importance in connection with the solution of problems in more
specialized fields of sociology. We do not, however, propose to
attempt to carry such structural morphology farther here. Before
leaving the treatment of social structure as such it will, however,
prove useful and illuminating to attempt to short-cut this process by
mobilizing available empirical and theoretical knowledge to give
some indications of the main lines of internal differentiation and
comparative variability of types of social structure.

There are two devices by which we can attempt to take such a short cut. The first is by applying the broad classificatory scheme we have developed to the assessment of the significance of certain empirical uniformities which are fairly well established in sociology. The essential point is that in certain crucial areas of social structure we do not find that empirically observable structures cover anything like the whole range of theoretically possible variability; possible, that is, according to purely logical permutations and combinations of structural components. Actual structures are, rather, concentrated in empirical "clusterings." In the first section of this chapter we will review certain highlights of evidence for the special importance of four such clusterings, those 1) of kinship, control of sex relations and socialization, 2) of the organization of instrumental achievement roles and stratification, 3) of the relation between power, force and territoriality, and 4) of the relation of the paramount integration of value-orientations to cognitive orientations and certain problems of personality adjustment in "religion." If the existence of such clusterings can be validated, even only in a rather rough way, this validation serves a two-fold purpose for the sociologist. On the one hand it justifies his short-cutting investigation of the *whole* range of structural possibilities and concentrating on a fraction of them; thus it enormously simplifies arriving at least at a first approximation of a systematic classification of empirically significant ranges of differentiation and structural variation of societies. On the other hand, it can serve as a highly important lead into the formulation, and hence testing, of fundamental dynamic generalizations, of laws of social process, since the explanation of *why* the logically possible range of variability is empirically restricted can be found only in terms of such laws.

The second short cut involves making use of certain of the positive theoretical results of the foregoing analysis. The whole nature of the theory of action in general, and hence of the theory of social systems, as here developed, is such that precisely with respect to variability of structure, patterns of value-orientation as the focus of institutionalization, *must* play a crucial role. Empirical demonstration that this was not the case would, in effect, be a refutation of the present general conceptual scheme, or the reduction of its ana-

lytical relevance to relative insignificance. We are, therefore justified in taking the possibilities of variation in fundamental value-
orientations, i.e., in pattern-variable combinations, as a point of
departure for developing a provisional classification of generalized
types of social system in structural terms. If this is taken as a point
of departure it is possible to introduce modifications of the purely
logical implications of such a classification, modifications which are
necessitated by what we know about the empirical interdependence
of patterns of value-orientation with the other components of the
social system. This attempt will be undertaken in the final section
of the present chapter.

In the middle section we will attempt to make the transition
between the problems presented by the empirical clusterings to be
reviewed here in the first section and the classification of total societies, by showing the importance of what we may call the adaptive
structures and the corresponding integrative imperatives of the particular social system for the limitations of compatibility of different
structural elements as parts of the same society.

§ SOME EMPIRICAL CLUSTERINGS OF THE
STRUCTURAL COMPONENTS OF
SOCIAL SYSTEMS

1. *Kinship Systems*

FROM a purely taxonomic point of view any considerable
prominence of kinship in social structures generally would seem
highly problematical. Elaborate as the classification under the first
heading in the scheme presented in the last chapter, Categorization of Objects, was, it got only so far as to *name* the principal
ascriptive foci of a kinship system, namely sex, age and biological
relatedness, without developing a classification under each or showing how they were combined, to say nothing of developing a classification of types of kinship structure themselves. In other words,
kinship in terms of the possible combinations of the general structural elements of social systems has a high degree of specificity. The
fact that kinship looms large in every known society means that a
great many other logically possible permutations of the structural

elements have either been eliminated or relegated to secondary positions in the social structure. This calls for explanation.

But not only do kinship systems, that is, prominent groupings in a population constituted on the basis of biological relatedness, exist but certain further general facts are highly significant. The first of these is that membership in a kinship unit and status within it is universally the primary mode of initial status ascription of the new-born infant in all known societies. Following this, a highly significant part of the socialization process almost always occurs within the kinship unit, with kinship personalities serving as strategically important socializing agents. Thus just as initial status is ascribed by birth in a kinship unit and relations to the rest of the social structure are initially mediated only through relation of that unit as a unit to the outside society, so child-care is a function everywhere ascribed to kinship units, and to various statuses within them. Details vary, especially the incidence of other agencies such as organs of "formal education" and various others such as health care, but the central fact remains.

Third, there is a universal relation between kinship structures and the regulation of erotic relations between the sexes. It is universally true that there is a taboo on incest, namely that sexual relations as well as intermarriage are, for at least the vast majority of the population, except for spouses forbidden within the conjugal family, and often within larger kinship units. It is unusual for the legitimacy of sexual relations to be confined to the marriage relationship, but there is *never* lack of discrimination with regard to sexual access to married persons; their spouses always have defined sexual privileges, and post marital sexual relations outside are most generally rather narrowly restricted both by eligibility of partners and by occasion.[1]

Finally, kinship units themselves, in spite of their many variations, fall within a narrow sector of the total range of structural variability of types of collectivities. In pattern variable terms, roles within them are always functionally diffuse and collectivity-oriented. Their constitution on the basis of biological relatedness precludes the primacy of universalistic orientations, and narrowly limits the

[1] Cf. G. P. Murdock, *Social Structure,* for the comparative evidence on this point.

relevance of achievement patterns, at least as criteria of membership, to the marriage selection process.

The important point is the near universality of the limitation of variability to such narrow limits both with respect to function and to structural type. Why is not initial status-ascription made on the basis of an assessment of individual organic and personality traits? Why is not all child care and responsibility sometimes placed in the hands of specialized organs just as formal education is? Why is not the regulation of sexual relations divorced from responsibility for child care and status ascription? Why are kinship units not patterned like industrial organizations? It is, of course, by no means excluded that fundamental changes in any or all of these respects may sometimes come about. But the fact that they have not yet done so in spite of the very wide variability of known social systems in other respects is none the less a fact of considerable importance.

The broad lines of the explanation of this particular clustering are fairly well known, though many details are still obscure. The most fundamental considerations probably have to do with the consequences of the plasticity, sensitivity and dependency of the human infant and with certain closely associated features of the place of "sex" in the need-structure of the human personality. Presumably there is continuity from sub-human origins in one critical respect, namely the centering of the earliest child-care on the mother. This fact, plus the disabilities of pregnancy and the fact that only recently has other than breast-feeding become widely feasible, lie at the basis of the differentiation of sex roles.

It seems, then, that the personality of the human infant has always developed in the context of certain crucially important early attachments, that to the mother looming by far the largest. Whatever the importance of these facts for the general possibilities of personality development, it seems that they are crucial for the perpetuation of kinship as a central focus of social structure. The most essential point is that the child grows up with a deeply rooted need for adult attachments which can serve as substitutes for his infantile attachments. Furthermore, this attachment system comes to be structured along the axis of sex discrimination. Surely, in spite of the apparently very great institutional plasticity of erotic need-structures, the great regularity with which homosexuality is tabooed, or at most permitted within very narrow limits, is a further fact which deserves to be ranked with those of initial status ascription, that of child care and the regulation of heterosexual relations as a central social uniformity. One essential point, then, is above all that the child has his erotic development channeled in the direction of normal heterosexuality and that this includes not only needs for erotic gratification in a specific sense, but for the placing at least of *some* erotic gratifications in the context of a diffuse heterosexual attachment. A stable attachment of a man to a woman with inclusion of sexual relations taken for granted, almost automatically results in a family. If this happens, the forces tending to integrate the child into the same unit are very powerful indeed.

It is a highly open question how far the human family has an "instinctive" basis. However that may be, there is a powerful complex of forces on the action level which, once the family is given, tends to perpetuate it. The essential point is that the conditions of socialization within a kinship unit predispose the child to assume both marital and parental roles at the relevant stage of his own life cycle. It is by no means out of the question that this basic complex of social structures and motivational forces should sometime be broken. Our knowledge is not yet sufficient to be able to say in much detail what the conditions necessary to break out of it would be, nor what would be its effects on personality and social structure. But, in spite of the enormous and highly significant variability of kinship structure itself, the persistence of the kinship complex throughout the range of variability of social structures in other respects is indicative of a powerful combination of forces.

The most recent large-scale demonstration of its power is the case of Soviet Russia.[2] There is nothing in Marxist ideology in favor of preservation of the family; indeed the balance is strongly the other way. In the early days of the revolution it was taken for granted that the family was mainly a "bourgeois prejudice" and was in process of immediately "withering away." Then came a very powerful reaction so that in legislative terms a far stricter level of official enforcement of family obligation than in most Western

[2] Cf. Alex Inkeles, "Some Aspects of Social Stratification in the USSR," *American Sociological Review*, Sept. 1950.

countries emerged. A possible set of forces operating to bring this about may be suggested, along with whatever may have seemed "good policy" to the top leadership. The basic need-disposition structure on which motivation for the familial roles of adults is built up is developed in the context of childhood attachments. Ambivalence relative to these attachments is, of course, the rule though varying in intensity. The revolutionary situation may well have given opportunity for expression of the negative side of the ambivalence. But it is well known that in situations of acute psychological insecurity there is a strong tendency to regression. A revolutionary period certainly creates a great deal of insecurity. It may well be, therefore, that the resurgence of a demand for, or at least a toleration of, strict family morality, involved a widespread regression to attachment needs with high security values. This interpretation, if correct, would illustrate the difficulty of "abolishing" such a deep-rooted complex of role-orientations as those underlying the place of kinship structures in societies.[3]

2. *Instrumental Achievement Structures and Stratification*

A second principal clustering which limits the variation of structures which might otherwise be formally possible, is that of the relation of instrumental complexes to stratification. The essential fact here seems to be that there are rather sharp limits to the independent variability of the instrumental structure and the distribution of facilities, on the one hand, the distribution of rewards on the other. The actual variability, that is, occurs within a "band" which is considerably narrower than the range of logically possible permutations and combinations.

The more "strung out" dimension of this band is the degree to which instrumental orientations are segregated out from fusions with expressive orientations and are differentiated. On this continuum, the modern Western type of occupational role structure stands near the pole of maximum segregation, while the situation characteristic of so many non-literate societies, where the over-

---

[3] A similar process took place in the French Revolution in connection especially with the attempt to abolish the legal distinctions between legitimate and illegitimate children. Cf. Crane Brinton, *French Revolutionary Legislation on Illegitimacy 1798-1804.*

whelming proportion of instrumental functions is carried out in kinship roles, stands close to the opposite pole. This is, to be sure, a highly significant range of variability in social structures and the differences along it are fundamental in a whole series of respects.

But the "band" is relatively narrow. This is a way of saying in figurative terms that there is not very much variability along another dimension. This dimension is the matter of the degree of *independence* of instrumental role allocation and hence distribution of facilities from prestige distribution, or allocation of rewards. Whatever the type of structure with regard to fusions and segregations, and the degree of functional differentiation of roles, these two tend to go hand in hand, to be closely integrated with each other.

There are two primary aspects of this integration. The first concerns problems internal to a universalistic, functionally specific, and affectively neutral sub-system of instrumental orientations. Here the *relational* reward system consists primarily of approval and esteem, and their obverses disapproval and disesteem, and the distribution of non-social reward-objects in accordance with their symbolic relations to an approval-esteem scale. The second concerns the response and love aspects of the reward system and its relation to the instrumental complex. The significance of kinship in this latter context is, because of the considerations just outlined, so great that it is above all a question of the relations between the instrumental complex and the family.

First, within the instrumental complex itself. With the elaboration of the division of labor there is an inherent tendency to differentiate along two axes both of which have inferiority-superiority implications. In the first place, achievement values cannot mean anything at all, if there is no discrimination between doing things "well" and doing them "badly." The capacity to do things *relatively* "well" (which is always at least implicitly a comparative judgment, relative to other actors) may be called "competence" or "skill." With any at all elaborate system of the division of labor there will inevitably be a considerable range of differentiation of levels of competence, especially when a system of different technical roles and not just one such role is considered.

Secondly, beyond rather elementary levels, instrumental role-differentiation requires organization. Organization in turn differentiates roles along the axis of "responsibility" for the affairs of the collectivity. It seems to be one of the best attested empirical generalizations of social science that every continuous organization which involves at all complex cooperative processes, is significantly differentiated along this axis, informally if not formally.

It goes almost without saying that the imperatives of effectiveness demand that with differentials of competence and of responsibility there should go differentials in facilities. It would clearly not be efficient to place the best tools in the hands of the least efficient workers in order to compensate them for their lower efficiency status, still less perhaps to entrust the most important facilities to those carrying the least responsibility. The latter is indeed strictly impossible because of the relational component in facilities themselves. Thus the "connections" necessary to adjust an organization to its social situation, can only serve this function if they are accessible to those exercising responsibility. There is, therefore, an inherent tendency to allocate greater facilities to those on the higher levels of competence and responsibility.

This tendency is *both* a functional imperative of effectiveness and efficiency of instrumental structures, *and* an inherent implication of the valuation of instrumental achievement. But the valuation of instrumental achievement *itself* means that achieving higher levels of competence and/or responsibility, and having larger facilities at one's command *are in themselves rewards,* and rewards which are inherently differential. It is literally impossible to have an instrumental system sanctioned by the valuation of achievement without the internal differentiation of the role and facility structure coming *also* to be a differentiation of rewards, an internal stratification. This conclusion follows directly from the fundamental theorem of institutional integration of motivation presented in Chapter II.

The only way to avoid this would be to suppress the valuation of the differences of competence or responsibility, including denial of their functional relevance. Here again the history of Soviet Russia is instructive. Marxist ideology, including Lenin's own statements, did radically deny that any competence above that of the ordinary "worker" was a legitimate basis of differential valuation.[4] But what has happened in fact is that, with the developing industrialization of the Soviet Union, both facilities and rewards have become markedly differentiated, including monetary reward. The fact that the Soviet industrial manager belongs to the "intelligentsia" while his American counterpart is called by Marxists a "capitalist" does not alter the essential structural situation. Both receive rewards greatly in excess of those going to ordinary workers. Whether in this respect the equalitarian ideal of communism will be realized in the future remains to be seen. Perhaps a sociologist is at least entitled to be skeptical.

This, of course, does not in the least mean that there is *no* room for variability in the relations between instrumental complexes and reward systems. There is very considerable room, but the fact remains that the "band" is far narrower than the permutations and combinations of the structural elements of such systems would by themselves lead us to believe had to be the case.

But this is not all. The same individual actor who is the incumbent of instrumentally oriented, e.g., occupational roles, also has certain expressive needs which are not gratified in that role. He is above all incorporated into other role systems where immediate gratifications and diffuse attachments and loyalties to individuals loom large. The relative exclusion of such orientations from an occupational role system is itself a prerequisite of the latter developing to a high degree of elaboration.

This is the essential basis for the segregation of kinship and occupational roles in "industrial" societies. But no such society so far known has shown strong signs of eliminating the kinship unit entirely or for a long period—as we illustrated by the case of Soviet Russia. In view of these facts it is not conceivable that, so long as there is a kinship structure, it should be totally unintegrated with the occupational structure. This integration above all concerns its relation to the reward system. The solidarity of the kinship unit is of such a character that if certain facilities and rewards are available to one member, they will have to be "shared" with the other members. It is strictly inconceivable that most of the men highly placed

[4] Cf. Barrington Moore, Jr., *Soviet Politics, the Dilemma of Power,* Chapter II.

in the occupational sphere, should fail to share what their incomes can buy, with their families if they have them, and perhaps still more fundamental, that they should not share their prestige. So long, that is, as there is a solidary kinship unit, it is impossible for the wives and children of those high and low in the occupational system to be equally treated, *regardless of their personal achievements*. In other words, these two basic components of the reward system of the society, occupational approval or esteem and the symbolic accoutrements thereof, and "emotional security," love and response in the kinship unit, must go together in some way. The consequence of this is that the combination of an occupationally differentiated industrial system and a significantly solidary kinship system *must* be a system of stratification in which the children of the more highly placed come to have differential advantages, by virtue of their ascribed kinship status, not shared by those lower down. Again this generalization is amply confirmed by the history of Soviet Russia. It is conceivable that this empirical generalization will some day be invalidated for instance by elimination of the kinship unit. But in the light of the historical persistence of this clustering, the question of *how* this would be possible is sharply posed.

If what has just been said is true of "industrial" societies, how much more so in the cases closer to the "fusion" end of the continuum referred to above. Indeed it can safely be said that in such societies, anything even closely approaching "equality of opportunity" to the degree to which that is characteristic of modern industrial societies, is out of the question. But unless the need for kinship solidarities can be radically reduced below, for instance, the present American level, there is an inherent limit to the development, not only of absolutely egalitarian societies, but even of complete equality of opportunity.

3. *Territoriality, Force and the Integration of the Power System*

A third very central empirical clustering in social systems concerns the power system. We have already shown the way in which instrumental orientations, through the relational focus of facilities, tend to focus on power as a proximate goal and how, since facilities and rewards are so intimately connected, and the power of one actor is *always* relative to that of another, power can readily become the focus of disruptive conflicts. Finally it was also shown that force in *one* primary context, namely that of the *prevention* of undesired action, is an ultimately effective means, and force is inherently linked to territorial location because it is a *physical* means.

This complex of facts is of such critical functional significance to social systems that it is safe to say that no paramount integrative structure of a society could perform that function effectively unless it were intimately tied in with the control of power relations in general and force in particular. No society can subsist unless there is a basis for "counting on" some control of the use of force, and unless disruptive conflicts which inevitably become "struggles for power" tending by progression along the gradient of resort to increasingly drastic means to eventuate in resort to force, are kept within bounds. If it is a partial social system which is in question an essential part of the problem of its relation to the society is that of its place in the power system.

Certain types of integrative structure are, of course, very directly organized about these foci. The ideal type case is what we refer to as the state, which is the equivalent for this area of the social structure of the kinship system and the system of stratification for the other two. There is a very wide range of variability with respect to the extent to which such a differentiated structure emerges. Among other things it is a function of the level of organization of the use of force, and of course its technology. This in turn is connected with the level of technology and organization in general—if there is a highly developed occupational system it is always possible that the organizational patterns which characterize it can be applied to organization of the use of force. We may say that the higher the level of organization the more potentially disruptive violent conflict can become, and therefore the greater the functional need for its control. But in any case force must be territorially organized. It is not possible to have a variety of different jurisdictions commanding force within the same territory without definition of their limits.

One concrete illustration of the importance of these considerations may be given. There seem to be certain elements of inherent instability in societies where the overwhelming bulk of the population is organized on the basis of peasant village communities.

One of the reasons for this is the fact that the village community as the primary focus of solidarity can only within very narrow limits be an effective unit for the organization of the use of force. It is, in the face of any more extensive organization, not a defensible unit. Hence there must always be a "superstructure" over a peasant society, which, among other things, organizes and stabilizes the use of force. The question is how far such a superstructure is, as it were, "organically" integrated with the self-contained village communities and often the level of integration is not high. This circumstance is of great significance for the history of China, and, for example, of Eastern Europe. Among many other things it has much to do with the striking fact that the Communist movement has had so much more success in peasant societies than in industrialized societies, which have a much firmer structure between the lowest level community unit and the paramount integration of the power system.

We may conclude, then, that societies where there is almost unrestricted freedom to resort to force, and above all where several agencies with independent control of organized force operate within the same territorial area, are as rare as societies where children are socialized without any reference to kinship relations or where the reward system is in inverse relation to the gradations of competence and responsibility in the principal areas of valued achievement.

4. Religion and Value-Integration

A fourth empirical clustering may be briefly delineated. In the first place there are certain types of situation of human life in any society which, though varying in specific structure, incidence and intensity in different societies have certain universal features. There is the limitation of the human life span and the universal experience of death, especially of premature death, not only as an expectation for the person who knows he is going to die, but as posing a problem of emotional adjustment to the survivors. The crucial significance of attachments to human individuals is such that death cannot be treated with indifference. Secondly, whatever the value system institutionalized in a society, the realization of the expectations which it defines is necessarily to some degree both uncertain and uneven. In part this results from the exposure of men to an external nature which is capricious and in some respects "un-friendly" in relation to human interests—the vagaries of the weather constitute one prominent example. But more fundamentally it results from the empirical impossibility of complete integration of *any* value-system with the realistic conditions of action. Every social system is in some degree malintegrated, which means that there is always a problem of the discrepancy between institutionally legiti-mized expectations and the actual outcome of events. There is always a problem of what attitude should be taken to what in terms of the current value system is undeserved suffering, and to the actual existence of unpunished behavior in contravention of the moral norms of the society, the "problem of evil." The moral econ-omy of a human society never has perfectly balanced books.

From what we know of the psychology of expectations and the consequences of frustration, it is clear that there are difficult prob-lems of adjustment in these areas. Just as it is not possible to be indifferent to the death of an object of intense attachment, so it is not possible simply to take the frustration of one's fundamental expectations with respect to values, as to what, for example, is fair, "in one's stride" as it were, saying, "what the hell." It is therefore imperative that there be some sort of socially structured orientation to these problems of discrepancy precisely between events and *institutionalized* expectations. This problem of the *Ausgleich*, the ultimate balancing of the motivational and moral economy, is the core of the significance of religion in a sociological context.

The phenomena in this field are exceedingly complex, and can-not be gone into in detail here. There is, of course, a very wide range of possible structures. But the essential point for present pur-poses is that whatever mechanisms of adjustment in this area exist in a society—and they must in the nature of the case be more than merely idiosyncratic to particular personalities—they must be socially structured, whatever these may be. They must in some sense and to some degree be integrated with the dominant system of institution-alized values. They cannot vary at random relative to it. There must also be some order of cognitive orientation which covers both areas and the relation between them; the problem of the "meaning" of the discrepancies cannot be simply ignored in the belief systems of the society. Furthermore, there must be some integration on the level of expressive symbolism. These problems will be further discussed below in Chapters VIII and IX, respectively.

Essentially the same order of analysis could be carried farther, not only by citing other empirical clusterings of the components of social structure, but by citing certain highly generalized relations of interdependence between the ones which have already been reviewed. Here only one illustration of this interdependence will be given, that of certain relations between religion and the power system.

The religious movement, because of its relation to general value integration, claims a paramount jurisdiction over human value-orientations, which must somehow be integrated with the values institutionalized in the state. Some of these movements, however, have, in their religious ethics, radically repudiated the use of force or more broadly concern with power.

Such movements face a basic dilemma. So long as they are alienated from the central institutional structure, the problems of power and force can be relegated to "Caesar" in the sense of Early Christianity. But if the movement becomes institutionalized as the dominant religion of a going society, it must somehow come to terms with these problems. The possibilities are various. The simplest solution structurally is for the religious movement to become merged with the "political" integrative structure of the society, but this is a solution which places peculiarly severe strains on the maintenance of what in this, as in perhaps other respects, are "other-worldly" values. But the structural segregation (not separation in the American sense) of church and state as in mediaeval Catholicism is not an easy and simple solution either. If the religion is highly organized as a church it *cannot* completely dissociate itself from responsibility in this context—hence we have such phenomena as the church "itself" repudiating the use of force, but heretics being burned at the stake by "the state" as soon as they had been condemned for heresy by an ecclesiastical court.

This "dilemma of institutionalization" relative to a religious value-system is one of the most important threads of analysis of social systems and will, in particular, be further analyzed in Chapter XI on Social Change below. Here it may be remarked that it is also very much of a dilemma for a "secular religion" like Communism which also repudiates coercion and the use of force, as a matter of ethical principle, *in the ideal state;* indeed this is perhaps the most definite item in the official Marxist forecast of what "communism" really will turn out to be. But as we all know, as a movement, not only in promoting the revolution within "capitalist" societies, but in the stage of "socialism" within the Soviet Union, far from repudiating the use of force, the Communist movement has magnified and glorified it. The obvious question is, how if at all will the transition be made.

These four examples of empirical clusterings of social structures are meant to be illustrative, not exhaustive. They are meant to show in the first place that the structural analysis of social systems is not merely a matter of spinning out the logical possibilities of the permutations and combinations of certain more or less arbitrarily defined structural components. We have taken a step toward bringing these components into connection with the problems of dynamic analysis, which is always the analysis of motivation in relation to personality structures and to situations. This is another way of saying that social systems must meet the functional prerequisites of their persistence as systems.

These empirical clusterings thus provide us with excellent approaches to the analysis of dynamic problems. It is well known that value-patterns in many cases vary beyond the limits of these clusters, as in the case of doctrines repudiating the use of force, as just noted. There is, therefore, a highly important set of problems which concern the possibilities of institutionalization of patterns along the edges of the "band" of historically given structures, and beyond those edges. Along the edges we are presented with what are, more or less definitely ready-made "experimental" situations, of which the Soviet regime is a grand-scale example.

That such situations should continually arise is indicated by evidence which will be presented later[5] that there are strong forces in all social systems making for commitment to "utopian" patterns of value-orientation, that is, patterns which are incompatible with the known conditions of effective long-run institutionalization. Thus it seems fair to say that in contemporary society advocacy of

[5] See below, Chapter VII.

complete abolition of the family, of absolute egalitarianism or of absolute repudiation of coercion, can be placed in this category.

However, it should be made *very clear* that it is dangerous to suggest that there is a rigid line at the edge of the band. On the contrary there is every reason to believe that the line is indefinite. Society is not a static thing, and some things certainly become possible at certain stages of its development which were previously not so; to take a simple example the modern scale of organization would probably not be possible without modern methods of communication and record keeping. But this indefiniteness of the line at any given time does not mean that "anything is possible" if some people only want it enough, and it most certainly means that if the line is to be importantly shifted, *specific* mechanisms to meet the relevant functional exigencies must also be developed. There must be a development of "functional alternatives" to the structures which have been eliminated.

§ THE CONSTITUTION OF EMPIRICAL SOCIETIES

THE implication of the foregoing review of empirical clusterings of the elements of social structure is that societies are subjected to certain functional exigencies without which we cannot account for the fact that the known range of actual social structures is only a fraction of those which would result from a random assortment of the permutations and combinations of their structural components. These exigencies are of two classes: first, the universal imperatives, the conditions which must be met by any social system of a stable and durable character, and second, the imperatives of compatibility, those which limit the range of coexistence of structural elements in the same society, in such a way that, given one structural element, such as a given class of occupational role system, the type of kinship system which goes with it must fall within certain specifiable limits.

The elements of social structure have been derived from two sources, the patterns of orientation of action, and the elements of the situation to which it is oriented. The relevance of the orientation elements to the organization of systems of action, including social systems, centers on the role of patterns of value-orientation, because it is in the selective dilemmas to which these patterns apply that the basic alternatives of such organization are to be found. We may say, then, that if the structure of social systems were solely a function of the "free choices" of their component actors, their main structural outline would be capable of description in terms of the patterns of value-orientation alone, and these in turn would be derivable from cognitive and expressive orientation patterns. The extent to which the structure of social systems is *not* derivable from cultural elements is therefore a measure of the importance of the determinants underlying what we have called the two classes of "exigencies" or "imperatives" to which they are subject in the realistic conditions of their operation as systems. These resultants of these factors may be considered as patterns of deviation from what would be the model of "perfect integration" in terms of the dominant pattern of value-orientation. Such patterns we may, relative to a given value system, call the *adaptive structures* of the social system. A complete account and classification of such structures cannot be worked out in the present state of knowledge. But the knowledge we do have can serve as a rough guide to the beginning of systematization.

We may then distinguish that part of the social structure which directly institutionalizes the dominant patterns of value-orientation of the culture; there is little doubt for instance that in the American case the core of this is the occupational system. But as a concrete sub-system of the social system even this cannot correspond exactly with the pattern-expectations of the value-system itself. There will have to be adaptive aspects even of this structure, which may be interpreted as modes of adaptation to the exigencies of institutionalizing the value patterns in question under the given conditions, that is to say, in the light of the strains to which the population in question are subjected, in these roles themselves, and in combining these with the other roles in which the same people are involved in other aspects of the society. In the American occupational case, for example, the simultaneous involvement of the same individuals in both occupational and kinship roles is one of the key problems.

Only in a limiting case, however, would the social structures which directly institutionalize the dominant value patterns, even with the above qualifications, meet most of the functional prerequisites of a going society. There will, then, in the same society, be other structures which are adaptive in a still broader sense, in that they are organized primarily by the institutionalization of patterns *other* than the dominant value patterns; this would be the case, for instance, with kinship in American society.

We have already presented evidence to indicate that the exigencies of a going society are such that it is exceedingly unlikely that any one consistently integrated pattern can cover the necessary range. There will, therefore, have to be institutionalization of secondary or subsidiary or variant value patterns, institutionalization of which is in a sense conditional, in that its application and hence legitimation is limited to certain contexts in such a way as to minimize interference with the main value pattern. The problem of integration posed by the necessity of "tolerating" and indeed institutionalizing patterns deviant from the main values is one of the main integrative problems for social systems, the more so, the more complex and differentiated their structure.

It is, therefore, possible to approach the analysis of types of social structure from the side of the patterns of value-orientation. By this procedure the first step will be to consider at what points in the system of foci of crystallization reviewed in the last chapter the primary foci of significance for the value-system in question will be found, and what the functional conditions of realization of the value patterns in question in that area are. How will these necessitate modification of the fully ideal pattern? Then the question will have to be raised, given what we know about the functional imperatives of social systems and their empirical working out, what *other* structures must also exist in the same social system, and how can these other structures be integrated with the central value-focus structures? This procedure will in fact be followed out in a sketchy way in the final section of the present chapter for each of the four main pattern-variable combinations for social value systems.

Before undertaking this task, however, it will be best to build a somewhat firmer foundation for it by inquiring more systematically about some of the minimum structural features of all societies and then showing how these provide starting points for further differentiation and variation. The contention will be that there are certain types of relationship which must find a place in any society, though their relative importance and their relation to others will vary widely. What we will be doing, then, is to approach the problem of the constitution of the empirical society from both ends, from that of certain functionally required minimum structures, and from that of the differentiation of types of value-orientation pattern, and the implications of implementation of these in a concrete social relationship system.

Throughout the discussion, in both contexts, the system of points of reference developed in the preceding chapter, particularly the fundamental outline of six categories presented on page 137, will be our primary guide. The question will always be, in the society we are describing, what structures are found which fit under each of the six categories, and of course the further elaborated sub-categories so far as differentiation goes far enough to make these relevant.

We may start by pointing out a conspicuous and apparently fundamental asymmetry in the relationship between ascriptive and achievement foci of status and role definition. There is, that is, a sense in which categorization in ascriptive terms apparently has a certain priority over that in achievement terms. There has to be an ascriptive base relative to which achievement-expectations are defined. When we combine these considerations with the implication of the universality of the kinship cluster, we may focus attention on a fundamental complex of social structures in which ascriptive criteria play a central part and which, so far as we know, is common, though with many variations, to all societies.

This is the cluster which in classificatory terms utilizes the qualities of age and sex, and in relational terms those of biological position and of territorial location as ascriptive points of reference. In the first instance on these bases kinship groupings are built up, with the conjugal family serving as the nuclear unit. Though there is enormous variation in the structure of kinship systems, there is constancy with respect to this focus.[6] Moreover, as was pointed out in the last section, this fact has further implications. This is true, first, because given the kinship unit, the status of the child in the wider

[6] On the whole subject of the variability of kinship systems and their relation to residential location see G. P. Murdock, *Social Structure.*

society must be predominately ascriptively defined, and indeed the wider the influence of kinship the more powerful the ascriptive emphasis generally. Secondly, in terms of the other pattern variables, there is an inherent relationship between this ascriptive emphasis and particularism and diffuseness. Particularism follows from the fact of ascription by *relational* criteria. Diffuseness follows from the fact that the kinship unit is not organized about specific functions, but about a generalized solidarity of those placed together by the relevant ascriptive criteria. Only with respect to the choice of marriage partners, under certain conditions, does this primarily ascriptive structure of kinship come to be broken through at certain points.

A central aspect of the diffuse ascriptive solidarity of kinship units is the fact that they constitute the units of residence of most normal populations. It is this circumstance which links biological relatedness as an ascriptive focus with territorial location. Hence, so far as the kinship unit is the unit of residence, we have kinship and community of residence directly linked together. In residential terms the community is a cluster of kinship units, or put a little differently the effective concrete kinship unit is at the same time the primary unit both of a kinship system and of a system of territorial organization of the population.

There are, of course, many exceptions to this pattern. Various population elements such as students, some specialized work groups, e.g. lumberjacks, monks and nuns, and military forces, do not "live" in kinship units. But there is no known society where living apart from kinship units is the primary pattern for the normal individual throughout the life cycle.

There are intricate inter-relationships between kinship and residence which need not concern us here.[7] But given the universality of this combination of the two structures it constitutes a focus from which ramifying structural relationships can be followed out. The combination, for instance, gives one component at least of the sociological setting of the problems of territorial mobility and stability of populations. It is above all because territorial mobility must either move kinship units as units, or set the individual into relationship

[7] Cf. Murdock, op. cit.

with a different set of kinship units that it acquires its sociological significance.

However, there are two directions of ramification which may be selected for comment here. They are essentially two fundamentally different ways of organizing kinship units into larger clusterings. The first of these is the ethnic group. An ethnic group is an aggregate of kinship units, the members of which either trace their origin in terms of descent from a common ancestor or in terms of descent from ancestors who all belonged to the same categorized ethnic group. It may according to the point of view either be regarded as an extension of kinship into larger aggregates or as the matrix, defined in terms of biological relatedness, in which a given kinship unit fits. An ethnic group is normally endogamous and recruitment is by birth, though, of course, assimilation by intermarriage or even other mechanisms is in a certain proportion of cases possible. The biological distinctness of an ethnic group will presumably only be significant to the social structure if the group is characterized by a distinctive social status in the larger social system, a status which is very often at least marked and symbolized by a distinctive cultural tradition.[8]

The second direction of ramification is the sorting out of kinship units relative to prestige status within the social system. This is what we call social *class,* a class being an aggregate of kinship units of approximately equal status in the system of stratification. Ethnic grouping and class can coincide where there is little or no class mobility. The Indian caste system is an approximation to this situation. But in the case of an "open" class system the distinction between the two is, of course, crucial; the ethnic and the class bases of differentiation cut across each other.

Within every society, therefore, it becomes necessary to ask what is its kinship system, what is the basis of its organization into communities at the various levels of inclusiveness, and is it differentiated into ethnic and/or class groups? What groups and on what bases and how related to each other? It is possible that there are functional equivalents of these structures. We have seen that in the case of kinship this is highly unlikely. In the case of community it would

---

[8] As in the case of the Jews. In the case of the Negro color as a visibility symbol in a sense takes the place of a distinctive culture.

appear to be strictly impossible. It is possible in the case of ethnic grouping, but only on the basis that the society as a whole constitutes a single undifferentiated ethnic group. It is, then, itself always an ethnic group relative to groups outside what has been treated as the same society, so we can say that in a strict sense this basis of organization is never absent. Theoretically all humanity *could* be a single ethnic group, but this seems rather remote. Similarly ethnic and class composition may in a limiting case coincide. But class differentiation within ethnic groups is the rule rather than the exception. Finally, some degree of prestige differentiation of kinship units, that is, of class differentiation, also seems to be universal.

The fact that these types of groupings are built about relationally ascriptive criteria has critical implications for the role-patterning within them. With the one exception of choice of marriage partner, membership in a kinship group can be only ascribed. Similarly with an ethnic group. In the case of a community, entry into the community may be voluntary, but *given* residence the rest is ascribed, e.g. liability to local taxes. This at least greatly narrows the range of achievement criteria. Secondly, residence either ensures or predisposes to diffuseness of role-obligations rather than specificity, since there is no way of ensuring that the exigencies of a situation from which either there is no escape, or only at the cost of changing residence, can be confined to any specifically defined context.

Therefore, we may say that membership in the four types of groupings, kinship, community, ethnic and class, should characterize every individual actor in every society and such groupings should, with the requisite qualifications, be looked for as part of the structure of every society. Moreover, these groupings will be patterned partly, if not wholly, in ascriptive terms; they will have important indeed usually predominant particularistic elements, and they will have diffuse emphases, if not without qualification.

What might be called a "minimum society" might as a structure be describable exclusively in terms of these four categories if the requisite discriminations of differentiated roles within each of them were made. It will be noted that *none* of them is organized primarily about the primacy of an orientation type.

The next set of questions concerns the differentiation of roles and sub-collectivities not only within these four groupings but in structural independence from any of them. These will, in the first instance, concern the areas open for, and the structures developed within sub-systems of, "private" instrumental and expressive orientation. At the lowest level of differentiation these would be purely "interstitial" to the ascriptive groupings, in which case such orientations would, in the ideal type case, be confined to representative roles on behalf of the sub-collectivity. This would, for example, be true of negotiating marriage arrangements between kinship groups or relations between adjacent communities.

But such structures may be more than interstitial. In such a case the structurally more primitive type is, as we have seen, the "ecological complex," for example, in the instrumental case a market nexus, in the expressive a network of "purely personal" friendships. Then, as a next step in structural elaboration, particularly in the instrumental case, there may develop collectivities characterized by primacy of an orientation type instead of an ascriptive basis of constitution. By far the most prominent of these is the instrumentally oriented organization.

Both within the ecological complexes and the collectivities constituted by orientation types a premium is placed on achievement criteria over ascriptive. Similarly there is much more scope for universalism, and in the instrumental types, instrumental primacy implies affective neutrality.

Both ecological complexes and their constituent orientation-primacy roles should, in these terms, if at all stabilized, be treated as parts of the structure of the social system, as, of course, are constituent collectivities organized on other than an ascriptive basis. They will still in a sense always be interstitial to the ascriptive groupings, but can, of course, develop to a point where they overshadow all except the broadest basis of community and of ethnic belongingness. This is, of course, the case in the "industrial" type of society.

The integrative structures fit into this schematization readily. The power-territoriality-force complex is of such importance that what is ordinarily considered to be a society will, if on a high level of differentiation, generally almost always be organized as a single collectivity on this basis, will, that is, be a "politically organized" society. There are rare cases, such as classical Greece, where a "family" of city-states rather than any one really constituted the society. But the relation of this overall political collectivity to the "private" spheres of the constituent actors, both individual and collective, constitutes a principal area of the structural features of any social system. As noted, this will almost always be closely integrated both with a territorial basis of community and with an ethnic tradition, as well as with internal differentiation on a class basis.

There is, however, as we have seen, a possibility that certain aspects of the integration of cultural orientations will be integrated in part separately from the political integration. This is the case when there is a "church" distinct from the state. It is also possible for cultural integration to belong almost wholly to a private and informal sphere without overall formal organization, as in the case of Hinduism in India, which for much of its history has coexisted with a plurality of political units.

Finally, what we have above called the "economies" of the allocation of facilities and of rewards as overall organizations must be treated as part of the structure of the society. As we have seen they must be closely integrated with each other and with the system of ascriptive traits. They are essentially to be regarded as modes of ordering the units of the system, the orientation-roles and the object-roles of the constituent actors both individual and collective. We can speak of differences in the degree of equality or inequality of the distribution of facilities and rewards, of degrees of stringency of control of this distribution, of relative prominence of individuals and of collectivities as units, and the like, and of equality and inequality of opportunity of access to both facilities and rewards, and degrees of mobility and immobility relative to ascriptive starting points.

The above considerations give us one frame of reference for treating the problem of structural differentiation of societies. Underlying all of the more elaborate types of differentiation are the fundamental ascriptive groupings of which, in turn, kinship and territorial location seem to be the most fundamental, though ethnicity and class rank close to them. There may be, as voluminous evidence from anthropological investigations shows, a wide variety not only of variations, but of structural elaborations in various directions, without breaking through the primacy of these ascriptive foci and the predominantly particularistic-diffuse role patterns organized about them—variation within these ranges is by and large characteristic of non-literate societies. In general both instrumental and expressive functions are carried out within the fused type of role-structure (Type 4, Chapter III, p. 87). Segregation of such interests is predominantly by occasion, not by role differentiation. The contexts of exchange transactions, mediating particular roles in relation to each other, are also predominantly included in the particularistic-diffuse role system, are institutionalized above all in terms of kinship relations or, as it has sometimes been put, the "fiction of kinship." The "economies" of the facility and reward systems are thus not structurally differentiated out, but are integral parts of the central ascribed role-systems themselves. There will, of course, inevitably be some "interstices" in such a system, but by and large this is the major structural type. Within it, let it be repeated, there is room for very considerable structural variation and elaboration.

A qualitatively new gradient of structural differentiation is, however, entered upon when two further closely interdependent developments take place. The first of these is the specialization of the roles of individual actors and of collectivities in relation to instrumental and expressive interests and functions as such, roles which are structurally *independent* of the ascribed diffuse solidarity groupings. The second is the growth of a nexus of "free" exchange relationships between these role and collectivity units where the settlement of terms is not fused into the particularistic solidary relationship structure, but is allowed to be independently variable. This, in turn, necessitates the institutionalization of rights to possessions, both as facilities and as rewards, on a basis which is more than just one aspect of an ascribed-particularistic-diffuse solidarity structure. This new gradient of differentiation is that usually regarded as constitutive of the more "advanced" types of society, and the process may be carried to greatly varying degrees of elaboration. It certainly, however, opens out possibilities of the arrangement of human affairs which are altogether absent from the other type, no matter how great the elaboration within it. Certainly it is connected with literacy on the cultural level, and the concomitant capacity for abstraction and for cumulative cultural developments.

Different types of value-orientation will, of course, have different selective emphases relative to the above structural possibilities. The way in which these selective emphases work out will be reviewed in the final section of the chapter.

The above applications of the classification on page 137 and following of the last chapter bring us relatively close to a system of categories necessary for the adequate empirical description of a society *as a system.* They have all been systematically derived from the fundamental components of action theory. As a first approximation they should be complete; and very definitely they are not ad hoc. They constitute a systematic outline of the structure of the system, in terms which can link quite directly with whatever dynamic knowledge we have available, and can serve as a highly important guide to research.

The next task will be to explore certain of the interconnections between these parts of the social system. The facts brought forward in the discussion of empirical clusterings will again serve as a guide.

§ THE STRUCTURAL IMPERATIVES OF A GIVEN SOCIAL SYSTEM

LET us go back to the problem of the subjection of a given value-orientation pattern to the exigencies of implementation in a given situation. An essential part of this situation is the nature of the other parts of the social system in which the pattern itself is institutionalized.

Action toward the implementation of a value-orientation pattern, that is, must not only be adapted to certain motivational and situational exigencies which are universal to the human species and hence to the existence of stable social systems at all, but must meet certain conditions of compatibility *within the same social system.* The former set have been called the universal imperatives, the latter imperatives of compatibility or the structural imperatives. Only the two together can give us the limits to ranges of social variability.

First let us discuss some of the problems of the modern type of "industrial" occupational structure. Its primary characteristic is a system of universalistic-specific-affectively neutral achievement-oriented roles. There must not only be particular roles of this type but they must fit together into complex systems both within the same organization and within the ecological complexes linking individuals and organizations together. It is out of the question for such a role system to be directly homologous with a kinship structure, so that it should be essentially a network of interlocking kinship units, as many other social structures, like the feudal, tend to be. It must for a variety of reasons be segregated from the kinship system, because certain ranges of freedom independently of kinship pressures, including freedom for mobility, i.e., change of status, are essential to it. These conditions would be incompatible with those essential to many types of kinship system. Indeed it can be said that the "conjugal" type of the latter, which isolates the conjugal unit from other solidarities to a high degree, is the only kinship type which interferes relatively little with an industrial economy. Hence we may say with considerable confidence to those whose values lead them to prefer for kinship organization the system of mediaeval Europe or of Classical China to our own, that they must choose. It is possible to have either the latter type of kinship system or a highly industrialized economy, *but not both in the same society*. Either one requires conditions in the corresponding part of the social structure, which are incompatible with the needs of the other. In other words, a given type of structure in any major part of the society imposes *imperatives* on the rest, in the sense that given that structure, if it is to continue, other relevant structures in the same society cannot vary beyond certain limits which are substantially narrower than are the general limits of variability of social structures in the relevant spheres.

A second example may be taken from the Chinese politico-cultural integration, the "bureaucratic Empire." This involved, it will be remembered, under the Emperor, a synthesis of religious and cultural authority in the hands of an appointive official group, trained in the Confucian classics, and selected by competitive examination. This selection was nominally open to all on a basis of complete equality of opportunity.

Actually, with few exceptions except in times of political disorganization, there was an effective monopoly of access to official position in the hands of a land-owning, town-dwelling "gentry" class. This class, though its informal privileges were in conflict with the strict implications of the Confucian value system, had an essential set of functions in making such a regime possible. The two were integrated in such a way as to block at least two important types of development, either of which would have destroyed the system. The first was a feudal system which would have led to an appropria-tion of governmental power on a kinship basis and thereby broken down the universalism and central control of the governmental apparatus. This was prevented on the one hand by depriving the influential elements of the gentry of the incentive to feudalize be-cause they were "on the inside" anyway, while on the other hand, the centrally controlling agency, through the power of appointment and related facilities, was in a position to play potentially dangerous elements off against each other.[9]

Secondly, however, this structure also blocked the development of anything like "capitalism" though in other respects the setting for the latter was highly favorable. It did this by control of the towns, through the residence there and the participation in governmental power of the gentry, and by the capacity to absorb upwardly mobile elements into its power orbit and way of life. Capitalism would have destroyed the Confucian synthesis by shifting the balance of internal power to a group which could not be integrated into the "humanistic universalism" of the diffuse politico-cultural type which was distinctive of the Chinese "literati." The state would have had to become bureaucratic in a sense resembling the Western types. This case, therefore, again illustrates the dependence of a key struc-ture of a society, the special Chinese type of "bureaucracy," on its relation to another structure, the status of the gentry class, and one which was not by any means in full conformity with the cultural value-pattern which gave the former its raison d'etre.

One more example may be briefly cited, this time of a case where structural incompatibility was a powerful dynamic factor leading to the breakdown of a notable social integration, that is, to an altered state of equilibrium of the system. This is the famous problem of the relations of church and state in mediaeval Europe. It is quite clear that culturally the Catholic church was essential to mediaeval civili-zation, it was its paramount cultural focus of integration. But it was institutionalized in terms of a hierarchy of priestly office, the func-tion of which was the implementation of the sacerdotal powers of

[9] Another important institution was equality of inheritance between sons, which weakened the long-term consolidation of the kinship interests.

the papacy. Centralized control was the very essence of the Catholic system. But the secular structure was organized on a feudal basis. The structural conflict focused on the fact that above all the essential facilities for the functioning of any organization were accessible only through feudal tenure. Every bishop and priest, therefore, was in an equivocal position, as a priest of the church and as a vassal of a feudal superior. The two roles were structurally incompatible.

In such a situation the very upswing of the power and the cultural prestige of the church in the 11th century could not but have a most corrosive effect on feudalism. But the dissolution of feudalism in turn strongly stimulated the forces which eventually destroyed the synthesis of mediaeval civilization. There was never more than a precarious balance between the church and the secular power structure, and this was fraught with high tensions. The victory of either would destroy the other. It is probably of fateful significance in Western civilization that it was a victory for the church, because if the balance had tipped the other way the hereditary principle in social organization would probably have been consolidated, not attenuated.[10]

Again as in the case of the empirical clusterings which define relative universals of social structure, the boundaries of the variations which the structural imperatives of compatibility permit are not rigidly fixed. Indeed, as the mediaeval case shows, a good deal of structural conflict can be tolerated at the price of strain and perhaps instability. But there are certainly limits to this tolerance, even though they may change with the change of ultimate social "resources." These structural imperatives, then, give us another way of narrowing down the range of social variability which it is realistically important to take into serious consideration. The two sets of limitations to empirical variability combined make at least an approach to the problem of systematic analysis of the general range of comparative social structure feasible.

§ PRINCIPAL TYPES OF SOCIAL STRUCTURE

WE MAY now return to the value-orientation side of the problem of classification of types of social structure. We will proceed

[10] The celibacy of the priesthood was probably an important factor, because it exempted the church from the full force of vested interests in heredity of status.

by taking up each of a series of value-orientation patterns in turn under the assumption that this pattern is the dominant value-pattern of a society. We will inquire first about its most direct institutionalization in a social structure, in what sector it can be most directly institutionalized, and broadly what type of structure is most likely to be found there. Note will also be taken of the types of adaptive structures most likely to be found within this area. Then we will inquire, in the light of the foregoing analyses, what principal additional adaptive structures are likely to be found in other sectors of the society, and within what ranges they must fall in order to meet the imperatives of compatibility, given the central value-institutionalization structure of the society. There will also be a brief noting of probable foci of strain, instability and susceptibility to processes of change.

Because of the central place of the pattern variable scheme in the theory of action, we will take the four fundamental value-orientation types of social values set forth in Chapter III in Table 2a as our point of departure. These, it will be remembered, are defined by the combinations of the two pattern variables of ascription-achievement and universalism-particularism respectively. The reasons why these two pattern variables have been given priority for this purpose have already been discussed.

In the light of the foregoing section it will be clear that, from the point of view of certain interests in comparative social structure, this approach will introduce what from some points of view may be regarded as a bias. Either universalism or achievement or both enter into three of the four combinations we shall treat. This means that societies which are organized to an overwhelming degree around the four types of relationally ascriptive foci we discussed in the last section, will automatically fall into one of the four types. But as shown, for example by Murdock's work, there is enormous structural variation in a whole series of respects within this type, and certainly in numbers of cases the great majority of known societies fall in this category. It may, therefore, be said that our approach here is biased in favor of stressing the importance of a small minority of known social systems which depart from this type.

There is probably involved here a difference in perspective and interest between the sociologist and the anthropologist. Many of the social variations in which the latter is most interested will not be brought out on this basis, though they can be treated by more detailed breakdowns in terms of the same conceptual scheme. It would seem also to follow that the differentiations in which the anthropologist was most interested were less likely to be functions in a high degree of major differentiations of value-orientation, though this factor is by no means to be excluded. But on the other side of the coin, the present approach serves to accent lines of fundamental structural differentiation which are in some sense of "evolutionary" significance. They are above all the types which tend to emerge when major types of cultural development in the literate cultures have occurred, the emergence of the religious systems, the development of science and the like, and these developments have had a profound relation to changes in the structure of society itself. Both types of interest belong legitimately within the theory of action and of social systems. Our present approach seems to be deeply founded in the structure of the theoretical scheme itself, as well as in empirical problems relative to the significance of types of variability among "civilizations" rather than among primitive cultures.

Obviously what can be presented in the remainder of the present chapter is a highly schematic introductory sketch and most definitely not a "treatise" on comparative social structure. Its intention is to indicate the feasibility of an approach to a problem which, since the breakdown of the older evolutionary sociology, has not been satisfactorily handled in a systematic way. Carrying the implications of this approach through to a high degree of empirical elaboration is an enormous task which cannot be attempted within the limits of the present work.

1. *The Universalistic-Achievement Pattern*

This is the combination of value-patterns which in certain respects introduces the most drastic antitheses to the values of a social structure built predominantly about the relationally ascriptive solidarities we have discussed, of kinship, community, ethnicity and class. Universalism has above all two major types of application by itself. In the first place it favors status determination, i.e., the allocation of personnel, allocation of facilities and rewards, and role-treatment on the basis of generalized rules relating to classificatory qualities and performances independently of relational foci. Sec-ondly, on the cultural level it favors a cognitive as opposed to an expressive interest. These emphases already involve a certain "ten-sion" relative to much of the "givenness" of social situations, such as kinship and community relations.

The combination with achievement values, however, places the accent on the valuation of goal-achievement and of instrumental actions leading to such goal achievement. The choice of goals must be in accord with the universalistic values. Therefore promotion of the welfare of a collectivity as such tends to be ruled out. The col-lectivity is valued so far as it is necessary to the achievement of in-trinsically valued goals. This is the basis of a certain "individual-istic" trend in such a value system.

The achievement element also has a further bearing on the problem of goal selection. If *any* goal is given, there is some kind of pressure to achievement; in precisely this sense achievement-orienta-tion is as it were an endemic and partly an actual aspect of any action system. But achievement-orientation as itself a fundamental value pattern, not as only instrumental to other values, implies that the *choice* of goals should embody this value, that the choice of goals and not merely the attainment of goals derived from other value-considerations should be regarded as an expression of the actor's achievement values. This, in the first place, eliminates tra-ditionalism as a criterion of goal selection. But it also seems to exclude a universalistically defined *absolute* goal system, because this is intrinsically capable of attainment once and for all, and such attainment would from then on deprive the achievement component of the value-system of its meaning. Only where such an absolute goal was defined as continually subject to threat even though at-tained would it fit.

At any rate, more congenial to the universalistic-achievement complex is a *pluralism* of goals with unity in the *direction* rather than the specific content of the goal-states. This is particularly con-genial to integration with inherently dynamic cultural patterns, such as those of science which do not admit of a final state of perfection.

Hence we may speak of the valuation of a pluralistic and/or individualistic system of goal-achievement through instrumental actions as the primary concern of people holding such a value-orientation pattern. This will lead to valuation of activities segregated from the relational solidarities—the primary focus of such a social system will hence rest in a differentiated instrumental complex, in occupational roles, in the ecological nexi of exchange, in possessions and in instrumentally oriented organizations. The combination of achievement interests and cognitive primacies will mean that it is a dynamically developing system, with an encouragement for initiative in defining new goals, within the acceptable range, and an interest in improving instrumental efficiency. This means that the instrumental complex will tend to be a progressively developing and differentiating system of the division of labor, hence of differentiated occupational roles. This is the type of structure central to what are often called "industrial" societies.

There will, in the nature of the case, be a number of adaptive aspects of such a structure. In the first place the goals of occupational aspiration, to say nothing of actual role-activity, cannot in a simple sense be the direct embodiment of achievement values in all cases, because they have to be realistically adapted to the exigencies of the actual occupational opportunity system in which, once an elaborate division of labor has become established, many things have to be done which, though necessary conditions of highly valued achievement-outcomes, it is not easy to value "in themselves." While in less elaborately differentiated systems these might be links in the chain of instrumental steps to a valued goal for the individual, when they are all a given individual does, the question of his motivation to do them becomes acute. The most obvious cases of this sort are found in the labor role. But there is an important component of this sort in two other types of occupational role, those involving collective responsibilities and those involving the facilitation of exchange functions where such a high premium is placed on the persuasion of the exchange partner. Thus both the executive and the salesman roles involve acceptance of conditions which may not be directly very meaningful in terms of individual achievement values. In the higher reaches the rewards are such that the strain may not be very serious, but even here this may be a factor in the tendency for "success" to become dissociated as a goal from its basis in valuation of intrinsic achievement.

One adaptive problem of such a system, then, is to integrate realistic achievement orientations in the actual occupational structure with what may be called intrinsic achievement values. There will inevitably be considerable discrepancies, which are bridged by the institutionalization of compensatory rewards, e.g., short working hours, and of the obligations, for example, of the adult male to have a regular job and earn a living, even though what he does is "not very interesting." A second adaptive context which may be mentioned is that concerned with the difficulty of implementing genuinely universalistic criteria of judgment of performance-qualities and achievements, so that the individual is put in the right place and his rewards are nicely proportioned to his actual achievements. In this sphere we find institutional patterns which seem directly to contravene the principles which would be deduced from the dominant value-orientation pattern. Examples are the prevalence of seniority as a criterion of status, promotion and privileges throughout much of industry, and the "tenure" system in the academic world and in civil service. These may be treated as adaptive structures which have the function of mitigating the structured strains inherent in the exposure of people to competitive pressures where detailed universalistic discriminations are impracticable. From this point of view such a system is subject to a delicate balance. On the one hand it must resort to adaptive structures which are in conflict with its major value patterns, because to push these patterns "to their logical conclusion" would increase strain to the breaking point. On the other hand, it must not let the adaptive structures become too important lest the tail wag the dog, and the major social structure itself shift into another type.

Along with the institutionalization of occupational roles, it is clear that such a social structure is also heavily dependent on the institutionalization of rights in possessions, that is property, and of the patterns of exchange within certain limits. The functional requirement is above all that possessions and exchange relationships should be sufficiently free from restrictions which would prevent an approach to an optimum development of a system of facilities for instrumental achievement, and a flexibility of rewards which can be proportioned to achievements.

Next, the reward system must be integrated with such an occupational structure. As noted above, this must take the form that achievements within the system should be valued, and that this valuation should be expressed in attitudes of approval and esteem and their antitheses properly distributed within the system. Non-relational rewards must, in turn, be symbolically integrated with these attitudes and their gradations. This implies, as noted above, a certain minimum of inequality, though its extent and exact content will vary with the specific achievement goals and reward symbols and the degree of differentiation of the occupational role system. In the most general terms it may be said that the basic reward in such a system is "success," defined as level of approval for valued achievement. There are, however, extremely complex problems concerning the integration of such a reward system, and above all the ways in which various expressive symbols can be integrated with the dominant value-attitudes.

Approval and esteem are sources of direct gratification but, as we have seen, of a specialized character. Above all, they exclude direct gratification of need-dispositions, other than the needs for approval and esteem themselves, in specific terms or in diffuse attachments. These and a variety of other considerations lead us to predict that as adaptive structures there will be institutionalized in this type of social system a variety of patterns at variance with the main universalistic achievement patterns. In the first instance these will be found in the kinship cluster which is above all built about ascriptive statuses and diffuse affective attachments. As noted above no industrial society has yet appeared which has come close to dispensing with kinship as a major part of the social structure. Perhaps two main things may be said of the type of kinship system which can best be integrated with the industrial type of occupational system. First the extent of solidarities must be limited so that the individual in his occupational role does not come into too drastic conflicts with his kinship roles. Very broadly this tends to be accomplished by confining the most stringent kinship obligations to the conjugal family of procreation, and isolating this in a relative sense from wider kinship units. Further, the involvement of the kinship unit with the occupational system tends to be primarily focused on the adult male. Especially with a system of formal education, which serves functions especially of technical training for occupational roles, and is, in one primary aspect, a kind of system of pre-occupational roles, the relative exclusion of minor children is relatively easy. The primary problems and strains center on the role of the wife and mother. The "easy" solution is for her to be completely excluded from the occupational system by confining herself to the role of housewife. In most industrial societies, however, there tends to be a good deal of adaptation and compromise relative to this solution. The second important feature is the accent on affectivity in the kinship system. This has partly the function of inhibiting the development of some of the kinds of kinship patterns which would be a threat to the operation of an individualistic type of occupational system. Partly, however, it serves as a counterbalance to the accent on neutrality in the occupational system in that it offers a field for diffuse affective attachments which must be inhibited in the occupational realm.

Thus from the perspective of the institutionalization of a universalistic achievement value system the kinship structure and the patterning of sex roles should be considered primarily as adaptive structures. There is, however, every indication that they are of such crucial functional significance to the motivational economy of the occupational system itself that their institutionalization is of high strategic importance. They cannot be left uncontrolled, and must in some fashion be integrated with the instrumental system. Because of the fundamental difference of patterning, however, the relation between the two structures is bound to be a major focus of strain in this type of society.

Just as the imperatives of such a social system impose rather strict limitations on the variability of kinship patterns, so also does it with respect to the smaller units of territorial community within the system. The primary basis for this is the imperative of free mobility within the occupational system which means that too close ties of community solidarity, which are inevitably diffuse rather than specific, can be a serious threat to the main system. Similarly with regional differentiations. Perhaps partly as a compensatory mechanism in this context such societies tend to develop intense diffuse affective attitudes of solidarity with reference to the largest unit of community, namely the nation. The connection between the development of industrialism and of nationalism is well attested. Soviet

Russia in this as in so many other respects, seems to be no exception, in spite of its "internationalist" ideology. At the other end of the scale the intensity of sentiment about the "American home" may well be another compensatory mechanism. One reason for this is that the conjugal family is the unit *both* of kinship and of community as local unit of residence. It, rather than the individual, must in certain respects be the unit of mobility. Its solidarity is less of a threat to universalism and achievement values than would be that of a larger unit of community as well as kinship.

Ethnic subdivisions within such a society are not, as such, in harmony with its main structural patterns and hence create strains. They do, however, often exist not only by "historical accident" such as immigration, but they persist in such a way as to suggest that they have functions. On the one hand for the members of a given ethnic group it may be suggested that they constitute a focus of security beyond the family unit which is in some respects less dysfunctional for the society than community solidarity would be; on the other, for the outsider they often seem to perform an important scapegoat function as targets for displaced aggression. Nationalism absorbs many of the motivational forces not only of community but of ethnic solidarity since the national is normally at the same time a territorial community and an ethnic unit.

Stratification in terms of an open class system seems to be inherent in this type of society. In order to accord at all with the major value patterns it must be open. But some form not only of class differentiation in the sense of differential rewards for individuals, but of integration in terms of styles of life including all members of the kinship unit seems to be inevitable. The basis of this is above all the fact that the family must be integrated into the reward system, and, therefore, that the differentials of rewards must be expressed in a style of life for the family as a unit, including women and children, and not only for the occupational status-achiever. There is, therefore, as noted above, an inherent limitation on absolute equality of opportunity in such a society.

Finally, too closely integrated a religious system would be dysfunctional in such a society. If the orientation of such a religion were strongly other-worldly it would undermine motivation in the central role system—if not this, it would, like Marxism as a "religion," tend to shift the balance over to the universalistic-ascriptive type to be discussed below. The pattern of religious toleration and a diversity of denominations as in the American case seems to be the least disruptive structure. The state in such a system, it may be remarked, tends to be regarded as any other collectivity, justified only in terms of its service to valued goal-achievement. It may very well be, then, that the problem of institutionalizing collective political responsibility is one of the most serious points of strain in such a social system. The primary diffuse solidarities of such a society then are family-home, class, community, ethnic group, religious denomination, and nation. There is also room for an ecological system of diffuse affective attachments. These are exceedingly prominent in the cross-sex relationships of the "dating" period with the attendant romantic love complex, but tend to be absorbed into the kinship unit by marriage. Intrasex friendship as diffuse attachment is much less prominent, probably because it can too readily divert from the achievement complex. Among men it tends rather to be attached as a diffuse "penumbra" to occupational relationships in the form of an obligation in a mild way to treat one's occupational associate as a friend also. It is thereby spread out, and does not form a focus of major independent structuring. The very fact that affectionate bodily contact is almost completely taboo among men in American society is probably indicative of this situation since it strongly limits affective attachment.

It may be suggested that expressive orientations are less dangerous—outside the family—in specific rather than in diffuse forms, and that this has something to do with the proliferation of "entertainment" in industrial societies. In these forms the actor can take his gratifications piecemeal, as it were, without incurring the obligations inherent in diffuse attachments.

In general, what place is occupied by the affective-expressive orientations constitutes a major adaptive problem for this type of social structure. The problem of the place of diffuseness is another such problem focus. Its connection with affectivity has already been dealt with. It recurs, however, in connection with the "political" functions, within organizations and within the society as a whole. Where the emphasis on specificity is strong, there will be strong inhibitions against letting approval pass too readily over into esteem, .

against imputing *general superiority* to an individual, a role or a class. This is one of the most important factors in the fluidity and openness of the class system of such a society. Similarly, of course, with general inferiority. It may, then, be suggested that leadership roles in such a society tend to be unstable, and a focus of a good deal of anxiety and aggression. This is one factor tending to throw the balance in an individualistic direction and toward an anti-authoritarian attitude.

It was noted above that in value-orientation terms there was a tendency for such a society to be individualistic rather than collectivistic in its emphases. This seems to be, above all, associated with the connection between universalism, achievement and specificity. The segregation from the fusions involved in diffuseness, either of generalized status ascriptions or of affective attachments, seems to be essential to the mobility of personnel and facilities and the allocation of rewards by achievements, which this pattern requires. Leadership roles, for example, are least questionable where the organization has specific achievement goals, rather than, as with a political organization, diffuse ones. This set of considerations may well, then, underlie the "economic" bias of American society, and the fact that political responsibility is a point of strain.

The collectivistic direction of emphasis, then, has a tendency to pass over into the universalistic-ascription type which will be discussed presently. First, however, a few more words may be said about some directions of variation of the universalistic-achievement type. First it is possible for the achievement goals to be non-empirical. Unless, however, as in the case of Calvinism, these non-empirical goals give rise to direct empirical implications (the Kingdom of God on Earth) which can be taken as the immediate goals, the effect is to displace the whole emphasis away from the occupational achievement complex and thus alter the character of the society profoundly. The activities oriented to the primary achievements can no longer be rational-instrumental but must assume a symbolic-ritual character. This possibility has probably been most fully realized in Catholic Christianity where the church has been an organization for the realization of non-empirical goals. This throws the main emphasis away from the secular instrumental complex and puts a premium on its stabilization through traditionalism and/or authoritarianism rather than its continuing development. By the same token the pressure against giving affectivity and diffuseness prominent places decreases. This may well have something to do with the fact that the Latin countries, with their Catholic background, have proved relatively unsusceptible to the development of industrial patterns and that in certain respects, in spite of their religious transcendentalism, they have leaned in a "hedonistic" direction.

2. *The Universalistic-Ascription Pattern*

It will not be possible to take space to treat the other three types of society as fully as was done with the Universalistic-Achievement type, but since a comparative base line has been established, it ought not to be necessary.

The universalistic element has the same order of consequences here as in the above case, but its combination with ascription gives it a different twist. First, the emphasis becomes above all *classificatory*. There may be a *secondary* achievement orientation in that the ideal state of affairs to which action is oriented may not exist in the here and now, in which case there is an obligation to attempt to bring it about. If it is present, conversely there is an obligation to defend it against threats. Achievements, however, are valued *instrumentally*, not in themselves. Because of the universalistic quality of the definition of the ideal state there is a strong tendency to dualism, to drawing a sharply absolute distinction between conformity with the ideal and deviation from it, and in action terms, being "for it" or "against it."

This dualism appears in two distinct ways. The first is the one just mentioned, the dualism of attitude toward particular persons, collectivities, etc. The second is a dualism of locus of application of the value pattern itself. On the one hand the existing institutional structure—or parts of it—may be felt to embody the ideal values and be sanctioned by them. On the other hand the ideal pattern may be set over against the existing pattern—an ideal state against a corrupt present. In either case the dualistic tendency is present though in a sense it seems paradoxical that the same type of value pattern can be involved in both extreme conservatism of certain types and extreme radicalism.

Because of the universalistic element there is the same emphasis on the sphere of occupation and organization and its independence of kinship or narrowly defined community. However, there are certain important differences. First, the strong emphasis on classificatory qualities tends, in terms of social structure, to become an emphasis on *status* rather than on specific achievements. Hence the inevitable elaborate differentiation of roles where achievements are concretely of high importance and where universalistic criteria apply to them, tends to work out to a status-hierarchy where the accent is on what a given actor *is* rather than on *what he has done.*[11]

Secondly, there is a strong tendency to collectivism because of the absence of valuation of the particularization of achievements. The ideal state tends to be defined as one enjoyed by the society as a collectivity, or to be achieved by it. Furthermore, it is easy to make the transition from an ideal state to be achieved, to the ascription of ideal qualities to the collectivity.

Third, there is a tendency to authoritarianism, in that the clear conception of what is ideal for all makes it natural for those who have roles enjoining collective responsibility to "see to it" that everyone lives up to the ideal, either directly, or in making the proper contribution to the collective achievement.

In more general terms, there is a strong tendency to give diffuseness priority over specificity. Status, then, tends not to be specific to a particular occupational role for instance, but tends to become very readily generalized relative to a general prestige scale. An aspect of this generalization of status is the tendency to ascribe qualities to the whole group to which an individual belongs. Since universalism precludes frank recognition of particularistic elements, the group, e.g. kinship or class, is held to have inherent qualities. Hence conceptions of aristocracy, and of ethnic, especially national qualities, are congenial to this orientation. Esteem tends to take precedence over approval in the reward system.

Perhaps it may be said that this type is subject to peculiarly drastic internal tensions. There seems to be an inherent connection between achievement, universalism and specificity which is broken

[11] This is the conservative case. In the revolutionary case the same kind of status hierarchy tends to appear in the revolutionary movement itself, the party.

through in this case. Actual achievement must play an important part, the more so the more differentiated the social structure. But the fact that achievement is not valued for itself is a source of strain. In one respect the accent on collectivism may be a manifestation of this strain in that it acts to inhibit the individualizing tendencies of an emphasis on achievement. Furthermore there are particularly strong inhibitions on affectivity, centering particularly on the "honor" of status, either within the society or as a member of it in general. Affective manifestations, therefore, tend to be relegated to even more secondary positions than in the first type. Especially, particularistic attachments are devalued. There is thus no real German counterpart of the American romantic love complex.

Because of the strong accent on the occupational system in this case, the limitations placed on the size of the kinship unit and its constitution are similar to those involved in the first type. There is, however, an important difference in the definition of familial roles. The primary focus of these differences lies in the importance of status-categorization in a diffuse sense, which above all works out in sharpness of categorization of the age and sex roles as they impinge on the internal structure of the family. Above all the feminine role tends to be defined in sharp contrast to the masculine. Because of the importance of discipline in the politico-occupational structures and the importance of affective needs, it seems likely that this type of society will have a strong accent on women as love-objects and as responsive, but not as having instrumental or moral capacities of a high order. Combined with the general emphasis on hierarchy and authority in this type of society, this would seem to suggest an authoritarian family structure, in which the wife was carefully "kept in her place." This is notoriously characteristic of the traditional German family structure.

The reader will recognize that many of the traits being sketched here seem to fit German social structure. Indeed "conservative" German society seems to be one of the best cases of this type where the accent is on the status quo. Nazism, on the other hand projected the ideal state into a political future ideal, conceived to be an emanation of the mystically ideal qualities of the German *Volk*. There are also certain respects in which Soviet Russia approximates this type.

Communism is a utopian ideal state of affairs to be realized by collective action. The primary status-focus revolves about the Party as the elite vanguard of the realization of the ideal.

It again may be emphasized that this ideal type tends to have a "political" accent as distinguished from the economic accent in the American case. This is associated with its diffuseness and the tendency to mobilize all resources in the interest of the collective ideal. The combination of this politicism and universalism have something to do with the tendency to aggressiveness of such societies. This is accentuated by the severity of internal strains and the tendency to project the attendant anxiety and aggression on the outsider. The very effectiveness of authoritarian measures in eliminating internal opposition probably contributes to this aggressiveness, in that it deprives the population of internal scapegoats which are both relatively "safe" and which are sufficiently important and formidable to be "worth while" to be aggressive about. The degree of internal tension is such that a low level of free floating aggression would seem to be out of the question.

It also follows from the general characteristics of this type that a particularly strong emphasis should be placed upon the state, as the primary organ of realization or maintenance of the ideal states of collective affairs. In a corresponding sense collective morality, as distinguished from individual morality, has a particularly central place. The wide range open to private interests in the first type is therefore felt to be a "low level of morality," defined by preoccupation with self interest as opposed to the common interest.

It appears from the above sketches that one way of broadly characterizing the differences between the achievement-universalistically and the ascription-universalistically oriented types of society is to say that the first is "individualistic," the second "collectivistic." This seems broadly true and significant. What we have done is to give a considerably fuller analysis of the factors underlying the application of these terms than is current in common usage. The same is true of the terms authoritarian and anti-authoritarian, which also broadly fit the contrast. Both pairs of terms should be understood to characterize derivative resultants of the major value-orientation components of the social system in relation to the imperatives of social integration.

3. *The Particularistic Achievement Pattern*

Turning to the third type which combines achievement values with particularism, we may start with the familiar implications of the achievement-orientation. The focus of this is the valuation of social objects for what they do rather than for what they are. The problems arise in connection with the content of what achievements are valued, and in what context of social relationships in other respects.

The shift from universalism to particularism precludes that the primary criteria of valued achievement should be found in universalistic terms such as efficiency or conformity with a completely generalized ideal. They must, on the contrary, be focused on certain points of reference within the relational system itself, or inherent in the situation in which it is placed. It may be presumed that, as defining role-expectations, these are in the first instance the relational bases for the categorization of objects, namely biological relatedness, territorial and temporal location. There are, then, certain "secondary" points of reference in the structure of social relationships themselves, notably membership in solidary collectivities as such and relations of superiority-inferiority.

The element of achievement which is combined with these particularistic emphases precludes that the orientation to them should be predominantly passive. The achievement emphasis then leads to the conception of a *proper* pattern of adaptation which is the product of human achievement and which can be maintained only by continuous effort and if not maintained must be reachieved. At the same time the relational focus precludes that this achievement orientation should set goals transcendent to the system.

The classical Chinese social structure seems to fit this pattern very closely. It can be said to have been organized primarily about the relational reference points of kinship, local community, continuity with ancestors, the ordering of hierarchical relationships, and a general orientation to collective morality emphasizing responsibility for the functioning of collectivities, all the way from the Emperor's responsibility for the society as a whole, to the father's responsibility for his family. Both instrumental orientations and "spontaneous" expressive orientations tend in such a system to be subordinated. Activities in which either is involved tend to be carried out within the diffuse solidary units which constitute the main structure, the instrumental activities on their behalf.

In the first place this whole structure fits with the well-known "familism" of Chinese society. There is a strong emphasis on the solidarity of the kinship unit, extending beyond the conjugal family. This extension is above all carried out in the temporal dimension to emphasize continuity with the ancestors, and hence responsibility toward them. The exigencies of maintaining continuity in kinship terms are, however, such that the female line of descent is drastically sacrificed to the male, female subordination is thus primarily an adaptive structure. The problem of equality of the statuses of brothers, however, seems to involve exigencies other than those primarily involved in kinship, namely, those of the achievement complex.

The kinship unit in China has also been extremely closely integrated with territorial community, which is one of the reasons why land has been of such overwhelming importance. In the first instance this has involved the family's land holding in the village community, but also the family burial grounds as symbolic of continuity with the ancestors. On a higher status level it has involved the kinship group's residence in the town as one of the cluster of gentry families of that town.

The differentiation of such a social system beyond the level of extreme localism, partly through the exigencies of integration of power, partly through the problems of cultural uniformity transcending the local unit, has involved also a hierarchical differentiation. This has tended to be directly institutionalized in a pattern congruous with that of kinship, first with reference to the patriarchal superiority of the land-owning gentry over the peasantry, partly with reference to more individualized achievement superiority and political authority.

The fact that Chinese society did not remain organized in feudal terms seems to be connected with the achievement component in the fundamental value-orientation which among other things derives from the fact that heredity of status is the *most* drastic antithesis of an achievement value. At any rate the top status elements under the emperor were structured in achievement terms through the examination system and the appointive status of the official. This involved an element of mobility and could symbolically set personal achievement goals before every Chinese boy. But the relative weakness of universalism in the general value-orientation was associated with the fact that it was a diffuse rather than a specific achievement pattern, attaining "superiority" rather than competence. We have already seen that the gentry class functioned as an adaptive structure as between this political organization and the rest of society.

This diffuseness in turn was connected with the fact that superiority of status was so closely connected with responsibility. In this sense the Chinese system tended to be both collectivistic and authoritarian. The weakness of universalism and the attendant specificity made it difficult for achievement to become individualistically oriented. There was a coincidence of superiority and responsibility in strictly collective terms. The fact of being particularistically bound within the relational system also contributed to the accent on traditionalism, the acceptance of a model of propriety which was permanently binding and which, since it was conceived to have been realized in the past, was to be continually re-achieved.

This type of system involves a far more unequivocal acceptance of kinship ties than is the case with either of the universalistic types. Kinship plays a central part in the whole hierarchical network of solidary collectivities, and is in a certain sense the prototype of them all. But orientations within the kinship unit are none the less structured in certain directions, notably in that spontaneous affectivity is strongly inhibited in favor of a "moralistic" attitude of responsibility for the interests of the unit. Anything like the American romantic love complex is excluded by this set of facts. Indeed spontaneous affectivity tends to be tolerated only as interstitial and constitutes one of the main foci for deviance.

Instrumental orientations must either be kept under control or strongly inhibited, because their individualistic trends could readily destroy the central collective solidarities. It is this above all which channels achievement in collective directions. But the strong inhibition on instrumentalism has the consequence that a certain primacy of symbolic actions develops, a "code of propriety" which is more ritual than instrumental. Indeed Confucian morality, in addition to its collectivistic trend, tends to this ritualistic propriety rather than to what to the Western mind is an "ethical" orientation to good works.

Thus the particularistic-achievement type of society has a collectivism in common with its exact opposite combination of pattern variables, because particularism inhibits the individualistic implications of achievement-orientation just as ascription inhibits those of universalism. On the other hand, by contrast with the rationalism of both the universalistic types, this type tends to be traditionalistic, in that its particularism precludes the placing of primary achievement goals outside the given relational system.

4. *The Particularistic-Ascriptive Pattern*

There remains the combination of particularism with ascription as the definition of a dominant social value-orientation pattern. This case has certain similarities with the one just discussed but also certain important differences. Because of its particularism it shares the tendency for the organization of the social structure to crystallize about the relational reference points, notably those of kinship and local community. But because of the ascriptive emphasis these tend to be taken as given and passively "adapted to" rather than made the points of reference for an actively organized system.

One might say with such an orientation there would be a preference for a minimum of differentiation beyond what was essentially given in the human situation. But because of such exigencies as those presented by the power problem this is seldom possible. Some integration beyond the local community both in power and in cultural terms is nearly inevitable. Such larger integrative and ecological structures tend, therefore, to be accepted as part of the given situation of life, and to have positive functions when order is threatened, but otherwise to be taken for granted. There is not the same incentive to use such structures as the political in order actively to organize a system, they are there first as given facts, second as insurance against instability.

The absence of the achievement emphasis even further inhibits the development of instrumental orientations and the structures associated with them than in the previous case. Work is basically a necessary evil just as morality is a necessary condition of minimum stability. Hence the overwhelming preponderance of emphasis is thrown in the expressive direction. These are above all the artistically oriented societies. They tend to be traditionalistic for two reasons, first that there is no incentive to disturb tradition; on the contrary a strong vested interest in its stability, second that there is a high elaboration of expressive symbolism which is in fact a system of conventions. It can only serve this function if the symbolic meanings are highly stabilized. Morality, therefore, tends to be focussed on the traditionalistic acceptance of received standards and arrangements.

Morality and responsibility tend to focus in two directions. The first is with reference to forestalling the dangers inherent in unregulated expressive orientations which, not only through aggression, but through attachments which conflict with a given order, can be highly disruptive. The second is with reference to situational dangers to the established order.

Such societies tend to be individualistic rather than collectivistic and non- if not anti-authoritarian, but in each case with important differences from the application of the same concepts where universalism is involved. The individualism is primarily concerned with expressive interests, and hence much less so with opportunity to shape the situation through achievement. There tends to be a certain lack of concern with the remoter framework of the society, unless it is threatened. Similarly, there is no inherent objection to authority so long as it does not interfere too much with expressive freedom, indeed it may be welcomed as a factor of stability. But there is also not the positive incentive to recognize authority as inherent that exists in the cases of positive authoritarianism. The tendency to indifference to larger social issues creates a situation in which authority can become established with relatively little opposition. Hence a susceptibility to "dictatorship" is not uncommon in such a society. The Spanish-American seems to be a good example of this social type.[12]

The foregoing has been a mere sketch of four types of social structure. In no sense does it pretend to be either a thorough and

[12] The author has been greatly sensitized to the special features of this type of social structure and its culture by Dr. Florence Kluckhohn, in many oral discussions, and in her *Los Atarquenos,* unpublished Ph.D. dissertation, Radcliffe College.

systematic analysis of each type individually or a careful and systematic comparison of them with each other. Above all it has not even begun to approach the difficult analysis of mixed and transitional cases, of which there are undoubtedly many. It has been presented here for a very specific purpose, to give a sense of concrete relevance to the claim that the categories of social structure developed in this chapter and the preceding ones do provide a starting point for systematic comparative analysis and eventually the construction of a typology of social structures.

This illustrative discussion has, we think, gone far enough to substantiate that claim. The types, not only in terms of direct spelling out of the implications of the basic value-orientations, but in terms of the adaptive structures which go with them, certainly make sense empirically. Even on such a superficial level as the present one they stimulate many insights and seem to make otherwise baffling features of certain societies understandable. When the same basic conceptual framework is applied systematically and in detail, with careful checking of empirical evidence, and when it is combined with a much more sophisticated analysis of motivational process, there is every reason to believe that a highly useful set of tools of comparative empirical analysis will prove to be available.

Now we must leave the analysis of social structure as such and proceed to further development of the theory of motivational processes in the social system, the processes both of its maintenance and of its change. In analyzing these problems the relation between the social system and its roles on the one hand, and personality on the other, will always have to be in the forefront of our attention.

VI

THE LEARNING OF SOCIAL
ROLE-EXPECTATIONS AND THE MECHANISMS OF
SOCIALIZATION OF MOTIVATION

THE social system is a system of action. It is a system of interdependent action processes. The structural aspects which have been singled out for attention in the three preceding chapters involve a certain mode of abstraction from this process. It is now necessary to fill in certain aspects of what has been abstracted from, to analyze certain aspects of the element of process itself in the context of the social system. For this purpose it is necessary to clarify further the concept of *mechanism,* which is here used in a sense parallel to its use in physiology and in personality psychology.

A process is any way or mode in which a given state of a system or of a part of a system changes into another state. If its study is an object of science any process is assumed to be subject to laws, which will be stated in terms of determinate interrelations of interdependence between the values of the relevant variables. Frequently, however, the laws governing a process are incompletely known, or even not at all. Then it may still be possible to *describe* the process in terms of the initial and the final states, and possibly intermediate stages or go a step further to state empirical generalizations about it.

A scientist studying the interdependences of variables generally isolates the particular process or class of them in which he is interested and treats it as a system. For some purposes, however, it is necessary to treat the process in question as part of a larger system.

When this is done in such a way that interest is focused on the significance of *alternative outcomes of the process* for the system or other parts of it, the process will be called a *mechanism*.

This concept is of the first importance in the present context. There is no reason to believe that there is anything relative about the *laws* of motivational process, beyond the sense in which all scientific laws are relative. But while the laws are not relative, the mechanisms of motivation are, because they are formulated with specific reference to their *significances* for a particular class of system. The particularly important point is that the mechanisms of personality as a system are *not the same* as the mechanisms of the social system, because, in the ways which have been set forth in this work and elsewhere, personalities and social systems constitute two different classes of system. In so far as "psychology" gives us completely generalized laws of motivational process they are as much and as directly applicable to processes of action in the context of the social system as anywhere else. But in so far as what psychology gives us is not laws but mechanisms, the high probability is that they are mechanisms of the personality as a system. In this case the presumption is that they are not directly applicable to the analysis of social process, but their content in terms of laws must be reformulated in terms of its relevance to the social system. Social systems thus do not "repress" or "project," nor are they "dominant" or "submissive"; these are mechanisms of the personality. But the motivational processes which are involved in these mechanisms also operate in social systems. We are profoundly concerned with these processes, but in their relevance to the mechanisms of the social system.

It is necessary to explain a little further just what this means. We may take for granted that motivation is *always* a process which goes on in one or more *individual* actors. We may speak of the "motivation" of a collectivity only in an elliptical sense as referring to certain *uniformities* in the motivations of its members, or to a certain *organization* of those motivations. But in order to select the relevant uniformities and patterns of organization, it is necessary to have criteria of relevance which are seldom if ever given in generalized knowledge of motivational process itself. It must be given in terms of mechanisms which involve, as part of their conceptualization, the specification of the types of consequences of alternative outcomes of the processes concerned which are significant to the social system. But in order to make this specification in turn we must be in a position to say in systematic terms what these consequences are. It is this circumstance which, in the present state of knowledge, gives the "structural" analysis of the social system a certain priority over its "dynamic" or motivational analysis. If we do not have the structural analysis we do not know where to begin dynamic conceptualization, because we are unable to judge the relevance of motivational processes and laws, above all to distinguish between mechanisms of personality and mechanisms of the social system.

The first task is to set up a classification of the motivational mechanisms of the social system and to relate this systematically to the classifications of the mechanisms of personality. In another publication[1] the mechanisms of the personality system have been classified in three categories, those of learning, of defense and of adjustment. Learning is defined broadly as that set of processes by which new elements of action-orientation are acquired by the actor, new cognitive orientations, new values, new objects, new expressive interests. Learning is *not* confined to the early stages of the life cycle, but continues throughout life. What is ordinarily called a "normal" adaptation to a change in the situation or the "unfolding" of an established dynamic pattern, is a learning process.

The mechanisms of defense are the processes through which conflicts internal to the personality, that is between different need-dispositions and sub-systems of them, are dealt with. In the cases of complete resolution of such conflicts the mechanisms of defense merge into those of learning. Finally, the mechanisms of adjustment are the processes by which the individual actor deals with elements of strain and conflict in his relations to objects, that is to the situation of action. He may thus face the threat of loss of an object of attachment, of frustration of the attainment of a goal through situational strains and the like. Again, with complete resolution of situational strains and conflicts the mechanisms of adjustment merge with those of learning. A completely successful substitution of a new object for one entailing severe conflict may thus obviate the need for dependency on the object the loss of which is threatened.

[1] Parsons and Shils, *Values, Motives and Systems of Action,* Chapter **II.** This chapter is of first importance as background for the present discussion.

This way of conceiving and classifying the mechanisms of personality functioning implies a most important assumption which should be brought into the open. Learning as conceived above is a process of *change* in the state of the personality as a system. Defense and adjustment are conceived as *equilibrating* processes, processes which counteract tendencies to change the system in certain ways. There is in this classification *no* class of mechanisms for *maintaining* a stable motivational process in operation. In other words, we are assuming that the *continuance* of a stabilized motivational process in a stabilized relationship to the relevant objects is to be treated as *not problematical.* This assumption, though seldom made explicit, seems to be of very general applicability in psychology. It may be compared to the first Newtonian law of motion, the law of inertia, which states that the *problems* for mechanics concern *not* what makes bodies move, but what makes them *change* their motion, in direction or velocity. We shall assume the motivational counterpart of the law of inertia in the present discussion, that it is change of intensity or "direction," i.e., orientation, of action which poses the problems for the dynamics of action theory. Hence for the social system as well as the personality we will *not* be concerned with the problem of the maintenance of given states of the social system *except where there are known tendencies to alter those states.* This principle gives us a clear criterion of what constitutes a motivational problem in the context of the social system.

Now it must again be remembered that motivational processes are *always* processes in individual actors. Therefore, the application of the above criterion means that the problems of the mechanisms of the social system arise where, from our knowledge of individuals, we have reason to believe that there are tendencies to alter established states of the social system. What, then, for our immediate purposes is an established state of a social system, or relevant subsystem?

The answer to this question is given in the basic paradigm of social interaction which has been discussed so often. An established state of a social system is a process of complementary interaction of two or more individual actors in which each conforms with the expectations of the other('s) in such a way that alter's reactions to ego's actions are positive sanctions which serve to reinforce his given need-dispositions and thus to fulfill his given expectations. This stabilized or equilibrated interaction process is the fundamental point of reference for all dynamic motivational analysis of social process.

It is certainly contrary to much of the common sense of the social sciences, but it will nevertheless be assumed that the maintenance of the complementarity of role-expectations, once established, is *not problematical,* in other words that the "tendency" to maintain the interaction process is the *first law of social process.* This is clearly an assumption, but there is, of course, no theoretical objection to such assumptions if they serve to organize and generalize our knowledge. Another way of stating this is to say that no *special mechanisms* are required for the explanation of the maintenance of complementary interaction-orientation.

Then what classes of tendencies *not* to maintain this interaction are there? Fundamentally they can be reduced to two. First it is quite clear that the orientations which an actor implements in his complementary interaction in roles, are not inborn but have to be acquired through learning. We may then say that *before* he has learned a given role-orientation he clearly tends to act in ways which would upset the equilibrium of interaction in his incumbency of the role in question. The acquisition of the requisite orientations for satisfactory functioning in a role is a learning process, but it is not learning in general, but a particular part of learning. This process will be called the process of *socialization,* and the motivational processes by which it takes place, seen in terms of their functional significance to the interaction system, the *mechanisms of socialization.* These are the mechanisms involved in the processes of "normal" functioning of the social system.

However, the problems of the socialization process are formulated on the assumption that the factors producing the equilibrium of the interaction process are stabilized with the exception that the requisite orientations for adequate functioning of a given actor in a given role have not yet been learned. But concretely this is not the case. Both within the individual actors as personalities and in the situation in which they act there are factors tending to upset the equilibrium. Changes in the situation as such may be said to present new learning problems and thus fall within the scope of socializa-

tion. But certain changes arising from the personalities of the interacting factors and their *reactions* to situational changes are another
matter.

We have seen that the very structure of the interaction process
provides the major dimension for the organization of such tendencies. They are tendencies to *deviance,* to depart from conformity with the normative standards which have come to be set up
as the common culture. A tendency to deviance in this sense is a
process of motivated action, on the part of an actor who has unques-
tionably had a full opportunity to learn the requisite orientations,
tending to deviate from the complementary expectations of conformity with common standards so far as these are relevant to the
definition of his role. Tendencies to deviance in this sense in turn
confront the social system with "problems" of control, since deviance
if tolerated beyond certain limits will tend to change or to dis-
integrate the system. Focusing, then, on the tendencies to deviance,
and the reactions in the social system which operate in the direction
of motivating actors to abandon their deviance and resume conformity, we may speak of the second class of mechanisms, the
mechanisms of social control. A mechanism of social control, then,
is a motivational process in one or more *individual* actors which
tends to *counteract* a tendency to deviance from the fulfillment of
role-expectations, in himself or in one or more alters. It is a re-
equilibrating mechanism.

The mechanisms of social control comprise aspects of the two
classes of mechanisms of the personality which have been called
mechanisms of defense and of adjustment. They constitute, that is,
defense and adjustment *relative* to tendencies to violate role-expectations. Psychologically the particularly close relationship to the superego is immediately evident. It should, however, again be emphasized
that though the mechanisms of social control comprise *elements* of
these personality mechanisms, they are *not* the same, but are mechanisms of the social system. Just what specific systematic interrelations exist will have to be explored in the subsequent analysis. Of
the two classes, however, for obvious reasons the mechanisms of
personality adjustment are *dynamically* the more closely related to
the mechanisms of social control. It is, after all, in the interrelations
with social objects that both the problems of adjustment of the per-

sonality and of control for the social system, arise. On the other hand *functionally*, the mechanisms of social control are more closely analogous with the mechanisms of defense, since both are concerned with the processes by which a system of action is internally integrated, and disruptive tendencies are held in check.

A word should also be said about the relations between the mechanisms of socialization and social control on the one hand and the allocative processes of the social system on the other. The allocation of personnel between roles in the social system and the socialization processes of the individual are clearly *the same processes* viewed in different perspectives. Allocation is the process seen in the perspective of functional significance to the social system as a system. Socialization on the other hand is the process seen in terms of the motivation of the individual actor. Learning to decide between alternatives of role-incumbency which the social system leaves open to the individual is certainly part of social learning and such decisions manifest the value-orientations acquired through socialization. The process of allocation of facilities and rewards on the other hand is from the motivational point of view a process of acquisition and loss of valued object-relations by individual actors. It is thus a process of "flow" in a stabilized situation (e.g., of "income") or it is a process of situational change requiring adjustment by the actor. The adjustments may be successfully learned through socialization mechanisms or they may be factors in producing tendencies to deviance and hence foci for the operation of mechanisms of social control.

The present chapter will be concerned with the processes of socialization and their mechanisms, leaving until Chapter VII the analysis of deviance and the processes of social control.

§ THE SOCIALIZATION OF THE CHILD AND THE INTERNALIZATION OF SOCIAL VALUE-ORIENTATIONS

THE term socialization in its current usage in the literature refers primarily to the process of child development. This is in fact a crucially important case of the operation of what are here called the mechanisms of socialization, but it should be made clear that the term is here used in a broader sense than the current one to designate the learning of *any* orientations of functional significance to the operation of a system of complementary role-expectation:. In this sense, socialization, like learning, goes on throughout life. The case of the development of the child is only the most dramatic because he has so far to go.

However, there is another reason for singling out the socialization of the child. There is reason to believe that, among the learned elements of personality in certain respects the stablest and most enduring are the major value-orientation patterns and there is much evidence that these are "laid down" in childhood and are not on a large scale subject to drastic alteration during adult life.[2] There is good reason to treat these patterns of value-orientation, as analyzed in terms of pattern variable combinations, as the core of what is sometimes called "basic personality structure" and they will be so treated here. Hence in discussing certain highlights of the socialization of the child, primary emphasis will be placed on this aspect of socialization in more general terms.

Before proceeding it may be emphasized that the socialization of the child is a case of socialization in the strict sense of the above definition, not of social control. What has sometimes been called the "barbarian invasion" of the stream of new-born infants is, of course, a critical feature of the situation in any society. Along with the lack of biological maturity, the conspicuous fact about the child is that he has yet to learn the patterns of behavior expected of persons in his statuses in his society. Our present discussion is not concerned with the fact that children, having learned these patterns, tend very widely to deviate from them, though this, of course, happens at every stage, but with the process of acquisition itself on the part of those who have not previously possessed the patterns.

As a mechanism of the social system, the combination of motivational processes in question must be conceived as a set of processes of action in roles which, on the basis of known facts about motivational process, analytical and empirical, tend to bring about a certain result, in the present case the internalization of certain

---

[2] The commonest apparent type of exception is that explained by ambivalence in an earlier orientation system. In such a case there may of course be dramatic changes of overt behavior.

patterns of value-orientation. This result is conceived to be the outcome of certain processes of interaction in roles.

In order to analyze the processes then, it is necessary to have two classes of information available. First we must have knowledge of the processes or mechanisms of learning from the point of view of the actor who is in the process of being socialized. Secondly, we must have in mind the relevant features of the interacting role system, which place the *socializee,* if the term may be permitted, in a situation which favors the relevant learning process. The assumption is that mechanisms of socialization operate only so far as the learning process is an integral part of the process of interaction in complementary roles. Thus not only the socializing agents *but the socializee* must be conceived as acting in roles. At the instant of birth, perhaps, the infant does not do so. But almost immediately a role is ascribed to him which includes expectations of his behavior. The behavior of adults toward him *is not* like their behavior toward purely physical objects, but is contingent on his behavior and very soon what are interpreted to be his expectations; thus *"the baby is expecting* to be fed." It is only when this mutuality of interaction has been established that we may speak of the socialization process. Purely physical care of the infant in which he has no role but is merely a passive object of manipulation is, if it ever exists, not socialization.

In *Values, Motives and Systems of Action* five cathectic-evaluative mechanisms of learning were distinguished and systemically related to one another. All of these are relevant to the present context and what they are and how related must be briefly reviewed here. In the background stand the cognitive mechanisms of discrimination and generalization. The five are reinforcement-extinction, inhibition, substitution, imitation and identification. The first three do not necessarly involve orientation to social objects, while the last two do.

Reinforcement-extinction is the name given for the most general relation between the gratifying-depriving features of the outcome of a behavioral process, and the strength of the tendency to repeat it under appropriate conditions. The broad law is that in general the receipt of gratifications will tend to strengthen the pattern while that of deprivations will tend to weaken it. This generalization should, of course, be carefully interpreted in the light of the many different meanings in the content of gratifications and deprivations and the complex interrelations of need-dispositions in the personality system as well as the significance of many variations in the conditions. A simple "hedonistic" interpretation is clearly inadequate.

The second mechanism is inhibition, which means simply the process of learning to refrain from carrying out the action motivated by a given need-disposition, in the presence of an appropriate opportunity for gratification, regardless of what happens to the "affect" involved. There is a fundamental sense in which inhibition is the obverse of, and inherently linked with, learning itself. For unless complete extinction of previous need-dispositions were immediately given with every new step of learning, learning would be impossible, for the attachment to the old pattern would be unbreakable. Inhibition is thus in one direction the process of breaking through motivational inertia.

The third general mechanism is substitution, which means the process of transferring cathexis from one object to another. Substitution obviously involves inhibition, in the form of renunciation of cathexis of the *old* object, but in addition it involves the capacity to transfer, to "learn" that the new object can provide gratifications which are more or less equivalent to the old. Thus in the most general terms "progress" in learning means, first, at least enough reinforcement to prevent extinction of motivations, second, capacity to inhibit the need-dispositions which block new orientations, and third, capacity to accept new objects, to substitute.

Closely connected with these cathectic-evaluative mechanisms are the primarily cognitive mechanisms of discrimination and generalization. Discrimination is the very first condition of the construction of an object-world, and must continue to operate throughout all learning processes. Generalization on the other hand, by providing awareness of the common attributes of classes of objects, is an indispensable condition of substitution, and of higher levels of organization of an orientation system. Above all, generalization is essential to the cathexis of classes of objects and even more of abstract categories and cultural objects, i.e., symbols, as such, hence to any process of successive substitutions building up to these cathexes, including processes of symbolization. Probably the acquisition of at all generalized patterns of value-orientation involves this mechanism deeply.

Imitation is the process by which *specific* items of culture, specific bits of knowledge, skill, symbolic behavior, are taken over from a social object in the interaction process. In one sense then it may be conceived as a process of short cutting the process of independent learning, in that alter is able to show a shorter and easier way to learn than ego could find by himself. Of course imitation presumably must prove rewarding in some sense if the act to be learned is to be reinforced. But above all imitation does not imply any continuing relation to the "model," or any solidarity attachment.

Identification, on the other hand, means taking over, i.e., internalizing, the *values* of the model. It implies that ego and alter have established a reciprocal role relationship in which value-patterns are shared. Alter is a *model* and this is a *learning process*, because ego did not at the beginning of it possess the values in question. Identification may be subclassified according to the type of values and the nature of the attachment to alter. The most important variations would be according to whether it was a specific or a diffuse attachment and whether it was an affective or love attachment or a neutral or esteem attachment. In any case this is obviously the most important of the learning mechanisms for the acquisition of value patterns.

We may now turn to the features of the interaction process itself, as a complementary role structure, which are important for the socializing effect of the operation of the learning processes just reviewed. The socializing effect will be conceived as the integration of ego into a role complementary to that of alter(s) in such a way that the common values are internalized in ego's personality, and their respective behaviors come to constitute a complementary role-expectation-sanction system.

The first point to mention is that, prior to and independent of any identification, alter as an adult has certain control of the situation in which ego acts, so that he may influence the consequences of ego's actions. Put in learning terms, he may use these to reinforce the tendencies of ego's behavior which fit his own expectations of how ego should behave, and operate to extinguish those which are deviant. Corresponding to the *learning* mechanisms of reinforcement-extinction, then, we may speak of *socialization* mechanisms of *reward-punishment*, the particular and specific orientations to ego's behavior which tend to motivate him to conformity and dissuade him from deviance from alter's expectations.[3] These are to be conceived in abstraction from alter's functioning as a model either for imitation or for identification.

However, rewards and punishments obviously operate to induce inhibitions and substitutions. The simplest motivation for an inhibition presumably is learning that gratification of a need-dispositon will bring deprivational consequences.[4] So far as these consequences have been imposed by a social object contingent on ego's action they constitute punishments. For substitution, on the other hand, presumably a combination of rewards and punishments is, if not indispensable in all cases, at least an optimum; namely the punishment of continued retention of the old object, combined with rewarding of cathexis of the new.

Secondly, alter may operate not only as a reinforcing-extinguishing agent but as a model for imitation. In addition to imposing contingent consequences on ego's specific acts he may hold up a model, which in turn becomes the focus of reinforcement-extinction processes, however actively they may or may not be carried out by alter's own action. In this case we may say that alter as an active model adopts the role of a "teacher" and because the term fits directly, we may speak of *socialization by "instruction"* as the implementation of the mechanism of imitation by the socializing agent. In the learning context the term imitation emphasizes what happens when *there is* a model for imitation. In the socialization context the fact that a model of a given type *is provided* to "instruct"

[3] It is of course possible for ego to reward or punish himself, *given* motivation to do so, which implies internalization of the relevant value-orientations.

[4] There are many complex problems of the psychology of learning involved here which it is desired to leave open: For example Solomon's studies of avoidance conditioning seem to show a quite different pattern from the "classical" reinforcement experiments. It is extremely important not to beg any of these questions. The aim of the present sketch is to place some of the problems of the psychology of learning in the context of their possible significance for the social system. This is done essentially by analyzing the role-structure of the socialization process. It is hoped that sufficient parsimony is observed on the psychological side to avoid commitment to dubious generalizations.

ego is just as much the focus of attention. Thus attention is directed to the specific role of *alter* as well as to ego's learning processes as such.

Finally, the mechanism of learning (generally *in addition* to the others in a complex process) may be identification. For identification to take place there must develop a further feature of the interaction relationship of ego and alter. In addition to what alter *does* in the sense of his overt discrete acts with their reward-punishment significance, and to what he *offers* in the sense of patterns for imitation, alter's *attitudes* toward ego become the crucial feature of the socialization process. We have seen at a number of points how crucial this step in the integration of an interactive system is. Indeed it is in this way that we have defined an *attachment,* namely an orientation to alter in which the paramount focus of cathective-evaluative significance is in alter's attitudes. Overt acts thereby come to be interpreted mainly as "expressions" of these attitudes, that is, as signs, or even more as symbols of them.

When a reciprocal attachment has been formed ego has acquired, as it was called in Chapter IV, a "relational possession." He acquires a "stake" in the security of this possession, in the maintenance of alter's favorable attitudes, his receptiveness-responsiveness, his love, his approval or his esteem, and a need to avoid their withdrawal and above all their conversion into hostile or derogatory attitudes.

The generalizations about motivational processes which are summed up in what is called the mechanism of identification apparently imply the extremely important generalization, we may perhaps say theorem, that value-orientation patterns can *only* be internalized from outside[5] through reciprocal attachments, that is, through ego becoming integrated in a reciprocal and complementary role relative to alter which reaches the level of organization and cathectic sensitivity which we call that of attachment and a common value pattern involving loyalty. The third of the basic classes of mechanisms of socialization, then, we may call the *mechanisms of value-acquisition* with all the implications as to the nature of the process, not only within the personality of ego, but in terms of his interaction with alter, which have been outlined above.

[5] There may, of course, be creative modifications from *within* the personality.

This sketch of the significance of the process of identification is extremely elementary and leaves many crucial problems unsolved. The stress has been placed on the building up of a pattern of values common to ego and to alter, ego being considered as acquiring the values from alter through identification. This leaves open, however, several crucial problems concerning the processes of differentiation of such a value-system. Above all the roles of ego and alter are generally complementary and not identical. There is, therefore, an element of *common value* but equally an element of *differential applicability* of the common value element to ego and to alter. Ego as a small child is clearly not expected to behave exactly as alter as an adult does. Furthermore, ego and alter may be of opposite sex, thus introducing a further differentiation.

On this basis we may distinguish the following elements in the value-patterns acquired by ego from alter through identification; a) the common value-orientation in sufficiently general terms to be applicable both to ego's role and to alter's and hence, presumably more broadly still, e.g., to the family as a whole, etc. This would take the form of allegations that such and such things are right or wrong, proper or improper, in rather general terms; b) alter's expectations—in value-orientation terms for *ego's* behavior in his role, e.g. differentiated from alter's by age and possibly by sex and perhaps otherwise; and c) the complementary expectations for the definition of alter's role.

There is still a fourth element involved in the possible differentiation from the roles of either ego or alter of third parties, e.g., the father if alter is the mother, and finally a fifth in that ego's role is not static but expected to change in the process of his "growing up" —so that a valuation relative to his own future is very much part of his value-acquisition. The complex problems involved in these differentiations will be briefly touched upon in the subsequent discussion but their analysis can at best only be begun.

Of course many features of the actual process of socialization of the child are obscure, especially the factors responsible for differences in outcome, and for pathologies. However, using the above conceptual scheme it will be worthwhile to attempt a brief sketch of some of the highlights which at least can provide the points of departure for some hypotheses, if not the codification of established knowledge. It should be remembered that our concern here is with the acquisition of value-orientation patterns, and factors which may be responsible for the internalization of different types of value-orientation pattern. Hence our primary focus will be on mechanisms of value-acquisition through identifications.

There are throughout two terms to the analysis, namely the role of the socializing agent and of the socializee. In the latter case there are three primary classical attributes of the infant, his *plasticity,* which is simply a name for his capacity to learn alternative patterns, his *sensitivity,* which may be interpreted to be a name for his capacity to form attachments in the above sense, and his *dependency.* The last is, given the first two, the primary "fulcrum" for applying the leverage of socialization. The infant, as an organism, is helpless and dependent on others for the most elementary gratifications of food, warmth and other elements of protection.

The socializing agent is, therefore, inherently in a position to begin the process of socialization by being the agent of rewards and, implicitly at first, then explicitly, of punishments. The beginning orientation of the infant very soon must include awareness of the role of the adult in this most elementary sense. It is, then, the securing of the leverage of the infant's motivation to secure the specific rewards of being fed, kept warm, etc. and avoid the corresponding deprivations[6] which constitute the first beginning of his

[6] Just as in the case of the more specific processes of learning, many problems arise concerning the more specific significances of particular infantile needs and their handling in the course of socialization, including degrees of leniency and severity with respect to such matters as weaning and toilet training and the significance of the timing of discipline in such areas. Again we cannot attempt here to go into these problems in detail but can only attempt to provide a general framework of role analysis within which these detailed problems may be approached. It may, however, be tentatively suggested that if the processes of identification are as important as the present approach seems to indicate, the presumption is that these specific details of child-training practice are likely to be primarily significant in their capacity as expressions of the attitudes of the socializing agents, rather than through their independent intrinsic effects. It seems probable that the strong emphasis on the latter in some circles has been colored by seeing the socialization process in terms of a reinforcement theory of learning alone without reference to the processes of interaction in roles which are of primary interest to the present discussion.

playing a role as distinguished from being merely an object of care.[7] Certain elements of this care come to be expected to be contingent on conformity with alter's expectations, starting with respect to such responses as crying, smiling, or coming to get something (after learning to walk).

It is probable that the basis of attachments begins to be laid down before much imitation occurs, because it takes considerable maturation before the infant has high capacity for imitation. It is probably of great significance that, except in disorganized conditions, there is relatively little direct and early frustration of the infant's fundamental physiological needs. The primary frustrations come with the necessity to make substitutions for the original objects—e.g., weaning. But certain other gratifications coming from pleasant physical contact and the like are especially likely to be contingent on the adult's attitudes toward the infant, and thus on his own behavior. This is probably a main basis of the strategic significance of erotic gratifications and needs in human personality, that their genesis in physical contact with the mother, through suckling, fondling, etc. is likely to be a most prominent focus of role-expectation *contingency* at an early stage of socialization. Then by a series of substitutions an adult structure of erotic need-dispositions gets built up.

In any case generalization from the particularity of rewarding acts on alter's part plus early dependence is the process of genesis of early attachments. Perhaps the first thing to be said about the earliest attachments is that they are in the nature of the case primarily affective if only because the infant does not yet have the capacity for inhibition which underlies affectively neutral orientations. It seems to be completely established that inhibition must be learned, and how, when, in what contexts and subject to what limitations is one of the most important problem areas of socialization theory.

Secondly, there is the question of the temporal priority of specific and diffuse attachments, in the pattern variable sense. Both are, if we assume reward-punishment for particular acts as the

---

[7] The existence of genetically inborn social-relational needs may remain an open question here. If they exist this provides additional motivation to role-assumption.

primary starting point, results of processes of generalization. But the generalization from the specific act to the category of action of which it is an example seems tentatively to be the more elementary one. Hence one would expect that an attachment to the mother as for example, the source of food gratifications, would be the first type of attachment. The generalization to a diffuse attachment in which she is the person who "cares for" ego, not merely in the sense of ministrations but of attitudes, requires a further step. The duality of meaning of the word "care" in the language would appear to be significant.

Granting both sensitivity and dependency, there is still a problem of the mechanisms by which this generalization takes place. It may be suggested that here again the erotic sphere plays a particularly strategic part. Precisely because of many of the practical exigencies of infant care, bodily contact with the mother plays an important part in the relationship. Though as psychoanalytic theory has emphasized, the oral, anal and even urethral zones have in early childhood special erotic potentialities, it may well be that the more significant property of the erotic sphere is its diffuseness. The specific acts of care, such as feeding, have in a certain sense an instrumental character; as such their significance may not be confined to the fact that they provide a favorable basis for building up response needs as distinguished from reward needs and generalizing these to the person of alter rather than to the particular context or class of acts. Much of the significance of the erotic sphere may thus rest on the fact that it is a favorable bridge between reward and response, in that, from the dependence on erotic rewards, especially the diffuser ones of affectionate bodily contact, the path to diffuse attachment can most readily be entered upon.

If this interpretation is correct, it would seem to follow that though specific fixation on specific erogenous zones would ordinarily occur in the normal socialization process to some degree, the more extreme fixations which play a prominent part in pathological syndromes should be treated as consequences of some disturbance of the normally more diffuse functions of erotic interest. It is suggestive that erotic fixation on parts of ego's own body may indicate disturbance of security of a diffuse erotic interest in relation to alter. This would make oral and anal eroticism more significant as secondary aspects of libidinal development than as the primary foci of it.

If the foregoing analysis is correct even the most elementary attachment of a specific response character means that the step to role-playing in the full social system sense has been taken. There is already a common value pattern shared by ego and alter, namely the valuation of their mutual attitudes of affection, such that particular acts are treated as "expressions" of the appropriate attitudes, not simply as discrete rewards and punishments. There are definite norms of appropriate behavior on *both* sides. The dependence of this development on capacity for generalization is clear.

Such an attachment means that the child is not merely receptive to the responses of alter, but has learned to respond himself, for example, by smiling and "cuddling up." But at about this point another of the most fundamental alternatives of socialization patterning opens out. The child has an obvious interest in eliciting both rewards and responses from the adult. But there is an enormous inequality in realistic capacity to perform. In this context the socialization process may take the turn of encouraging ego in passivity, an orientation which is in a sense appropriate to his helplessness, or it may encourage him in building up the more symmetrical reciprocity of receptiveness and response, if not of concrete reward-actions. Indeed it would seem that because of the inherent inequality in the latter sense the only real possibility for motivating an active orientation lay in encouraging responsiveness as well as receptiveness on the child's part, that is, rewarding it *both* with discrete acts and with enhanced receptiveness and responsiveness on alter's part. It is clearly through internalization of the values expressed in attitudes along this dimension that orientation, in terms of the variable of ascription-achievement, tends to be built up. This may, for instance, be extremely important to the development of the achievement values of American Society.

It seems highly probable that early diffuse attachments, particularly to the mother, constitute the focus of what is sometimes called the security system of the child. Security in this sense may be taken to mean that there is a certain stabilization of his system of orientation, by virtue of which the child is able to develop a certain tolerance of frustration. But the price of this security is, in the early attachments, a certain enhancement of dependency. This may be culturally variable in that the presence of mother surrogates mitigates the degree of dependency on the one attachment, but ordinarily this does not involve a difference of *pattern* as between the objects of attachment from which new values could be learned.

The tolerance of frustration, which becomes possible within a diffuse love attachment, seems to provide a major clue to the further significance of such an attachment, namely as a lever for imposing the learning of new values. Part of the frustration to which a child is exposed is inherent in the physical and other aspects of the situation, but a substantial part of it consists of disciplines, whether administered to the child deliberately or not, which may be considered to be mechanisms of socialization.

The uses to which the leverage of frustration tolerance is put will vary with the nature of the roles for which individuals are being socialized, which in turn are very different in different societies. Making allowance for this variability, however, we may concentrate the discussion on some considerations relevant to the processes of acquisition of some of the value-patterns not directly involved in the diffuse love relation of mother to small child. These are above all the independence necessary to an autonomous achievement orientation, the capacity for affective neutrality, for universalism and for functional specificity independent of the direct gratification interests of childhood, especially in affectively neutral contexts. These are admittedly value-patterns of particular significance in the adult role-system of our own society, but they have varying kinds of relevance in other societies.

Success in making the transition from dependent status in a diffuse mother attachment to a more "grown up" stage depends on two primary sets of conditions. The first is the combination of objects of identification offered by the situation in which the child is placed, the value patterns they embody, and their relations to each other in the earlier stages, especially the relations of the two parents. The second is the set of conditions which provide a psychologically favorable situation for the process of identification to operate.

The second is not primarily our concern but a few things may be said about it. The first of these favorable conditions apparently is adequate security in the above sense. In the first instance this centers on the mother. One may, however, say that, for the father to serve as an important identification object, he must be included in a solidarity system with the mother, so that neither is the child excluded from the mother-father solidarity nor the father from the mother-child solidarity—for purposes of simplicity we may omit reference to siblings. It is from his inclusion in this diffuse solidarity system, the family as a collectivity, that the child derives his primary "support."

Secondly, there must be an imposition of disciplines which, given the starting points, constitute frustrations of the child's already established need-dispositions, especially certain needs for immediate gratification, and his dependency needs. It may be surmised that these will include not only ad hoc frustrations but will, at critical points, include failure of alter to respond to ego's established expectations; what had become established as legitimate expectations from alter at one stage of childhood, are not responded to at the next stage.

Ego may respond to these frustrations with adjustive mechanisms; indeed, to some degree he certainly will. But these must not become frozen in combination with defense mechanisms so that the socialization process is blocked, so that, for instance, alienative need-dispositions become established. It would seem, then, that certain adjustive responses to the pressure of frustration of expectations would have to be treated permissively, in the sense that they are "tolerated" by alter without jeopardizing ego's security. If the attachment were specific to the need-disposition context in question, alter's failure to reciprocate would necessarily jeopardize the security of the attachment, but by virtue of the latter's quality of diffuseness it is possible for alter to show in *other* ways that the attitude of love has not been disturbed. Just what the balance in detail of failure to reciprocate, of permissiveness, and of expression of diffuse love should be, will vary with the kinship system and the roles for which ego is being socialized. It also involves problems of psychological process on which our knowledge is fragmentary, and the available evidence cannot be reviewed here.

Finally, it may be said that the frustration involved in the refusal to reciprocate ego's expectations must be balanced by a promised reward for the fulfillment of alter's expectations, that is, for learning the new orientation. If a diffuse love attachment is already given, and if we maintain that relational rewards are by this time the most fundamental, we may see that specific significances attach at this later stage to the attitudes of approval and esteem on the part of alter. These can above all be the conditional elements in the reward system which are manipulated by the socializing agents, along with specific gratification-rewards.

In our own society, particularly, this throws a considerable light on the problem of "conditional love." If capacity for independent achievement is to be learned, there must be a conditional element in the reward system. Ideally it is not the parent's love attitude which is conditional, but his approval for specific performances. A capacity to segregate these two aspects would be a condition of parental adequacy. But under certain conditions this segregation will tend to break down, and the love, not merely the approval, become conditional. This may be expected, if it is sufficiently severe, to have pathogenic consequences for the child.

It may be noted that these four prerequisites, security, discipline (implying frustration), permissiveness, and affectively neutral relational rewards are also characteristic of the psychotherapeutic process, and in this capacity are deeply involved in the equilibrium of the social system. There are fundamental differences which will be commented upon at the proper points, but it is important to note that socialization, psychotherapy and other mechanisms of social control are intimately interdependent. These relationships will be further analyzed in the following chapter and in Chapter X below.

Within this framework it is interesting to look at the possible significance of the differentiation of the two parental roles in the socialization process, above all with reference to the question, why is a father important? Even if his participation in the routine care of the child is minimal! That he is extremely important is indicated again by the erotic factor and by the intricate geometry of sex role identification and of erotic attachments. It is highly suggestive that normal heterosexuality is institutionalized in all known societies, hence that homosexuality is with few exceptions tabooed, and that there is a universal incest taboo within the principal solidary kinship group, which universally includes the conjugal family. We presume that to a significant degree this patterning is learned through socialization, is not therefore a sample manifestation of the "sexual instinct."

Precisely in this connection the *difference* between psycho-therapy and socialization is suggestive. The small child whose security rests primarily on his attachment to his mother has not yet learned the value-orientations of higher levels of maturity. We may suggest that acceptance of certain pressures to take further steps in maturing, with their attendant frustrations, is in such circumstances less disturbing if the responsibility for the pressure can be divided between the parents and hence does not come primarily from the central love-object. With all the variability of sex role from society to society, it can be said to be universally true that the adult mascu-line role is less implicated with detailed child care than the femi-nine, and is more implicated with prestige and responsibility in the wider society beyond the narrow kinship circle.

The fact of the father's solidarity with the mother makes it pos-sible, therefore, for him to be the symbolic focus of certain pressures on the child. The situation can be defined in the terms that, "you have to do this because your father wants you to," and the mother will support the father in this but still be less directly involved. Security in the mother relation is less likely to be jeopardized by this pressure because she does not have to take the full onus of the pressure on herself. There is, of course, room for wide variations in the ways in which this influence is concretely exerted and the responsibilities are divided, but this seems to be a common element.

It seems to be significant that in the geometry of erotic attach-ments, in the case of both sexes, the sacrifice of the erotic element in the attachment to the mother seems to figure prominently in the "price" which has to be paid for growing up. It is a critical fact that children of both sexes start with a primary attachment to the mother which, since Freud, we know contains a prominent erotic element. The boy has to renounce the erotic element of his mother-attach-ment in favor of an adult heterosexual attachment which must, however, be *outside* the family of orientation. The heterosexual orientation remains, but the particular object, indeed *class* of ob-jects in the case of the mother surrogates, e.g. older sisters in our society, other kinswomen in others, must be renounced. Generally this renunciation must be in favor of a generation mate. The common phenomenon of men being sexually interested in younger women, but seldom older women, might even be interpreted as a reaction formation against incestuous wishes, connected as they are with dependency needs. Seen in this perspective the Oedipus conflict of the boy may be regarded as connected with the pressure to renounce in certain respects the expectations of his infantile attachment-role vis-à-vis his mother, rather than with sexual rivalry in the ordinary sense. The father is symbolically identified as the source of the pressure, in part no doubt because the boy cannot bring himself to believe that his mother would "do this to him." In the more general sense of course both parents are merely manifesting their attitudes of what is expected of a "big boy."

It may be presumed that in this situation the relational rewards mentioned above are above all connected with the masculine role-identification of the boy, they thus not only include accepting the generalized values of both parents, which it may be presumed in the normal case they share, but involve particularizing those values in application to himself by his coming to understand that he must grow up to be a man, in a *normative* sense. It is the *approval and esteem* of both his parents for his demonstrations of masculinity which forms one of the main foci of his socialization at this point. He therefore identifies with his father in a double sense; first, in that he shares the values in general and for his age group of both parents, and second, that he accepts the norm that their application to him should be in the differentiated role of a boy as distinguished from that of a girl. In our society at least the prolonged "latency period," with its evidences of compulsive masculinity, and its strict segregation of the sexes, not by adult decree but by peer-group pressure, as socially patterned phenomena, strongly suggests that the learning process in this case is heavily involved with complicated adjustive processes.

The case of the girl shows an interesting combination of similarities and differences. The "danger" of retaining her infantile status is not that of identification with the wrong sex role, but failure of capacity to form an adequate attachment to the opposite sex. Her father is presumably the prototype of the masculine object for her as he is for her brother. But again the incest taboo forbids a simple transfer of erotic attachment from the mother to the father, there must be renunciation first of the mother attachment, second of an infantile erotic attachment to the father, and then development of a mature attachment to a man. This involves a complex combination of identifications with the mother and with the father. In terms of sex role, of course, the prescription is for acceptance of the role of the mother, hence identification with her in this sense. But there must still be the process of emancipation from the infantile mother-attachment. It may be presumed that identification with the father plays a crucial part in this, but because of the complementarity of the sex roles it may be relieved of certain of the pressures operating in the case of the boy. It may be presumed that because of the pressure to renounce the mother-attachment there is a tendency to transfer the erotic needs to the father, but this in turn is inhibited by the implications of the incest taboo. It may well be that this blocking is a fundamental focus of feminine resentments against men. But the important point is that for the girl as well as the boy the father constitutes an important focus of the pressure to grow up, to renounce infantilism, and hence to learn the value orientations of the adult world of the society; in both cases attachment to the mother is a barrier to this learning, and the father's intervention constitutes a lever to pry the child loose from this attachment.

It may be inquired what, from the present point of view, is the crucial difference between the role of sexuality in the infantile mother-attachment and in normal adult sexuality? Adult sexuality is fitted into a context of acceptance of adult values and roles generally while infantile sexuality is not. On the infantile level eroticism is an integral part of, and symbolizes, the total role in which security rests; on the adult level it is put in its proper place in the larger complex of values and roles. A man is "worthy" to enjoy an erotic love relationship only in so far as he lives up to the general value-pattern for the masculine role in the society, as he attains requisite levels of competence, responsibility, etc. Similarly a woman must accept her familial role, her attachment to a fully masculine man not a mother figure, and the responsibility of socializing her children in terms of the general value system, as a condition of being loved in the sense which is an altered repetition of the infantile prototype. It is this integration of the erotic needs with the adult value-system of the society which defines the essential difference between normal adult sexuality and "regressive" sexuality. At the same time the powerful force of erotic need-dispositions on the normal adult levels testifies to their crucial role in the socialization process. It is at least strongly suggestive that though these needs can be shaped and integrated with adult roles they are too deeply rooted to be eliminated. The relevance of this situation to the prevalence of the empirical clustering of social structures about the kinship system, which we discussed in the last chapter, is evident.

An essential part of this process is the progressive introduction of new patterns of value-orientation. The stress on particular patterns will vary greatly in different social systems, and their incidence will be differently distributed between different roles. But the greater responsibility of the adult in all societies, as compared with the child, means above all that the capacity for inhibition, hence for affectively neutral orientations, and for achievement must be developed to some important degree. Also universalism is by no means negligible in any society, for example, with reference to technical efficiency.

It may be suggested that identification with the father is critically important, especially with reference to these components of a value-orientation system in all societies, but the more so the more these latter value-patterns are institutionalized. There are also crucial questions as to how far the mother role must also be altered in conformity with varying emphases on different components in the system of value-orientation. The necessity of this is given in the requirement that both parents share a common value system and in its terms show solidarity vis-à-vis their child. Only this solidarity permits the leverage of socialization relative to the early mother-attachment to operate.

One of the most interesting features of the socialization process of the child, as reviewed in terms of the acquisition of value-orientations as formulated by the pattern variables, is the hierarchy of capacity for and incidence of the principal value-patterns. From this point of view the affective orientations are the first and in a sense easiest to acquire because of their direct relation to infantile dependency and gratifications. Affective neutrality is more difficult, and needs to be motivated by diffuse affective attachments. At the same time it requires emancipation from too great exclusiveness of these attachments. Universalistic orientations would appear to be the most difficult to acquire. Activity-passivity, which is related to achievement-ascription, and specificity-diffuseness on the other hand are not so directly related to this hierarchical scale except that one may perhaps say that passivity is more "primitive" than activity, and that affective specificity is more primitive than affective diffuseness, since it involves a lower level of generalization.

This hierarchy clearly is related to the phenomena of regression which have concerned personality psychologists so greatly. The orientation element, which is most difficult to acquire and which in a sense depends on the most complex set of prerequisite conditions, is, at least under certain types of strain, likely to be the first to break down. Furthermore it is one with relation to which the socialization proces is most likely to go wrong, since it involves the most complex prerequisite and hence around which more of the neurotic type of defensive and adjustive mechanisms are likely to cluster.

This structure of the value-orientation patterns relative to the socialization process, sketchy as its presentation has been, is clearly of the first importance for understanding the functioning of social systems, of different types. It is clear from the preceding chapter that different types of society and sub-system, because their role-orientation patterns are built up of different combinations of the pattern variables, impose very different sorts of strain on the socialization process and on the personality types which result from it. They are, hence, vulnerable to different types of strain in different ways.

§ BASIC PERSONALITY STRUCTURE: MODAL CLUSTERING AND DIVERSITY

WE HAVE seen that each one of the pattern variables is intimately involved in that aspect of the socialization process which concerns the acquisition of value-orientation patterns. It has been possible, in a rough way, to show that each of them may present crucial alternatives at different stages of the socialization process, and that it is within the possibility of variation of the role taken by alter to swing the balance one way or the other. Of course what has been presented above is in this respect a very crude sketch. These alternatives in fact appear not once but many times, and there are very complex combinations of influences emanating from the role-expectations of the various socializing agents. But this sketch has been sufficient to show the relevance of the pattern-variable scheme to the analysis of socialization, and the kind of theoretical approach which would be indicated to carry the analysis farther with genuine empirical rigor.

It follows, then, from the above analysis that in principle any one of the major pattern variable combinations can become internalized as a result of socialization processes and presumably, though this question has not been explored here, without a primary part being played by recourse to the operation of mechanisms other than the learning mechanisms, that is, without "neurotic" complications. At least the indications are very strong indeed that there is *no one* humanly "normal" pattern of internalized value-orientation so that all others could be considered to be "neurotic" deviations from it; for example some pattern of the "mature personality" *in general.*

It seems to be without serious qualification the opinion of competent personality psychologists that, though personalities differ greatly in their degrees of rigidity, certain broad fundamental patterns of "character" are laid down in childhood (so far as they are not genetically inherited) and are not radically changed by adult experience. The exact degree to which this is the case or the exact age levels at which plasticity becomes greatly diminished, are not at issue here. The important thing is the fact of childhood character formation and its relative stability after that.

Secondly, if the above account of the process of value-acquisition is correct only in its broadest lines, it follows that the combination of value-orientation patterns which is acquired *must in a very important degree be a function of the fundamental role structure and dominant values of the social system.*

This statement needs to be qualified in two ways. First, as we shall show presently, it cannot be a function *only* of this fundamental role structure. Secondly, the roles in which socialization takes place are predominantly kinship roles, and we have seen that these are in certain structural respects among the less variable as between primacies in the values of the pattern variables.

We are then justified in concluding that the weight of evidence is strongly in favor of the existence and importance of an element of "basic personality" as Kardiner has called it, which is a function of socialization in a particular type of system of role relationships with particular values. Patterns of value-orientation play a peculiarly strategic part *both* in the definition of role-expectation patterns and in personality structure. Hence it may be concluded that it is the internalization of the value-orientation patterns embodied in the role-expectations for ego of the significant socializing agents, which *constitutes the strategic element of this basic personality structure*. And it is because these patterns can only be acquired through the mechanism of identification, and because the basic identification patterns are developed in childhood, that the childhood structure of personality in this respect is so stable and unchangeable.

The value-orientation patterns are so crucial in this regard because they are in fact the principal common denominator between personality as a system and the role-structure of the social system. If the whole analysis of action systems presented up to this point is correct this *must* be the strategic set of features of personalities which is most directly shaped by socialization processes. The same analysis of action, however, enables us to introduce certain very important qualifications and limitations relative to the concept of basic personality structure.

The most important is that such a concept must be interpreted to refer to a *component* of the normal personality structure in a society, not to that personality structure as a concrete entity. Secondly, such a personality structure cannot be uniform for a whole society, but it must be regarded as differentiated with regard to those status-differentiations in which kinship groups function as units within the same society, and also by sex within the same classes of kinship units.

We assume that all normal early socialization of children occurs within the context of kinship, though often, of course, supplemented by other agencies such as schools and peer groups. The fundamental lines of differentiation in socialization patterns will then be by sex within any given status group, and relative to the more general role-structure in which the parents are involved. The fact that it is the status differentiations which involve kinship units as units which are significant means that class, community and ethnic differences would be the most important within the same society. We must speak, then, of broad differentiations of basic personality structure between major types of societies, and of narrower differentiations by these status categories within the same society.

But even so the basic personality structure will be *only one aspect* not only of the total concrete structure of the personality, but of its concrete value-orientation aspect. This is because of a variety of factors. In the first place no two human organisms are alike by genetic constitution. Therefore the same influences operating on different genetic material will not necessarily bring about the same result. It is a case analogous to that of the same beam of light refracted through different prisms; the spectra will not be identical.

But, secondly, it is the concrete constellation of reciprocal role relationships which constitutes the socializing influence, and within the same broad status groupings of the society these are different in a variety of ways. One of the most obvious is the age, sex, birth-order composition of kinship units. Even though there is a broad similarity of pattern, in detail the relationship of a first child and a second child to the mother is never identical, first, because the mother is older when the second child is born, second, because of the presence of the first child. The relation of a second child to the mother is never quite the same if the first is a brother as it is if it is a sister, and so on. These variations may be almost random within certain status-groups, and their consequences thus "iron out," but they nevertheless produce differences of result for people who are, broadly, being socialized for the same adult roles. There is also, thirdly, the fact that the individual idiosyncrasies of the socializing agents enter in. It is the concrete reciprocal role relationship to the particular person in the particular situation which influences the learning process, and this may be more or less "typical," no two cases are absolutely identical.

It must be kept in mind that a personality is a distinctive action system with its own focus of organization in the living organism and its own functional imperatives. Given the initial diversity of genetic constitution, plus the diversity of situational influences, *including* the combination or role-interactions, it would be strictly impossible for socialization, even in a relatively uniform milieu, in terms of major differentiations of social structure, to produce a strictly uniform product. The diversity of personality structures of those occupying the same status in the social structure, which is one of the best attested facts of clinical observation, is thus not fortuitous but is fundamentally grounded in the nature of the relations between personality and the social system. The two systems of action are inextricably bound together, but they *not only are not, they cannot be identical* in structure or in the process of functioning.

This diversity of personality structures relative to the role structure of the social system implies that we cannot rely on the building up of basic personality structures alone to explain the fundamental motivational processes of social systems. There are, it would seem, three further places we must seek. The first of these is to the capacity of the individual to make rational adaptations to the exigencies of his situation. This capacity is clearly along with genetic endowment a product of the processes of socialization in which identifications and value-acquisition will have played a prominent part. Once *given* the value-orientation patterns of the personality as internalized these processes of rational adaptation are not theoretically problematical to the sociologist and will not be further treated here.

Second we must look for additional mechanisms of socialization than the acquisition of basic value-orientations as sketched above, and third, where motivation to deviance exists, for mechanisms of social control. The latter will be deferred to the following chapter, but before approaching the former a few further remarks may be made about types of basic personality structure and their relations to the distribution of variations from them.

The facts concerning the nature of the acquisition of value-orientations, which we have reviewed, make it quite clear that the empirically observed diversity of concrete personality types cannot, relative to the dominant value-pattern system of the society or subsystem of it, vary at random. The point of reference for analyzing the distribution will, of course, have to be the relevant institutional-ized pattern-type. This, it is to be remembered, will always be differentiated by sex role. The "modal personality type" for a social system or sub-system then will be that which predisposes to con-formity with the major role-expectations of the sex role patterns in that part of the society, will be that is, the type which, in personal-ity terms, is most congruous with these expectations.

The variability from this modal type may be, in principle, ana-lyzed with respect to any one or any combination of the pattern variables. Where the modal type is achievement-oriented some individuals may incline to passivity; where it is also universalistically oriented some may, while retaining the achievement-orientation, incline to particularism and so on. Hence the permutations and combinations of Table 2 should be kept in mind for reference purposes in this type of analysis. The strength of the socialization mechanisms is, however, sufficiently great so that it would seem very improbable that the completely antithetical types would be as common as those which varied from the modal type with respect to one, or possibly two, of the variables.

In addition to this general consideration, however, something can be said about specific factors which would tend to influence the distribution of more or less variant[8] types. Of these, three may be mentioned. First, the source of the deviation from the modal type may have been an identification with a model alternative to that which might be regarded as normal. Of course in these terms there are many different shadings possible because of the diversity of concrete adult personalities in any child's situation. But some of these alternatives may be relatively definitely structured. Perhaps the most obvious of these possibilities is the identification with a model of the wrong sex, so far as sex-role orientations are concerned, since both sexes are so readily available and so crucially important. This is apt to be a highly complicated matter, with, for instance, connections with the problem of homosexuality. But apart from such considerations, the value-pattern elements in the character for example of the parent of opposite sex may be taken over instead of

[8] The term *variant* in a meaning similar to this has been used by Florence Kluckhohn. Cf. "Dominant and Substitute Profiles of Cultural Orientation," *Social Forces*, May, 1950.

those of the parent of the same sex. Thus in a given population one would expect to find that a certain proportion of the men leaned toward the value-patterns appropriate to the feminine role in that society or sub-system and vice versa. For example, in a sector of our own society, where universalistic-specific values are particularly prevalent, a minority of men might lean more in the particularistic-diffuse direction, hence be more inclined to assume roles primarily emphasizing informal organization.

Cross-sex identification is, of course, by no means the only possibility of finding an alternative role model. There may well be other, slightly variant persons of the same sex.[9] Here perhaps particularly uncles, aunts and substantially older siblings may be highly important if they are substantially different from the parent of the same sex. Also in a complex and heterogeneous society like our own, an identification process started in such a direction may well take on association with various sub-cultures within the society, including perhaps the ethnic. Such a society offers a rich fund of alternative value-patterns, often without being defined as radically deviant.

The second direction in which the distribution of variant personality types may be organized is that of the "hierarchy of regression possibilities" discussed above. The important process here would not be regression itself, but the failure in the course of socialization to make some of the last steps successfully. This would seem to apply particularly to universalistic orientation trends and the affectively neutral-specific combination. Regression to particularistic orientations is one of the most important possibilities in a universalistically oriented role-system, and further "overemotional" types in situations which call for affective neutrality are familiar. A failure on these levels may, of course, be a result of failure in the early years to achieve a diffuse affective attachment to the mother, but it might be manifested in these other types of orientation context. It should be kept in mind that the relevant structure of the regression hierarchy will vary according to the value-orientation pattern in question; it is not constant for all types, not even for the sex roles within a social sub-system—thus the manifestation of affec-

[9] Which may, of course, relative to the modal type, include the parent of the same sex.

tivity by crying in certain types of situation is "childish" for a man, but not for a woman. It must, of course, also be kept in mind that we are here speaking of regression in relation to the order and conditions of acquisition of value-orientation patterns, not of object-attachments as such. Though the two are, of course, closely related, the fact that psychoanalysts particularly so often have the latter in mind when speaking of regression should not be a source of confusion. Indeed the failure to distinguish these two things is characteristic of much psychoanalytic thinking. The capacity, through generalization, to abstract a value-orientation pattern from the original object through identification with which it was first acquired, is obviously one of the most important results of successful socialization.

It is highly probable that no process of socialization occurs without an important part being played by the special mechanisms of defense and adjustment. But this exposition has deliberately attempted to abstract from such considerations in order to throw the operation of the mechanisms of socialization into full relief. It seems obvious, however, that in seeking role-models alternative to the parent of the same sex and in failing to attain what is for the role system in question the normal order of steps of value-acquisition, that it is extremely likely that such mechanisms will be involved in the total process in important ways. Here attention will, however, be called to only one important aspect of their operation. We have seen that conformity-alienation is inherently a primary dimension of all interaction systems. The assumption of a role by the socializee means ipso facto that he comes to be faced with a conformity problem, and therefore the development of an alienative predisposition toward alter's expectations is always an immediate possibility. Those elements of such alienation which are built into the personality in the course of the elementary socialization process we may call the *primary* alienative (and conversely conformative) need-dispositions. Both the mechanisms of defense and those of adjustment, where such a need-disposition exists, may be various. These will be analyzed more fully when the problems of deviance and social control are taken up. But here it may merely be noted that alienation is always a possible product of something going wrong in the process of value-acquisition through identification.

It may be presumed that in the genesis of alienative need-dispositions the negative affect is in the first instance directed against the object of attachment as a person. But the phenomenon of interest here is the more generalized alienation from the value-patterns involved in the role-expectation. This, then, would motivate the actor to avoid conformity with these patterns, whenever encountered, either by withdrawal or by actively seeking a counter-orientation. This can be a source of motivation to seek alternative identifications and may also reinforce regressive tendencies. In any case the possibilities of primary alienation are among the most important factors giving *direction* to the distribution of variability from the modal personality type.

What will be called *secondary* alienation is not built into the primary value-orientation patterns of the personality, but is a consequence of the fact that a personality with a given value-orientation pattern in his character structure is faced, *in a specific role,* with role-expectations which are uncongenial to his need-dispositions and that, therefore, he is motivated to try to avoid conformity with them, though of course this component of his motivation may be outweighed by others such as a fear of the consequences of sanctions.

Even without primary alienative need-dispositions the diversity of personality types within a given role-system is such that further mechanisms would be necessary in order to secure the level of uniformity of behavior which is required by most roles in a social structure. There are three sets of facts, however, which cut down considerably the need for further mechanisms on the socialization level. These may be briefly mentioned before taking up the latter.

First, there are the mechanisms of social control, which operate to secure conformity with role-expectations in spite of need-dispositions to avoid that conformity. The simplest and most obvious of these are the reward-punishment mechanisms which may give sufficient rewards for conformity and punishments for deviance to tip the balance in favor of conformity. This aspect of reward and punishment will, however, have to be taken up later.

Secondly, to a widely varying degree for different roles and in different social systems, there is institutionalized a range of toleration, so that conformity does not need to mean absolute uniformity of behavior. Put a little differently, along with prescriptions and prohibitions, there are also permissions. Very often, however, there is a certain relativity in the permissiveness in that there may be, as some anthropologists say, "preferred patterns," that is, a hierarchy among the permitted ones. Perhaps the most important case of this is that where there are differentiated levels of achievement within a role, as is true for example of most modern occupational roles. Then there will be differential rewards correlated with the differential achievements, so that the actor whose grade of achievement is low, while he may not be deviant, is still "paying a price," in that he fails to get the higher rewards, both, for example, in money earnings and in approval. Finding his place on such an achievement ladder may, however, constitute a tolerable adjustment for a variant personality, and this is an important kind of flexibility in the relation between the social system and the individual. Of course this is still more sure where the place occupied within the permitted range is a "matter of taste" without clear hierarchical distinctions.

Finally, the third element of flexibility is the very important one, which again varies from society to society, of the existence of a system of *alternative role-opportunities* so that there is no one set of role-expectations which every individual who starts at a given status-point must conform with or pay the cost of deviance in sanctions. There seems to be little doubt that in a complex and mobile society like our own, one of the major sorting-out factors between alternative role-opportunities is to be found in differences of the value-orientation patterns of different personalities. When the major family status factors have been taken into account, and such obvious performance-capacity factors as I.Q., there is still a substantial residual variance with respect to occupational career orientation.[10] It seems highly probable that one of the major factors in this residual variance is the variability of basic personality structure within the population concerned, which is not a function of the modal role-expectation patterns of their initial status.

[10] This has been clearly demonstrated in an unpublished study of the social mobility of high school students in the Boston area by S. A. Stouffer, Florence Kluckhohn, and the present author.

§ THE SITUATIONAL ROLE-SPECIFICATION OF ORIENTATIONS

THESE three types of mechanism of accommodation in the social system to the non-role-adapted diversity of personality types do not, however, even taken together, account for actual motivation to the degree of conformity with role-expectations normally found in a stable social system. In addition to sheer rational adaptation to the exigencies of situations, there is still another highly important set of mechanisms of socialization which may be called the situational role-specification[11] of orientations.

It may be recalled that the constellation of value-orientation patterns, which we have called basic personality structure, has in particular two features. First, being defined only in pattern variable terms, it is extremely general. Second, the identifications out of which it has been constructed are *early* identifications, which in the great majority of cases are superseded before adulthood. These two facts are closely connected. If there are general criteria of maturity, one of the most important is probably the combination of the stability of basic orientation patterns with relative flexibility of object choice, and action patterns, that is, relatively high capacity for substitution and reality testing. In this sense, as well as in the sense that attachments have concretely changed, it is necessary for the adult to become emancipated from his childhood identifications.

But in this transition it is necessary for the actor to acquire more specific orientations relative to the specific situations and expectations of his adult roles; there is a further process of socialization on a new level. A very important part of this consists in the acquisition of the more complex adult culture of sophisticated knowledge, technical skills, and canons of expressive orientation, tastes and standards of taste. It may be presumed that in detail the paramount learning mechanism in these acquisition processes is imitation, since in the higher societies the level of complexity and sophistication of what has to be learned is such that individual creativity as the *primary* process is out of the question. It is, of

[11] Specification and specificity in the present usage should not be confused with specificity in the pattern variable sense. The context should make the distinction clear.

course, above all about this complex cultural content that the processes of formal education come to be organized.

But this is not to say either, that identification ceases to be an important learning mechanism on this more mature level, or that it is only specific cultural content which still has to be learned.

First let us taken an example, which will be developed more at length in a later chapter in other contexts. Suppose we have an individual in whom the general value-orientation pattern of achievement-universalism, specificity, neutrality and collectivity-orientation is well established in his basic personality structure. First, as a male, he must learn that a man is expected, when he "grows up" to become the incumbent of an occupational role, to "do a job," to "earn his living" and very probably to support a family. He learns that the occupational system is hierarchically graded, and that if he is properly ambitious for "success" he should aim to reach one of the higher levels in the occupational system. We have, then, the connection of a highly generalized achievement-orientation with the much more specific, but still very generalized goal of *success* in an occupational system.

The basic personality orientation patterns are indeed a function of the social system in which the individual was socialized. But they are too general directly to embody the specific structure of the situation as a complex of alternative role-opportunities or the specific cultural definitions of what constitutes occupational success. The father may, in this respect, also be a highly important role model, but much more in terms of his specific role in the occupational system and his specific attitudes toward his own and other occupations and toward the specific context of what is meant by success. If the father were an American physician on the one hand, or a Chinese gentleman-scholar on the other, it would make a very important difference on this level, in part at least, independently of the father's significance as a primary role-model on the level previously discussed. Resorting to an alternative role model would, on this level, not have quite the same significance as on the primary level. For example, in American society upward mobility is to a degree institutionalized. If a father in the lower status levels is ambitious for his son, and other conditions are given, he might well be a highly appropriate primary role model and a completely inappropriate secondary role model for the son.

The degree of specificity of the orientation may be still further increased. Within this rather general orientation to occupational success the individual in question may incline toward a professional career and within that toward the medical profession. In this case he must, of course, orient himself to an extremely complex process of formal training, but also toward the definition of the specific role of physician (and the many sub-types within it), to what success in medicine or the relevant branch means, and the like.

Or we may take a different example. A need-disposition for diffuse affective attachments is presumably a component of the basic personality structure of all normal people in our society. But besides this orientation structure, much needs to be learned for adjustment, for example, to the role of marriage in our type of society. The predisposition to seek an object of the opposite sex and to fuse erotic gratifications in the diffuse attachment may be regarded as given in the basic personality structure. But the status of marriage, the responsibility for children, the standards with respect to an acceptable home, the mores with respect to the style of life of a married couple, and all the rest are *not* directly derivable from the basic personality structure. Certain patterns in basic personality structure are, of course, important prerequisites for a successful marriage, but the specific definition of the role and its specific values is another matter.

Every society then has the mechanisms which have been called situational specifications of role-orientations and which operate through secondary identifications and imitation. Through them are learned the specific role-values and symbol-systems of that particular society or sub-system of it, the level of expectations which are to be concretely implemented in action in the actual role.

Relative to the orientations of basic personality structure these are much more specific. But they are generalized in another sense in that they inculcate definitions of expectation which apply to *all incumbents of the type of role in question* in the particular social system. Thus this set of mechanisms has two primary functions. First is the *specification* of more generalized motivational orientation patterns to the point where they connect up with the sufficiently concrete definition of the situation in the actual social system actually to motivate conformity with concrete role-expectations. The second is, in combination with the system of sanctions and mechanisms of social control, to counterbalance the variability of basic personality structure, so that a level of uniformity emerges which would not be possible were concrete adult role-orientations a simple and direct manifestation of the basic personality structure.[12] Of course this second function, the motivation of uniformity of role-behavior, is only possible because there is an important range of flexibility in the average personality. The "determination" of character in the early process of basic personality formation is not a pre-determination of all future behavior in detail, but only of a basic directional orientation. There is still considerable plasticity so that, when allowance has been made for ranges of toleration and alternatives of role-opportunity it is only those toward the extremes of the range of variability of basic-personality structure who are *not variant but deviant,* in the sense that their need-dispositions not merely make it a bit harder to conform, but psychologically impossible. Of course this line between the variant and the deviant is, in most societies, by no means rigid and many factors of post-childhood experience may throw the balance one way or the other. There are also mild and/or temporary deviances which do not place the individual in an irrevocably deviant role, but may afford some relief from the pressures to conformity.

It is to be presumed that with respect to the role-specification mechanisms as with respect to those of value-acquisition, there is, in a given social role-system, a hierarchy of learning stages. Thus from a variety of points of view in our society experience in the course of formal education is to be regarded as a series of apprentice-

[12] It may be noted that neglect of such considerations is one of the most serious shortcomings many of the views current in the "Culture and Personality" school of thought where there is an attempt to connect culture patterns and child training practices in such a direct way. First, this view does not allow for the fundamental fact of the variability of basic personality structures as a direct result of socialization in the *same* "culture" or structured role system. Secondly, however, it fails to see the significance of the second great class of socialization mechanisms. It tends to think of the role-behavior of the adult as the *direct* "acting out" of need-dispositions on the basic personality structure level, thus treating institutions apart from the details of child-training practices as epiphenomena. This view is implicit in Kardiner's concept of the distinction between "primary" and "secondary" institutions.

ships for adult occupational roles, even apart from the degrees to which the actual content of instruction, e.g., arithmetic and linguistic skills, can be directly used there. Thus to a much higher degree than in the family, in school the child learns to adjust himself to a specific-universalistic-achievement system. He is brought into explicit competition with his classmates, and his standing with respect to the achievement orientation pattern is overtly symbolized in grades, as well as in the other rewards and punishments administered by the teacher, and in her attitudes. So far as the child accepts the role-expectations of the school system, attainment of good marks, which is one form of success, becomes what may be called a *situationally generalized goal*. This is a point at which a great many possible motivational factors may converge. One child may become highly interested in the subject-matter he is learning itself, another more interested in the favorable attitudes of the teacher, still a third in surpassing his classmates. But these different motivations may all converge on a common direction of actual behavior, namely the striving for marks. This illustrates how the social system operates to socialize different personality orientations so that in spite of the diversity of their basic personalities, they may still fulfill the same set of role-expectations, at least within the limits of tolerance. Of course it must not be forgotten that there are those who fail to fulfill these expectations altogether. But that is another story.

There is, then, a sense in which the school system is a microcosm of the adult occupational world, and experience in it is a main field of operation of the second stage mechanisms of socialization, the specification of role-orientations. There are, of course, a whole series of stages within this before full adult status is achieved. Here only one further aspect will be mentioned, that of the place of new identifications. It seems probable that the predominance of women teachers in the early grades in American school systems is important not merely because of the fact that on comparable levels of training and technical competence they can be secured to work for less pay than men, and thus save economy-minded school boards and taxpayers money. There is probably considerable significance in the role of the woman teacher as an object for identification, obviously a significance connected with the process of emancipation from earlier attachments to the mother.

It is suggested that this importance lies in a delicate balance between similarities to and differences from the mother. The fact of being a woman and of having a kindly, protective attitude toward the children is the most important similarity. A woman can by and large permit herself greater tenderness and solicitude than can a man. But there are also striking differences. The teacher is responsible for a class of some twenty or more children. They are almost of an age and therefore much more directly in competition with each other than siblings are, even in large families. The teacher cannot give each one the solicitude that would be normal in a mother. Moreover the relation is focused on the specific content of the curriculum; it is not general supervision and care, and it is sharply restricted to the school period. It is much more universalistic in content and specific in focus than the relation to the mother. Moreover the child does not have the same level of rights by ascription that he has vis-à-vis his mother; he can more readily be held to achievement standards.

We know that dependence on the mother is particularly intense in the American kinship system, and we also know that emancipation from that dependence is particularly important for the adult in an achievement-oriented individualistic society. Too abrupt and drastic a transition might involve intolerable strain with neurotic consequences. The woman teacher as an identification figure may therefore perform a very important function in American socialization.

To connect with the mother it is significant that the teacher be a woman; but it may be equally important that she should not be *too much* like the mother, or there would not be any new element in the pattern of her influence on the child. Perhaps this situation has something to do with the prevalence of the "irrational prejudice" against married women as teachers. Symbolically at least, since they are or should be mothers, for teachers to be married women might be dimly felt to be too close an assimilation between the mother role and the teacher role. Perhaps the traditional American "old maid" school teacher has her functions.

Finally, it may be remarked that a very important step in respect to identifications as well as otherwise comes with the transition to "secondary" education, now usually in Junior High School. This is the breaking up of the one class per school grade into a different class —and teacher—for each subject. Then the child no longer has the one identification figure for his school life, he can no longer speak of "my teacher" but only of "my English teacher" and "my science teacher." This is another big step toward the acquisition of universalistic orientations, in that the focus is on competence in the subject matter rather than the more diffuse, general, and hence parent-like superior knowledge and standing of the teacher. The teacher approaches the role of a technical expert, not of a general prestige and authority figure. It is perhaps significant, that it is at this point that the American child generally first encounters men as teachers to a significant degree.

It should be clear that socialization does not in this sense cease with the attainment of adult status. Societies differ a great deal of course in the degree to which they call upon their members for major role changes after the childhood period, but many, like our own, do so to a considerable extent. Even to take one nearly universal example, namely marriage, the content of the role is continually changing, partly as a function of the individual's own age and that of his spouse. The childless stage of marriage means in fact a different role from that which is assumed with the advent of children. The number and ages of the children change the character of the role, as of course happens drastically in our society when the "stage of the empty nest" is reached. Similarly in those occupational roles which have a typical "career line," the expectations shift quite substantially as new stages in the career are reached. Here one of the most important problems of adjustment is that concerned with starting a career in a position of low responsibility and in the course of it coming to assume large responsibilities. In one phase it is a shift from subordination to many people to superordination over many. It is well known that such shifts place considerable strains upon individuals, but it remains a fact that many accomplish them successfully; they can hardly do so without undergoing a complicated learning process.

Finally, many societies are involved in processes of social change. Such changes may, even over the span of active adult life, be considerable, so that the expectations of an early period must be considerably readjusted to meet the requirements of a later one. Here again the process can be successful only through the operation of learning mechanisms in the context of socialization, of further role-specification of orientations.

§ AN EXAMPLE: THE "PROFIT MOTIVE"

IN CONCLUSION we may develop a somewhat fuller illustration of the operation and functions of the mechanisms of situational role-specification of orientations by examining certain aspects of the place of the so-called "profit motive" in modern liberal societies. The popular term is placed in quotation marks because in the light of the present theoretical analysis of role-motivations it is apt to be somewhat misleading. Some psychologists have spoke of a primary acquisitive drive or instinct. Whatever the major orientation pattern of the modern "businessman" may be, it is not in any simple sense a manifestation of such a drive.

The profit motive is rather, in the above sense, a situationally generalized goal which is learned in the course of what has been called the secondary socialization process. It is not general to human beings, but is very specifically culture-bound to certain types of roles in specific social systems. It is not bound to any particular basic personality type,[18] though in certain respects it is certainly more congenial to some than to others. Its situational generalization, however, has precisely the function of making it a possible common orientation of action deriving from a diversity of "psychological" motivational roots, and combinations of them.

The structural focus of the orientation to profit is, of course, the phenomenon of instrumental exchange, which, as we have seen, has some place in every social system. Since there is in the structure of the situation inherent motivation to secure relatively advantageous terms in exchanges—not to be so oriented in any sense could be compatible only with the extreme of masochism, or of drastic other worldliness, and even there one might say that the masochist sought advantage in what others considered to be disadvantageous.

[18] One of the cruder versions of the idea that it does manifest such a type is the conception of some psychoanalytic amateur sociologists that "capitalism" is a manifestation of the "anal character." There is certainly a grain of truth in this idea, but hardly more. It completely overlooks the focal problems of the organization of the social system.

In any case, then, in this most general sense the profit motive is "endemic" in all social relationship systems.

However, differentiation of the instrumental complex, its segregation from diffuse solidarities and above all the development of money, enormously extends the range of relevance of exchange. The availability of money as a generalized medium of exchange makes it possible through the securing of advantageous monetary terms to enhance the means available to gratify all need-dispositions with reference to which purchasable means may be important. In a market economy like ours the range of monetary purchasability is extremely wide. It is particularly important to be clear that the relevance of this range of exchangeability has virtually *nothing* to do with what is ordinarily considered the "ethical quality" of the goals to which monetary resources are a means. Thus *every* religious movement seeks to "raise money," that is to make a profit, for its particular purposes, just as much as the man who wants to bet his earnings on the races or to drown his sorrows in drink. To have more money rather than less is simply, with only a few exceptions, to be in a more advantageous position to realize *whatever* goals the actor may have in mind. In this sense the "profit motive" is nothing but a primary aspect of what may be called "practical rationality."

But, of course, this is not all. Means-objects inevitably acquire symbolic significance, and the quantifiability of money as a possession means that money lends itself peculiarly to the symbolization of prestige. Since it is useful, in one sense its possession is inevitably a reward as well as being a facility for the attainment of other rewards. Hence money, income, or wealth, i.e., resources convertible into or measurable in money terms, are, in an economy with a high development of monetary exchange, an important reward symbol. As such profit may be a measure of otherwise valued achievement acquisition, or it may be a direct goal of success-striving, so that other forms of achievement content become instrumental to monetary gain.

Further, there are complex relations between money as a reward symbol and other components of the reward system, money as a symbol of achievement being one. Another obvious one is the connection between monetary resources and the style of life, in such a way that money is the means of purchasing valued items of the style of life, but conversely, the display of style of life items may be a way of telling the public that one has a large income—the case which Veblen called "conspicuous consumption." Incidentally among certain Bohemian groups this relationship is inverted, the style of life is, among other things, meant to advertise that the actor is contemptuous of the "flesh pots" of the bourgeois world, that he accepts and glorifies "honorable poverty."

Whatever the range of variability with respect to these symbolic significances of money income and earnings, there is in a developed market economy—even in socialism—as we have noted, a strong tendency for integration of the income scale with the general prestige scale of the social system. This aspect must in turn be integrated with certain possibilities of orientation to monetary gain, which are inherent in the structure of the situation in a system of instrumental division of labor. The following possibilities may be noted:

1) The interest in gain may be a purely personal orientation, the actor merely taking advantage of an opportunity presented in the situation. Such opportunities necessarily arise in a money economy.

2) It may become a feature of an institutionalized role for an individual who is as such a unit in an ecological complex of market relationships. There are two principal sub-types of this, a) where he is an artisan or independent professional practitioner who has to engage in financial transactions for disposal and acquisition of facilities, but these are conditional to his main occupational goal which is to "produce" or to "provide service"; and b) where he is an independent "businessman," e.g., a merchant, whose role is institutionally defined as to "make money."

3) It may be orientation in a membership role within a collectivity. In *any* collectivity, most roles are not primarily oriented to profit-making; they are oriented rather to cooperation in the sense of Chapter III. Cases would be professional technicians or ordinary "workers." Only certain representative roles, which are concerned with mediation of the affairs of the collectivity vis-à-vis the outside situation can be oriented to profit. These again are of two main types. a) In a collectivity which as a unit is *not* oriented to profit,

the problems of exchange for disposal, remuneration and provision of facilities still remain. Roles may be specialized relative to these functions. When it becomes an obligation of the role to secure advantageous terms on behalf of the collectivity, the incumbent is oriented to profit. Examples would be the treasurer of a university or a hospital. b) In a collectivity, which as a unit is oriented to profit, a "business firm," profit has primacy as the paramount obligation of the top executive roles. But in both these cases profit-making becomes the role-obligation of a role *on behalf of* the collectivity; it is not orientation to "personal gain" in the usual sense.

The question of the orientation of the individual actor to the collectivity in which he participates presents still a further structural aspect of the problem. He must secure his personal remuneration and must settle terms with the collectivity, with respect to the assumption or continuation of his role within it. This is, of course, the place where *personal* orientation to profit can operate in relation to organizations in the occupational world. There is naturally a connection between the "value" of a man's services to the collectivity and the terms he is able to secure for his services to it. But the connection is seldom simple and direct, and certainly when he occupies one of the above two types of roles he generally does not put his earnings on behalf of the firm or organization directly into his own pocket.

There is, thus, a whole range of possible significances of orientation to financial "gain" in a market economy. But the most important common denominator of these is not motivational in the usual sense, it is not a "propensity of human nature." It is, rather, an aspect of the structuring of the situation of action. It concerns a highly generalized mode of action in which a highly generalized class of advantages is to be sought, which funnels all manner of motivations into a common channel. On the level of structure there is a wide variety of different role elements which are articulated in different ways into the monetary market system. These are, first, the purchasing interests of "consumers," a purely "instrumental" interest. Second, the disposal interests and facility-procuring interests of independent "producers," though they may be only secondarily oriented to "making money." Third, the interests of employed persons in securing income through the contract of employment. Fourth, the orientation of independent individuals to making money "on their own." Fifth, the role of conducting market transactions on behalf of an organization, though the organization is not primarily profit-oriented and sixth, the corresponding type of role where the organization is primarily profit-oriented. Only four and six are in any usual sense "capitalistic" or "profit making" orientations.

But in addition to these aspects of the problem we have the symbolic place of money income in the reward system of the society, as a symbol of achievement and of success, and of course as a means of exercising power.

We can speak properly of individuals as oriented to profit, then, so far as by socialization they have become integrated within this system of role-expectations and situational opportunities. Within any given role in the system there is room for a variety of different nuances of personal orientation, of different attitudes toward money in each of the many different respects in which it enters into the structure of the situation. But as the basis of a uniformity of the orientation of action the profit motive is a situationally generalized goal, its generality comes from its place *in the definition of the situation,* and the integration of this with the individual's orientations, not from any pre-socialization features of the motivation of the individual.

It is, furthermore, not of the same order of generality as the orientation-directions which are grounded in the elementary structure of the interaction relationship, such as the need-dispositions for affection, for security or for a sense of adequacy. It is precisely this difference which justifies treating the profit motive as a "secondary" product of the socialization process. There are many societies where, even in the most general non-monetary sense, orientation to favorable exchange terms has a relatively minimal significance. For it to acquire a significance remotely approaching that in the modern industrial type of society, *even in its socialist version,* means that relatively specific features of the specific social structure have to be incorporated into the orientation of the personality on the secondary socialization level. There has to be a role-specification of orientations going far beyond the most generalized basic personality orientations of the primary socialization level, and to a certain extent cutting across them. It is by such mechanisms that motivation adequate to the more detailed role expectations of a social system, perhaps particularly those involved in the adaptive structures which are not direct manifestations of the primary value-orientations, are built up.

The above, as has several times been noted, treats only one half of the problem of motivational process in the social system. The other half is the analysis in motivational terms of the sources of tendencies to deviance, and the mechanisms of their control. To this we now turn.

VII DEVIANT BEHAVIOR
AND THE MECHANISMS OF SOCIAL CONTROL

IT HAS been evident from the beginning of this work that the dimension of conformity-deviance was inherent in and central to the whole conception of social action and hence of social systems. One aspect, that is, of the common cultural patterns which are part of every system of social interaction, is always normative. There is an expectation of conformity with the requirements of the pattern, if it be only in observing the conventions of a communication pattern, for example, by speaking intelligibly. The complementarity of expectations, on which such great stress has been laid, implies the existence of common standards of what is "acceptable," or in some sense approved behavior. In the preceding chapter we have dealt with the processes by which motivational structures required for behavior in conformity with such normative social expectations are built up. We must now turn to the other side of the coin, the processes by which resistances to conformity with social expectations develop, and the mechanisms by which these tendencies are or tend to be counteracted in social systems.

It is a cardinal principle of the present analysis that all motivational processes are processes in the personalities of individual actors. The processes by which the motivational structure of an individual personality gets to be what it is are, however, mainly social processes, involving the interaction of ego with a plurality of alters. Thus the sectors of the motivation of the individual which are concerned with his motivation to deviant behavior, are the outcome of his processes

249

of social interaction in the past and the whole problem must therefore be approached in social interaction terms. In the analysis of deviance as well as of socialization we must focus on the interactive processes as it influences the orientation of the individual actor in his situation and in orientation to the situation itself, including above all the significant social objects, and to the normative patterns which define the expectations of his roles.

Deviance and the mechanisms of social control may be defined in two ways, according to whether the individual actor or the interactive system is taken as the point of reference. In the first context deviance is a motivated tendency for an actor to behave in contravention of one or more institutionalized normative patterns, while the mechanisms of social control are the motivated processes in the behavior of this actor, and of the others with whom he is in interaction, by which these tendencies to deviance tend in turn to be counteracted. In the second context, that of the interactive system, deviance is the tendency on the part of one or more of the component actors to behave in such a way as to disturb the equilibrium of the interactive process (whether a static or a moving equilibrium). Deviance therefore is defined by its tendency to result either in change in the state of the interactive system, or in re-equilibration by counteracting forces, the latter being the mechanisms of social control. It is presumed here that such an equilibrium always implies integration of action with a system of normative patterns which are more or less institutionalized.

It is clearly the conception of deviance as a disturbance of the equilibrium of the interactive system, which is the more important perspective for the analysis of social systems. But we must still be quite clear that it is essential to be able to follow this analysis from the level of ascertaining uniformities in the processes of change in the structure of the social system, to that of analyzing the relevant motivational processes in the personalities of the individual actors. Hence there is always *also* a reference to the first context implied.

It should also be made clear that there is a certain relativity in the conceptions of conformity and deviance. These are concepts which refer to problems of the integration and malintegration of social systems and sub-systems. It is therefore not possible to make a judgment of deviance or lack of it without specific reference to the system or sub-system to which it applies. The structure of normative patterns in any but the simplest sub-system is always intricate and usually far from fully integrated; hence singling out one such pattern without reference to its interconnections in a system of patterns can be very misleading, e.g., the judgment that a person who tells a "white lie" as a way out of a conflict situation is a "dishonest person." Similarly the concrete individual actor never acts in one role only, but in a plurality of roles and situations, with complex possibilities of variation in the expectations and tensions to which they subject the actor. Furthermore, there is the problem of the time sector which is taken as relevant to the analysis of a system. Actions are mortised together in time sequence as well as in other respects, and conflicts can focus on time-allocation as well as on the conflicting claims of different interaction-partners.

These are all problems of the first importance and must be made as clear and explicit as possible. Nevertheless the fact remains that all social action is normatively oriented, and that the value-orientations embodied in these norms must to a degree be common to the actors in an institutionally integrated interactive system. It is this circumstance which makes the problem of conformity and deviance a major axis of the analysis of social systems. The fact that in its working out it is highly complex, does not imply that it can be safely ignored or cannot be satisfactorily analyzed. The crucial significance of this problem focus derives as we have seen from two fundamental considerations; first that the frame of reference of action makes the concept of orientation a primary focus of analysis and second, the fact that we are dealing with the "boundary-maintaining" type of system, which defines what we must mean by the concept of integration of the system.

§ INTERACTION AND THE GENESIS OF DEVIANT MOTIVATION

LET US go back then to the fundamental paradigm of social interaction including the assumption, stated at the beginning of the last chapter, that a stably established interactive process, that is, one in equilibrium, tends to continue unchanged. We will further assume that ego and alter have, in their interaction, developed mutual cathectic attachments to each other, so that they are sensitive to each other's attitudes, i.e., attitudes are fundamental as sanctions, and that the interaction is integrated with a normative pattern of value-orientation, both ego and alter, that is, have internalized the value-pattern. We have stated many times that such an interaction system is characterized by the complementarity of expectations, the behavior and above all the attitudes of alter conform with the expectations of ego and vice versa.

This paradigm provides the setting for the analysis of the genesis of motivation to deviance. Let us assume that, from whatever source, a disturbance is introduced into the system, of such a character that what alter does leads to a frustration, in some important respects, of ego's expectation-system vis-à-vis alter. This failure of the fulfillment of ego's expectations places a "strain" upon him, that is, presents him with a problem of "adjustment" in the terms which we have used. There are always, we may presume, three terms to this problem. First ego's expectations in the interaction system are part of his own system of need-dispositions which in some sense press for gratification. Second, these expectations are organized to include an attachment to alter as a cathected object, and third the value-pattern governing the relationship has been internalized and violation of its prescriptions is directly a frustration of some of ego's need-dispositions. In so far as the adjustment problem is "serious," in that alter's disturbing behavior is more than momentary and in that it touches some strategic area of ego's orientation system, ego will be forced to restructure his orientation in one or more of these three respects. He can first restructure his own need-dispositions, by inhibition and by one or more of the mechanisms of defense, such as simply repressing the needs which are no longer gratified. He can, secondly, seek to transfer his cathexis to a new object and relieve the strain that way and, finally, he can renounce or seek to redefine the value-orientation pattern with which alter is no longer conforming.

In any one or more of these three directions there may be resolution of the strain by a successful learning process; ego may learn to inhibit his need-disposition, he may cathect a new object which will fulfill his expectations, or he may extinguish or alter the value-pattern. This would be the obverse of alter abandoning his changed behavior. In either case equilibrium would be re-established, in one case with a changed state of the system, in the other with a restoration of the old state.

But another outcome is possible, and in many cases very likely. That is that, in one or more of the above three respects, a "compromise" solution should be reached. Our primary interest is not in the internal integration of the personality but in ego's adjustment to social objects and to normative patterns. Hence first, ego may not abandon his cathexis of alter by substituting an alternative object, but may retain his cathexis, but this cathexis can no longer be "undisturbed." Ego must have some reaction to the frustration which alter has imposed upon him, some resentment or hostility.[1] In other words the cathectic orientation acquires an ambivalent character, there is still the need to love or admire alter, but there is also the product of his frustration in the form of negative and in some sense hostile attitudes toward alter. In so far as this happens of course ego is put in an emotional conflict in his relation to alter. Similarly, the integration of ego's expectations with the value-pattern has been disturbed by alter's failure to conform with it, the pattern may be too strongly internalized for ego to be able to abandon it and accept one in conformity with alter's behavior. Here again ego may develop an ambivalent attitude structure, at the same time adhering to the normative pattern and resenting the "cost" of this adherence in that it involves him in conflict with alter and with aspects of his own personality.

There are many complications involved in the possibilities of handling the strains inherent in such an ambivalent motivational structure. For our purpose, however, they may be related to two fundamental alternatives. The first is repression of one side of the ambivalent structure so that only the other side receives overt expression. If it is the negative side which is repressed, ego will continue to be attached to alter and/or to be motivated to conform with the normative pattern in question. If the positive side is repressed, conversely ego will tend to abandon his attachment to alter, in the sense of giving it overt expression, and to refuse to conform with the normative pattern. The second fundamental possibility is for ego to try to find a way to gratify both sides of his ambivalent motivation

[1] Another very important phenomenon of reaction to strain is the production of phantasies.

Presumably in the same concrete relationship this is impossible[2] since the two are in conflict. But in a more extensive and complex interaction system there may be such possibilities either because contexts and occasions can be segregated, or because it is possible to find alternative objects for one or both sides of the need-disposition structure. This latter possibility will become very important to the discussion of the social structuring of deviance later in this chapter. But for the present let us adhere to the simpler case.

The negative component of such an ambivalent motivational structure relative to a system of complementary expectations will be called an *alienative* need-disposition, the positive component, a *conformative* need-disposition. It should be noted that in these theoretical terms alienation is conceived *always* to be part of an ambivalent motivational structure, while conformity need not be. Where there is no longer *any* attachment to the object and/or internalization of the normative pattern, the attitude is not alienation but *indifference*. Both social object and pattern have become only neutral objects of the situation which are no longer a focus of ego's cathectic need-system. The conflict in such a case would have been solved by full resolution, through substitution of a new object, through inhibition or extinction of the need-disposition, and/or through internalization of a new normative pattern.

Where alienative motivation is present, but the conformative component is dominant over the alienative, we may speak of *compulsive conformity*, where on the other hand the alienative component is dominant over the conformative, we may speak of *compulsive alienation*. The psychological reasons for using these terms are not far to seek. The essential point is that ego is subject not only to a strain in his relations with alter, but to an internal conflict in his own need-disposition system. Precisely because he has a negative feeling toward alter, but at the same time a powerful need to retain his relation to alter and to the normative pattern, he must "defend himself" against his need to express his negative feelings, with the attendant risk of disturbing his relation to alter still further or provoking him to retaliatory action, in the more extreme case, of losing

---

[2] It is of course possible within limits through time allocation. At certain times ego's resentment may break through into hostile acts (including verbal) and the positive attitude then regain ascendancy.

alter. This is, indeed, in relation to social interaction relationships, the basis of the defense mechanism of reaction formation. The pattern is to "accentuate the positive," to be compulsively careful to conform with what ego interprets as alter's expectations (which by institutionalization are also his own) so as to minimize the risk of disturbing the relationship still further.

Conversely, if the alienative component is dominant, the fact that the attachment to alter as a person and to the normative pattern is still a fundamental need, means that ego must defend himself against the tendency to express this need-disposition. He must therefore not only express his negative reaction, but be doubly sure that the conformative element does not gain the upper hand and risk his having to inhibit the negative again. Therefore his refusal to conform with alter's expectations becomes compulsive. This defense against the repressed component is in both cases the primary basis of resistance against the abandonment of "symptoms," even though they involve ego in serious negative sanctions in his social relationships.

It is here that we have the focus of the well-known vicious circle in the genesis of deviant behavior patterns, whether they be neurotic or psycho-somatic illness, criminality or others. It may be presumed that the reaction of ego to the change in alter's behavior, which resulted in resort to adjustive and defensive mechanisms involving ambivalence, will be in some way complementary to the change alter introduced. For example, alter, instead of recognizing the merit of a piece of work ego has done, may have shown marked disapproval, which ego felt to be in contravention of the value-pattern with respect to competent achievement shared by both. Ego reacted to this with resentment which, however, he repressed and became compulsively anxious to secure alter's approval. This compulsive element in ego's motivation makes him excessively "demanding" in his relation to alter. He both wants to be approved, to conform, and his need for approval is more difficult to satisfy because of his anxiety that alter may not give it. This in turn has its effect on alter. Whatever his original motivation to withhold the approval ego expected, ego has now put him in a position where it is more difficult than it was before for him to fulfill ego's expectations; the same level of approval which would have sufficed before is no longer sufficient. Unless a mechanism of social control is operating, then, the tendency will be to drive alter to approve even less, rather than more as ego hopes. This will still further increase the strain on ego and intensify his resentment, hence, if the alienative component does not break through, it will add to the compulsiveness of his motivation to seek approval through conformity with alter's expectations. The pressure of ego's conflict may also of course lead to cognitive distortion so that he thinks that alter's expectations are more extreme than they really are, and that therefore he is being held to intolerable standards.

This is the essential structure of the generation of cumulative motivation to deviance through the interaction of complementary ambivalences in the motivational systems of ego and alter. Of course this is a highly simplified and abstract paradigm. The "direct line" of development of the vicious circle could not empirically proceed far without some modification for two sets of reasons. First the need-dispositions of ego and alter which are the focus of the developing conflict are only parts of a complicated system of need-dispositions in the personalities of each. The alterations in these parts growing out of the interaction process would lead to repercussions in the rest of the personality systems which would modify the development of the interaction itself. Secondly, the interaction of ego and alter on which we have focused is only a sector of a larger system of social interaction which involves other actors than ego and alter, and perhaps their interaction in other roles. These complications must duly be taken into account, and are of course extremely important for the mechanisms of social control. But the vicious circle in the interaction of two actors is the fundamental paradigm of the genesis of the motivation for deviant behavior.

§ THE DIRECTIONS OF DEVIANT ORIENTATION

WE MAY now return to the question of what are the most important further differentiations in the direction of deviant motivation itself, whether it be in the compulsively conformative or alienative direction. Two such further differentiations appear to be particularly important. In the first place, the differentiation between activity and passivity, is of generally recognized psychological significance.[3] If the conformative and the alienative types each be subdivided according to whether the orientation is primarily active or passive, we derive the following four-fold classification:

	ACTIVITY	PASSIVITY
Conformative Dominance	Compulsive Performance Orientation.	Compulsive Acquiescence in Status-Expectations.
Alienative Dominance	Rebelliousness.	Withdrawal.

This classification is of interest, not only because of its direct derivation from the analysis of the interaction paradigm, but because it restates, from the motivational point of view, in essentials the classification put forward some years ago by Merton in his well-known paper on Social Structure and Anomie.[4] What Merton calls

[3] There may be a variety of aspects and sources of this distinction. For present purposes it may, however, be regarded as a direct derivative of the fundamental paradigm of interaction itself. The conformity-alienation dimension of possible deviance concerns, as we have just seen, the orientation of any actor to the pattern aspect of the established system of expectations—or any part of it—which is institutionalized and internalized in the interaction system. Activity-passivity, on the other hand, is the dimension concerned with one primary aspect of the mutual orientation of ego and alter to each other *as objects*. The point of reference is, as always, a stabilized system of interaction. The concept of "activity" defines deviation from the role of an actor in this stabilized process in the direction of taking more "initiative," of taking a larger degree of control over the interaction process, than the role-expectations call for. "Passivity," on the other hand, is the obverse, it is the direction of taking less initiative, of letting alter control the situation and himself, to a larger degree than the role-expectations call for.

There is a third dimension of the possibilities of deviance, which will be discussed presently. This concerns relative primacies, in the orientation of the actors, as between the pattern element and the social object element of the inter-action system. A stabilized interaction system always involves a balance between these. This balance can be upset, on the one hand by giving a greater primacy to the pattern—either by insisting on conformity or by alienative resistance to it—on the other hand to orientation to alter as a social object positively or negatively. All three of these dimensions are thus grounded in the essential structure of the interactive relationship system.

[4] Revised and extended version in his *Social Theory and Social Structure*, Chapter III.

"conformity" is clearly what we here mean by the equilibrated condition of the interactive system without conflict on either side or alienative motivation. Merton's "innovation" and "ritualism" are our two compulsively conformative types, while "rebellion" and "retreatism" are clearly the two alienative types. Since Merton's paradigm was formulated in terms of relations to institutionalized goals and means, it is interesting to find that the active emphasis puts the primary stress on goals—as its relation to the achievement pole of the pattern variable of ascription-achievement would lead one to expect—while the passive emphasis puts the stress on means. In each case, however, we may infer, the compulsive element puts a strain on genuine conformity with institutionalized expectations, but in the two cases the primary incidence varies. We may surmise that Merton's paradigm is most readily applicable to a social system where achievement values are prominent, then because achievement goals are highly institutionalized, the actively ambivalent person can find the easiest "way out" in accentuated goal striving. Where ascriptive values were institutionalized, especially in combination with particularism, this outlet would largely be closed. Because of this element of culture-boundedness of the Merton paradigm, and because of the inclusion of the motivational element, we may presume that the version presented here is the more general one, of which Merton's is a very important special case.

The second further differentiation of the directions of deviant motivation which needs to be introduced concerns the possibility of differentiation between focusing on one or the other of the two fundamental components of the interactive system beside ego's own need-disposition system, namely alter as a person, i.e., a social object, and the normative pattern which integrates their interaction. Both are, as in the case of ambivalence, inevitably involved. But there may be dominance of compulsive concern in one direction or the other. The introduction of this further differentiation yields the eightfold classification presented in Table 4.

Where the conformative element is dominant and ego's primary concern is with his relations to alter as person, anxiety focuses on disturbance of the relation, on the possibility that alter may turn his favorable attitude into an unfavorable one and may aggressively punish ego or withdraw from the relationship. There are, fundamentally, two ways in which ego can seek to cope with the situation, in relation both to his own anxiety and to alter. He may, if he is actively oriented, seek to put alter in a position where it is impossible for him to do anything but fulfill ego's expectations, that is, to *dominate him.* If, on the other hand, he is passively inclined, he may seek to protect his interest in the relationship by acquiescing in

TABLE 4

	ACTIVITY		PASSIVITY	
Conformative Dominance	Compulsive Performance Orientation		Compulsive Acquiescence	
	Focus on Social Objects	Focus on Norms	Focus on Social Objects	Focus on Norms
	Dominance	Compulsive Enforcement	Submission	Perfectionistic Observance (Merton's ritualism)
Alienative Dominance	Rebelliousness		Withdrawal	
	Aggressiveness toward Social Objects	Incorrigibility	Compulsive Independence	Evasion

alter's every wish, lest failure to do so jeopardize the relationship, that is, he may be *submissive* to alter.

If the alienative component of ego's motivation is dominant he is by definition less concerned with preserving alter's favorable attitudes than he is with expressing his alienative need-dispositions. Hence in the active case he will tend to act *aggressively* toward alter, to "pick a fight" with him relatively regardless of the risk of alienating alter, to seek a "showdown." If, on the other hand, he is passively inclined, his tendency will be, not aggressively to force a "showdown" but to avoid exposure to uncongenial expectations on alter's part, to be *compulsively independent,* in the extreme case to break the relationship altogether by withdrawing from it. The four cases may be grouped together by saying that both dominance and submission are expressions of a compulsive dependency need, to avoid losing alter as an object at almost any cost, while aggressiveness and passive compulsive independence have in common that they are motivated by a compulsive need for independence, a need to avoid giving way to the dependency need at almost any cost.

Turning to the cases where the normative pattern is the primary focus of the conflict, on the conformative side we may differentiate according to activity and passivity, a compulsive need to enforce the norm on alter, and a compulsive need for perfectionistic observance on the part of ego himself. An alternative to compulsive enforcement on alter is, for the actively oriented, to develop a compulsive achievement drive for himself. He may of course manifest both tendencies as in the familiar case of the compulsive achiever who is merciless in his demands on his subordinates. The passively inclined will tend to evade demands for active achievement or control and focus his compulsiveness on the details of conformity-expectations.

Finally, where the alienative component is dominant, the active type is the "incorrigible," the one who flouts rules and laws apparently "for its own sake," whose attitude is "try and do anything about it." The passive type on the other hand tends to evasion of conformity with the normative pattern, to do his best to avoid situations in which the expectations can be implemented, or sanctions applied.

These are, of course, definitions of the direction of deviant tendencies. First it must not be forgotten that they are *always* relative to a particular set of complementary role-expectations, to a particular alter or class of alters, and to a particular normative pattern or sub-system of them. In some cases the ambivalence may, in the personality of the actor, be highly "localized" in its application. But it may also under certain circumstances become more or less highly generalized, transferred by substitution from the original objects and normative patterns. In the extreme cases we may have personalities with a highly generalized need-disposition for rebellion or for withdrawal. It is not possible to go into all the complications here.

Secondly, of course, the actual behavior patterns which will result are not a function only of the ways in which deviant motivation comes to be built into the motivational structure of the personality, but of the nature of the situations in which the actors are placed. As noted, this always involves third persons, and also a variety of features of the normative pattern system and the sanction system. What we have presented is only the barest beginning of a dynamic analysis of these complex processes. Some of the further complications will have to be analyzed as we proceed.

The differentiation between alter as a social object and the normative pattern itself as a focus of strain and of compulsive motivation throws light on a common differentiation in psychological discussion. We may say that the need for *security* in the motivational sense is the need to preserve stable cathexes of social objects, including collectivities. Tendencies to dominance or submission, aggressiveness or compulsive independence, then, may be interpreted as manifestations of insecurity. The need for a feeling of *adequacy* on the other hand, we may say, is the need to feel able to live up to the normative standards of the expectation system, to conform in that sense. The compulsive enforcer, the perfectionist, the incorrigible and the evader, then, could be interpreted as motivated by a sense of inadequacy. Of course both are concretely involved in every action system. Many complex resultants are possible. But these seem to be the fundamental points of reference for analysis of these processes. Insecurity and inadequacy are by the same token the primary foci of anxiety.

The distinction is of course analytical. Probably a stable interactive relationship without common value-patterns is not empirically possible, hence both aspects are always involved in the same concrete relationship. Nevertheless it is an analytical distinction of far-reaching importance in the theory of action and can help us greatly to focus our analysis both of the sources of alienative need-dispositions and of the directions and mechanisms of deviant behavior tendencies. We may say then in general terms, that alienation from social objects tends to focus on problems of security, on anxiety about being able to count on their receptiveness-responsiveness or their love, approval or esteem, while alienation from normative patterns as such tends to focus on a problem of adequacy on one or both sides of the interactive relationship, that is, ego's own capacity to fulfill the expectations of conformity, or alter's capacity (including motivation) to do so, or both. In the case of threats to security the focus of anxiety is the problem "can I count on him, or might he 'let me down'?" In that of threats to adequacy the focus is on the other hand the problem "Is there any use in trying?" either because "I don't think I can do it" or "Even if I do, he probably won't do his part" so that expectations of the rewards of conformity may be frustrated. In both cases alienation should be regarded as a reaction to "disillusionment," the feeling that it just isn't any use in ego trying to do his part, because "what do I get for it?"

It should be kept clear that the problem of adequacy is not restricted to the cases where achievement-orientations as distinguished from ascriptive are involved in the normative patterns in question. There may be very important performances involved in living up to an ascriptive pattern, as of the obligations of a given status. Of course where the value-pattern itself places a special emphasis on achievement as such the problem of adequacy is accentuated, and alienation from achievement-expectations may be a particularly important possibility.

There is an important source of asymmetry in the motivational structure of the need for security. This is the consequence of the overwhelming importance of infantile dependency, and hence of the asymmetrical structure of early attachment relationships. We may say that very generally there are underlying need-dispositions to regress into passive dependency. It would seem that on the whole compulsive independence is more common as a reaction formation against these passive dependency needs than the other way around, dependency needs as a reaction formation against independent, assertive needs. However important such a generalized source of "skewing" of the logical possibilities of deviant orientation, it is certainly overlaid by the pressures of particular types of social situations and cultural patterns. For example the reaction to latent dependency needs may be particularly important in the dynamics of a society like our own where the expectations of individualistic achievement are particularly pronounced.

There is an important relation between the classification presented in Table 4 and the pattern variable affectively-neutrality. This becomes evident with respect to dominance and submission.

In both cases ego's primary concern is assumed to be to protect himself against threats to disrupt the relationship. To do this he tries to manipulate sanctions, to make it "worth while" to alter to fulfill his expectations. These sanctions can, however, assuming that attitudes are the crucial ones, be of two main types according to the affectivity-neutrality variable. On the positive side they are the responsiveness and love attitudes, on the one hand, those of approval and esteem on the other. Domination through love seems to be what happens in what is sometimes called "maternal overprotection." On the other hand the "authoritarian" father presumably dominates mainly through the affectively neutral sanctions.

The relation to value pattern elements also differs according to the affectivity-neutrality variable. Where the affectivity pole has primacy the dominant values must be those of expressive symbolism. Where, on the other hand, neutrality has dominance they will be either instrumental or moral. On this basis the types where the focus of compulsive motivation is on norms may also be subdivided; thus compulsive enforcement may be that of standards of taste, as in the case of the mother who is very rigid in enforcing good manners on the part of her child, or it may be on standards of efficiency or of morality. An example here would be a parent who held his child to excessively high standards of achievement, e.g., punishing him for making only a normal record in school and the like.

The specificity-diffuseness variable is of course also involved in the definition of the sanctions which operate in these compulsive motivation systems in interaction. The character of the motivational picture will vary also as a function of this variable.

It was shown in the last chapter that internalization of these generalized normative patterns involves the process of identification with the relevant significant alters. In the light of its relevance to the problem of alienation it should be clear how important is the basic classification of types of attachment and hence of modes of identification, in terms of these two pattern variables of specificity-diffuseness and of affectivity-neutrality. A normative pattern is not an actor, it cannot react to ego's action, only another actor, an alter, can do that. The normative pattern cannot, as an object of cathexis, therefore be a source of direct and immediate gratification, it serves gratification interests only indirectly through organizing and stabilizing ego's own personality system and through influencing the gratifications he receives in interaction with the situation, notably of course the alters in it. Perhaps this is what primarily we mean as the significance of the "internalization" of patterns as distinguished from the "enjoyment" of cathected social and physical objects.

The implication of these considerations would seem to be that where orientation to a normative pattern as such has clear primacy over that to alter as a person, the orientation will have to be affectively neutral. Conformity with the pattern cannot be immediately and directly gratifying in itself. But the most direct and immediate rewards which are possible for conformity are the attitudes of the significant persons, alter's and ego's own, that is, their approval and esteem. This is of particularly crucial significance to the problem of social control since approval and esteem, both external and internal, that is, ego's own self-approval and self-esteem, may be regarded as the first-line stabilizing or control mechanisms of the social system, that is, the most immediate mechanisms of motivation to conformity with normative patterns. The establishment of sensitivity to the attitudes of approval and esteem, again both external and internal, is one of the most fundamental requirements of adequate socialization of the individual and serves as the central core of his system of motivation to conformity. It is here, then, that the alienative need-dispositions are most directly dangerous to the stability of a social system. They will consist in "not caring what they think," or at least turning to alternative persons with other attitudes for approval and esteem.

There is, however, a complex kind of interdependence between these attitudes of approval and esteem and the types of attachment where affectivity has primacy, the receptiveness-response and love types, as they have been called. The probability has been pointed out in the last chapter that only the establishment of such attachments provides an adequate motivational basis for the acceptance of the affectively neutral types of orientation, hence for the higher levels of disciplined organization of the personality which is in turn essential to adequate performance in many roles in a complex social system. This indeed itself constitutes a form of organization and of focusing of gratification interests, especially in the diffuse love type, where a fundamental reciprocity of orientation is established, which can form a highly important stabilizing factor in some parts of social systems, and plays a particularly important part in the socialization process. Hence the type of alienation where the focus is on the actor as a person rather than on the normative pattern, is also highly important. It takes the form of aversions to particular types of expected specific receptiveness and response, and to the personality of alter as a whole, in the extremer cases what we would call "hate."

There are certain important empirical connections which can immediately be discerned when these variations in the character of the sanction system are taken into account. In general the normative patterns defining the larger framework of the social relationships system tend to be affectively neutral, particularly where certain kinds of value system such as our own universalistic achievement pattern predominate. In such a case the most imperative demands for conformity would appear to be found relative to the patterns themselves, that is, to "impersonal" expectations as of efficiency in achievement, acting "according to the rules" and the like. It would seem likely, then, that the pressures of the system of social control would tend to deflect deviant tendencies into channels which would be relatively less threatening to the system. In general deviance relative to persons in intimate relationships is probably less threatening than relative to value-patterns as such. Furthermore, the withdrawal direction is less threatening when alienation predominates than is the rebellious direction. Hence compulsive independence would be expected to be very common in such a social system, especially since submissiveness contravenes a fundamental implication of the value system relative to independence.

Perhaps two further aspects of the psychology of deviant behavior should be briefly commented upon before turning to a more explicit and systematic discussion of certain situational problems. It is clear that, whichever of the basic alternatives in dealing with them is taken, the presence of important alienative need-disposition elements implies an important element of conflict on the personality level in the social system. This means that either the alienative or the conformative need-disposition elements must frequently be repressed, or at least relatively dissociated from whichever is the dominant orientation component. It is well-established that, if the relevant need-disposition has not been fully extinguished, it will tend to find some outlet, however indirect. The mechanisms of displacement and projection perhaps formulate the most important types of such outlet. But the very fact that the connection between the object of a displaced affect and the need-disposition from which it arises—and even more so in the case of projection—is intrinsically so loose, means that there is normally a considerable instability in the object-cathexes and motivational imputations involved. This seems to be the most important basis for the existence of what is often called "free-floating" affect. By virtue of the fact that the appropriate need-dispositions exist, and that their normally appropriate object-cathexis is blocked, such affect may be conceived as "seeking" a second-choice appropriate object. There is a certain relative unsatisfactoriness in any such choice which is available, hence readiness to transfer to still another. The affect may be love-readiness, aggression, passive evasiveness relative to norms, or any one of a variety of other types. But the common feature is the fluidity and instability of the cathexis. In turn the urgency of the need for cathexis may lead to a compulsive intensity of the cathexis once achieved, the very intensity of which, however, is a symptom of its instability. The relevance of such considerations to such phenomena as romantic love attachments or group prejudice scarcely needs to be pointed out. In general it comprises the cases where the affective intensity can be shown to be "over-determined" relative to any intrinsic significance of the object.

Secondly, the elements of conflict involved in the presence of alienative need-dispositions clearly have implications for the structure of cognitive orientation. The obvious point is the relevance of the mechanism of rationalization to coping with the attendant strain on the cognitive level. Rationalization is an adjunct and instrument of repression in that cognitively it denies the existence of a conflict and attempts to present a consistent picture in accord with approved normative standards of proper motivational orientation. There are many possible "devices" to which rationalization may resort in order to make the actor's behavior and attitudes plausible and acceptable, such as the appeal to "extenuating circumstances," the imputation of exaggerated deviance to alters and the like, but they have in common an element of cognitive distortion of what, in

terms of the cognitive culture which is predominantly institutionalized, is the appropriate and adequate explanation and justification
of action. Again the relevance of these considerations to the genesis
and structuring of ideologies needs no further comment at this time.

§ SOME FURTHER SITUATIONAL ASPECTS OF THE GENESIS AND STRUCTURING OF DEVIANCE

WE MUST now supplement the above considerations about
the roots of alienative need-dispositions in the personality, and the
processes of mutual stimulation of these alienative tendencies in the
interaction process with an analysis of certain crucial features of
normative patterns themselves and their variability. The problem of
conformity cannot be dissociated from a consideration of that with
which conformity is expected.

The most fundamental classification of the components of normative patterns which is derived from the pattern variable scheme
need not be further discussed just now. Here only a few observations on points of relevance to the present context are necessary. The
first point to emphasize is that the ways in which "pressure" is
exerted on the motivational system of the actor will vary as a function of the kind of pattern with which he is expected to conform.

This is in the nature of the case a very complicated field. Yet
considerations such as those advanced in the last chapter relative to
the process of socialization would make it seem likely that in spite
of socio-cultural variations some types of value-pattern impose inherently greater strains on most human beings than others; some
such factor is for example essential to the meaning of the concept
of regression. For present purposes we need not consider whether
the principal sources of these strains are to be found in constitutional features of the human organism or in certain constants of the
process of socialization. A good example is the degree of stress on
affective neutrality.

There is a sense in which as we have seen, all normative patterning involves an element of affective neutrality, in that as was
noted, conformity with a normative pattern cannot in itself be a
source of direct and immediate gratification. However, some types
of normative pattern impose the disciplines of affective neutrality
far more stringently and over far wider segments of the action system

than do others. Some on the other hand seem more concerned with the organization of and selection among direct gratifications, rather than their postponement or diversion from particular contexts. These are above all the patterns which organize social relationships to a high degree about diffuse love attachments, and further stabilize expressive activities in terms of relatively definite and rigorous systematization of expressive symbol and action systems, as for example in a large amount of ritual and etiquette. On the other hand our own society, with its very strong instrumental emphases and very long-range planning, puts a strong accent on affective neutrality and requires exceptionally high levels of discipline in certain respects.

Somewhat similar considerations, as we have seen, apply to achievement patterns and to universalism. Indeed in this respect the latter is probably the more fundamental. This seems to derive above all from the fact that universalistic requirements cut across the particularism of attachments to persons. The fundamental importance of the latter in all human socialization seems to be established beyond question. Hence where patterns involve a prominent universalistic emphasis, it is necessary not merely to inhibit certain "natural" cathectic tendencies, but to transcend them, in the sense of developing a capacity of cathexis of all members of a universalistically defined class of social objects and correspondingly to internalize the valuation of abstract principles. This latter step is thus, in the universalistic case, possible only through a special elaboration of the development of "secondary" motivational structures.

The upshot of all this is that one focus of strains consists in the difficulty of conformity with the expectations involved in the particular type of pattern in question. In general this difficulty can be analyzed in the same fundamental terms which were used above. It will, that is, involve elements of ambivalence and conflict.

It is highly probable that there is a commonly human component in this motivational difficulty of fulfillment of certain types of expectations, but it is equally clear there is a component deriving from particular combinations with other elements. One example will suffice to illustrate the point. American society certainly requires an exceptionally high level of affectively neutral and universalistic orientations, both of which are, it would appear, intrinsically difficult of attainment. But because of the conditions of socialization in the isolated conjugal family, it seems probable that particularly middle class males develop a strong dependently tinged love need. This is itself a powerful lever for motivating the acceptance of disciplines. But this is a source of additional strains because in so many of the crucial masculine roles in our society this is almost the last need which can be directly gratified. Indeed the opportunities for gratification of a dependency component are inherently extremely limited for the American adult, except in deviant patterns. The American must therefore go farther in the process of socialization than many others for two sets of reasons: first, because he must reach higher levels of affective neutrality and universalism, and second, because he has a more strongly developed set of dependence needs from which he must become emancipated. This seems to be one of the focal points of strain in American society.

There is a second important range of problems concerning the difficulty of conformity with a normative pattern which focuses in the nature of the pattern itself. This concerns the question of how far the expectations of conformity are or are not specific and detailed. We have emphasized the importance of the fact that all normative patterns are to an important degree generalized relative to the particularity of the situations in which they apply. But there are enormous variations in the degree to which this is true. In proportion as the pattern becomes more generalized and hence "abstract" the problem of "interpretation" becomes accentuated. In other words, the actor faces the problem not only of living up to the expectations of his role, assuming that he knows exactly what they are, but of knowing just what is expected of him. In a society like our own there is an extensive proliferation of highly generalized rules and hence of difficulties in their interpretation. It may be noted that one of the primary functions of the legal profession is to advise clients on what their rights and obligations are. That the client should know them without expert advice is by no means to be taken for granted in a complex society, especially where certain aspects of the normative pattern system, those embodied in the formal law, are being continually changed by new legislation as well as by other processes.

Psychologically the importance of this element of indefiniteness of expectations which derives from the generality of norms, lies in the element of uncertainty which it introduces into the orientation system. To the relevant degree the actor is confronted with an "unstructured" situation in which he must take responsibility for an independent solution. We know that this factor is particularly difficult to tolerate for some types of personality, especially we may surmise, the compulsive conformists. By increasing anxiety, the impact of indefiniteness of expectations in this sense may be a factor in deepening the vicious circle of progressive motivation to deviance. It may also provide loopholes for those whose motivational pattern leans to non-conformity, in that the very indefiniteness of the expectation makes it impossible to draw a rigid line between conformity and deviance, since this is a matter of "interpretation." In particular it is possible to utilize such a loophole to go a little farther in each of a succession of instances until imperceptibly the "spirit" of the norm comes to be violated even though no one has been able unequivocally to point out where the "letter" was transgressed.

It may be pointed out that one important aspect of this problem of specification of expectations concerns distribution of activities between occasions. One of the reasons for its importance is that every social system has certain "safety valve" patterns, situations and occasions where there is an element of extra "permissiveness" or license for behavior which would on other occasions not be tolerated. A good example is the tradition of Hallowe'en in our society, with its greater permissiveness for mildly aggressive and destructive "pranks" than is ordinarily granted. Such extra permissiveness stands in a certain sense in contravention of some of the more general normative patterns of the society and raises the uncomfortable question of whether the society "really means it" that conformity with the general rule is expected. The point is that if there is special permissiveness on some occasions, why should it not be extended to other occasions? In such cases normally there is clearly a limit beyond which the behavior in question would become seriously threatening to the stability of the social system. But this "limit" is a more or less broad zone; it is not a clearly defined line.

An important special case of the indefiniteness of expectations concerns those roles where there is a graduated scale of possible achievement or performance. Here the potentially disturbing question is "how much is enough?" In the nature of the case not everyone can be capable of the highest achievement, even if what this consists in is clearly defined. But there is an expectation that one must "do his best." The problem is always to some degree open whether falling short of a level higher than actually achieved was due to factors the actor could not be expected to control or whether he "didn't try hard enough."

It seems clear that this type of normative expectation pattern sharply accentuates what has been called the problem of "adequacy" by the very fact that adequate performance is not specifically defined but only by such vague formulae as "doing your best" or "making the most of your opportunities and resources." We may surmise that in such a situation the active compulsive conformist, the compulsive performer, will tend to be unduly "ambitious," to try to do so much that there can be no possible doubt that it is enough. The passive compulsive conformist on the other hand will tend to try to cut down the definition of enough to terms which in his anxiety he feels able to cope with, perhaps by laying overly strong emphasis on perfection in minor details at the cost of the larger achievements. The overtly alienative types on the other hand will find in this situation loopholes for justifying an achievement drive to goals or by means which are dubiously within the rules, or altogether outside, or for taking a "sour grapes" attitude that they "never had a chance." These latter cases of course in their alienative attitudes shade into repudiation of the whole system.

What has been outlined above takes account only of the most elementary beginnings of the complexities of the normative pattern system with which an actor may be confronted. A next step in complication is taken when in addition to the problem of interpretation of specific expectations there is introduced the problem of the applicability of alternative norms. This type of problem is most clearly seen in the case of a developed legal system, where quite clearly one of the most important functions of the courts is to determine which of a plurality of rules or precedents "governs" in a particular case. This possibility of "conflict of rules" is inherent in the nature of a system of generalized norms, and becomes a more acute problem in proportion to their generality and complexity. This is because generality implies abstractness, and abstractness means that one rule does not alone "cover" the concrete case, since the case will inevitably have a variety of aspects to which a corresponding variety of generalized norms is relevant. But if more than one norm is intrinsically applicable it is clear that there must be some order of precedence among them.

The general impossibility of "having your cake and eating it" which underlies the general significance of the pattern variables in systems of action is particularly relevant here. In any at all well integrated institutional system the major decisions of precedence will be made for the individual actor through the institutionalization of norms and hence lie beyond his control. Thus although both the particularistic loyalties to kinsfolk and the universalistic obligations to reward technical competence are institutionalized in our society, an actor who is in a position of responsibility in an occupational organization is not at complete liberty to favor his relatives at the expense of people of superior technical competence. But this major settlement of the order of precedence of normative patterns, which is essential to social stability, does not go all the way. There are still areas of genuine doubt open to the decision of the individual actor, within which his own need-disposition structure may swing the balance between alternatives. This accentuates the "unstructured" character of the situation, posing problems again for the compulsive conformists and providing loopholes for the alienated. It is important to note that we are not yet here speaking of the cases where there is a conflict between clearly defined expectations, but only of that where there is a lack of clear definition of what the expectations are.

The facts we have just reviewed about the indeterminacy often present in the normative definition of expectations, raise certain problems about the operation of sanctions.

The most fundamental distinction relative to sanctions which we have made is that between the specific, discrete acts of alter which influence ego's situation of action on the one hand, and alter's attitudes toward ego and his actions on the other. Attitudes as sanctions imply either attachment to alter as an object of cathexis or internalization of the normative pattern alter is "enforcing" or both. They constitute the central core of the sanction system of a role complex and organize it into a system. Through them specific sanction-acts acquire, in addition to their "intrinsic" significance the "meaning" of expressions of these attitudes. From the point of view of the stabilization of the reciprocal interaction system, alter's acts then either "confirm" ego's feeling that his actions are "right" and manifest the "proper attitude" or serve as a warning that they are "wrong" and alter expects him to "mend his ways."

All this is stated in terms of the "norm" of a fully integrated and stable interaction complex. But there is a variety of ways in which rifts in this integrated structure may develop on the side of the sanction system. They are essentially to be interpreted in terms of the elements which have already been discussed. Alter is subject to the same kinds of strain, deviant need-dispositions, uncertainty, lack of definiteness of expectations and the like as is ego. Therefore, in addition to the fact that ego is faced with an unstructured situation in terms of the normative pattern system itself, there is the possibility that alter's reactions to ego's action will be systematically biased relative to the norm.

It has been clear at many points that under certain conditions the interactive system operates to organize the motivational systems of the actors in such a way as to build up motivation to conformity with the expectations of a shared system of normative patterns, and that sanctions in such a "normal" case operate to reinforce this motivation. But the factors we have just discussed open the door to a range of variability on ego's part where within limits the question of conformity vs. deviance cannot be unequivocally settled. The question is whether alter's reactions are such as to tend to "bring ego back" toward the modal point in the range relative to the normative pattern structure, or to motivate him to diverge more widely toward one extreme of the range, with the possibility of a vicious circle developing which carries him "over the line."

It is clear from our discussion of alienation that an element of motivation to conformity is always present and important. Then the question is whether the sanction system operates to strengthen this element of an ambivalent structure of need-dispositions or to weaken it and/or strengthen the alienative component. The problem is far too complex to permit doing more than indicating a few starting points here.

The most important consideration for present purposes is the effect of the indeterminate elements of the pattern and of sanctions on the tendency of ambivalent motivation in the interaction process to lead to a cumulatively deepening vicious circle of intensification of the alienative components. Under what conditions will this vicious circle operate and under what different conditions can sanctions operate to nip such developments in the bud. First we may say that an element of unstructuredness in the expectation system, deriving either from indefiniteness in the definition of normative patterns or their application, or from uncertainty as to how alter will react to a given action of ego's or both, opens the door to the beginning of a vicious circle. This is simply because action is allowed to deviate further from a modal norm without counteracting forces coming into play than would otherwise be the case. Here we see immediately that from the point of view of stability as such there are certain advantages in the type of social pattern which maximizes the detailed specification of role-expectations.

We may assume that if alter's motivational pattern is fully integrated with the norm and has sufficient "resiliency" not to be thrown out of equilibrium by the strain put upon it by ego's incipient deviance, the sanctions he will impose will tend to be such as to tend to re-equilibrate ego's action with the norm. There is of course a wide range of variation of the possible specific elements involved, but broadly we may assume first that on the one hand alter will tend to act in such a way as to influence ego's situation in the direction of making it advantageous for ego in reality terms to return to conformity, and second that alter's attitudes will be such as, without ambivalence, to show his disapproval of the direction ego's action is taking. At the same time, there will tend to be acts on alter's part which serve as mechanisms of tension release to ego, such as "laughing off" ego's compulsive exaggerations of an issue, of insistence on his own "rights" in the situation, or perhaps his compulsively conscientious insistence on too literal fulfillment of his obligations. Of course a variety of combinations of these three types of sanction elements may be involved.

On the other hand, if alter's own motivational structure is ambivalent with reference to the relevant conformity problem, he and ego may start "working on each other" in such a way as to build up the vicious circle. It would seem that this can work out through either of two principal types of process, with enormous variations in detail. In the first place they can tend to become "partners in crime." Alter's and ego's alienative need-dispositions, that is, may match each other, so that instead of imposing negative sanctions for ego's deviant tendencies, and driving ego to alienation from him, alter tends to act in such a way as to reward them. This may provide sufficient impetus to the already incipient trend, to cancel out the effect of negative sanctions from other quarters and build up an emotional vested interest in the deviant patterns through the alienative need-dispositions underlying them.

The second type of process operates through the intensification of conflict. Alter's ambivalent structure may be such that he is compulsively driven to impose unduly drastic negative sanctions on ego as a defense against his own repressed deviant need-dispositions and to deny him opportunities of tension release. If there is in ego an already established alienative need-disposition, this exaggerated punishment of the manifestations of his alienative needs may accentuate the conflict and actually stimulate the alienative need. This is usually, one may surmise, further accentuated by ego sensing that alter is ambivalent and somehow "secretly" approves his deviant tendencies and would like to reward them. The effect of this process of intensifying the conflict is to block the "road back" for ego, to make it most difficult to resolve his conflicts in a conformative direction. It is clear, in the light of the discussion above, that it is the compulsive conformist types of personality which as alters are likely to have this kind of effect on ego.

There are of course many further possible complications of the vicious circle process. A person who is in conflict will attempt a variety of "escape" maneuvers, one class of which will be, in the light of the strain in his relation to the one alter, to turn to another. It is thus, as we have noted, often possible to gratify both sides of an ambivalent need-disposition structure in a limited way by cathecting different objects in terms gratifying to each side. In determining such outcomes much will depend on the structure of the situation and of the sanction system outside the particular ego-alter relationship we have singled out for analysis. A strained relationship with any one alter can often be counteracted by "good" relationships in other directions. At present, however, it is not possible to attempt to follow out all these complications. All we can do is to point out that the outcome will depend on ego's place in the total relevant interaction system, not merely on his particular relation to one alter. Furthermore, the interaction in question is a process in time, and much will depend on the sequence of the various phases of the temporal process, especially the timing of the incidence of various sanctions from various quarters on ego. Thus one consequence of secrecy is to delay or eliminate some otherwise operable sanctions.

In any case, and whichever of these main routes to deviance has been taken, the essential phenomenon from the motivational point of view is the emotional "investment" of the actor in his deviance. Internally this is what, in the particular case of the neuroses, psychiatrists often call his "secondary gain," which he cannot give up without help because of the serious disturbance of the internal "economy" of his personality which this would entail. Externally, vis-à-vis alter, the counterpart of secondary gain is the expectation of frustration by significant alters if the deviant pattern is given up. This expectation may be grossly unrealistic; indeed, when severe conflict is involved an element of distortion of reality is inevitable. But this is not the point; the anxiety resulting from such expectations is real enough. The compulsively independent person for example is afraid to enter into attachments because of the expectation that alter is likely to "let him down" in some way. The compulsive nonconformist equally is afraid to live up to institutional expectations for fear he will in fact be punished rather than rewarded for it—the question is always in some sense "what does it get me?"

It would seem that underlying this expectation of deprivation is always some prototype of a previous deprivation experience. Ego at some time actually did feel that an object of attachment let him down—whether he was realistically justified in this feeling or not. This would thus seem to be the primary basis of the significance of childhood experiences, as emphasized in psychoanalytic theory, that they provide the early prototype of the deprivational experiences (and of course also gratifications) around which anxiety (and hope) focus. Unless these anxieties about repetition of the feared deprivation are somehow allayed, it is not motivationally possible for ego to give up his deviant need-dispositions, because to him the alternative means the expectation of actualization of the dreaded eventuality.

This problem of the secondary gain of deviance is a primary focus of the mechanisms of social control as we shall see later. In terms of the structure of what, in the present sense is the sanction system, these mechanisms must operate in one of two fundamental ways. The first is to "nip in the bud" the incipient tendencies to deviance, so as to prevent the building up of a vicious circle. The second is to "break through" the vicious circle, by somehow lessening ego's investment in his alienative need-dispositions. As mechanisms of the social system it is clear that the structure of alter's role vis-à-vis ego is the focus of both orders of mechanism of social control. A mechanism of social control after all only acquires a function when ego "has a problem" in the sense that he cannot without difficulty be expected to overcome the tendencies to deviance by himself by "will power."[5] It is the impact on him of his relations to others which is the focus of the problem. But in analyzing this we must always bear in mind that the distinction of ego and alter is *only* a distinction between points of reference. Every alter who may be an "agent of social control" to ego, is at the *same time an ego* who may have his own problems of tendencies to deviance. The full analysis of the problem can only be attained on the level of treatment of the interactive system *as a system,* not by isolating any one personality. This is the fundamental difference between the sociological and the "clinical" point of view.[6]

In all this, of course the "reality factors" in the situation must not be overlooked. On the more naïve level, actual deviance as distinguished from motivation to deviance, is a function of whether it is realistically possible to "get away with it," or whether in some sense it "pays." It is of course possible, and frequently happens, for the sheer compulsion or the severity of sanctions to forestall the acting out of deviant motivation and to limit its consequences in various ways. In the last analysis force is an infallible means of the prevention of any human action, as we have pointed above. These aspects of the problem should by no means be minimized, and will

[5] Of course coercive measures of various sorts can operate to prevent ego from acting out his deviant need-disposition without altering their structure. Thus the custodial hospitalization of chronic mental patients may prevent them from disturbing others in their normal interactive circles.

[6] This is not to say that the theory of personality does not involve factors independent of the interactive system.

be given some further attention below. But from the point of view of the central dynamics of the social system they are not the core of the problem. The core is to be found in the balance of forces which is involved in the building up and the counteraction of motivation to deviance, that is, of the alienative component of the need-disposition system. This follows from the whole conception of the social system set forth in this work. If any empirical justification of this statement is needed at this point perhaps mention of the enormous and tragic willingness of compulsively motivated people to "punish themselves" in the sense of incurring sanctions and deprivations which, if they were "sensible," they could easily avoid, will suffice.

There is one further point about the system of sanctions which needs to be made before taking up the matter of role conflict itself. This is that the immediacy and the certainty of sanctions has a significance similar to that of the degree of the definiteness of expectations. Uncertainty as to how alter will react is a factor in the "unstructuredness" of the situation which is directly comparable with and often concomitant with uncertainty as to what the normative pattern itself requires. Indefiniteness in the normative pattern will be conducive to reciprocal uncertainty about sanctions on both sides of the interactive relationship; this is one of the main reasons why it is so important.

There is, however, another crucial factor in uncertainty of sanctions, namely the adequacy or inadequacy of communication. Alter's reaction, that is, is a function of what he believes he is reacting to. In the extreme case therefore sanctions will drop out completely if alter is not aware of what ego has done. Such phenomena as the anonymity of urban society find part of their importance here. But short of this extreme, alter's cognition of ego's action may be partial or distorted or both, either because of his own motivation to distort or because of other impediments to full communication. This is a fact which obviously contributes to the possibility of vicious circles getting under way, since they may go some distance before alter's awareness of the situation permits his "normal" reaction pattern to come fully into force. By this time it may be too late for it to have the effect which it would have had at an incipient stage. The problem of the "levels" at which cognitive processes operate is particularly important here. Sometimes alter may "sense" a feature of ego's orientation which he cannot "pin down" in explicit cognitive terms. How far this is adequate cognition is a complex and open question.

The remoteness which is antithetical to immediacy of sanctions may be of at least two types, first to immediacy in time, second, to that in the relationship system. It seems to be well established in learning theory that the timing of contingent gratifications and deprivations is a highly significant feature of the learning process. If the consequence in the form of alter's appropriate reaction is too long delayed—as for instance by difficulties of communication—the effect may be very different, particularly in weakening the control effect from that of the same reaction at an earlier time. This is obviously because the forces favorable to the deviant pattern may have had a stronger effect the longer they have operated without counteraction.

The concept of "closeness" of social relationship is not a simple one. But there seem to be no doubt that alters are differentiated in terms of their degrees as well as types of significance to ego, and that the force of a sanction is therefore a function of its source in this respect as well as in others. Of the many significant problems in this area only one of special sociological significance will be mentioned. "Formal organization," means the allocation of both expectation-definition and enforcement functions to differentiated roles. The incumbents of these roles cannot, in the nature of the case, stand in close "primary" relationships to more than a small minority of those to whom their decisions and actions constitute important definitions of the situation and sanctions. They must by and large come to be accepted by virtue of extensive generalization to the authority of generalized normative patterns as such and the acceptance of status-definitions independently of the personality of the incumbent. These alters, the persons in authority whom ego does not "know personally" play a crucially significant part in the sanction system of any complex social system and the problems of the motivational mechanisms involved in the acceptance of their "authority" are of central significance for many of the problems of social control. It may be that the well-known phenomena of the discrepancies between formal and informal organization can be fruitfully approached in terms of the motivational difficulties involved in social control "at a distance." We shall maintain that this is the case and that the conflicts over the formal sanctions of formal organization and informal participations should be treated as special cases of role conflict.

§ ROLE CONFLICT AND THE GENESIS
OF DEVIANCE

THE consequences of the factors in the genesis of deviant motivation and behavior so far dealt with may be and often are compounded by the factor of role conflict. By this is meant the exposure of the actor to conflicting sets of legitimized role expectations such that complete fulfillment of both is realistically impossible. It is necessary to compromise, that is, to sacrifice some at least of both sets of expectations, or to choose one alternative and sacrifice the other. In any case the actor is exposed to negative sanctions and, so far as both sets of values are internalized, to internal conflict. There may, of course, be limited possibilities of transcending the conflict by redefining the situation, as well as of evasion as for example through secrecy, and segregation of occasions.

Role conflict in this sense is continuous with the elements of uncertainty and malintegration which have already been discussed. This is particularly true of the conflict of rules, and of exposure to alters who though not explicitly deviant, "stretch a point" in their reaction to ego. The beginnings of a role conflict may thus be present in the difficulty of living up both to the expectations of one alter who interprets a norm in the direction of a "perfectionistic" compulsive conformity pattern, and those of another who is also in close interaction with ego, and who stretches the same normative pattern to the verge of active rebellion, both of them expecting active reciprocation from ego.

There is a certain endemic potentiality of role conflict inherent in the fact that any actor has a plurality of roles, which involve differences of pattern, thus of relations to alters whose interests and orientations mesh with ego's in different ways. These differences have to be adjusted by an ordering or allocation of the claims of the different role-expectations to which the actor is subject. This ordering occurs by priority scales, by occasion, e.g., time and place, and by distribution among alters. There are thus always a variety of activities which have their appropriate partners, which would not be appropriate with other partners, and which have their appropriate time and place. This allocative ordering of any given actor's role-system is often delicately balanced. Any serious alteration in one part of it may encroach on others and thus necessitate a whole series of adjustments.

In the present context it is particularly important to note that a deviant motivation component relative to one set of role-expectations will have a tendency to upset this delicate balance. Thus a compulsive need to excel in an occupational role may cause the actor to encroach on times appropriately allocated to kinship roles, and make him feel that he is exposed to a conflict of expectations as between his boss and his wife. This may in turn accentuate elements of strain in his marital relationship with the possibility that this should lead to stimulation of the deepening of the vicious circle from there on.

But the source of the conflict may not be ego-made. It may be imposed upon the actor from the malintegration of the social system itself. Not all social malintegration belongs in this category, there may for example be conflicts between groups with no overlapping membership. But, even here, in the pattern sense, there may well be role conflict because only part of the role-pattern defining participation in each group justifies the expectations of the group vis-à-vis the adversary group. This would, for example, be the case in white-negro relations in the South (and in less accentuated form throughout the United States). This may be put as a conflict of roles in that for example the white man has in his role as American citizen internalized participation in the universalistic values of the wider society, the "American creed," but also as a Southerner in the pattern of "white supremacy." The conflict can, however, be mitigated in that he relatively seldom has to act in roles where the significant alters hold up the conflicting expectations to him in such a way that he must directly choose. He deals universalistically in some contexts for example vis-à-vis white colleagues in his occupational sphere, and particularistically vis-à-vis negro-white situations. This segregation is essential to minimize the strain. This situation may be regarded as a main basis of the Southern resentment against "northern interference" in the race problem. It introduces an active conflict of the expectations of significant alters whose differences cannot be ignored. This forces a decision which the segregation of contexts has tended to make it possible to evade.

The significance of role conflict as a factor in the genesis of alienative motivation should be clear from the above. Exposure to role conflict is an obvious source of strain and frustration in that it creates a situation incompatible with a harmonious integration of personality with the interaction system. There must be external frustrations, internal conflicts or both, in the severer cases always both. Indeed what, on the interaction level if not the fully developed social role level, is exposure to conflicting expectations of some kind may be presumed to be the generic situation underlying the development of ambivalent motivational structures with their expression in neuroses, in deviant behavior or otherwise.

When, however, the element of conflict is present on the level of institutionalized role-expectations, a further element is introduced which can be of great significance. The fact that both sides of the conflicting expectations are institutionalized means that there is the basis for a claim to *legitimacy* for both patterns. As distinguished then from alienative need-dispositions which are clearly stigmatized by the moral sentiments common to ego and alter, and later, hence are the foci of feelings of guilt and shame, there is the possibility of the justification of the alienative as well as the originally conformative motivation.

On one level this should serve as a factor in the intensification of internal conflict, and therefore call for greater pressure to resort to defensive and adjustive mechanisms. An example would be the "touchiness" of the Southern white with regard to outside interference. But the obverse of intensification of conflict is that in a certain sense the defenses against overt deviance are greatly weakened if the alienative need-disposition (from the point of view of one of the given expectation patterns) is given a basis of legitimation. Both internal sanctions and those from significant alters are weakened. Then on the one hand role conflict can be seen to be very important as a source of motivations leading to social change, through some sort of undermining of the motivational bases of an established order which includes the provision of motivationally acceptable alternatives. On the other hand this possibility is potentially so dangerous to the stability of a given institutional system that it may be presumed that one of the major functions of the mechanisms of social control is to forestall the establishment of a claim to legitimacy for the expression of need-dispositions which are alienative relative to the major institutionalized patterns of the social system. Of course the establishment of such a "functional need" of the social system does not in any way explain the actual structures and processes related to it. But it does serve to focus our attention on certain points in the motivational equilibrium of the social system in such a way that our attention will be called to certain problems of the determination of processes which might otherwise have been overlooked.

§ THE SOCIAL STRUCTURE OF DEVIANT BEHAVIOR TENDENCIES

WE MAY now turn to a consideration of the principal ways in which the factors in deviant behavior which have been reviewed tend to "structure out" in types of concrete pattern forms in the social system. Since deviance is always relative to a given institutionalized value-pattern system the starting point for this analysis is to be found in the classification of the main directions of deviant orientation developed in the earlier part of the chapter.

It will be held that the cases of conformative dominance, where the compulsiveness of conformity and the accompanying skewing of orientation shows the presence of alienative motivational components are definitely to be treated as deviance. The overtly alienative and compulsively conformative tendencies are most emphatically part of the same dynamic system and must be treated together.

We then of course differentiate deviant orientations further according to the active-passive distinction, and for certain purposes still further according to whether the primary focus is on alter as a social object or on the value-pattern itself.

We will first take up the case of purely individualized deviance, that is, the deviance of ego which is not shared by alter. We will then proceed to consideration of the case where two or more actors share a deviant pattern, thus forming a sub-collectivity over against those who remain integrated with the institutionalized system. We shall also consider the corresponding compulsively conformative types.

Finally we will be concerned with the further factor of indeterminacies, conflicts and differences of level of institutionalization of the value system and its attendant ideology, providing a basis for a claim to legitimacy for the deviant sub-collectivity.

First then, let us assume that an overtly alienatively oriented ego is isolated in that the significant alters in his situation are all oriented to conformity with the institutionalized expectations. There is no company available to constitute the nucleus of a deviant sub-group nor any alternative institutionalized pattern which is congenial to legitimacy.

Even under these highly simplified assumptions we can recognize the roots of certain empirical types of deviant patterning in a society like ours. In a very broad way we may say that the actively alienated person is predisposed toward individualized crime. By virtue of his active orientation he is inclined to defy sanctions, to challenge others to "do something about it." This of course leaves altogether open the question of what specific kinds of norms he is oriented against, and what other motivational complications may be involved. It should also be clear that such a person is not necessarily deviant in all respects. In particular, his active orientation may well be part of the institutionalized culture—he may be very much achievement-minded, but be under compulsion either to achieve goals defined as illegitimate or to achieve acceptable goals by means which are in contravention of the institutionalized normative patterns.

On the other hand the passively oriented anti-conformist may be predisposed to such a pattern as "hoboism," to a maximal avoidance of implication in the positive expectation system of the society. The hobo, we may presume, is above all concerned to protect his freedom, and is willing to pay what others would consider an exorbitant price for it. Above all he wants to be let alone to live his own life the way he wants to live it without recognizing any obligations to anyone. The person who has economic resources for a comparable freedom without sacrificing ordinary living standards may be a psychologically comparable case; this is perhaps one factor in "Bohemianism." Perhaps it would be legitimate to place the schizophrenic as the extreme case in this direction, in that he cuts himself off from the ordinary interactive relationship nexus to an extreme degree and retreats virtually completely into his own private world.

In both these types of cases we have abstracted from complicating combinations with other orientational factors. Illness, in our society, is undoubtedly motivated to a high degree and therefore may legitimately be regarded as a type of deviant behavior. There is little doubt that illness belongs predominantly in the passive-alienative category. But there seem to be at least two other features of the sick role. First there is an element of dependency, which in terms of our analysis means an element of conformative motivational orientation. Illness is predominantly a withdrawal into a dependent relation, it is asking to be "taken care of." It uses disability as the basis of legitimation of this claim. Since, unlike hoboism, illness implies the assertion of a claim upon others, it provides, as we shall see, a point of "leverage" for social control which is not so readily available without the underlying conformative motivational structure. Put a little differently, the sick person emphatically does not "burn his bridges" vis-à-vis the institutionalized system. Furthermore the combination of both a dependency need and an alienative element in a generally passive orientation is psychologically readily understandable. Indeed it is hard to see how one could exist without at least some admixture of the other.

In an actively oriented personality, similarly, the occurrence of a strong aggressively alienative element is also certain to be combined with a conformative aspect of the need-disposition structure. The acting out of the actively defiant component in social situations, however, obviously maximizes the pressure of the sanction system, since the rebel virtually makes it impossible for others not to try to suppress his deviance. Such a role as that of illness, in which the passive avoidance of obligations and overt dependency on others are combined, is therefore closed to him. But a motivational equivalent of the combination of alienative and conformative elements in illness is possible if the rebel can "team up" with others. This possibility will be taken up presently.

The individual who has strong compulsively conformative need-dispositions constitutes a type whom it is more difficult to identify in the usual terms as clearly deviant. As we have seen, however, he does definitely skew his behavior relative to institutionalized expectations. The actively oriented sub-type seems to have in our society at least two principal variants, or foci of emphasis, as we have seen. One is the compulsive achiever who places excessive demands on himself and on others, and who may also show his alienative motives by excessive competitiveness, an incapacity to tolerate normal challenges to his security and adequacy. The other focus is the enforcement of his will and of normative patterns on others. He is the person who makes it his business to see that others toe the mark in excess of normal institutional expectations. The passive type on the other hand is best represented by the perfectionist or ritualist in Merton's sense. He evades normal fulfillment of expectations by making every excuse not to "stick his neck out."

The next factor to be taken up is the possibility that ego can team up with one or more alters. In the active overtly alienative case this is exemplified above all by the criminal or delinquent gang. Such a gang has two obvious advantages over the situation of the individual criminal who "goes it alone." First, organization is by far the most effective way of coping with the overt sanctions which this pattern of deviance is the most certain to provoke. Second, ego and alter obviously by their partnership in crime reinforce each other's alienative need-dispositions. This greatly weakens the attitudinal sanctions of the normal institutionalized structure in that each has an alter to whom he can turn for approval of his action to offset the disapproval of the rest of society.

But more than this the deviant is thereby enabled to act out *both* the conformative and alienative components of his ambivalent motivational structure. To do this he must of course make the substitution of the pattern of the deviant sub-culture for that of the main social system. But having done this he can be compulsively conformative *within* the deviant sub-group at the same time that he is compulsively alienated from the main institutional structure.

The most important point is the opportunity provided by the existence of a deviant collectivity for ego to be overtly alienatiye vis-à-vis the relevant parts of the instutionalized system and at the same time conformative vis-à-vis the expectations of fellow gang members. Here the compulsive quality of the need to conform should be kept in mind. This fact may have an important bearing on various features of such delinquent sub-culture groups, such as the extreme concern with loyalty to the group and the violence of the condemnation of "ratting." The need for ego to feel that he is a member of a group which is genuinely solidary and which he can "count on" is compulsively intensified.

This may become a peculiarly acute focus of strain for another reason. Our previous analysis would suggest that if the alienative need-disposition is combined with a strongly active orientation, the conformative component would, in relation to persons, tend to be oriented in a dominating and norm-enforcing direction. But clearly too widely distributed dominance is incompatible with the functional needs of a solidary group. The very fact that such a group must enforce a stringent discipline because it is in danger vis-à-vis the outside society, may mean that it is peculiarly shot through with internal strains, because more than in most groups it selects members who have a need to dominate which under the conditions of the group many of them cannot express. There is an impression that overt struggles for leadership break out especially readily in such groups and that they are peculiarly subject to "fission." If this is true it may be associated with this situation.

There seem to be two main directions in which such tension may be mitigated. One is to "sublimate" the need for active conformism from dominance over persons within the group into the channel of excelling in the types of achievement which, in terms of the group norms, are the most valued. This may have something to do with the motivation to extraordinary risk-taking in such groups—such achievement is of course also a possible path toward the validation of a claim to leadership, that is, to a dominant role within the group. The second direction is the recruitment into the group of persons who are suited to play roles complementary to those of some of the more dominant group members. This phenomenon would seem to be very common; the presence in such groups of rather passively inclined and generally obedient types, who tend to be submissive to the dominant members. In certain sectors of the society such roles may be alternatives to that of illness.

Thus from a certain point of view the roles of passively isolated avoidance-withdrawal and of active "criminal" destructiveness and rebelliousness may be considered the polar antithesis in the structure

of deviant behavior. When the conformist component of the ambivalent motivational structure is given opportunity for acting out
along with the alienative, the former pattern tends to shift into the
pattern of illness, the latter into the criminal or delinquent gang
or sub-culture. These, however, are clearly ideal types and fail to
take account of many complicating factors. Thus it is altogether
possible for the passively inclined personalities to form a sub-cultural
group which instead of actively defying the institutionalized patterns and their personal bearers, asks essentially to be "let alone"
to work out their patterns "in their own way." This seems to be the
case with various exotic religious sects. Such roles may well be
alternatives to that of illness. They also usually involve elements of
active defiance here and there, but very likely as a secondary phenomenon. This would be true, for example, of Jehovah's Witnesses.
This is understandable in the light of the general ubiquity of
ambivalence in the motivation of deviance.

To attempt to enter into the many possible complications of this
order would, however, lead too far afield for the very general purposes of the present analysis. We have so far introduced two major
components in the structuring of actual deviant behavior; first, the
basic nature of the alienative need-disposition structure, and second,
the availability in the social situation of roles which would mesh in
with the complementary need-dispositions of others, especially in
such a way as to enable the deviant to "eat his cake and have it" in
the sense that within limits both sides of the ambivalent structure
can be acted out. This is the salient feature of illness and the delinquent gang as deviant patterns. Hoboism and individual criminality are perhaps less important empirically precisely because they
do not permit such a combination to a comparable degree.

These two patterns are susceptible of further differentiation in
terms of whether the primary alienative orientation is directed
against normative patterns as such or against social objects, e.g.,
persons. With respect to individualized crime the obvious distinction is that between crimes against persons and crimes against "law
and order" or objects that symbolize normative rules. The prevalence
of crimes against property in the pattern of urban delinquency is
highly suggestive in this connection. This focus of differentiation
can be readily extended to the delinquent sub-culture. One type of

gang may be more concerned with punishing the types of people (including collectivities such as rival groups) who have incurred the wrath of its members. Another type may be more oriented to stealing. Most cases are presumably mixed, but the question of relative primacy may nonetheless be significant.

With regard to the passively oriented types, again the distinction seems significant. Hoboism in our society, and such variants as Bohemianism, seem to be above all oriented to passive evasion of obligations to live up to "the rules." Perhaps the schizoid direction of mental pathology on the other hand is more focused on avoidance of attachments to persons.[7] When we turn to the types which combine outlets for both alienative and conformist components, again a distinction seems important. Illness seems particularly to involve orientation to dependency on persons, for understandable reasons perhaps mainly "mother figures" or physicians as "father figures." The conformative component may on the other hand be expressed more in relation to the adequacy context in terms of a passively ritualistic conformism with pattern expectations, thus being a "good patient."

This is clearly a complex field. There are many possible subtle combinations of the motivational elements we have considered here. They can, however, be used to generate hypotheses which should to a significant degree prove susceptible of empirical test.

The compulsive conformist does not face the same problems of overtly breaking with the institutionalized value system as in the alienative case, indeed by definition the balance of motivational forces is opposed to this. There is, however, the possibility that such compulsive conformists will interact with each other in such a way that, relative to the main institutionalized value-pattern the expectation-sanction system becomes skewed so that there will be a typical pattern of deviance which is reinforced in the same way as in a deviant sub-culture, but without overt break by the formation of a new collectivity.

Certain features of the dynamics of group prejudice seem to fit here. Vis-à-vis the members of an outgroup, our major value-patterns

---

[7] Demareth's findings are suggestive here. Cf. N. J. Demareth, *Adolescent Status and the Individual*, unpublished Ph.D. dissertation, Harvard University, 1942.

call for an attitude of universalistic evaluation and treatment and tolerance for their own achievement-goals and needs within certain limits. Since Jews are admitted as legitimate members of the society the major value-pattern prescribes this type of attitude on the part of Gentiles toward Jews. What we call anti-Semitism constitutes in this respect a deviation from conformity with these features of the institutionalized value-system, especially in a particularistic direction.

The hypothesis that the displacement of aggression on the Jew as a scapegoat object plays a part in anti-semitism has become almost a commonplace of social science. But from the point of view of the Gentile group this constitutes deviant behavior since the Jew is by the main value-pattern entitled to the same universalistically tolerant behavior as any fellow Gentile. Hence there is a strong pressure to "rationalize" his special treatment by such allegations as that he "does not compete fairly," and that he cannot be counted upon to be honest or loyal. Discrimination against him is thereby subsumed under the universalistic value system. So long as this type of legitimation is accepted and mutually reinforced within the Gentile group, or a sub-collectivity within it, we can have a reinforced pattern of deviant behavior without any individual having to accept the normal price of deviance in the form of an overt break with his institutionalized role and the risk of negative sanctions. Indeed, if the process goes far enough it is the person who conforms with the main value-pattern who is subject to negative sanctions.

The compulsive conformist is in this situation able to accomplish the same splitting of the components of his ambivalent motivation as in the case of the member of the delinquent gang. The latter had to transfer his conformative needs to the deviant sub-group. The case of the anti-Semite is the obverse—the displacement of his alienative needs outside the group onto a scapegoat outgroup.

An analogous type of process would seem to be involved in what is sometimes called bureaucratic "ossification." According to Merton's description of the bureaucratic personality, he would in our terms be characterized as predominantly a passive compulsive conformist. If the situational exigencies of role-performance in certain types of organization, and/or the process of selective recruitment of personnel in such roles, operate consistently in the direction of putting a premium on skewing the main achievement-values in the direction of "playing safe" and "not sticking one's neck out," there may well be a cumulative process, so that the "bureaucratic sub-culture" becomes in fact deviant without any overt break with the main institutionalized values. It would seem that such a process of cumulative skewing offered one very important possibility for social change since it avoids or minimizes some of the most obvious re-sistances to such change.

What happens to the alienative component of the motivation in this case is less obvious than in that of anti-Semitism. It would seem that it was concentrated on passive resistance to the fulfillment of the normal expectations of the role. Once again this shows that the passively oriented person is not under the same pressure to split ambivalent needs as is the active.

We may now turn to the question of the significance of the availability of a claim to legitimacy for the pattern of deviant be-havior. It should first be pointed out that this is a relative matter, since on one level the very existence of complementary roles in-volves values common to the interacting role-partners. Thus the willingness of an alter to take care of a sick person represents in itself a partial legitimation of the latter's illness; he is not in this particular relationship to be "punished" but "helped." Similarly in the delinquent gang the "partner in crime" is the focus of a partial legitimation. The gang has its own code and sanctions. Without the support of this partial legitimation the motivation to the pattern would be greatly weakened.

The problem hence concerns the extension of the claim to legitimacy to a wider field. In the case of illness this is blocked by the conditional nature of the legitimation of the sick role which is granted in terms of the wider value-system. The claim to be taken care of is made contingent on admission that it would be a good thing to get well as expeditiously as possible. In the case of the de-linquent gang on the other hand the legitimation is limited to the sub-culture, which by definition is in overt conflict with the wider value-system.

There seem to be two main possible types of situation which would further the extension of this claim to legitimation of an alienative pattern. One is the existence in the actual social situation of a conflict of patterns, such that ego is in a position to select a legitimate alternative to the one against which he is alienated. If this alternative is part of the expectation system of the actual inter-action complex in which ego is involved, he is already subject to role-conflict in the sense discussed above and the present analysis thus constitutes a continuation of the discussion of that subject. He may deal with the conflict by seeking to escape the interaction situation in which the original pattern is institutionalized and move into the one in which the alternative prevails—a very common process in a complex society.[8]

The second type of situation is that in which there is a suffi-cient indefiniteness in the definition of the original pattern-expec-tations so that it is possible for ego without overt deviance to "interpret" the pattern in conformity with his deviant needs. These two are of course ideal type cases. In fact alternative expectation patterns normally shade into each other without sharp discontinui-ties, especially along certain paths of transition. Thus a certain "liberalism" of religious orientation may be an alternative to "fun-damentalism." Ego's parental home may be strongly fundamentalist in its orientation, but his parents value education highly. This enables him to go away to college where he comes into contact with a liberal set of expectations. If he can segregate this college situa-tion from his parental home, e.g., by not talking about it when he is home for vacations, he can make the transition without an open break which would entail an overt definition of his attitude by his parents as deviant. He has achieved a legitimation of what in terms of the parental values was a deviant need-disposition. In general the presence of these bridges of common value-orientation between alternative patterns is one of the most important phenomena in this field.

The legitimation of a deviant pattern immediately shifts it from the status of an individual to that of a collective phenomenon.

---

[8] This is one of several points at which the theory of "reference groups" be-comes of great importance to the analysis of social systems. Ego is conceived as standing at the point of intersection between a system of interactive participations. Within limits the institutionalized patterns of his roles permit him freedom of choice as to which shall have priority. Beyond these limits conflicting expectations may be forced upon him. The structure of alternatives open to him is an essential component in the determination of his behavior. Cf. Merton and Kitt's paper in Merton and Lazarsfeld, Eds., *Continuities in Social Research.*

Those whose orientations reciprocally legitimate each other constitute a collectivity which is a sub-system of the social system. It is obvious that when an individual has attained this type of interactive support it becomes immensely more difficult to undermine his motivation to deviance. Very simply his deviance is strongly rewarded.

In general two other sets of factors contribute to the further strengthening of deviant motivations which have an anchor in legitimation within a collectivity. The first of these is the degree of difficulty of stigmatizing the sub-culture pattern as illegitimate in terms of the wider value system. This is a function of the relative prominence of what have been called the "bridge" elements between the two value-systems. Thus at one end of the scale the delinquent sub-culture, though it may have a strongly enforced code within itself, is relatively weak in bridges to the wider value system. The elementary security of property and the person are such widely and deeply institutionalized values that delinquent gangs do not readily find allies outside their own numbers. Moreover, on the relevant levels, these value-patterns are not seriously ambiguous. At the other end of the scale a "leftist" political movement has many such bridges. Most of the "ideological issues" which define the difference of value systems concern highly abstract and general formulae which are open to much "interpretation." Moreover, many of the abstract formulae, such as the desirability of "social justice," of "democracy" or of "peace" are shared in common. Who is to say whether one interpretation is more legitimate than the other? Movements which exploit the generalities and ambiguities of dominant value-systems and their accompanying ideologies are hence particularly difficult to control by any means which involves depriving them of the claim of legitimacy.

The second set of factors which further the claim to legitimation is that involved in the development of a strong defensive morale of the deviant group. This is the homologue of the secondary gain of the individual neurotic, and may in fact be psychologically continuous with it in that the mutual support of the group members in their deviance adds both to their investment in the maintenance of the deviant pattern and to the risks of abandonment of it. This is true on rational levels, but also on non-rational and unconscious levels. The anxiety as to what would happen if the deviant pattern were abandoned is greatly strengthened by clear and unequivocal attitudes on the part of the other members of the group; ego would be clearly a traitor who was guilty of letting them down if he abandoned them or questioned the legitimacy of their position. This situation tends to favor transferring ego's security needs to his fellow group members; in short, attaching the motivational factors involved in any institutionalized role-system, to conformity with the norms of the deviant sub-cultural collectivity.

To a certain degree these two factors in the legitimization problem are antithetical to each other, in that defensive morale is in part a function of the clear definition of conflict, thus of having "burned bridges." The deviant sub-group which is making the most of its claims to legitimacy will not in general tend to maximize the possibilities of heightening the defensive morale of its members by accentuating the radicality of their differences from the main value-system too much. However, especially by the path of interpretation, there is an important possibility of making the best of both these worlds, namely by turning the tables on the wider society and declaring the latter's value-orientations to be illegitimate in its own terms. The full-fledged revolutionary or prophetic religious movement generally does just this. But even so this procedure is seldom carried out as radically as might be thought possible. The fact that ambivalent motivational structures are involved is clearly shown by the very common vacillation between on the one hand an attitude almost of pleading to the outgrouper to recognize the devotion of the deviant to the "real" values of the society and their applicability to him, and on the other the expression of violent aggression toward the same outgroupers. For example the Communists certainly often quite self-consciously exploit the patterns of freedom of speech and the like in liberal societies, but certainly in the rank and file there is widespread feeling that in justice they have a right to expect every "consideration" from the law. But at the same time that they insist on this right they indulge in wholesale denunciation of the "system" of which it is an institutionalized part. The rationalistic tendencies of our common sense thinking easily obscure the ambivalent character of the motivations involved in such a movement. It scarcely seems possible, considering the processes of recruitment and the position of such a movement in our society, that very many of its members should be anything but deeply ambivalent about the position they have taken. This ambivalence would be expected to be manifested in inconsistencies of attitudes and behaviour as well as in the well-known fierce defensiveness whenever the legitimacy of their position is questioned. Where the Communist ideology has been institutionalized in a Communist state the situation may, of course, be quite different.

With reference to the claim to legitimacy, there is one further consideration of such general significance that it requires a brief discussion here. This is the place occupied in all cultural traditions of complex societies by a "romantic-utopian" element which is partly and in some sense equivocally institutionalized. The origins of this element appear to lie in the fundamental fact that every social system imposes disciplines on its component individual actors, and that these disciplines are never completely and fully accepted in the sense that they are fully integrated in the personality structure of the actors without alienative elements and hence ambivalence. There is always the element of wishing that this did not have to be, and there are always elements of fantasy about states of affairs where the frustrating restrictions do not apply, where everything is, in this wish-fulfillment sense, as it "ought" to be. What the content of this romantic-utopian element will be will depend on what particular disciplines are enforced in the society and the complex psychological reactions to these disciplines at all levels of the process of socialization.

The ways in which such elements may be handled in a cultural tradition are also various. Some of them may be expressed in artistic form in such a way as to divorce them drastically from the possibility of the implication of commitments in action. However important and authentic the frame of reference of the "problem of meaning" undoubtedly is in relation to religion, the displacement of frustrated wishes into the transcendental sphere seems to be one exceedingly common if not universal component of religions, for example the conception of a state where complete and perfect psychological security will exist, where the infallible love of God makes up for the deficiencies of finite human love, or where the element of coercion which to some degree seems to be inherent in human societies, is thought to be totally absent.

Some of these elements, however, find their way into definitions of the desirable in concrete social relationships, and under certain circumstances the ethically obligatory. They seem to play a prominent part in most "charismatic" religious and political movements, certainly in the Western world. The fact that much of our cultural tradition derives from the institutionalization of the values and ideologies of such movements—notably the various branches of Christianity and the rationalistic-revolutionary "ideas" of the Enlightenment—means that these elements have played a very prominent part in the cultural tradition of Western society.

This, in addition to the high incidence of generality of norms implied in a universalistic value system, is one of the principal reasons why the element of generality and ambiguity is so prominent in our patterns of value-orientation. An open break with the symbolic formulae on which great social structures have been founded would involve a very high cost indeed. The easier way has been to meet the exigencies of realistic situations by interpretation, thus the wish to be free from any coercion whatever, and the idealization of such a state, shifts into some such conception as "freedom under law."

This adaptation by interpretation, however, leaves what may be called a latent reservoir of legitimation possibilities in the more radically romantic or utopian elements of the cultural tradition. A movement which utilizes these can attach in many cases to exactly the same symbols as the institutionalized culture uses. Thus such symbols as freedom and justice may receive interpretations incompatible with the functional needs of the institutionalized order. But, precisely in terms of the approved cultural tradition, it is not possible to stigmatize these interpretations out of hand as illegitimate. Taking advantage of these latent legitimation possibilities is one of the most important characteristics of deviant movements.

This becomes all the more important when it is seen that such definitions of the situation may well have important correspondences with the motivational patterns present in a population. The alienative elements are part of it. But it is particularly important that linking with firmly established symbols of the cultural tradition makes it possible to a degree to eat your cake and have it. The basic pattern is to put the established values and status-persons "in the wrong" with respect to what purports to be the value-system they themselves subscribe to. This can be particularly effective, not only because general formulae have to be restricted in a realistic direction by interpretation, but because every complex social system is in fact shot through with conflicts and adaptive patterns with respect to whatever value-system it may have. The utopian deviant can then almost always derive a profound self-justification from the question "do you really mean it?" with respect to the obligation to conform to an ideal pattern. He puts himself in a highly favorable light by saying or implying "You merely pay lip service to this ideal, I will show that I really intend to act upon it." It may be suggested that this is one of the points at which the modern liberal-individualistic type of society is most vulnerable to a breakdown of its system of social control. The diversion of deviant motivational elements into alternative channels would seem to be particularly important in such a society.

Before closing this section it should be noted that the above discussion of the social structuring of deviant behavior has been illustrated almost entirely in terms of the American or at most the modern Western institutional structure and value-system. It would lead too far afield to attempt to develop corresponding illustrations of the main deviant possibilities for other principal types of social structure. There is no reason to doubt that the conceptual scheme developed here for statement of the problems and approach to their solution is, with proper adaptation, equally applicable to the analysis of deviance from any type of value pattern and within any type of institutional structure.

In many other respects the above analysis is very incomplete. It should suffice, however, to show how the analysis of the genesis and consequences of deviance can be fitted into the general scheme of the analysis of social systems with which we are concerned.

§ THE MECHANISMS OF SOCIAL CONTROL

THE theory of social control is the obverse of the theory of the genesis of deviant behavior tendencies. It is the analysis of those processes in the social system which tend to counteract the deviant tendencies, and of the conditions under which such processes will operate. Like the theory of deviance, it must always be stated relative to a given state of equilibrium of the system or sub-system which include specification of the normative patterns institutionalized in that sub-system, and the balance of motivational forces relative to conformity with and deviance from these patterns.

Hence the stable equilibrium of the interactive process is the fundamental point of reference for the analysis of social control just as it is for the theory of deviance. But our attention will be focused on one aspect of the interactive process, the forestalling of the kinds of deviant tendencies we have analyzed earlier in the chapter, and the processes by which, once under way, these processes can be counteracted and the system brought back, in the relevant respects, to the old equilibrium state. This latter is, of course a theoretical point of reference. In empirical fact no social system is perfectly equilibrated and integrated. Deviant motivational factors are always operating, and become established so that they are not eliminated from the motivational systems of the relevant actors. In that case the mechanisms of social control account not for their elimination but for the limitation of their consequences, and for preventing their spread to others beyond certain limits.

There are such close relations between the processes of socialization and of social control that we may take certain features of the processes of socialization as a point of reference for developing a framework for the analysis of the processes of control. The preventive or forestalling aspects of social control consist in a sense of processes which teach the actor not to embark on processes of deviance. They consist in his learning how not to rather than how to in the positive sense of socialization. The re-equilibrating aspects on the other hand are a special case of the learning process in that they involve the unlearning of the alienative elements of the motivational structure.

Perhaps the key to the relationship of the two sets of processes is to be found in the fact that both socialization and social control consist from one point of view in processes of adjustment to strains. the strains either may eventuate in deviant motivation or, previous strains already having done so, a secondary strain may be introduced into the system by the pressure on it of the established deviant motivations.

Strain, we may assume without going into all the psychological complexities, provokes four main types or components of reaction namely anxiety, fantasy, hostile or aggressive hitting-back or hitting-out reactions, and defensive measures in the sense of attempts to limit the deviation from ego's expectations and/or restore the status quo ante. Indeed all the reactions may on one level be interpreted in the latter light, but at a more differentiated level it is useful to distinguish these elements. Effective measures of control must in some sense operate on all these elements of the motivational structure.

One whole important class of such measures operates only on the level of dealing with overt behavior. These are the measures which by compulsion, and by appeal to rational decision through coercion or inducement, prevent certain actions or deter from them or from carrying them beyond narrow limits. The empirical significance of these aspects of the social control system is not to be doubted, but our concern is with the subtler underlying motivational aspects.

The first element of any social control mechanism in the latter sense may be called "support." Its primary direct significance is in relation to the anxiety component of the reaction to strain, to give a basis of reassurance such that the need to resort to aggressive-destructive and/or defensive reactions is lessened. Support may be of various kinds, but the common element is that somewhere there is the incorporation or retention of ego in a solidary relationship so that he has a basis of security in the sense of the above discussions. The stability of the love attitudes of the mother in critical phases of socialization is one fundamental type of case. The collectivity-orientation of the therapist, his readiness to "help" and his "understanding" of the patient is another. These types differ fundamentally as role-pattern types and yet they have this common element. In one sense the consequence of support is to localize the focus of strain, by making it possible for ego to feel that his insecurity is not "total" but can be focused on a limited problem area for adjustment.

Quite clearly, however, the element of support cannot be unconditional in the sense that *whatever* ego does is met with a favorable response from alter; in that case there could be no control exerted over ego's motivation; he would be directly rewarded for continuing and possibly extending his deviance.

Support could not be effective as reassurance if there were no element of permissiveness relative to the pattern system from which ego deviates. We may say that people under strain are, whether alter is fully aware of it or not, expected to deviate in some ways and to some extent, to do and say things which would not be tolerated if the circumstances, or their own states were wholly normal. (The child is understood to be under strain in "having to learn.") In general this permissiveness is to be interpreted as toleration of "natural" reactions to the frustration of expectations. These will of course be of one order if alienative motivation has not become established, and of another order if it has. This is the basis for a fundamental differentiation of types of mechanisms of social control, namely, whether it is necessary to cope with the vicious circle phenomena or not.

Permissiveness, must, however, be strictly limited if it is not to lead to the encouragement instead of the forestalling of the vicious circle. Hence there is a balance between areas of permissiveness and of restriction on it. The most fundamental form of the latter may, in the light of our analysis, be seen to be the refusal of alter to reciprocate certain of the expectations which ego develops under the pressure of his anxiety, his fantasies, his hostility and his defensiveness. Indeed support itself is in one sense a refusal on alter's part to "justify" ego's anxieties by reacting as ego fears that he might. Similarly, alter will refuse normally to reciprocate ego's hostility by being hostile in return, or will for example not accept either dominance or submission from ego. The most fundamental difference between a vicious circle-building reaction on alter's part and a social control reaction seems thus to be the combination of permissiveness with the discipline of refusal to reciprocate. Exactly in what areas this combination will operate and how the balance will be held will vary with the nature of the strains to which ego is exposed and with the role structure of the interaction system. There is, however, the common element that the refusal to reciprocate, like the support, is legitimized in terms of the institutionalized value patterns which in this case we may assume ego has previously internalized.

With respect to all three basic aspects, support, permissiveness and restriction of reciprocation, there is a further important distinction between the extents to which alter's action is consciously manipulative or is not. Many of the most fundamental elements of social control are built into the role structure of the social system in such a way that neither ego not alter is conscious of what goes on. Their functions are wholly latent functions. On occasion, however, one or more of them may be manipulated with greater or less awareness of what the actor is doing. These are deliberately imposed sanctions, and may touch any one of the three aspects of the control problem we have distinguished. Again in line with our previous analysis we may hold that the most fundamental elements of this manipulation concern the "relational rewards," that is, alter's attitudes of love, approval and esteem. There are of course other extremely important aspects of the control relationship, notably the control of communication, but the attitude elements must, it is clear, have a critically important place.

The process of psychotherapy is the case in our own society where these fundamental elements of the processes of social control have been most explicitly brought to light. For certain purposes, as we shall point out a number of times, it can serve as a prototype of the mechanisms of social control. It should not, however, be forgotten that psychotherapy has a number of special features not shared by many other mechanisms involving the same fundamental elements. First, it is carried out in a professional role of a specialized type, and qualifications must be made for the differences of this role structure from those involved in many other types of social control. Secondly, in its classic form, it is carried out in a one-to-one relationship of two persons, not a group interaction process, whereas many mechanisms operate through more complex group situations. Third, the cultural patterns of scientific knowledge of psychological processes and, hence, the value-standards of scientific objectivity play a prominent role not to be found in many other cases, and, finally, the therapist extends his conscious manipulation of the situation and of the reward system in the light of his own theory, much farther than the case for many other types of mechanism.

It should immediately be evident on general grounds that the most fundamental mechanisms of social control are to be found in the normal processes of interaction in an institutionally integrated social system. The essentials of these processes have been analyzed and illustrated throughout the earlier chapters of this work. Hence it is necessary here only to add a few points. The central phenomena are to be found in the institutional integration of motivation and the reciprocal reinforcement of the attitudes and actions of the different individual actors involved in an institutionalized social structure. These considerations apply to any one pattern of role-expectations. But institutionalization has integrative functions on various levels, both with reference to the different roles in which any one actor is involved, and to the coordination of the behavior of different individuals. The latter has been dealt with in a number of contexts.

A few remarks, are, however, in order in the former context. The individual engages in a wide variety of different activities and becomes involved in social relationships with a large number of different people whose relations to him vary greatly. One of the primary functions of institutionalization is to help order these different activities and relationships so that they constitute a sufficiently coordinated system, to be manageable by the actor and to minimize conflicts on the social level. There are two particularly interesting aspects of this ordering. One is the establishment of a time schedule so that different times are "set aside" for different activities, with different people. "Time off" from occupational obligations on Sundays, holidays, vacations, etc. is one example. The fact that there is a time for each of many different activities—and also a place—keeps the claims of each from interfering with those of the others. In fact a society so complex as ours probably could not function without relatively rigid time scheduling, and the problem of the cultural values and psychological need-disposition structure of such a time organization is of great importance. We know that in many societies the motivational prerequisites for fitting into such a time-orientation do not exist.

A second major area is the establishment of institutionalized priorities. Especially in a relatively free and mobile society it is inevitable that people should become involved in situations where conflicting demands are made upon them. It is quite obvious that such situations are sources of serious potential conflict. This can be minimized if there is a legitimized priority scale so that in choosing one obligation above the other the individual can in general be backed by the sentiments of a common value system. It is indeed in areas where this scheme of priorities is indefinite or not well integrated that loopholes for deviance are most common. One example of such a potential conflict may be cited. A physician has peculiarly sharply emphasized obligations to his patients. But he also has important obligations to his family. Far more than in most occupations he is often called away at times when the family has important claims on him—meal times, evenings when social engagements may be scheduled, etc. The institutionalized expectation of the priority of the claims of patients is indispensable to the physician in dealing with his wife on such an occasion. As Merton has so well analyzed, the exposure to situations of such conflict without clearly institutionalized priorities of obligations is a very important aspect of *anomie*.

The above considerations do not however concern mechanisms of social control in a strict sense though they describe essential aspects of the background on which we must understand the operation of such mechanisms. When we turn to the consideration of normal social interaction within such an institutionalized framework as a process of mutually influenced and contingent action we see that a process of social control is continually going on. Actors are continually doing and saying things which are more or less "out of line," such as by insinuation impugning someone's motives, or presuming too much. Careful observation will show that others in the situation often without being aware of it, tend to react to these minor deviances in such a way as to bring the deviant back "into line," by tactfully disagreeing with him, by a silence which underlines the fact that what he said was not acceptable, or very often by humor as a tension-release, as a result of which he comes to see himself more nearly as others see him. These minor control mechanisms are, it may be maintained, the way in which the institutionalized values are implemented in behavior. They are, on a certain level, the most fundamental mechanisms of all, and only when they break down does it become necessary for more elaborate and specialized mechanisms to come into play.

Beyond the scope of such mechanisms there are points in the social system at which people are exposed to rather special strains. In a good many such cases we find special phenomena which have been interpreted to function at least in part as mechanisms for "coping" with such strains with a minimum of disruptive consequences for the social system. Two types may be briefly discussed.

One is the type of situation where because of uncertainty factors or specially acute adjustment problems there is exposure to what, for the persons concerned, is an unusual strain. In general the field of religion and magic yields many examples of this. The problem of uncertainty in the health field and of bereavement are good examples. The reactions which such unusual strains tend to produce are of the character noted above. They both include potentially disruptive components and are unstructured in relation to the social system. In the case of uncertainty, as in gardening in the Trobriands, one of these may be discouragement, a general tendency to withdrawal. Similarly in the case of bereavement, there may be a loss of incentive to keep on going. Ritual on such occasions serves to organize the reaction system in a positive manner and to put a check on the disruptive tendencies.[9]

One aspect of such ritual patterns is always the permissive one of giving an opportunity for "acting out" symbolically the wishes and emotional tensions associated with the situation of strain. It provides opportunities for a permissive relaxation of some of the disciplines of everyday life which are characterized in part by a relatively strict pressure to reality-orientation. But at the same time it is by no means a completely free and untrammeled opportunity for expression. Action is on the contrary strictly channeled into culturally prescribed forms, which prevent "wandering all over the lot." It is a conspicuous feature of such rituals that they are communally prescribed and thus give the support of emphasizing group concern with the situation. They also symbolically assert the dominant value attitudes, thus in the case of death for instance the importance of the survivors going on living in terms of that value system, redefining the solidarity with the deceased in these terms: it is "what he would have wished."[10]

[9] Almost the classic analysis of this type of function of ritual is Malinowski's analysis of funeral ceremonies in *Magic, Science and Religion*. As Kroeber, *op. cit.*, notes, however, there are still important problems of the universality of the relationship between such strains and ritual which must be further studied.

[10] We shall discuss in the next two chapters some of the ways in which the religious orientation of a society can be of the first importance with reference to its general system of values in the secular sphere. The control mechanisms in certain areas of special strain tend in turn to be integrated with both. This is the essential difference between the view of religion taken here and that of Kardiner in *The Individual and His Society*. The latter tends to treat it overwhelmingly as a

A slightly different type of structuring of behavior which is certainly in part significant as a mechanism of control is what may be called the "secondary institution." The American youth culture is a good example. Like ritual it has its conspicuous permissive aspect, so much so that it shades over into explicit deviance. In this permissive aspect it also may be regarded as primarily a "safety valve" of the social system in that attempting to keep youth completely in line with adult disciplines would probably greatly increase the strains of their position. But it also has more positive control aspects. One of these is the integration of the youth culture with major institutional structures, mainly in the field of formal education. This not only brings it under direct adult supervision, but it legitimizes some of the patterns, for example athletics and dances. In spite of the deviant fringe, the existence of such a legitimized core undoubtedly keeps down the total amount of deviance.

Finally there are certain "self-liquidating" features of the youth culture which are relatively hard to identify but probably quite important. In a variety of ways, through the experience of youth culture activities and relationships the individual in the optimum case goes through a process of emotional development to the point where he ceases to need youth culture and "graduates" into full adult status. Of course in this as in many features of our social control system there are innumerable "miscarriages." But broadly speaking it is extremely probably that on the whole the net effect tends to be emotionally "maturing." For example, the very insistence on independence from adult control accustoms the individual to take more and more responsibility on his own. In the youth culture phase he tends to substitute dependency on his peer group for that on the parents, but gradually he becomes emancipated from even this dependency. Similarly in the relations of the sexes the youth culture offers opportunities and mechanisms for emotional maturation. The element of rebelliousness against the adult world helps to emancipate from more immature object-attachments, while certain features of the "rating and dating" complex protect the individual during the process of this emancipation from deeper emotional involvements

---

"projective system" which expresses motivational elements which are blocked by the disciplines of secular life. This is undoubtedly *one* major aspect of the matter, but only one.

than he is yet able to accept. The very publicity of such relationships within the peer group serves as such a protection. Thus the youth culture is not only projective but also exposes the individual passing through it to positively adjustive influences.[11]

It will be noted that the above mechanisms operate within the framework of socially legitimated interaction. Within the normal processes of nipping of minor deviances in the bud of course no differentiated social structures are involved at all. In the case of "safety-valve" mechanisms like ritual, and of secondary institutional patterns, there are special social structures. These entail a limited permissiveness for modes of behavior and types of emotional expression which would be tabooed in ordinary everyday life, e.g., the display of "grief" at funeral ceremonies. But this permissiveness is rather narrowly limited, and it is of the greatest importance that it operates within a system of interaction which is continuous with the main institutionalized social structure, differing from it only with respect to occasion, or as in the case of the youth culture, to stage in the socialization process. The behavior is emphatically not stigmatized as deviant, but is legitimized for people in the relevant situations. They are treated in the present context because of their relevance to the control of *potentially* deviant motivational elements.

Thus it is clear that some balance of permissiveness and its restriction is maintained. Support is clearly given through the institutionalized legitimation of the patterns in question and the resulting solidarity. Generally speaking, however, there is little conscious manipulation of sanctions.

It has been noted several times that secondary institutions like the youth culture shade into actual deviance.[12] It may next be noted

[11] Suggestive evidence of the importance of the youth culture in this connection is given in Demareth's study of a sample of schizophrenics. An early "maturity" of interests combined with lack of participation in youth culture activities was highly characteristic of the group. Not one of the 20 had established satisfactory heterosexual relationships on a youth culture level. It may well be that without the youth culture there would be many more schizophrenic breakdowns. See N. J. Demareth, *Adolescent Status and the Individual,* unpublished Ph.D. dissertation, Harvard University, 1942. It is also suggestive that one element of alcoholism for men may be connected with over-involvement in the youth culture and failure to become emancipated from it at the proper time. The alcoholic may be in part an adolescent who is unsuccessfully trying to be an adult.

[12] It may be remarked that this is true not only of the "frivolous" youth culture which has been predominant in the United States, but also of the "serious"

that there are in a complex society many phenomena which are either on the edge of deviance or in important respects shade off into what is definitely deviant. These resemble secondary institutions except that the legitimacy of their broad status is more in question, the society often being seriously divided about it. One of the most striking of these is gambling. E. C. Devereux has recently made by far the fullest sociological study in this field yet attempted.[13] The conclusion of a careful analysis is that it would be seriously disruptive to the society either to attempt to suppress gambling radically or to remove all the restrictions on it. On the one hand gambling performs important functions for large classes in the population, very similar to those of magic, as a kind of acting out of tensions which are symbolically at least associated with the economic sphere. On the other hand the values and sentiments which in one connection justify or rationalize the objections to gambling play a highly significant role in the general value system, and full permissiveness to gambling could not be allowed without undermining these values in other important spheres.

It may be that in view of this situation, to call gambling a "mechanism of social control" is stretching a point. But the existence of such behavioral phenomena, is intimately connected with the problem of social control, and not merely in the aspect of deviance from certain values. At the least it can probably be said that it is not *merely* a symptom of social disorganization, but of a social structure which is sufficiently elastic, even at the expense of serious cultural conflict, to relieve strains by permitting a good deal of this type of behavior, and yet to keep it sufficiently within bounds so that it is not too disruptive in the opposite direction. Devereux's analysis at least suggests that it is a mechanism for expressing and thus releasing strains related to the economic context which, if this outlet were completely closed, might be diverted into other more

---

youth culture. This undoubtedly played an important part in the Nazi movement in Germany, and in this as in other countries contributes significantly to the recruitment of radical political movements and some religious sects. It is interesting that the deviant fringe of the frivolous youth culture shades off into delinquency, crime, etc., while that of the serious version shades into movements for social change which strongly emphasize the claim to legitimacy.

[13] See E. C. Devereux, Jr., *The Sociology of Gambling*, unpublished Ph.D. dissertation, Harvard University, 1949.

dysfunctional channels. It is notable that gambling of certain sorts like "playing the numbers" is particularly prevalent among the economically disadvantaged groups.

Whatever the verdict on the basis of better knowledge on the question of the functional significance of such semi-deviant activities as gambling may turn out to be, this case calls attention to a most important more general consideration. This is the functional importance to the society of certain phenomena which from one point of view constitute imperfections in its cultural or institutional integration. One of these is the delicate balance involved in our pattern of religious toleration. Certainly in a broad sense religion is closely related to the integration of the social system, and the ideal type of a fully integrated society of a certain kind would have one completely integrated religious system. This is true, but at the same time the attempt to integrate the religious structure of our society in that way, unless it came about by a gradual process probably involving profound changes in other respects, would undoubtedly be highly disruptive, perhaps to the point of precipitating civil war. In the circumstances the very looseness of the religious integration is functionally important.[14]

Other examples which have been or will be discussed are the limitations on formal controls and status-rankings. There are many others. In such a situation there is great functional importance in relative insulation of many sub-systems of the larger society from each other by occasion or otherwise. In the absence of such insulating mechanisms it would not be possible to prevent the conflicting elements from direct confrontation with each other, resulting in the transformation of a latent into an open conflict.

In personal relations "tact" is such an insulating mechanism. It consists in the calculated avoidance of expressing certain sentiments and of the raising of certain questions which, if they had to be directly faced, might disrupt the relationship system. There is a gradual shading off from tact to the "white lie" which makes it pos-

[14] The individualism of a social system which institutionalizes a universalistic-achievement value system precludes religious integration of the type either of an authoritarian established church or of the traditionalistic fixity of many non-literate religions.

sible, often by tacit mutual agreement, to keep potentially conflicting things apart.

Anonymity also serves this function. In general the segregation of both activities and population elements does so. It is true that this segregation often breaks down social controls which operate successfully in smaller less internally differentiated communities. But there is another side to the picture; they also make possible the coexistence of potentially conflicting elements. The importance of this for the kind of flexibility which permits change is clear. Traditionalism in the sense which is obstructive even of desirable changes is very generally associated with a kind and degree of integration which mobilizes the full force of control mechanisms against almost any kind of innovation. A society in which there is a good deal of "disorganization" and "pathology" is almost certainly the necessary price of dynamic openness to progressive change. The balance between flexibility and disorganization is delicate.

With consideration of the functional significance of insulation we have introduced mechanisms which presuppose that alienative motivation relative to some parts of the social structure has come to be established. The first class of mechanisms we shall consider in this connection are, given its existence, concerned with *limiting* its impact on the rest of the social system.

The *insulation* mechanisms just spoken of may thus be interpreted as having the function of preventing potentially conflicting elements in the culture and social structure from coming into the kind of contact which would be likely to lead to open conflict or to exacerbate it—conflict is kept relatively latent. These apply in so far as a structuring on the collective level has already taken place. The mechanisms which may be summed up as *isolating*, on the other hand, have the function of forestalling even this structuring, and the development of appropriate cultural patterns around which it could be built. There are therefore two primary facets, the prevention of the formation of group structures with their greater intrenchment of deviance, and the prevention of a successful claim to legitimacy except perhaps in specifically limited ways.

The two leading patterns in our society which exemplify this set of mechanisms in different ways are those of crime and of illness.

In the case of crime the primary emphasis is on the deprivation of the claim to legitimacy, and even where the prevention of group structures has not been successful the illegitimacy of the acts generally has been maintained. Thus it is important to realize that the purely negative aspect of criminal behavior is only part of the story. The criminal is not merely one who refuses to conform, but in refusing to do so in certain ways he is placed by others in his situation in a specific institutionally defined role. That is, both the role expectations applied to the performer of a criminal act from then on and the sanction system are quite specifically structured so as to "push" the deviant into a certain type of position.

Undoubtedly the structure of this sanction system in the case of crime has deterrent effects, except in the cases where the vicious circle of motivational structuring discussed above has gone too far for them to be effective. But it may be asked why, apart from merely keeping the criminal out of circulation, does society go on punishing even where the vicious circle exists and it will not "cure" the criminal. Durkheim was the first to point out clearly that punishment had another highly significant set of functions than the immediate "protection" of society. It is, in a sense, a ritual expression of the sentiments which uphold the institutionalized values which the criminal has violated.[15] This ritual expression serves to consolidate those sentiments and above all to strengthen them in that part of the population which has positive but latent motivations to the deviance being punished. Punishment is thus a kind of declaration that "you are either with us or against us," and tends to mobilize the sentiments of solidarity with the group in the interest of continuing conformity. A good deal of it therefore is not directed at the criminal himself, but at the others who potentially might become criminals. Of course where the underlying sentiment system in the populations contains serious elements of ambivalence, punishment may well take on the character of "overreaction." Furthermore, because it so drastically deprives the deviant of support and narrows if not eliminates the sphere of permissiveness the criminal role is in general not conducive to reintegrating the deviant with the social system. Both confession of guilt and expiation through punishment may, however, operate in this way if the break is not too drastic.

[15] See Emile Durkheim, *Deux lois de l'évolution pénale.*

An extreme case of this isolating function characteristic of our type of criminal role seems to be found in some cases of the use of black magic or sorcery in non-literate societies. It is often extremely difficult to draw the line between social legitimation of such activities and their illegitimate use in connection with deviant private interests and grudges. But there do seem to be cases where the fact that a man has been attacked by sorcery is subtly legitimized by the community and its support withdrawn from the victim. The sanctioning of counteractive white magic in the community may be considered in such a context as a declaration in favor of the victim rather than his attacker. Warner goes so far as to suggest that the psycho-somatic consequences of this isolation or withdrawal of support by the community account for the apparently authenticated cases of actual death by black magic.[16]

The definition of acts as criminal is the type case of the very broad category of mechanisms of control of the most familiar kind, where normative patterns are "enforced" by the attachment of specific negative sanctions to their violation, and by the differentiation of roles with the specific functions of implementing this enforcement, administrative officials of various sorts, including policemen, courts, and the like. The importance of these mechanisms is of course not to be underestimated. How they operate is, however, in general terms so well known, that it is not necessary to discuss them further here. It is through their relation to the subtler types of control mechanism that the problems of greatest sociological interest arise. Among the most important functions of such enforcement agencies is the limitation of the spread of the deviant tendencies which they define as illegitimate.

One difficulty of organized enforcement measures may be pointed out here. The specialization of the enforcement roles brings their incumbents into close connection with criminals who are themselves generally organized. If crime is important enough to necessitate elaborate enforcement organization it is unlikely that the interaction will be entirely one sided. It is likely that "concessions" to the criminal element will be made which from the point of view of the "function" of the enforcement agency must be defined as "corrup-

[16] See W. Lloyd Warner, *A Black Civilization.* See also E. E. Evans-Pritchard, *Azande Witchcraft,* and Clyde Kluckhohn, *Navaho Witchcraft.*

tion." The enforcement agent is in a position similar in some respects to the foreman in industry. Such corruption is likely to appear wherever enforcement on a recalcitrant population is necessary, e.g., in dictatorships.

In the ideal type case it may be said that the definition of the deviant as a criminal overwhelmingly emphasizes the negative side. It constitutes a kind of extrusion from the social group, with little concern for his return. He is used rather in a sense as a "scapegoat" on whom to project sentiments in such a context as to strengthen the institutionalized values. What happens to *him* becomes secondary. Certain modern trends of criminological practice, where the "remedial" aspect enters in, however, shade over into the case of illness.

As will be analyzed in some detail in Chapter X, the sick role is also an institutionalized role, which shares certain characteristics with that of criminality but also involves certain very important differences. Instead of an almost absolute illegitimacy, the sick role involves a *relative* legitimacy, that is so long as there is an implied "agreement" to "pay the price" in accepting certain disabilities and the obligation to get well. It may not be immediately obvious how subtly this serves to isolate the deviant.[17] The criminal, being extruded from the company of "decent" citizens, can only by coercion be prevented from joining up with his fellow criminals, for the various types of reasons and with the results discussed in the last section. The conditional legitimation of the sick person's status on the other hand, places him in a special relation to people who are not sick, to the members of his family and to the various people in the health services, particularly physicians. This control is part of the price he pays for his partial legitimation, and it is clear that the basic structure resulting is that of the dependence of each sick person on a group of non-sick persons rather than of sick persons on each other. This in itself is highly important from the point of view of the social system since it prevents the relevant motivations from spreading through either group formation or positive legitimation. It is especially important that the motivational components which cannot be expressed in the deviant behavior itself, in this

[17] So far as illness is *motivated* it may be considered a type of deviant behavior.

case tend to tie the sick person to non-deviant people, rather than to other deviants, unlike the delinquent gang as analyzed above.

But again, the sick role not only isolates and insulates, it also exposes the deviant to reintegrative forces. Through psychotherapy, whether it be deliberate or not, in the sick role an actor is exposed to a situation where forces can be brought to bear which are capable of breaking through the vicious circle of the generation of deviant motivation. The role of therapist, therefore, can in a certain sense serve as a prototype of the mechanisms of social control in this more radical sense. It is quite clear that much of the therapeutic effect is attributable to certain of the features of institutionalized role of the physician (in modern Western society) and only part of it to his deliberate therapeutic measures.

It is partly because of its intimate involvement in the motivational balances of the social system that the role of the physician will be more fully analyzed in Chapter X below. Hence, only a few highlights of its social control aspect will be mentioned now, to be more fully examined at that time. The criminal role, precisely because of the overwhelmingly negative character of its emphasis, tends notably to fail in this respect. Above all two factors are lacking which come into the therapeutic relationship, first the element of support in exchange for the obligation to get well, the positive attitude of helping the patient with its various ramifications in accepting him as a person and understanding rather than condemning him. Secondly, therapy provides permissive opportunities for expressing under carefully controlled conditions the distorted and alienative components of the patient's motivational system.

In other words to a considerable degree the criminal tends to be "written off" so far as a constructive social role is concerned, the sick person is not. Some would say that in the shift from the definition of many deviant acts as criminal, to that as pathological, an element of "softness" enters in which makes control ineffective. This is by no means certain, but in any case presents problems beyond the range of the present discussion. At least the pathological definition would appear in general to provide much greater opportunity for reintegration than the criminal even though its preventive functions may not be so effectively performed. Also it may be remarked that there may be some serious difficulties in the attempt to combine the two to the degree which has become common in recent criminological practice. It is not, however, possible to explore this problem further here.

Just as the isolation of the individual deviant may be regarded as the extreme form of insulation of potentially conflict-producing elements from other parts of the social system, so there is every reason to believe that therapy in the context of the medical or most closely related types of relationship is not an isolated phenomenon. This would be more likely to be the case if psychotherapeutic effects were solely a function of the deliberate operations of the therapist as an applied scientist. But we shall see in Chapter X that this is most definitely not the case.

If the therapeutic effect of the doctor-patient relationship is "built into" the social structure of that relationship independently of deliberate planning, it should be built into other parts of the same social structure. That this is true in some degree of such phenomena as "faith healing," and in non-literate societies of magical treatment of the sick, has come to be widely recognized. But the identification of cognate elements of our own social structure may be facilitated by a more explicit analysis of the structural factors which are conducive to this functional result.

This can be stated as an application of the general conditions of the reintegration processes of social control as outlined at the beginning of the present section. First, the collectivity-orientation of the therapist and the definition of his function as to "help" the patient give the basis for the element of support. Second, the definition of the patient as "sick" gives the basis for the element of permissiveness, he cannot be "held responsible" for his condition and/or certain things he says and does in it. Third, however, certain of the professional features of the role enable the therapist to refuse to reciprocate many of the patient's tendencies in interaction with him, notably through the pattern elements of specificity and affective neutrality. Finally, his definition as a technically competent expert gives him the opportunity to manipulate the reward system. His approval in particular has meaning to the patient because of his professional authority, which is anchored in the values of the social system.

An essential part of the leverage of the therapeutic process is the discrepancy between the patient's own definition of the situation—in "transference"—and the standards institutionalized in the professional role.

Details of the structure will vary enormously but it is suggested that functional equivalents of these four features of the physician's role can be found in a wide variety of other parts of the social structure.[18] The problem then is to apply these generalized patterns with the appropriate modifications more widely to a variety of phenomena outside the therapeutic field. The unit of the reintegrative process need not be the individual actor—it may be a sub-collectivity such as a deviant gang.

The generality of application of the first criterion scarcely needs further comment. Complete break with institutionalized values is not a common phenomenon but a limiting case, and the closest approaches to it are those which involve being "pushed out" as in the case of the criminal, rather than purely spontaneous alienation. Very generally then it is safe to assume that there are analogues to the element of support given by acceptance of an obligation to help the sick person to get well. The question is how these opportunities are mobilized in actual control mechanisms. Space will not be taken to go fully into these here. It may, however, be suggested that some of the rationalistic and utopian elements of the value tradition have this significance in reverse, as it were, in that they have sufficient common ground with the institutionalized values so that by "interpretation" it is possible to find a bridge back to these more generally institutionalized values. Thus both individuals and movements which start out relatively radical have a tendency to the attenuation of this radicalism and to a relative assimilation to the going system. What is widely decried in radical circles as the tendency to "sell out" may from the point of view of the system as a whole be interpreted as a process of "getting well." Essentially the same may be said of many sectarian movements in religion. Though from the point of view of their fanatical adherents "secularization" is by definition giving in to the devil, from the point of view of the social system it may indicate the progressive ascendancy of the institutionalized values.

[18] Some aspects of these problems have been previously analyzed in the author's paper "Propaganda and Social Control," *Essays*, Chapter XIII.

In this connection it should be noted that as the dynamically related opposite of this, religious movements and often their political derivatives have a very general tendency to define the issue between "god" and "mammon" or "spirituality" and "materialism," as though there were no positive moral values whatever involved on the side opposed to the particular movement in question. The institutionalized values are from this perspective not values at all, but only "self-interest" or the temptations of the "flesh." It may be strongly surmised that the very radicality of this repudiation of the institutionalized values against which such movements are in revolt involves a reaction-formation against the values to which adherents of the movement are in fact deeply attached. It is positive evidence of the above contention. Such reaction-formation is necessary because the definition of the situation is often such that a deviant movement must not only attack the "abuses" of the system it opposes but precisely its highest achievements and the values which underlie them. Thus some branches of Christianity have attacked not only prostitution and sexual license, but the highest ideal of conjugal love, conceding only that "it is better to marry than to burn." The very value conflict necessitated by such repudiations helps explain the radicality of such movements once well embarked on the vicious circle of deviance. Nevertheless the common value element which makes a bridge back possible is always present to a significant degree.

The refusal to reciprocate deviant expectations seems to be most definitely institutionalized in our society relative to "private" motivations in the universalistic and functionally specific patterns of office and status and their consequent separation of the "office" or other institutionalized status from the "person" of the incumbent. The office gives him the justification of not responding in kind to many things the people he has to deal with do and say. This is even true of political and executive office which must carry routine responsibilities for going decisions. But there are also institutionalized in our society various judicial organs which are kept farther aloof from the give and take, the courts being the most conspicuous example. The relative inaccessibility of a high executive seems to be important in this general connection, because he can then choose his own ground in dealing with most others, and can use them in the context of his "office" in both senses, where the dignity and authority of his status is symbolically emphasized.

Barnard, in discussing the process of executive decision, lays considerable stress on the importance of the decision when and whether, and when *not* to decide.[19] It may be surmised that very often the decision not to decide is in effect the refusal to be "drawn in" to a reciprocity of interaction which would, if participated in too much, jeopardize the dignity and independence of the office. It is also well known that the executive must take great care in the regulation of his personal relations, particularly if they are with people with whom he also has official dealings. In general, this insulation from particularistic reciprocities may be held to be one of the very important functions of the institutionalization of universalistic and functionally specific patterns. It puts the incumbent of a status institutionalized in such a pattern in a position to exercise certain types of both manifest and latent control functions which would not be possible in another type of role.

The element of permissiveness is also prominent at various points in our society as well as in the religious and magical rituals of other societies, as already noted. Perhaps the most conspicuous example is the institutionalized right of "partisanship." In the political area this is particularly marked, of course. People are not merely permitted but positively encouraged to let their views be known and to discuss them with a high degree of freedom. This is also a conspicuous feature of our educational system, in that both students and colleagues are encouraged to state their views. The confession in certain religious organizations, particularly of course the Roman Catholic church also belongs here. Many types of organization also attempt, probably increasingly, to set up channels for the expression of grievances and suggestions. Also counseling systems which directly permit such expression under the guarantee of anonymity are becoming more common.

Another feature which is connected with permissiveness is the projection on important figures and institutional symbols of attitudes which are more or less unrealistic and not in the long run tenable. These are both positive and negative. The high executive in par-

[19] *The Functions of the Executive.*

ticular is blamed for many things for which he could not possibly be responsible, but equally "gets the credit" when things go well.

In both these respects permissiveness in our society goes so far that, if attention were directed only to what is said and done within its sphere, it would hardly seem possible that the society could survive. Thus one political party during a political campaign solemnly assures the public that their opponents are totally unfit to govern, that the values they represent are antithetical to all "true" Americanism, etc. But when their rivals come into office nevertheless, on the whole the excitement subsides, and the members of the first party somehow find it possible to go on living in the society and performing their normal role-obligations. Even a President of the opposite party is still the President of the United States with all the dignity of that high office.

This suggests that there is not only permissiveness, but a set of mechanisms which tend to counteract and limit that permissiveness. One set of these prevents certain elements of the institutional structure as noted above from being "drawn in" to the controversies. Office is never treated exclusively as the "political plum" of a partisan group but has its aspect of responsibility for the common welfare. In a certain sense attainment of office tends to "acculturate" successful candidates to its expectation system so that they do in fact play the role to a significant degree.

Furthermore, in certain contexts and on certain occasions the actions and words of persons in office are ceremonialized as expressing the sentiments and values common to the group as a whole. In function relative to the sentiment systems of the people involved these may sometimes be compared to the "interpretations" of the psychotherapist.

It will also be shown in Chapter X that collectivity-orientation plays a very important part in validating the position of the therapist. It may be suggested that this is capable of generalization, that throughout the social system the elements of collectivity-orientation have important functions in the more general contexts of social control. It is first notable that *within* organizations, authority is always institutionalized in collectivity-oriented terms, even though the organization-purpose is primarily defined in self-oriented terms as in the case of a business firm.

Secondly, it is certainly important, that as distinct from political parties which closely approach the definition of wanting to "get into office" as such, political office itself is strongly defined, whatever the behavorial pattern, ideally in collectivity-oriented terms. Third, there are, even in a "capitalistic" society, very important organizations and structures which are also defined in collectivity-oriented terms, as devoted somehow to the common welfare. Certainly in terms of social control one of the most important classes of these is the university. Its role as the carrier of the institutionalization of much of the cultural tradition which will be discussed in the next chapter, would almost certainly not be possible without this feature of its pattern, with its intimate connection with the values of ob-jectivity and impartiality.

On the other hand it may well be that one of the important reasons why the business class has failed to consolidate its position as a national elite in a sense closely approaching that of a "governing class" is that its primary role has been defined in "self-oriented" terms, thus exposing it too readily to the charge that power would not be exercised as "responsibility" but as exploitation. The public confidence necessary to facilitate a "therapeutic" function may be incompatible with such a definition of the role. A deviant movement which opposes the "profit system" on moral grounds has relatively easy going if there is nothing to counteract the profit symbol.

It is not meant to press the similarity between psychotherapy and other mechanisms of social control too far. Certainly there are just as important differences as there are similarities, but the relationship seems to be sufficiently close, and the common factors sufficiently general, so that these similarities can provide important leads to the recognition and analysis of the operation of control mechanisms which as such are by no means obvious to common sense. What we have presented is, however, only a few suggestions about the problems. An immense amount of research will be necessary in this field.

The most important general conclusions are that without deliberate planning on anyone's part there have developed in our type of social system, and correspondingly in others, mechanisms which, within limits, are capable of forestalling and reversing the deeplying tendencies for deviance to get into the vicious circle phase which puts it beyond the control of ordinary approval-disapproval and reward-punishment sanctions. The therapeutic function is perhaps the best understood case of which this is true. But it has been shown that this therapeutic function is not by any means dependent only on applied science, but also on certain features of the social structure. It is argued that if this be true it would be very strange if these broad features and their broad functional significance were confined to the one very specific context of illness and its treatment. It has been possible to suggest a few avenues of extension of the relevance of these features, but not to analyze them adequately.

There is no pretense that in this final section of a long chapter anything like justice has been done to the exceedingly complex subject of the mechanisms of social control. It has been possible to do no more than scratch the surface. Fragmentary as it is, however, this treatment will have served its purpose if it has been possible to show with some convincing illustrations, that there are in fact important unplanned mechanisms in the social system which in a sense "match" the inherent tendencies to socially structured deviance, with some few intimations of the directions research must take if it is to unravel the intricacies of the operation of these mechanisms.

In conclusion, perhaps a few general summary propositions, which bring together what is most essential in this analysis, may be stated.

1. The conformity-deviance "dimension," or functional problem, is inherent in socially structured systems of social action in a context of cultural values as analyzed in this volume.

2. The relevance of tendencies to deviance, and the corresponding relevance of mechanisms of social control, goes back to the beginning of the socialization process and continues throughout the life cycle.

3. Except in a highly qualified sense at the very beginning of life the tendencies to deviance are not random relative to the structure of the cultural norms and the social action-system, but are positively structured.

    a. The need-dispositions of personality structure are a resultant of interaction in the socially structured role system from birth on, and whether conformative or involving an alienative component relative to role-expectations, are structured relative to the role system of the society. This structure of need-dispositions may be taken at any moment in time as one of the components determining the behavior of the individual.

b. Whatever the "fit" or lack of it between structure of need-dispositions and role-expectations, individuals in social situations are exposed to a whole series of "structured strains" which may further accentuate the difficulty of conformity. Such strains tend to be reacted to in terms of a special set of psychological propensities and mechanisms, the mechanisms of defense and of adjustment. This set of circumstances further structures the tendencies to deviance.

4. The tendency to deviance is finally also conditioned by the objective opportunities provided in the social system, in the structuring of which the "loopholes" in the system of social control are particularly important.

5. Every social system has, in addition to the obvious rewards for conformative and punishments for deviant behavior, a complex system of unplanned and largely unconscious mechanisms which serve to counteract deviant tendencies. Very broadly these may be divided into the three classes of a) those which tend to "nip in the bud" tendencies to development of compulsively deviant motivation before they reach the vicious circle stage, b) those which insulate the bearers of such motivation from influence on others, and c) the "secondary defenses" which are able, to varying degrees, to reverse the vicious circle processes.

6. Structured deviant behavior tendencies, which are not successfully coped with by the control mechanisms of the social system, constitute one of the principal sources of change in the structure of the social system. This set of problems will have to be taken up in Chapter XI below.

APPENDIX

Since the completion of the manuscript of this chapter, there have been some further developments in the underlying paradigm for the analysis of deviance and social control. Rather than attempting to revise the manuscript to make a place for them, it seems best to state them in extremely succinct fashion in a brief appendix to it.

It will be remembered that four essential conditions of successful psychotherapy were stated above, which served as prototypes of the corresponding elements in other mechanisms of social control. These were support, permissiveness for the expression of deviant expectations, denial of reciprocity for these deviant expectations, and conditional manipulation of sanctions, notably the relational rewards, in this connection. The question arises of what the systematic relations between these elements may be, and what in turn is the relation of the resulting paradigm to that defining the directions of deviant orientation.

The element of support clearly concerns the mutual cathexis of the actors in an interactive relationship. The therapist, for example, supports his patient so far as he cathects him, that is, holds the positive attitude toward him which is relevant to the role in question. He treats him as a full-fledged member of the collectivity, which in this case is that composed of therapist and patient. This appropriate measure of support may be deviated from in either of two directions. On the one hand under-support consists essentially in withdrawal of the positive cathexis, or its conversion into hostility. This is essentially what psychiatrists mean by "rejection." On the other hand, support may be given, but by reciprocating alter's deviant expectations or overtures in contravention of the normative pattern defining ego's role. In this case, again to use psychiatric terminology, the therapist will have allowed himself to be "seduced" by the patient.

Rejection places the patient outside the solidary interactive relationship altogether. Openness to seduction, the therapist's seducibility on the other hand, disturbs the equilibrium by creating a strain between the cathectic aspect of the relationship and the normative pattern structure, which certainly should be conceived to be internalized in the therapist, and presumably to some degree in the patient.

This set of circumstances establishes a relation between support and its directions of deviance on the one hand, and the permissiveness-denial of reciprocity pair of conditions on the other. These latter two conditions together define the optimum balance of attitudes relative to the normative pattern itself. Permissiveness, if it is to have positive therapeutic effect, is conditional on it not involving the therapist in reciprocation of the deviant expectations. Then the proper attitude with respect to the normative pattern also may be deviated from in either of two directions. On the one hand the requisite permissiveness may not be granted, the norms may be over-literally and stringently enforced. On the other hand reciprocity may be granted where it should not be, that is, there may be an avoidance of taking responsibility for upholding conformity with the norm.

The purport of these considerations is that effective social control is dependent on an integration of two main factors, the cathexis of the individual actor as a social object, that is, of support, and taking responsibility for upholding of the normative pattern. Each may be deviated from in either a "too much" or a "too little" direction. Hence, according to whether the cathectic aspect or the "pattern responsibility" aspect is the primary focus, there are four primary ways of deviating from this optimum balance, two in the negative, "rejecting" direction, two in the direction of "overfulfillment" of alter's expectations. These relations may be diagrammatically represented as follows:

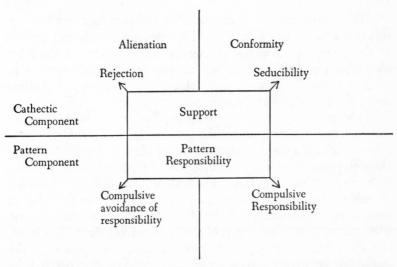

It will be seen that this paradigm is built on two of the fundamental variables which entered into the eightfold table of directions of deviance given on page 259 above, namely conformity and alienation on the one hand, social-object focus and pattern focus on the other. If the third of the variables included in the table is introduced, it has the effect of subdividing each of the four types of deviance from the optimum attitude pattern for social control into two sub-types. It is clear that, by this path we arrive again at the same list of eight major directions of deviant orientation which was set forth in the previous table, as follows:

	ACTIVE FORM	PASSIVE FORM
Rejection	Aggressiveness	Withdrawal
Seducibility	Dominance	Submission
Compulsive responsibility	Compulsive Enforcement	Perfectionism
Compulsive avoidance of responsibility	Incorrigibility	Evasion

The fourth element of the social control paradigm was the conditional manipulation of rewards. This does not as such find its place in the above classifications, but serves as a link between the other elements. The bestowal and withholding of such sanctions can be used as an instrument to swing a balance in situations of uncertainty at various stages of the process in question.

It seems to be a very important conclusion that analysis of the directions of deviance under the pressure of strains on the interactive relationship, and analysis of the conditions of reducing strain through processes of social control, have turned out, independently, to involve the same fundamental paradigm. The difference between the approaches in the two cases lies primarily in the fact that in developing the paradigm of the directions of deviance, following Merton, we laid, after the conformity-alienation dimension itself, our stress on the activity-passivity distinction, and introduced the distinction between focus on social objects and on patterns, only as a "secondary" basis of variation. In the paradigm for the analysis of mechanisms of control, on the other hand, this latter proved, along with conformity-alienation, to be the major axis. Only when this fact was seen, and the third variable of activity-passivity also introduced, was it possible to see that the two paradigms directly converge with each other. Both in fact are ways of stating both the conditions under which strain will be imposed on an interactive relationship, and under which such strain can be mitigated. Or, put a little differently, one states the conditions of strain, the other the conditions of successful re-equilibration of the interactive system when subjected to conditions of strain.

It should be clear from the discussion throughout Chapter VII that use of psychotherapy as an example is for purposes of convenience only. The paradigm we have set forth is of general significance for analysis of the mechanisms of social control. It is above all important to note that it is independent of the particular role structures of the interaction relationship.

VIII BELIEF SYSTEMS AND THE SOCIAL SYSTEM: THE PROBLEM OF THE "ROLE OF IDEAS"

THE most fundamental relations of the cultural tradition to the social system have already been set forth. Indeed these are so fundamental to any analysis of any phenomena of action, that it would have been altogether out of the question to attempt to carry the theory of the social system to the points reached in the foregoing chapters without working out these fundamental problems of the place of cultural patterns. Hence the task of this chapter and the following one is, taking these fundamentals for granted, to develop certain more specific problems of the interdependence of the cultural elements with those of the other components of the social system somewhat farther.

We have seen that the patterns of value-orientation are particularly central to the social system. Because of this fact, and of the way in which we have developed its implications through use of the pattern variable scheme, it may be said that, except for the context of social change which will be taken up in Chapter XI, we have already, on the level appropriate to the present study, covered the field of the sociology of value-orientations. Hence this and the following chapter will concentrate on the other two principal components of cultural traditions, the present one on systems of beliefs or ideas, and the following on systems of expressive symbols. First, however, a brief recapitulation of the general place of culture in action systems and the bases of the classification of its components will help orient the reader to the subsequent discussion.

Culture, in terms of the conceptual scheme of this work, consists, as we have seen, in patterned or ordered systems of symbols which are objects of the orientation of action, internalized components of the personalities of individual actors and institutionalized patterns of social systems. The terms in which cultural phenomena are analyzed are, as is the case with any other components of the phenomena of action, theoretical constructs which the social scientist uses to order his observations, formulate his problems and provide a conceptual framework for his interpretations. The general maxim that "all observation is in terms of a conceptual scheme" applies to the observation of what we call cultural patterns just as much as to any other aspect of systems of action. It is a set of abstractions from the concrete phenomena of social action processes.

The keynote of the conceptualization we have chosen is that cultural elements are elements of patterned order which mediate and regulate communication and other aspects of the mutuality of orientations in interaction processes. There is, we have insisted, always a normative aspect in the relation of culture to the motivational components of action; the culture provides *standards* of selective orientation and ordering.

The most fundamental starting point for the classification of cultural elements is that of the three basic "functional" problem-contexts of action-orientation in general, the cognitive, the cathectic and the evaluative. It is fundamental to the very conception of action that there must be pattern-complexes differentiated with respect to each of these major problem contexts. These considerations provide the basis for the initial classification of cultural pattern types, namely belief systems, systems of expressive symbols, and systems of value-orientation.

The fundamental relation of belief systems to social action processes can be most clearly brought out by referring back again to the paradigm of interaction. We pointed out in introducing that paradigm in Chapter I that one of the fundamental functions of the common culture which develops was communication. Without a sharing and a relative stability of meanings, the complementarity of expectations would not be possible. This applies preeminently but not exclusively to cognitive symbol systems. Furthermore even in this aspect of the culture a normative element is always present in the orientation, since observation of the conventions and standards of the language and belief system is a condition of communication.

In general action terms "reality-testing" is the obviously paramount function of cognitive orientation. This includes of course the accuracy and adequacy of the cognition of alter as an object—and ego's own self-knowledge. But in the context of interaction there is another aspect, the sharing of beliefs. Beliefs like other elements of culture, are internalized as part of the personality of the actor who holds them. That there should be a common belief system shared by ego and alter is in certain respects as important as that the beliefs should be adequate to reality outside the particular interaction system. Because of this duality of functional reference it is not uncommon for cognitive distortions to have positive functions in an interaction system and thus for them to be resistant to correction in terms of pressures of reality. Put a little differently, if ego and alter share a distorted belief—about the physical environment or about third parties, if ego corrects his belief to bring it closer to reality while alter does not this introduces a strain into the relations of ego and alter.

This integrative function of common beliefs in systems of interaction will concern us at many points in the present chapter, but in so far as the cognitive interest has clear-cut primacy the primary focus is "existential." The primary "pure type" of cognitive orientation, then, is what we may call the system of *existential beliefs*. It is necessary then to subdivide this category into empirical and nonempirical beliefs. The distinction is simply that ideas or beliefs will be called empirical when, in terms of the major orientations of the cultural tradition of which they are a part, they concern processes which are defined as subject to understanding and manipulation in a pattern of "practical rationality," that is, in terms of what we call empirical science and its functional equivalents in other cultures.[1] Contrasted with empirical beliefs or ideas in this sense are

[1] The work of Malinowski, among various others, can be held effectively to have disposed of the allegation, represented by Lévy-Bruhl and his followers, that primitive man had a "pre-logical" mentality such that what we call empirical knowledge and the corresponding rational techniques had no place in his thought or action. Every culture includes an element of "empirical lore" which is the

non-empirical beliefs concerning subjects which are defined as beyond the reach of the methodology of empirical science or its equivalent in the culture in question.[2]

Empirical ideas or beliefs may be subdivided according to the classes of objects to which they apply. In terms of the theory of action these are the classes of objects in the situation of action as they have been discussed in the foregoing chapters. For present purposes we may distinguish four main classes, namely physical objects (including organisms) or "nature," individual actors, or personalities, collective actors or collectivities and cultural objects themselves. For certain purposes it may be important to distinguished organisms from other physical objects, as we have seen in the classification of points of reference for the categorization of actors as objects in Chapter IV above. Empirical beliefs about all classes of objects, however, have in common the fundamental fact of the relevance to their cognition of the methodological canons of science, though these are often not explicit in the culture in question.

The category of non-empirical beliefs is avowedly residual. That there should be such a category as part of a cultural tradition seems to be inherent in the frame of reference of action. In its existential reference we may refer to this as the "philosophical" belief system of the culture. It includes beliefs about "supernatural" entities: gods, spirits and the like, and about alleged properties of natural objects, personalities and collectivities, which are not subject to what, in the culture in question, are the canons of empirical knowledge (i.e., the cognitive value-standards). In terms of modern science, they are beliefs which are neither verifiable nor disprovable by the procedures of science, which thus cannot be relegated to the categories of ignorance and/or error according to its standards.

As we have said there may be a primacy of purely cognitive in-

---

precursor of what we call scientific knowledge. Cf. B. Malinowski, *Magic, Science and Religion.*

[2] This is not of course to say that the actors in another cultural tradition are aware of and apply *our* canons of scientific relevance and validity. It is rather to say that in every system of action there is to be found the *equivalent* of the line we draw between empirical and non-empirical ideas. Thus Malinowski's Trobriander, though he believes magic to be essential to the success of his gardening, does not *confuse* the efficacy of magic with that of empirical technology. He does not beleve it is possible to make up for bad technology by more and better magic.

terest in relation to patterns of cognitive orientation. The type of actions which meets this criterion has been called "investigation." If the problems under investigation are empirical we may speak of "scientific investigation"; in so far as they are non-empirical we may speak of "philosophical investigation." In the latter will be included investigation of the logical and epistemological presuppositions of empirical knowledge so long as it is not questions of verifiable empirical fact and its theoretical generalization which are at issue.

Cognitive primacy is also, as we have seen, maintained in a relative sense when a specific goal is given, and the problem is raised of the most effective ways of attaining that goal, and of the "cost" involved in terms of the sacrifice of alternatives. This is what we have called instrumental orientation. Given the goal, the action *problem* is still purely cognitive, and the solutions are hence subject to the primacy of cognitive standards with appreciative and/or moral considerations being subordinated. Apparent exceptions are accounted for by the fact that the particular goal must fit into a larger orientation system, and that in the cost of attaining a goal may be included the sacrifice of appreciative or other evaluative interests. Once these questions are raised it is of course not possible to decide them according to purely cognitive criteria, but cognitive criteria are decisive in determining what the issues are, and what the price of attaining the goal will have to be.

This introduction of expressive and evaluative considerations, when the means to a given goal are being weighed, indicates the next important elaboration of the analysis of belief-systems. This is the point at which a cognitive problem is no longer purely existential but involves, in Max Weber's term, a "problem of meaning." A problem of meaning in this sense always *includes* existential problems, empirical and/or non-empirical. But *in addition* to the existential problem is that of "what of it?" from the point of view of bearing of the existential considerations on the *interests* of actors, individual and/or collective. Because of inherent features of the structure of action systems, this meaning-reference has in turn a double aspect, a cathectic and an evaluative aspect. The first consists in the assessment of the cathectic significance for the relevant actors, of the actual or alleged existential states of the situation, past, present, or predicted future, an assessment which in the last analysis is referable to what we have called the gratification-deprivation balance of the personality. The second concerns the evaluative assessment of its bearing on the value-realization of the action-system in question. So far as an individual actor is fully integrated, that is, his motivational needs and his values are fully synthesized, the cathectic and evaluative aspects come to the same thing. In the case of a collectivity, however, there may have to be sacrifice of the interests of some component individuals in the interest of the collective values.[3]

It seems justified to adopt the term *evaluative* beliefs as parallel to that of existential beliefs. When, therefore, a problem of meaning in the above sense is involved in addition to the existential problem of "what is the state of affairs," we shall speak of evaluative belief systems.[4]

It will, therefore, prove necessary to treat belief systems in terms of a double classification. On the one hand we must distinguish empirical and non-empirical references, on the other hand, existential and evaluative significance or relevance to the system of action. The combination of empirical and existential is clearly the case of science and its proto-scientific counterparts. That of non-empirical and existential we have already designated as philosophy, also, of course, making allowance for the fact that below certain standards of explicitness and logical articulation it might be better to speak of proto-philosophy.

When we turn to the evaluative category we may make a parallel distinction. Where the primary reference is empirical we may speak of *ideology*. The only difficulty with this term is that it refers primarily to the belief system shared by the members of a collectivity, and for some purposes it may in the theory of action be important to speak of this aspect of the belief system of an individual actor. When the individual actor is the point of reference we shall try to avoid this difficulty by speaking of a "personal ideology." Finally, when the primary reference is non-empirical we may when the problems of meaning are of paramount significance speak of *religious ideas,* as distinguished from philosophical.

[3] This is essentially the distinction which Pareto made between "utility" *for* and *of* a collectivity. Cf. *The Mind and Society,* Vol. IV and *Structure of Social Action,* Chapter VII.

[4] This is essentially what Kluckhohn (in his chapter in *Toward a General Theory of Action*) means by Value-Orientations as distinct from Values.

According to this view, then, there is a fundamental symmetry in the relations, on the one hand, of science and ideology, on the other of philosophy and religious ideas. In both cases the transition to the evaluative category means a change in the "stake" the actor has in the belief system, it means the transition from acceptance to commitment. The primary question is no longer that of interest in whether a proposition is "true," but, in addition to that, in a commitment to its implications for the orientation of action as such. We have, thus, by another route, come back to the distinction made in Chapter II between acceptance of a cultural pattern and commitment to it. This has very important implications for differences in the relation of the pattern in question, in this case a belief system, to the action system, notably for what is meant by its institutionalization in a social system.

We shall deal with each of these four major types of belief system in turn, coming at the end of the chapter to a brief discussion of the problem of general classification of types of belief system on another plane, that of orientation content.

§ EXISTENTIAL EMPIRICAL BELIEFS AND THE SOCIAL SYSTEM

OUR treatment of empirical belief systems will be divided into four parts. First will come a brief discussion of the general status of empirical knowledge in social systems. Second, a very important special case will be taken up, that of the institutionalization of scientific investigation as a type of role-function. Third, a few problems about the application of empirical knowledge on the scientific levels in practical affairs will be discussed and finally, fourth, there will be a discussion of social ideologies.

There can be no possible doubt of the importance of "empirical lore" as part of the cultural tradition of every social system. Without a relatively high development of this component, we could not speak of a human society at all. Language and the transmissibility of culture of course open up the possibility of the cumulative growth of empirical knowledge or lore.

Throughout a very large proportion of human societies, however, notably but by no means exclusively in non-literate societies, there are, as compared to the development of modern science, sharp restrictions on the rate of the development of empirical knowledge and even on the acceptance of available knowledge or its use in instrumental contexts. These restrictions seem to have to do primarily with the integration of such knowledge with the other elements of action in such ways that investigative interests are inhibited.

The very immediacy and urgency of practical instrumental needs itself constitutes a basis of inhibition. The conditions of scientific advance seem to lie in two main directions: first, the abstraction and generalization of knowledge, and second, the development of special investigative procedures. Neither of these is possible to a high degree under the pressure of immediately urgent practical needs. Under such conditions the development of knowledge will tend to be tied down to the immediately relevant context, and to readily available procedures. It takes the specialization of roles in these directions to make notable and rapid developments possible. But in "primitive" conditions this possibility is not even cognitively realized, to say nothing of the other institutional prerequisites being absent.

Closely related to these considerations are those involved in the need of the social system for stabilization both of its relationship system and of its cultural orientations. To take one example, the prevalance of magic in non-literate societies seems to be associated with the element of uncertainty in the success of practical endeavors. But precisely because magic provides a non-empirical cognitive orientation to the unknown and uncontrollable factors in the situation, which is in certain respects motivationally gratifying and functionally positive for the social system, the existence of magical beliefs, as Firth clearly points out,[5] inhibits the development of rational empirical knowledge, because the two are in direct competition and are incompatible with each other. In other words, a system of empirical beliefs, which is bordered on every hand by magical beliefs, is by that fact strongly inhibited from further development. It tends to be stabilized in a status quo.

The same is true of various other aspects of a complex socio-cultural system. There is, as we have seen, always a set of vested interests in the maintenance of a status quo. Development of em-

[5] Cf. Raymond Firth, *Primitive Economics of the New Zealand Maori,* Chapter VII.

pirical knowledge is always upsetting to some vested interest. Hence, unless it is positively institutionalized in itself, it is likely to develop only slowly and sporadically, in spite of the fact that on the other side there is an obvious interest in its development. Perhaps above all it is relevant to note that magical beliefs shade into and are integrated with religious beliefs. The latter are apt to be strongly institutionalized in a social system and strongly integrated with the power and reward systems of the society. Unless the religious system is itself both strongly dynamic rather than traditionally oriented, and is dynamic in a manner favorable to empirical investigative interests, it also is likely to have an inhibitory effect on the growth of the empirical stock of knowledge.

Closely associated with these aspects of the problem is that of the ways in which instrumental and investigative interests are bound in with predominantly expressive interests. The very immediacy of instrumentally urgent needs mentioned above is likely to be associated with a general orientation to immediate gratifications and expressive activity, and hence to the relative minimization of the kinds of discipline which are associated with, indeed essential to, a high development of instrumentally oriented action-patterns. The primary disciplines in non-literate societies, as in many literate ones, are more likely to be associated with such affective-diffuse types of role-obligation as those of kinship than with the universalistic, specific and affectively neutral patterns of the modern type of occupational role. It is in the very nature of the higher developments of empirical knowledge, that the pursuit of investigative problems must be universalistically oriented, that the reaching of remoter implications implies a high level of affectively neutral discipline, and that specialization—hence specificity of role function—is essential to success. The very fact that this type of role pattern does not develop on a large scale except under rather special conditions has much to do with the relative stagnation of the development of empirical knowledge in so many societies.

In view of these facts, the high development of science in our own type of society poses important problems of the relation of the investigative interest to the rest of the social system. To this problem we now turn.

1. *The Institutionalization of Scientific Investigation*

THE difference between science and empirical lore, and the corresponding difference between scientific investigation and empirically cognitive problem-solving on a common sense level, are gradual and in a sense relative. What was the technical science of yesterday has in certain respects become the common sense of today —as in the case of the heliocentric theory of the solar system or the germ theory of disease. But though the borderline is indistinct, in fundamental pattern there is a sharp difference. The generality of science far transcends the boundaries of particular practical fields of instrumental interest, and cuts across many of them. The role of the scientist becomes technical and his specialized interests and procedures are of "no use" except for his own specialized purposes. The knowledge he possesses is only with difficulty if at all accessible to the untrained layman. The ultimate judgment of it must lie with his professionally qualified peers. Thus, the status of any given item of knowledge, as belonging to science or to common sense, may be doubtful. And the variations between these two types is a matter of degree. But the distinction is nonetheless vital.

The basic norms of scientific knowledge are perhaps four, empirical validity, logical clarity or precision of the particular proposition, logical consistency of the mutual implications of propositions, and generality of the "principles" involved, which may perhaps be interpreted to mean range of mutually verified implications.[6] Very specific propositions of particular fact may be held to be verified with a certainty approaching absoluteness. The more general the proposition the less that order of approach to certainty in the sense that it is inconceivable that it should ever have to be modified, is possible. But science "progresses" in proportion as it is possible to relate very particular facts to generalized systems of implication.

[6] The reader may for purposes of orientation to the general nature of science and its processes of development, be referred to James B. Conant, *On Understanding Science*. Some of the best treatments of sociological problems relative to science are to be found in R. K. Merton, *Social Theory and Social Structure*, Part IV. Also the author's *Structure of Social Action*, especially Chapters I and XIX contains some relevant discussions. Cf. also "The Institutionalization of Social Science and the Problems of the Conference," Chapter XIV of *Perspectives on a Troubled Decade*. Published by the Conference on Science, Philosophy and Religion, 1950.

Hence it is not possible to use only the one criterion. It would be generally admitted that analytical mechanics before the relativity and quantum era was in some sense a more "advanced" science than botanical taxonomy, even though the "meaning" of many of the generalized propositions of mechanics was in certain respects seriously in doubt, and taxonomy ordered enormous numbers of facts, with very little in its logical structure which was questionable or controversial.

There is, therefore, not merely the question of whether or not a given item of knowledge "belongs" to science, but implied in the term used above, "basic norms," is the implication that there are levels of scientific advancement. Moreover this advancement does not consist only of discrete additions to existing knowledge of facts, but of the relation of this knowledge of fact to systematization and generalized theoretical analysis. This gives us the sense in which science, specifically on the cultural level, is a dynamic thing. Its inherent structure is one of variant levels of advancement. Such a type of culture element contains, in its relation to action, an inherent element of instability. There is always the possibility that someone will make a new discovery. This may be merely a specific addition to knowledge of fact, in which case it will simply be fitted in with the rest in its proper place. But it may be something which necessitates the *reorganization* to a greater or less degree, of the systematized body of knowledge.

This growth-oriented dimension of scientific knowledge as a part of culture is of particular interest here. For this ties in with action; scientific innovation is not a culturally automatic process, but is an action process, and as such involves all the fundamental elements which are relevant to the analysis of action-processes.

There is, however, as Kroeber has brought out with particular clarity,[7] an inherent element of "cultural structure" which provides a partial but very important set of determinants of this process. For precisely as a cognitive system the body of scientific knowledge, in any given field at a given time, is definitely structured. Advance does not and cannot take place in random fashion in all directions at once, i.e., unselectively. It is structured by the intrinsic cultural features of

[7] See A. L. Kroeber, *Configurations of Culture Growth,* and *Anthropology,* 1948 Edition.

that knowledge. Certain problems are inherent in this structure. Facts which are discovered may be more or less relevant to these problems. Even if discovered by chance, the consequences of a discovery are thus a function of the way in which it fits into the structure of existing knowledge, and its problem-structure. The possibilities inherent in any given knowledge-system and related problem-structure are not random and infinite, but finite and specifically structured. There will then be a determinate process of working out the possibilities inherent in a knowledge structure the building of which has once begun, until these possibilities have finally become exhausted. Kroeber uses this type of analysis most convincingly to show that creativity in scientific advance, as well as for example in the arts, is not a simple function of the supply of biologically gifted individuals, but depends on the job there is for them to do. By exactly the same token it cannot be simply a function of favorable states of the social structure. This is authentically a *cultural* factor.

Empirical knowledge is an essential part of all action, particularly when the instrumental aspect is highly developed. There is hence an inherent interest not only in the application of such knowledge, but in its further development. But at the same time we have seen that there are strongly counteracting factors of such a character that unless investigation becomes the primary technical function of specialized roles, the advancement of knowledge is often very slow and halting. Perhaps the most fundamental reason is that for the "practical man" the primary focus is on the attainment of the immediate goal itself, and knowledge constitutes simply *one* of the available resources for achieving it. But, furthermore, practical action tends, for a variety of reasons, to be imbedded in a matrix of non-rational orientation patterns (including the functional equivalents of magic) which, because they are not directly empirically grounded, can only be stabilized by being traditionalized. Indeed the general pressure toward stabilization of a system of action militates against the advancement of knowledge because this obviously has many repercussions besides making the effective attainment of the particular goal more feasible. Also the practical man does not have a direct interest in the further ramifications of a scientific body of knowledge beyond his immediate sphere of practical interest. All this is attested by a considerable amount of tension between scientists and practical men even in the fields where science has been most successfully applied.

These reasons why the practical man develops resistances to himself pushing the advancement of empirical knowledge forward are also in turn connected with the fact that beyond certain points this advancement only becomes possible through the kinds of technical means which involve specialization of roles. Knowledge itself becomes technical, and takes long training to master. Furthermore, investigation is a process which requires special skills which in certain respects go beyond the mastery of the bases in established knowledge from which any given phase of the process starts. Hence the above considerations about the way in which changes in empirical knowledge impinge on any system of social interaction, become even more cogent when the place in a differentiated instrumental complex of the specialized role of scientific investigation is taken into account.

First, the technical nature of specialized science means that there develops what may be called a communication gap. The scientist is inevitably dependent on "laymen" for support and for the provision of facilities. But in circumstantial detail the layman is not technically competent to judge what the scientist is doing, he has to take it "on authority." This general situation is accentuated by the fact that there is often a large gap between the frontiers of scientific investigation and the practical results which the practical man can most readily appreciate, understand and use. This is particularly because the cognitive structure of science is such that the ramifications of scientific problems cannot be restricted to the solution of the kind of applied problem area in which a practical man is interested. He, therefore, from his own perspective often does not have the basis for seeing that what the scientist is doing is of "any use."

Such a communication gap between roles always creates a problem of control. Besides the question of why an activity should be supported, which doesn't seem to be of any particular use, there are two types of foci of anxiety. In the first place the scientist must do a good many things which impinge upon others. Partly these things are just "queer" and their motives seem to be unfathomable. But sometimes they are potentially dangerous to some laymen, e.g., explosions in the chemical laboratory, and partly they impinge on touchy areas of sentiment. Thus, the dissection of cadavers by anatomists and medical students long had to be carried out surreptitiously and today, with all the prestige of medical science, some religious groups permit autopsies only in the few cases where it is legally required. The activities of the Society for Prevention of Cruelty to Animals in trying to limit the use of animals in scientific research are well known. Scientists may also impose burdens on the layman if only by even asking him to give some of his time for a purpose which as a layman he does not understand. This is frequently the case in social science research, e.g., in interviewing subjects.

Along with having to secure facilities from others in ways which impinge on their interests and sentiments, the scientist is faced with a good deal of anxiety about the implications of the results of his work. This is particularly true because the crucial significance of generality of implication of science means that it is not possible to limit these implications to the solution of clear-cut and limited practical problems. This is perhaps particularly important in relation to the ideological, philosophical and religious fields. The motives of adherence to ideological and religious ideas are usually differently structured from those of belief in the simpler bits of empirical lore; the very fact that the elements of the situation involved present such extremely difficult cognitive problems and yet the affective interests in a clear-cut definition of the situation are so strong, makes that clear. But certainly no large-scale development of science is possible without some important impingement and hence in part an upsetting effect, on ideological and religious positions which play an important part in the cultural tradition.

In general the practical man is hedged in by considerations which make only relatively ad hoc and limited resources available for him to make use of. Where the operations of scientific investigation may involve far-reaching repercussions on the sentiment system of a society, it is unlikely that the major impetus for such a development will come alone or even primarily[8] from practical "interests." At the least practical interests will have to be combined

[8] The wielder of political power is the most obvious exception since he often cannot avoid such repercussions.

with a cultural situation which lends prestige to the relevant types of activity on bases other than their promise of improvements of practical efficiency.

This appears very definitely to be the case with science. The place of science in Western society is part of the ascendancy of a cultural tradition which involves a high valuation of certain types of rationality of understanding of the empirical world, on grounds apart from the promise of practical applicability of the results of that understanding. Once such valuation is established and built into the institutional system, it comes to be strongly reinforced by the practical fruits, once science has been permitted to develop far enough so that these fruits have become relatively impressive. In all probability only when such a combination has become firmly established does it become possible for scientific investigation to acquire the level of prestige which it has enjoyed in the modern Western world. But even here there are many elements of ambivalence in public attitudes toward science and the scientist, which are expressed in much irrational and some relatively rational opposition to his role.[9]

The obverse of this is that there is a strong non-rational element in the popular support of the scientist. He is the modern magician, the "miracle man" who can do incredible things. Along with this in turn goes a penumbra of belief in pseudo-science. Scientists themselves are, like other people, far from being purely and completely rational beings. Their judgment, particularly toward and beyond the fringes of their technical competence, is often highly fallible, and things are said in the name of science which are very far from meeting the standards of scientific demonstrability, or short of that, showing the degree of tentativeness and suspension of judgment which is indicated in the light of the deficiencies of the evidence. From this professionally internal penumbra there is a shading

[9] Thus an article in the Vienna *Presse*, which the author happened to see while in Austria in the summer of 1948, argued with the utmost seriousness that it would have been a good thing for civilization had the Church in the long run won out against Galileo, that is, had the development of modern science been suppressed. The argument was that science had opened a Pandora's box with the contents of which humanity was unable to cope, and a kind of intellectual authoritarianism which would limit investigation to fields known to be "safe" was the only solution. Who is to say that there is no force in such an argument?

off into the ideas about scientific matters current among the lay public, where pseudo-science is much more prolific. It is important to note that the conditions under which science could have a well-established place in the social system are such that the presence of this pseudo-scientific penumbra seems to be inevitable. It can, of course, to a degree be limited and controlled, and in fact is, but it seems unlikely that it can be eliminated.

In the broadest possible sense, the most important feature of the Western cultural tradition as a bulwark of science is its strong universalistic trend. This means in the first instance a strong emphasis on the importance of knowledge, an emphasis evidenced for instance in the stress on rational theology in all the most important branches of Christianity. That the hospitality to science was greatly increased in the "ascetic" branches of Protestantism, as compared to the Catholic tradition, is shown by Merton's analysis of the religious situation in England at the time of the great scientific developments of the 17th century.[10]

The valuation of knowledge in a secular direction greatly increased in post-mediaeval times, connecting with the revival of interest in and prestige of the traditions of classical antiquity. Eventually, in the Western world the doctrine that a gentleman ought to be an educated man, first as part of his ascribed aristocratic role, gradually shifted until it has at least become true in more recent times that an educated man was to be considered a gentleman, that is, knowledge became the most important single mark of generalized superiority. This is, of course, a highly schematic statement of a very complex development.

The primary core of the Western tradition of higher education as the mark of the gentleman was in its earlier phases humanistic rather than scientific, though the place of mathematics is of considerable importance. But the great tradition of humanistic learning shares many features with science, above all the respect for impartial objectivity and hence for evidence; in the first instance shown in the concern for the authenticity of historical and literary texts, which is by no means so prominent in many other great literate traditions. The humanistic scholar in this sense was in many respects

[10] Robert K. Merton, *Science and Society in 17th Century England.*

the precursor of the scientist and is of course today his colleague in the most highly educated sector of the population.

In the most modern era this cultural tradition has above all become embodied in the university as its principal institutionalized frame. Not least important of the facts about the modern university is that it combines the highest levels of development of the functions of pure scientific investigation in the same basic organizational complex with the humanistic branches of learning which have formed the primary core of the most highly rationalized part of the great expressive cultural tradition of the West. This includes, of course, theology as the rational foundation of religious beliefs. Furthermore, of course, it is highly significant that a large part of the fundamental training function of the major branches of applied science, especially in medicine and engineering, has become an integral part of the university.

Apart from the institutionalization of the specific role of the scientist as such, which will be commented upon presently, this situation has the great importance of directly integrating the role of the scientist with those of the other principal "experts" in major branches of the cultural tradition. The scientist has the support of being considered part of the same cultural complex which includes the humanities. Not least important, he shares with them the function of educating the primary elite elements of the oncoming generation in the society. In so far as the doctrine is upheld that in general the "leading men" of the society should be educated men in the modern sense, their elite status carries with it commitment to a value-system of which the values of the scientist, and the valuation of his activities and their results, form an integral part. This integration of science, both with the wider cultural tradition of the society, and with its institutional structure, constitutes the *primary* basis of the institutionalization of scientific investigation as part of the social structure. It means that the scientist shares the status in the universities with the other key groups who are primary culture bearers and on terms such that the values of science come to be inculcated in the value-system of society generally through the education of its primary elite elements. Without this it is highly doubtful whether even at its most recent stages of development, the interest of practical men in the fruits of science could alone long sustain scientific investigation as the function of a major type of specialized social role.

In more specific terms, it is first important to note that status on the faculty of a university gives the scientist a clearly institutionalized role with all its concomitants. In terms of modern organization in the occupational field, it gives him both a source of remuneration for himself and of course his family, and a "market" for his products, through putting him in relation to students and professional colleagues and providing or encouraging publication channels for his work. It provides him by and large with the increasingly necessary but expensive facilities for his work, and the framework of the all-important cooperative relationships with colleagues and others. By giving him an "orthodox" occupational role, it gives not only him, but members of his family, an acceptable status in the society, e.g., he "earns a living." Moreover, the university, both through its general prestige and sometimes through specific administrative action, serves to protect his freedom to carry out his function in the face of forces in the society which tend to interfere with it.[11]

The occupational role which the scientist occupies, with its center of gravity in the university, is an integral part of the general occupational system. Moreover it is of the special type we have above called a professional role.[12] The fact that it shares the pattern elements of universalism, affective neutrality, specificity and achievement orientation with the occupational system in general does not require special comment here. But it is worth while to call attention to the fact that as a professional role it is institutionalized predominantly in terms of collectivity—rather than self-orientation.

There seem to be two primary contexts in which self-orientation in the scientific world would tend to be seriously dysfunctional. One

[11] The fact that mechanisms of social control sometimes fail to operate successfully is no evidence that they do not exist, or are not effective in other connections.

[12] There are, of course, many possibilities of dysfunctional phenomena developing when scientific investigation is thus institutionalized. Thus exposure to the criticism of colleagues may be associated with a tendency to sterile pedantry and perfectionism in detail which sacrifices the importance of bold ideas. In general the minimization of refined competitive ratings in university faculties— the treatment of the "company of scholars" as a "company of equals"— may be interpreted to be an adaptive structure with the function of counteracting some of these dysfunctional tendencies. Cf. Logan Wilson, *The Academic Man.*

is the implication of the saying "knowledge is power." It is indeed true that in a sufficiently large number and strategically important type of cases the discoveries of the scientist would, if uncontrolled, put him in a position to interfere with the interests and sentiments of others. These others, the "public," are in need of protection in the whole field of the uses of science. A major factor in this need lies in the gap in communication between expert and layman occasioned by the technical character of science. The layman is unable to protect his own interests in a "market situation." Thus, in a certain sense, the scientist is institutionally endowed with authority, he is recognized as "an authority" in his field, and the general analysis of the functional reasons for the association of other-orientation with authority applies.

The second dysfunctional possibility is that of the "monopolization" of knowledge in its bearing on the process of scientific advancement itself. Such monopolization would not only restrict the rate and spread of scientific advance, by making it more difficult to build on what others had done, but it would also seriously interfere with the social control mechanisms of science internal to itself. It is a cardinal fact that the scientist is, through discussion and publication, exposed to the criticism of his professional colleagues to an unusual degree, including the checking of his results through replication on the part of others. The idea that a "scientist's theory is his castle" which must not be trespassed upon, except on terms laid down by himself, would be incompatible with this discipline which is so important to the maintenance of standards of objectivity.[13] Finally, it should not be forgotten that the scientist requires "privileges" from his fellow men. Collectivity-orientation certainly does much to validate his claims to them. Thus, when the social scientist requests information in an interview the subject may very likely ask, "why do you want to know this?" The legitimation, which must be explicit or implicit in the answer, is that it is in the interests of the advancement of knowledge, not the personal "axe to grind" that the interviewer may conceivably have. Often explicit safeguards

[13] This is what Merton, "Science and Democratic Social Structure," op. cit., Chapter XII, calls the "communism" of science. He gives an admirable functional analysis of its significance.

against misuse of information, i.e., generally "personal" or "partisan" rather than scientific use, have to be given.

The above discussion has dealt only with certain aspects of the institutionalization of the process of scientific investigation in a social system. It has not treated the very complex problems of the repercussions of the results of this process in the rest of the society; something about this subject will have to be said in Chapter XI below in connection with the problems of social change. It has, however, become evident that, important as the cultural aspects of science are, the concrete processes of its development will depend very heavily on the ways in which these are related to the other elements of the social system, some of which, of course, consist in other than scientific aspects of the cultural tradition. The possibilities inherent in a cultural configuration are, as Kroeber has so brilliantly shown, one essential element of scientific development. But these possibilities may remain undeveloped unless the cultural pattern element comes into the proper articulation with the institutional structure of the social system.

The most important single consideration is that the function of investigation, above all in "pure" science, should become the primary functional content of a system of fully institutionalized roles, roles which are necessarily occupational in type. This requires the support of an institutionalized cultural tradition broader than that of science itself, as well as of the more immediate patterns defining the relevant role-type. It involves all the elements of the social system which are relevant to the place of that cultural tradition in the society, in its non-scientific as well as its scientific aspects. The "obvious" intrinsic merits of science, as seen by the modern rational mind, are by no means sufficient to account for the fact that the scientist has in fact acquired a fully institutionalized role in modern Western society.

2. *The Institutionalization of Applied Science*

JUST as scientific investigation, though an inherent possibility of rational action, does not develop far unless it is institutionalized as part of the role structure of the social system, it cannot be taken for granted that even available scientific knowledge will be utilized in practice unless the roles in which it is utilized are equally institutionalized. An example of this institutionalization, that of modern medical practice, will be analyzed in some detail in Chapter X below. Here only a few brief remarks about the setting of the problem will be introduced.

In the first place very generally the kinds of technology in which sophisticated science plays an important part are those which take the "long way around." They involve approaching the attainment of an empirical goal by the use of elaborate equipment, training of personnel, and complex organization. They develop to any great extent only when there is a basis for the acceptance of the disciplines necessary for the functioning of that type of social structure. Not least of these is a fundamental fact about the instrumental division of labor. This is the very simple fact that the incumbent of the ordinary differentiated role in such a system cannot, in the nature of the case, have a direct gratification-interest in the immediate results of the bulk of his activity in the role. He must work for goals of which others are the primary direct beneficiaries, often even then only after a long series of further steps in the process of "production" following his own contribution. He must look for his own gratifications in two other directions. First, he has "remuneration" for his role-activities, which in a complex society like ours above all takes the form of money income contingent on his role performances but also includes various symbolic rewards such as prestige and honors. Secondly, he has the gratifications derivable from the activities themselves, including the complex of social relationships in which they are performed. These we call by such terms as pride of workmanship, concern with self-respect and with the approval and esteem of others. They involve the cathexis of affectively neutral value patterns. Of course the affectively positive cathexis of persons with whom there are occupational associations is also very generally involved, but this must be a specifically limited and controlled cathexis if it is not to interfere with occupational performance.

The acceptance of scientifically grounded technologies in general fits into this context. It involves pressing these general features of an elaborate division of labor farther than they would otherwise be pressed. Above all, perhaps, it is important that the persons who must in the nature of the case perform the roles of implementing the technological ideas, cannot normally themselves be the immediate beneficiaries of the results. Hence the problem of motivating such innovations must be approached in the same general terms as those of motivating any further elaboration of the division of labor. It must either be in terms of the "self-interest" of the incumbent in possible remuneration, which almost always involves an uncertainty factor, or it must be in terms of the motivational significances of achievement values or collectivity obligations without direct regard to the enjoyment of the immediate results. Very generally it may be said that the latter class of motivational elements almost certainly outweigh the former in significance.

The applied scientist, if we may call him such, is subject to most of the difficulties which beset the investigator. There is the same communication gap, in that his technical competence can be appreciated by the layman only in the light of results which can only be demonstrated after he has been "given a chance," or through non-logical mechanisms associated with the prestige of his knowledge, its sources and associations. There is the same set of factors which everywhere operate to oppose innovation because it threatens to upset the equilibrium of an established system of social interaction. As a major aspect of this, there is the fact that the applied scientist must often "interfere" with the interests and senti-ments of those on whom his activities impinge, who are sometimes the direct beneficiaries of his functions and sometimes not.

These are the types of considerations which help to account for the fact that in most societies technological innovation has, in spite of its obvious benefits, often been surprisingly slow and halting, and that even in our own, where it has become institutionalized to a very high degree, it generates very substantial resistances in many fields. These resistances imply in general that there will be a high degree of technological development only where there is the same type of support from a broader general cultural tradition, and its principal modes of institutionalization as we discussed for scientific investiga-tion itself. Here we may again note that in our society the highest levels of technology are rooted in the universities, and share the sup-port of the latter with scientific investigation as such. In the case of medicine, which will be discussed below, it is not too much to say that American medicine scarcely could be said to have come of age as a field of applied science until, not much more than a generation ago, it became established that the norm for medical education was the *university* medical school, and that the norm again for medical research was to be found in the laboratories of such schools and of the teaching hospitals associated with them. Thus the scientific focus of medical practice, the training of the practitioner, the fountainhead of scientific innovation directly applicable in medicine, and the general cultural tradition of which all science is a part, have become organized about the university as the principal trustee of that tradition, as the focus of its institutionalization. What is true of medicine is broadly true of the other principal fields of applied science.

In addition, of course, the institutionalization of applied science requires a direct role structure which is "adequate" to its functional needs. In the modern Western world this has taken place mainly in terms of the professional type of role. It will be argued in Chapter X in connection with the specific material about medical practice that, by and large, the conditions necessary for the application of science to practical affairs on a large scale would not be compatible with any other of the major types of role structure. The reasons for this contention will be summed up and generalized after the evidence on this particular professional group has been presented.

In general, then, we may hold that applied science, like scientific investigation itself, requires quite definite conditions in the structure of the social system, as well as the cultural prerequisites in the form of the adequate state of existing knowledge. Knowledge does not "apply itself," no matter how advantageous to the society the results may, to our Western mind, appear. It gets applied only through the mechanisms of institutionalization of roles within which the requisite combinations of motivational and cultural elements can develop. Only by becoming in this sense incorporated into the structure of the social system, thus coming to constitute *more* than a body of "ideas," does empirical knowledge acquire the basis for a major influence on action.

3. *The Institutionalization of Ideologies*

IN DEALING with scientific investigation we were concerned with a type of action where cognitive interests had unquestioned primacy. In the case of the practical applications of science a goal is given, but subject to this given goal, on the instrumental level cognitive interests still have primacy. When we move to the consideration of ideologies we are no longer dealing with cognitive primacy, but with evaluative primacy. It may be noted that it is impossible for there to be a type of belief system where expressive interests have clear primacy, for there the cognitive interest would be subordinated to the expressive and we would have a system of expressive symbols, not of beliefs. The cognitive interpretation of the meaning of these symbols on the other hand would, as a type of action interest focus, become a process of investigation which would bring it over into the realm of cognitive primacy again.

An ideology, then, is a system of beliefs, held in common by the members of a collectivity,[14] i.e., a society, or a sub-collectivity of one—including a movement deviant from the main culture of the society—a system of ideas which is oriented to the evaluative integration of the collectivity, by interpretation of the empirical nature of the collectivity and of the situation in which it is placed, the processes by which it has developed to its given state, the goals to which its members are collectively oriented, and their relation to the future course of events. In so far as the cognitive interest has clear primacy the belief system is scientific or philosophical. Such belief systems may contribute to the building of an ideology, indeed always do, but solely as an object of such a paramount interest the belief system does not constitute an ideology. Similarly so long as it concerns only interpretation of a situation in terms relevant to the attainment of a given specific goal, e.g., victory in war, the belief system is a set of instrumental beliefs. To constitute an ideology there must exist the additional feature that there is some level of evaluative commitment to the belief as an aspect of membership in the collectivity, subscription to the belief system is institutionalized as part of the role of collectivity membership. There is a great variation in the mode of this institutionalization as well as its degree. It may be completely informal, or it may be formally enforced as subscription to a specified text with sanctions for deviance enforced by a specific agency. But as distinguished from a primarily cognitive interest in ideas, in the case of an ideology, there

---

[14] Since our concern is with the social system we shall not deal here with personal ideologies.

must be an obligation to accept its tenets as the basis of action. As distinguished from a purely instrumental belief there must be involvement of an idea that the welfare of the collectivity and not merely attainment of a particular goal hinges on the implementation of the belief system.

What we are here calling an ideology has its central focus in the empirical aspects of the interpretation of the nature and situation of the collectivity. But it is in the nature of the case that these empirical elements should be combined with and shade off into non-empirical elements at the points where justification of the ultimate goals and values of collective action become involved. A system of religious ideas, on the other hand, rests primarily on the non-empirical premises of its belief system and "works back" as it were, from these to their implications for the empirical nature and situation of the collectivity.

The statement that the orientation of an ideology is toward the "evaluative integration of the collectivity" is in need of interpretation. By this is not meant that the actor who subscribes to the belief system needs to have a sophisticated theory of what integrates the collectivity, but only that it is felt that the welfare of the group is bound up with maintenance of the belief system and its implementation in action. It can readily be seen that a belief system toward which such an attitude is held in common must in fact acquire integrative significance for the collectivity.

The primary emphasis of this volume has been on the integration of social systems at the level of patterns of value-orientation as institutionalized in role-expectations. These patterns of value-orientation are elements of the cultural tradition, but are only part of it. Man is a cognizing animal, and so his values do not exist apart from beliefs which give them cognitive meaning. The dimension of cognitive orientation to the situation is just as essential to a total system of cultural orientation as is that of value-orientation to the choice-alternatives of action, and is analytically independent of it, but of course also interdependent with it.

Furthermore, of course, the general strain to consistency in a cultural tradition, the more so the more highly "rationalized" it is, means that in general the value-orientations tend to be relatively consistent with the belief system. The question of cause and effect is not at issue just now, interdependence may be assumed.

Since there must be relative consistency in the value-orientation patterns of a collectivity—though perfect consistency is not possible —this consistency must extend to the system of beliefs which give cognitive meaning to these value-orientations, again imperfectly to be sure. If ideological beliefs and value-patterns are, as assumed, interdependent, relative stability and consistency of the belief system has the same order of functional significance as do stability and consistency of the value-orientation patterns. Hence there must be a set of beliefs, subscription to which is in some sense an obligation of collectivity membership roles, where the cognitive conviction of truth and the "moral" conviction of rightness are merged. Again this integration may well be and generally is, as we shall show, imperfect. An approximation to it is, however, of high significance to a social system.

Ideology thus serves as one of the primary bases of the cognitive legitimation of patterns of value-orientation. Value-orientation patterns, it will be remembered, always constitute definitions of the situation in terms of directions of solution of action-dilemmas. It is not possible in a given situation to give primacy both to technical competence independent of particularistic solidarities, and to the particularistic solidarity, and so on through the list of dilemmas. So far as this is possible in empirically cognitive terms, an ideology "rationalizes" these value-selections, it gives reasons why one direction of choice rather than its alternative should be selected, why it is right and proper that this should be so.

The importance of this function of cognitive legitimation may be derived from two sources, the general importance of cognitive orientation in action, and the need to integrate this with the other components of the action system. Given the importance of the cognitive interest, cognitive deficiencies in the belief system constitute a source of strain. The relative significance of the value-of "truth" in a value system may vary over a wide range. But it cannot be said that a human action system can exist in which in a radical sense "it does not matter" whether the cognitive propositions which are current in the society are believed to have *any* cognitive validity in any sense. Such a situation would be radically incompatible with the empirical relevance of the frame of reference of action.

As we have seen the sharing of common belief systems is a condition of the full integration of a system of social interaction. Cognitive differences are thus sources of strain, but so also are cognitive inadequacies.

The "trend to rationality" has a status in the frame of reference of action which is cognate with that of the "optimization of gratification." By definition it is nonsensical within the frame of reference to conceive an actor as preferring an increment of deprivation to a gratification unless there were a balancing gratification elsewhere in the system. Similarly, when confronted by a choice between a more and a less adequate belief according to cognitive standards, it is nonsensical, in terms of the frame of reference, to conceive the actor as preferring the less adequate, that is "error" to 'truth." This is true unless the strain introduced by the feeling of cognitive inadequacy is balanced by an interest in another direction which would have to be sacrificed—e.g., in the sharing of beliefs.

Rationalization is in this sense an inherent "directionality" of the action process, like entropy in classical mechanics. It is so in the nature of the conceptual scheme, *not as an empirical generalization*. This poses the problem, as in the case of gratification, of the balances of forces which may facilitate this process, impede it or even counteract it. But it *always* requires motivational "force" to impede or counteract the tendency to rationalization. The empirical problems are to locate the relevant forces in the action system and their relations to each other. It is thus quite possible for the cognitive interest to be drastically inhibited by its relations to other elements of action, as we have repeatedly pointed out. Furthermore there may be very powerful and hence effective motivations to cognitive distortion. But nonetheless belief in cognitive validity is a functional necessity of action systems. Further, where that belief is possible only at the sacrifice of cognitive value standards, this fact constitutes an element of strain in the action system in question.

The significance of the function of legitimation comes to a head in the relation of ideology and religious ideas to the social system. This is simply because when we speak of ideologies we are dealing with a case where the cognitive interest does not have the degree of segregation from other elements of the action system which is possible in the cases of investigation and instrumental application of knowledge in specialized roles and with respect to specific goals. Cognitive legitimation of value-orientations is a matter of the integration of cognitive values with the other elements of the social system.

The cognitive content of ideologies may involve any one or all of the classes of situational objects discussed above, namely physical objects, personalities, collectivities and cultural objects. Beliefs about the world of nature are certainly an essential part of the cultural tradition of any social system, and necessarily acquire ideological as well as purely cognitive-investigative or instrumental significance. The elaboration and generalization of this belief system is particularly important. Only in a few societies, of course, are sophisticated scientific levels of such elaboration of high ideological significance. The importance which such belief systems have acquired on the ideological level is one of the salient facts of the modern world. Beliefs about the heliocentric view of the solar system, about Darwinism and the principle of natural selection, about genetics and the problems of human inequality will serve as examples.

There is a special significance of the content of scientific knowledge in the ideology of scientists as members of professional collectivities. Tentativeness is, of course, an essential part of the value system which governs the role of the investigator. But equally the acceptance of evidence in accord with the canons of investigation, and of the implications of such evidence, is part of that same value system. Hence in a special sense, subject of course to the ultimately tentative character of all scientific findings, there is an *obligation* on the scientist to accept the validity of scientific findings and theories which have been adequately demonstrated. The extreme skeptic of the variety who when faced with the direct evidence stubbornly insists that "there ain't no such animal" cannot be a good "citizen" of the collectivity of scientists. Thus not only is there in the value-system of science commitment to the canons of scientific procedure, but there is commitment to a system of belief-content which is part of the obligation of the role of scientist. The fact that the beliefs may be modified in the light of new scientific evidence does not alter this.

In spite of the importance of beliefs about empirical "nature" in the general cultural tradition, and their special importance for the ideology of natural scientists, for understandable reasons the more prominent content of social ideologies is to be found in beliefs about personalities, collectivities and cultural objects. Indeed we may say that the social ideology focuses in beliefs about the collectivity itself, with the other content-categories entering in largely in terms of beliefs about the significance of and the relations of personalities and cultural objects to the collectivity. Thus the problem of "collectivism" vs. "individualism" as an ideological problem concerns the mode of integration of the individual personality system with the collectivity.

In general it is clear that the *cognitive* standards of ideological legitimation of value-orientations must be the same as the canons of scientific validity. By definition the most developed *empirical* knowledge in any field at a given time is the state of science in that field. Hence the ultimate authority for the validity of any ideological tenet as a cognitive proposition must be a scientific authority. But the very fact that ideology unlike science has as integrative functions in the social system involving relations to many other interests than the cognitive interests of scientists, means that these standards will very generally not prevail in the determination of what beliefs will actually be held. If they do not, there have to be adjustive mechanisms which are homologous with the mechanism of rationalization in the personality system.

Because of the central place of the sciences of action in relation to the subject matter of social ideologies, the problem of the relations of the social sciences to ideology is as is, of course, well known particularly acute. Even more than in the case of natural science, because of this fact the high development of social science is subject to a special set of conditions of integration in the social system.

It may be noted that an ideology is an empirical belief system held in common by the members of *any* collectivity. The focal type of case of course is the ideology which serves to legitimize the value-orientation patterns central to a stable society. These are, in the most fully institutionalized sense, the established beliefs of the social system. In any complex social system there will, of course, be differentiation on the ideological level between various sub-collectivities of the larger society. There is room for a considerable amount of this differentiation without any of the sub-ideologies being treated as explicitly deviant.

In the last chapter, however, in dealing with deviant behavior we called attention to two types of cases of variability beyond the range of this order of sub-collectivity differentiation. The first is what was there called the deviant sub-culture. Here, as illustrated by the case of the delinquent gang, there is an explicit lack of appeal to legitimation in terms of the values and ideology of the wider society, there is an open "state of war." But within the deviant collectivity there is very definitely a value-system and hence an ideology. This ideology will always include a diagnosis of the basis for the break with the main society and its value system. For example, there will be such beliefs as that "you can't win" in the wider society, that "they're out to get you" and the like. It will also involve an ideology of the relationship system within the deviant collectivity, as for instance to why leadership and discipline should be accepted, and as to why "ratting" cannot be tolerated. In such cases of an open break with the value-system and ideology of the wider society we may speak of a "counter-ideology."[15]

The second case is that of the deviant movement which seeks legitimation in terms of the institutionalized value-system, but by giving its own "interpretation" of the value-system and its accompanying ideology. This is in general what "radical" movements do. Precisely because of the tension involved in the degree of break with the main society to which they have become committed, the ideological preoccupations of the members of such movements are likely to be very intense. They have both the interest in convincing themselves and in winning proselytes. It is crucially important for them to believe and to convince others that the aspects of the established society—such as "capitalism"—against which they are in revolt, can be defined as illegitimate in terms of a common set of beliefs and values.

In the light of the tensions involved in these situations and the motivational elements which are, as was shown in the last chap-

[15] In a sense similar to Lasswell's use of the term "counter-mores."

ter, likely to be involved in either of these two types of deviance, it is not surprising that the beliefs of such deviant collectivities often show signs of compulsiveness in the psychological sense. The believer must be protected against any challenge to his belief, not least from within himself. On high levels of generalization, as in the thought of radical "intellectuals," this is very likely to take the form of the "closed system." There are likely to be pseudo-logical devices by which the general formulae of the belief system can be believed to yield a "satisfactory" answer to any question, so that the possibility of damaging evidence turning up need not be a source of anxiety. Of course, compulsive conformity with an insti-tutionalized ideology may lead to the same order of cognitive distor-tion. The antithesis to the orientation of science is too patent to need elaboration.

These two cases of the ideology of more or less explicitly deviant collectivities serve to call attention to some of the bases of cognitive distortion in conformist ideologies. In *Motives, Values and Systems of Action* (Chapter III) it was shown in some detail why it was not possible, in a complex social system, for a single pattern-consistent system of value-orientation to be completely and evenly institution-alized in all of the roles within the social system. Because of the intimate relation between value-orientation patterns and ideologies, this element of imperfection of integration in the value-system will pose cognitive problems on an ideological level. For example in our society the universalistic achievement values embodied in the occu-pational system are undoubtedly very strongly emphasized. But at the same time kinship ties and the solidarities which are most closely connected with kinship are also highly valued. There is an element of rank-ordering of these values but it is not fully adequate to solve the conflicts. Thus we have more deviation from the ideal of equality of opportunity than we feel altogether comfortable about.

It was stated that, in the nature of the case, integration of the social sysem is the primary function of its common ideology. Hence where there is an element of malintegration in the actual social structure the tendency will be for the ideology to "gloss it over" and "play it down." Fully to "face-up" to the reality of the im-portance of conflicting elements in the value-system and in the realistic situation, e.g., with respect to the prevalence of some types of deviant behavior, would be a threat to the stability of the society. In these respects, relative to conflicting elements within the social system, ideologies have functions directly homologous with those of rationalization in the personality system.

It may be noted that this statement applies just as much to the ideology of a deviant movement (or sub-culture) as it does to that of a stabilized social system. There may, in fact, be even stronger pressure to selectivity of emphasis in such an ideology than in an "official" one, because of the greater insecurity of the position of the adherents of the movement, both with respect to their own internal conflicts and with respect to legitimation vis-à-vis the larger society.

A second source of the cognitive distortion of ideologies lies in the needs of "mass psychology." The importance of this set of factors will vary greatly with the character and size of the collectivity in question. But in so far as the ideology must serve to unify large numbers and these are not competent in the intellectual fields covered by the ideology, there will ordinarily be a tendency to "vulgarization" in the well-known ways. Oversimplification is perhaps the keynote of this distortion. Very simple slogans and pat formulae will tend to have a prominent role, and will gloss over the intellectual complexities of the field.[16]

Finally, the strongly evaluative reference of ideologies tends to link in with the "wishful" or romantic-utopian element of motivation which is present in every social system. There will generally, it may be inferred, be a tendency to ideological distortion of the reality in the direction of giving reign to the wishful element. In the case of the ideological legitimation of the status quo it will tend to overidealization of that state of affairs. In the case of a deviant movement it will tend to include a romantic-utopian component in the definition of the goals of the movement. Conversely there is a tendency to paint the contrast of the idealized state of affairs, and what it is compared with, in exaggeratedly black and white terms. To a "conservative" ideology there tends to be a sensitivity about any suggestion of imperfections in the status quo. To the "radical" the institutional status quo against which he is in revolt may appear

---

[16] The phenomena of "sharpening" and "leveling" familiar in the work of social psychology are prominent here.

to be very nearly radically evil, precisely because of the probability that he is compulsively motivated to rejection of it because of the part played by his genuine attachment to the status quo.

It is likely, then, that ideologies will become the symbolic battleground of some of the principal elements of tension and conflict within a social system. In the nature of the case, there would seem to be an inherent tendency to polarization, to the development of vicious circles which is part of the general vicious circle tendency analyzed in the last chapter. By the same token this process of ideological polarization must be subject to mechanisms of social control. Traditionalization and authoritarian enforcement are obvious possibilities, it may be surmised. Another in the modern type of society operates through the linking of ideologies with the institutionalized pursuit of the intellectual disciplines dealing with their subject matter.

In this perspective it becomes clear that the social sciences have a particularly crucial, and in certain respects precarious position relative to the ideological balance of the social system. On the one hand the more important social ideologies cannot avoid concern with the subject matter of the social sciences, nor can the latter simply avoid problems which touch on ideological interests. But on the other hand, the circumstances in which ideologies are developed and operate are such, that it seems practically impossible to avoid the presence of an important area of conflict between the two major types of cognitive interest. The cognitive distortions which are always present in ideologies, often compulsively motivated, will tend to be uncovered and challenged by the social scientist. Some of the results may be accepted, but only painfully and with allowance for a process of assimilation and adjustment over time. Because of this situation there will, more or less inevitably, be a tendency for the guardians of ideological purity in a social system to be highly suspicious of what social scientists are doing.

Indeed it is not surprising that the two non-rational mechanisms of stabilization of ideological orientations, which we have several times mentioned, traditionalization and authoritarian enforcement of an "official" creed, are so very commonly encountered in this field. The "liberal" pattern of freedom of thought, which both permits ideological controversy and free interplay between the scientific and the ideological levels, is the exception, and certainly depends for its stability on a rather delicately balanced combination of conditions in the social system. It may, however, also be a highly important condition for many elements of the potentiality of growth of societies, as it is obviously a prerequisite for the flourishing of social science.

§ THE RELATION OF NON-EMPIRICAL BELIEFS TO THE SOCIAL SYSTEM

NON-EMPIRICAL belief is, as has been noted, a residual category. But, in the light of the development of modern philosophy, it may be claimed that this is more than just an arbitrary assumption. At many points in the theory of action the methodological canons of modern science are found to constitute a fundamental *substantive* point of reference. This is true of the standards of instrumental efficiency of action, and of the judgment of cognitive distortion in relation to rationalizations and ideologies.

Science may thus be treated as the major axis of our analysis of cognitive problems. In so far as this is the case it is legitimate to use it as a negative as well as a positive point of reference, to define deviations as well as correspondences.

In these terms the first major distinction to be called attention to is that between deviation from the standards of empirical science *within* the scope of their applicability, and problems and beliefs which fall *outside* the scope of scientific applicability. The former comprise the categories of ignorance and error.[17] The one important thing to establish about them here is that the beliefs which fill these gaps in positive empirical knowledge are not properly *non*-empirical beliefs but are *scientifically inadequate* empirical beliefs. They may be summed up in the category of "pseudo-science."

Non-empirical beliefs by contrast concern those cognitive problem areas which are inaccessible to scientific method or the equivalent cognitive value-standards in the culture in question. These may be classed in two categories. The first is the "problem of knowledge," the second the problem of cosmology, or that of "being." The essential fact about the problem of knowledge in the

[17] This problem area has been exhaustively analyzed in the *Structure of Social Action*, and need not be further gone into here.

present context is that science yields substantive empirical knowledge which is evaluated by a given set of the canons of its validity. From a logical point of view, then, scientific knowledge becomes a closed system which it is not possible to break out of by scientific procedures. In scientific terms it is possible only to add to the fund of scientific knowledge itself, to refine and perfect within the closed circle.

What is left unanswered is the radical question of "How is empirical knowledge itself possible?" What are the conditions in the nature of the universe on which it depends? This is, of course, the question to which Kant addressed himself, and which has pre-occupied the modern theory of knowledge. It is not our province to go into the technical philosophical problems of epistemology, but merely to note that this problem area constitutes one of the two major foci of the boundaries of scientific-empirical belief systems. In every system of non-empirical beliefs there will, if rationalization has proceeded far enough, be beliefs as to the grounding of empirical knowledge and its relations to non-empirical knowledge. An example is the theory of the relations between revelation and natural reason, which has played such an important part in much of Christian theology.

The second problem area is that of cosmology or being. Science of course gives us substantive knowledge of empirical phenomena. But it is only here that the philosophical problem begins. It is essentially the problem, *given* empirical belief-systems and their place in human action, what are the *implications* of these facts for the cognitive problems which are not solved by scientific procedures? Are the other aspects of experience besides empirical cognition relevant to a "theory" of the nature of the cosmos? Is "nature," perhaps defined as that which is knowable by empirical science, the whole of "reality"? What is the relation of "life" to inanimate nature, of human personality to the organic world, etc.?

This is in a sense an area of "problems of meaning." But this sense of the term should be distinguished from the sense in which that term was used in the preceding section. There the key fact was the bearing of a belief on the *interests* of actors, specifically the cathectic and evaluative interests. Here the context is so far purely cognitive. But it does involve the extension of the area of cognitive interests beyond the circle of empirical knowledge and problems, to include the substantive problems of "what of it" in a cognitive sense.

It could be argued from a certain point of view that the above very brief statement of the main non-empirical problem areas is "culture bound" because empirical science does not have the same relative position in other cultures as it does in that of the modern Western World. This is, of course, empirically true, and yet it does not seem to be a serious source of difficulty. The question at issue is not the relative empirical importance of the different components of the cultural tradition, but the definition of their logical and theoretical relations to each other. There is every reason to believe that the same fundamental components can be found in all cultures. If science (i.e., empirical knowledge) is such a universal component, no matter how primitive its development in some cultures, there should be no *theoretical* objection to using it as a point of reference for the definition of its relations to other components within the frame of reference of action. Only the strictly positivistic position, which claims that there is no other cognitive orientation but that of science, hence that all of what are here called non-empirical beliefs should be classed as error, seems to be really culture-bound in this sense.

In principle the same order of problems arise in defining the relations of philosophy, as non-empirical cognitive orientation, to social systems as must be faced in the case of science. We may speak of them under the three corresponding headings, of the problem of the institutionalization of philosophical investigation itself, of the institutionalization of "applied philosophy" and, finally, of the evaluative synthesis between non-empirical beliefs and the non-cognitive interests of action. This latter category, which we shall call that of *religious ideas*, corresponds to that of ideology on the empirical side. It will receive the bulk of our attention in the following discussion.

Philosophical investigation, as distinguished from the general imbeddedness of philosophical problems and considerations in any system of action, can, it would seem, proceed only under conditions if anything even more specialized than those underlying the development of scientific investigation. For the most part there would, in this field, seem to be no "practical utility" of specialization which corresponds closely with that to be derived in the instrumental division of labor from specialization which reaches the point of differentiating out the investigative function to the point of its becoming the content of a special role-type. In general it seems safe to say that differentiation of specialized cognitive roles in the sphere of religious interest is probably a prerequisite of extensive development in the philosophical direction. This is essentially because the cognitive problems inherent in the problems of the "meaning" of a religious tradition usually constitute the principal points of departure for a movement of philosophical speculation.

The case of classical Greece might at first sight appear to be an exception to this statement. It is true that the development of Greek philosophy itself took a secularizing direction, and that the Greek Polis was notable for the lack of special influence of a priestly class, especially as compared with the other societies in the Near East in the period. Nevertheless the special religious aspect of the Polis is a feature of it well known to historians. There is a sense in which every citizen was a priest. And certainly the ideational content of the religious tradition, as set down in the Homeric poems and in Hesiod, and elaborated in the later literature, especially the drama, was most intimately involved in the development of philosophy. It is probably fairest to say that the Greek case was characterized by a special kind of religious development, not that it occurred independently of religion. On the other hand the place of the religious background in the two other most prominent movements of philosophical speculation we know, that of Hinduism and Buddhism in India, and that of the Western World, is too obvious to need further comment.

The Western case, however, in its modern phase, presents a further complication. Building on the Greek heritage, sophisticated empirical knowledge and its systematization by the 16th century reached a point where the problem of knowledge relative to the canons of science began to assume a central place. It may be presumed that the prominence of this point of reference was dependent both on a prior development of empirical knowledge, and on a religious tradition in which the problem of the status of empirical "nature" had a prominent place. At any rate the "philosophy of science" is obviously of central importance in modern Western philosophy.

Perhaps even more, then, than in the case of science, the development of philosophy depends on its articulation with a favorable cultural tradition. But at least as much as in the scientific case it must be a special kind of a cultural tradition. It must be one in which the values involved in cognitive endeavors as such have a high place, and which at the same time can tolerate considerable departures from strict traditionalism. As we shall see, because of the prominent part played by expressive interests and by certain types of symbolism in religion generally, there tends to be a very strong strain to traditionalism in the religious field, and anything approaching ascendancy of a class of religious specialists in the social system often has the effect of traditionalization of virtually the whole of the culture. Thus there is a sense in which the professional philosopher is apt to be even more disturbing and threatening to the other elements of the society on which his thought impinges, than is the case with the scientist.[18]

Generally speaking the resistances to the development of philosophy as a specialty are so formidable that it would appear that only a cultural tradition, in which the pressure to the solution of non-empirical cognitive problems is very strong, could counteract them. This pressure can also, of course, be aided by a balance of power within the society such that the classes with the strongest interest in checking philosophical developments are in turn checked by a delicately balanced relation to others.

Thus in India the great philosophical development, culminating in the Buddhist movement, seems to have been associated with a balance between the two associated but distinct classes of the Brahmans and the Ksatriyas. After the latter were substantially eliminated by foreign invasion the philosophical development soon practically stopped, and the religious tradition became the highly stereotyped one we know as Hinduism. In the case of Christianity it is very doubtful whether a rational theology, which could form the seeding bed of a great philosophical tradition, could have gotten really started if the philosophical tradition of the Greeks had not

[18] *Even* in Greece, Socrates was condemned to death.

been still alive in the territory into which the movement spread, and certain elite classes thus been committed to a favorable attitude toward philosophy.

These problems are of great significance for the whole question of the "role of ideas" in social change. If the culture and social structure of the Western World had not developed in such a way that scientific investigation had become institutionalized in a distinctive pattern of specialized roles, science, which after all is a body of "ideas" and nothing else, could not have acquired the enormous influence which it is now having on social developments, both through technological applications and through its relation to ideologies. Similarly, if a body of religious *ideas* is to have a great influence on social change, its "chances" are at least greatly enhanced, if as a cognitive structure it has acquired the levels of clarity, logical articulation and profundity of reasoning and insight, which it seems probable that only a sophisticated tradition of professional philosophical thinking can give. It is no more likely that the great influence of Christianity, of Hinduism or of Buddhism would have come about *only* through the activities of the "practical men" of religion, the administrators of cults, of church organizations, the curers of souls, or even the prophets, than is the case with the practical men of everyday affairs, who we all agree would not by themselves have created modern science. The fact that the solutions of the cognitive problems are "there" to be found, and that it would from some point of view "be a good thing" if they were found, does not account for the fact that a great tradition of ideas in fact develops.

The problem of "applied philosophy" as homologous with applied science presents considerable difficulties, and only a few tentative suggestions can be offered here. Perhaps the simplest type of case is that where the philosophy is on the border lines of science rather than of religion. Indeed the logician and the mathematician are so much on this border line that it is often unimportant to attempt to distinguish them from scientists. The application of their work is in the first instance to science itself, then in turn to practical affairs as part of science. But the fundamental sociological problems are the same as in the case of science.

A different case is that of the relation of philosophy to ideologies. Precisely because the ideological uses of scientific ideas are apt to be general rather than specific, and because of the evaluative element in ideologies, it is natural that in a society where there is a developed philosophical tradition, there should have to be some kind of articulation between the philosophical tradition and the current ideologies. In the Western World philosophy has, of course, played a very important part in the genesis of ideologies. All extensive and highly articulated ideologies root in the doctrines of some branch of the philosophical tradition and tend to borrow prestige from it.

This relation is particularly important because of the central position of the subject matter of the social sciences in the content of modern ideologies. The social sciences have not so far been as well articulated as the natural sciences, nor as firmly grounded in empirically established knowledge. This situation, combined with the inherent involvement in evaluative problems, has helped account for the prominent place of philosophical ideas in ideological movements. Indeed, it is only recently, if now, that it has come to be no longer possible to say in social science circles that "it all depends on your conception of human nature."[19] The meaning of such a statement traditionally has been that a philosophical interpretation of the nature of man, independent of scientific evidence, a "philosophical anthropology," is the ultimate determinant of ideological beliefs in the social field.

The sense in which there is often dubiously legitimate "intrusion" of philosophical considerations into the proper field of science, particularly social science, in relation to ideologies, should not be allowed to obscure the positive functions of philosophy in this connection. It can rather generally be said that given the state of social science knowledge, in many fields up to the present, and certainly for the past, philosophical articulation of many problem areas has been the *only* alternative to either traditionalization or authoritarian enforcement as a stabilizing mechanism. A relatively high intellectual level of the philosophical tradition may thus in this connection have played a very important part as a protection of the "liberal" tradition in Western culture. The essential point is that the inherent nature of the problems leads into high levels of complexity.

[19] This was a favorite statement of the late Professor H. J. Laski.

It is quite beyond the powers of the "man in the street" to deal with such complex cognitive problems in any orderly way which has a semblance of rationality. The social sciences have not yet contributed nearly as much as they are intrinsically capable of. Philosophy has filled the gap which would otherwise have had to be filled by one or the other of the predominantly non-cognitive mechanisms.[20]

These considerations are extremely important to an understanding of the place of the "intellectuals" within the social system. Their presence is, of course, possible and important only when there is a highly elaborated cultural system in the belief area. Science, applied science, ideology, philosophy and religious beliefs are all necessarily articulated with one another, and in certain respects shade off into each other. The institutionalization of any one of these types of cognitive interest, in relatively specialized roles, is possible only with the presence of a "penumbra" of beliefs and persons holding them and/or interested in them, who do not quite belong to the core of the role type. There are the "core" professional scientists, the amateur scientists, and the public "interested in scientific ideas." There is established scientific knowledge, tentative ideas at the forefront of scientific growth and the fringe of pseudo-scientific beliefs, some of them held by scientists themselves. Similarly there are "ideologists" closely identified with the revelant scientific fields, and others who are only "spokesmen" for partisan interest groups. There are highly technical professional philosophers and an immense welter of people who talk the language of philosophy with greatly varying degrees of competence and cognitive

---

[20] Competent observers seem to be of the opinion that in the recent Communist movement there has been a marked decline in the intellectual level of Marxist thought as compared with the days of the revolutionary ferment, before and shortly after the Russian Revolution. It may be suggested that this is probably partly at least a result of the extent to which the Communist parties have resorted to authoritarian enforcement of doctrinal orthodoxy, relatively regardless of cognitive considerations. This is a loss to the "liberal" tradition of Western thought even though the Marxists who have been "squelched" would have written far more which was properly considered philosophical rather than scientific. The point is the cutting off of the opportunity and the social conditions for cognitively interested activity in any form. To the present-day Communist the relevant question about a proposition's "rightness" is not, can it be defended on intellectual grounds, but is it in accord with the official party line? The belief in Stalin's infallible *intellectual* superiority may be regarded as a compensatory mechanism.

disinterestedness. Over against the mass of the population who have only secondary symbolic and instrumental interests in cognitive problems this whole group should, in certain respects, be classed together. Many of the features of their belief systems are not in strict accord with the cognitive standards of the core professional groups. Nevertheless it is probable that the currency of such pseudo-scientific and pseudo-philosophical beliefs, and of a class of people who more or less specialize in purveying them, generally has positive functional significance for the type of social system in which science and philosophy are institutionalized. They help to absorb and channel the strains which are inevitably involved in the existence of specialized and esoteric cognitive activities in a society. It is also, of course, evident that they can constitute the principal sources of ideological legitimation of deviant movements.

Religious Belief Systems

RELIGIOUS beliefs may here be characterized as the non-empirical homologue of ideological beliefs. By contrast with science or philosophy the cognitive interest is no longer primary, but gives way to the evaluative interest. Acceptance of a religious belief is then a commitment to its implementation in action in a sense in which acceptance of a philosophical belief is not. Or, to put it more accurately, a philosophical belief becomes religious in so far as it is made the basis of a commitment in action. This seems to be the primary meaning of Durkheim's dictum about religion "c'est de la vie sérieuse." Religious ideas may be speculative in the philosophical sense, but the attitude toward them is not speculative in the sense that "well, I wonder if it would make sense to look at it this way?"

Religious ideas, then, may be conceived as answers to the "problems of meaning" in *both* of the senses discussed above. On the one hand they concern the cognitive *definition of the situation* for action as a whole, including the cathectic and evaluative levels of interest in the situation. This they share with ideological beliefs. On the other hand, however, they also must include the problems of "meaning" in the larger philosophical sense, of the meaning of the objects of empirical cognition, of nature, human nature, society, the vicissitudes of human life, etc. From the point of view of integration of the social system, therefore, religious beliefs constitute the paramount focus of the integration of the cognitive orientation system in its implications for action.

Evaluative orientation has been treated throughout this volume as the synthesis of the cognitive and the cathectic interests of actors. In relation to a total system of action, a personality or a social system, we have spoken of this as the *moral* aspect of orientation interest. Religious beliefs then are those which are concerned with moral problems of human action, and the features of the human situation, and the place of man and society in the cosmos, which are most relevant to his moral attitudes, and value-orientation patterns.

It is this connection with the moral aspect of integration of the system of action, in its social system rather than its personality application, which constitutes the basic insight of Durkheim's analysis of the sociology of religion in the *Elementary Forms of the Religious Life*. The same thing was clearly seen, though not made quite so explicit, by Max Weber. Religious beliefs, then, are systems of cognitive orientation relative to problems of meaning in the double sense noted above, and acceptance of which is treated as a moral obligation by the actor. This *may* be a purely personal obligation, but the case of interest at present is that where it is a part of *social* morality, that is, the belief system is institutionalized as part of the role-system of the collectivity, whether it be a sub-collectivity or a total society.

It is apparently the combination of the moral-evaluative aspect of religious orientations, with certain features of the philosophical nature of non-empirical belief systems, which underlies the place in religions of the conception of the "supernatural." Put very briefly, the moral aspect yields what Durkheim called the sacred character of entities with a specifically religious significance. These are, as he said, entities toward which men show the same fundamental attitude of respect which they show toward moral obligations. In so far as these entities have cognitive significance then, they must be connected with the cognitive legitimation of moral norms and sentiments. They must be concerned with the explanation of the *meaning* of these norms and obligations. By virtue of their sacredness these entities are assimilated to moral norms, and sharply distinguished from instrumental facilities toward which a very different attitude is held.

As Durkheim pointed out, many empirical entities like material goods, buildings, places, clothing, and certain individuals at least under certain conditions are objects of this attitude of respect for the sacred. But in so far as this attitude is cognitively rationalized, it does not tend to be in terms of their empirical properties in the context of the "order of nature" in the sense of the range of ideas from empirical lore to science. It is rather in terms of a "world" of entities distinct from the empirical, or at least of "principles" which are not directly involved in the conception of an empirical world. These entities serve somehow to explain the "meaning" of the sacredness of sacred things, and their relation to ordinary human interests. Since philosophy very generally conceives of non-empirical entities and forces which are different from the empirical order of nature, the "reality" underlying and explaining the sacredness of sacred things is located in this "area." These two circumstances taken together seem to constitute the principal basis for the genesis of the conception of a "supernatural" order, which is in some sense distinguished from or set over against the "order of nature." The supernatural order thus gives cognitive meaning to the moral-evaluative sentiments and norms of an action system, not in the sense that either the sentiments or the cognitive beliefs have causal priority but that they tend to be integrated with one another, and that this integration is importantly related to the stabilization of the system.

This is only the simplest and most elementary account of the factors in this aspect of the situation of the social system. It does not in the least imply that only when there is a sophisticated conception of the "order of nature," in the sense in which that has developed within Western science and philosophy, does this analysis apply. It means only that the distinction between the order of nature and the supernatural in Western thought is a kind of methodological prototype of the relationship, an analytical model. On both sides there may be a low level of cognitive organization, as would be true of many if not most non-literate societies. Also, of course, the conceptions on the two sides and that of their relation to each other may be very different from that in Western thought.

In most Oriental philosophies, for example, the "supernatural" is held to be immanent rather than transcendental in our sense. Philosophically the duality then applies to realms or phases of "manifestation" rather than to the philosophical conception of more ultimate "reality." But the duality on this manifestation level still needs to be rationalized in cognitive terms. There may even, as in Marxist thought, be an attempt to fuse the two, projecting the "supernatural" into a conception of the "dialectic" process of history. The fundamental criteria embodied in the conception of a system of entities, which are not strictly "scientifically" knowable and which serve as the cognitive rationalization of moral sentiments of a collectivity, still apply. In this sense there is a component of religious belief, as well as of ideology, in Marxism, as to be sure there is also in liberal individualism. In so far as ideology ranges into philosophical problem areas, where beliefs cannot be directly derived from the empirical beliefs of the culture, it merges into religious belief. The conception of religious belief put forward here is thus by no means identical with what is traditionally called religion in our own culture.

A further set of circumstances important to the understanding of the place of religious beliefs concerns what Max Weber called the moral "irrationality" of the situation of human life. The conceptual scheme developed in this volume, with the broad empirical verification it receives in many directions, tends to confirm his view that in terms of *any* pattern-consistent value-orientation system there are bound to be situations and circumstances which make complete realization of the expectations developed, when that value system is internalized and institutionalized, impossible. This problem has been extensively analyzed in Chapter III of *Values, Motives and Systems of Action,* and at various points in the present volume and the main reasons for the above statement need not be repeated here. The consequence is that in any case there are considerable elements of frustration and conflict left over relative to any given institutionalized value system. Perhaps to our optimistic mentality the most difficult thing to realize is that this is *especially* true if the value system is consistent and highly institutionalized—though it is, of course, also true of "disorganized" societies. But clearly the "optimum" situation for human adjustment, if indeed such an optimum can be defined at all, does not lie at the pole of maximum institutionalization of a rigorously consistent value-system.

There is always a complex variety of mechanisms in the social system which mitigate the severity of these frustrations and conflicts. Some of them have been briefly touched upon in analyzing the mechanisms of social control. Thus premature death, if not the mortality of men in general, is surely a frustrating phenomenon, not only prospectively for the victim but for the survivors who have been attached to him. It is a situation calling for an emotional readjustment, and a cognitive rationalization. Similarly discrepancies between effort and reward, the fact that conformists with normative expectations do not always fare better than those who do not conform, and many other types of cases. Above all the "problem of evil" and the problem of "meaningless" suffering are focal points in this situation of strain.

If this general analysis be accepted, then it seems to follow that man's knowledge of the empirical world, and the expectations oriented to and by his knowledge, cannot alone constitute adequate mechanisms of adjustment. Any other adjustment patterns, however, must involve a cognitive component, as well as an evaluative, in that it is precisely the failures of the actual situation to conform with evaluative sentiments which constitute the focus of the adjustment problem.

The pressure in such a case is to a cognitive-evaluative orientation scheme, which can comprise *both* the successfully institutionalized and expectation-fulfilling aspects of the value-system, *and* the "irrational" discrepancies. It seems almost inevitable that such an inclusive orientation scheme *must* include reference to supernatural entities in the above sense. Just what the place of this reference may be, how related to the conception of the order of nature, and just what the structure of attitudes toward institutionalized social obligations will be, is subject to wide variations, only a few of which can be briefly mentioned here.

For sociological purposes it is, as so often, convenient to take the orientation to the given institutionalized order of things as the major point of reference, realizing of course that this orientation may in turn be in part a result of prior religious orientations. The complications arising from this fact will be dealt with briefly below.

In these terms the system of institutionalized values may be basically accepted or rejected. In the former case the problem is that of how the discrepancies between expectations in terms of the institutionalized value-system and the actual course of events are handled in the belief system. There seem to be two *primary* possibilities. In the first case the conception of a supernatural order is utilized in order to delineate a "compensatory" re-equilibration, an *Ausgleich* in a transcendental sphere, in the commonest case, in a life after death. Then it is possible to conceive that unmerited good fortune and undeserved suffering will be compensated somewhere. The popular conceptions of Heaven and Hell obviously fit into this pattern. By this means the moral economy of human society is rounded out, and the sources of strain involved in "meaningless" discrepancies between what the institutionalized system through its ideology says ought to happen to people, and what in fact does, are ironed out.

In such a case, of course, the question remains open of how solid the basis of credibility in this compensatory balancing out may be. This type of pattern also probably tends to be associated with a relative traditionalized stabilization of the social system, the institutionalized expectations of which are fundamentally accepted. This pattern seems to be the fundamental one of institutionalized Catholic Christianity, in so far, that is, as the given institutional order really is accepted. In the earlier phases of Catholicism, and in sectarian movements within the church from time to time, the balance has tended to shift to radical rejection of the institutionalized order, making the earning of salvation the overwhelmingly dominant orientation, and treating conformity with institutionalized expectations as altogether secondary if not reprehensible. A similar pattern with certain differences has also existed within Lutheran Christianity.

The second possibility is that where the institutionalized system itself is conceived as containing the potentiality of improvement in such a way as progressively to reduce the area of such discrepancies. This is in general the solution of the modern Western "progressive" orientation. It tends to project the compensation of the discrepancies, not into a transcendental sphere, but into a *future* state of the social system itself. Since, however, this future state almost inevitably must wait for full realization until after the lifetime of the current generation, the question of the personal compensation of living individuals remains imperfectly solved. It somehow has to take the direction of the internalization of norms in such a way that gratification is derived from the feeling of contributing to the realization of a "worth-while" goal, even though the individual actor himself will not experience its realization. Hence, though usually submerged, there tends in fact to be a non-empirical element in the cognitive rationalization of such an orientation, a belief in the "supernatural" possibilities of social development itself.

It is important to note that the above two orientations are in a kind of direct competition with each other, in that projection of compensation for discrepancies into a transcendental sphere or state can readily be interpreted to mean that any attempt realistically to reduce the discrepancies themselves is either superfluous or somehow contrary to a sacred order of things. Thus, for example, in many of the more conservative Catholic societies high mortality in the earlier years of life tends to be accepted as "God's will," which it either is not possible to attempt to do anything about or, even, it is held, might be contrary to religion to do so. The "progressive" attitude that premature death is a problem to be solved by medical or other measures is clearly in conflict with this resigned acceptance. At the same time the discrepancy problem is sufficiently serious so that it cannot be assumed that the "progressive" orientation is always adequate to achieve a general minimization of tension. It is, however, intimately associated with the levels of rationality found in the cultural belief system generally, notably in the place given to science and to its technological applications.

There is, empirically, a gradual shading off from either of the above two types of acceptance of the institutionalized value system, into its rejection. This is in the nature of the case since the problem of discrepancy is the starting point of the present discussion, and while value patterns may be accepted, not everything which empirically happens within the system where they are institutionalized can be. Rejection, when it begins to predominate, may, like acceptance, be oriented in either one of the two major directions which have been discussed. In the one case rejection of the institutionalized value system may be rationalized in terms of transcendental considerations, in the sense that man's relation to the "supernatural" world takes evaluative priority over his relation to the empirical including the social situation, *and the two are held to be in fundamental, irreconcilable conflict.* In the most usual senses this is the case where "salvation" from the "world" is conceived to be the essential goal of human life, and the "world" is held to be, not merely of secondary value, but positively "evil." This is the definition of the situation for the radical religions of salvation. In its most radical form this position would, of course, if taken literally, eliminate all motivation for the fulfillment of role-expectations in the secular social community. It has most frequently appeared as the ideal orientation for a select religious elite rather than for the "laity."

The other basic type of orientation is to project the alternative to the rejected institutionalized order into the empirical social world itself. In the nature of the case this must be a *future* social order, since by definition the orientation is in conflict with the existing society. It may or may not coincide with an actual or alleged previous state. This is the "revolutionary" solution.

In this case, as in that of "progressivism," the question arises of how far this "utopian" future state is cognitively rationalized in terms of empirical considerations. Precisely because, in the Western World, revolutionary utopianism has arisen in a cultural milieu in conscious opposition to the transcendentalism of traditional Christianity, it has tended to be in the "positivistic" tradition itself, and claim to state a position demonstrable by the methods of empirical science. It seems, however, legitimate to suggest that in fact a supernatural order in the above sense plays a central role in this type of orientation, that the "dialectic" and other such entities are more like "providence" than the proponents of "scientific socialism" are wont to admit. Certainly by the criterion we have set forth above, the attitude of respect, they qualify as sacred entities.

The supernatural element may, of course, be explicit. This was the case with Calvinism, in the aspects to which Max Weber called attention. The essential cognitive pattern is the belief in a Divine mission of man, to work for the establishment of the Kingdom of God on Earth. Though the conception of salvation is very much part of Calvinist theology, it is pushed out of the position of constituting a direct goal of action. As decided by God through Predestination it becomes the badge of membership in the appointed company of saints who share the responsibility for implementing the Divine will. The field of action, then, is exclusively oriented in "this world" with the sole exception of the very scant Calvinistic forms of religious observance of which *teaching* the true doctrine is the central focus, though prayer plays a certain part.

The existence of conceptions of a supernatural order raises the question of what types of *action* exist in relation to it. The general integration of cognitive orientation and the goal-directedness of action is such that beliefs in a supernatural order could not very well have the importance which is here being attributed to them, unless they figured in goal-directed action.

What type of action will "make sense" depends of course on what the nature of the supernatural order itself is believed to be. There seem to be three principal types of such "techniques" of directly putting the actor into relation to supernatural entities. The first is ritual, which depends on the conception of the relevant aspects of the supernatural as constituting an order the "laws" of which can be understood and adapted to, in a way which is essentially analogous to instrumental manipulation of the empirical world. Then, the problem is to "do the right thing" in order to bring about the desired goal-state. If the right thing is done this will come about automatically through the operation of the mechanisms and processes of the supernatural order. Ritual may be classed as religious in so far as the goal sought is non-empirical, magical, so far as it is empirical.

The second type of action may be called *supplication*. It depends on the conception of the relevant supernatural entity as itself an actor who must make a decision about what to do in relation to ego. Ego's "technique" then is to try to influence the decision in a direction favorable to the realization of his goal. Prayer in the Christian sense obviously falls in this category, but so does most "sacrifice." For this to make sense the supernatural must be conceived as a "personal," decision-making entity.

Finally the third type, "contemplation" operates on the actor's own state of mind in such a way as to make him "receptive" to the supernatural influence. It may have more of a cognitive emphasis in the direction of coming to "understand," or more of an expressive emphasis on a state of feeling. This type tends to be associated with the conception of the supernatural as impersonal and diffuse, not as operating according either to the pattern of decision-making of actors or to "laws" on the analogy of empirical nature, but as something qualitatively different from either action or nature. It is the conception most conspicuously found in the "mystical" religions such as early Buddhism and Taoism.

Closely related to all three of these techniques, but particularly important in relation to contemplation, is the whole field of techniques of control, which in the most general way may be said to be oriented to the prevention of "interference" from the personality, from the body and from others, with the proper relation to the supernatural. These techniques may take the form of deliberate frustration of major gratification needs. Only when they go beyond the point of imposing disciplines, to that of inflicting 'mortification," should they properly be called "asceticism." Admittedly the line is exceeding difficult to draw, empirically at least.

All belief systems naturally consist of symbols. However, the question arises of whether there may not be certain special features of the place of symbolism in systems of religious belief, which require at least calling attention to.

For this purpose we may return to the methodological canons of science as our major point of reference for the analysis of belief systems in general. The stricter doctrines of scientific methodology would seem to hold that *only* the observational results of very strictly defined operational procedures could legitimately claim to constitute "reality" references as such. Everything else is "construction" on the part of the scientist, most of which of course comes from the cultural tradition in which he works. This everything else, of course, includes the logical framework of "conceptual schemes" within which observations are made and interpreted. But very generally in the history of science it contains much more; it contains whole systems of "models" of "what the empirical entities are like." Thus protons and electrons have been conceived as miniature spherical particles, the atom as a miniature solar system. The introduction of such "realistic" models is psychologically the essential aspect of the "reification" of scientific theories, and the models constitute in practice an essential element of the belief systems which in a cultural sense we call science. These reified "models" of aspects of the empirical world may be said to constitute "intermediate symbolism." They are not the methodologically purified minimum verified content of scientific knowledge, but something in addition which aids in "grasping" that minimum content, which makes the ideas of science "credible." Once established in a scientific tradition such intermediate symbolism may on occasion constitute a serious barrier to further scientific progress.

That these models have been in some sense "believed in" by scientists of the highest levels of professional respectability is beyond question. In all probability the strict observance of the canons of the methodological purists is, as a standard for the actual belief systems of working scientists, psychologically impossible. But in any case if such models play an important part in science itself, it is quite clear that this part is greatly enhanced in the popular belief systems about the empirical world. Even within the sphere of those popular beliefs most nearly sanctioned by science certainly there is an enormous amount of such intermediate symbolism. Thus presumably the man in the street does not really "believe" that most "solid" objects contain far more "empty space" than they do "matter."

The symbolism which is so prolifically developed in religious belief systems should in its cognitive references be considered as intermediate symbolism in this sense. "Anthropomorphism" and "animism" are obvious examples. The psychological functions of believing that God is "an old man with a long white beard" or that the "devil" has horns and a tail are altogether similar to those of believing that an electron is a spherical solid particle of "matter," that is, a little round ball. It makes it possible to have a concrete image to fill an essential place in the cognitive orientation system.

However, intermediate symbolism seems to be more extensively proliferated in the religious field than in the empirical, for two sets of reasons. In the first place, the imposition of strictly cognitive standards of the acceptability of concrete images is more difficult in the non-empirical field than in the empirical. Logical reasoning is available as a cognitive controlling device, but direct observation in the scientific sense by definition is not. In the second place, religious beliefs are evaluative in orientation as well as cognitive. They are a way of ordering the whole action system in certain respects, and hence the kind of cognitive primacy which might maximize control in terms of cognitive standards is seldom present.

Nevertheless, in the religious traditions where there has developed a philosophical tradition of a sophistication at all comparable with that of modern science, much at least of this intermediate symbolism has dropped away. Thus Plato no longer believed in the existence of the Homeric Gods in a literal sense, and certainly not in all the tales that were told about them in the mythological tradition. Similarly in sophisticated Christian theology anthropomorphism has been pretty well eliminated, though not, of course, in popular belief. In general it may be said that in religious systems which have reached sophisticated philosophical levels, there is an inevitable tension between the philosophical objections to elaborate intermediate symbolism and the popular need for it. More will have to be said about this subject in connection with expressive symbolism below.

Before discussing such symbolism, however, a final word must be said about the other side of the "causal chain" as between religious beliefs and the institutionalized social order. The starting points which we took in analyzing the problems of religious belief systems were, following Max Weber, the inevitable discrepancies between the expectations institutionalized in a social value system, and certain features of the actual course of events. The relation between them is such that the religious belief system not only "rationalizes" an existing and independently given set of institutionalized value-orientations, it must to a greater or less degree be itself constitutive of it. This much follows directly from the tendency to pattern-consistency in the cultural tradition as a whole.

There is, however, as we have seen, always more or less tension involved in such actual relationships within the social system. This tension may, under certain circumstances, work out so that a system of religious beliefs, for example one oriented to radical salvation, becomes the cultural focus of an important movement of social change. In so far as such a movement becomes a collectivity and wins converts there immediately arises the question of the consequences of the institutionalization of these beliefs and the value-orientations implied in them for the collectivity and for the social system beyond it. In so far as the belief system becomes institutionalized, belief in the transcendental locus of values and goals becomes itself part of the social situation, and, therefore, paradoxically it would seem, part of the *empirical* world. Members of the society face the very practical fact that conformity with the expectations defined by the transcendentally oriented religious beliefs is institutionally expected and all the principal elements of the sanction system come to be mobilized about the upholding of this conformity. "Worldly interests," are thereby inevitably enlisted in the motivation of religious conformity, but by the same token, the pursuit of religious values inevitably becomes implicated in worldly affairs, for example, if religion is taken seriously enough, the "church," or its functional equivalent, inevitably acquires prestige and power in a "worldly" as well as a "spiritual" sense. The outcome is likely to be a highly unstable equilibrium in which it is unlikely that the religious orientation itself will remain entirely unchanged for long. This "paradox of institutionalization" applies equally to radically utopian belief systems and the corresponding value-orientations. The problems of this area will be somewhat further discussed below in connection with social change, but in the main they must be relegated to the more specialized study of the sociology of religion.

§ THE INDEPENDENCE AND INTERDEPENDENCE OF BELIEF SYSTEMS AND VALUE-ORIENTATIONS

BELIEF systems and systems of value-orientation are both parts of the cultural tradition and, as such, there is pressure for them to form a consistent system of patterns. They are, however, anchored as it were in different foci of the action system. Belief systems involve an independent orientation to a "reality" which has properties independent of the actor who attempts to understand it cognitively. He cannot by willing or wishing make it what he would like it to be but must, in the structure of his beliefs, in some sense "adapt" himself to it. Patterns of value-orientation, on the other hand, formulate the directions of choice in the dilemmas of action. They are "guided" by beliefs, but only partially determined by them since they are ways of organizing the *totality* of interests involved in the system of action, interests which are cathectic and evaluative as well as cognitive. The commitment involved in a value-orientation is not only a commitment to accept cognitively the logical consequences of a set of cognitive beliefs, though it may and almost always will include this, but it is *also* a commitment to a selection among the opportunities for gratification possible in the situation, the striving for some but equally the sacrifice of others which, with a different value-orientation, might have been possible. Value-orientation patterns are, as we have seen, points at which organization relative to all the dominant factors of the action system come to focus, adaptation to "reality" through cognition, the gratification-interests of the actor, the commitment to patterns of expressive symbolism, and the functional exigencies of the social interrelationship system.

In judging the mutual interdependence of beliefs and value-patterns it is, however, important to distinguish two fundamental types of "reality," that is, classes of object, to which the beliefs are oriented, namely, physical objects and social objects or systems of action. The essential point is, of course, that in the case of physical objects what the objects *are at any given moment* is not in any sense a function of beliefs. In so far as they have been modified by previous action, are, that is, to some extent, "artifacts," this modification process has, of course, been a function of action, and hence of the beliefs of the agent of this modification as one element of action. Social objects, on the other hand, are at a given moment partly a function of *their* beliefs (not those of the observer). In the case of the individual actor it is his beliefs, in that of a social system, those shared by its constituent actors. This difference in turn defines a fundamental difference in possibilities of influence of the two classes of objects. A physical object may be modified by the action of a human being upon it, and this action may be influenced by *his* beliefs. But it cannot be modified by attempting to alter *the object's* beliefs, since it has none. A social object may, however, be modified not only by a process involving the beliefs of the actor attempting to modify it, but by his attempting to alter *its* beliefs since these constitute one critical aspect of what the social object *is*.

In relation to physical objects, then, human beliefs can basically vary only with reference to two sets of considerations. The first of these is the cognitive validity of the beliefs, the second their "meaning" for human interests. The cognitive processes are, as we know, interdependent with the other elements of motivational process so that concrete beliefs about physical objects may, as we have seen, be distorted by the influence of the non-cognitive components of action. Thus, whether external nature is or is not "controllable," and to what degree in the interest of human goals, is a purely cognitive problem, and beliefs about it are correct or incorrect. However, as a function of *other* than cognitive interests there may be "biases" introduced into cognitive belief systems in this sphere, including those which are a result of value-orientations. Thus, a universalistic achievement value-orientation will tend to maximize if not exaggerate belief in the controllability of external nature because of the interest in achievement. On the other hand, a particularistic-ascriptive value-orientation will tend to lack interest in such controllability and may well be combined with a belief system which underrates the degree to which this is possible. The case is similar with the problem of "human nature" in the sense of the organism, e.g., as to how far its impulses or other processes are understandable and controllable and by what means. Modern medicine is a dramatic example of the maximization of belief in controllability of organic processes.

The dimension of belief in whether nature or human nature is basically favorable to human interests, is "good" or "evil," introduces the evaluative factor in the sense of the above discussion. Such a question is not answerable only in cognitive terms but only by referring a cognitive belief to an evaluative context, namely by assessing the probable consequences of the state of affairs formulated in the belief system for certain non-cognitive interests, cathectic and/or evaluative.

When we turn to beliefs about social objects a further complication is introduced, by the fact already noted that its beliefs are partly constitutive of the social object itself. Here also, however, the same fundamental discrimination must be made. There are purely cognitive elements in such belief systems, which are beliefs relative to the nature and functioning of action systems. In a social ideology there is always a system of explicit or implicit sociological propositions which must be assessed by standards of cognitive validity. In terms of the analysis in previous chapters we may say that these concern the adaptive problems of the social system relative to a given pattern of value-orientation. How far and under what conditions is it possible to institutionalize the values in question?

But we cannot say that the cognitive element in the concrete evaluative belief system is simply "determined" by or identical with the value-orientation patterns, in this case any more than in that of physical objects. In such a case there would be no possible basis for a distinction between utopian patterns of ideology and realistic patterns. Because, however, of the place of culture in action systems the value-orientation element may in this case have a more prominent part in the determination of the *total* orientation to social objects than in the case of physical objects. In fundamental theoretical principle, however, the relation between the independence and the interdependence of the two components of culture is the same in both cases.[21]

Finally, a further word may be said about certain relations of selective "affinity" between types of evaluative belief systems and particular patterns of value-orientation. We may illustrate in terms of the ways in which belief systems have handled the problems of discrepancy between institutionalized expectations and the actual outcome of events. In the first place we may say that, as argued above, the decision whether or not the *Ausgleich* can be "projected" into a transcendental sphere clearly is a function of the belief system, of the status of the supernatural world in that system. However much belief in such a supernatural world may involve "wishful thinking," the two phases must be considered interdependent, not the beliefs purely a "projection" of gratification interests or vice versa. Such a belief system, firmly entrenched, would, however, seem necessarily to lead to a lessening of incentive to the "progressive" direction of solution of the dilemma of discrepancy. In general we may say it will tend to lessen the emphasis on the value of achievement in secular social action. In fact we do find a correlation be-

[21] The problems just discussed are important to the position taken by Florence Kluckhohn in her paper, "Dominant and Variant Profiles of Cultural Orientation," *Social Forces*, May, 1950. We feel that in certain respects Dr. Kluckhohn's very suggestive analysis suffers from her failure to discriminate belief systems and value-orientation patterns and to make allowance for their independent variability.

tween a firmly institutionalized belief in supernatural compensation and an ascriptive emphasis in the institutionalized value-system. Thus mediaeval European society elevated the hereditary principle to a very high level in its secular value-system. The progressivism of the modern Western world seems to be dependent on, as well as a determinant of, the "this-worldliness" of our belief systems.

Similarly, where radical rejection of an institutionalized order is involved, we may suppose that value-orientations and cathectic considerations in certain cases have a certain primacy over the belief system itself. The circumstances in which such a movement arises at least strongly conduce to an element of cognitive distortion because of the prominent part played by ambivalent motivations. However, the strong tendency of such a movement is in its belief system to define an ideal state as drastically contrasting with the institutionalized order which has been rejected. This conception of an ideal state in turn, as embodied in the ideology of a revolutionary movement, strongly tends to favor a universalistic-ascriptive value-pattern, with all the implications for its institutionalization which we have reviewed above.

Hence we must conclude that the belief system element of the cultural tradition has a "strain to consistency" with the value-orientation element. It is obviously impossible for them to vary at random relative to each other. But value-orientations are anchored in interest complexes in a different way and on a different level from belief systems so that it is equally impossible to derive the belief system of a society by treating it as a simple "projection" of its value-orientation patterns on "reality" or vice versa to deduce the value-orientation patterns from the belief system without regard to the function of the latter in integrating the other components of the system of action.

IX EXPRESSIVE SYMBOLS AND

THE SOCIAL SYSTEM: THE COMMUNICATION OF AFFECT

THE field of expressive symbolism is, in a theoretical sense, one of the least developed parts of the theory of action. It will not, therefore, be possible to present as well worked-out an analysis of its place in relation to the social system as has been done for belief systems.

Expressive symbols constitute that part of the cultural tradition relative to which expressive interests in the sense defined in Chapter II have primacy. In the "purest" form they constitute the cultural patterning of action of the expressive type where the interest in immediate gratifications is primary and neither instrumental nor evaluative considerations have primacy. It should immediately be pointed out that this does not in the least imply that such expressive interests are in any sense crudely "hedonistic." They consist in the primacy of the interest in immediate gratification of *whatever* need-dispositions are relevant in the action context in question. These may be need-dispositions to care for others, or to "create" highly abstract ideas or cultural forms. The essential point is the primacy of "acting out" the need-disposition itself rather than subordinating gratification to a goal outside the immediate situation or to a restrictive norm. The "quality" of the need-disposition is not at issue.

Expressive action, in our central paradigm, as a type of action, occupies a place parallel with that of the instrumental type. Like all action it is culturally patterned or formed. Expressive symbols then

384

are the symbol-systems through which expressive action is oriented to the situation. Again like all of culture it has a normative aspect. As this has been stated above, there are appreciative standards in the cultural tradition by which expressive interests and actions are judged. These standards constitute the essential ordering principles of systems of expressive symbols.

In expressive action as such, systems of expressive symbols, including the relevant appreciative standards, have a place homologous to that of belief systems in instrumentally oriented action. They constitute the cultural element which has primacy in the patterning of the concrete action processes. Cognitive patterns, or beliefs, may themselves become the focus of a special type of instrumental activity which we have called investigation. Similarly, expressive symbol systems may themselves be developed as the goal of a type of instrumentally oriented activity, which may be called "artistic creation." This must be clearly distinguished from expressive action itself, which is "acting out" *in terms of* a pattern of expressive symbolism, not the process of deliberately creating such a pattern.

Of course only a small part of the expressive symbolism of a culture is the product of deliberate artistic creation just as very much of its cognitive orientation patterning is not the result of scientific or philosophical investigation, but has grown up "spontaneously" in the course of action processes where other interests have had primacy.

Finally, just as cognitive and evaluative interests may be fused in ideological and religious belief systems, so expressive and evaluative interests may be fused in relation to systems of expressive symbols. Where this evaluative interest involves symbolic references to a supernatural order we will speak of religious symbolism. Where it does not, we shall speak simply of evaluative symbolism, as in the case of symbolic acts of solidarity with the other members of a collectivity or the symbolization of an attachment to a social object.

As we have stated, expressive symbolism is the primary cultural component in any form of expressive action, and is involved in some way in all types of action. But in attempting to analyze the most important modes of relation of systems of expressive symbolism to the social system, it seems best to start, once more, with the paradigm of social interaction. In this connection we have pointed out repeatedly that specific actions and expectations tend to become organized and generalized around the reciprocal attitudes of ego and alter toward each other, and toward the common cultural patterns which define the situation for the interaction process.

Expressive symbolism is that part of the cultural tradition most directly integrated with the cathectic interests of the actor. In so far as it is the reciprocity of attitude which becomes the primary focus of these cathectic interests, it follows that expressive symbolism will tend to be organized relative to these attitudes as a point of reference.

From this point of view the concrete expressive symbols which are part of the process of interaction serve a threefold function, as do all elements of culture: 1) they aid in communication between the interacting parties, in this case the communication of cathectic "meanings"; 2) they organize the interaction process through normative regulation, through imposing appreciative standards on it; and 3) they serve as direct objects for the gratification of the relevant need-dispositions. The special feature of this aspect of culture is the differentiation of a system of symbols with respect to all of these functions, from other elements of culture through the primacy of the expressive interest.

The most important starting point of our analysis is the recognition that the organization of orientations within the interactive relationship about reciprocity of attitudes *already and in itself*, constitutes the development of an expressive symbol-system. This is because the particular discrete act acquires a *meaning* which in some way involves a reference beyond the "intrinsic" significance of the particular act itself. It is fitted into a context of association in such a way that the whole complex of associated acts is invested with a cathectic significance. Once this has happened it is no longer possible to isolate the specific act from the complex in which it has become embedded; it has acquired a meaning which is added to its immediate intrinsic significance.[1] Thus the response of the mother to the crying of a child comes, apparently very early, to be felt as

[1] It thus fulfills Durkheim's main criterion of a symbol, that its meaning is "superadded" to its intrinsic properties.

"symbolic" of her attitude toward the child, not merely as an instrumental measure of relieving the particular distress which occasioned
the crying. We may say, then, that the prototype of the expressive
symbol, within the context of interaction, is the *symbolic act*. It also
follows that in a stabilized interaction system all acts have this
symbolic quality to some degree, all serve as expressive symbols.
They are the modes of gratification of ego's need-dispositions and at
the same time signs to alter of what ego's attitudes toward him are.

In order to understand the significance of this it is exceedingly
important to see the problem in the context of the reciprocal symmetry of interactive relationships. It is an unreal abstraction to consider only that the symbolic act is of gratificatory significance to ego
and symbolic significance to alter, because in the nature of the interactive process it must acquire *both* types of significance for *both* ego
and alter. We may speak of this as the internalization of the expressive symbolism in a sense directly parallel to that in which we have
spoken of the internalization of moral norms. Ego's act has an
acquired gratificatory significance to alter, because in addition to
whatever intrinsic significance it may possess, it has the meaning of
a manifestation of ego's attitudes toward alter, and hence shares the
affective significance which the whole complex of these attitudes
and their manifestation have. By a process of "association," then,
ego's symbolic act is a focus of gratification, if it indicates the attitude for which alter "hopes," and it is deprivational if it frustrates
his hopes. Similarly such acts become the focus of anxieties. Thus
the fact that the act is an expressive act for ego, that is that it grati-
fies a need disposition of his, and that it is also oriented toward alter,
means that in a stabilized interaction relationship it must acquire an
expressive significance for alter. It must be cathected and its performance on ego's part become directly either gratifying or deprivational to alter.

If we regard symbolic acts occurring within the interaction
process as the focus of the genesis of expressive symbolism, we can
then proceed to analyze the generalization of this symbolic significance, that is of symbolization of the relevant attitudes, to objects
other than acts. Such objects, it is evident, come to be drawn into
the associational complex which is organized about the reciprocal
attitudes of ego and alter. Our classification of the objects in the

situation gives us the basis for such an analysis of generalization. In the first place ego and alter themselves, as objects to each other, come to be drawn in. In so far as they are treated as actors, it is their acts which are the symbols. But these acts may be "interpreted" as manifestations of action-relevant qualities. The feeling, then, that alter is an "honest man" or a "very friendly person" may be generalized in this direction.

Secondly, the bodies of ego and alter as a special class of physical objects are obviously so closely associated with their action that their features inevitably acquire symbolic significance and come to be cathected. Physical traits such as stature, body shape, hair color, facial features and the like are involved. Fundamental aspects of the significance of the anatomical differences of the sexes also fit into this context. This is in all probability the case with the basic erotic symbolism which has played such a prominent part in psychoanalytic theory. The penis, for example, is a feature of the body around which a whole complex of sentiments may cluster, both in relation to ego's own attitudes toward himself, and to those of alter. Thus the insistence in Freudian theory that many other objects should be treated as symbols of the penis is correct but is only one side of the picture. There is every reason to believe that the penis is itself a symbolic object to a high degree and that a substantial part of its psychological significance is to be interpreted in the light of this fact. In more general terms it may perhaps be said that "one way" symbolic significance, as exemplified in the case of Freudian sexual symbolism, constitutes a limiting case. The more general case is the symbolic or associational *complex* in which in some sense and to some degree every item symbolizes every other. Thus elongated objects may symbolize the penis but in turn the penis symbolizes the "masculinity" of its possessor and the whole complex of qualities and attitudes comprised under this term.

Third, there is the whole realm of physical objects besides the organisms of ego and of the relevant alters. These are the physical objects which constitute the immediate physical environment of the interaction process and which are involved in it, instrumentally or otherwise. One of the most obvious examples is clothing. Because of its direct relation to the body, and the fact that visual impressions of the body include clothing, clothing becomes one of the main foci of sentiments associated with the body. In addition clothing is considerably more subject to manipulative modification than are most of the features of the body itself, and hence presents a highly suitable medium for expressive purposes. Very similar considerations apply to the premises in which important activities take place, such as the home, and to its furnishings and utensils and the like.

Finally cultural objects themselves are of course also drawn into the association complex. The type of case of particular relevance here is that of the symbolic creations which have no "use" beyond their expressive significance. The ideal type is that of "works of art." There is always a physical aspect of a concrete work of art, but the more essential one is the cultural. In the pure type of the work of art the physical object, or even the concrete action process, e.g., in the case of "playing" a musical composition, would not be cathected but for its significance in the context of expressive symbolism.

If this approach to the problem of expressive symbolism is accepted, then there should be two primary bases of classification of types of such symbolism which cross-cut each other. The first has just been reviewed, namely, the classes of objects to which such symbolic significance has become or may become attached. The second is in terms of the fundamental types of attitudinal orientation around which the interaction process itself comes to be organized. In so far as alters are the direct objects of orientation we have called these the types of attachment and classified them in terms of the two pattern variables of affectivity-neutrality and specificity-diffuseness. The four major types, then, are receptiveness-response, love, approval and esteem.

We may, then, speak of any symbolic entity, an act, a quality of personality or of the organism, a physical object or a cultural pattern, as symbolic of any one of these four basic attitude types. This may be illustrated for two types of relationship, an erotic love relationship and one organized about attitudes of esteem.

The love relationship is defined as diffuse and affective. The affectivity specifically includes, though in such a case it cannot be confined to, mutuality of erotic gratifications. Erotic gratifications here specifically involve certain types of somatic stimulations and processes. Hence in the erotic aspect of the relationship the bodies of the parties have particular significances. The first aspect, then, of the expressive symbolism is the organization of the erotically significant features of the body of each around the "genital" level of erotic gratification. This means a certain symbolic priority of genital intercourse over other possibilities of mutual erotic gratification; rather generally these are standards of *taste* with respect to the expression of this relative to other elements of the total erotic complex. Some other practices such as kissing, and some other elements of "foreplay" may be allowable, but only in the proper manner and on the proper occasions. Others, what are usually called the "perversions," tend to be tabooed.

There is further, most emphatically a complex of expressive symbolism in terms of the regulation of occasions and the physical setting and associated physical objects for erotic activities. Privacy for all the specifically erotic activities is felt in our society to be extremely important. "Aesthetically" attractive surroundings are also generally involved. Clothing acquires high significance, including just the proper occasions and manner for its removal.

But quite clearly if the relationship is a *love* relationship, the associated expressive symbolism will not be confined to acts and occasions of immediate erotic gratification. It will include such symbolic acts as affectionate or endearing speech, exchange of gifts of various sorts, sharing of gratificatory activities in other connections, such as entertainment, acting and dressing to "please" the other and a whole variety of other symbolic acts and their associated contexts.

In its involvement in the social system in a larger way the erotic love relationship is universally associated with marriage, reproduction, and parenthood. The complex of expressive symbolism, therefore, extends beyond the context more immediately relevant to erotic gratification or even individual mutuality of diffuse love-gratifications. The erotic love relationship becomes a major nucleus of the kinship system with all that that implies. The erotic relationship itself is thus tied in with the acceptance of the parental roles and their responsibilities.

With this step, the expressive symbolism of the particular erotic relationship merges into that integrated with and part of the culture of a larger collectivity, the kinship unit. The orientation to "romantic love" is only partially isolable. As a part of our culture its symbolism is thus part of the larger complex of the symbolism of the sex roles generally and of the kinship system. In part this attitude of romantic love constitutes a field of partial and sometimes radical deviance from the completeness of that integration, for example in the youth culture aspects, which attempt a kind of "artificial" isolation from the possible implications for marriage and later parenthood. This relative isolation is to be analyzed in the general terms used in the analysis of structured strains in the social system and of tendencies to deviance.

It is not necessary to follow these problems further here. The important point is to show the organization of the system of expressive symbols about the attitudinal structure of the relationship and the cathectic interests involved in it. From this point of view the erotic activities themselves, in addition to their significance as direct sources of gratification, constitute an integral part of the system of expressive symbolism. This is indeed the main sense in which they must be said to be a function of something other than "primary drives." Essentially the same can be said about the erotically relevant features of the organism. The penis, the breast, etc., are expressive symbols and a large part of their erotic significance derives from this fact. They can, of course, be the referents for further elaborations of symbolization, as is well known. But these primarily erotic references of the system of expressive symbolization, are continuous with a much more widely ramifying complex, which extends to all aspects of the behavior relevant to the interaction and to all classes of objects involved in the behavior.

Essentially similar considerations apply, with the appropriate differences, to the cases where an attitude of approval or esteem is the primary basis of organization of the interactive relationship. A good example is the relation between teacher and student, let us say in a technical field of professional training. In so far as the relationship is one of a particularized attachment, it focuses, on the student's part, on "admiration" for the teacher's competence and performances in the field. The counterpart on the teacher's part is "respect" for the student's ability and "promise," and for his performances in the course of training. Here, though in another context the actions may be of primarily instrumental significance, they also have an aspect as expressive symbols.

This is essentially what is implied in the affectively neutral aspect of the attachment pattern. In other words, the expressive symbolism in this case belongs to the evaluative category, not the cathectic or pure-type expressive. This fusion of evaluative and cathectic elements is the fundamental basis of the motivational integration involved in the institutionalization of affectively neutral patterns, as has several times been pointed out. The relevant symbolization has the same fundamental characteristics.

Given this framework, however, the essential structure of the complex of expressive symbolism is the same as in the case of the erotic love relationship. Particular acts acquire symbolic significance relative to the cathectic elements of the attachment. In the first instance we may say these will consist in acts of valued professional achievement. These acts may be directly experienced by the student, as in hearing a lecture, watching and participating in the conduct of a seminar discussion, or watching the actual operation of a bit of research technique. It may then extend to the appreciation of the symbolic products of such activity, notably of course reading what the teacher has written.

Again, the complex will tend to be extended to other objects in the context of the teacher's activity, to the organizational setting in which he works and his role in it, to premises, the buildings, rooms and their contents. How far this will extend will depend both on the intensity of the cathexis and on how far it is limited to approval in the specifically professional context, or becomes a diffuse attitude of esteem, which will therefore mean admiration not only for the teacher's professional competence and achievement, but for him more generally as a man. In that case there is very likely to be a cathexis of a variety of aspects of the teacher's general style of life, his tastes in clothing or in literature or hobbies, a predisposition to think well of his wife and many other things.

In such a case the student will tend to become sensitized to the attitudes of the teacher toward him, and to interpret acts of attention to him personally as expressions of this attitude, or of course lack of attention where it might have occurred as expression of a negative attitude. This will in the first place center in acts which may be interpreted as direct recognition of his own achievements or qualities, such as a high grade on a paper, or praise for a piece of work. But it may extend to other objects not intrinsically connected with professional achievement, such as an act of kindness or consideration. The dynamic relations of the sentiments of approval and esteem and those of friendliness are so close that it is difficult for them not to occur together to an important degree.

In both types of relationship context there is a process of selection of appropriate symbolization of the relevant attitudes from among the possibilities available in the situation. This selection process ranges from the lending of symbolic significance at the "core" to the intrinsically strategic acts and objects, to the cathexis of more and more "arbitrarily" associated parts of the context. In the affectively positive case the "intrinsic" elements are those which, apart from special processes of symbolic association, are features of the object's and of ego's relation to them which are the focus of their capacity to produce direct gratifications for him. This capacity may, as is certainly true in the erotic case, be the consequence in important part of previous symbolic associations; this is what was meant by saying above that the erotically significant parts of the body and the acts of erotic gratification themselves constitute expressive symbols. But at any given stage of the development of an action system, certain gratification-opportunities will have particularly strategic significance in the relationship context in question, and there will be more and more shading off from these to the increasingly "arbitrary" fringes of the association complex.

In the affectively neutral case, similarly, the core will be the endowment with cathectically symbolic significance, of the acts and objects which are intrinsically essential to the fulfillment of the relevant role-expectations. In the case discussed above, that consisted essentially in professional performances themselves and the objects instrumentally essential to them, or produced by them. From this core there is again a shading off into more and more remote ranges of an associational complex, until the cathexis, for example, of the teacher's taste in neckties has very little intrinsically to do with the admiration of his professional competence, but may yet come to be of considerable symbolic significance.

The status of the selectively cathected acts and objects as expressive symbols has, as in the case of the other elements of culture, a tendency to become institutionalized. Whatever the complicated balance of psychological forces involved, the confining of approved erotic gratification to "normal heterosexual" activities may be regarded as primarily a case of the institutionalization of a pattern of expressive symbolism in this area, which is nonetheless learned and institutionalized for the fact that it is so nearly universal as the norm in human societies. Similarly the admiration of competent professional achievement is again in one aspect a pattern of institutionalized expressive symbolism where the professional role itself is institutionalized.

Institutionalization, however, does not apply only to the core of the association complex. Various elements of context are also involved. A good example in the erotic case is the imperative of privacy for sexual activities. For the professional case, that a teacher should dress in accord with the "dignity" of his position is an example.

With institutionalization there is always an evaluative element introduced into the orientation of the actor to and through the expressive symbolism, *in addition* to that involved in the symbolization of affectively neutral patterns. Thus a student may, through his previous socialization, have acquired an affectively neutral need-disposition to admire competent professional performance in a field. But if he enters into an institutionalized relationship to a teacher he assumes an additional obligation to respect his teacher's professional "authority." The respect for competence becomes an institutionalized common value of the collectivity to which they *both* belong. This should, therefore, not be confused with the evaluative element involved in the discipline necessary to accept an affectively neutral orientation at all. Institutionalization, however, is of course the mechanism of stabilization of the symbol system on a cultural basis, so it can be transmitted as an organized entity.

§ EXPRESSIVE SYMBOLISM AND COLLECTIVITIES

INTERACTIVE relationships and the reciprocal roles of the parties constitute, on the relevant level, the units of which all social systems are composed. But certain further considerations come to be involved on the higher levels of organization of collectivities. With extension of the role system beyond the particular interactive relationship, the problem arises of the extent to which expressive symbolism is commonly shared within the wider role system. There is further the question of whether or not the symbolism is directly integrated with the common values which are constitutive of the collectivity and may, therefore, be considered to be symbols of the solidarity of the collectivity. On these two bases three major types of expressive symbolism extending beyond the diadic relationship need to be distinguished. First are those symbols which are shared by the different sub-units of the social system, individual actors or sub-collectivities, without implying the existence of a bond of solidarity between them. These may be said to constitute the "common style" of these units within what in this respect is a common culture. Thus there may be common elements of style in the house furnishings of many different households, without this in any direct way symbolizing the solidarity of these households as members of the same collectivity.

Secondly, there may be symbolism which is essentially symbolism of the collectivity as such, not merely the common symbolism of its sub-units. This, however, needs to be subdivided into two classes, according to whether it is "purely expressive" or is evaluative in emphasis, according that is, to the affectivity-neutrality variable. The purely expressive type then would constitute the "acting out" of the need-dispositions constitutive of the collectivity, the "feeling of solidarity" of its members, but without direct involvement of morally evaluative considerations, except in that, through institutionalization, participation, i.e., acceptance of such symbolism becomes an obligation of collectivity membership. Family "observances" as of Thanksgiving and Christmas would be a good example of this type. These occasions may have other, namely religious, connotations in the cultural tradition, but in contemporary society much of the strictly religious connotation is subordinated to this direct familial expressionalism. This is also a prominent aspect of birthday celebrations and other anniversaries. They are thus ways of affirming the solidarity of the collectivity, but belong in the category of "recreation" not of Durkheim's *vie sérieuse*.

From these types of observance must be distinguished collective "rituals" where the attitude of moral respect is predominant, which are therefore marked by "solemnity." These types of expressive symbols may be considered as manifesting and regulating the common moral sentiments or need-dispositions of the members of the collectivity. It is this type which Durkheim so clearly illuminated in his analysis of religious ritual in its symbolic aspects. However, from the present point of view by no means all collectively moral expressions of solidarity should be called religious. In order to differentiate what does and does not belong in the religious category it is necessary to carry the analysis of possible relations of expressive symbolism to the collectivity a step farther.

In discussing belief systems in the previous chapter the distinction was made between ideologies and religious belief systems. Both were, to be sure, characterized by the fusion of cognitive and evaluative interests, and thus distinguished from scientific and philosophical beliefs as such. However, religious beliefs were distinguished from ideological by the non-empirical cognitive references involving relation to a supernatural order. This supernatural order in turn was related to the "rationalization," that is, the cognitive legitimation, of those phases of human experience which did not fully fit with the institutionalized expectations embodying the dominant value system.

Parallel with the cognitive problems of meaning involved in these areas of experience run a series of cathectic or emotional problems of "adjustment." These experiences are difficult to "take" precisely because they involve the frustration of established and legitimized expectations. But from the expressive point of view these phenomena must be placed in a still wider context.

It is inherent in the view of social action taken here that all such action involves tensions and the necessity of the imposition of frustrations and disciplines of the most various sorts. This fact underlies the occurrence of a variety of rhythmic cycles of effort and rest, of discipline and permissive release and the like. Sleep is clearly one of the most fundamental of these tension release phenomena, which though it has biological foundations is nevertheless profoundly influenced by interaction on socio-cultural levels.

Affective primacy is characteristic of the above phenomena. Like all the fundamentals of behavior orientation, these rhythms come to be built into the structure of social systems, so that certain of these predominantly affective release phenomena come to be collectively shared, and the requisite expressive symbolism institutionalized on the bases discussed above. There are, however, areas where the adjustment problems are particularly crucial from the point of view of the stability of the social system, and where the emotional adjustment aspect is particularly intimately connected with the belief system in the area of the "supernatural." It is this sphere of fusion of religious beliefs and the expressive symbolism of affective adjustment which is the religious sphere of expressive symbolism as such.

This religious sphere was defined in the last chapter as involving the legitimation of orientations, on occasion, *both* within the sphere of institutionalized value-orientations which constitute the framework of the main social structure, and in the areas of discrepancy relative to the institutionalized expectations. We may, therefore, have religious symbolism expressive of the solidarity of the main institutionalized collectivities. We also have religious symbolism which serves as an institutionalized channel for the adjustment of emotional strains in the discrepancy areas.

The first was what Durkheim regarded as the core type of religious ritual, the symbolic expression of the solidarity of the group. The second was the type especially emphasized by Malinowski, the type case being the funeral ceremonial. In this case it is not primarily an expression of the common moral sentiments of the collectivity, though that is also generally involved, but an expression of the adjustment of individuals under strain in such a way that their orientation is kept in line with an institutionalized pattern. Solidarity, however, as we have seen provides the element of support in this process of social control. The religious type of expression of group solidarity is to be distinguished from collective solidarity symbolism which is evaluative in emphasis, but not religious in that there is no reference to legitimation in terms of a supernatural order. Examples would be a patriotic observance, such as that of the Fourth of July in this country, or the ceremonial of a university Commencement.

In all of these cases, as in that of the diadic interactive relationship, we may regard the symbolic act as the core phenomenon. The essential point is that the need-dispositions which are being symbolically manifested are those which involve the institutionalized and internalized common value-orientations which constitute the collectivity. This gives a strong premium on performance of these symbolic acts in common, so that the sharing aspect is itself directly symbolized.

But as in the diadic case, the associational complex extends beyond the symbolic acts themselves. First it should, of course, be noted that cognitive orientation patterns are an integral part of concrete acts. Hence the beliefs in terms of which the acts are given meaning are themselves, in one aspect, *also* expressive symbols; they must be cathected as part of the total complex. This is particularly important in the case of many religious beliefs because of the prominence of what we have above called "intermediate" symbolism in that field.[2] Indeed it is frequently the case in this field that for a particular belief pattern its significance as a complex of expressive symbols has primacy over the strictly cognitive aspect. Broadly speaking this may be said to be true of "mythology" in the religious field as distinguished from "dogma." When it is said that a myth "explains" the meaning of a ritual, for instance, frequently the ritual activity consists in dramatic portrayal of certain mythological characters and their activities. The mythological personages themselves are to a high degree expressive symbols on which certain need-dispositions of the members of the collectivity are "projected." Their significance lies in their appropriateness in this context rather than in the strictly cognitive validity of any propositions.

As in the diadic cases analyzed above, the complex of symbolic association then extends to other aspects of the total action complex, to places, buildings, occasions, and physical objects which, for instance, serve as ritual paraphernalia. The whole associated complex comes to be cathected and the appropriate attitudes applied to all the objects within it. It is essentially by this process that physical objects, vestments, edifices, etc., come to be treated as sacred objects in a religious sense.

We find, then, that the collective aspect of expressive symbolism involves a whole series of differentiations of types. There is the uniformity of style within a collectivity. Then there are the modes of expression of collective sentiments, which are subdivided into the directly and primarily expressive, and the evaluative or moral. The latter in turn may or may not be primarily religious, and both may

[2] See above, Chapter VIII, pp. 376-378.

be oriented more to the expression of sentiments relative to established routine orientations, or to adjustment to the discrepancies from institutionalized expectations.

§ ROLE DIFFERENTIATION WITH RESPECT TO EXPRESSIVE SYMBOLISM

THE above treatment of the most general relation of expressive symbolism to collectivities was confined to the "common" aspects, to the respects in which symbolic acts and the other symbolic objects are shared by all members of a given collectivity. But in this as in other respects there tend to be internal differentiations of interest and hence of role as between different members and classes of members of any given collectivity. There are two types of such differentiation which will be briefly treated here. The first concerns the respects in which the acts and other elements of the associated symbolic complex, which have special symbolic significance in the collectivity in question, come to be allocated to specialized roles, and to the actors who perform them. With respect then to symbolic as well as to instrumental significance to the collectivity, there is a "division of labor" which underlies the structure of the system of expressive symbolism itself. Secondly, expressive symbolism generally is "embedded" in concrete action, and is ancillary to whatever interests may be dominant in that concrete activity. But just as there may be a specialization of interest in cognitive problems as such, so "aesthetic" or appreciative problems may become the focus of a specialized interest. This interest becomes that in creating new patterns of expressive symbolism, and in evaluating those which exist or are in process of creation. Like cognitive specialization in turn the aesthetic interest may come to be the primary determinative focus of a class of specialized roles. At this point we may speak of the emergence of the "artist" as a specialized role type homologous with the specialists in cognitive interests, the scientist or the philosopher.

To some significant degree every role which is intrinsically differentiated from other roles is by the same token a specialized symbolic role. This follows from the fact that the role is a crucial unit in the action; it and the incumbent are objects which as such acquire symbolic significances in the expressive "economy." Here as elsewhere there is a complex relation between the symbolic significance of the role, and of the actor who plays it as a personality.

Since the role is from one point of view the principal focus of expectations in the interaction process, the considerations about the relation of expressive symbolism outlined above apply directly here. From this point of view the role is an organized complex of particular acts, organized in such a way that reciprocal attitudes can become significant. Indeed the organization of particular acts relative to other actors, the emergence of attitudes as crucial, and the symbolic significance of roles are all part of the same complex, and are inseparable from one another.

Then the analysis of symbolic roles as foci for the organization of expressive symbol systems, must follow the general analysis of the bases of role-differentiation within social systems, as these have been set forth above. Within this it is the paradigm of cathectic or expressive orientations which should form the focus.

In current psychological terminology, roles, and their incumbents as persons, become the objects of "projection" from the need-disposition systems of other actors. The phenomenon has been classically demonstrated in the case of the "transference" which occurs in the relation of patient to psychotherapist. In this case, however, the projected role of the therapist is in sharp contrast to his institutionalized role, and this duality forms a principal "lever" for the psychotherapeutic process.

The projections in question may or may not be integrated with the institutionalized role structure, and there may be more or less well-marked duality phenomena as in the case of psychotherapy. But in any case the tendency will be for the expressive symbolic significance of roles to follow the main lines of differentiation which are inherent in the differentiations of the social structure generally.

The first type of case we may call attention to is the expressive aspect of leadership roles. In the ideal type the common value sentiments which constitute the collectivity are projected upon the leader as a symbolic embodiment of these values. In so far as this symbolic complex is well integrated, loyalty to these values, to the collectivity, and to the leader in his role become indistinguishable.

The degrees and ways in which symbolic leadership is combined in the same role with instrumental executive functions can vary considerably. But even the instrumental leader will tend to have at least some directly expressive functions. Most generally his presence, and his performing of symbolic acts will be an essential part of all collective symbolic action, e.g., celebrations or ceremonials. In general the symbolization connected with these activities will be organized around a symbolic role or system of them as a focus. The leader will "preside," he will say the symbolically crucial things, his physical position will be symbolic as, e.g., seated at the center of the "head table," and a whole variety of other symbolic associations will be organized around his role.

It is furthermore significant that this expressive element of leadership, as in the case of the instrumental aspect of the executive role, has both an internal and an external-representative aspect. The position and the actions in his role of an expressive leader serve to symbolize to outsiders the nature and the solidary sentiments of the collectivity he represents, and to organize its relations to other collectivities. All of this is of course clearly evident in various aspects of international relations. Certain symbolic acts can only be performed by a "chief of state," regardless of the question of who holds the "real power." Protocol in international gatherings is indispensable because it is impossible to avoid having almost any accidental happening come to be interpreted as "significant" when the persons involved are playing to such a high degree symbolic representative roles. The only alternative to exposure to possibly deleterious consequences in such a situation is careful regulation of the symbolic aspects themselves, as in setting the order of precedence.

It is possible for the symbolic aspect of a role to become rather highly differentiated from the instrumental aspects. The "toastmaster" at a dinner, which is essentially a demonstration of collective solidarity in the recreational context, may not be a "leader" in any of the other principal respects, but may be able to organize and canalize collective symbolism in the appropriate context very successfully—he may for example command certain types of humor as a technique of tension release. It is also possible for specialized expressive leadership roles to develop in relation to the solemn affirmation of solidarity. It is common for example for "elder statesmen," who are no longer actively influential in instrumental ways, to be brought forward on such occasions. The British monarch is, of course, a stock example of this differentiation of the expressive aspect. The distinction between "reigning" and "governing" is essentially that between expressive leadership and the executive role in the instrumental complex. Similarly religious leadership may be relatively segregated from the other aspects of group solidarity except for the solidarity of the religious collectivity itself. An extreme instance of this was the position of the "official" Shinto priest in Japan, for example, on the village level. He was apparently deprived of almost all influence in general collective affairs, his role being defined as almost purely "ceremonial." In any other connection he was not even a particularly respected figure.

These extreme segregations are, however, exceptional. At the very least we can say that executive leadership must carry with it a very significant expressive aspect. The strains and tensions involved in complex organization are such that the expressive aspect must be organized. The existence of a well-integrated system of expressive symbolism is a highly important mechanism of social control in that it "channels" the directly cathectic elements relative to action in the collectivity.

This functional imperative, however, does not preclude that there should be a relatively elaborate differentiation of sub-systems of expressive symbolism, including several symbolically significant roles relative to the same collectivity-organization context. The case of the Prime Minister and the King in England is merely one case in point.

Max Weber's famous category of charismatic leadership belongs directly in the present context. The charismatic leader plays an expressive leadership role where moral authority is claimed, that is, where the symbolization is evaluative and not only expressive. Whether this role is that of leadership in a deviant sub-culture in conscious opposition to the institutionalized value-system, or in a collectivity within the institutionalized system, is secondary. But the primacy of charisma means that the immediate expressive significance of the role takes precedence over its instrumental functions in the collective division of labor. This may be interpreted as the main significance of such religious maxims as "take no thought for the morrow." To do so would take the orientation off the purely expressive plane and introduce instrumental considerations into it, considerations which are felt to be inappropriate. The "routinization of charisma," then, is the process by which a primarily expressive orientation comes to be adjusted to the exigencies of a continuing situation which must in the nature of the case involve instrumental considerations. In such a case the pattern of charismatic leadership must give way to one in which executive aspects play a critical role. If a purely symbolic-role type survives, it must be segregated from the executive and "neutralized" as it were. This has often happened in the "ritualization" of religious movements.

With respect to symbolic roles as in other contexts of expressive symbolism the problem of "duality" is of fundamental significance. On the one hand expressive symbolism constitutes the cultural pattern system around which institutionalized gratification interests are organized, and which gives these interests a certain stability. At the same time, on the other hand, the need-disposition systems of personalities are imperfectly integrated. The elements of these systems which are not fully in accord with the institutionalized patterns hence also seek expression. Sometimes they do so in explicitly deviant forms, sometimes interstitially to the main institutionalized system of expressive symbolism. But sometimes such elements come to be "superimposed" on the institutionalized meanings of established symbols. This is perhaps peculiarly important in the case of symbolic roles.

Insecurity in the psychological sense is one of the persistent and ubiquitous aspects of the malintegration of social systems. Put a little differently we may say that in most social systems there are incompletely gratified needs to feel that "everything will be all right." It is very natural indeed that these needs should be projected on persons who occupy expressive leadership roles. There is, then, very generally an exaggerated trust or expectation that the leader will "take care of everything" in such cases. He becomes, even if not in a strictly religious sense, a kind of "savior." In such a case the question of whether or not the leader "delivers" may become acute. As was noted in the discussion of ideologies in the last chapter, the strains involved in such expectations may be lessened by displacing the fulfillment of the expectations outside the immediate field of action, either into the future, as in the case of the leader of a movement for reform, or into a transcendental sphere, as in the case of many religious movements.

The obverse of this romantic-utopian element[3] in expressive symbolism is what may be called "scapegoat" symbolism. In this case it is the negative affect, which is not fully institutionalized, which is projected onto a symbolic object. Persons performing differentiated roles, particularly those carrying responsibility, are often appropriate targets for such projection.

It is necessary to distinguish, relatively to any given collectivity, internal and external scapegoats. Solidarity is an essential common denominator of all collectivities. Hence the type case of internal threat is that from the member who breaks the solidarity. There is therefore a focus of negative affect on the "traitor," the "disloyal" member of the collectivity. Sanctions against disloyalty on an institutionalized and realistic level will be found in all stable collectivities though their exact nature varies over a very wide range. But just as insecurity in the above sense tends to motivate to exaggerated trust in and adulation of leaders, it also motivates to the search for scapegoats on whom actual troubles can be blamed, and anxiety about future troubles justified and legitimized. We are so familiar with these phenomena as in the case of "witch-hunts" that further comment seems to be unnecessary.

In the light of the analysis of compulsive ambivalent motivation in Chapter VII above, the mechanisms operating in these cases of romantization and scapegoating of expressive leaders can be generalized. For the person acting under what we have called strain, whether it be that directly imposed by the failure of fulfillment of his expectations or compounded by the internal conflict of ambivalence, expectations become "skewed" from the normal, which in this case we may define as the institutionalized pattern. There is always the dual aspect of this, the need to express the resentment or hostility which frustration arouses, and the need to protect by defensive-adjustive measures the cathectic investment in the disturbed orientation pattern and relationship. Since this orientation is most fundamentally organized in terms of the complementarity of expectations,

[3] This element, it will be remembered from Chapter VII, is associated with patterns of compulsive motivation.

ego in response to strain attempts to redefine his expectations of alter. There will, then, be both a compulsively alienative component in this definition, and a compulsively conformative one. In the alienative context ego will tend to express hostility toward alter and expect to be reciprocated, while in the conformative context he will compulsively skew his conformity with what he defines as alter's expectations and expect this to be reciprocated by positive attitude sanctions on alter's part.

It seems correct to say that what is usually meant by the mechanism of "projection,"[4] as a mechanism of defense, consists essentially of such an expectation of alter's behavior which, because it is inappropriate to alter's orientation system and to the situation, is not in fact acted upon by alter, that is, is not reciprocated. Alter is always, in an established interaction system, a symbolic figure to ego. What projection in this case does is to shift the symbolic meaning of alter and his attitudes, to redefine the symbolism. Alter becomes the source of the disturbance on which ego's resentment focuses, and/or the person who expects and should reward ego's skewing of his conformative orientation. It was, in ego's distorted definition of the situation, alter who, because he was angry at ego, placed the strain upon him and disturbed his expectations. It is because alter expects the value patterns to be lived up to in compulsively literal form, that ego must distort the normal patterning of his action in a compulsive direction. From this point of view the primary factor in projection is the failure of ego's expectations to be reciprocated. Then the gap in meaning between the expectation and the actual behavior of alter is filled by the imputation of behavior to alter (including attitudes and intentions), which he does not actually perform or have.

Further complications are of course introduced by the operation of the mechanisms of repression and displacement. The object of ego's projection need not be the actual and immediate agent of the imposition of strain on him. Indeed it is almost impossible to keep the balance of expressing both the conformative and the alienative orientation components equally toward the same object. One, then, must be repressed. Repression, however, is seldom complete, and

---

[4] This interpretation of the concept of projection was called to my attention by Professor R. F. Bales.

one of the obvious possible outcomes is the displacement of the repressed affect on a substituted object. Hence the tendency, as we noted, for symbolically prominent figures to function as "lightning rods," catching much of the displaced and hence relatively free-floating affect which is present in the social system.

We may add one further consideration. Though much repressed affect may be relatively free floating, it does not follow that just any object can function equally well as an object of displacement. There must be a certain symbolic appropriateness. Relatively little is known about the laws of symbolic association which define the various categories of appropriateness, that is the gradients of symbolic generalization. However, certain types of generalization in this field are relatively well known on a concrete level. Thus for example it is well known that hostility tends to be displaced from parents to authority figures generally. Especially relative to socialization in certain types of kinship system, in a *projective* sense it may be true that all masculine authority roles are held by "father figures." But it is extremely important to distinguish the truth of such a statement as applying to the projective symbolic significance of such roles for large parts of a population, and the actual institutional structure of such roles. Thus it is quite impossible for an executive in a modern occupational organization to have a role which is in fact structurally identical with the father role in the kinship system in the same society.[5]

Projective symbolism in this sense is by no means confined to what can readily and clearly be defined as "pathological" phenomena, such as the adulation of heroes and scapegoating. Much of it comes to be built into the actual social structure, especially in those patternings of activity which are especially significant as expressions of strain in rituals and what we have called "secondary institutions." The significance of family relationships in early socialization is such that the projective symbolization of family members is particularly likely to appear in such a case.

One example in the field of secondary institutions is that of the American youth culture. Here it is not without significance that the most prominent class of undergraduate college social clubs are

---

[5] In general what may loosely be called "psychoanalytic sociology" has tended to pass over this extremely important distinction.

called fraternities and sororities. Members address each other as "brother" and "sister," especially on ceremonial occasions. It is certainly significant that these are symbolized as groups of "siblings" *without* the participation of parent-symbols. The "old grads" are not referred to as "fathers" but are "older brothers." There is to be sure, sometimes the vaguely benevolent figure of the "house mother," but emphatically never a "house father." In the light of the functions of the youth culture in the process of emancipation from dependence on the conjugal family, particularly the parents, this symbolization is clearly appropriate and significant.

In some other cultures, familial symbolism is very much more integrally built into the social structure. The case of the Roman Catholic Church is a particularly noteworthy one. Secular prestige figures are, in Catholic societies, generally not endowed with the projective status of family figures; and kings are not fathers and queens are not mothers in general. The church, however, is organizationally separated from secular society, and by its own symbolization it is a family "writ large." God of course is the Father, but the priest as his vicar is also explicitly called Father. The Virgin assumes the Mother role,[6] and religious orders consist of Brothers and Sisters. There is an interesting sense in which it may be said that Catholicism, while recognizing that in secular life the individual must become emancipated from his childhood role in the family and assume both non-familial roles and parental roles within the family permits, indeed enjoins, that, in his religious capacity as a member of the church, the lay Catholic symbolically *remains a child.*

Closely related to this religious extension of the symbolic familial role to other relationships is the provision of symbolic families. This is a feature of monarchical regimes generally. In England a very important place is occupied, not merely by the King, but by the Royal Family as a whole. It is a kind of prototype of what a family should be, especially perhaps since the reign of Victoria. All the crucial events within the Royal Family are followed with the strongest interest by the general public; indeed, there is a vicarious participation in its life by the whole nation. It is not surprising that the selection of a Queen should be treated as a matter of legitimate public concern, and not merely the private affair of the royal suitor.

[6] There is also the Mother Superior of a Convent.

§ THE ROLE OF THE ARTIST

IN THE above treatment one type of differentiation of roles with respect to expressive symbolism was discussed, namely, that in which the role itself was an integral part of the general system of expressive symbolism of the culture. We must now turn to the second type noted above, that where the incumbent of a differentiated role becomes not so much himself a symbol, as a specialist in the creation and manipulation (application) of expressive symbols. We find here a direct parallel to the creation and application of beliefs by the scientist or philosopher and the applied scientist. The term artist is generally used to designate both types, but differentiated as the "creative" artist and the "performer."

As we have noted above, expressive symbolism like cognitive beliefs is "originally" and "normally" embedded in the ordinary processes of action. The ordinary person who acts, and surrounds his action with objects in accord with a definite expressive "style" is no more an artist in the present sense than is the peasant who possesses knowledge about his soil, seed, fertilizer and crop pests and uses this knowledge in a practical way, a scientist. In both cases the use of the cultural pattern may be very skillful and "sound," but this is not the criterion. The criterion is rather specialization of role with respect to the relevant aspects of the cultural tradition itself. In a strict sense then the creative artist is the person who specializes in the production of *new patterns* of expressive symbolism, and the performing artist is the person who specializes in the skilled implementation of such symbolism in an action context. Both are "experts" with respect to a particular phase of the cultural tradition.

As is the case with any other type of specialty, this artistic type arises through differentiation relative to the other components of the total action complex. Once differentiated, furthermore, there is the same order of problem of the relation between the technical function of the role and its relational context which exists with respect to other differentiated roles.

Placing the problem in this frame of reference at once directs our attention to the problems of disposal and of remuneration, as well as to the provision of facilities. There are two primary aspects of the disposal-remuneration problem of exchange relations. The first is the question of disposal on terms which will enable the artist to acquire the means for meeting his other wants, which is a condition of his being able to specialize. This aspect is of course to be analyzed in the same theoretical terms as apply to any other specialized role, though of course the concrete conditions involve many special features in this case.

The second aspect is that of the appreciative or expressive side of the disposal and remuneration relationships. This is the problem of the relation of the artist to his "public." It is a very striking fact that in spite of the notorious "individualism" of artists, at least in the modern Western world, there is among them a very deep concern with communicating, with making an impression on a public. The expressive symbolism of art is not a "private" matter at all but is part of a culture. When it does become purely private and the individual ceases to try to communicate, he is a schizophrenic, not an artist, which is a very different type of social role, though one may shade into the other.

Though there are many different variations, in broad terms this is the basis of the institutionalization of the role of the artist. He supplies a want or meets a need in his public, and on the expressive level he receives "appreciation" and admiration in return. He is highly sensitive to the attitudes of the significant others among his public. He has a responsibility for the maintenance of the standards which have been established, both to other persons and to himself, because these are institutionalized standards. The same basic mobilization of motivational elements which applies to other institutionalized roles also applies to this one. There are, of course, many specific differences, but they are not relevant at this level.

There is a particular combination of expressive and instrumental elements of orientation in the role of the artist which is important to understanding some of the peculiarities of the role. For himself and for his public the artist is engaged in creating expressive symbols. But it is precisely the difference in one respect between sophisticated art and purely "spontaneous" expressive activity that there is a "technical" aspect of the artist's work which is directly comparable with other techniques. This aspect of his activity is instrumental. It depends on knowledge and skill in exactly the same fundamental sense as does industrial technology, or the technology of scientific research. The artist must accept severe disciplines, must spend much time in study and practicing his skills. But his goal is to produce appropriate patterns for the expression of affect, to "stir up" his audience or public. There seems to be an inherent tension between these two aspects of the role, which is not present for the scientist, because the content of the latter's goal is not of the same order of direct cathectic significance. How much certain aspects of the situation in the Western world are culture bound it is difficult without careful comparative study to say. However, the well-known association of art with "Bohemianism," with the repudiation of many of the main institutionalized patterns of ordinary life, is clearly very much less marked in the case of science. It may at least be suggested that in a society where affectively neutral patterns are institutionalized to such a high degree, the expressive interests of the artist come more drastically into conflict with the main institutional structure than do the interests of the scientist. In more expressively oriented societies the conflict is presumably not so acute, but conversely the opportunity for the scientist is less well developed.

The parallel between the role of the artist and of the scientist extends to the structure of the continuum between the "pure" creative artist and the corresponding types of application. Corresponding to the professions in which science is applied, like medicine or engineering, we may distinguish the performer of sophisticated works of art, who is himself a trained "professional." Of course only some among the media of artistic expression admit of specialized performance. The principal examples in our culture are music, the theater and the dance whereas some forms of literature, painting, sculpture and architecture do not admit of a separate role of performance. In their essentials the specialized roles of performers in these fields are similar in structure to that of the creative artist himself. There are, of course, often transitional types between the two as well. Thus a great concert musician or conductor is certainly "creative," but in a sense parallel to that in which a great surgeon is.

"Pure" art, whether as practiced by the creative artist or the performer, is parallel to specialization relative to non-evaluative cognitive orientation, to belief systems. As we have seen evaluative symbolism, religious or not, is not "purely" expressive. We can, however, have specialization in the creation and performance of evaluative symbolism as well as of "pure art." The core of Greek art seems in these terms to have been evaluative in its original setting, to have been both civic and religious in different contexts. Similarly religious art has played a very prominent part in Western culture. A distinction should, however, be made between artistic creation which is itself an act of religious devotion, as in the building of cathedrals, and the use of religious symbolic *content* in artistic creations, as is the case with so much of Renaissance art. A good deal of the latter should not be called religious art in a full sense. It shades over into "pure" art.

In the above sense, the actual conduct of collective ceremonials may in certain cases be treated as artistic performance of a special type. Much of the "embellishment" of religious ritual is clearly art in this sense. Thus the singing of a Bach mass as part of the religious service itself is an integral part of the religious expression. But the singing of the same mass in a secular concert hall may be an act of a quite different order. Similarly, Lincoln's Gettysburg address as originally delivered was not "literature," it was an act of expressive symbolization of the collective need dispositions of the nation, or at least the North; it was part of a collectivity ceremonial. It has, however, to a certain degree become divorced from this context and come to be treated as "art."

Thus in addition to the creative artist and the artistic performer we may speak of the ceremonial performer, who manipulates artistic symbolism in an evaluative context, where its meaning in terms of explicit common values is directly symbolized.

The distinction is paralleled by that between modes of participation of the public or audience. The standards of pure art in this sense are institutionalized only in "acceptance" terms. As we ordinarily put it, we are "pleased" or "moved" by a work of art or its performance. But this attitude does not have specifically binding implications for our action beyond this specific context. In general, attendance at performances, or paying attention to art as such, is treated as voluntary.

The most essential modification of this occurs when adherence to a set of artistic standards becomes itself the primary symbol of belonging to a sub-cultural group. This tends to be true of the "coteries" of the art world, the schools and the "little revues." This is the elevation of what in terms of the general cultural tradition is a secondary basis of institutionalization into a primary basis for a special sub-culture, one which, however, in the nature of the case could not become a primary basis of institutionalization of a society. It is directly paralleled by the "sects" of intellectuals who share a common belief system differing from the diffuser general ideology of the society.

Where, however, expressive symbols become an integral part of the primary orientation system of a collectivity, the mode of institutionalization is that of commitment, not of acceptance only. A far severer set of sanctions is mobilized for conformity and against deviance, and there is pressure for a far closer integration of the expressive symbolism with the major value-orientations of the collectivity. Thus, characteristically in the Soviet Union, literature, which merely tries to portray human beings, their feelings and conflicts, is distinctly frowned upon. Art must be "proletarian," it must serve the cause of the Revolution directly. Anything which does not have such a direct relation to the major values of the society is "frivolous" or possibly counter revolutionary.

There is a whole class of phenomena which fall in between the attribution of symbolic significance to roles which are not primarily expressive in their functions, and the primarily expressive role-system comprising the artist and his public. Perhaps the most conspicuous of these is the role of the propagandist, who is consciously using available expressive symbolism or creating new symbols, in order to manipulate the attitudes of a public. Whenever a leadership or executive role is performed in such a way that the symbolic aspects of the role are not merely accepted, but explicitly arranged for and manipulated, the leader is in some degree in this sense a propagandist. He is appealing to the sentiments of his constituency by to some degree redefining the situation in symbolic terms. The "pure" artist on the other hand, we may say, is not oriented to the influencing of the attitudes of his public in other than expressive terms, but only to giving "form" to their expressive interests. The symbol systems with which the artist operates are, however, deeply involved in the equilibrium of the whole attitude system. It is an easy transition from pure art to their use in such a way as to attempt to influence attitudes in a direction favorable to particular courses of action in other than purely expressive contexts.

Thus both expressive leadership and artistic roles tend to become involved in "propaganda" activities. Frequently the expressive leader provides the principal legitimation of the propaganda, it is for instance promulgated in his name, while the artist contributes to the "technique." Thus the practice of a political figure, e.g., the late President Roosevelt, having key speeches at least partly written by a literary artist (Robert E. Sherwood) is a case in point. Propaganda in this sense may, of course, have the most varied expressive content and may serve the most varied ends. A class of great significance in our own society is that of advertising appeal. But of greater significance is the proselytization of orientations where evaluative symbolism and beliefs are involved, in the political and religious movements which have a strong "charismatic" tinge.

It should be clear from the whole of the foregoing analysis that at many points a very intimate fusion occurs between cognitive orientation patterns, i.e., belief systems, and expressive symbols. Indeed there is always both a cognitive and an expressive aspect to any set of symbols. Only in some types of "ideas" do the cognitive interests and value-standards have clear primacy, so that the criteria of cognitive adequacy, clarity, logical consistency and respect for evidence are prominently involved. In all of what have been called evaluative beliefs, this aspect is not clearly primary, but yet it may have considerable significance. However, starting with evaluative beliefs, the expressive interest acquires great significance, and in many ideological and religious belief systems the specific symbols become to a very great extent expressive symbols. This is particularly true where intermediate symbolism in the sense discussed in the last chapter is prominently involved, but it may also be true of highly abstract concepts or generalizations, such as the concept of Divine Grace, or of the Dialectic. Where such abstract entities are treated as expressive symbols, however, there is almost certain to be a "vulgar" concretization of them so that more tangible symbolic entities enter in. Thus in popular Catholicism the conception of intercession by a Saint is common, the saint being a greatly humanized and concretized figure. Similarly in vulgar Marxism, the conception of the "imperialist circles" who are responsible for opposing the course of the revolution contrary to the will of the "people" is such a concretized symbol, as indeed is that of the "people" itself.

Toward the pole of mythology, however, as was noted in the last chapter, cognitive criteria as such tend to be subordinated and the expressive elements to take precedence. The very common situation in non-literate cultures where certain institutions are "explained" by the "fact" that a certain mythological figure did so and so in the remote past certainly belong in this category.

It is also, however, possible for expressive symbolism to develop certain types of refinement and "abstraction" so that rather than concretization taking place as in the creation of personal figures, certain rather abstract symbolic patterns become a primary orienting framework. One of the principal examples of this appears to be the traditional Chinese system of symbolic orientations. The "conceptions" of Tao, Yang and Yin are certainly not anthropomorphic or otherwise concretized. But Granet[7] seems to be quite correct in his contention that these are not "concepts" in the sense of Western philosophy. We may call them highly abstract expressive symbols, and speak of the Chinese orientation as one in which, in the primary evaluative symbol system, the expressive element has primacy over the cognitive. This interpretation fits with the particularism, traditionalism, and "ritualization" of traditional Chinese society.

§ EXPRESSIVE SYMBOLISM AND THE REWARD SYSTEM

IN CHAPTER IV above the concepts of facilities and of rewards were treated, along with the conception of the allocation of personnel among roles, as the primary foci of the allocative processes of the social system. Both belong to the category of "possessions," that is, of entities, rights in which are transferable from one actor to another through the process of "exchange." Possessions are facilities in so far as their primary significance to actors lies in their instrumental uses, while possessions are rewards in so far as their significance is expressive, that is, so far as they constitute objects of direct gratification without regard to their instrumental uses. It goes without saying that the same concrete objects may be, and very

[7] *La pensée chinoise.* He uses the term *emblèmes.*

generally are, both facilities and rewards. The distinction is analytical, not concretely classificatory.

It was argued above that the "core" of the reward system in a social system is to be found in the attitudes of actors toward each other. These attitudes were called "relational possessions" in that ego can "give" or "withhold" a favorable attitude from alter, he can make it contingent on alter's performance in a variety of respects and he can choose objects on which to bestow it. He can also control his unfavorable attitudes, he can "get mad" or blame alter for actions—or qualities—which he dislikes. Attitudes are thus contingently controllable. They are also as we have seen the core of the system of mutually oriented expectations in the interaction process. Hence so far as ego entertains a legitimized expectation of alter's attitudes toward him we may speak of his having a "right" to that attitude. The conditions on which alter may legitimately change his attitude toward ego are institutionally defined just as are the conditions on which he may legitimately dispose of a physical object in his possession. Hence we may say that the conditions of holding and of transfer of relational possessions are institutionally regulated, and hence the allocation of such possessions is so regulated.

Finally, it was further argued that all other rewards must tend to become symbolically integrated with relational possessions. This is not in the least to say that many objects other than actors do not have cathectic significance which can vary independently relative to that of the attitudes of actors. It is only to say that the significance of other actors, and the cultural patterns directly integrated with their attitudes, is so great that the cathectic significance of these other objects, e.g., food objects, cannot be independent of the system of relational possessions without also being interdependent with it. The attitudes of persons from whom one receives food, to whom one gives food, and with whom one eats food, are an integral part of the symbolic complex relative to food habits. It is, for instance, well known to how great an extent commensality serves as a symbol of solidarity, and its denial as a symbol of the lack of solidarity.

The initial treatment of expressive symbolism in the present chapter took its departure from essentially these considerations. It will be remembered that it was held that the focus of the whole system of expressive symbolism is the symbolic act relative to one or more alters, and that the primary symbolic reference of the symbolic act is the attitude of the actor performing it. Other symbols, physical or cultural, become organized into an associated complex relative to this attitudinal core of the symbolic system. We may say, then, that *one* major element of the value of a reward may always be traced back to the ways in which it symbolizes the attitudes of significant actors, alter or ego himself, individual or collective.

But this is not merely one major element in the value of the reward. It is quite clearly that element which is most crucial to the structure of the social system. For it is elements of stability in the mutuality of orientation of interactive relationships which essentially constitute the structure of the social system. Its stability depends on the integration of the interests of actors with the patterning of the interaction process. If interests in objects other than the attitudes of actors cannot be integrated with this mutual attitude system, such interests must constitute threats to the stability of the social system. This is simply an aspect of the fundamental theorem of the institutional integration of motivation which was developed above in Chapter II.

Mutually oriented attitudes in the social system are, as we have seen, extremely complex and varied. We have found, however, that the main types may be classified in terms of the two pattern variables of affectivity-neutrality and specificity-diffuseness, yielding the four familiar types of receptiveness-response, love, approval and esteem. We may, then, classify expressive symbols as patterns of the reward system according to which of the four attitude types they symbolize, as was developed above.

Every social system must be characterized by some ordering of its reward system, that is, of allocation of the possession of expressive symbols relative to positive and negative attitudes. At the core, that is, with relation to the attitudes themselves, this involves coordination of the criteria of legitimate claim to a positive attitude, and of legitimation of changes in the attitudinal system. There are two main types of these changes, first, transfer of an attachment from one object to another, for instance, of love where the attitude is of such a character as to preclude it being held toward an indefinite plurality of objects at the same time. The second type is the shift from positive to negative attitudes toward the same object—through a point of balance between the positive and the negative components, of course.

Beyond the core there must be an ordering of the symbolic significances of other objects relative to the attitudinal focus. Since almost all objects associated with action acquire symbolic significance to some degree, there must be common symbolic meanings of these objects relative to the attitudinal system.

This imperative may first be applied to the category of purely expressive as distinguished from evaluative symbolism. This in turn falls into the two sub-classes of attitudes of affective attachment and style pattern symbolism.

The positively affective as distinguished from the affectively neutral attitudes toward actors have a strong tendency to be associated with particularism. Hence the problems of order in relation to them tend to be concerned with three foci. The first is the definition of the legitimate content of such symbolism itself, the second of the legitimate objects of attachment, the processes of their selection, degrees of exclusiveness, etc., and the third the limits on the expressive interests and obligations thus assumed. One of the most conspicuous examples of this ordering is to be found in the institutionalization of kinship relationships, and the associated fields of the regulation of courtship and erotic relationships generally. The strong sanction of legitimacy on marriage, and at most permission of a secondary status to other bases of erotic relationship, the taboo on homosexuality, and the institutionalization of affectional relationships between parents and children, and between siblings all belong in this category.

One of the most important facts in this field is that most societies do not permit that expressive symbolism in the erotic, or even the affectional sphere, should be purely expressive except within quite narrow limits, it becomes evaluative, and even frequently directly religious in reference. In other words, this is a doubly strong institutionalized sphere. This strongly suggests that the allocation of this class of rewards is of great functional significance to the social system, a suggestion which is confirmed by such facts as the ubiquity of sexual jealousy.

What is true of individual actors as objects of attachment and the expressive symbolism focusing on such an attachment is also true of collectivities. Here the focal problem for the social system is the allocation of loyalties among the different collectivities in which the component individual actors have roles, and the symbolization of these loyalties. For example, a society focused on kinship solidarity to the extent of that of classical China, is not, without drastic reorganization of its reward system, able to develop strong loyalties to other types of collectivity which differ greatly in their structure, particularly those institutionalizing universalistic standards. So long as the kinship symbol system remains intact, and its expressive significance untouched, it is not possible to reward individuals adequately to motivate loyalty to other types of collectivity.

An obverse type of situation is found in our own society. Particularly between men, we institutionalize a diffuse "friendliness" among occupational associates, to a markedly higher degree than is the case, for example, in most European countries. This is symbolized in such ways as the use of first names, various informal social relationships such as "having a drink" together, and often a "kidding" relationship. But such expressive orientations are not permitted to go too far in particularistic exclusiveness; there is an obligation to manifest them relatively impartially toward all associates or colleagues, and the corresponding expressive symbols and rewards are organized in this way. The conspicuous thing about this pattern is the limit placed on its particularism and hence its integration with the universalism of the occupational system. It readily becomes evident how breaking through these limits could be threatening by providing occasions for "favoritism" in the instrumental aspects of the same concrete relationships.

The allocation of the symbolism of attachment to individuals and to collectivities shades off into that to physical and cultural objects. Here, of course, the significance of the allocation problem depends very heavily on the scarcity factor. This aspect calls attention to a very important dimension of the reward system, namely, the differential distribution of valued expressive symbols.

The case of the erotic attachment is a good point of departure for discussing this. The approximate equality of numbers of the sexes means that if the main basis of erotic rewards is institutionalized in monogamous marriage there can be a presumption of equal distribution of these rewards through the allocation to each person of one mate. This does not, of course, mean that there will not be any differentiations of desirability, but that with respect to the fundamental difference between having and not having access to a spouse there will tend not to be a major differentiation. In a society, on the other hand, where polygyny is institutionalized, probably universally plurality of wives tends to become a status symbol, and the poorer and less influential elements are excluded from this reward, and by a still further consequence a certain proportion of low status men are excluded from marriage altogether. It may also be noted that such a situation would tend to skew the internal structure of the kinship unit in a "patriarchal" direction, because on the one hand in the upper groups wives could be played off against each other while in the lower, the draining off of desirable women would create a tendency for men to seek wives from lower statuses than their own.

It is clear that in this context, as well as those discussed in a previous section, the symbolic structure may become skewed as a consequence of projective needs resulting from strain and ambivalence. One of the most obvious cases is that of the place of symbolism in sexual jealousy. Here the primary focus is, of course, on the loyalty of the partner. Compulsiveness is manifested in the insistent demand for proof of that loyalty, and the demands tend to become such that unless alter is himself submissively oriented, it is not possible for him to satisfy them, if then. Ambivalence explains the readiness with which love can alternate with aggression toward the object. But the most essential point for the present context is that the normal expressive symbolism of the love attitude is shifted so that excessive acts of devotion are required to prove loyalty, and their omission is projectively interpreted as showing the absence of the expected loyalty. Where such motivation exists there may be an extra drive for some persons to attempt to control a larger sector of the relational reward system than by their institutionalized status they are entitled to. This may, as in the case of jealousy just discussed, take the form of monopolizing more of the devotion of a single love object than is legitimate, or it may take the form of attempting to establish such relations with a larger number of objects than the actor is legitimately entitled to. The latter type of factor is involved in "Don Juanism" and in the needs of the "preda-tory" glamor girl type to command the devotion of whole coteries of men.

The second type of purely expressive symbolism with respect to which the allocative problem arises is composed of physical and cultural objects in their "style pattern" significance, both the style of the object itself and the symbolic significance of possessing that object, in certain quantities and qualities, as part of the style of life of the actor in question. The ordering of this aspect of the reward system involves some rather complex considerations.

In the first place, as is true of relational rewards as such, access to non-relational expressive symbols is a function of power. The most obvious aspect of this in a society like our own is access through purchasing power. Hence so far as purchasing power is, for whatever reasons, differentially distributed, it must result in dif-ferential access to valued expressive symbols. The differential access in turn introduces an inevitable status-comparative dimension into the organization of this aspect of the reward system. Other things being equal having greater access to the possession of expressive symbols means that one has a more highly valued and privileged position with respect to the reward system, one can acquire more and "better" things. What is true of purchasing power is also true with certain modifications of political power. Here the style factor appears in access to elements of the style of life which are differen-tially accessible to persons at different power levels. Thus the sym-bolization of occupying the top executive's office with its better furnishings and the like would fit here.

In both respects, by virtue of this comparative dimension, style symbolism necessarily becomes in one aspect *status* symbolism in the hierarchical sense. This is in the nature of the case since the person higher up in the scale, since he has command of more pur-chasing power, or more political power, is by definition in a "better" position than the one lower down. Hence obviously it is imperative that such style symbolism should, in access terms at least, be legiti-matized and institutionalized. The actor in question must "have a right" to live the way he does.

This hierarchical aspect of the style system is always present, but "other things" are at best only approximately equal, so this factor is cross cut by another set of considerations. *Given* differential access to expressively symbolic objects, how this access is used is subject to performance criteria and contingent sanctions in terms of appreciative standards, that is, in terms of canons of "taste." So far as expressive orientation is concerned, the level of access through power may be treated as an ascribed base, but how this access is used is subject to achievement by the individual actor. Therefore there tends in every reward system, relative to the levels of access to style-objects, to be independent variability with respect to standards of taste. In this way the nouveau riche may be guilty of "vulgarity," while the impoverished aristocrat, with his greatly inferior resources, displays "exquisite taste," and thereby symbolizes a superiority which is not fully impugned by the greater power of the other.

Style symbolism thus permeates the whole social structure. It has a pronounced element of desirability and its objects are inherently scarce. Hence their allocation must be institutionally regulated in the social system. However, regulation in terms of power of access is only one form of regulation. That in terms of realization of standards of taste is another which cross cuts the first. It can in certain respects serve to offset the prestige-implications of differential access, and thereby serve as an independent balancing force in the system of social stratification.

Both, of course, are subject to projective distortion of the main institutionalized values. On the one hand this projective distortion relative to well-established standards of taste is the main feature of the vulgarity of the *parvenu*. He does not yet feel secure in his enhanced status position and therefore tends to distort style symbols from their more intrinsic expressive significance in relation to disciplined appreciative norms, into predominantly status symbols. Since his need to symbolize his status is compulsive, he is apt to be somewhat undiscriminating in his choices of ways to do it, to go in for "extremes" and for quantity rather than quality. Persistence of a residue of lower status style patterns is also common. On the other hand, especially for groups with an ascribed status position in a society where achievement criteria are strongly institutionalized, it is common for the projective distortion of style symbolism to operate in the obverse way. In this case the actor tends to compen-

sate for the dubious legitimacy of his ascribed position by emphasizing his superiority of taste to the vulgar multitude who are
engaged in achievement activities. Since at the top of the scale of
stratification in an achievement system, there must be a modification of the incidence of achievement values, it is suggestive that
patronage of the arts, which is a prominent interest of such groups,
constitutes an important mechanism for legitimatizing the status of
the elite groups.

We may now turn to the affectively neutral components of the
reward system which focus on the attitudes of approval and esteem.
Attention has been called a number of times to the fact that these
are more directly relevant to the institutionalization of the larger
structures of the social system than are the affective attitudes,
mainly because of the inherent limitations on securing immediate
gratification from the cathexis of generalized patterns, and of the
necessity for certain types of discipline in acting in accord with
those patterns, notably but by no means exclusively perhaps universalism and achievement-orientations. We have also called attention to the great importance of the development of sensitivity to
these attitudes in the course of the socialization process.

The attitude of approval is relevant wherever the contingency
element operates in social interaction, wherever there is a question
of conformity with an expectation, where that is, there is a possibility of failing to conform. Then alter can reward ego for conformity with his expectation by his approval, and punish him
for non-conformity by his disapproval. The place of the normative
pattern comes in essentially as the *generalization* of these expectations. Clearly, then, the institutionalization of attitudes of approval-
disapproval is in certain respects the focus of the institutionalization
of the reward system generally. It is the sine qua non of social
stability.

In this most general sense the relevance of approval rewards
applies to conformity with the expectations of any role in any social
system. Another aspect emerges, however, with extension of the
range within which opportunities for performance and its valuation
open up. The crucial transition is that between living up to the
norms defining specific traditionalized expectations of the given
role in which ego happens to be placed, and having his status itself

become contingent on his performance. Then the incidence of approval rewards is no longer confined to symbolizing that ego is a "good" whatever it is, a good boy, a good servant or peasant or what not. Approval then becomes the symbolic focus of reward for having achieved beyond what was ascribed to an initial status. It is here that the peculiar dynamics of the reward system of an achievement-oriented social structure open out.

We may focus the consideration of these problems on the concept of "success."[8] Success is, in a situation where achievement goals are paramount, the measure of the degree of attainment of the valued goals. These may of course be of the most varying content. Our concern here, however, is not with this content, but with certain generalized aspects of the organization of such goal-striving in social systems. Since, we are assuming, achievement goal-striving takes place in the context of social relationships, we must first make clear that the valuation of the attainment of the goals is a *common* valuation not peculiar to ego. This is the basis of the relevance of alter's approval, and indeed only this gives much of the force to ego's own self-approval and hence his motivation to achievement, in that, namely, his success is measured by himself in terms of an internalized common value-pattern. Hence we may say that the source of gratification is never the attainment of the goal alone but the achievement as measured in terms of a value-standard, which gives both ego's and alter's approval its relevance as a reward. The striving for goal achievement and the striving for approval are thus inseparable in an integrated social structure.

In the pursuit of achievement-goals and of approval there is an inherent comparative "better or worse" dimension. Ego can and does measure his achievement by intrinsic standards without reference to the achievement of an alter, but if many are striving for the same goals, it is inevitable that in some sense they should be judged as doing better or worse by the same standards, ego that is should excel alter or vice versa. Thus approval as a reward has an inherent dimension of differential distribution; it cannot be distributed equally to all performers in an achievement system without vitiating the whole meaning of the system.

[8] It will be remembered from Chapter VI that success is a "situationally generalized goal."

Finally, if a system of approval rewards is to be integrated in a social system, this comparative dimension implies that it will be a source of strain if to some degree different lines of achievement are not reduced to a common denominator. The very fact that actors are sensitive to approval and disapproval means that for those in different lines of goal-striving it cannot be indifferent whether attainment in one line is or is not more highly approved than in another. It is inherent in a social system with a developed division of labor that there should be a wide variety of concrete goal striving activities. These must be ordered into some sort of a system, including an ordering of their precedence in the approval scale. There must be higher and lower achievements.

Actual intrinsic achievement, or lack of it, and the approval or disapproval of actors do not, however, stand alone in the symbolic complex of which achievement values are the center. In the nature of the case other entities of possible symbolic significance are involved. In the type of case with which we are concerned a system of monetary exchange is generally involved, and, as part of it, money remuneration in occupational roles. It seems almost inevitable that the level of money remuneration should become a symbol in this complex. Money has the one particularly striking property of unambiguous quantitative measurability. Therefore, precisely in the hierarchical aspect of an achievement system, comparative level of money remuneration very readily becomes a major symbol of success. This symbolic association is further encouraged by the fact that money remuneration is a necessary common denominator as between different classes of concrete achievement goals. Hence, it can at least be said that where there is an at all well integrated system of the valuation of different achievements, it is highly important for the differentiation of monetary rewards to be integrated with it. In so far as money income is treated as a symbol of success, it is clearly a source of strain if the relation is reversed, the higher the achievement the less the money income.

There are other "auxiliary" symbols of success than money income. Clearly in a differentiated achievement system organization occupies a prominent place. Hence status in organizations is certain to acquire symbolic significance in this context. The connection between income and status in organization, which in one aspect is position in the power system, with power as a basis of access to symbols of the style of life, is obvious. Other types of "informal" power status may also have a comparable significance, though they are generally not so highly visible, a factor of great significance for symbolization.

The attitude of approval must have visible signs to which to attach itself, since in the nature of the case it is a *contingent* attitude. Often actual intrinsic achievement is difficult for alter to judge, because of communication difficulties, lack of technical competence, inaccessibility for observation and such factors. Hence especially for purposes of the broader comparisons, it is very easy and to some degree essential, for alter's attitudes of approval—and to some degree ego's own—to be made contingent on ego's acquisition of *symbols* of achievement as well as achievement itself. This fact automatically makes the acquisition of such symbols in some sense a meaningful goal for ego.

In an institutionally integrated system of action achievement, approval of achievement, and the principal symbols of achievement should be integrated together in an inseparable complex. Above all acquisition of the symbols of achievement should be possible only by the appropriate achievement. But short of this level of integration there is the possibility of a rift between them. It becomes realistically possible to acquire money without a requisite level of valued achievement, and also to acquire status in organizations, etc. We do not need to go into the various features of the social system which make the occurrence of such opportunities possible and to some degree inevitable.

At this point there is a particularly important opening for the operation of projective distortions. The actor with compulsive motivations, above all when they center on the adequacy problem as it was called in Chapter VII, may have a compulsive need for approval, including self-approval. This need is not likely to be satisfied by direct achievement alone. The tendency is to distort the definition of the situation by making doubly sure that one is approved. The opportunity to accumulate more than a due measure of the symbols of achievement presents a very ready outlet for this compulsive motivation. We may surmise that in such an achievement system, the persons who are unduly concerned with money rewards[9] and with their power position have a prominent component of this type of compulsive motivation.

This would above all be true of those with active motivation to compulsive conformity with the success goal. Where there is a trend to passivity, it takes the form of a striving for undue "security" in the common-sense meaning of the term. This for instance can be found in trying to be over-certain of the stability of even a modest income, as well as in the perfectionism of detail which sacrifices the central achievement goals for assurance of immunity from active disapproval.

Thus the attitude of approval and its negative constitute another primary focus of the expressive-symbolic reward system. It is the center of a symbolic complex which includes money income and power position and which has to be integrated with the symbolism of the style of life. The whole complex must be organized and ordered as a central part of the integration of the social system. In this ordering the dimension of differential reward relative to the value system occupies a central place.

Finally, the attitude of esteem differs from that of approval by its diffuseness. For this reason it is the paramount focus of the scale of prestige in a society which is the core of the system of stratification. Attitudes of approval can be segregated by context. It is possible to approve one act of ego and disapprove another, to consider him to be a highly competent technician and a bad administrator at the same time. But in the social system there is a functional problem comparable to that of reducing particular achievements to a common denominator which was just mentioned. To some degree, as measured by the dominant value system, there must be an over-all judgment of a human being; it is this which we mean by the esteem in which he is held. Far less than in any other of the cases of relational rewards can the bases of the attitude of esteem be left uninstitutionalized in a society. This fact is the main functional basis for the existence of social stratification as an essential feature of every social system.

The diffuse breadth of the factors which must be integrated in

[9] It is, we may surmise, essentially this phenomenon to which Elton Mayo referred when he spoke of "the acquisitiveness of a sick society." Cf. *Human Problems of an Industrial Civilization.*

a judgment of esteem is such that stratification is inevitably an important focus of strain in a social system. It will suffice to mention, for our own society, the problem of integrating the individualistic achievement aspects of the occupational system, and the solidarity of the kinship system, as that problem was discussed in Chapter V. It is this sort of functional problem which makes the phenomena of social class such an important field for sociological study.

As in the case of approval rewards, those of esteem are obviously linked with a symbolic complex which extends well beyond the central value-foci which provide the direct standards of esteem. This is particularly true of style symbolism because of its visibility and its relative controllability by the individual or the small sub-collectivity.

It would be possible to go much *farther into detail* in the theory of social stratification, especially in analyzing the ramifications of the complex of esteem-symbolism, and in analyzing the types of malintegration to be found in systems of stratification, the factors involved in them and the adaptive structures which are for understandable reasons particularly prominent in this area. These problems, important as they are, will have to be left to the more specialized theory of stratification, which is one principal branch of the theory of social systems.

More generally, the present chapter has been a sketch. As it was noted at its beginning, the theory of expressive symbolism is one of the least satisfactorily developed parts of the theory of action generally, and of social systems in particular. The reader will note, however, that we have been able to contribute more to the problems of the relations of certain known types of expressive symbolism to the social system, than to the systematization of the field on the cultural level itself. Indeed there is an urgent need for more work, which is only very partially the province of the sociologist, on the laws and types of symbolic patterning and association. The contrast with the cognitive field is striking. We have a very well-developed knowledge of the structure of belief systems as such, but a very fragmentary one of the structure of systems of expressive symbols. It may be safely predicted that advances in this field will contribute very greatly to the advance of the sciences of action.

X

SOCIAL STRUCTURE AND DY-
NAMIC PROCESS: THE CASE OF MODERN MEDICAL
PRACTICE[1]

WE HAVE followed a long and complicated course in working through the derivation of the major structural outlines of the social system from the action frame of reference, in the analysis of the central place of patterns of value-orientation in this structure, in the analysis of the motivational mechanisms of social process, and that of the involvement of cultural patterns other than those of value-orientation in the social system. It will perhaps help the reader to appreciate the empirical relevance of the abstract analysis we have developed if, in addition to the illustrative material which has been introduced bearing on many particular points, we attempt to bring together many if not most of the threads of the foregoing discussion in a more extensive analysis of some strategic features of an important sub-system of modern Western society.

For this purpose we have chosen modern medical practice. This field has been a subject of long-standing interest[2] on the author's

[1] For general comparison with this chapter the reader may be referred to L. J. Henderson, "Physician and Patient as a Social System," *New England Journal of Medicine*, Vol. 212, May 2, 1935, 819-23.

[2] The most important phase of this interest was concerned with a field study of medical practice which was carried out mainly in the Boston area several years ago. A variety of circumstances prevented the completion of that study and its publication in the intended form. Hence the opportunity has been taken for the formulation of some of the most important of the results in the context of their relevance to the present work. Of course the earlier interpretations have been considerably modified by subsequent theoretical development and by other ex-

428

part as a result of which he has a greater command of the empirical material in this field than in most others. But it also provides an excellent opportunity to illustrate some of the interrelations of the principal elements of the social system which have been reviewed in more abstract terms. A highly distinctive cultural tradition, certain parts of modern science, provides a central focus for the activities of the medical profession. We have already seen that there are important problems of the modes of institutionalization of such a cultural tradition. This institutionalization fits into the functional context of a ubiquitous practical problem in all societies, that of health, and is specially organized relative to distinctive role patterns and value-orientations in our own society. Finally, as has already been brought out briefly, the bearing of the therapeutic process on the problems of deviance and social control is such that adequate analysis of the motivational processes involved has implications reaching far beyond the particular field to throw a great deal of light on the general motivational balance of the social system.

§ THE FUNCTIONAL SETTING OF MEDICAL PRACTICE AND THE CULTURAL TRADITION

IN THE most general terms medical practice may be said to be oriented to coping with disturbances to the "health" of the individual, with "illness" or "sickness." Traditionally the principal emphasis has been on "treatment" or "therapy," that is, on dealing with cases which have already developed a pathological state, and attempting to restore them to health or normality. Recently there has been increasing emphasis on "preventive medicine," that is, controlling the conditions which produce illness. For our purposes,

perience, notably training in psychoanalysis. It is, however, of considerable interest that it was in connection with the earlier study of medical practice that the beginnings of the pattern variable scheme were first worked out.

There has been fragmentary previous publication of results in three places, the papers "The Professions and Social Structure" and "Propaganda and Social Control," *Essays*, Chapters VIII and XIII, and "Education and the Professions," *Ethics*, Vol. 47, 365-369.

The original study was assisted financially by a grant from the Harvard Committee on Research in the Social Sciences. This assistance is hereby gratefully acknowledged.

however, the therapeutic functional context will present sufficient problems.

A little reflection will show immediately that the problem of health is intimately involved in the functional prerequisites of the social system as defined above. Certainly by almost any definition health is included in the functional needs of the individual member of the society so that from the point of view of functioning of the social system, too low a general level of health, too high an incidence of illness, is dysfunctional. This is in the first instance because illness incapacitates for the effective performance of social roles. It could of course be that this incidence was completely uncontrollable by social action, an independently given condition of social life. But in so far as it is controllable, through rational action or otherwise, it is clear that there is a functional interest of the society in its control, broadly in the minimization of illness. As one special aspect of this, attention may be called to premature death. From a variety of points of view, the birth and rearing of a child constitute a "cost" to the society, through pregnancy, child care, socialization, formal training and many other channels. Premature death, before the individual has had the opportunity to play out his full quota of social roles, means that only a partial "return" for this cost has been received.

All this would be true were illness purely a "natural phenomenon" in the sense that, like the vagaries of the weather, it was not, to our knowledge, reciprocally involved in the motivated interactions of human beings. In this case illness would be something which merely "happened to" people, which involved consequences which had to be dealt with and conditions which might or might not be controllable but was in no way an expression of motivated behavior.

This is in fact the case for a very important part of illness, but it has become increasingly clear, by no means for all. In a variety of ways motivational factors accessible to analysis in action terms are involved in the etiology of many illnesses, and conversely, though without exact correspondence, many conditions are open to therapeutic influence through motivational channels. To take the simplest kind of case, differential exposure, to injuries or to infection, is certainly motivated, and the role of unconscious wishes to be injured or to fall ill in such cases has been clearly demonstrated. Then there is the whole range of "psycho-somatic" illness about which knowledge has been rapidly accumulating in recent years. Finally, there is the field of "mental disease," the symptoms of which occur mainly on the behavioral level. Of course somatic states which are not motivationally determined may play a larger or smaller part in any or all of them, in some like syphilitic paresis they may be overwhelmingly predominant, but over the field as a whole there can be no doubt of the relevance of illness to the functional needs of the social system, in the further sense of its involvement in the motivated processes of interaction. At one time most medical opinion inclined to the "reduction" of *all* illness to a physiological and biological level in both the sense that etiology was always to be found on that level, and that only through such channels was effective therapy possible. This is certainly not the predominant medical view today. If it ever becomes possible to remove the hyphen from the term "psycho-somatic" and subsume all of "medical science" under a single conceptual scheme, it can be regarded as certain that it will not be the conceptual scheme of the biological science of the late nineteenth and early twentieth centuries. It is also certain that this conceptual scheme will prove applicable to a great deal of the range of social action in areas which extend well beyond what has conventionally been defined as the sphere of medical interests.

The fact that the relevance of illness is not confined to the non-motivated purely situational aspect of social action greatly increases its significance for the social system. It becomes not merely an "external" danger to be "warded off" but an integral part of the social equilibrium itself. Illness may be treated as one mode of response to social pressures, among other things, as one way of evading social responsibilities. But it may also, as will appear, have some possible positive functional significance.

Summing up, we may say that illness is a state of disturbance in the "normal" functioning of the total human individual, including both the state of the organism as a biological system and of his personal and social adjustments. It is thus partly biologically and partly socially defined. Participation in the social system is always potentially relevant to the state of illness, to its etiology and to the conditions of successful therapy, as well as to other things.

Medical practice as above defined is a "mechanism" in the social system for coping with the illnesses of its members. It involves a set of institutionalized roles which will be analyzed later. But this also involves a specialized relation to certain aspects of the general cultural tradition of modern society. Modern medical practice is organized about the application of scientific knowledge to the problems of illness and health, to the control of "disease." Science is of course a very special type of cultural phenomenon and a really highly developed scientific level in any field is rare among known cultures, with the modern West in a completely unique position. It may also be noted that scientific advance beyond the level to which the Greeks brought it is, in the medical field, a recent phenomenon, as a broad cultural stream not much more than a century old.

We have dealt at some length in Chapter VIII with science as a general feature of the cultural tradition, and with some of the conditions of its application to practical affairs. This need not be repeated here. We need only note a few points particularly relevant to the medical field. First, it should be quite clear that the treatment of illness as a problem for applied science must be considered problematical and not taken for granted as "common sense." The comparative evidence is overwhelming that illness, even a very large part of what to us is obviously somatic illness, has been interpreted in supernatural terms, and magical treatment has been considered to be the appropriate method of coping with it. In non-literate societies there is an element of empirical lore which may be regarded as proto-scientific, with respect to the treatment of fractures for instance. But the prominence of magic in this field is overwhelmingly great.

This, however, is by no means confined to non-literate cultures. The examples of traditional China and our own Middle Ages will suffice. Where other features of the cultural tradition are not favorable to the traditionalized stereotyping which we think of as characteristic of magic in the full sense, we find a great deal, and sometimes predominance, of health "superstition" in the sense of pseudo rational or pseudo scientific beliefs and practices.

In the light of these considerations it is not surprising that in a society in which scientific medicine has come to be highly institutionalized, popular orientations toward the health problem are by no means confined to the scientific level. There is much popular health superstition, as evidenced by such things as the "patent medicines," for example the widely advertised "Dr. Pierce's Golden Medical Discovery," and many traditional "home remedies." Furthermore in the health field there is a considerable fringe of what are sometimes called "cults." Some religious denominations, of which Christian Science is perhaps the most conspicuous example, include a religious approach to health as an integral part of their general doctrine. Then there is a variety of groups which offer health treatments outside the medical profession and the professions auxiliary to it like dentistry and nursing. These are apt to include complex and bewildering mixtures of scientifically verifiable elements and various grades and varieties of pseudo-science.[3]

Finally the institutionalization of science is, as the analysis of Chapter VIII would lead us to expect, far from complete within the profession itself. There are many kinds of evidence of this, but for present purposes it is sufficient to cite the strong, often bitter resistance from within the profession itself to the acceptance of what have turned out to be critically important scientific advances in their own field. One of the classic cases is the opposition of the French Academy of Medicine to Pasteur, and for some time the complete failure to appreciate the importance of his discoveries. A closely related one is the opposition of the majority of the surgeons of the day to Lister's introduction of surgical asepsis. The conception of "laudable pus" is an excellent example of a medical "superstition."

It goes without saying that there is also an important involvement of expressive symbolism in medical practice. Rather, however, than attempting to review it at this point it will be better to call attention to certain aspects of it as we go along.

§ THE SOCIAL STRUCTURE

THE immediately relevant social structures consist in the patterning of the role of the medical practitioner himself and,

---

[3] An excellent and very detailed analysis of one of these border-line groups is given in the study by Walter I. Wardwell, *Social Strain and Social Adjustment in the Marginal Role of the Chiropractor,* unpublished Ph.D. dissertation, Harvard University, 1951.

though to common sense it may seem superfluous to analyze it, that of the "sick person" himself. There is also a range of important impingements of both roles on other aspects of the total structure of the social system which will have to be mentioned at the appropriate points.

The role of the medical practitioner belongs to the general class of "professional" roles, a sub-class of the larger group of occupational roles. Caring for the sick is thus not an incidental activity of other roles—though for example mothers do a good deal of it—but has become functionally specialized as a full-time "job." This, of course, is by no means true of all societies. As an occupational role it is institutionalized about the technical content of the function which is given a high degree of primacy relative to other status-determinants. It is thus inevitable both that incumbency of the role should be achieved and that performance criteria by standards of technical competence should be prominent. Selection for it and the context of its performance are to a high degree segregated from other bases of social status and solidarities. In common with the predominant patterns of occupational roles generally in our society it is therefore in addition to its incorporation of achievement values, universalistic, functionally specific, and affectively neutral. Unlike the role of the businessman, however, it is collectivity-oriented not self-oriented.

The importance of this patterning is, in one context, strongly emphasized by its relation to the cultural tradition. One basis for the division of labor is the specialization of technical competence. The role of physician is far along the continuum of increasingly high levels of technical competence required for performance. Because of the complexity and subtlety of the knowledge and skill required and the consequent length and intensity of training, it is difficult to see how the functions could, under modern conditions, be ascribed to people occupying a prior status as one of their activities in that status, following the pattern by which, to a degree, responsibility for the health of her children is ascribed to the mother-status. There is an intrinsic connection between achieved statuses and the requirements of high technical competence, as well as universalism and competence. In addition, of course, there is pressure in the society to assimilate the medical role to others of similar character in the total occupational system.

High technical competence also implies specificity of function. Such intensive devotion to expertness in matters of health and disease precludes comparable expertness in other fields. The physician is not, by virtue of his modern role, a generalized "wise man" or sage—though there is considerable folklore to that effect—but a specialist whose superiority to his fellows is confined to the specific sphere of his technical training and experience. For example one does not expect the physician as such to have better judgment about foreign policy or tax legislation than any other comparably intelligent and well-educated citizen. There are of course elaborate subdivisions of specialization within the profession.

Affective neutrality is also involved in the physician's role as an applied scientist. The physician is expected to treat an objective problem in objective, scientifically justifiable terms. For example whether he likes or dislikes the particular patient as a person is supposed to be irrelevant, as indeed it is to most purely objective problems of how to handle a particular disease.

With regard to the pattern variable, self vs. collectivity-orientation, the physician's role clearly belongs to what, in our occupational system, is the "minority" group, strongly insisting on collectivity-orientation. The "ideology" of the profession lays great emphasis on the obligation of the physician to put the "welfare of the patient" above his personal interests, and regards "commercialism" as the most serious and insidious evil with which it has to contend. The line, therefore, is drawn primarily vis-à-vis "business." The "profit motive" is supposed to be drastically excluded from the medical world. This attitude is, of course, shared with the other professions, but it is perhaps more pronounced in the medical case than in any single one except perhaps the clergy.

In terms of the relation of the physician's occupational role to the total instrumental complex there is an important distinction between two types of physicians. One of the "private practitioner," the other the one who works within the context of organization. The important thing about the former is that he must not only care for sick people in a technical sense, but must take responsibility for settlement of the terms of exchange with them because of his direct dependence on them for payment for his services, and must to a high degree also provide his own facilities for carrying on his function. It is a crucially important fact that expertness in caring for the sick does not imply any special competence one way or another in the settlement of terms of exchange. It may or may not be a good social policy to have the costs of medical care, the means of payment for it and so on settled by the members of the medical profession, as individuals or through organizations, but such a policy cannot be justified on the ground that their special training gives them as physicians a technical competence in these matters which others do not have.

An increasing proportion of medical practice is now taking place in the context of organization. To a large extent this is necessitated by the technological development of medicine itself, above all the need for technical facilities beyond the reach of the individual practitioner, and the fact that treating the same case often involves the complex cooperation of several different kinds of physicians as well as of auxiliary personnel. This greatly alters the relation of the physician to the rest of the instrumental complex. He tends to be relieved of much responsibility and hence necessarily of freedom, in relation to his patients other than in his technical role. Even if a hospital executive is a physician himself he is not in the usual sense engaged in the "practice of medicine" in performing his functions any more than the president of the Miners' Union is engaged in mining coal.

As was noted, for common sense there may be some question of whether "being sick" constitutes a social role at all—isn't it simply a state of fact, a "condition"? Things are not quite so simple as this. The test is the existence of a set of institutionalized expectations and the corresponding sentiments and sanctions.

There seem to be four aspects of the institutionalized expectation system relative to the sick role. First, is the exemption from normal social role responsibilties, which of course is relative to the nature and severity of the illness. This exemption requires legitimation by and to the various alters involved and the physician often serves as a court of appeal as well as a direct legitimatizing agent. It is noteworthy that like all institutionalized patterns the legitimation of being sick enough to avoid obligations can not only be a right of the sick person but an obligation upon him. People are often resistant to admitting they are sick and it is not uncommon for others to tell them that they *ought* to stay in bed. The word generally has a moral connotation. It goes almost without saying that this legitimation has the social function of protection against "malingering."

The second closely related aspect is the institutionalized definition that the sick person cannot be expected by "pulling himself together" to get well by an act of decision or will. In this sense also he is exempted from responsibility—he is in a condition that must "be taken care of." His "condition" must be changed, not merely his "attitude." Of course the process of recovery may be spontaneous but while the illness lasts he can't "help it." This element in the definition of the state of illness is obviously crucial as a bridge to the acceptance of "help."

The third element is the definition of the state of being ill as itself undesirable with its obligation to want to "get well." The first two elements of legitimation of the sick role thus are conditional in a highly important sense. It is a relative legitimation so long as he is in this unfortunate state which both he and alter hope he can get out of as expeditiously as possible.

Finally, the fourth closely related element is the obligation—in proportion to the severity of the condition, of course—to seek *technically competent* help, namely, in the most usual case, that of a physician and to *cooperate* with him in the process of trying to get well. It is here, of course, that the role of the sick person as patient becomes articulated with that of the physician in a complementary role structure.

It is evident from the above that the role of motivational factors in illness immensely broadens the scope and increases the importance of the institutionalized role aspect of being sick. For then the problem of social control becomes much more than one of ascertaining facts and drawing lines. The privileges and exemptions of the sick role may become objects of a "secondary gain" which the patient is positively motivated, usually unconsciously, to secure or to retain. The problem, therefore, of the balance of motivations to recover, becomes of first importance. In general motivational balances of great functional significance to the social system are institutionally controlled, and it should, therefore, not be surprising that this is no exception.

A few further points may be made about the specific patterning of the sick role and its relation to social structure. It is, in the first place, a "contingent" role into which anyone, regardless of his status in other respects, may come. It is, furthermore, in the type case temporary. One may say that it is in a certain sense a "negatively achieved" role, through failure to "keep well," though, of course, positive motivations also operate, which by that very token must be motivations to deviance.

It is inherently universalistic, in that generalized objective criteria determine whether one is or is not sick, how sick, and with what kind of sickness; its focus is thus classificatory not relational. It is also functionally specific, confined to the sphere of health, and particular "complaints" and disabilities within that sphere. It is furthermore affectively neutral in orientation in that the expected behavior, "trying to get well," is focused on an objective problem not on the cathectic significance of persons,[4] or orientations to an emotionally disturbing problem, though this may be instrumentally and otherwise involved.

The orientation of the sick role vis-à-vis the physician is also defined as collectively-oriented. It is true that the patient has a very obvious self-interest in getting well in most cases, though this point may not always be so simple. But once he has called in a physician the attitude is clearly marked, that he has assumed the obligation to cooperate with that physician in what is regarded as a common task. The obverse of the physician's obligation to be guided by the welfare of the patient is the latter's obligation to "do his part" to the best of his ability. This point is clearly brought out, for example, in the attitudes of the profession toward what is called "shopping around." By that is meant the practice of a patient "checking" the advice of one physician against that of another without telling physician A that he intends to consult physician B, or if he comes back to A that he has done so or who B is. The medical view is that if the patient is

---

[4] This it will appear later is particularly important to the therapeutic process. It is not to be interpreted either that the cathectic significance of persons has no part in the etiology of illness or that cathexis of the physician as an object does not occur—but it is controlled.

not satisfied with the advice his physician gives him he may properly do one of two things, first he may request a consultation, even naming the physician he wishes called in, but in that case it is physician A not the patient who must call B in, the patient may not see B independently, and above all not without A's knowledge. The other proper recourse is to terminate the relation with A and become "B's patient." The notable fact here is that a pattern of behavior on the part not only of the physician, but also of the patient, is expected which is in sharp contrast to perfectly legitimate behavior in a commercial relationship. If he is buying a car there is no objection to the customer going to a number of dealers before making up his mind, and there is no obligation for him to inform any one dealer what others he is consulting, to say nothing of approaching the Chevrolet dealer only through the Ford dealer.

The doctor-patient relationship is thus focused on these pattern elements. The patient has a need for technical services because he doesn't—nor do his lay associates, family members, etc.—"know" what is the matter or what to do about it, nor does he control the necessary facilities. The physician is a technical expert who by special training and experience, and by an institutionally validated status, is qualified to "help" the patient in a situation institutionally defined as legitimate in a relative sense but as needing help. The intricacy of the social forces operating on this superficially simple sub-system of social relations will be brought out in the following analysis.

§ THE SITUATION OF MEDICAL PRACTICE

A. *The Situation of the Patient*

THE first step is to go more in detail into the analysis of relevant aspects of the situation in which the doctor and the patient find themselves. This will provide the setting in which the importance of the broad patterning of both physician's and patient's role can be interpreted, and will enable us to identify a series of mechanisms which, in addition to the physician's deliberate application of his technical knowledge, operate to facilitate his manifest functions in the control of disease, and to promote other, latent functions which are important to the social system.

First, it must be remembered that there is an enormous range of different types of illness, and of degrees of severity. Hence a certain abstraction is inevitable in any such general account as the present one. There is also a range of different types of physician. It will, therefore, be necessary to concentrate on what can be considered certain strategic and typical features of the situation of both.

It will be convenient first to take up the salient features of the situation of the patient and his "lay" associates, particularly members of his family. These may be classified under the three headings of helplessness and need of help, technical incompetence, and emotional involvement.

By institutional definition of the sick role the sick person is helpless and therefore in need of help. If being sick is to be regarded as "deviant" as certainly in important respects it must, it is as we have noted distinguished from other deviant roles precisely by the fact that the sick person is not regarded as "responsible" for his condition, "he can't help it." He may, of course, have carelessly exposed himself to danger of accident, but then once injured he cannot, for instance, mend a fractured leg by "will power." The exhortation to "try" has importance at many peripheral points in the handling of illness, but the core definition is that of a "condition" that either has to "right itself" or to be "acted upon," and usually the patient got into that condition through processes which are socially defined as "not his fault."

The urgency of the need of help will vary with the severity of the disability, suffering, and risk of death or serious, lengthy or permanent disablement. It will also vary inversely with the prospect, as defined in the culture, of spontaneous recovery in terms of certainty and duration. But a sufficient proportion of cases is severe in one or more of these senses, and unlikely to recover spontaneously, at least soon enough, so that the feeling of helplessness and the need of help are very real.

The sick person is, therefore, in a state where he is suffering or disabled or both, and possibly facing risks of worsening, which is socially defined as either "not his fault" or something from which he cannot be expected to extricate himself by his own effort, or generally both. He is also likely to be anxious about his state and the future. This is a very different kind of "need" from that of a person who merely "wants" something that he can be permitted to have if he can "swing" it independently, such as a new car, or even if he "needs something," such as adequate food, if he can reasonably be expected to procure it by his own efforts, as by working for it, and not being lazy or shiftless. In a special sense, the sick person is "entitled" to help.

By the same institutional definition the sick person is not, of course competent to help himself, or what he can do is, except for trivial illness, not adequate. But in our culture there is a special definition of the kind of help he needs, namely, professional, technically competent help. The nature of this help imposes a further disability or handicap upon him. He is not only generally not in a position to do what needs to be done, but he does not "know" what needs to be done or how to do it. It is not merely that he, being bedridden, cannot go down to the drug store to get what is needed, but that he would, even if well, not be qualified to do what is needed, and to judge what needs to be done. There is, that is to say, a "communication gap."

Only a technically trained person has that qualification. And one of the most serious disabilities of the layman is that he is not qualified to judge technical qualifications, in general or in detail. Two physicians may very well give conflicting diagnoses of the same case, indeed often do. In general the layman is not qualified to choose between them. Nor is he qualified to choose the "best" physician among a panel. If he were fully rational he would have to rely on professional authority, on the advice of the professionally qualified or on institutional validation.

This disqualification is, of course, not absolute. Laymen do know something in the field, and have some objective bases of judgment. But the evidence is overwhelming that this knowledge is highly limited and that most laymen *think* they know more, and have better bases of judgment than is actually the case. For example the great majority of laymen think that *their* physician is either the best or one of the few best in his field in the community. It is manifestly impossible for the majority of such judgments to be objectively correct. Another type of evidence is the patterning of choice of physician. A very large proportion of people choose their physicians on the basis of the recommendations of friends or neighbors who "like

Dr. X so much," without any sort of inquiry beyond that as to technical qualifications, even as to the medical school from which he holds a degree or the hospital at which he interned.[5] There must be some mechanisms to bridge this "gap." There must be some way of defining the situation to the patient and his family, as to what is "the matter with him" and why, what his prognosis is, what burdens will have to be assumed in recovery. There must be some mechanism for validating the "authority" of the physician, who only in special cases like the military services has any coercive sanctions at his command.

In this connection it should be noted that the burdens the physician asks his patients and their families to assume on his advice are often very severe. They include suffering—you "have to get worse before you can get better" as for instance in the case of a major surgical operation. They include risk of death, permanent or lengthy disablement, severe financial costs and various others. In terms of common sense it can always be said that the patient has the obvious interest in getting well and hence should be ready to accept any measures which may prove necessary. But there is always the question, implicit or explicit, "How do I know this will do any good?" The one thing certain seems to be that the layman's answer to this cannot, in the majority of severe and complex cases, i.e., the "strategic" ones, be based primarily on his own rational understanding of the factors involved and a fully rational weighing of them. The difference from the physician in this respect is often a matter of degree, but it is a crucially important difference of degree.

Finally, third, the situation of illness very generally presents the patient and those close to him with complex problems of emotional adjustment. It is, that is to say, a situation of strain. Even if there is no question of a "physic" factor in his condition, suffering, helplessness, disablement and the risk of death, or sometimes its certainty, constitute fundamental disturbances of the expectations by which men live. They cannot in general be emotionally "accepted" without the accompaniments of strain with which we are familiar and hence without difficult adjustments unless the patient happens

---

[5] One physician, a suburban general practitioner, told that in several years of practice only one patient had asked him from what medical school he had graduated.

to find positive satisfactions in them, in which case there is also a social problem. The significance of this emotional factor is magnified and complicated in so far as defensive and adjustive mechanisms are deeply involved in the pathological condition itself.

The range of possible complexities in this sphere is very great. The problems are, however, structured by the nature of the situation in certain relatively definite ways. Perhaps the most definite point is that for the "normal" person illness, the more so the greater its severity, constitutes a frustration of expectancies of his normal life pattern. He is cut off from his normal spheres of activity, and many of his normal enjoyments. He is often humiliated by his incapacity to function normally. His social relationships are disrupted to a greater or a less degree. He may have to bear discomfort or pain which is hard to bear, and he may have to face serious alterations of his prospects for the future, in the extreme but by no means uncommon case the termination of his life.

For the normal person the direction of these alterations is undesirable, they are frustrations. Therefore it is to be expected that two types of reaction should be prominent, a kind of emotional "shock" at the beginning of illness, and anxiety about the future. In both cases there is reason to believe that most normal persons have an unrealistic bias in the direction of confidence that "everything will be all right," that is they are motivated to underestimate the chances of *their* falling ill, especially seriously ill (the minority of hypochondriacs is the obverse), and if they do they tend to overestimate the chances of a quick and complete recovery. Therefore even the necessary degree of emotional acceptance of the reality is difficult. One very possible reaction is to attempt to deny illness or various aspects of it, to refuse to "give in" to it. Another may be exaggerted self-pity and whining, a complaining demand for more help than is necessary or feasible, especially for incessant personal attention. In any case this factor reinforces the others. It makes it doubly difficult for the patient to have an objective judgment about his situation and what is needed. Whether they pay explicit attention to it in any technical sense or not, what physicians do inevitably influences the emotional states of their patients, and often this may have a most important influence on the state of their cases.

In this connection perhaps a few words may be said about the relation of the medical situation to death. As was noted in Chapter VIII death, and particularly premature death, is one of the most important situations in all societies, demanding complex emotional adjustments on the part of the dying person, if the probability is known to him in advance, and on the part of the survivors. This is so important that in no society is there an absence of both cultural and social structuring of ideas about death, attitudes toward it, or behavior in the presence of imminent death or its recent occurrence. Moreover the "death complex" is never purely instrumental in its patterning. It is a central focusing point for expressive symbolism.

American culture in general seems to have a strong "optimistic bias," one aspect of which is the "playing down" of death, the avoidance of too much concern with its prospect or its implications, and, when it must be faced, "getting it over with" as rapidly as possible. For example, we have relatively slight and probably decreasing emphasis on mourning. Our tendency is to "get on with living" as nearly in the usual pattern as possible. In the light of psychological knowledge and the evidence from comparative cultures it seems highly likely that this attitude is maintained only by virtue of strong disciplines which repress preoccupation with and anxiety about death. It may also mean that "grief reactions" are more frequently repressed than in other societies.

In a society normally at peace, death in most cases is preceded by illness, which links it very closely with the sick role. This is hence a point at which more or less free-floating anxieties about death have an opportunity to focus. Moreover, the physician is brought very closely into contact with death. He is often present at a death bed, and he is the first one to whom people look for structuring the situation in relation to their anxieties about the possibility of death; if the clergyman comes in it is usually later than the physician. It is striking that the medical is one of the few occupational groups which in our society have regular, expected contact with death in the course of their occupational roles, the clergyman, the undertaker, and in certain ways the police, being the other principal ones. The military in our society are a special, though sociologically extremely interesting case, because for us war is an exceptional "crisis" situation, not part of the normal life of the society.

It is to be presumed that this association with death is a very important factor in the emotional toning of the role of the physician. If he is not in general tending in our society to take the place formerly occupied by the clergy, an assertion often made, but subject to considerable qualifications, he at least has very important associations with the realm of the sacred. In this connection it is interesting to note that the dissection of a cadaver is included in the very first stage of formal medical training, and that it tends to be made both something of a solemn ritual, especially the first day, on the part of the medical school authorities, and medical students often have quite violent emotional reactions to the experience. It may hence be concluded that dissection is not only an instrumental means to the learning of anatomy, but is a symbolic act, highly charged with affective significance. It is in a sense the initiatory rite of the physician-to-be into his intimate association with death and the dead.

Indeed, this is confirmed by the fact that historically the medical profession had to wage a long and sometimes bitter struggle to secure the right to dissect cadavers as a regular part of medical training—at one time they secretly raided cemeteries for the purpose.[6] Even today some religious bodies strongly oppose autopsies except when they are required by the law of the state where there is suspicion of foul play.

To come back to the main theme. There are two particularly important broad consequences of the features of the situation of the sick person for the problem of the institutional structuring of medical practice. One is that the combination of helplessness, lack of technical competence, and emotional disturbance make him a peculiarly vulnerable object for exploitation. It may be said that the exploitation of the helpless sick is "unthinkable." That happens to be a very strong sentiment in our society, but for the sociologist the existence of this sentiment or that of other mechanisms for the prevention of exploitation must not be taken for granted. There is in fact a very real problem of how, in such a situation, the very possible exploitation is at least minimized.[7]

[6] Cf. Shryock, Richard Harrison, *The Development of Modern Medicine.*

[7] It is interesting to note that even leftist propaganda against the evils of our capitalistic society, in which exploitation is a major keynote, tends to spare the physician. The American Medical Association tends to be attacked, but in general not the ideal-typical physician. This is significant of the general public reputation for collectivity-orientation of the medical profession.

The other general point is the related one that the situation of the patient is such as to make a high level of rationality of judgment peculiarly difficult. He is therefore open to, and peculiarly liable to, a whole series of irr- and non-rational beliefs and practices. The world over the rational approach to health through applied science is, as we have noted, the exception rather than the rule, and in our society there is, even today, a very large volume of "superstition" and other non- or irrational beliefs and practices in the health field. This is not to say that the medical profession either has a monopoly of rational knowledge and techniques, or is free of the other type of elements, but the volume of such phenomena outside the framework of regular medical practice is a rough measure of this factor. This set of facts then makes problematical the degree to which the treatment of health problems by applied science has in fact come to be possible. It can by no means be taken for granted as the course which "reasonable men," i.e., the normal citizen of our society will "naturally" adopt.

The above discussion has been concerned primarily with the sick person himself. But in some cases, e.g., when he is an infant or is in a coma, the patient himself has nothing whatever to say about what is done to him. But short of this, the patient tends to be buttressed by family members and sometimes friends who are not sick. Does this not vitiate the whole argument of the above discussion? Definitely not. It may mitigate the severity of the impact of some of the features of the patient's situation, in fact, it often does. But in the first place laymen, sick or well, are no more technically competent in medical matters in one case than the other. The need of help is also just as strong because the solidarity of the family imposes a very strong pressure on the healthy members to see that the sick one gets the best possible care. It is, indeed, very common if not usual for the pressure of family members to tip the balance in the admission of being sick enough to go to bed or call a doctor, when the patient himself would tend to stand out longer. Furthermore the emotional relationships within the family are of such a character that the illness of one of its members creates somewhat different emotional problems from the patient's own to be sure, but nevertheless often very severe ones, and sometimes more severe, or more difficult for the physician to cope with. It is not, for instance, for nothing that pediatricians habitually mean the mother, not the sick child, when they say "my patient." To anyone schooled in modern psychology the emotional significance of a child's illness for the mother in our society scarcely needs further comment. Hence we may conclude that the basic problems of the role of the patient himself are shared by the others in his personal circle with whom the physician comes into contact in his practice. Sometimes the role of these others is to facilitate the work of the physician very significantly. But it would be rash to assert that this was true very much more often than the reverse. In any case it is quite clear that the role of family members does not invalidate the significance of the situation of the patient for the character of medical practice, as outlined above.

B. *The Situation of the Physician*

THE role of the physician centers on his responsibility for the welfare of the patient in the sense of facilitating his recovery from illness to the best of the physician's ability. In meeting this responsibility he is expected to acquire and use high technical competence in "medical science" and the techniques based upon it. The first question to ask about his situation, therefore, concerns the relation of these technical tools to the tasks he is called upon to perform and the responsibilities he is expected to live up to.

In a certain proportion of cases the doctor has what may be called a perfectly straightforward technological job. His knowledge and skill give him quite adequate tools for accomplishment of his ends, it is only necessary to exercise sufficient patience, and to work steadily and competently at the task. This would, it is true, leave the "penumbra" of emotional reactions of patients and their families for him to deal with, and his own emotional reactions to such things as severe suffering and imminence of death might well pose certain problems of emotional adjustment to him. But with these qualifications it would be much like any other high level technical job.

But in common with some and not other technical jobs there is in this case a shading off into cases with respect to which knowledge, skill and resources are not adequate, with hard, competent work, to solve the problem. There are two main aspects to this inadequacy. On the one hand there are cases, a good many of them, where the upshot of a competent diagnosis is to expose a condition which is known, in the given state of medical knowledge and technique, to be essentially uncontrollable. This is true both in the individual case and generally. Though there is a fundamental relationship between knowledge and control, this is a general and not a point-for-point relationship. Optimistic biases are very general and fundamental in human social orientations, perhaps particularly in our society and certainly in relation to health. It is, therefore, very common that the initial effect of a given advance in knowledge is to demonstrate the impossibility of controlling things which were thought to be readily controllable, to expose unfavorable factors in the situation which were not previously appreciated, and to show the fruitlessness of control measures in which people had previously had faith.

This has been the case with many advances of medical science. For example, about in the 1870's many people, both in the medical profession and outside it, had a strong faith in the efficacy of various drugs in the treatment of pneumonia. Sir William Osler, one of the most eminent physicians of his day, undertook against strong opposition in the profession to show that this faith was not well founded. He claimed, and his claim has been scientifically validated, that there was not a single case of the use of drugs in this connection which was—apart from psychological considerations, we would now add—not either useless or positively harmful. It must of course be remembered that serum treatment, sulfa drugs and penicillin had not been discovered at that time. Hence the net effect of Osler's "campaign" was to reduce what had been thought to be the area of rational control of disease, yet it represented definite scientific advance.[8]

The same can be true in the individual case. The patient and his family may know only that he has abdominal discomfort, has been losing weight and lacks energy. Diagnostic procedure reveals an advanced, inoperable cancer of the stomach with a hopeless prognosis. "More" is definitely known than before, but hope has been destroyed. The remarkable advances of medicine in the past two generations have significantly narrowed the range of cases of this sort. But they are very far from having eliminated them, and it

[8] Cf. Harvey Cushing, *The Life of Sir William Osler*.

seems quite definite that there is no early prospect of their elimination.

These inherent frustrations of the technical expert acquire special significance because of the magnitude and character of the interests at stake. The patient and his family have the deepest emotional involvements in what the physician can and cannot do, and in the way his diagnosis and prognosis will define the situation for them. He himself, carrying as he does responsibility for the outcome, cannot help but be exposed to important emotional strains by these facts.

The absolute limits of the physician's control—which of course are relative to the state of medical science at the time and his own assimilation of it—are not the only source of frustration and strain. Within these limits there is a very important area of uncertainty. As in so many practical situations, some of the factors bearing on this one may be well understood, but others are not. The exact relation of the known to the unknown elements cannot be determined; the unknown may operate at any time to invalidate expectations built up on analysis of the known. Sometimes it may be known *that* certain factors operate significantly, but it is unpredictable whether, when and how they will operate in the particular case. Sometimes virtually nothing is known of these factors, only that the best laid plans mysteriously go wrong. In general the line between the spontaneous forces tending to recovery—what used to be called the *vis medicatrix naturae*—and the effects of the physician's "intervention" is impossible to draw with precision in a very large proportion of cases.

The great importance of the uncertainty element is evident even if attention is confined to the physiological-biochemical levels of analysis of medical problems. In the first great era of modern scientific medicine explicit attention was almost in principle confined to this level. In the light of subsequently acquired knowledge of the psychic factor in disease, a very substantial proportion of the uncertainty factor when attention was thus narrowed must have consisted in the impingement of psychological elements on the disease process, which at that stage were not understood at all. Taking explicit account of these, to the extent that this has so far become possible, helps to reduce the range, but again by no means eliminates it. One of its effects, like that of all scientific advance, is to increase awareness of the vast extent of human ignorance, even in the most sophisticated fields of applied science.

The primary definition of the physician's responsibility is to "do everything possible" to forward the complete, early and painless recovery of his patients. The general effect of the existence of large factors of known impossibility and of uncertainty in the situation with which he has to cope is to impose strain upon him, to make it more difficult for him to have a "purely rational" orientation to his job than if his orientation were such as to guarantee success with competent work. This is true of his own orientation without taking account of reciprocal interactions with his patients and their intimates.

But the function of "doing everything possible" is institutionalized in terms of expectations, and these expectations are most vividly and immediately embodied, besides in the physician's own attitude system, in the attitudes of precisely this group of people. But compared to most such groups their involvement is, because of the considerations analyzed above, peculiarly intensive, immediate, and likely to contain elements of emotional disturbance which are by definition, tendencies to deviant behavior. Hence the elements of strain on the physician by virtue of these impossibility and uncertainty components of his situation are particularly great. Non- and irrational mechanisms were noted as prominent in the reactions of sick people to their situations, and those of their families. In spite of the discipline of his scientific training and competence, it would be strange if, in view of the situation, physicians as a group were altogether exempted from corresponding tendencies. In fact that magic frequently appears in situations of uncertainty is suggestive. In a later section the problem of the functional equivalents of magic in actual medical practice will be taken up briefly. However, it is clear from the above that quite apart from the operation of so-called psychic factors in the disease process itself, the strains existing on *both* sides of doctor-patient relationship are such that we must expect to find, not merely institutionalization of the roles, but special mechanisms of social control in operation.

Factors of impossibility, and uncertainty in situations where there is a strong emotional interest in success, are common in many other fields of applied science—the military field is an outstandingly important example. There are, however, certain other features of the situation of the physician which are not common to many other fields which share those so far discussed. The engineer, for example, deals primarily with non-human impersonal materials which do not have "emotional" reactions to what he does with them. But the physician deals with human beings, and does so in situations which often involve "intimacies," that is, in contexts which are strongly charged with emotional and expressively symbolic significance, and which are often considered peculiarly "private" to the individual himself, or to especially intimate relations with others.

One whole class of these concerns the body. For reasons which undoubtedly go very deep psychologically, certain of the sentiments relative to what Pareto called the "integrity of the individual" are focused on the "inviolability" of the body. Their structuring will vary greatly according to the society and culture. But the amounts and occasions of bodily exposure and of bodily contact are carefully regulated in all societies, and very much so in ours. To see a person naked in a context where this is not usual, and to touch and manipulate their body, is a "privilege" which calls for explanation in view of these considerations. The case of exposure and contact when the patient is of opposite sex is, it should be clearly kept in mind, only one case in a wider category, though it is a peculiarly dramatic one. In our society there is no doubt that there are also very strong sentiments regulating physical contact between men, and between women as well. Furthermore, as to exposure, it may not, for instance, be "shameful" for a man to appear in public without his trousers, as it might be for a woman without either skirt or slacks, but it would certainly expose him to ridicule, and this also is certainly an expression of important sentiments. It is clear, in the light of the discussion in the last chapter, that both the parts of the body themselves, and acts of exposure and of bodily contact are expressive symbols of highly strategic significance.

It is essential for the physician to have access to the body of his patient in order to perform his function. Indeed, some of his contacts, as in the case of a rectal or a vaginal examination, would not be permitted to any other person by most normal individuals, even to a sexual partner. Various others would be permitted only to special intimates.

Along with all this goes the problem of sentiments toward "injury" of the body. Certainly many complex anxieties center about this in many respects. It is, for example, noteworthy how many people have really severe anxieties about the insertion of a hypodermic needle even when this has become such a commonplace in our society. Obviously the problem of securing consent to surgical procedures and many types of diagnostic procedures—such as the use of a gastroscope or a bronchoscope—is not to be too easily taken for granted. The essential point in all this is that these are no simple matters of weighing a rationally understood "need" against an equally rationally assessed "cost" in the form of discomfort or inconvenience, but very complex non- and irrational reactions are inevitably involved with the typical, not only the "abnormal" patient. The fact that these elements are organized and controlled does not make them unproblematical. On the contrary, in the light of the *potentialities* of disturbance, the fact of successful control presents peculiarly important sociological problems.

Similar considerations apply to the physician's need of access to confidential information about his patient's private life. For reasons among which their place in the system of expressive symbolism is prominent, many facts which are relevant to people's problems of health fall into the realm of the private or confidential about which people are unwilling to talk to the ordinary friend or acquaintance. Some of these concern only "reticences" about himself which are not specially bound up with intimate relations to others. A man will often, for example, hesitate to tell even his wife—even if he is on excellent terms with her—about many things which might well be of symptomatic significance to a physician. Others concern the privacies of intimate personal relationships, not only, but perhaps particularly those with sexual partners. Such information, however, is often essential to the performance of the physician's function. His access to it presents the same order of problems as does access to the body.

Modern developments in psychology, particularly psychoanalysis, have made us aware that in addition to resistances to access to the body, and to confidential information, anyone taking a role like that of the physician toward his patients is exposed to another sort of situational adjustment problem. That is, through processes which are mostly unconscious the physician tends to acquire various types of projective significance as a person which may not be directly relevant to his specifically technical functions, though they may become of the first importance in connection with psychotherapy. The generally accepted name for this phenomenon in psychiatric circles is "transference," the attribution to the physician of significances to the patient which are not "appropriate" in the realistic situation, but which derive from the psychological needs of the patient. For understandable reasons a particularly important class of these involves the attributes of parental roles as experienced by the patient in childhood. Transference is most conspicuous in "psychiatric" cases, but there is every reason to believe that it is always a factor in doctor-patient relationships, the more so the longer their duration and the greater the emotional importance of the health problem and hence the relation to the physician.

If all these factors be taken together it becomes clear that, in ways which are not true of most other professiosnal functions, the situation of medical practice is such as inevitably to "involve" the physician in the psychologically significant "private" affairs of his patients. Some of these may not otherwise be accessible to others in any ordinary situation, others only in the context of specifically intimate and personal relationships. What the relation of the physician's role to these other relationships is to be, is one of the principal functional problems which underly the structuring of his professional role.

If the features of the situation of the patient, the sick person, his intimates, and the physician, which have been reviewed, are taken together, they seem to present a very considerable set of complications of the functioning of medical practice on the level of human adjustment. These complications are not ordinarily taken account of in the simple common-sense view of the obviousness of the expectation that knowledge of how to cope with situations which are distressing to human beings will be applied to the limit of the availability of trained personnel and other necessary resources. They present another order of functional problems to the social system.

The severity of these functional problems is such that it can confidently be expected that a whole series of specific mechanisms has developed which can be understood as "ways" of meeting the strains and overcoming the obstacles to the effective practice of scientific medicine which would exist if these mechanisms did not operate. We must now turn to the analysis of a variety of these mechanisms.

§ THE FUNCTIONAL SIGNIFICANCE OF THE INSTITUTIONAL PATTERN OF MEDICAL PRACTICE

THE analysis of this problem may be centered about the pattern variables and the particular combination of their values which characterizes the "professional" pattern in our society, namely, achievement, universalism, functional specificity, affective neutrality and collectivity-orientation, in that order.

The most fundamental basis for the necessity of a universalistic-achievement and not a particularistic-ascribed structuring of the physician's role lies in the fact that modern medical practice is organized about the application of scientific knowledge by technically competent, trained personnel. A whole range of sociologically validated knowledge tends to show that the high levels of technical training and competence which this requires would not be possible in a relationship system which was structured primarily in particularistic terms or which was ascribed to incumbents of a status without the possibility of selection by performance criteria. This would drastically alter the bases of selection for the personnel of the profession, the focusing of their ambitions and loyalties and many other things. The tendency would be toward nepotism, the hereditary principle, etc.[9] It is furthermore of the first importance

[9] This is not to say that relatively high levels of technical competence cannot ever be attained or maintained in a context of particularistically ascribed role patterns. A notable example is that none of the Roman Generals who won her empire was a professional soldier in our sense. All were aristocrats to whom military activity was ascribed, and who held military command as part of a largely ascribed political career. But even Roman conquest was not applied science in quite the sense or degree that modern medicine is. Certainly no society is known with the high general level of institutionalization of very high technical competences of the applied science type in which they were usually structured in particularistic-ascribed patterns.

that only this patterning is congruent with the structuring of the rest of the occupational world in modern Western society, particularly with the general world of science in the universities, and its application in other professional roles.

This last is a particularly important point. The tendency of particularistic structuring is to develop solidarities which, through contributing to the integration of the social situation *within* the solidary group, tend to do so at the cost of deepening the separations between such groups, even generating, or contributing to, antagonism and conflict.

A basic fact about science is that the structure of "pure" scientific disciplines cuts across the structure of the fields of application of science to practical affairs. The term "medical science" is thus a somewhat equivocal one, it is not the designation of a single theoretically integrated discipline, but of a field of application. Many different sciences find applications in the medical or health field, physics, chemistry, the whole gamut of biological sciences, psychology and, we can now see, sociology, though the latter is little recognized as yet. A particularistic structuring of the medical profession would almost certainly operate to emphasize and institutionalize the distinction between the medical and the non-medical even more than has actually been the case. Pasteur was initially repudiated by the medical profession in considerable part because he was not a physician but "only" a chemist—how could anything medically important come from anyone who was not a member of the "fraternity"? This repudiation of Pasteur is rightly regarded by modern physicians as a very unfortunate aberration, a refusal to recognize the "intrinsic" merits of a contribution regardless of its source. But particularistic bases of status-ascription, of solidarity, etc., *inherently* cut across the intrinsic structure of science. If they were the predominant institutional focus of the physician's role it is hard to see how the Pasteur case could fail to become the rule, which would come to be ideologically glorified in the profession as a proper protection of its "purity" against gratuitous interference by "outsiders."

The universalism of the medical role has, however, also another type of functional significance. In the light of the considerations brought forward in the last section it is clear that there is strong pressure to assimilate the physician to the nexus of personal relationships in which the patient is placed, quite apart from the specific technical content of the job he is called upon to perform. In so far as his role can be defined in unequivocally universalistic terms, this serves as a protection against such assimilation, because personal friendships, love relationships and family relationships are overwhelmingly particularistic. However, this aspect of the functional significance of universalism is closely bound up with that of functional specificity and affective neutrality. Its significance will be more advantageously discussed when the bearing of these two pattern elements has been made clear.

In its relation to technical competence, universalism is, as has been noted, linked to functional specificity. A generalized "wisdom" which is genuinely universalistic but not specialized for any particular context is conceivable, but it is certainly not the basis of the competence of the physician who is a specialized expert in a specifically defined, if broad and complicated field. But the definition of the physician's role in this respect is not relevant only with relation to the specificity of his competence, but also of his legitimate scope of concern. Specificity of competence has primarily the function of delimiting a field so that it is relatively manageable, so that competence will not be destroyed by "spreading too thin." Specificity of the scope of concern, on the other hand, has the function of defining the relationship to patients so that it can be regulated in certain ways and certain potential alternatives of definition, which might be disruptive, can be excluded or adequately controlled.

In terms of the features of the situation discussed above, functional specificity is an important element in overcoming potential resistances to the physician, in that through it the limits of his legitimate claims on the patient are defined, and thereby anxieties about the consequences of the special privileges accorded to him are allayed. The role conforms strictly to the criterion of the burden of proof being on the side of exclusion. If the patient asks why he should answer a question his doctor puts to him, or why he should submit to a given procedure, the answer is in terms of the relevance of his health problem—"if you want to get well, you have to give me the information I need to do my job," etc. If it cannot be justified by the relevance to the health problem it is "none of the doctor's business."

The obverse of permissions on the basis of positive relevance to the health problem is some sort of assurance that information or other privileges will not be used for other purposes, or that access to the body will not be used to exploit the patient, or to distort the relation in another direction, e.g., in the direction of mutual sexual attraction.

One of the most prominent mechanisms by which this is brought about is the segregation of the context of professional practice from other contexts. The doctrine of privileged communications is one of the best examples. That what the doctor learns about his patient's private affairs in the course of his duties is confidential and not to be divulged is not only one of the strongest tenets of professional ethics, but is protected by law against the claim to testify in court. Another significant example is the rule that physicians do not care for members of their own families except in essentially trivial illnesses. Not only might their emotional involvements distort their judgment, but they might well come to know things about which it is just as well for them not to know.

Even where there is both a professional and a non-professional aspect of the relationship of the physician to the same persons, there is a definite tendency to segregate the two aspects. For example one physician expressed a strong dislike of being asked for professional advice on social occasions, e.g., the lady sitting next to him at dinner asking what she should do about some illness of her child. His usual response was to ask her to come to his office and discuss it. It might be argued that his interest was in the fee, but the same thing is to be observed where no fee is involved.

One of the most conspicuous cases of the operation of segregation is where a potential sexual element enters in. For example a general practitioner whose office was in his home, and who had no office nurse or dressing room, reported that he habitually stepped out of the office to allow a female patient to get ready for a physical examination. When, as occasionally happened, the patient started to disrobe before he had time to get out of the room, he found it definitely embarrassing, though the same patient disrobed on the examining table did not embarrass him at all. The essential point is that for most men "woman in the same room undressing" usually means potential sexual relations, for the physician "woman on the examining table" means a professional job to do. Naturally, ensuring the right behavior in each context requires a learning process and a system of control mechanisms.[10]

These examples show that segregation operates not only to maintain functional specificity, but also affective neutrality by defining situations which might potentially arouse various emotional reactions as "professional" and thereby mobilizing a system of sanctions against "inappropriate" reactions. The importance of functional specificity is to define, in situations where potential illegitimate involvements might develop, the limits of the "privileges" in the "dangerous" area which the physician may claim. The pattern of affective neutrality then defines his expected attitudes within those limits.

The case of situations which might easily arouse sexual attractions is a particularly vivid one in our society. It should be noted that breakdown of the controls insuring affective neutrality in that connection is important not only to the doctor and the patient, but would often also involve the interests of a variety of third parties, since each tends to be involved in erotic relations with others whose interests would in turn be affected. In other words the toleration by a husband of his wife privately seeing a doctor and the lack of jealousy of their husband's female patients on the part of the doctors' wives are important conditions of medical practice. Occasionally disturbances in this area do occur, but their relative infrequency and the quickness with which they are stigmatized as "pathological" is indicative of the effectiveness of the control system.[11]

[10] The testimony of a considerable number of physicians interviewed is that in the early stages of medical education sexual arousal to some degree is not uncommon, but that the relevant occasions soon become "part of the day's work." Also by no means the only problem of control is the "protection" of the woman patient from the physician's "taking advantage" of her. Quite frequently it is the other way around, including the possibility of his susceptibility being used for blackmail. One of the prominent hospitals justified the policy of having a nurse present on such occasions by saying "it is at least as much for the protection of the doctor as of the patient." This nurse is graphically referred to as a "nurse-chaperone."

[11] One particular case has been reported to the author of a husband who would not allow his wife to go to a male obstetrician. The physician reporting it assumed this attitude to be pathological. But it is pertinent to note that it was not very long ago when attendance at childbirth by a male physician was not tolerated in most of Western society.

There is a good deal of folklore current in such places as the pulp magazine literature and burlesque stage humor about the special opportunities of the

This problem of emotional involvements is not, however, confined to the sexual aspect. It also includes likes and dislikes on another level. An eminent surgeon, for instance, was acutely aware of the emotional reaction provoked in himself by seeing a patient through a long and difficult convalescence from a severe and dangerous operation—one case was a nine-year-old boy. He said he would distrust his own judgment if he had to decide to operate a second time on such a case: He was afraid he would lean over backwards to spare the patient the suffering he knew would be involved, even in a case where he also knew the operation would probably be best for the patient in the long run. It is also important that doctors should not let their personal dislikes of particular patients be expressed in a poorer level of treatment or even positive "punishment." And doctors would scarcely be human if they did not take a dislike to some of their patients.

The argument of the last few pages may be summed up in the proposition that one principal set of functional significances of the combination universalism, functional specificity, and affective neutrality, is to enable the physician to "penetrate" sufficiently into the private affairs, or the "particular nexus" of his patients to perform his function. By defining his role in this way it is possible to overcome or minimize resistances which might well otherwise prove fatal to the possibility of doing the job at all.[12]

This importance is not, however, confined to the overcoming of potential resistances. It is also evident that these pattern elements are "for the protection of the physician" in a broader sense than in the case of the "nurse-chaperone" as she is sometimes actually called. The obverse functional danger to that of refusal to admit to the sphere of private affairs is that this admission should be too thorough, that the role of the doctor should be assimilated to that of other "significant persons" in the situation of the patient, that he really should become a personal intimate, a lover, a parent, or a per-

---

doctor for sexual gratification. It might be that "where there is smoke there is fire." But the available evidence points to the probability that this expresses a wish-fulfillment projected on the physician's role, rather than a shrewd guess as to what actually happens.

[12] It is interesting to note that the social or psychological research worker faces similar problems in his relations to people he wishes to interview or observe. The cognate features of his role have the same order of functional significance.

sonal enemy. All these roles are, it will be noted, defined in terms of the opposite combination of the values of the pattern-variables being discussed from that which characterizes the professional pattern.

A good many instances were collected by the author in which physicians had been put in positions where there was a "pull" to assimilate their roles to patterns of this type, particularly that of a "personal friend" of the patient. There are various complicating factors but in general it can be said that there was a marked tendency for the physician to feel uncomfortable. Asked why it was undesirable to allow the assimilation to take place, the usual answer ran in terms of the difficulty of maintaining "objectivity" and "good judgment" in relation to the job. There is every reason to believe that there was an element of correct insight in the testimony of these doctors, none of whom incidentally was a psychiatrist or psychiatrically trained. It is, however, difficult to judge how far this is a rational appraisal of the situation and how far a rationalization of other factors of which the respondent was not explicitly aware.

The enormous recent development of psychotherapy, and increase of our knowledge of the psychological aspects of human relations relative to it, calls attention to another most important aspect of this whole situation. Through the mechanisms of transference the patient, usually without knowing what he is doing, not only has certain resistances, but he actively attempts by projection to assimilate his physician to a pattern of particularistic personal relationship to himself. He attempts to elicit the reaction which is appropriate to his own need-dispositions. Though this is most conspicuous in psychiatric cases, as noted, there can be no doubt that it is also of the greatest importance throughout the field of doctor-patient relationships.

In the first place it is necessary for the physician to be protected against this emotional pressure, because for a variety of reasons inherent in his own situation it is not possible for him to "enter in" to the kind of relationship the patient, usually unconsciously, wants. Above all this functional specificity which permits the physician to confine the relationship to a certain content field, indeed enjoins it on him, and affective neutrality which permits him to avoid entering into reciprocities on the emotional level, serve to bring about this protection. The upshot is that he refuses to be "drawn in" and has institutional backing in his refusals of reciprocity.[18]

But, in addition to this, our knowledge of the processes of psychotherapy reveals another important dimension of the situation. That is, the same features of the physician's role, which are so important as protection of the physician himself, are also crucially important conditions of successful psychotherapy. Psychotherapy, as we have seen, becomes necessary when the control mechanisms inherent in the reciprocities of ordinary human relationships break down. One of the most important features of neurotic behavior in this sense is of course the involvement in vicious circles, so that the social pressures which ordinarily serve to keep people "in line" and bring them back if they start to deviate, serve only to intensify the recalcitrant reaction and to drive the individual farther from satisfactory behavior. If these vicious circles are to be dealt with there must be an "Archimedean place to stand" outside the reciprocities of ordinary social intercourse. This is precisely what the patterning of the physician's role provides. Whether it is love or hate which the patient projects upon him, he fails to reciprocate in the expected terms. He remains objective and affectively neutral.[14] The patient tries to involve him in his personal affairs outside the health field and he refuses to see his patient except at the stated hours in his office, he keeps out of his sight so as to avoid opportunities for reciprocal reactions.[15] Finally, the discrepancy between the transference reactions and the realistic role of the physician provides one of the most important occasions for interpretations which can bring the patient to new levels of insight as part of the process of emotional readjustment.

An essential part of what the psychiatrist does is to apply direct knowledge of the mechanisms of neurotic behavior to the manipula-

[18] The fact that his role is collectively-oriented, on the other hand, tends to draw him in and has to be counteracted by these other factors.

[14] "Countertransference" of course occurs, but the therapist is expected to minimize and control it, not just "let himself go."

[15] Many specific points in the details of psychotherapeutic and psychoanalytic technique are controversial within the relevant professional groups. The present discussion is not meant to take a position on such questions as to whether it might or might not under certain circumstances be better to get the patient off the couch into a face-to-face position. It is meant only to call attention to certain general features of the psychotherapeutic situation.

tion of his patient. Increasingly, however, psychiatrists are becoming aware of the importance of the structuring of their own roles as part of the therapeutic process. But it is quite clear that the basic structuring of the physician's role in our society *did not come about through the application of theories of the ideal situation for psychotherapy*. It was a spontaneous, unplanned development of social structure which psychiatry has been able to utilize and develop, but which originated independently of its influence.

There is a most important implication of all this. Psychiatry is much more recent than organic medicine, and today constitutes only a fraction of the total of medical practice. But the continuity between them in function must be, and historically has been, much greater than the usual explicit interpretations allow for. If the structure of the physician's role has the kind of functional significance for deliberate psychotherapy which has been outlined here, it must have some effect on the mental state of the patient whether it is used for deliberate psychotherapy or not. And there is every evidence that it does. Psychotherapy to the militantly antipsychiatric organic physician is like theory to the militantly antitheoretical empirical scientist. In both cases he practices it whether he knows it or wants to or not. He may indeed do it very effectively just as one can use a language well without even knowing it has a grammatical structure.[16] But the general conclusion is that a very important part of non- and prepsychiatric medical practice is in fact "unconscious psychotherapy" and that this could not be true if the institutional structure of the physician's role were not approximately what it has here been shown to be.[17]

---

[16] This has sometimes been called the "art of medicine."

[17] Two formulae are more or less current among physicians which show an inadequate understanding of the situation. One is that the doctor is the patient's "best friend." He is, in terms of willingness to help him. But a relationship of friendship is not confined to a functionally specific context, nor is it affectively neutral. A friend does not have the "place to stand" outside certain reciprocities. The other is current among certain psychoanalysts, "the doctor is the father." It is true that the father role is perhaps the most immediately appropriate *transference* role to a male analyst, especially if there is a considerable age differential. But when a son misbehaves a father reacts with anger and punishment, not affectively neutral "understanding." A father can also be called upon to help where a physician can legitimately refuse. It is precisely the *differences* from friendship and familial roles which are the most important levers for the psychotherapeutic process.

This brings us to the last pattern element, collectivity-orientation. It is this which is distinctive of professional roles within the upper reaches of our occupational system, especially in the contrast with business. Indeed one of the author's principal motivations in embarking on a study of the medical profession lay in the desire to understand a high-level occupational role which deviated from that of the businessman who, according to certain theorists, represented the one strategically crucial type of such role in modern "capitalistic" society.[18]

It was noted above that the sick person is peculiarly vulnerable to exploitation and at the same time peculiarly handicapped in arriving at a rationally objective appraisal of his situation. In addition, the physician is a technically competent person whose competence and specific judgments and measures cannot be competently judged by the layman. The latter must therefore take these judgments and measures "on authority." But in the type case there is no system of coercive sanctions to back up this authority. All the physician can say to the patient who refuses to heed his advice is "well, it's your own funeral"—which it may be literally. All this of course is true of a situation which includes the potential resistances which have been discussed above.

These different factors seem to indicate that the situation is such that it would be particularly difficult to implement the pattern of the business world, where each party to the situation is expected to be oriented to the rational pursuit of his own self-interests, and where there is an approach to the idea of "caveat emptor." In a broad sense it is surely clear that society would not tolerate the privileges which have been vested in the medical profession on such terms. The protection of the patient against the exploitation of his helplessness, his technical incompetence and his irrationality thus constitutes the most obvious functional significance of the pattern. In this whole connection it is noteworthy how strongly the main reliance for control is placed on "informal" mechanisms. The law of the state includes severe penalties for "malpractice" and medical associations have relatively elaborate disciplinary procedures, but these quite

[18] See "the Professions and Social Structure," *Essays in Sociological Theory*, Chapter VIII, for a general analysis of the relations between business and the professions in our social structure.

definitely are not the principal mechanisms which operate to ensure the control of self-orientation tendencies. The significance of this will be discussed below.

Here it may be noted that the collectivity-orientation of the physician is protected by a series of symbolically significant practices which serve to differentiate him sharply from the business-man. He cannot advertise—he can only modestly announce by his "shingle" and the use of his M.D. in telephone directories and classified sections, that he is available to provide medical service. He cannot bargain over fees with his patients—a "take it or leave it" attitude is enjoined upon him. He cannot refuse patients on the ground that they are poor "credit risks." He is given the privilege of charging according to the "sliding scale," that is, in proportion to the income of the patient or his family—a drastic difference from the usual pricing mechanism of the business world. The general picture is one of sharp segregation from the market and price practices of the business world, in ways which for the most part cut off the physician from many immediate opportunities for financial gain which are treated as legitimately open to the businessman. The motivational significance of this difference will have to be discussed below.

It is also interesting to note, following up the earlier remarks about "shopping around," that the definition in terms of collectivity-orientation is expected to be reciprocal. The most usual formulation for this is that the patient is expected to "have confidence" in his physician, and if this confidence breaks down, to seek another physician.

This may be interpreted to mean that the relationship is expected to be one of mutual "trust," of the belief that the physician is trying his best to help the patient and that conversely the patient is "cooperating" with him to the best of his ability. It is significant for instance that this constitutes a reinforcement of one of the principal institutional features of the sick role, the expectation of a desire to get well. It makes the patient, in a special sense, responsible to his physician. But more generally, it has been pointed out before that collectivity-orientation is involved in all cases of institutionalized authority, that is authority is an attribute of a status in a collectivity. In a very special and informal sense the doctor-patient relationship has to be one involving an element of authority—we often speak of "doctor's orders." This authority cannot be legitimized without reciprocal collectivity-orientation in the relationship. To the doctor's obligation to use his authority "responsibly" in the interest of the patient, corresponds the patient's obligation faithfully to accept the implications of the fact that he is "Dr. X's patient" and so long as he remains in that status must "do his part" in the common enterprise. He is free, of course, to terminate the relationship at any time. But the essential point is the sharp line which tends to be drawn between being X's patient, and no longer being in that position. In the ideal type of commercial relationship one is not A's customer to the exclusion of other sources of supply for the same needs.

Finally, there is a most important relationship between collectivity-orientation and psychotherapy, conscious or unconscious. There are differences of opinion among psychiatrists on many subjects, but so far as the author knows, none on this point—that therapeutic success is not possible unless the patient can be brought to trust his physician. This is particularly important because it can safely be said that there is no important class of psychological disturbances which do not have, as one important component, an impairment of the capacity to trust others, essentially what, in Chapter VII, we called a sense of insecurity. This element of distrust then tends to be projected onto the physician in the transference relationship. If the role of the physician were defined in self-orientation terms it could hardly fail to invite deepening of the vicious circle, because the patient would tend to see his own neurotic definition of the situation confirmed by the institutional expectation that the physician was "out to get everything he could for himself." In this as in other contexts it is of the first importance that the institutionalized definition of the role is such as to counteract these transference tendencies of the patient, thus to set up a discrepancy between his neurotic expectations and reality which is as difficult as possible for him to avoid understanding. In view of the immense importance of what has here been called the element of unconscious psychotherapy in non-psychiatric medical practice, the element of collectivity-orientation is certainly one of the keystones of the institutional arch in this respect.

§ SOME SPECIAL PROBLEMS

A FEW special problems may now be taken up which illustrate in still other contexts connected with medical practice the
usefulness of the type of analysis which is here being employed. The
ones which will each be briefly discussed here are, the part played
by certain pseudo-scientific elements even within the profession
itself, the predominance of informal internal controls and the resistance to outside and to formal control, and the problem of the
comparative motivational patterns of the medical and business
world.

We may go back to the discussion of the element of uncertainty
which looms so large in medical practice. This element, and that of
impossibility, the border lines between them often being indistinct,
places serious strains on a well-integrated balance of need, skill,
effort, and expectations of result.[19] Within this situation there is a
variety of motivational factors operating to drive action in one direction, namely, "success" of the therapeutic enterprise. The physician
himself is trained and expected to act, not merely to be a passive
observer of what goes on. The patient and his family are also under
strong emotional pressures to "get something done." There is on
both sides, in Pareto's terms, a "need to manifest sentiments by
external acts."

One of the best types of examples of this situation is that where
a decision to perform a surgical operation is in the balance, and
where, from a technical point of view, there is a genuine uncertainty
element involved. The surgeon must weigh the risks of operation
against the risks of delaying operation or deciding not to operate at
all. In general it is clear that there tends to be a bias in favor of
operating. After all the surgeon is trained to operate, he feels active,
useful, effective when he is operating. For the patient and his
family, in their state of anxiety and tension also, inactivity, just

---

[19] Durkheim, in his classic interpretation of the nature of *anomie* in *Suicide*,
was one of the first to analyze correctly the nature of the strains involved in
upsetting a normal balance in the relation between effort, skill, and expectation
of result. His analysis is further generalized by our treatment of the complementarity of expectations in interactive relationships and the motivational consequences
of disturbances of this complementarity.

waiting to see how things develop is particularly hard to bear. A decision to operate will, in such a situation, almost certainly "clear the air" and make everybody "feel better." At least "something is being done." It is also probable that American culture predisposes more to this pattern of activity than most others, and that this has much to do with our tendency to glorify the surgeon, who is indeed a kind of culture hero.

This problem of the bias in favor of active intervention, of giving the benefit of the doubt to operating in surgical cases, underlies the problem of "unnecessary operations" about which there has been a good deal of discussion in medical circles. It is true that, in the situation of individual fee-for-service practice, the surgeon has a direct financial incentive to be biased in favor of operating. In the folklore of the subject, however, whatever tendency to unnecessary operations there may be, tends too immediately to be ascribed to this financial incentive. It is forgotten that there are other powerful motives operating in the same direction. In such a situation it would take far more refined research methods than have yet been applied to the problem to discriminate the effects of the two factors. One may thus be warned against glib, easy interpretations of the "obvious" motivation of a pattern of action, where it can be shown that *one* motivational factor operates in the right direction.

It is suggested that the situation of surgical practice, where the uncertainty factor is almost inevitably great, predisposes to a bias in favor of active intervention. Since the motivation for this bias tends to be strongly shared by patients and their families, its existence is obscured since there is no conspicuous group whose conscious interests are injured by it to protest. But this particular version of the bias is by no means isolated. A second conspicuous phenomenon is the existence of a pattern of "fashion change," even within the medical profession as such, which, however, is far less conspicuous than the related health "faddism" current among the general public.[20]

This phenomenon is easy to observe only in temporal perspec-

[20] An excellent place to study the latter is in the field of health advertising. For an analysis of one such "fad," cf. L. J. Henderson, "Aphorisms on the Advertising of Alkalis," *Harvard Business Review*, Autumn, 1937, Vol. 16, pp. 17-23.

tive. A technical innovation in the medical field will for a time be slow in "catching on." When, however, it begins to be accepted, it will spread very rapidly and be utilized on almost every possible occasion where an at all plausible case for it can be made. This continues until the point is reached where it becomes "oversold" and a reaction sets in. Its use will then fall off, probably to a level below its intrinsic merits, and after a series of narrowing fluctuations it will tend to settle down to a well-established place in the professional "repertoire."

The phenomenon was perfectly described, without the slightest awareness of its sociological implications, by two surgeons writing in a medical journal, discussing a new operative technique for the removal of the prostate gland. But the same tendency can be observed in many cases, e.g., "focal infection," the use of the sulfa drugs recently, psycho-somatic interpretations in many fields. The important point is that the "irrational" element in the belief in the efficacy of *any one* technique or diagnostic idea, which we see must be interpreted as a reaction to strain, is only temporary, but *at any given time*, there is always a group of such ideas current in the profession. By the time that rational criticism and experience have succeeded in "finding the proper level" for one, another has arisen to take its place.

The general phenomenon then is an "optimistic bias" in favor of the soundness of ideas or efficacy of procedures. Since the basic normative pattern by which such ideas are measured is that of science, there are strong pressures toward the elimination of the bias in any particular case. But as a general phenomenon it persists—it is a pseudo-scientific element in the technical competence of the medical profession which is more than simply an expression of the relative lack of scientific development of the field; it is positively motivated.

The question arises of whether it has positive functions, or as the "rationalistic" tendency of thought goes, is simply an "imperfection" to be eliminated. Comparative perspective is very helpful in answering this question. Malinowski among others has shown that magical beliefs and practices tend to cluster about situations where there is an important uncertainty factor and where there are strong emotional interests in the success of action.[21] Gardening and deep-sea fishing are examples he analyzes. It is suggestive that pseudo-science is the functional equivalent of magic in the modern medical field. The health situation is a classic one of the combination of un-certainty and strong emotional interests which produce a situation of strain and is very frequently a prominent focus of magic. But the fact that the basic cultural tradition of modern medicine is science precludes outright magic, which is explicitly non-scientific. The result is a "bias."

It may be safely inferred that there is an important element of positive functional significance in this. The basic function of magic, according to Malinowski, is to bolster the self-confidence of actors in situations where energy and skill *do* make a difference but where because of uncertainty factors, outcomes cannot be guar-anteed. This fits the situation of the doctor, but in addition on the side of the patient it may be argued that *belief* in the possibility of recovery is an important factor in it. If from purely a technical point of view both the individual doctor and the general tradition are optimistically biased it ought to help, through a "ritual" demonstra-tion of the will to recover and that there *is* a chance.[22] Of course this argument must not be pressed too far. Too many conspicuous failures of optimism to be justified by events could have a shatter-ing effect on just this confidence. The functional needs of society call for a delicate balance in this as in many other fields.

Modern medical practice is, as has so frequently been pointed out, overwhelmingly oriented to science. Science in turn attempts to make the state of its knowledge as clear and rationally explicit as possible. One would think that this type of pattern would run through the whole social complex of medical practice. There is a certain formal precision and clarity about the existence of a system of formal rules of behavior and formal mechanisms for their enforce-ment which seems to bear a certain relationship to scientific pre-cision, so that on the basis of "cultural congruence" one might expect

[21] See B. Malinowski, *Magic, Science and Religion*. Kroeber, *Anthropology*, 1948 Ed., pp. 604, questions the universality of this relationship, but not that it exists in many cases.

[22] It may be suggested that reference to this context constitutes a significant, if not well understood undertone, in the physician's so frequent insistence that his patients should have "confidence" in him.

a system of bureaucratic-legalistic social organization to be particularly congenial to a scientifically trained profession.

Broadly the facts do not bear out this expectation. A certain jealous guarding of their independence from outsiders might be expected from such a professional group, indeed they do tend to do so vis-à-vis the state and, ideologically at least, vis-à-vis any other potential source of "lay control."[23] But perhaps the most conspicuous fact is that even their own professional associations do not play a really important part in the control of medical practice and its potential abuses through formal channels. It is true that medical associations do have committees on ethics and disciplinary procedures. But it is exceedingly rare for cases to be brought into that formal disciplinary procedure. Thus the well-known reluctance of physicians to testify against other physicians in cases of malpractice, in the courts, has its parallel in the reluctance of physicians to resort to the formal disciplinary procedures of their own associations, which do not involve "washing their dirty linen" before laymen.

It is suggested that behind this conspicuous tendency lie factors which are common throughout the occupational world, but perhaps in certain respects especially prominent here. The general tendency is to fall considerably short of living up to the full "logical" implications of the dominant culture pattern in certain crucial respects. It is suggested that this derives from the fact that it is not possible to "apply" the dominant cultural pattern literally and without restriction and not generate strains which in turn would produce responses which would be more disruptive than certain "mitigations" of the rigorous applications of the pattern itself. This deviation from the dominant pattern is what we have called an adaptive structure.

The physician is expected to act responsibly in a situation where the interests of others are very vitally affected, and in ways where

[23] The qualification "ideologically" is necessary here. Almost all medical education, by explicit sanction of the organized profession, is now in the hands of Universities. Ultimate legal control of the university is usually in the hands of boards of trustees, not one of which is composed of a majority of medical men. Much the same is true of the government of hospitals. Yet many medical men, who never think of protesting against this situation, roundly assert that any change which will subject medical men to the authority of laymen in any respect is "in principle" intolerable.

it is not by any means always probable that the reaction of these others to things going wrong will be "reasonable." The resources he has available to do his job are by no means fully adequate. He inevitably makes mistakes, and his mistakes may on occasion have very serious consequences. Moreover, it may be peculiarly difficult to explain many situations where things go wrong to people not technically competent or familiar with the peculiar circumstances of medical work and whose emotions are wrought up. Even within a medical society formal procedures necessarily abstract from the subtleties of the particular situation.

It may therefore be suggested that reliance on informal controls, even though greater formalization would be more "logical," may have its functional significance. As one physician put it, "Who is going to throw the first stone? We are all vulnerable. We have all been in situations where what we did could be made to look very bad." Formalization inevitably gives a prominent role to "technicalities" of definition. It always opens the door for the "clever lawyer" whether he be a District Attorney or merely the "prosecutor" of the medical society's own Committee on Ethics. Undoubtedly a certain amount of abuse does "get by" in the present situation which "ought not to" and would not in a well-run formal system of control. But it is at least possible that the strong reliance on informal controls helps to give the physician confidence, and a certain daring in using risky though well-advised procedures, which he would not be so ready to do in a more thoroughly bureaucratized situation.[24]

Finally, a brief discussion may be devoted to the problem of the sociological interpretations of the motivation of the physician in his professional role which can supplement the discussion of the "profit

---

[24] In this connection it should be noted that some branches of medicine show a willingness to have their work exposed to professional criticism which is rarely matched in other professions. The practice of surgery is, within the profession, essentially public, and has the further check of the pathological laboratory and the autopsy. But it is interesting that it is only professionally public, laymen are generally excluded from the operating room. The author's observations suggest one possible factor in this. The families of patients undergoing an operation are generally emotionally "wrought up" to a high degree. The atmosphere of the operating room, on the other hand, is in general a "work-a-day" atmosphere, with calm technical comment and discussion, and often a good deal of joking. Much of this could not fail to appear to the emotionally disturbed relative as frivolity or callousness—the doctors "don't care what happens to my wife."

motive" in Chapter VI. Because of the prominence in their own ideology of the difference between "professionalism" and "commercialism," and the general popular tendency to think of all businessmen as "heartless egoists" and medical men as "altruists," the discussion may center on this issue. This tendency is deeply grounded in the total "ideology" of our society with its roots in the utilitarian pattern of thought. It can be shown to be quite definitely wrong in this case.

It is quite true, as has been pointed out in the discussion of the pattern of collectivity-orientation above, that the medical man is expected to place the welfare of the patient above his own self-interest, financial or otherwise. He is also explicitly debarred, in the code of medical ethics, from a whole series of practices which are taken for granted as quite legitimate for the honest and upright businessman, such as advertising, price-competition, refusing to take patients on the ground that they are not good "credit risks," etc. Thus the physician is both debarred from a variety of immediate opportunities for financial gain which are open to the businessman, and is positively enjoined to promote the welfare of his patients. It is not these facts which are at issue, but the interpretation of their meaning for motivation and the mechanisms of social control.

It is quite possible that a selective process operates so that a career in medicine appeals to a more "service oriented" type of personality than does a career in business. But even if this is a factor of considerable significance it is certainly not the only or even the principal one. For the question arises, would it really be to the self-interest of the normal physician to ignore the code of his profession and to garner the financial rewards from advertising, from increasing his practice by undercutting the rates of his colleagues, and from excluding the bad credit risks. In general, assuming that the situation is institutionally well integrated, this would not be to his interest. For such action would impinge on both the interests and the sentiments of others in the situation. The consequences would take the form of a loss of professional standing which in turn would, if it went far enough, begin to show in quite tangible forms. Desirable connections from financial, as well as other points of view, would become more difficult to form, or be endangered, such as hospital staff appointments or referrals of patients from other physicians. A staff appointment might be terminated, or not renewed. In the extreme case there might be the threat of disciplinary action on the part of the medical society. All along there would be a jeopardizing of the easy informal "belongingness" to a group who understand each other as to proper conduct.

In other words, the collectivity-orientation of the professional pattern has become built into a set of institutionalized expectations of behavior and attitude. In conformity with the basic theorem of the institutional integration of motivation discussed in Chapter II, both self-interested and "altruistic" elements of motivation have thereby become channeled into the path of conformity with these expectations. Therefore the seeming paradox is realized that it is to a physician's self-interest to act contrary to his own self-interest—in an immediate situation, of course, not "in the long run."

The difference between the professional pattern and that of the business world in this respect, which turns primarily on the variable of self- vs. collectivity-orientation, is thus in the first instance institutional and not motivational. Whatever differences there may be from a psychological point of view between the typical motives of physicians and of businessmen, must be analyzed with this in mind, taking it as a starting point. It is a particularly vivid example of the importance of the sociological analysis of the social system for formulation of the problem of the analysis of motivation when the generalization of the implications of that analysis is to be extended beyond the single individual to problems of significance to the social system.[25]

§ SOME THEORETICAL CONCLUSIONS

IN THE foregoing discussion we have not attempted to give anything like a full coverage of the facts relevant to the analysis of medical practice as a social system, and its place in the larger social system. We have, for example, not dealt with the processes of recruitment and training of the profession. We have not more than hinted at its very complex internal differentiations, or the large field of professional organization. Above all we have dealt only with a

[25] This problem is somewhat further discussed in the two papers, "The Professions and Social Structure" and "The Motivation of Economic Activities," *Essays in Sociological Theory,* Chapters VIII and IX.

kind of ideal type of the situation in a way which has ignored a whole range of what, relative to the technical and ethical standards of the best of the profession, are sub-standard and deviant practices. We have, however, presented enough material to justify certain conclusions which are of central significance to the present work. Our object was not to give a complete empirical review but only the facts most directly relevant to some of our main theoretical interests.

The case selected for presentation was that of an occupational role. We are accustomed in the common sense of our culture to think of such a role in terms of the instrumental division of labor, a view which is correct and sound enough. We are accustomed to think of the incumbent of the role as "having something to sell," in this case a service, to people who have a need and know how to go about meeting that need. The place of technical competence based on scientific training is also in a broad way understood on a common-sense basis.

In common-sense terms, however, it is far from possible to give an adequate account of how these functions of purveying a service to those who need it can in fact be effectively carried out under the actual conditions of the concrete social system. We have seen that with respect to the problems of health, as to many others, the treatment of practical problems in terms of applied science is not to be taken for granted, but is subject to special conditions in the cultural and social systems. We have seen that medical practice must be a part of the general institutionalization of scientific investigation and of the application of science to practical problems, which is a characteristic feature of modern Western society.

In general in the instrumental division of labor, on the grounds we have adduced throughout this work, the institutionalization of all the roles in ways of which common sense is not at all or only very vaguely aware, is a functional requirement of the effective performance of the role. We have not taken space to demonstrate that the role of physician, simply as one of the general class of occupational roles, is institutionalized, and what this institutionalization consists in; that can be taken for granted.

We have, rather, concentrated on certain special features of the roles of both parties to the doctor-patient relationship, and their relation to certain special features of the conditions in which the performance of medical service takes place. There are perhaps two most general conclusions from consideration of these special features in terms of the conceptual scheme of this work. The first of these is that successful performance of those functions of medical practice, which are obvious to common sense, depends on a whole series of conditions, the necessity for which is not obvious. The second conclusion is that the ways in which both roles are institutionalized are related to aspects of the motivational balances of the social system, both in direct relation to health and in broader respects, in ways which are altogether inaccessible to common sense, and which admirably illustrate the general analysis of that motivational balance of social processes which was presented in Chapters VI and VII above.

With respect to the first context, the role of being sick as an institutionalized role may be said to constitute a set of conditions necessary to enable the physician to bring his competence to bear on the situation. It is not only that the patient has a need to be helped, but that this need is institutionally categorized, that the nature and implications of this need are socially recognized, and the kind of help, the appropriate general pattern of action in relation to the source of help, are defined. It is not only the sick person's own condition and personal reactions to what should be done about it which are involved, but he is placed in an institutionally defined framework which mobilizes others in his situation in support of the same patterns which are imputed to him, which is such an important feature of his role. The fact that others than the patient himself often define that he is sick, or sick enough for certain measures to be taken, is significant.

On the other side of the relationship, the collectivity-orientation of the physician, and its universalism, neutrality and specificity, make it possible for the things he has to do to perform his function to be made acceptable to the patient and his family. These include validation of his professional authority and justification of the "privileges" he must be accorded.

A central aspect of this phase of the problem is that certain of the features of the role structure on both sides of the relationship are essential to bringing together the cultural and the situational elements of the action complex. It is possible to have a sick role, and to have treatment of illness institutionalized, where the role of therapist is not of the modern professional type. Treatment by kinsmen is a common example. But if, as in our society, the primary cultural tradition defined as relevant to health is science, it is not possible to have the role of therapist institutionalized in the same pattern terms as those of kinship. Hence in addition to the *sick* role we may distinguish the role of *patient* as the recipient of the services of a scientifically trained *professional* physician. The definition of the sick role as that of potential patient is one of its principal characteristics in our society.

Finally, on this level we have shown that certain deviations from the ideal type of institutionalization of science and of rational action are found in the field of medical practice. These deviations are of two types: first, a deviation from the ideal type of the institutionalized belief system in the form of the prevalence of an element of pseudo-scientific belief in the efficacy of measures, a deviation which is continuous with the wider deviations to be found among the lay public. The second type of deviation is on the level of social organization, and was illustrated by the case of the conspicuous reliance within the profession on informal sanction systems where from a "rational" point of view formal disciplinary machinery would be more appropriate. Both of these are to be regarded as adaptive phenomena of the general type we have often spoken of.

We may express the second main conclusion by saying that the sick role, including its aspect as patient, and the role of physician, both have latent functions with respect to the motivational balance of the social system which are of considerable significance. Some of the most important keys to the understanding of these latent functions are to be found in the psychiatrist's own analyses of the processes of psychotherapy, but the significance even of these for the social system is only brought out when they are seen in their more general setting in the theory of the social system. Other elements necessary to the understanding of these functions are derived from the analysis of institutional structure, in its application to these roles and their interaction, and from bringing out the common elements as between the processes of the interaction of physician and patient, and those operating in a variety of other types of situation.

The essential assumption in this connection is that illness is, in one of its major aspects, to be defined as a form of deviant behavior, and that the elements of motivation to deviance which are expressed in the sick role are continuous with those expressed in a variety of other channels, including types of compulsive conformity which are not socially defined as deviant. Because of the element of fluidity in so much of the motivation to deviance, or more generally the reactions to strain, it is possible to regard illness as belonging to a system of alternative channels for the "acting out" of such motivational elements, hence as an integral part of a larger dynamic system of motivational balance.

Seen in this perspective, both the sick role and that of the physician assume significance as mechanisms of social control, not only within the bounds of the common-sense definition of the traditional functions of the physician, but much more broadly, including intimate relations to many phenomena which are not ordinarily thought to have any connection with health.

The sick role is, as we have seen, in these terms a mechanism which in the first instance channels deviance so that the two most dangerous potentialities, namely, group formation and successful establishment of the claim to legitimacy, are avoided. The sick are tied up, not with other deviants to form a "sub-culture" of the sick, but each with a group of non-sick, his personal circle and, above all, physicians. The sick thus become a statistical status class and are deprived of the possibility of forming a solidary collectivity. Furthermore, to be sick is by definition to be in an undesirable state, so that it simply does not "make sense" to assert a claim that the way to deal with the frustrating aspects of the social system is "for everybody to get sick."

These two functions of the sick role operate even if no therapeutic influence is exerted, and their importance to the social system should not be underestimated. On this ground alone it is legitimate to question the adequacy of the common assertion that the increase in the proportion of mental illness is necessarily an index of increasing social disorganization. The fact may be provisionally granted, though because of shortcomings of the statistical information and of the fact that many conditions are now diagnosed as mental illness, which would not have been a generation ago, it might be questioned. In any case such an increase need not, as is very commonly asserted, be a direct index of increasing general social disorganization. It is quite possible that it constitutes the diversion into the sick role of elements of deviant motivation which might have been expressed in alternative roles. From the point of view of the stability of the social system the sick role may be less dangerous than some of the alternatives.

However, obviously in addition to this insulating function of the sick role, there is its reintegrative influence. The significance of this is greatly enhanced by two factors. The first is that deliberate psychotherapy is, even within the role of the physician, not an isolated phenomenon, but may be regarded as the specialization of features of that role which are present in what has sometimes been called the "art of medicine." All good medical practice therefore, we have maintained, has been and is to some degree psychotherapy. Psychotherapy as a mechanism of social control, therefore, builds on and extends what must be regarded as an "automatic" or latent set of mechanisms which have been built into the role of physician independent of an application of theories as to what psychotherapy, or social control processes, should be. Deliberate psychotherapy is, to use a graphic metaphor, only the part of the iceberg which extends above the water. The considerably larger part is that below the surface of the water. Even its existence has been largely unknown to most psychiatrists, to say nothing of laymen. It consists in certain institutional features of the physician's role in its particular form of meshing with the sick role.

But even more important is the second fact, the continuity of the fundamental processes of psychotherapy with the general processes of "coping" successfully with the psychological consequences of the exposure of people to strain in social relationships. This means not only that, as just stated, the motivational materials which enter into illness are continuous with those expressed in many other forms of deviance, but also that the mechanism of control of psychotherapy is one of a much larger class of such mechanisms. In turn, a clue to what these are is provided by the element of unconscious psychotherapy we have shown to be present in the doctor-patient role relationship. The elements involved have been discussed with examples in the latter part of Chapter VII and need not be repeated here.

A very important set of problems arises, however, with respect to the generality of that analysis. The modern physician's role constitutes a very distinctive type of social structure. It is far too distinctive alone to form the basis for the generalizations about the relations between motivation to deviance and the mechanisms of social control which we have set forth. But we have shown that it is possible to modify our analysis of the factors involved in the motivational processes to take account of variations of role structure. In other types of roles some of the things which happen in psychotherapy are clearly not possible; thus in general parental roles are not capable of reintegrating the deviant once the vicious circle of alienation has reached the neurotic stage of elaboration. But in spite of this fact the fundamental processes involved in normal socialization and those involved in psychotherapy have crucially important elements in common, along with the obvious differences. Focusing attention on these common elements thus makes it possible to pose in a sharply meaningful way such questions as that of the significance of the existence of two parents, whereas there is normally only one psychotherapist. Similarly we have tried to show that in much magical and religious ritual, in secondary institutions, and in much of the wider institutional patterning of the social system, there are latent functions of social control, the operation of which must be understood to an important degree in the same fundamental terms as are involved in the operation of psychotherapy.

Thus the analysis of modern medical practice has not only given us a "case study" of a type of social structure which is interesting and significant in itself, and as a way of applying a theoretical paradigm for the analysis of social structure. More than that it has opened a "window" which can be used for the observation of balancing processes within the social system, which have generalized significance far beyond the "room" within the larger edifice of society into which this particular window opens.

XI THE PROCESSES OF
CHANGE OF SOCIAL SYSTEMS

IN THE foregoing chapters of this work we have been concerned with two fundamental areas of theoretical problems. The first of these has been the attempt to work out a conceptual scheme in which the major structural components of the social system could be identified, described and their interrelations in systems, both as internally differentiated and as variable from case to case, worked out. The second major problem area of our concern has been the analysis of motivational processes within the system. In order to make our treatment logically complete, we must now turn briefly to a third set of problems, those concerned with processes of change of the system itself, that is, processes resulting in changes in the structure of the system.

For reasons which we must now try to make clear, the treatment of this third set of problems comes in the present scheme *logically* last, and presupposes some level of theoretical solution of the other two. This is true so far as the central point of reference is, as we have consistently attempted to make it, the concept of *system*. It is, of course, entirely possible and appropriate to theorize about many *particular* processes of change within social systems, without attempting to build up a theory of the processes of change *of* social systems as systems. It is this latter task which logically presupposes a theory of social structure and a theory of motivational process within the system.

§ THE PROBLEM OF THE THEORY OF CHANGE

BEFORE clarifying this statement further it is necessary to distinguish clearly between the processes *within* the system and processes of change *of* the system. It is very common to confuse these two things under the term "dynamic." For the purposes of our conceptual scheme the distinction derives from the concept of equilibrium and the way in which this has been used in the present work. Beyond the most general meaning of the concept of equilibrium, the meaning which is most directly applicable here is that applying to what we have called a "boundary-maintaining" system.

It has been clearly and repeatedly brought out that it is essential to the conception of the interaction process put forward in this work, and of the theorem of the institutional integration of motivation which was directly derived from that conception, that the stabilization of the processes of mutual orientation within complementary roles is a fundamental "tendency" of interaction. We have used the conception of such a stabilized interaction process throughout as the major point of reference for the analysis of motivational process. This is another way of stating that we have treated the continuation of such a stabilized process without change in the structure of the roles, as not problematical for the theory of social systems. It was clearly recognized in Chapter VI, where this proposition was first stated, that this was *a theoretical assumption, not an empirical generalization*. But as such it is one of the central strategic elements of the present conceptual scheme. It was, however, also recognized that the equilibrium formulated in these terms could be a moving equilibrium where certain orderly processes of empirical change were going on.

Seen from this point of view, the theory of motivational process *within* the system is built about the processes of maintenance of equilibrium. Besides the unproblematical continuance of interaction which was assumed to go on, this maintenance of equilibrium, as we have seen, revolves about two fundamental types of process. The first of these are the processes of socialization by which actors acquire the orientations necessary to the performance of their roles in the social system, when they have not previously possessed them; the second type are the processes involved in the balance between the generation of motivations to deviant behavior and the counterbalancing motivations to restoration of the stabilized interactive process which we have called the mechanisms of social control.

The special methodological significance of this approach to the analysis of motivational process, i.e., of "dynamics," lies in two interrelated sets of considerations. The first of these is the implication of the fact that we are dealing with the boundary-maintaining type of system. The definition of a system as boundary-maintaining is a way of saying that, *relative to its environment,* that is to fluctuations in the factors of the environment, it maintains certain constancies of pattern, whether this constancy be static or moving. These elements of the constancy of pattern must constitute a fundamental point of reference for the analysis of process in the system. From a certain point of view these processes are to be defined as the processes of maintenance of the constant patterns. But of course these are empirical constancies, so we do not assume any inherent reason why they have to be maintained. It is simply a fact that, as described in terms of a given frame of reference, these constancies are often found to exist, and theory can thus be focused on the problems presented by their existence. They may cease to exist, by the dissolution of the distinctive boundary-maintaining system and its assimilation to the environment, or by transformation into other patterns. But the fact that they do exist, at given times and places, still serves as the theoretical focus for analysis.

Theory, relative to such systems, is directed to the analysis of the conditions under which such a given constant system pattern will be maintained and conversely, the conditions under which it will be altered in determinate ways. This, we may surmise, is the fundamental basis of the assumption of our "law of inertia" of social process.[1] What this theorem does is to state the fundamental point of reference for the theoretical analysis of process in the social system. The analysis of the conditions or factors affecting motivational process is always stated in terms relative to this point of reference. The *problem* is always some version of the problem why, given a certain change in the relevant conditions, the constant pattern which is the point of reference is altered in a certain way or, conversely, why it fails to be altered in the face of certain alterations in

[1] This conception is similar to that of homeostasis in physiology.

the conditions. The latter question is always implicit in the problem structure, the problems of theory, that is, revolve about the conditions of maintenance and alteration of equilibria which are defined as the empirically observed pattern-constancies of a boundary-maintaining system. The essential point is that for there to be a theory of *change* of pattern, under these methodological assumptions, there must be an initial and a terminal pattern to be used as points of reference. We have given an example of processes of change in this sense in our analysis of the socialization of the child. Clear definition of the patterns into which he is being socialized is, within our conceptual scheme, a logical prerequisite of successful analysis of the process by which the necessary conditions of action within that pattern come to be established.

The second set of considerations constitute implications of the fact that we are operating on the level of theory which we have called "structural-functional." The two are interdependent in that for such theory to have relevance it *must* apply to a boundary-maintaining type of system, because only in this way can the system to which such a theory is applied be delimited. But, in addition to this fact, the crucial characteristic of structural-functional theory is its use of the concept system *without a complete knowledge of the laws which determine processes within the system.*

The gap produced by our fragmentary knowledge of laws is filled, or better, bridged, in two ways. The first is the use of structural categories. By their use we are enabled to achieve a systematic and precise description of the states of systems, of the variations in the state of the same system through time and of the similarities and differences between different systems. Such description is couched in terms which we have excellent reason to believe will connect directly with, if not incorporate, the values of the most significant variables of the theory of action. This, along with the possibility of taxonomic systemization, is the fundamental reason why it has been so important to *derive* our categories of the structure of the social system from the essential features of the frame of reference of action itself. As the case of the classical mechanics so clearly shows, it is in terms of the logical requirements of the frame of reference that the fundamental variables of the theoretical system are defined.

Structural categories can, however, in combination with certain other things, carry us beyond description as such. If they describe the structure of an empirical system in generalized terms, we can, by going back to the relevant aspects of the frame of reference, say something about what we have called the "functional prerequisites" of empirical systems, and developing further from there, about what, in Chapter V we have called the "imperatives" of the particular type of empirical system. If, then, we can regard certain structural features of the system as empirically *given,* the relevant facts are not merely of descriptive significance. We can make inferences from them, at least to the extent of saying that if these facts are given the range of variation of other facts about the same system must be limited in certain respects. It is this type of reasoning which we employed in Chapter V to approach the orderly analysis of types of social system. It should be clear that when we say that a structure in the social system is empirically given, e.g., the "conjugal" type of kinship structure, we mean that the processes within the relevant sub-system of the society may be assumed to be in a sufficiently stable state of equilibrium so that within a defined range of variation in other respects this structure, i.e., this "system pattern," can be assumed to be constant. Obviously the use of structural categories for explanatory purposes in this way is dependent on the assumption that the constancy of pattern to which we have referred has some empirical significance. But if this were not true we clearly would not be dealing with a boundary-maintaining type of system at all.

In our two chapters dealing with motivational process we were able to go an important step beyond reliance on structural imperatives alone for explanatory generalization. We used the analysis of structure in the interactive process, notably the structure of roles, and the institutionalization and internalization of patterns of value-orientation in the definition of role-expectations, to define the problems of motivational process in interactive relationships in such ways that the orientation variables of the theory of action enter both into the motivational process in the personalities of individual actors and into the social structure in definable ways. Above all, using these patterns of value-orientation as our major point of reference, their acquisition for the analysis of socialization, and conformity with them as the major axis of variation for that of deviance and social control, we were able to work out a substantially complete *paradigm* of motivational process within the social system.

It is extremely important to be clear that what we have presented in these two chapters is a paradigm and *not a theory,* in the usual sense of the latter term as a system of laws. This is almost another way of saying that we have had to formulate the concepts of motivational process as *mechanisms,* not as laws.

It is indeed the use of the concept of mechanism with its consistent reference to relevance to the system, which has enabled us to achieve *systematization* in this field on the paradigmatic level.

To say that we have achieved a paradigm and not a theory is not to say that *no* knowledge of laws is involved. For example, the statements to the effect that strain, defined as some combination of one or more of the factors of withdrawal of support, interference with permissiveness, contravention of internalized norms and refusal of approval for valued performance, results in such reactions as anxiety, phantasy, hostile impulses and resort to the defensive-adjustive mechanisms, are definitely statements of laws of motivational process. Without a good deal of such knowledge the paradigm would not be possible. But this knowledge is, relative to the empirical problems to be solved, fragmentary and incomplete. The paradigm primarily accomplishes two things. First, it serves to mobilize such knowledge of laws as we have in terms of its relevance to the problems of the explanation of processes *in the social system.* Secondly, it gives us canons for the significant statement of problems for research so that knowledge of laws can be extended. Thus for a complete account of the processes of socialization of the child we need to know much more of the relations between certain variations in the character of the parental roles, and the processes of determination of alternative outcomes in the personality structure of the child. To state the problem in terms of specific characteristics of the roles of the parents as conceptualized in the terms set forth in this work is a very different thing from merely inquiring, "what kinds of influences of parents are important?" as so much of psychiatric theory has done. In so far as it does not directly incorporate knowledge of laws, then, a paradigm is a set of canons for the statement of problems, in such terms as to ensure that the answers to the questions asked will prove to be of generalized significance, because they will state or imply definite relations between the fundamental variables of a system.

It is of the greatest importance to note that the paradigm of motivational process we have set forth *is independent of the particular structure of roles* in an interaction process. It is a generalized paradigm which can be used to analyze any motivational process in any role system. It is this generality which makes it possible to incorporate what knowledge of laws in the field of motivational process we have, and to state problems of research—the answers to which should be capable of incorporation into a general body of laws. At the same time, however, the system of structural categories in terms of which the particular roles are analyzed has a comparable order of generality and the two elements of theory are parts of the same more general system, the theory of action. It is this which makes it possible to think that the present work constitutes a step toward the development of a generalized theoretical system.

It is a necessary inference from the above considerations that *a general theory of the processes of change of social systems is not possible in the present state of knowledge.* The reason is very simply that such a theory would imply complete knowledge of the laws of process of the system and this knowledge we do not possess. The theory of change in the structure of social systems must, therefore, be a theory of particular sub-processes of change *within* such systems, not of the over-all processes of change *of* the systems as systems.

But by the same token it should be clear, that so far as our knowledge goes beyond description and sheer empirical generalization it is always to some degree knowledge of processes of change. It is not possible to segregate *theoretical* knowledge of the laws of the processes within systems, and of their processes of change. They are both different contexts of *application* of our knowledge of the relations between variations of conditions and the outcomes of processes going forward under the conditions in question. When, therefore, we combine our knowledge of structural imperatives in the above sense, our paradigmatic knowledge of motivational process, and our fragmentary knowledge of laws, we do in fact have considerable knowledge of many processes of change, and the progress of research will steadily increase it.

We have been speaking of theoretical knowledge of processes of change within the theory of social systems in the sense of this work. There are two other types of knowledge which have a bearing on the empirical understanding of such processes in the concrete which must be mentioned to avoid possible confusion.

The first of these is sheer empirical generalization. It is quite possible, indeed common, to know that certain processes of change do in fact typically take place under certain conditions without being able to deduce the pattern of the processes and of their outcome from knowledge of the laws of a system. It is also possible to have considerable knowledge about variations in conditions and a variety of specific consequences of such variations for the system. A familiar example of this type of knowledge is knowledge of the outline of the biological life cycle. There is, in biological science, *no general theory* of the life cycle, by which growth, its cessation at maturity, senescence and finally death can be systematically explained in terms of general laws. But it is known *that* organisms go through this typical cycle, and its broad division into phases is established on the level of empirical generalization. There is much theoretical knowledge of various processes within the organism, some of which bears on the shift from one phase of the cycle to another, for instance regarding the effects of sex hormones on the organism, following the maturation of the gonads. There is also considerable knowledge of the consequences of disturbances of the normal cycle, as through various kinds of malnutrition. But a general theory of the life cycle is still lacking.

Though it has frequently been claimed by such authors as Spengler, or the older evolutionists, to exist, the present evidence indicates that there is no over-all simple empirical pattern of the development of social systems generally through a series of phases which is comparable to the biological life cycle. At least one major reason for this would seem to be the part played in social systems by culture, and the facts, first, that culture does not develop in a single linear pattern, and, second, that it can be acquired by diffusion so that any internal developmental process can be profoundly influenced from outside in ways to which organisms are not susceptible of influence.

There are, however, typical processes of change from given

starting points in social systems which can be identified by empirical generalization. We have made use of these in our discussion of the empirical clusterings of the elements of social structure in Chapter V, and will comment on some of them further below.

The second type of knowledge, and hence of explanatory hypotheses which can bear on the concrete problems of change in social systems, derives from the analysis of the empirical significance of variables which are not part of the theoretical system with which we have been working. There are two classes of such variables. These are the variables which concern the constitution of the organism so far as it is independent of the factors of orientation of action, and those which concern the physical environment. It is clear that they are logically independent of the theory of action, but equally clear that their impingement on concrete systems of action is of the first order of empirical significance. A third set of variables, those involved in the cultural factor, is in a different status. The theory of culture is an integral part of the theory of action. But there are phases of it which should not be regarded as parts of the theory of the social system, but as data for that theory. This concerns the existence and possible influence of inherent "configurations" of the development of culture pattern systems, as this process has been analyzed by Kroeber.[2]

It should be quite clear that throughout this work we have deliberately refrained from attempting to deal with the influence on concrete social phenomena of the variables of genetics or physiology or of the variables of the physical aspects of the situation. We have been exceedingly careful to keep the place for dealing with their empirical influence open, and at many points have clearly delineated this place. Above all various fundamental aspects of these two categories have found a place in our system of points of reference for the analysis of the orientation of action. But quite clearly *we have advanced no theory* of the interdependence of social action processes and the biological and physical factors of their determination. This would be an exceedingly important task for social science, and the failure to attempt it here is in no way meant to imply a suggestion that it is not important. The only remark in order is that it is much more likely to be done successfully if the theory of

[2] Cf. *Configurations of Culture Growth.*

action itself is well developed, so that the nature of articulation can be precisely formulated, than if, as has been the rule in the past, such theories are motivated largely by a conviction that these non-action variables are "very important" and therefore the person interested in them chooses to deal exclusively with them without explicit reference to the categories of the theory of action.

It should be made very clear, then, that the theory of action, so far as it is in any sense a logically closed system, which is an open question, can be so *only* on an analytical level, most definitely not as a system of empirical generalizations.

It is a notable fact, which may be mentioned here, that where attempts have been made to formulate generalized theories of the processes of change in concrete social systems, they have very frequently laid the primary emphasis on these variables outside the system of action orientation. It is inevitable in view of the logical structure of these outside variables that these theories should be built about the variables included in the two categories of heredity and environment in the biological sense. In this class should above all be placed the whole class of theories sometimes called those of "Social Darwinism," which attempted to treat the development of societies in terms of the application of the law of natural selection. The difficulties which these theories as general theories of social process have encountered are so well known that they need not detain us further here.[3] The environmental emphasis is found, for example, in the case of the climatological explanations of social change.

Quite clearly, unless the analysis of social systems in terms of the theory of action is fundamentally wrong or purely epiphenomenal so as to be of no independent empirical relevance, such theories of social process, exclusively formulated in terms of biological variables or those of the physical environment, could not be empirically satisfactory. But this fact should not blind us to the importance of the variables themselves. Particularly the field of population is undoubtedly of great significance as a field of articulation of the theory of action and that of the genetic constitution of human organisms, and the variations and distribution of variations of this constitution

[3] The problem is analyzed in *The Structure of Social Action,* Chapter III and passim.

in terms of interdependence with the processes of the social system as formulated in action terms. Somewhat similarly the field of human geography may be conceived as the primary field for the formulation of the interdependences between social action and the physical environment.

The case of cultural factors is, as we have noted, somewhat different. Culture is an integral part of action as here conceived. The essential point here, however, is that the theory of the social system, as a branch of the theory of action, is not directly concerned with the dynamics of culture any more than it is with the theory of personality as such. It assumes certain facts about culture as given and investigates the significance of these facts for the processes of the social system. It is not a theory of culture in the sense in which that will be discussed in the next chapter. But we have given ample proof of the importance of very detailed and explicit concern with many of the problems of culture for the theory of the social system.

There is a certain parallel with respect to generalization about social change in the concrete sense between heredity and environment theories on the one hand and cultural theories on the other. It is logically possible, that is, to escape certain implications of our imperfect knowledge of the laws of social process, if one assumes explicitly or implicitly, that, subject to certain pre-action conditions in the environment and the organism, *process of change* in the social system is exclusively determined by its culture and the configurational processes of culture development. This was indeed the primary logical basis of the seeming adequacy of most evolutionary theories of social development, in that the essential factor was held to be the cumulative development of empirical knowledge. Somewhat similar tendencies with emphasis on other elements of the cultural tradition have appeared, differing greatly among themselves, in the theories of such diverse authors as Leslie White, Sorokin and Ruth Benedict.

§ THE GENERAL NATURE OF CHANGE IN SOCIAL SYSTEMS

WE MAY take for granted, then, that when we discuss the theory of change in social systems, for our purposes we are abstracting from the influence of variability in biological constitution or in the physical environment. Though in a strict sense even within these limitations we have asserted that a general theory of the change of social systems is not possible, we can still say a number of empirically relevant things about the general *nature* of such processes, which derive from the fact that they are processes occurring within the social system. These general considerations can serve as a background for the discussion of a few selected empirical processes in the latter part of the chapter.

The first consideration involves what we may call the phenomenon of *vested interests*. This derives from the nature of the processes of equilibrium in a boundary-maintaining type of system. The specific application of the idea of equilibrium which is of concern to us is one aspect of the phenomenon of institutionalization. Institutionalization produces, as we have seen, a form of the integration of the need-dispositions of the relevant actors with a set of culture patterns which always include in one sense patterns of value-orientation. We have defined strain in the technical sense of our discussion as disturbance of the expectation system which is an essential part of this integration. Strain in this sense *always*, i.e., by definition, sets up re-equilibrating processes. In terms of personality as a system this is precisely what is meant by the mechanisms of defense and of adjustment. It is thus in the nature of this type of integration of the action system that it should be resistant to change in certain respects. So far as it impinges on institutionalized patterns of action and relationship, therefore, change is never just "alteration of pattern" but alteration *by the overcoming of resistance*.

There is one apparent exception to this. Certain processes of empirical change are themselves institutionalized. There are in turn two types of cases of this. One of these is exemplified by the institutionalization of scientific investigation as this has already been analyzed and will be further below. Here the institutionalized value patterns will allow for and directly promote change in the cognitive *content* of the relevant part of the culture. Hence the resistance to change of which we are speaking would in this case focus on any attempt to stop the equilibrated process of change by stabilizing not the action process but the cultural content. We shall discuss some further implications of this case in a later section. It is one we pri-

marily had in mind in saying that the equilibration of social processes could take the form of a moving, not a static equilibrium.

Though it is not as such a process of change in the structure of
the larger social system, the second type can be exemplified by socialization. We have assumed, that at various stages the child
does reach a relatively stabilized pattern of interaction with the parents, for example, in the early love-attachment to the mother. For
the process of socialization to proceed further, however, this equilibrium must be upset. Strain, that is, must be imposed, and a new
equilibrium signifying the internalization of new value patterns,
attained. Here we find in the social system specific mechanisms
which first impose the strain, that is, "pry" the child loose from his
equilibrated orientation, and secondly, provide ways of "coping"
with the strain so that neurotic motivational structures are not built
up—in the "normal" case, of course. In the sub-system of the family
this is, of course, a process of social change, and similar processes
operate in the wider system.

The term vested interests seems appropriate to designate this
general resistance to change which is inherent in the institutionalization of roles in the social system. The term interest in this usage
must, of course, be interpreted in the broad sense in which we used
it in Chapter II. It is not confined to "economic" or "material" interests though it may include them. It is fundamentally the interest
in maintaining the gratifications involved in an established system
of role-expectations, which are, be it noted, gratifications of need-
dispositions, not of "drives" in the simple hedonistic sense. It clearly
includes the interest in conformity with institutionalized expectations, of the affectively neutral and often the moral type. Of course
it also includes the interest in the relational rewards of love, approval and esteem. The phenomenon of vested interests, then, may
be treated as always lying in the background of the problem of
social change. With the exception of processes of institutionalized
change, change in the social system is possible only by the operation of mechanisms which overcome the resistance of vested interests. It is, therefore, always essential explicitly to analyze the structure of the relevant vested interest complex before coming to any
judgment of the probable outcome of the incidence of forces making
for change. These considerations will often yield the answer to the

questions of why processes of change either fail to occur altogether or fail to have the outcomes which would be predicted on a common-sense basis.

The next main consideration is that on general grounds we are able to say that there are no one or two inherently primary sources of impetus to change in social systems. This is true both in general and with reference to particular types of social system. The "dominant factor" theories, which were so popular a generation ago, that is, with reference to the priority of economic factors, of the genetic constitution, of organisms or of "ideas," have no generalized basis in the theory of the social system.

The impetus to a process of change may perfectly well originate in the development of a cultural configuration, such as a development of science, or of religious ideas. It may also perfectly well originate in a change in the genetic constitution of the population, or a shift in the physical environment such as the exhaustion of a strategic resource. If a primary origin lies in the field of technological applications of scientific knowledge there is likely to be a development of science itself in the background, though certainly the process of invention is in important respects independent of that of science. Another very important possibility lies in the progressive increase of strains in one strategic area of the social structure which are finally resolved by a structural reorganization of the system. The conception of strain developed in this study is such that strain is not itself a "prime-mover," it is a mode of the impingement of other factors on an interaction system. But a structured strain may well be the point at which the balance between forces tending toward re-equilibration of the previous structure and toward transition to a new structure may be most evident.

As our knowledge of the laws of social process develops we will be able to say more and more about the conditions under which certain types of states of affairs in various parts of social systems, and in the external variables impinging on them, tend to lead to various types of change. But the view that there is no simple intrinsic priority in the factors of the initiation of change is inherent in the conception of the social system which we have advanced here. The central methodological principle of our theory is that of the interdependence of a plurality of variables. At a variety of points empirical relationships between these variables can be demonstrated which, as in the case of the empirical clusterings we have reviewed, limit the range of logically possible variability. But these limitations must be empirically demonstrated. To lay down a general theory of the priority of factors in social change is, in the present state of knowledge, to beg the question of the empirical interdependences which have yet to be demonstrated. We, therefore, put forward what we may call the conception of the plurality of possible origins of change with the understanding that change may originate in any part of the social system described in structural terms or in terms of variables, and that restrictions on the generality of this statement may be introduced only as the outcome of empirical demonstration that relations of interdependence are such that certain parts cannot be independent sources of the impetus to change.

Probably considerably more important than the problems of the initiating factors of processes of social change, are those concerned with tracing the repercussions of a change once initiated throughout the social system, including the "backwash" of modification of the original direction of change. It is here above all that the conception of the social system as a *system* is crucial. The combination of our scheme for the analysis of the structure of the system with the paradigm of motivational process gives us a genuinely technical basis for tackling such a problem, for asserting some propositions about such repercussions and for locating the problems which cannot be solved without further empirical investigation.

In addition to the arbitrariness of the assumptions as to what were the most important prime movers of change made in so many of the early generalized theories of social change, such theories have almost uniformly committed the error of postulating the continuance of a trend without taking account of the interdependence of the factors involved in the trend with the other variables in the social system. This has been particularly conspicuous in the case of the theories which have placed primary emphasis on the development of empirical knowledge as a linear evolutionary process.

It is, of course, evident and important that such general theories of social change have had a strong ideological character and that the motivations for their acceptance have not been organized according to the highest levels of the discipline of scientific investigation. It is further true that the theorists at the time did not have at their disposal anything like the resources for analysis of social systems which we now have, so that many features of such theories which are unacceptable to the contemporary social scientist are quite understandable in the light of the historical circumstances at the time. But these facts do not alter the great importance of making the fullest possible use of our own available resources for refinement of the analysis of such processes.[4] Rather than attempting to develop this very fundamental point further in abstract terms, we shall presently analyze a few examples of types of process of change which can illustrate how the analysis of repercussions can be carried out.

For such an analysis we have certain resources which we can utilize. First, we can describe the initial state of the system, into which the process of change enters, in precise and technical terms, which among other things can clearly reveal whether the empirical evidence is adequate. Secondly, in the same terms, those describing the structure of a social system, we can specify what has changed into what and through what intermediate stages. If the process has only begun we can specify its direction relative to the various parts of the system.

Third, we can invoke our knowledge of the two classes of structural imperatives of social systems, the general ones and those peculiar to the specific type of system. In these terms we can ask whether the change tends to violate any of these imperatives, to jeopardize the motivational needs of important groups in the population, to weaken the controls over important parts of the power system, to upset the balance in the reward system in specific ways, or to introduce a structure which is incompatible in certain respects with other concrete structures in the system. When any of these

[4] Of course shift in the character of ideologies, which in turn is in part, though only in part, a function of the development of scientific knowledge, has played an important part in shifting the climate of opinion of social science in the past two generations. On the technical side the statement of Pareto in *The Mind and Society* is probably still the best statement in general methodological terms of the significance of interdependence of variables in a system for analysis of the problems of change. Pareto's views on these subjects are summarized in the *Structure of Social Action,* Chapters V-VIII, especially VII.

"problems" can be precisely identified and stated we can then proceed to analyze the processes of adaptation and adjustment which ensue from the introduction of a change.

For this purpose the paradigm of motivational process is fundamental. Because of the phenomenon of vested interests, as we have called it, we may assume that the introduction of the change in the relevant part of the system imposes strains on the actors in those other parts on which the change impinges. The reactions to these strains constitute the tendencies to re-equilibration of the system, that is, to the elimination of the change and the restoration of the state of the system before its introduction. But these forces may be "coped with" so that the change becomes consolidated and perhaps extended. But unless the system is in the relevant respects exceedingly loosely integrated, this consolidation will mean that the other parts of the system than the original area of change have also been changed, so that eventually what is reached is a new state of the system as a whole. It may also, of course, mean that the strains are only partially coped with so that chronic states of tension come to be institutionalized and more or less stabilized.

§ THE DIRECTION OF CHANGE IN SOCIAL SYSTEMS

BEFORE going on to the analysis of a few concrete types of process of change, we may discuss briefly the problem of whether on general theoretical grounds we can say anything at all about directions of change in social systems. Though obviously this subject must be treated with great caution, there are certain implications of the general nature of action and of social systems which can be brought to bear on it. In so far as the theory of action is able to demonstrate its empirical validity at all, these considerations must be of some empirical significance.

Action is, as we have seen, a set of *oriented* processes. The concept of orientation is inherently a *directional* concept. There are furthermore, it seems, two fundamental aspects of the orientation of action, two major vectors of its directionality, namely, that of gratification and that of patterning, or organization, of value-realization as we might put it.

The first of these we have conceptualized as the trend to the optimization of gratification.[5] *By definition,* in the theory of action it does not make sense for an actor to seek deprivation and avoid gratification. What in common-sense terms is interpreted to be action not oriented to gratification or positively seeking deprivations must be interpreted in one of two ways. It may be simply a matter of terminology, as when in certain religious patterns of thought "spiritual" needs are set over against worldly gratifications. But in action terms we have no hesitation in speaking of the *gratification* of "spiritual" need-dispositions, provided we are able to give a satisfactory account of the sense in which these are need-dispositions. The second interpretation is that in terms of strains and conflicts within a system of action. In this sense an act of suicide would not be interpreted as motivated by a simple wish to die, but as what was felt by the actor to be the least intolerable resolution of an intolerable conflict situation, therefore, as in some sense a minimization of relative deprivation. We may presume that most such conflicts are internal to the personality, but in principle the action of the suicide is similar to that of the man who would face certain death or bring it on himself rather than face the certainty of prolonged torture. The situation of the suicide is in that sense *to him* desperate.

There is one fundamental reason, however, why the trend to the optimization of gratification cannot serve as a canon for defining a fundamental directionality of change for *social* systems generally.[6] This reason is that the social system transcends the life span of the individual actor and is in certain other respects independent of particular individual actors, whereas gratification is inherently a state of the individual actor, of his personality as a system. This is in fact the old dilemma of hedonism. There is literally no way of making the transition in gratification-deprivation terms from the individual actor to the social system. There is such a thing as integration of a social system, but most specifically and definitely there is no such thing as a state of gratification of social systems. If there is no such thing as such a state, obviously there can be no trend to quantitative

[5] Most fully discussed in *Values, Motives and Systems of Action,* Chapter II.

[6] This reason was clearly understood by Durkheim, probably for the first time within what may broadly be called the "utilitarian" and biological orientations of modern social thought. He stated it in the *Division of Labor* in his analyses of the reasons why the desire to increase "happiness" could not account for the development of the division of labor.

increase in it. The state of gratification of individuals on the other hand is a function of their integration in a *particular* social system, hence this cannot be made a canon of the direction of change of social systems generally, of the transition from one type to another.

There is, however, one important inference from this position which should be explicitly stated. This is that the point of reference for the analysis of "cultural relativity" must be the institutionally integrated social system as an ideal type, not any empirical social system. Where the actual social system deviates from this ideal type of integration, the trend to the optimization of gratification can and does operate as a factor of change, because of the discrepancy between what, in that particular social system, are the ideal patterns for given groups in the population, and the actuality. Analysis of this aspect of the process must, of course, take full account of the immense complications of the motivational process with which modern psychopathology among other things has made us familiar. But the general principle is clear. The drive toward the optimization of gratification is, because of its significance to motivational process, a fundamental aspect of the tendencies to change from one particular type of social system to another. But it cannot be the source of the general directions involved in the succession of patterns of change over a series of type changes. For the understanding of this latter aspect it is necessary to turn to other features of the total system of action.

The only alternative lies in the cultural component of orientation. It is after all one of the critical properties of culture that it is transmissible without loss. Whereas the state of gratification of an individual actor cannot be transmitted to his successors, his culture, his knowledge, his moral standards and his expressive symbols can be transmitted. Thus a change in the cultural tradition can be perpetuated and can serve as a base for further changes. There is, as has long been recognized, in culture the possibility of indefinite cumulative development.

We have classified the content of the cultural tradition under the three headings of belief systems, systems of expressive symbols and systems of value-orientation. Of these three, in cultural terms as such it is clear that systems of value-orientation are the least independent, because they are the patterns of articulation between the cultural orientation system and the other components of action. This is particularly true of moral value-patterns on the social level because of their special involvement in the structure of social systems. It is often for this reason convenient for the sociologist to take moral value-patterns as his primary point of reference in the cultural tradition for many purposes, but in terms of the longer run perspectives of change it seems more important to consider the significance of the possibilities of cumulative development of belief systems and systems of expressive symbols. It will, of course, be understood that the implications of these developments cannot be fully institutionalized in social systems without articulation with the exigencies of social systems through the appropriate patterns of moral value-orientation.

Of the two, by far the more obvious case is that of belief systems. Here there seems to be no doubt that there is an inherent factor of the directionality of change in social systems, a directionality which was classically formulated by Max Weber in what he called the "process of rationalization." In Chapter VIII above we have shown the principal ingredients which must be taken into account in formulating such a conception. The older evolutionary theories erred in confining their attention to empirical science, and in failing to take account of the complex interdependences of the development of science itself with the rest of the social system. But there was undoubtedly an element of substantial truth in their views.

In addition to science itself, however, the non-empirical elements of cognitive orientation must be taken into account. There is indeed an ultimate strain to consistency in the total system of cognitive orientation in a society, and developments in science will have their long-run repercusions on philosophy, ideologies, and religious beliefs as well as vice versa. But this does not mean that science is the only significant reference point for the analysis of cognitive orientations and that it is safe to treat the other components of a total system of cognitive orientation simply as dependent variables relative to science.

Making allowance for this factor, however, we may speak of the process of rationalization with considerable confidence as a general directional factor in the change of social systems. We have repeatedly shown that there can be no simple general linearity of the empirical developmental process in these terms. Above all the vested interest phenomena in this field are very powerful and seriously inhibit the development of belief systems. But this does not invalidate the very great importance of this directional principle.

The question of the significance of systems of expressive symbols as a source of directionality of change must be answered very much more tentatively. As elements of the cultural tradition expressive symbols share the fundamental property of transmissibility. There are, however, reasons for believing that the empirical obstacles to cumulative development are more serious than in the case of belief systems. This is essentially because of their fundamental functions in shaping the expressive interests of actors, and therefore their intimate connection with the specific cathectic orientations of actors. We have several times called attention to the connection between expressive primacy and particularism, hence involvement in a particular relational system. It would seem that there was connected with this, a whole complex of factors making for stabilization through traditionalization, which did not operate so strongly in the case of beliefs.

This empirical aspect of the question is not, however, the main one. That concerns, rather, the question of whether and how far in the inherent cultural character of expressive symbolism there is a basis for cumulative development. The answer would seem to be that there must be. But we know too little about the principles of symbolic organization to be able to say with any confidence just what the pattern of such cumulation may be.

Two questions may be raised. The first is that of whether and/ or how far cognitive processes of rationalization themselves operate within the complex of expressive symbolism, so that in certain respects the fundamental processes of cumulation in this field are an aspect of those in the cognitive field. Such studies as that of Max Weber in the sociology of music[7] would suggest that there is something in this possibility. The second question is whether, independently of cognitive rationalization, there is any unitary process in the expressive field, or whether it must be understood to be in-

---

[7] Printed in the *second* German edition of *Wirtschaft und Gesellschaft*.

herently pluralistic. To this question there does not seem to be a satisfactory answer available in the present state of knowledge. It may very well be, however, that the recent emphasis on the pluralism of expressive orientations is related to a phase of development of our own culture and of the social sciences within it, and will prove in the long run to be untenable. Such attempts as that of Northrop[8] suggest the possibility of working toward the introduction of a more coherent order into this field.

We have, then, the virtual certainty that there is an inherent factor of the general directionality of change in the process of rationalization, and the probability that there is an at least partially independent one involved in the processes of development of systems of expressive symbolism. One of the most important questions about the latter is whether the higher developments in that direction are in conflict with the higher reaches of rationalization or can in certain respects be fused with them. This, along with the questions of internal differentiation of each type of trend, must be left to much further analytical and empirical work.

Finally, we should be quite clear that when we speak of such a directional trend of change in social systems, *we are not directly stating an empirical generalization*. Perhaps the best model we have is that of entropy in classical mechanics. Entropy, like rationalization, is an inherent trend of change, so far as the system is isolated and so far as certain obstacles to development of the process do not operate. We have seen repeatedly that in social systems a very large class of obstacles may operate to block the process of rationalization. Directly in the field of beliefs themselves we have spoken of traditionalization and authoritarian enforcement. More indirectly we are aware of the operation of the mechanism of rationalization in the psychological sense and the analogous mechanisms involved in the formation of ideologies on the social system level. In other words, the statement of such a trend in itself says nothing about the empirical process by which it may work out, or fail to do so.

It not only says nothing directly about the empirical process, but it in no way says that the trend may not under certain circumstances be reversed. In physics it is by no means impossible for the

[8] *The Meeting of East and West.*

entropy of a system to be reduced instead of being increased. But this reduction of entropy must be accounted for by the introduction of new energy into the system from outside. Similarly if the level of rationalization of a social system is reduced, which is empirically entirely possible, a problem is posed. It is necessary, we may say, that new, relatively unrationalized orientation "material" should be introduced into the system from outside.[9] By thus reducing the general level of rationalization of the system, the process of rationalization could, as it were, get a new start. Indeed in Weber's view this was the primary reason why, in spite of the place he gave to the process of rationalization, a generally linear conception of the evolution of social systems could not be upheld. Of course similar considerations will apply to an independent directional trend in the field of expressive symbolism, so far as this can be demonstrated.

In spite of the fact that such directional trends cannot be interpreted as simple empirical generalizations, their theoretical significance should not be underrated. They give to the theory of change in social systems a logical framework which would not otherwise be present. Indeed, some such logical construct as this seems to be essential to a conceptual scheme which points toward the development of a theoretical system. Process, as conceived in such a system, cannot be simply random change from one state of the system to another. It must, through time, have direction, and what we are attempting to do is to say something about that direction. The fact that we have had to look on the cultural level and not in the narrower sense the motivational level for that direction for the social system is a fact of the first importance. That personalities are above all oriented to the optimization of gratification as their fundamental directional principle, while social systems are oriented to cultural change, is an inference from, and a way of stating, the mutual independence of the two classes of system. It is a further validation of the importance of the symmetrical asymmetry of the pattern variable scheme on which we have laid so

---

[9] In Max Weber's scheme this, we may infer, was one of the theoretical functions of the concept of *charisma*, to serve as the conceptualization of the source of new orientations on which the process of rationalization was then conceived to operate.

much stress from time to time. The difference goes to the deepest roots of the theory of action.

§ SOME SPECIFIC EXAMPLES OF PROCESSES OF SOCIAL CHANGE

THE main part of this final section will be concerned with a sketch of the analysis of three types of process of large scale change in societies as a whole, in order to illustrate the nature of the problems faced by the sociologist in attempting to carry out such an analysis. Before entering upon these, however, it will be useful to call attention to the fact that even in a relatively stabilized society, processes of structural change are continually going on in many sub-systems of the society, many of which are institutionalized. In other words stabilization and change are relative to the problems on which the observer focuses his attention; a complex social system is not either stabilized or changing as a whole, but in different parts and different respects, always both.

A good example of a changing sub-system within a larger system is the conjugal family. A fundamental part of this process of change is imposed by non-action variables, through the unfolding of the biological life cycle, thus though biological factors do not alone account for the birth of children, once born and accepted, their biological maturation proceeds inexorably. Thus because the parents are continually growing older and children are growing up, the family cannot be a statically stabilized system.

The feature of the family as a changing system on which we have focused attention is the process of socialization. This process must quite strictly be considered as orderly process of change, one which is largely institutionalized, *in the family as a system, not only in the personality of the child.* As the child grows older and becomes more socialized, obviously his roles in the family change. It is further an obvious inference from the complementarity of role-expectations that if the child's role changes, that of the parents must also change in complementary fashion, if the family as a system is not to be disorganized.

All the fundamental ingredients of the theory of change in social systems are thus involved in the analysis of what is now sometimes called the family cycle. In the discussion of the socialization of the child in Chapter VI above we focused attention on the process as one of changing the role of the child. We saw that there are resistances to this change on his part, that is, he develops a vested interest in a given stabilized pattern of interaction and has to be "pried" out of it. We saw that this involved strain, and that the child tended to react to this strain with anxiety, with phantasies, with hostility and with defensive-adjustive mechanisms. We saw that a certain combination of treatment, deliberate and otherwise, on the part of the parents could overcome these resistances and create a situation favorable for identification and thus for the acquisition of the requisite value-patterns. The main ingredients of this treatment were support, permissiveness, denial of certain reciprocities and manipulation of sanctions through conditional approval and disapproval for performance.

In its fundamentals the same set of considerations also applies to the parents. They too acquire vested interests in the maintenance of their own roles in the early stages of socialization; the parent who is reluctant to let his or her child "grow up" is a well-known phenomenon. Growing up of the child thus imposes strains on the parents too, with the typical manifestations of strain. There must be mechanisms of social control operating on the parents as well as on the child. Misfiring of the process of socialization may very well be accounted for by compulsive motivation on the part of the parents which accentuates their vested interests and makes them insensitive to the normal mechanisms of control.

Thus we see that the normal conjugal family should be regarded as undergoing a process of institutionalized change as a system, not, except for certain limited perspectives, as a statically equilibrated system. This is, of course, true of many other sub-systems in larger societies. A society like our own is, for example, full of continually rising and declining organizations. Such organizations are, independently of larger processes of change in the society as a whole, often involved in processes of growth or decline. The same fundamental considerations which apply to the family as a changing system also apply to such organizations. Rather than developing further examples on this level, however, it seems best to turn to the problems presented by change in the society as a whole considered as a social system.

1. *Institutionalized Rationalization and "Cultural Lag"*

In Chapter VIII above we discussed at some length the institutionalization of scientific investigation itself and of the application of scientific knowledge in technical fields. This was more fully elaborated in Chapter X for the particular field of medical practice. Obviously one fundamental feature of the institutionalization of science and its application is the introduction of a continual stream of factors of change into the social system. The present problem is how this stream of innovation affects parts of the social system which are not directly involved in the process of its introduction.

In the above discussions we have stressed the fact that the institutionalization of both types of process creates strains in their immediate environments. It is by no means to be taken for granted that because in terms of our dominant value system, scientific advance is a "good thing," either the processes by which this is accomplished or the application of the results will be easily and "automatically" accepted. On the contrary there are many strains and resistances. Some of these are associated with the communication gap between the specialist and the "laity," some with the special "privileges" required by the investigator or the applied scientist, some with his interference with established ways of doing things or thinking, and some with the fact that he introduces changes which if adopted require the abandonment of established ways in which there is a vested interest. All of this is compounded by the fact that what this type of specialist does is very generally associated with situations in which the non-specialists are themselves under strains which predispose them even less to "rational" acceptance than would otherwise be the case. This was particularly vividly illustrated in the case of illness.

The repercussions of the changes introduced by scientific and technological advance can be followed through two principal channels. The first of these starts with the structure of the economy of instrumental orientations within which the role in which the changes originate and receive their first applications is located. The second concerns the cultural aspects, the belief systems and the systems of expressive symbolism, and hence the rewards, with which the earlier phases of the process of rationalization were integrated. We shall discuss each one of these in turn.

We may distinguish three principal types of repercussion in the instrumental complex. The first is the restructuring of occupational roles themselves. This has a positive aspect in that by virtue of the new knowledge and techniques new roles are created, or old roles are redefined with respect to technical content. For example in the scientific field, only in fairly recent years did such a thing as a "nuclear physicist" exist. William Welch was the first professional "pathologist" in the history of American medicine, and only about the turn of the last century did the role of "sociologist" emerge. Similarly in technological fields the role of I.B.M. operator had to await the invention and production of the machines he operates and obviously before the days of the typewriter there was no such thing as a typist.

The tendency, of course, is for these new technical roles to develop by extension of familiar roles. The role of professor, of course, existed long before there were any professors of sociology, and the latter was assimilated to the wider role category. But the interdependence between the technical function of a role and the definition of role-expectations in value-orientation terms is sufficiently close so that very considerable adaptations and adjustments are necessary with changes in technical content. There are many different respects in which the role of a professor of sociology must differ from that of a professor of classics even in the same university with the same basic social structure and cultural traditions. Both his teaching and his research must be different.

The obverse of the creation of new roles is the rendering of old roles and role-content obsolete. This is obviously the well-known phenomenon of technological unemployment. For a variety of reasons it is difficult for the same personnel to take over the new knowledge and techniques, and very frequently they are superseded before the normal turnover through superannuation solves the problem. Obviously they have a strong vested interest in their ways of doing things, in their status and in its remuneration, so that there is a strong tendency for the incumbents of the roles which are superseded, or are threatened with supersession, to resist the introduction of such changes. A society where rapid technological change is going on would be expected to show many signs of strain centering about this process, and of defensive behavior on the part of groups which are threatened with supersession or less drastic upsetting of their established ways. This may indeed be interpreted as one of the primary sources of the "security mindedness" which is so prominent in certain sectors of our society.[10]

Of course it follows from our general analysis that these reactions to the threat of change will vary greatly, both as a function of the impact of the change, and of the ways in which it is handled. Where care is taken that communication is adequate, where support is given in the form of reassurance that fundamental securities are not threatened, and where alternatives are opened, the resistance can often be successfully overcome. But in any case such change imposes strains on important groups in the population which may have more or less serious consequences.

The second type of repercussion in the instrumental complex consists in the impact of technological change on the character of organizations rather than of particular roles. There are many possible phases of such impact, but one particularly important one may be singled out. This is the fact that, though with many individual exceptions, technological advance almost always leads to increasingly elaborate division of labor and the concomitant requirement of increasingly elaborate organization.[11]

The fundamental reason for this is, of course, that with elaborate differentiation of functions the need for minute coordination of the different functions develops at the same time. An excellent example is the minuteness of specifications which must be followed in the production of complicated machinery, such as an airplane engine.

---

[10] An excellent analysis in detail of the repercussions of technological change in stimulating restriction of production and the consolidation of informal organization resisting change is given in Roethlisberger and Dickson, *Management and the Worker*, especially the study of the "bank-wiring" room.

[11] In this as in other respects Durkheim's insight was far in advance of that of the utilitarian individualists. For example, he correctly argued that far from the growth in the functions of the state being in some sense in conflict with an increasing "individualistic" division of labor, it was a necessary concomitant of this development. We may merely add that what is true of the state is also true of the development of organization in the sphere of private enterprise.

Quite clearly adherence to such minute specifications cannot in general be left to the unregulated and voluntary "self-interest" of the incumbents of the various roles. There must be a complex organization of supervision to make quite sure that exactly the right thing is done. Almost as important is the temporal coordination of the many functions. Feeding the various parts into the process in such a way that a modern assembly line can operate smoothly requires very complex organization to see that they are available in just the right quantities at the right times and places.

Change in the structure of organizations, like change in the content of particular roles, imposes strains. There are complex vested interests in the maintenance of an organization as it is which must be overcome. One of the most important phases of this process of change is concerned with the necessity of formalization when certain points of complexity are reached. Smaller and simpler organizations are typically managed with a high degree of particularism in the relations of persons in authority to their subordinates. But when the "distance" between points of decision and of operation increases, and the number of operating units affected by decisions with it, uniformity and coordination can be attained only by a high degree of formalization which requires profound changes in the structure of the organization itself, that is, of the roles within it. Again there is the problem of the processes by which these changes are introduced and the attendant strains coped with. Failure of the mechanisms of control to operate properly may mean that the process of development itself comes to be blocked.

Finally, the third type of repercussion of technological change on the instrumental economy is that on the composition of the system of facilities and through it on the power structure. The introduction of new physical facilities, in the form of equipment and machinery and the like, is obvious. Another phase is change in the physical resources which are strategic. Thus the internal combustion engine made liquid fuels, especially oil, of a strategic significance which they had altogether lacked before, and today uranium deposits have become a strategic resource whereas quite recently they were of no significance except to a very few scientists.

But for the social system still more important is the shift in the significance of types of skill and competence, and in the control of certain types of organization. It is probably not too much to say that one of the most fundamental social changes in the United States in the past two generations concerns the repercussions of this process on the power system and through it the system of social stratification. In what might be called the "independent business" era of our national development, which roughly closed with World War I, the individual owner-manager entrepreneur was perhaps the most strategic figure in the instrumental economy. Capital and enterprise were more important than high technical competence, and organizations were simple enough to be created and managed almost ad hoc by the entrepreneur himself.

The development of technology and its repercussions have, however, led to a great change in this situation, which has two primary aspects. The first of these is the fact that the highly trained and specialized technician has acquired a strategic place in the structure of industry, which is far different from that of the ad hoc "inventor" of earlier days whose invention was more or less complete at one stroke. Not the least important aspect of this is the fact that the pure scientist has more and more been drawn into the sphere of practical affairs. In this sense we may say that the instrumental system has become "professionalized" to a degree which was not foreseen by the businessmen of the turn of the century.

Secondly, organization itself has become enormously elaborated and formalized, with the "executive" or "manager" taking the place of the earlier "entrepreneur." The latter was the classical "capitalist" not the former. In this sense, then, we may say that the instrumental system has tended to become "bureaucratized."

These two processes mean that the center of gravity of power has shifted drastically. This shift has a great deal to do with the fact that the "business elite" of the great era of capitalistic expansion during the period following the Civil War failed to become consolidated as anything closely approaching a "ruling class" in American society.

We see, then, that the institutionalization of science and technological change has led to a complex series of repercussions within the instrumental complex itself which have fundamentally altered its structure; however much other processes may have been concretely involved in the historical changes, these certainly were. We may now speak briefly of the repercussions on the adaptive structures outside the instrumental complex. The most important of these probably is kinship. Here the broad lines of the process of repercussion are well known.

Only a few highlights can, however, be mentioned. In the broadest terms it would seem that the development has strongly accentuated the general trend to isolation of the conjugal family, above all because professionalization and bureaucratization have both operated to accentuate the universalistic-specific-achievement patterning of an increasingly large proportion of occupational roles. The mere decline of the proportion of the gainfully employed engaged in agriculture to well below 20% (compared with India's 85% or more) is sufficient indication of this, but it has also operated in many other occupational fields. This obviously means that family and occupational unit must be sharply segregated, and that the processes of allocation of personnel within the occupational system must be relatively independent of kinship solidarities.

This segregation and isolation of the conjugal family in turn has had repercussions on the feminine role; on the whole, at least temporarily, probably increasing the sharpness of sex role segregation and having much to do with the emergence of such phenomena as the glamor pattern. It has increased strains on the feminine role and hence produced or accentuated certain strain-reaction patterns. It certainly had much to do with the precipitate decline of birth rates until quite recently. These factors in turn have presumably had further repercussions on the processes of socialization of children which cannot be very well followed out in the present state of knowledge.

Another well-known aspect, of course, is the alteration in household technology, through the utilization of technological innovations to make operation of the household easier. With respect to the higher income groups this partly at least balances the decline in the availability and quality and the greatly increased cost of domestic service, which is probably itself to an important degree a consequence of the changes in the labor role which have resulted largely from the technological revolution.

Repercussions of technological change on religious organization or other non-instrumental features of the social structure are more difficult to trace and we shall not attempt to do so here. It may merely be mentioned that with greatly increased spatial mobility the structure of communities has greatly altered. Furthermore it would seem probable that the maintenance of relative ethnic separateness is becoming more difficult.

We may now turn to a few of the cultural aspects of the process of repercussion. We may start with the style of life aspects of the system of expressive symbolism. The very mechanical gadgets which the development of technology has made available in quantity of course become expressive symbols and play their part in the prestige system. The family car or cars, the refrigerator, the washing machine, and now the television set of course all have this aspect to their significance. Associated with this is the fact that, except perhaps at the very top, numbers of domestic servants have lost their significance as symbols of status.

In certain respects, however, there are interesting phenomena which are associated with the strain incident to change. A social system undergoing such change is presumably subject to considerable mobility so that the upper groups contain a considerable number of parvenus who do not have well settled standards of taste. There appears to be an interesting dichotomy in this field in that on the one hand there is a strong demand for "antiques," that is, for style-objects the acceptability of which is unequivocally validated in traditional terms, and on the other hand, a demand to be "up to the minute" in following the latest new styles, for example, in house furnishings. Such a dichotomy is suggestive of insecurity.

Another interesting phenomenon is the clinging to expressive symbols in a prestige context which once had an instrumental use but no longer do so. The cult of the horse is an outstanding example. While the horse has been almost eliminated from our technology, interest in horses, in racing and even in fox hunting is still a symbol of considerable importance in certain circles. Fox hunting is particularly interesting in the United States because of its association with British aristocracy, which as a social structure can have no place in the American system of stratification, but can as it were serve only as a wish-fulfillment symbol for those who have certain dissatisfactions with their place in the system, perhaps because having reached what is in a certain sense the top there is nowhere further to go.

Expressive symbolism of this type really includes the patterns of entertainment in the society. Here technological change has made many things possible which earlier were not, such as the movies, radio and television. But there are other orders of repercussions as well. Here it may merely be suggested that a certain trend toward "hedonistic" forms of entertainment, especially perhaps in the spectator role, have something to do with the impact of the severe disciplines of a highly technological and bureaucratic occupational system where above all affective neutrality is rigorously enforced. Also, we have noted, such entertainments may be less threatening to the system than would be affective outlets which entail the formation of diffuse attachments.

Another exceedingly important aspect of the expressive symbolism of the entertainment field lies in the ways in which entertainment provides outlets for the phantasy life of the population. It is well known that phantasy is one of the most important features of psychological reaction to strain. Certainly much of the outlet that children find in the "comics," and in radio programs especially designed for them, concerns vicarious gratification of the phantasies produced in the process of socialization. But fundamentally the same considerations apply in the adult world. The movies and a good deal of magazine literature and the novel, as well as the notorious soap opera, are cases in point. A substantial part of the strain, which is expressed in this sometimes bizarre phantasy life, is presumably the product of the processes of change which are necessitated by technological development.

The discussion of deviance and social control above should make it clear that it is dangerous to pass a functional judgment on these phenomena without giving consideration to their relations to strain. The essential problem probably is that of how far they fall within the range of permissiveness which should be considered normal to people under certain strains, and how far they lead into a vicious circle of gratification of deviant wishes, and hence to undermining of the main value system. The judgment of the "view with alarm" school is almost certainly not to be accepted literally without discount.

It is also clear that such phenomena as the scapegoating involved in much of "group prejudice" and in the tendencies to "witch-hunting" for "disloyal" elements are related to the strains produced by such processes of change. Problems of the determination of the incidence of such phenomena, of just how threatening they are to the stability of the system, and of what mechanisms of control operate and how effective they are, are obviously very complex and cannot be gone into here.

Turning to the relational reward aspect of expressive symbolism it is clear that the process of technological change inevitably results in a continual reorganization of this system. The changes in the instrumental complex which have been outlined themselves constitute, in one aspect, changes in the fundamental reward system of the society. New types of technical role-content and of role patterns acquire strategic significance in the system, and old ones become obsolete or are lowered in relative significance. Organizations are continually restructured, old ones die out or decline while new ones rise, and the role structure within those which continue is altered. Finally, new types of facilities acquire significance and hence their possessors power and prestige. The fact of the integration of all these things in the reward system constitutes one major facet of the vested interests structure and hence of the strain occasioned by the processes of change.

It is probable that the strains imposed by these processes much more than any inherent "conflict of interest" is the primary factor in the genesis of so-called "class-conflicts" in modern Western society. In England it was the agricultural laborers who felt their livelihood threatened by machinery who constituted the spearhead of radical movements rather than the "proletariat" as such.

These phenomena are, however, exceedingly complex and above all are relative to the particular social structure in which the process of change occurs. Frustration, we must remember, is always *relative* to expectations. It is this circumstance which serves to explain why movements for radical change have so often centered in relatively privileged groups who by common sense standards are "well off."

They have become accustomed to rising levels of expectation, and certain features of the established order have seemed to stand in the way. Thus the French Bourgeoisie in the Revolution had not been in a declining situation with respect either to standard of living or to power before 1789, on the contrary. The continuance of the old regime interfered with the projections of the line of their rise rather than with their current status. Similarly, labor organization has ordinarily been spear-headed by the "aristocracy" of labor, not by the most "exploited" groups. The pattern is essentially, "since so much has already proved possible, why can we not go farther?"[12]

It is a striking fact that in the United States the reactions to the strains of technological development have not tended to become organized about class conflict, contrary to the Marxist predictions. The first factor in the explanation of this fact is the relative weakness of a pre-industrial status elite—except in the South—which could identify its interests with resistance to *any* further change. In Europe the tendency has been for the threatened elements of the "capitalist" class to form an alliance with the pre-industrial elite groups which stood over against the "people." In this country the threatened elements have not had this group to ally with, and this circumstance has left the door open to a successful transition *within* the industrial elite. In very schematic terms we may say that the "technicians" and the "managers" have taken over from the entrepreneurs without the struggle erupting into violence.

At the other end of the scale there have also been factors which prevented the consolidation of the "proletarian" elements into a solid opposition to the "interests." The open frontier, the scarcity of human as opposed to natural resources, etc., have been very important. In addition the influx of immigrants at the bottom of the scale has, by giving ethnic differences a certain priority over class solidarity, served to prevent such a structure of conflict. These circumstances, combined with the very rapidity of technological de-

---

[12] This phenomenon may be interpreted as a case of "relative deprivation" as that concept was developed by Stouffer and his colleagues in *The American Soldier* and further refined by Merton in his paper in *Continuities in Social Research* (Edited by Merton and Lazarsfeld). For example, Stouffer et al. found that there was more dissatisfaction about promotion opportunities in the Air Force than any other branch of the armed services, but at the same time the Air Force had by far the highest actual rate of promotion.

velopment itself and the fact that there was not the same structure of "interests" to combine against, have served to maintain American labor as essentially part of the relatively integrated system rather than having it become a tightly organized "interest group" standing over against "the system."

If this interpretation has any validity, the supreme importance of this situation for the position of the United States in world affairs scarcely needs further comment.

To bring up these considerations, however, is to run somewhat ahead of the more rigorous analysis. Whatever the outcome in these specific respects, it is clear that technological change of the sort just sketched must have considerable repercussions on the structure of the reward system, and thus on the system of stratification of the society. It would above all appear to be extremely clear that if the United States is to remain a highly dynamic technologically changing society, as it has been for several generations, it must retain a "loose" system of social stratification. It seems to be a justified conclusion that a "tightening" of this system very far in either a "conservative" direction which would deny the opportunity for newly rising elements to "take their place" in the reward system, or in the "radical" direction which would drastically cut down the rewards open to *any* elite elements, would be likely to have a seriously disturbing effect. Similarly the extreme rigidities of Soviet society would seem, if long combined with rapid technological development, to be likely to develop very high tensions which might result in a "blow-up," or in a suppression of the technological development itself.

We may now turn to the repercussions of the processes of change we are considering through the channels of the belief system. In the first place technological development and science are, particularly in the present phase of their development, inherently linked together. In earlier times there has been a great deal of technological development which was essentially independent of science, but for present purposes we may confine our attention to the integrated complex. It is the "ideas" of science which constitute the primary source of initiation of change in the more general belief system of the society. There are in turn two primary directions in which their repercussions may be traced, that of religious ideas and of ideologies.

It is hardly too much to say that the "warfare of science and religion" has been the dominant note of the relevant part of the intellectual history of the Western world since the emergence of theoretical science to high maturity in the seventeenth century. The relations between them have of course been by no means simple. But the combination of the fact that religion belongs to the *vie sérieuse*, that it is, that is to say, evaluative, and that what we have called intermediate symbolism has played such a prominent part in religious orientations, has made it inevitable that a really large scale development of science and the diffusion of its orientations into popular thinking, should have profound repercussions on religious belief and should encounter formidable resistances in religious quarters.

Analyzed in terms of the theory of action, the relationships have been far from simple. There has inevitably been much strain on both sides, with the typical manifestations of strain in the form of compulsive attachment to certain symbols. Thus "fundamentalism" has been a persistent feature of one major wing of religious opinion, and militant "positivism" the complementary feature of one wing of scientifically oriented opinion. There has in these terms been both much "pseudo-religion" and much "pseudo-science" promulgated in the name of each body of cultural belief.

Though by no means all of the cognitive justification can be found on one side, the profundity of the contributions of modern science to man's cognitive orientation to his world in general is such that it can scarcely be entertained as a serious possibility that religious belief systems formulated in the first three centuries A.D., or even in the thirteenth century, could be cognitively tenable without the slightest modification in the twentieth. The attempt to maintain them unchanged must, therefore, in an important measure be a phenomenon of "fundamentalism" that is of the defensive primacy of vested interests, in this case expressive-evaluative in primary content, over the institutionalized cognitive standards of the society. In simpler words, anxiety about the consequences of altering religious belief prevents unbiased consideration of the arguments for any *particular* current formula which purports to "reconcile" science and religion, including that of declaring religious belief in general to be "tender-minded nonsense."

The consequence of this process of repercussion along with the others has necessarily been to alter the position of religious orientations, and of the cognate collectivity organizations in the society. It is, for example, extremely difficult to see how the dynamic of technological-scientific development of our society could possibly be reconciled with the dominance of a religious ethic and organization which was, like the Catholic or Lutheran churches, oriented to safeguarding the spiritual interests of the population according to a completely stabilized system of religious belief. Cases where such a situation approximately prevailed, as in rural Ireland or French Canada, or in rural Prussia, could only subsist by virtue of elaborate insulation from the main currents of social change in the Western world. Broadly, even in these islands, the maintenance of such insulation has proved in the long run impossible.

It may be noted that the vulnerability of traditional religious belief systems to the repercussions of the development of science has been a major factor in setting the stage for the major ideological structuring of Western society, the polarization of the "progressive" or "rationalistic" wing and the "conservative" or "traditionalistic" wing. This polarization has had a different incidence within the different sub-societies within the Western world. It has been less pronounced in the United States than in most of Europe, to an important degree because American sectarian Protestantism has relative to both Lutheranism and Catholicism carried many of the seeds of the process of rationalization within itself, and because its organization relatively to the rest of the social structure has made it impossible, as for instance in Catholic countries, for "religion" to present a united front against the "progressive" forces. We have no counterpart, for instance, of the inherent assumption of most continental Europeans that, to be in any sense "on the left" must mean to be anti-religious on principle.

Finally, the repercussions of the process of rationalization on ideology have certainly been profound in the Western world. It would seem in the first place that the differentiation of secular ideology from religious belief systems, which had barely begun by the sixteenth century and really gathered force only in the eighteenth, should be regarded as part of the fundamental process we are concerned with.

The general tendency to line "science" and its implications, real or alleged, up with the "progressive" cause, is perhaps the most important broad generalization which can be made. In general this has been associated with espousal of the groups in the social system which were struggling for enhancement of their positions in the prestige and power systems, the bourgeoisie at one phase, the "proletariat" at another, and not least important perhaps the scientists and technologists themselves.

The linking with the interests of various groups within the social system and the strains which they were under has, of course, meant that reactions to strain have played a prominent part in the progressive as well as the conservative ideologies. This fact has had much to do with the prominence of utopian elements in these ideologies, and with the part played by varying degrees and modes of alienation from the institutionalized system itself. They have of course ranged from mild progressivism to radical revolutionism with a definite gradualness of transition between the various gradations.

A word may be said about one particularly interesting phase of this development which was briefly mentioned in Chapter VIII, namely, its association with the development of social science. In a very schematic sense, it may be said that the secularization of social thought made *some* cognitive stabilization of ideological beliefs from other than religious sources urgent, and we have seen that philosophy has played a very important part in this respect. But the general prestige of science in secular thought has been such that the attempt to extend it to the field of human behavior was inevitable.[13] The fact of its being rooted in ideological interests to this extent, to the sociologists of knowledge, explains many of the complex vicissitudes to which social science has been subjected in the course of its development. It is both needed and demanded as an inevitable extension of an established cognitive orientation pattern, but at the same time it encounters serious resistances. Some of these are par-

[13] The common German methodological doctrine of a generation and more ago, that human behavior and culture were not subject to "laws" in the sense of the natural sciences, but were uniquely individuated phenomena may, in part, be regarded as a defensive rationalization against this pressure. It was drastically disposed of by Max Weber.

ticularly frustrating because they come from the "friends" of social science who have acquired a vested interest in ideological pseudo-science. It is not surprising that these difficulties have not been confined to the acceptance of social science by those outside the profession but have, for reasons with which we are familiar, deeply penetrated the profession itself. A certain proportion of these difficulties have, however, been overcome. So far as this is the case, the definite establishment of results of social science is bound to have complex further repercussions on the social system in other respects. One set of these repercussions concerns the implementation of social science knowledge in its appropriate technology through the type of channels which were analyzed above. But perhaps not less important is the effect on the structure of the belief systems of the society as such, particularly through "taking the wind out of the sails" of an important part of the ideological pseudo-science which is inevitably current. The case of medical knowledge in its organic aspects should serve to warn us that it is highly improbable that pseudo-scientific beliefs in the fields of competence of the social sciences will quickly or completely disappear from the society, even where much genuinely validated social science knowledge exists. But by the same token, it is equally highly improbable that this development will be without significant effect on ideological belief systems.

The foregoing is an exceedingly sketchy outline of a very complex subject. It makes no pretense to completeness or technical precision. It is introduced merely to illustrate that the conceptual scheme of the present volume, which has been developed primarily in terms of its bearing on the equilibrating processes of the social system, can readily be applied to the analysis of the processes of change. Because a system is encompassed in a process of institutionalized change, it does not cease to be a system. The scientific-technological "core" of the process of change we have attempted to trace is interdependent with all the other parts of the society in which it takes place. If any approach to solution of the problem of how it will affect the total society over a long period is to be attained, the *only* way to proceed outside of sheer "intuition" is to attempt to trace meticulously the repercussions of the changes through the various parts of the system, and back again to the locus of the original changes. We are in a position to do that only in the most fragmentary fashion in the present state of knowledge. But at least we have a theoretical canon of what *needs* to be done and some fairly detailed standards for a judgment of how far what we can do falls short of these needs.

If one broad generalization about the type of process which we have attempted to trace can be hazarded, it is that the society in which it has become institutionalized is in a relatively precarious state of moving equilibrium with respect to the process. This equilibrium can break down in either of two main directions, both of which if they occur should be interpreted as consequences of the fact that strain in certain parts of the system has mounted to points which cannot be coped with short of major alterations of the moving equilibrium state. One of these centers on the mounting resistance of the "vested interest" elements to further change, so that the essential process itself is finally choked off and the society stabilized on a traditionalistic basis. This, fundamentally, seems to be what happened in the society of later Mediterranean Antiquity partly at least under the influence of Christianity. The other direction is that of mounting strain in "progressive" sectors so that a radically alienated revolutionary movement develops. Though proclaimed and threatened for a long time this has not yet happened in any major industrialized country of the Western world, least of all in the most highly industrialized, the United States. But what some of the processes involved in that alternative are and what some of their consequences might be will be developed in the final sections of this chapter. However, both types of deviation are continually occurring in sub-sectors of our society. The question is whether they are likely to come to dominate the society as a whole.

2. *The Ascendancy of the Charismatic Revolutionary Movement*

The other two types of process of change which we intend to discuss can be treated considerably more briefly. The first is the sudden alteration in the major balance of equilibrium of the social system by the ascendancy of a "revolutionary" movement which organizes a set of alienative motivational orientations relative to the main institutionalized order. The second is the process by which such a movement, once in the ascendancy, comes to be adapted to the exigencies of long-run continuance as "setting the tone" for the society. These are, of course, fundamentally phases of the same process. Furthermore certain of the main outlines of the process in both phases are the same whether the movement in question be a "political" movement to reorganize secular society, as in the cases of the Nazi and Communist movements in our own time, or a movement for religious salvation in terms of a transcendental religious value system, as in the case of early Christianity.

We may lay down four major broad sets of conditions which must be present if such a movement is to spread widely and gain ascendancy in the social system, and then illustrate briefly by the case of the Nazi movement in Germany. All of the conditions are familiar from our previous analysis and we need only to bring them together in their relevance to the present context.

The first condition is the presence in the population of sufficiently intense, widely spread and properly distributed alienative motivational elements. These will, as we have seen, be manifestations of strain, the possible origins of which are various and cannot concern us here. Such strain and its manifestations will, however, we have made clear, not be random relative to the structure of the social system in which they occur, but will constitute alienation from particular institutionalized patterns, and from symbols associated with those patterns. It will, therefore, not be randomly distributed in the social system, but the alienative motivation will cluster about particular points of strain. The implications of its existence for the stability of the social system will depend on this distribution. It will specifically depend on how significant withdrawal of support from institutionalized values at these particular points will be.

Such alienative motivation is a prerequisite of the development of a revolutionary movement. But as such it is only a potentiality for change and its "force" may be dissipated in a variety of ways, through phantasies, through crime, mental disease and psychosomatic illness to mention only a few possibilities. Obviously "coping" with it is a primary function of the mechanisms of social control. But if these fail the second prerequisite of such a movement may develop, namely, the organization of a deviant sub-cultural group or movement. Such a development greatly strengthens such a tendency and may make it possible to exploit latent alienative motivation of the requisite types in other sectors of the population. Combining in a solidary group, we will remember, enables the deviantly motivated to evade a large proportion of the sanctions of normal social interaction, since they associate so largely with each other. They reinforce each other's deviance by providing an alter for ego's expectations, who will reciprocate them in the positive direction. Moreover, they make it possible to split the ambivalent motivational structure, expressing the negative, alienative side vis-à-vis the institutionalized structure, and the positive within the sub-cultural group in the form of compulsive conformity with the claims of the group. Solidarity will be further enhanced if expressive leadership can be developed so that the solidarity is directly symbolized and organized. The frequency with which the compulsive conformist element includes dependency and hence probably submissiveness to authority facilitates this.

If, however, the culture of the deviant group, like that of the delinquent gang, remains merely a "counter-culture" it is difficult to find the bridges by which it can acquire influence over wider circles. This bridge is above all furnished by the third element, the development of an ideology—or set of religious beliefs—which can successfully put forward a claim to legitimacy in terms of at least some of the symbols of the main institutionalized ideology. The features of the ideologies of complex societies which present an opening for this have already been discussed. Ideological formulae are often highly general and susceptible to "appropriation" by a not too drastically deviant movement. There are serious strains and inconsistencies in the value-implementation of any complex social system; therefore, it is always possible to take advantage of the inevitable phenomena which do not square with the dominant values. Sentiments in favor of "social justice" thus have a hard time to defend the treatment of the Negro in the United States, or the "exploitation" of colonial territories by "imperialist" powers. The derivation of the ideologies of the revolutionary left from that of "democratic liberalism" in the Western world is obvious, and can be followed out in detail. The possession of such an ideology which incorporates symbols of wide appeal in the population, and with respect to which the going system is vulnerable, is an essential condition of the deviant sub-culture becoming a movement which can hope to attain ascendancy in the society as a whole.

The fourth set of conditions concerns the stability of the aspects of the social system on which the movement impinges, and their relation to the equilibrium balance of the society. For obvious reasons the focal point here is the organization of the power system, with particular reference to the state. One suspects that the fundamental reasons why the revolution of the left has not yet succeeded in any highly industrialized country lies in this set of circumstances more than any of the other three. For example, in pre-revolutionary Russia, and in China there was a very small governing group set over against an enormous mass of politically "inert" peasants, inert, that is, except for their susceptibility to being swept up in a protest movement against the existing state of affairs. In such a state the power structure is peculiarly unstable, and can be "pushed over" by what is virtually a coup d'etat, especially when it is under such strains as result from defeat in war and hence shaken loyalty of the masses of an armed force.

The political case is not, however, the only one. The "conquest" of the Roman Empire by Christianity was by a quite different process where it may be held the primary part was played by the need of a dictatorial regime for legitimation in a situation of general disorganization.

To turn to the case of Germany. To account for the existence of widespread alienative motivation is scarcely a problem in any society which has been undergoing a very rapid process of industrialization. Probably it was more intense and widespread in Germany than elsewhere because of the relatively rigid status-structure of German society which had greater difficulties in adapting to change. At any rate because there had been no "bourgeois revolution" in Germany and the pre-industrial elites were in a particularly strong position there, they were a focus of strain, as witnessed by their susceptibility to "anti-capitalistic" symbolic appeals. Because of the presence of these upper groups the "industrialists" were in a far more equivocal position than in the United States, and tended to "team up," e.g., the common German formula of the "feudalization of the bourgeoisie." Another focus of strain was certainly in the lower middle class which had had traditionalized status and vested interests unknown to us. Of course there were obvious complementary strains in the labor groups, which were expressed in the formation of a political labor movement which could be exploited as a "threat" by the conservative groups under strain.

The German soil after the first world war was highly receptive to the organization of "patriotic" agitational groups with a nationalistic orientation. The defeat, the militaristic tradition, and the possibility of serving as a patriotic underground vis-à-vis the occupying powers gave them their opening. There were in the beginning many of these semi-underground groups, some engaged in political assassination. Because of the displacement of the older ruling groups from power their activities had partial legitimation in internal politics as well as in the context of defiance of the enemy. The Nazi movement then spread especially by bringing in all sorts of idle and dissident groups.

Resting partly on German military and authoritarian traditions, the movement developed a very tight internal organization and soon there emerged a highly efficacious expressive leader in the person of Hitler, who was a "little man," a war veteran and in other respects a suitable spokesman, not excepting his great capacity for propaganda activity and for organization on certain levels.

The ideological basis was provided by a highly ingenious combination of the appeals of nationalism and of "socialism," which had hitherto been defined as antithetical, the former belonging to the "right" the latter to the "left." At the very least we may say that the inclusion of socialism in the ideological formula served to neutralize the left and to mobilize the immense reservoir of anti-capitalistic sentiment from the right and large parts of the left behind the single movement. For a variety of reasons "liberalism" had been considerably weaker in Germany than in the rest of the Western world, and this, plus the existence of a strong Communist movement as a foil, created a highly favorable situation from the propaganda point of view.

Finally, the power structure in post-war Germany was certainly highly unstable. Not only was there the presumption against the elements in power because they had collaborated with the enemy and even more had adopted his formula for government, but the class system was out of balance with government. This is because the top elements had been excluded from government, but their position in society left essentially unshaken.

Severe economic depression, especially because it came *after* substantial economic recovery from the chaos of post-war inflation, added to the general strain. Finally, the treatment of Germany by the victorious allies was notably indecisive and vacillating. It is highly probable that this was more important than either severity or generosity; it created a situation where agitation for revisionism had an excellent chance in Germany, and the elements in power were highly vulnerable to such agitation.

In any case we all know the outcome, the accession of Hitler to power in 1933 and his consolidation of that power until the Party had complete control. The process we wish to try to trace in the next section had no opportunity to go far in Germany because its extreme of military expansionism led to the blowup and extinction of the movement by military defeat. Whatever new combination of the ingredients which went into the Nazi movement may come about in the future, it is unlikely that just the same kind of movement will arise in Germany again.

The above has been an exceedingly bare sketch, but it is sufficient to indicate some of the principal ways in which the factors abstractly dealt with in this work operated to make the ascendancy of the Nazi movement possible.[14]

3. *The Adaptive Transformation of a Revolutionary Movement*[15]

We will follow the same procedure used under (2) above and first lay down a series of conditions which generally must operate in the course of such a process, and then illustrate it briefly from one case. Since the revelant development in Nazi Germany was cut

[14] The analysis of this process is carried into somewhat further empirical detail in Talcott Parsons, "Democracy and Social Structure in Pre-Nazi Germany," *Journal of Legal and Political Sociology*, Vol. I, 96-114.

[15] Much the most sophisticated treatment of this problem in generalized terms in the sociological literature is still Max Weber's discussion of the "routinization of *charisma*" at various places in his works, but especially *Wirtschaft und Gesellschaft*, Part III, Chapter X. Only a brief résumé is included in the part translated as *The Theory of Social and Economic Organization*, Chapter 3, Sects 10-12.

off short, we shall take the case of Soviet Russia since in the thirty-fours years since the Revolution it has gone far enough for certain things to emerge clearly.

The first set of conditions concerns the fact that, since the revolutionary (or religious) belief system always to an important degree contains utopian elements, there must, in general, be a process of "concession" to the development of "adaptive structures." Exactly what these will be, in what order and through what processes, will vary a great deal, as a function of the content of the ideology, and of the degree to which it is utopian. Even where that degree is not extreme, however, the tendency is strongly, because the dominant motivational pattern of a revolutionary movement is compulsive, for its leaders to be oriented to "principles" and thus to be reluctant to make the "normal" concessions to the exigencies of an operating social system, which are always necessary. For a religious movement which has not gained ascendancy in the society as a whole, and for a revolutionary movement out of power this problem can, of course, be postponed. Thus in early Christianity it was possible for St. Paul to counsel simply "remain in that state in which you were called" because Christians as such had no control over the larger affairs of the society. In the middle ages the Church, however, could not avoid responsibility for those affairs, it was a "power" whether it liked it or not.

The points at which we are most certain that such adaptive processes must take place are those of the principal empirical clusterings of social structure which we discussed in Chapter V. We were careful not to exaggerate the degree of rigidity within such spheres but it is still true that probably most if not all radical movements in the Western world have contained a strong utopian element relative to some of them as their limits can be judged by the available evidence. Certainly the equivalent of the Marxist treatment of the family as a "bourgeois prejudice" has appeared many times. So also has radical egalitarianism which denies the legitimacy of any differential reward, and often also of institutionalization of property at all. Similarly organization of the power system, especially relative to the use of force, has often been declared to be radically evil and acquiescence in any kind of authority backed by coercive sanctions radically unacceptable. The problem of the paramount focus of value-integration raises special difficulties which will be mentioned presently. This involves what happens to the ideology itself in the long run.

A second set of conditions is closely related but should be distinguished. It concerns the consequences of the fact that the motivational composition of a revolutionary movement is always to an important degree ambivalent in structure. We have seen that participation in the movement itself permits a certain easing of the conflict by splitting of the components. But this is clearly only a partial resolution and is generally attended by clear evidence of operation of the mechanisms of defense and adjustment, for example in the compulsive cognitive distortion of the reality of the institutionalized order against which the movement is in revolt, which we have discussed. Thus to the early Christians the "world" was as such radically evil.

Ascendancy of the movement necessitates, for the participants who come over from the "opposition" phase to that of control, a reorganization. The "system" is no longer "theirs" but "ours." It has to be made to work, but above all in the present context, the pressure of not giving way to certain older established conformative needs, because of their incompatibility with uncompromising hostility to the established order, is relaxed. The sparse conformity-opportunities of the opposition movement are now broadened out to include the possibilities of a whole society which, since it is controlled by the movement, is to a degree legitimized. In a sense, then, the basic conflict comes to be transferred from the form, the movement vs. the society, to that between the "principles" of the movement and the temptation of its members to use their control of the society to gratify their repressed need-dispositions some of which are precisely needs of conformity with the patterns of the *old* society which they have tried to abolish. This process of the re-emergence of needs to reinstate elements of the old order under the guise of the revolutionary regime is one of the main sources of the tendency to "mitigate" the radicality of the revolution. It is particularly facilitated by another very common feature of the situation of a revolutionary regime, namely, that of finding itself in conflict with the outside world, so that the old dissociation between movement and patriotism is reversed, and often "restoration" can occur under the guise of patriotism. It may be that this transformation will be sufficient to destroy the ascendancy of the revolutionary ideology, at least partially, but more often it is not if there is continuity of regime.

There is a problem complementary to that of the re-emergence of repressed conformity needs in the revolutionary group, namely, that of the "disciplining," in terms of the revolutionary values, of the population over which the movement has gained ascendancy but which did not participate in the movement. This accounts in large part for the extreme concern of revolutionary regimes with "education."

But it also is very much involved with the reasons why one phase of utopian belief is almost always bound to be abandoned in the very early stages of a revolutionary regime, namely, the belief in the illegitimacy of coercion. Sometimes, as in the case of Communism, this belief is projected into the indefinitely future state of "communism" itself and a great show made of legitimizing coercion in order to reach this goal, with the allegation that it will no longer be necessary when the goal is reached, but it is hardly to be supposed that this attitude can be maintained without considerable strain. At any rate both in the interests of controlling its own following in their tendency to "backslide" and in the interest of "domesticating" the non-revolutionary population, it is typical of such regimes that they resort to coercive measures to a far higher degree than in most normally stabilized societies.

The necessity of coping with these aspects of the situation, plus the fact that the main problem of the movement is no longer "propaganda" to secure voluntary support, probably has much to do with the well-known fact that the old leaders of the movement tend to be supplanted during the phase of consolidation of the movement and altogether different types to emerge. Parallels can be only very approximate, of course, but perhaps it is not merely sacrilegious to suggest a parallel between Marx and Jesus, Lenin and St. Paul and Stalin and Constantine. The same doubts as to how far Constantine was "really a Christian" may be and have been voiced as to whether Stalin is "really a communist."

This whole set of circumstances may be summed up by saying that there is a sense in which gaining ascendancy over a society has the effect of "turning the tables" on the revolutionary movement. The process of its consolidation as a regime is indeed in a sense the obverse of its genesis as a movement; it is a process of re-equilibration of the society; very likely to a state greatly different from what it would have been had the movement not arisen, but *not so greatly* as literal interpretation of the movement's ideology would suggest.[16]

There is one final phase of the process which may briefly be mentioned. The type of motivational structure which is involved in attraction to and participation in a revolutionary movement *over against* an institutionalized system, obviously cannot be that which the "new society" tends to develop in its members through socialization. The revolutionary values necessarily become those of an "orthodoxy," and the tendency will be to socialize to conformity with them in the same fundamental sense as is true of any stabilized society. Thus to be a Christian in the first century A.D. and in Mediaeval France meant two quite different things, just as to be a communist in the United States and in Soviet Russia today are different things. Quite clearly it would be utterly impossible for a society to become stabilized on the basis that a fundamentally ambivalent motivational structure toward its central values, and ideology became the norm. Just how the founders become role models for identification on the new basis and how other phases of the process work out are highly problematical. But in this case as in many other respects a revolutionary movement must pay the price of success. It cannot both have the cake of the motivational advantages of revolt, and eat it by being the focus of institutionalization of an orthodoxy too. In sum, it ceases to be a revolutionary movement.

Stress on these re-equilibrating aspects of the process of course in no sense means to imply that no fundamental changes are ever introduced by revolutionary movements. But it does mean that these movements are subject to a dynamic of developmental process which involves certain fairly precisely definable exigencies. It very clearly means that no revolutionary movement can reconstruct society according to the values formulated in its ideology without restriction.

Just as a revolutionary movement can and does result in the

[16] Perhaps the best available general statement of this point is to be found in Pareto's *The Mind and Society*.

introduction of permanent change, so also in its residue it often leaves certain unresolved strains which may be the starting points for further dynamic processes. One of these is concerned with the tensions involved in maintaining the ideology intact, including its utopian elements, and yet making the indispensable concessions to the exigencies of operating as a society. As noted in Chapter VIII, in this respect a transcendental system of religious beliefs has an advantage over a secular ideology in that it can project the *Ausgleich* of discrepancies into the transcental sphere while for the secular ideology the future is the only recourse. Without this resource the really radically utopian ideologies may well have to give way to pressure after a struggle. Early Christianity had a firm belief in the eschatological Second Coming and the realistic Day of Judgment. This belief survived through a long series of postponements, the last major one being that to the millennial year. Since then, except for a few splinter sects, the belief has disappeared from Christianity. It seems probable that the final state of "communism" will suffer a similar fate, and very likely much more rapidly.

The central facts about the Soviet Union which are relevant to this process have already been cited at various points, particularly in Chapter V, and need only to be briefly recapitulated. The abandonment of the immediate abolition of coercion came very early, indeed, the semi-military organization of the party and its discipline was carried over more or less intact into the new regime. But in the early part of the Revolution there was certainly a widespread expectation that men now at last were "free" and could quite literally do what they pleased. Perhaps the most crucial step came after the attempt on Lenin's life, which became the occasion for the institution of the Terror as a deliberate policy which has never been relaxed since. It may perhaps be held that the tension between the drastic evaluative repudiation of coercion in the ideal state and the drastic way in which the regime has employed it for its own ends is in certain ways the deepest source of long-run tension in Russian Communism. Its importance is easily overlooked in the short run view, especially by persons inclined to a certain popular type of "debunking" cynicism to the effect that what men profess to believe is not important, it is only their "interests" which determine their action. This view can definitely be shown to be unsound in the light of sociological theory and empirical evidence.

The revival of fundamental institutions, which in the ideology have been declared to be "bourgeois prejudices," is in some respects the most striking single feature of Soviet development. This process culminated in the mid 1930's, that is, close to twenty years after the original revolution. The most conspicuous cases are the family, differential rewards in the occupational system, the new system of stratification, and the revival of a system of law.[17] It will be noted that private enterprise in the economy has not been mentioned among these. The N.E.P. phase came considerably earlier than the other revivals and was liquidated before these were well under way. But we have consistently argued that this aspect of the organization of the instrumental complex is *not* a fundamental institution in the same sense that coercive governmental authority, the family, differential rewards and stratification are. The revival of formalism in education, especially the use of disciplines and sanctions, is another phenomenon which deserves important emphasis.

This process should be regarded as involving a combination of the first two general trends mentioned above, the need for adaptive structures in the light of fundamental functional requirements of the social system, and the re-emergence of conformity needs associated with the old society as such. It may be suggested that the peculiarly rigid authoritarianism of the Soviet regime involves a good deal of the latter, and is not merely a matter of the exigencies of survival in a world which both internally and externally is troubled. Very obviously the fusion of the Soviet Regime with Russian nationalism and many things associated with this is a very conspicuous phenomenon. To take one small detail, the conspicuous role of the military and the tendency to extension of the military pattern of visible symbolization of rank, would seem to be very much an old regime trait which could not be readily derived from the exigencies of implementing revolutionary communism in any complex society.

The case of religion is a complex one. Though certainly important concessions to traditional religion have been made, these do

[17] Cf. Harold J. Berman, *Justice in Russia.*

not apparently constitute invasions of the revolutionary program in the same sense or to the same degree as the others. The compromise has been greatly facilitated by the traditional Russian pattern of state control of the church and there seems to be general agreement that the Orthodox Church in Russia does not as an organization have any greater degree of independence than other organizations.

It is obvious that this is a sphere in which there are very drastic inherent limits to concession. The regime in the nature of the case cannot simply abandon its adherence to the Marxist ideology, however much the latter may be bent and twisted. The whole historic relation of Marxism and Christianity is such that it is impossible for the regime to say that "religion is the pillar of the Soviet State," as has actually officially been said of the family. What can be done is only to "concede" a certain place to traditional religion. That this concession has proved necessary is, however, a fact of the first importance. It is not impossible that this might prove to be a very important focus for the organization of opposition.

It is very clear that such a society as that of Soviet Russia is shot through with exceedingly severe internal tensions. Indeed, it is highly probable that both the external expansionism which is of course legitimated by the ideology, and the drastic pace of internal industrialization are, in an important part, expressions of these tensions. Letting things "settle down" in either of these respects might become highly dangerous to the stability of the regime simply because emergency does produce a kind of integration, and probably a state of continuing emergency is less threatening than its relaxation would be.

The longer run prospect is, of course, obscure. It is altogether possible that some internal fissure in the unity of the regime might develop, particularly but by no means exclusively over the problem of succession to Stalin. If the regime itself does not fall apart it is certain that a very complex process of adjustment will have to occur in the next generation or two in the relation between the ideology and the realities of the social system. This particular sociologist's prediction is that "communism" will not be realized and that the increasing realization that there is no prospect of its realization will force far-reaching modifications in the ideology. Indeed, it is difficult to see how once the phase of dynamic expansionism, internally and externally—and no matter how far it extends it cannot last forever—is over, the belief system can hold up. Again, let us note, the Christian recourse of projection of the reconciliation of discrepancies into the transcendental world is closed.

This problem is connected with another. Industrialization itself, by its very success, probably generates another order of very important strains. We may put this in formal terms by saying that industrialization shifts the emphasis from the universalistic-ascriptive to the universalistic-achievement pattern. As we have seen this implies a kind of "individualism" which it will be exceedingly difficult to reconcile with the present character of the regime. It may be expected that the problems implicit in this tension will become acute particularly in connection with the status of the "intelligentsia." But greater freedom for the intelligentsia *must* include freedom to criticize the official version of the ideology. The intrinsic vulnerability of the official ideology is, however, so great, that in turn it is difficult to see how this freedom can be granted. What the outcome of this dilemma is likely to be will have to be left for future analysis —or the event—to decide.

The illustrative material presented in the latter part of this chapter has deliberately been confined to the analysis of processes of change on the largest scale in highly complex societies. In general the problem of the status of theoretical analysis of change in partial social systems is not a source of difficulty. We have stated before, and repeat, that so far as we have sound knowledge of the interdependence of variables, this knowledge is applicable to the understanding of processes of change as well as of process within equilibrated systems. The difference is *not a theoretical difference at all,* but depends on the empirical problems which are at issue, and the scientific resources available to solve them. These resources are obviously classifiable as (1) prior available knowledge of empirical fact, (2) theoretical resources for organizing description, stating problems and hypotheses, and analyzing implications and, finally, (3) techniques of empirical research for ascertaining the relevant facts where they are not already available.

It is processes of change in social systems as a whole, that is, of societies, which are problematical. The above treatment has been designed to illustrate two things. First, it brings home the fact that, as was stated at the beginning of the chapter, we do *not* in the present state of knowledge possess a *general* theory of the processes of change in societies as a whole. Therefore what we have been able to outline is not an "explanation" of such processes in a complete sense, but only a partial explanation in terms of certain elements. But, secondly, we hope we have been able to show that the theory of social systems in its present state is by no means devoid of relevance to the analysis of such processes of change, processes which pose precisely the most difficult empirical problems we have in our field. We very definitely have *something* to say about these problems. We can distinguish elements in them which we know to be of strategic importance, and we are by no means completely in the dark about many quite specific propositions about many of these elements. For example, whether or not it is possible completely to abolish coercive power from a society, or to do without any inequality in social stratification in an industrial society, is *not* simply a matter of opinion, in which the social scientist who takes the position stated here is merely "stating one view." The question of what elements in an ideology are utopian is, with a certain margin of error, a scientifically answerable question, and with it the question of the probable consequences of attempting to institutionalize such values literally in a large-scale society.

Above all, the treatment of the society deliberately and systematically *as a social system,* taking care to consider every problem indicated by the conceptual scheme as being germane to the functioning of a complete social system, constitutes an extremely powerful instrument of analysis in this connection as in so many others. It permits us to mobilize and apply, in the proper place and order, the empirical and theoretical knowledge we possess. But just as important, it forces us to recognize the gaps in our knowledge, to locate the unsolved problems, and to attempt to state accurately just what these problems are, and what we need to know in order to solve them. Thus, while we repeat we do not have a complete theory of the processes of change in social systems, we do have a canon of approach to the problems of constructing such a theory. When such a theory is available the millennium for social science will have arrived. This will not come in our time and most probably never. But progress toward it is much more likely to be assured and rapid if we know what we want and need. We submit that, without conceiving the problems in terms of the social system as a conceptual scheme, it is not possible to know what you want and thus even to measure progress toward the goal of attaining such a theory.

Perhaps one final word may be permitted. It has persistently been alleged that the "structural-functional" approach to the problems of theory in the sociological field suffers from a "static" bias. It has been held that the problems of change were outside its purview and since, the argument runs, these are obviously the really important problems, such a theory only succeeds in cutting itself off from genuine empirical relevance. Perhaps the first major example of large-scale processes of change introduced above, that of the processes of change arising from the institutionalization of science and technology, will serve to convince the reader that the author is aware of the fact that we live in what is sometimes called a "dynamic" society. Perhaps, even, it is not too much to hope that this chapter as a whole will convince him that there is a certain falsity in the dilemma between "static" and "dynamic" emphases. If theory is *good theory*, whichever type of problem it tackles most directly, there is no reason whatever to believe that it will not be *equally* applicable to the problems of change and to those of process within a stabilized system.

XII
CONCLUSION: THE PLACE OF SOCIOLOGICAL THEORY AMONG THE ANALYTICAL SCIENCES OF ACTION

THE substantive task of the present volume has been accomplished as far as it will be until the preparation of a revised edition is undertaken. It remains only to point up a very few main considerations which are relevant to the interpretation of what has been attempted, and hence of the relative success which the attempt has achieved, and then to discuss briefly the problem of classification of the sciences of action.

First a few final words may be said about what order of theoretical task has in fact been undertaken. The volume is unequivocally meant as an essay in *systematic* theory. It is not an attempt to formulate a theory of any particular concrete phenomenon, but is the attempt to present a logically articulated conceptual scheme. The title of the book, *The Social System*, is meant to emphasize this systematic reference. Social systems are empirical systems, but it is by virtue of their relevance to an articulated conceptual scheme that such empirical systems are classed together and made subject to a uniform analytical procedure within an explicitly defined frame of reference. Furthermore, the status of the book as an essay in theory *construction* justifies the two facts that, first, it has not attempted systematic codification of available empirical knowledge and, second, it has not tried to present a critical evaluation of the literature of theory itself in the field.

The book is thus an essay *in* systematic theory but the suggestion is quite explicitly repudiated that it attempts in one sense to present a system *of* theory, since it has been consistently maintained that in the present state of knowledge, such a system cannot be formulated. Put a little differently, it is a theory of systems rather than a system of theory. It attempts to represent the best attainable in the present state of knowledge with respect to the theoretical analysis of a carefully defined class of empirical systems. It is fully recognized that this theory is fragmentary and incomplete. But at the same time, the concept of system as a guiding conceptual scheme is of the first importance as an organizing principle and a guide to research. It may thus be said that the concept of a theory of systems is the most strategic tool for working toward the attainment of a system of theory. The general character of this particular theory of systems has been quite sufficiently discussed so that further elucidation is unnecessary. The general relations between structural categories, the general and special imperatives of social systems, the paradigm of motivational process and the "growing points" of research relative to these elements of theory have been repeatedly stated.

§ THE PLACE OF SOCIAL SYSTEMS IN THE GENERAL THEORY OF ACTION

IT HAS further been made quite clear that the theory of social systems is, in the sense of the present work, an integral part of the larger conceptual scheme which we have called the theory of action. As such, it is one of the three main differentiated sub-systems of the larger conceptual scheme, the other two being the theory of personality and the theory of culture.

The interdependence of the three has constituted a major theme of the whole present analysis. This has been fully and systematically set forth in *Values, Motives and Systems of Action* as well, and need not be recapitulated in detail here. It should, however, be quite clear to the reader that without a fundamental clarification of the relation of social systems to these other branches of the theory of action, the level of clarity in the analysis of social systems which has been attained in the present work would not have been possible.

By this is meant a clarification going well beyond what is now current in even the best literature of the subject. In this connection the experience of the author in connection with the development of the present volume, which was cited in the preface, may appropriately be recalled. A draft of about three-fourths of what had been planned had already been written when, in connection with the work going on in the general theory of action in collaboration with Professors Shils, Tolman and others in the fall of 1949, certain fundamental new insights concerning the relations between cultural and motivational elements in action generally developed. The work which was done in following up these insights, the results of which are documented in *Values, Motives and Systems of Action,* was not primarily and directly concerned with the theory of the social system as such, but with the general frame of reference of action. Theoretical developments from these starting points touched the fields of personality and of culture just as much as they did that of the social system. Yet the implications of that work for the theory of the social system were so far-reaching that, when work on the present book was resumed, it became necessary to start entirely anew, and it turned out that only a small proportion of the old manuscript, most of it consisting of illustrative material, could be made use of without complete re-writing. In other words, work on the general frame of reference of action necessitated a radical reorganization of thinking about the theory of the social system. Nothing could illustrate more vividly the fact that the theory of the social system is not a wholly independent conceptual scheme.

It will hence be clear to the reader why the implications of this situation have had to be so consistently followed through in the present work. We cannot speak of the structure of the social system in theoretical terms at all without speaking of the institutionalization of cultural patterns, notably of course patterns of value-orientation. If we are to do so sensibly we, of course, must know whereof we speak with respect to what the patterns which are institutionalized in fact are, in some sense also how they can be classified and otherwise analyzed. Similarly we have consistently maintained that the motivational processes of the social system are *always* processes within the personalities of the component individual actors. If the implications of such a statement are to be carried through it is obvious that we must know quite definitely what we are talking about when we speak of a personality system and its motivational processes. We cannot rely on common-sense levels of insight for this purpose; the problems become definitely technical.

It is fundamentally because, for the theory of the social system, the solution of these problems goes back to the general frame of reference of action that the anchorage of the present book in that general frame of reference is of such fundamental importance, and that important developments on the general level have proved to have such profound repercussions on the subject-matter of this volume.

If the ultimate unity of the theory of action as a conceptual scheme has been strongly emphasized by these theoretical developments, it is perhaps almost equally important that the mutual *independence* of personality, culture and social systems as sub-systems of action has been strongly confirmed. The insight of what is here considered the best tradition of sociological theory, that as a conceptual scheme it cannot legitimately be "reduced" in either direction is thus justified, and its grounds immensely clarified. On the one hand, the treatment of social systems only as "resultants" of the functioning of personalities in the sense common to writers with a "psychological" point of view, is clearly inadequate most fundamentally because it ignores the organization of action about the exigencies of social systems as systems.[1] On the other hand, to treat social systems as only "embodiments" of patterns of culture, as a certain trend of thought common among anthropologists has tended to do,[2] is equally unacceptable to the theory of the social system.

The mere assertion of the theoretical independence of the social system in both these directions has served an important function in the development of social science in that it has enabled sociologists to focus their attention on problems which would not have had justice done to them either in terms of psychology or of cultural anthropology. But, even in the thought of Durkheim, whose insight was probably the deepest in this respect, many aspects of the theo-

[1] Though perhaps generally now considered to be out of date, the book of Floyd H. Allport, *Institutional Behavior,* is one of the most vivid illustrations in the literature of what, in these terms, is the wrong way of conceiving the relations between the psychological and the sociological levels of the analysis of action.

[2] This trend is commonly associated in particular with the name of Ruth Benedict.

retical relationships involved in the combination of this aspect of independence with the equally important interdependence of these three system concepts, remained unclarified. The present work and that on which it rests in the more general theory of action may be said to have gone considerably farther in the clarification of these relationships. We are now in a position not merely to assert that a combination of independence and interdependence must be recognized, but to state on a certain level precisely in what this consists. We know just what we mean by the institutionalization of patterns of culture, and by the sense in which the structure of the social system is and is not an embodiment of a set of such patterns. We know certain of the most fundamental elements of personality as a system of action and its interrelations with the social system. We know that they *both* go back to the fundamental processes of interaction between actors, that in this one sense personality is just as much a "social" phenomenon as is the social system. We know certain fundamental relations between the institutionalization and the internalization of culture. Above all, perhaps, we know that the fundamental *common sector* of personalities and social systems consists in the value-patterns which define role-expectations. The motivational structures thus organized are units *both* of personality as a system and of the social system in which the actor participates; they are need-dispositions of the personality and they are role-expectations of the social system. This is the key to the "transformation formula" between the two systems of personality and social system. It is maintained that, in spite of the many brilliant insights bearing this relationship, especially in the works of Durkheim and of Freud, in terms which are both precise and highly generalized this set of relationships has never been so clearly understood before. This fundamental relationship between need-dispositions of the personality, role-expectations of the social system and internalized-institutionalized value-patterns of the culture, is the fundamental nodal point of the *organization* of systems of action. It is the point at which both the interdependence and the independence from each other of personality, social system and culture focus. If the nature of this organization is not clearly understood and formulated with theoretical precision, confusion on this fundamental subject will inevitably spread in all three directions and poison the whole theory of action.

It is a new level of clarity about this fundamental phenomenon, which more than any other factor has made the present level of analytical refinement of the theory of the social system possible.

§ THE THEORY OF ACTION AND THE NATURAL SCIENCES

THE clarification of the general theory of action and of the place of the theory of the social system in it, which has just been discussed, makes it possible to say something relatively systematic about the field of action generally.[3]

We may start with the general relation between action and "nature." It does not need to be emphasized that human action is in the most various ways profoundly influenced by the physical, chemical and biological properties both of the environment and of the organism itself. The question is that of the theoretical relevance and adequacy of the conceptual schemes of what, in this sense, are the "natural sciences" for full analysis of the phenomena of action. There is ample evidence of the inadequacy or inconvenience or both of these conceptual schemes for this purpose and thus of the independent justification of the action frame of reference.

The relevance of the action frame of reference is anchored in three fundamental considerations. The first is that the concern of the sciences of action is with the *relations* on a certain level of the concrete entities, which in their biological relevance are called organisms, to their environments. The conceptual scheme is, that is, wholly and fundamentally relational. The individual "actor" is a name for the same concrete entity as the organism, but seen as a unit in this relational context.

However, only a certain aspect of the concrete relations of the organism-actor to the environment is abstracted as being of interest to the theory of action; this is the aspect we call "action" or "behavior." There is, obviously, as of central concern to the biological sciences, a continual physico-chemical interchange between organism and environment, with reference, for example, to heat, and to the chemical interchange involved in food-intake and elimination

---

[3] The following discussion may be considered to be a revision of the scheme presented in Chapter XIX of *The Structure of Social Action*. It will be evident that it constitutes a revision rather than a drastic repudiation of that scheme.

of waste products and in respiration. This, however, is not action, or behavior, however much it may be empirically *dependent on* action. Action involves not a biochemical conceptual scheme but an "orientational" scheme as this conception has been developed here and elsewhere. Its units are conceived in terms of a specifically relational frame of reference which is *peculiar* to organisms as units, and not one which is common to organisms and all other physico-chemical systems. In this sense behavior is a phenomenon of higher-order organization in the world of nature than is the "functioning" of organisms. Or, put somewhat differently, the physico-chemical interchange of organism and environment is change over the boundaries of the organism as itself a *system,* the internal processes and equilibrium of which are of primary interest to the scientist. Physiology, as the most fundamental biological sub-science, is, we may suggest, essentially the science focused on the boundary-maintaining properties of the organism as a physico-chemical system.

But for the theory of action the organism is *not a system, but a unit point of reference.* The focus of interest for the theory of action is not in the internal equilibrating processes of the organism as a system, but in the equilibrating processes involved in its relations to an environment or situation in which other organisms are of crucial significance. It is *this relational system which is the system of action,* not the organism as a system. It is particularly important here to avoid an insidious version of the fallacy of misplaced concreteness which has been particularly common among psychologists. This is the conception that "the organism" is a concrete ontologically real entity and that somehow its internal physico-chemical processes, and their interchange with the environment are the "real thing" whereas behavior is a kind of resultant or epiphenomenon. It is exceedingly difficult for persons who think in this way to become aware that biological theory is abstract in exactly the same sense as any other scientific theory. Therefore, the organism in this sense is no more an ontological reality than is the famous particle of Newtonian physics. Pari passu the organism, as the boundary-maintaining physico-chemical system, *is in absolutely no sense more or less real than the system of action.* Both stand on fundamentally the same footing. Both are systems conceived in terms of a conceptual scheme. Both are subject to empirical verification in the same senses.

Underlying much of the psychological bias referred to above within the theory of action has been this biological bias, the tendency to think that only the internal system of the organism is somehow "real" while its relational system is not.

A system of action, then, is a system of the relations of organisms in interdependence with each other and with non-social objects in the environment or situation. It is in order to keep this system distinct from the organism as a physico-chemical system that we prefer, instead of referring to the "behavior of the organism," to speak of the "action of the actor," and instead of using the term environment, to speak of the "situation of action." We do not wish to quarrel about words, but we do submit that use of the biological terminology is frequently associated with genuine confusion of the frames of reference.

The second fundamental feature of systems of action is that as relational systems, they are boundary-maintaining systems. We have given ample justification for this statement earlier in this work and elsewhere. It is this property of systems of action which *states* the analytical independence of the frame of reference of action from that of biological theory. If this were not the case, there would be no point in complicating matters by using this additional frame of reference for the analysis of concrete organisms as behaving entities. The lack of empirical success of attempts to "reduce" most action phenomena to biological terms is well known and need not be further discussed here. Suffice it to say that this statement that systems of action are boundary-maintaining systems has the same justification that any fundamental methodological assumption about a scientific conceptual scheme has. It is *not* as such an empirical generalization, but is logically prior to all empirical generalizations which are stated in terms of the theory of action.

Finally, the third fundamental consideration touches the much discussed "subjective point of view," namely, the study of action "from the point of view of the actor." Contrary to the view held by the author in the *Structure of Social Action* it now appears that this postulate is not essential to the frame of reference of action in its most elementary form. It is, however, necessarily involved at the levels of elaboration of systems of action at which culture, that is shared symbolic patterns, becomes involved. It is, that is, a consequence of the fact that action comes to be oriented in terms of symbols which also serve to communicate with other actors.

Another way of looking at the postulate is to consider the implications of the fact that scientific investigation is itself a process of action. Precisely, in terms of our present conceptual scheme, if the object of investigation is a physical object—which includes organisms—there is no process of social interaction between ego and the object. The object, that is, does not *re*act to ego's action in terms analyzable in terms of the theory of action. But if the object is a social object, the process of investigation is itself a process of social interaction, and must be understood in the appropriate terms. Such interaction, however, in terms of the present conceptual scheme clearly involves communication. It is not possible in these terms to interpret alter's behavior in terms of the action frame of reference without communicating with him, without "understanding his motives" in the full sense of the theory of action as we have developed such a conception. This is essentially what is meant by the subjective reference or the subjective point of view of the theory of action.[4]

It is, of course, possible to remain a behavioristic purist and avoid this subjective reference, but only in one of two ways. The first is to repudiate the action frame of reference altogether and attempt to maintain a biological frame of reference. The other is to use the action frame of reference, but to keep the elaboration of the theory of action to pre-symbolic, that is pre-cultural levels.[5] The issue of

[4] It might well be argued that social scientists often do not interact with their subjects, but only objective courses of behavior or their results are studied. For the historian or archaeologist, indeed, since the subjects are generally dead, direct interaction is impossible. But this is not a valid objection. Inscriptions, historical documents and artifacts are clearly interpreted in terms of what they were supposed to have "meant" to the authors and users. The question asked is of the order of "if he were available to be interviewed about this what would he probably tell me?" Since he is not available for interview, the scientist resorts to the next best, the reconstruction from the available data of what he probably would say. The case of statistical and other data about "objective" behavior is not fundamentally different. The frame of reference in which such data are placed and interpreted is in general that of action which includes implicit if·not explicit reference to what the actors in question "meant by it" when they did what the observations record as having happened.

[5] This is essentially what Professor Skinner does (Skinner, B. F. *The Behavior of Organisms*) and is also perhaps the major trend in the thinking of Hull and his more rigid disciples. There is no possible objection to this if all that is sought is the explanation of animal behavior—and the corresponding components

"behaviorism" then really boils down to that of whether it is possible to handle the more differentiated levels of the frame of reference of action with the precision and care which the scientist attempts to attain. As in other branches of science "the proof of the pudding is in the eating."

§ THE CLASSIFICATION OF THE SCIENCES OF ACTION

WE MAY now turn to the problem of the internal division of labor between the sciences of action. We shall consider only those which have a claim to the status of analytical sciences in the sense that, whatever their specialization of interests in relation to classes of empirical phenomena, their primary claim to independent status as sciences rests on their concern with and responsibility for a relatively independent and distinctive conceptual scheme. Such a conceptual scheme need not be a closed system, but we will set up as a criterion that it must not simply be an "application" of a more generalized scheme.

In these terms the theory of action clearly differentiates most broadly into the theory of personality as a system, the theory of social systems and the theory of culture. There are, however, certain problems concerning the implications of this differentiation which need to be taken up.

The theory of personality as a system seems to coincide, with one exception which will be taken up presently, with the field of psychology as a discipline. Perhaps, it would be better to say it coincides with what psychology from our point of view ought to be, and it seems on the whole is tending toward. There are two primary strictures on the suggestion that this formula is descriptive of the present focus of psychology. The first is the persistence of the tendency to regard psychology as essentially a biological science. The

---

of human behavior—on levels where symbolism and culture are not involved. Indeed careful attention to the phenomena on this level can make very important contributions. The position becomes objectionable only when it is elevated into the dogma that the introduction of the symbolic-cultural levels, and with them the "subjective reference," is "unscientific," and should properly condemn those who venture into these, admittedly difficult, fields to the category of the "tender-minded" with the implication that their findings are almost certainly their own "wish fulfillments."

problem this raises can, it would seem, be satisfactorily handled by analogy with the physical sciences. There is, of course, no question whatever of the overwhelmingly great importance of the interdependence between the organism as a biological system and the personality as a system of action. But for the reasons we have just reviewed, this interdependence does not justify treating personality as simply an "extension" of the organism. The fruitful analogy is that with the status of bio-chemistry relative to the biological sciences. There is obviously room for specialization in the field of "psycho-biology," and in fact much of it of the most fruitful kind exists both in "physiological psychology" and in the field of "psycho-somatic" medicine. But we must insist that the legitimacy, promise and importance of this field does not justify treating the theory of personality as a branch of biological science, or putting the center of gravity of the theoretical interests of psychology into the biological sciences. This is a problem which the members of the psychological profession must ultimately face more squarely than they have hitherto done.

The second stricture consists simply in the fact that genuinely systematic treatment of personality *as a system* on the action level or any other for that matter, has not as yet been common among even the most eminent theorists in the field. The situation is parallel to that in the social system field, where Pareto stands almost alone in his clear and explicit conception of the social system. Even Freud, though it may be said that the conception of personality as a system was definitely emergent from his work, did not use it as a definite guiding conception, and he never fully disentangled the action aspects of personality from the biological. Furthermore, adequate treatment of personality as a system has had to await clarification of its relations to the social system and to culture. We may hope for rapid advance in this direction from psychologists, but what may be called bio-psychological eclecticism remains more typical of psychologists who are not either behaviorists or biologists than does systematic personality theory.

The exception referred to above, to the appropriateness of the definition of psychological theory as the theory of personality as a system, concerns the problem of where the study of certain fundamentals of action process which underlie all organization of action in systems belongs, the field that is of what is sometimes called "behavior psychology," which includes the field of "simple learning." The present view is that this belongs more appropriately in psychology than in any other of the theoretical sciences of action. This is essentially because the processes in question are prior to and underlie the organization of action in more complex systems, either personality or social. This is precisely the kind of thing which can be most fruitfully studied on pre-symbolic levels. Usually this implies that the experimental situation is one in which social interaction and its variability are not crucial—as is obviously true of most animal learning study, though such studies of animal imitation as those of Miller and Dollard raise other questions. But even on this level variability on both the social system levels and the cultural level are not likely to be problematical. The focus of interest is in the underlying action process itself.

As an analytical discipline, then, we would here define psychology as the science concerned with the elementary processes of action and their organization in personalities as systems. The status of social psychology raises special problems which can best be taken up after the problem of the theory of the social system has been discussed.

The theory of the social system is, as we have seen, in a certain fundamental sense, directly parallel to that of personality, though the relation of personality to the organism means that the relations of the two systems are only partly symmetrical. It would, therefore, seem logical that there should be an analytical science of social systems which was correlative with psychology as that of personality systems. This is in a broad sense an acceptable view, but there are complications touching the problems of the status of economics and political science which we must take up.

The advances in the theory of the social system which have been documented in the present work make it possible to clarify further a view of the proper status of sociological theory with which the author has been concerned for a number of years. It was first tentatively stated in the final chapter of the *Structure of Social Action*, and a further revision of it was stated in the paper on *The Position of Sociological Theory* (*Essays*, Chapter I). The focus of this view has been on the importance of institutions and institutionalization as the primary concern of sociology as a science. In the earlier version also the property of "common value-integration" was strongly emphasized.

If a sphere for sociological theory as a distinctive conceptual scheme is to be delineated, it must be either the theory of the social system as a whole, or some special aspect of the theory of the social system rather than the whole of it. First, we may suggest that the former formula might or might not be interpreted to include a "theory of culture." The problem of the status of such a theory will be taken up presently. Let it be said here only that the treatment of the involvement of culture in the social system is not in this sense a "theory of culture" any more than that of the involvement of personality and motivational process has to be psychology in the sense just stated.

The choice between the broader and the narrower views of the scope of sociological theory just stated does not involve this question, but turns essentially on that of the status of economic theory. The broader view would treat economic theory as "applied sociology" while the narrower would not. The narrower is the view taken here. It is consistent with the view that the central concern of sociological theory is with the phenomena of institutionalization.

It has been brought out in Chapter IV above that within the institutionalized framework of a social system where the instrumental division of labor was sufficiently elaborated, there could be a peculiar quantification of control of facilities through the processes of exchange, by means of what was called "purchasing power." This peculiar quantification is an emergent phenomenon appearing at certain levels of differentiation of social systems, and coming to be of high significance only within a relatively limited, though very important, class of social systems. It is the processes of equilibration of a system of such exchange-oriented actions which constitute the focus of economic theory as a conceptual scheme.

As a theory of process, economic theory depends on the relevance of the processes of decision-making to the determination of prices and quantities in the system of exchange. Hence within an economy where freedom for decision to operate is sufficiently broad this decision-making process is at least one primary process by which the allocation of resources, i.e., in our terms of facilities, comes about.

This economic process may be the resultant of large numbers of discrete decisions by participants in the market. But it may also be a centralized decision process carried out by a government planning body. The functional significance of the economic process for the social system in either case is a matter of its relevance to the allocation of facilities.

The *combination* of study of the functional significance of the process and its analysis in terms of a given conceptual scheme, however, depends on its analysis in terms of the famous "postulate of economic rationality." This can only be interpreted to mean that the science of economics has little *explanatory* relevance to the processes of allocation of resources in a "traditionalistic" economy where only "drift" leads to alteration of the allocation system. At most it can serve only a "criterion" function by measuring the actual allocation against a standard of what in some sense would be an "economically rational allocation."

The postulate of rationality, however, occupies a somewhat curious status in the theory of action. It is a clear implication of the theory of action on both the personality and the social system levels, that "rational action" is a type which presupposes a certain mode of the *organization* of all the elements of action. It is something which is possible within the limits imposed by value-orientation patterns and by the situation, and by a certain mode of integration of motivational elements. On the personality level, that is, rational action is a type which exists within certain limits of the organization of personality. On the social system level, correspondingly, there is scope for rational adjustments within certain limits imposed by the institutionalized role-system.

Three levels of the organization of rational action in action systems may be distinguished. The first of these, the most elementary, is that involving the mobilization of resources for the attainment of a single given goal, by an individual actor or a collectivity. This is essentially what, in the *Structure of Social Action* was called a "technology," the analysis of the patternings of action relative to such a single given goal. Technology always involves two aspects or sets of factors, those pertaining to the conditions of success, and those concerning the "cost," which is ultimately the sacrifice of alternative goals involved in the expenditure of resources for the one in question. "Efficiency" is the measure of the effectiveness of a technological process relative to its cost.

The second level of organization introduces considerations of "economy," which consists in the process of the allocation of resources relative to a plurality of alternative goals. Here cost is not a constant but a variable in that there is explicit consideration not merely of the minimization of expenditure compatible with effectiveness, but of allocation of resources between alternative goals. This is what the decision-making process does with the facilities of the social system.

The third level of organization of rational action is concerned not with economy but with the maximization of power in the political sense. Here the orientation is to the maximization of total command of facilities in the social system held by one actor, individual or collective, relative to others. There is hence, as we pointed out in Chapter IV, no inherent limitation of scope, but anything, especially in the sphere of relational possessions, which can have significance as a facility, may become involved in the political power system.

Technology and economy on the basis of the individual personality can be said to constitute psychological problem areas, whereas the relational character of political power makes it impossible to consider it wholly from a psychological point of view. On the social system level, on the other hand, technology can be the analysis of the goal-orientation of a collectivity as an organization, which involves its role structure, and hence involves problems of institutionalization, whereas economy involves the interrelations of a plurality of actors individual and/or collective. This perspective, however, involves a specific institutionalized limitation of scope.

Hence we may say that the implications of the postulate of rationality are within certain limits psychological, that is, they rest in the theory of personality, but that economics as a *social* science is concerned with the phenomena of rational decision-making and the consequences of these decisions within an institutionalized system of exchange relationships. This is, within the theory of action, such a highly distinctive complex that the claim of economic theory to autonomy with respect to it seems quite justified.

The case of political science is a wholly different one. Variant definitions of its scope are current within the profession itself. Here we are concerned only with the claim that it should be organized about an analytical theoretical scheme of a scope and character parallel to that of economic theory. The only current formula for this claim is that it should be treated as the theory of power. In this connection one fact will strike the reader immediately, namely, that in technical elaboration as a conceptual scheme, there is no such thing as a theory of power which is remotely comparable with economic theory. We believe that the above analysis (Chapter IV) has given the fundamental reason for this fact, namely, that power in the political sense is inherently diffuse as contrasted with the specificity of economic power. This means that a theory of political power must in the nature of the case take into account *as variables,* most of the variables of the social system.

In view of this fact it is in fact appropriate to treat political science as the discipline concerned with political power and its use and control, but because of the diffuseness of political power this makes it a synthetic science in the social system field, not one built about a distinctive *analytical* conceptual scheme, that is, a strictly limited set of variables. The common designation as the field of "government" comes relatively close to this conception.

In the light of these considerations we may come back to the question of the scope of sociological theory. Institutionalization of cultural patterns means, as we have often emphasized, in the integrated sense internalization of the same patterns in the personality. Psychologically an internalized pattern is no longer an object of the situation. It is not possible to treat it as an instrumental means or condition. There is a specific mode of cathectic integration of the actor's need-dispositions with an internalized pattern. This fact has a fundamental methodological significance. It means that the orientation of "instrumental rationality" *cannot* be the attitude defining the actor's orientation to internalized patterns.

We derive, then, a most significant complex of relationships. The value-integration of the social system is defined by the system of patterns of value-orientation which have become institutionalized to constitute the definitions of its constituent role-expectation patterns. The institutionalization of these patterns in turn means that typically they have become internalized in the personality systems of the actors in the social system and this fact in turn means that their relevance to the determination of behavior cannot be primarily through the "mechanisms" of instrumental rationality but *must* be through what are sometimes called the non- and irrational mechanisms of the functioning of personality.

This is the fundamental reason why the sociologist cannot follow the lead of economics or indeed of the whole of utilitarian theory in his fundamental account of the motivational forces in institutional behavior, and why the concepts of modern "dynamic psychology" have come to be of such critical importance to him. This again is why a sociological theory which can get beyond structural description and the classifications of "formal sociology" must be adequately integrated with the theory of personality precisely in the modern psychological sense.

Sociological theory, then, is for us *that aspect of the theory of social systems which is concerned with the phenomena of the institutionalization of patterns of value-orientation in the social system,* with the conditions of that institutionalization, and of changes in the patterns, with conditions of conformity with and deviance from a set of such patterns and with motivational processes in so far as they are involved in all of these. As motivational processes these cannot be the processes of rational action in the economic sense, but involve the processes of value-acquisition through identification and of deviance and social control as these have been analyzed above. Since we have only indicated where economics and political science fit in, the present volume can, in these terms, be regarded rather strictly as a contribution to sociological theory.

It is hoped that it will be entirely clear to the reader that this view does not constitute the "reduction" of sociological theory to psychological terms, but the extension of the structural aspect of that theory to an explicit statement of its concern with motivational process within the context of the functioning of the social system as a system. The processes are, as has been repeatedly stated, exactly the same concrete processes which are involved in the functioning of personalities as systems. But their context of theoretical relevance is that of the social system as a system and not of the personality as a system.

Now we are in a position to say something about social psychology as a discipline. We would interpret its place as that of an interstitial mediating field between sociology and psychology in a sense directly analogous to that of biochemistry or of psychobiology or physiological psychology. We could say, then, that the social psychologist is not directly concerned with the analysis of the structure of social systems, but with motivational processes and personalities in their specific relations to and interdependence with the structure of social systems, notably, that is, their bearing on the explanation of socially structured and "mass" phenomena.

It follows, however, that social psychology as a theoretical discipline should not have the same *order* of independent theoretical significance as does either psychological theory or sociological theory. Above all there can be no such thing as good social psychology without explicit and systematic reference to the sociological aspects of the theory of social systems. Without that it becomes merely a cover for a "psychological bias" in the interpretation of social phenomena. The only alternative to this view is to hold that since all action is "process of the mind" or "behavior" there is no place for a distinct theory of the social system at all. The unacceptability of such a position is, in the light of the whole above discussion, abundantly clear.

Finally, we may say a word about the implications of the relations between culture and social systems for the classification of the sciences of action. There is, in our opinion, an important place for a "theory of culture" as part of the theory of action, which is quite definitely not sociological theory in the sense in which this has just been defined. This is what, according to the present trend, anthropological theory is tending to become. According to this view culture, as an empirical phenomenon, is not more independent of personalities and social systems than are social systems of personalities. As part of the theory of action, then, the theory of culture must be the theory concerned not only with the properties of culture as such but with the interdependence of patterns of culture with the other components of systems of action. It is, of course, concerned with the structure of systems of culture patterns, with the different types of such systems and their classification. But it is also concerned with their involvement in social systems and personalities, and with the implications of this involvement for their maintenance as "living" cultures in action systems, and for their tendencies of change. The focus, however, is always on the culture pattern system as such, and neither on the social system in which it is involved, nor on the personalities as systems.

Only by some such definition of its scope can anthropology become an analytical empirical science which is independent both of sociology and of psychology. This view gives it a scope which partly justifies the breadth of the term Anthropology, because of the involvement of culture both in personalities and in social systems. The alternative is to take the name literally and make it the "science of man." As a theoretical science this is scarcely to be seriously considered, for surely physical anthropology as human biology is not theoretically a distinctive science. And surely the anthropologist is not going to try to absorb all of humanly significant biology, including all the medical sciences, all of psychology and all of sociology, to say nothing of history, economics and political science. It might be possible to make it a synthetic empirical science of man, drawing on these many theoretical sciences, but not itself an independent theoretical science. But as an alternative to this the above offers a definition of the possible theoretical scope of anthropology which is compatible with those of the other sciences of action which have been advanced here. Furthermore it is clear that such a theoretical science is needed in order to complete the roster of the theoretical sciences of the field of action. The place of culture is of such fundamental importance that we cannot afford to have it omitted.

One other point needs to be made. Anthropological theory defined in this way should be clearly distinguished from what in Germany have been called the *Geisteswissenchaften*, or are sometimes called the "formal" disciplines. These deal with analysis of the content of cultural pattern systems for its own sake without regard to their involvement in systems of action. Thus, logic or mathematics, the methodology of scientific theory, or the analysis of art forms fall in this category. Clearly the anthropological theorist must lean on these disciplines just as the psychologist must lean on the biologist. But anthropological theory as here conceived clearly belongs to the sciences of action, not to these formal disciplines.

The above has been a highly schematic classification of the theoretical sciences of action. Naturally it is not expected that the actual fields of empirical interest and research activity of persons belonging to the various disciplines will follow such a scheme with neat precision. Indeed this would be altogether incompatible with the nature of a vital growing scientific tradition. But this fact does not in the least diminish the importance of clarity about these fundamental points of reference around which the theoretical content of the sciences of action is organized. The disappearance of the relevance of the major distinctions of such a scheme will mean that theory itself has evolved to an altogether new level.

Also we have confined our attention to the sciences which are primarily organized about a distinctive theoretical scheme on an analytical level. This clearly precludes the inclusion of history as standing on the same level. In so far as history is a social science and not one of the humanities, it clearly is not organized about any one of these distinctive schemes unless it be that of the social system as a whole. It seems better to conceive history as a synthetic empirical science which is concerned with the mobilization of all the theoretical knowledge which is relevant in the explanation of processes in social systems and in cultural change in the past. There are, besides political science, according to the view of it as stated above, several others of these synthetic disciplines dealing mainly with contemporary phenomena such as population studies, "regional studies" —if it be a discipline at all—or "international relations."

We have now reached the end of our long analysis of the complexities of the social system. In conclusion, it may be appropriate to quote part of the closing paragraph of the *Structure of Social Action* written fourteen years ago in 1937.

"It is not, therefore, possible to concur in the prevailing pessimistic judgment of the social sciences, particularly sociology. . . . Notable progress on both empirical and theoretical levels has been made in the short space of a generation. We have sound theoretical foundations on which to build."

This statement seems to have been amply justified by the event. Further empirical progress has certainly been made in the intervening years with many students contributing to it. Similarly on the theoretical side, which has been our concern in the present book. *The Structure of Social Action* proved, as it was hoped that it would be, only a beginning. If the theory of the social system had not advanced notably since it was written, the present book would not have been possible. By the same token, the present effort is only a link in a much longer chain. We can have full confidence that many further links will be forged, and soon.

INDEX

IN THE Preface and at various points throughout this book it has been noted that many of the background concepts important to the book are more fully discussed in the monograph of Parsons and Shils' *Values, Motives and Systems of Action* in *Toward a General Theory of Action* (Parsons and Shils, editors, Harvard University Press, 1951). For the convenience of the reader who wishes to follow up some of the problems involved in the definition and use of these concepts this note is inserted.

In the nature of the present work, only limited attention could be given to many of the psychological concepts most relevant to it. Fuller discussion of these will be found above all in Chapter II of the monograph, "Personality as a System of Action," and in briefer form, in the "General Statement," Part I, Chapter I of the volume. The strategic concept *need-disposition* will be found defined and analyzed in both these places, and its relation to other motivational concepts like "drive" discussed. In the same chapter the reader will find a considerably fuller discussion of the mechanisms of personality, with an attempt at their systematic classification, than has been possible here. Further, the concept *optimization of gratification* is defined and elucidated in that chapter.

Also, the very central concepts of *interaction*, the "paradigm" of interaction, and the related concept of *double contingency* are discussed at several places in the other volume, notably in a separate section of the "General Statement" and in a section near the end of Chapter I of the monograph. The application of this analysis to the theory of personality is discussed particularly in the sections of Chapter II on "The Articulation of Personality and Social Systems" and "Need-Dispositions and Role-Expectations."

The reader who may be concerned about the use of the concept *system,* on both the theoretical and the empirical levels, will find a discussion of the meaning of systems of theory in the Introduction to the monograph (not the Preface to the volume) and one of the nature of empirical systems, and the classification of types of them, as the last section of Chapter I of the monograph.

Finally, the "pattern variable" scheme, its derivation from the frame of reference of action, and the way in which it is involved in personalities as well as in social systems, is more fully discussed in Chapter I of the monograph than in the present volume. The attention of the reader is particularly invited to the section "The Interrelations of the Pattern Variables" where the concept of *symmetrical asymmetry* is discussed.